GO MATH!

Middle School | Grade 8

COMMON CORE EDITION

Edward B. Burger • Juli K. Dixon
Timothy D. Kanold • Matthew R. Larson
Steven J. Leinwand • Martha E. Sandoval-Martinez

Authors

Edward B. Burger, Ph.D., is the president of Southwestern University, a former Francis Christopher Oakley Third Century Professor of Mathematics at Williams College, and a former vice provost at Baylor University. He has authored or coauthored more than sixty-five articles, books, and video series; delivered over five hundred addresses and workshops throughout the world; and made more than fifty radio and television appearances. He is a Fellow of the American Mathematical Society as well as having earned many national honors, including the Robert Foster Cherry Award for Great Teaching in 2010. In 2012, Microsoft Education named him a "Global Hero in Education."

Matthew R. Larson, Ph.D., is the K-12 mathematics curriculum specialist for the Lincoln Public Schools and served on the Board of Directors for the National Council of Teachers of Mathematics from 2010-2013. He is a past chair of NCTM's Research Committee and was a member of NCTM's Task Force on Linking Research and Practice. He is the author of several books on implementing the Common Core Standards for Mathematics. He has taught mathematics at the secondary and college levels and held an appointment as an honorary visiting associate professor at Teachers College, Columbia University.

Juli K. Dixon, Ph.D., is a Professor of Mathematics Education at the University of Central Florida. She has taught mathematics in urban schools at the elementary, middle, secondary, and post-secondary levels. She is an active researcher and speaker with numerous publications and conference presentations. Key areas of focus are deepening teachers' content knowledge and communicating and justifying mathematical ideas. She is a past chair of the NCTM Student Explorations in Mathematics Editorial Panel and member of the Board of Directors for the Association of Mathematics Teacher Educators.

Steven J. Leinwand is a Principal Research Analyst at the American Institutes for Research (AIR) in Washington, D.C., and has over 30 years in leadership positions in mathematics education. He is past president of the National Council of Supervisors of Mathematics and served on the NCTM Board of Directors. He is the author of numerous articles, books, and textbooks and has made countless presentations with topics including student achievement, reasoning, effective assessment, and successful implementation of standards.

Timothy D. Kanold, Ph.D., is an award-winning international educator, author, and consultant. He is a former superintendent and director of mathematics and science at Adlai E. Stevenson High School District 125 in Lincolnshire, Illinois. He is a past president of the National Council of Supervisors of Mathematics (NCSM) and the Council for the Presidential Awardees of Mathematics (CPAM). He has served on several writing and leadership commissions for NCTM during the past decade. He presents motivational professional development seminars with a focus on developing professional learning communities (PLC's) to improve the teaching, assessing, and learning of students. He has recently authored nationally recognized articles, books, and textbooks for mathematics education and school leadership, including *What Every Principal Needs to Know about the Teaching and Learning of Mathematics*.

Martha E. Sandoval-Martinez is a mathematics instructor at El Camino College in Torrance, California. She was previously a Math Specialist at the University of California at Davis and former instructor at Santa Ana College, Marymount College, and California State University, Long Beach. In her current and former positions, she has worked extensively to improve fundamental pre-algebra and algebra skills in students who have historically struggled with mathematics.

© Houghton Mifflin Harcourt Publishing Company • Image Credits: (Timothy D. Kanold) © Photo courtesy of Tim Kanold; (Juli K. Dixon) © Photo courtesy of Juli Dixon; (Martha E. Sandoval) © Carlos Delgado/AP Images for HMH.

Program Reviewers

Sharon Brown
Instructional Staff Developer
Pinellas County Schools
St. Petersburg, FL

Maureen Carrion
Math Staff Developer
Brentwood UFSD
Brentwood, NY

Jackie Cruse
Math Coach
Ferrell GPA
Tampa, FL

John Esser
Secondary Mathematics
Coordinator
Racine Unified School District
Racine, WI

Donald Hoessler
Math Teacher
Discovery Middle School
Orlando, Florida

Becky (Rebecca) Jones, M.Ed.
NBCT EA-Math
Orange County Public Schools
Orlando, FL

Sheila D.P. Lea, MSA
Ben L. Smith High School
Greensboro, NC

Toni Lwanga
Newell Barney Jr. High
Queen Creek Unified School District
Queen Creek, AZ

Tiffany J. Mack
Charles A. Lindbergh Middle School
Peoria District #150
Peoria, IL

Jean Sterner
Thurgood Marshall Fundamental
Middle School
Pinellas County Schools
St. Petersburg, FL

Mona Toncheff
Math Content Specialist
Phoenix Union High School District
Phoenix, AZ

Kevin Voepel
Mathematics & Professional
Development Coordinator
Ferguson-Florissant School District
Florissant, MO

UNIT 1

Real Numbers, Exponents, and Scientific Notation

MODULE 1 Real Numbers

MODULE 2 Exponents and Scientific Notation

MAJOR CLUSTERS ■
SUPPORTING CLUSTERS ■
ADDITIONAL CLUSTERS ■

UNIT 2
COMMON CORE

Proportional and Nonproportional Relationships and Functions

 MODULE 3 **Proportional Relationships**

 MODULE 4 **Nonproportional Relationships**

MAJOR CLUSTERS ■
SUPPORTING CLUSTERS ▪
ADDITIONAL CLUSTERS ■

 **MODULE 5** **Writing Linear Equations**

 **MODULE 6** **Functions**

MAJOR CLUSTERS ■
SUPPORTING CLUSTERS ■
ADDITIONAL CLUSTERS ■

UNIT 3 Solving Equations and Systems of Equations

COMMON CORE

MODULE 7 Solving Linear Equations

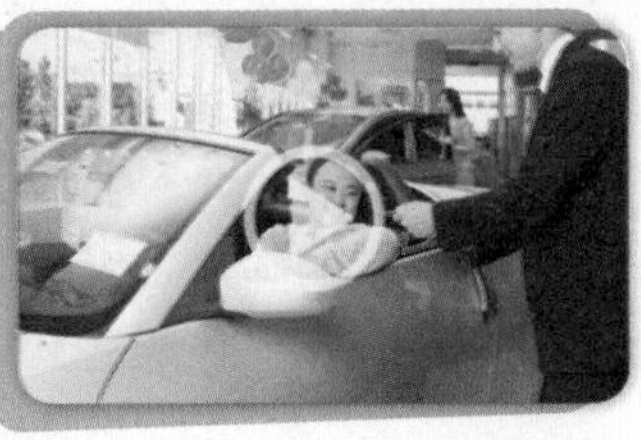

CLUSTER

MODULE 8 Solving Systems of Linear Equations

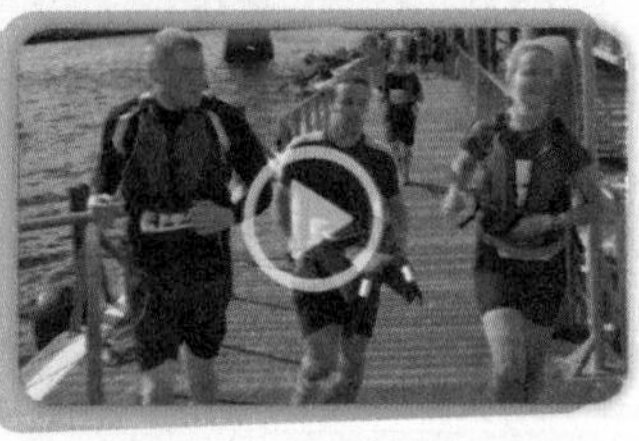

CLUSTER

MAJOR CLUSTERS ■
SUPPORTING CLUSTERS ■
ADDITIONAL CLUSTERS ■

MODULE 9 Transformations and Congruence

CLUSTER

MODULE 10 Transformations and Similarity

CLUSTER

MAJOR CLUSTERS ■
SUPPORTING CLUSTERS ■
ADDITIONAL CLUSTERS ■

UNIT 5 Measurement Geometry

MODULE 11 Angle Relationships in Parallel Lines and Triangles

CLUSTER

MODULE 12 The Pythagorean Theorem

CLUSTER

MAJOR CLUSTERS ■
SUPPORTING CLUSTERS ■
ADDITIONAL CLUSTERS ■

© Houghton Mifflin Harcourt Publishing Company • Image Credits: (t) ©Nifro Travel Images/Alamy Images; (b) ©Yuri Arcurs/Shutterstock

MODULE 13 Volume

MAJOR CLUSTERS ■
SUPPORTING CLUSTERS ■
ADDITIONAL CLUSTERS ■

UNIT 6 Statistics

MODULE 14 Scatter Plots

MODULE 15 Two-Way Tables

MAJOR CLUSTERS ■
SUPPORTING CLUSTERS ■
ADDITIONAL CLUSTERS ■

Common Core Standards for Mathematics

Correlation for *HMH Go Math* Grade 8

Standard	Descriptor	Taught	Reinforced
8.NS THE NUMBER SYSTEM			
Know that there are numbers that are not rational, and approximate them by rational numbers.			
■ CC.8.NS.1	Know that numbers that are not rational are called irrational. Understand informally that every number has a decimal expansion; for rational numbers show that the decimal expansion repeats eventually, and convert a decimal expansion which repeats eventually into a rational number.	SE: 7–9, 12, 15–17, 18	SE: 13–14, 19–20
■ CC.8.NS.2	Use rational approximations of irrational numbers to compare the size of irrational numbers, locate them approximately on a number line diagram, and estimate the value of expressions (e.g., π^2).	SE: 10–12, 21–23, 24	SE: 14, 25–26, 26A–26B
8.EE EXPRESSIONS AND EQUATIONS			
Work with radicals and integer exponents.			
■ CC.8.EE.1	Know and apply the properties of integer exponents to generate equivalent numerical expressions.	SE: 33–35, 36	SE: 37–38, 38A–38B
■ CC.8.EE.2	Use square root and cube root symbols to represent solutions to equations of the form $x^2 = p$ and $x^3 = p$, where p is a positive rational number. Evaluate square roots of small perfect squares and cube roots of small perfect cubes. Know that $\sqrt{2}$ is irrational.	SE: 9–11, 12	SE: 13–14
■ CC.8.EE.3	Use numbers expressed in the form of a single digit times an integer power of 10 to estimate very large or very small quantities, and to express how many times as much one is than the other.	SE: 39–41, 42, 44A–44B 45–47, 48, 50A–50B	SE: 43–44, 49–50
■ CC.8.EE.4	Perform operations with numbers expressed in scientific notation, including problems where both decimal and scientific notation are used. Use scientific notation and choose units of appropriate size for measurements of very large or very small quantities (e.g., use millimeters per year for seafloor spreading). Interpret scientific notation that has been generated by technology.	SE: 51–53, 54	SE: 55–56
Understand the connections between proportional relationships, lines, and linear equations.			
■ CC.8.EE.5	Graph proportional relationships, interpreting the unit rate as the slope of the graph. Compare two different proportional relationships represented in different ways.	SE: 83–85, 86, 168, 170	SE: 87–88, 171–172

■ MAJOR CLUSTERS   ■ SUPPORTING CLUSTERS   ■ ADDITIONAL CLUSTERS

Standard	Descriptor	Taught	Reinforced
■ CC.8.EE.6	Use similar triangles to explain why the slope m is the same between any two distinct points on a non-vertical line in the coordinate plane; derive the equation $y = mx$ for a line through the origin and the equation $y = mx + b$ for a line intercepting the vertical axis at b.	SE: 71–73, 74, 82A–82B 101, 103, 104, 364–365, 368A–368B	SE: 75–76, 106, 368

Analyze and solve linear equations and pairs of simultaneous linear equations.

Standard	Descriptor	Taught	Reinforced
■ CC.8.EE.7	Solve linear equations in one variable.	SE: 197–199, 200, 203–205, 206, 355, 358, 363–364, 366; *See also below.*	SE: 201–202, 207–208, 359–360, 367–368; *See also below.*
■ CC.8.EE.7a	Give examples of linear equations in one variable with one solution, infinitely many solutions, or no solutions. Show which of these possibilities is the case by successively transforming the given equation into simpler forms, until an equivalent equation of the form $x = a$, $a = a$, or $a = b$ results (where a and b are different numbers).	SE: 215–217, 218	SE: 219–220
■ CC.8.EE.7b	Solve linear equations with rational number coefficients, including equations whose solutions require expanding expressions using the distributive property and collecting like terms.	SE: 197–199, 200, 203–205, 206, 209–211, 212, 357, 358	SE: 201–202, 207–208, 213–214, 359–360, 220A–220B
■ CC.8.EE.8	Analyze and solve pairs of simultaneous linear equations.	SE: 228–231, 232; *See also below.*	SE: 233–234; *See also below.*
■ CC.8.EE.8a	Understand that solutions to a system of two linear equations in two variables correspond to points of intersection of their graphs, because points of intersection satisfy both equations simultaneously.	SE: 227, 232	SE: 233–234
■ CC.8.EE.8b	Solve systems of two linear equations in two variables algebraically, and estimate solutions by graphing the equations. Solve simple cases by inspection.	SE: 235–238, 240, 243–246, 248, 251–254, 256, 259–261, 262	SE: 241–242, 249–250, 257–258, 263–264
■ CC.8.EE.8c	Solve real-world and mathematical problems leading to two linear equations in two variables.	SE: 230–231, 232, 238–239, 240, 246–247, 248, 254–255, 256	SE: 233–234, 241–242, 249–250, 257–258, 264

8.F FUNCTIONS

Define, evaluate, and compare functions.

Standard	Descriptor	Taught	Reinforced
■ CC.8.F.1	Understand that a function is a rule that assigns to each input exactly one output. The graph of a function is the set of ordered pairs consisting of an input and the corresponding output.	SE: 153–157, 158, 161	SE: 159–160, 165–166, 166C–166D

■ **MAJOR CLUSTERS**   ■ **SUPPORTING CLUSTERS**   ■ ADDITIONAL CLUSTERS

Standard	Descriptor	Taught	Reinforced
■ CC.8.F.2	Compare properties of two functions each represented in a different way (algebraically, graphically, numerically in tables, or by verbal descriptions).	SE: 85, 86, 116–118, 167–169, 170	SE: 87–88, 120, 171–172
■ CC.8.F.3	Interpret the equation $y = mx + b$ as defining a linear function, whose graph is a straight line; give examples of functions that are not linear.	SE: 95–97, 98, 107–108, 110, 113, 117, 162–163, 164, 166A–166B	SE: 99–100, 111–112, 119, 165–166

Use functions to model relationships between quantities.

Standard	Descriptor	Taught	Reinforced
■ CC.8.F.4	Construct a function to model a linear relationship between two quantities. Determine the rate of change and initial value of the function from a description of a relationship or from two (x, y) values, including reading these from a table or from a graph. Interpret the rate of change and initial value of a linear function in terms of the situation it models, and in terms of its graph or a table of values.	SE: 77–79, 80, 83, 86, 102, 104, 108–109, 110, 114–115, 117–118, 127–129, 130, 133–135, 136, 167–168, 169, 170, 172A–172B	SE: 76, 81–82, 87, 105–106, 111–112, 119–120, 131–132, 137–138, 171–172
■ CC.8.F.5	Describe qualitatively the functional relationship between two quantities by analyzing a graph (e.g., where the function is increasing or decreasing, linear or nonlinear). Sketch a graph that exhibits the qualitative features of a function that has been described verbally.	SE: 173–175, 176	SE: 177–178

8.G GEOMETRY

Understand congruence and similarity using physical models, transparencies, or geometry software.

Standard	Descriptor	Taught	Reinforced
■ CC.8.G.1a	Verify experimentally the properties of rotations, reflections, and translations: Lines are taken to lines, and line segments to line segments of the same length.	SE: 279–281, 282, 285–287, 288, 291–293, 294	SE: 283–284, 289–290, 295–296
■ CC.8.G.1b	Verify experimentally the properties of rotations, reflections, and translations: Angles are taken to angles of the same measure.	SE: 279–281, 282, 285–287, 288, 291–293, 294	SE: 283–284, 289–290, 295–296
■ CC.8.G.1c	Verify experimentally the properties of rotations, reflections, and translations: Parallel lines are taken to parallel lines.	SE: 279–281, 282, 285–287, 288, 291–293, 294	SE: 283–284, 289–290, 295–296
■ CC.8.G.2	Understand that a two-dimensional figure is congruent to another if the second can be obtained from the first by a sequence of rotations, reflections, and translations; given two congruent figures, describe a sequence that exhibits the congruence between them.	SE: 305–307, 308	SE: 309–310

| --- | --- | --- | --- |
■ CC.8.G.3	Describe the effect of dilations, translations, rotations, and reflections on two-dimensional figures using coordinates.	SE: 281–282, 287–288, 293–294, 297–300, 316–317, 318, 321–323, 324	SE: 283–284, 289–290, 295–296, 301–302, 319–320, 325–326
■ CC.8.G.4	Understand that a two-dimensional figure is similar to another if the second can be obtained from the first by a sequence of rotations, reflections, translations, and dilations; given two similar two-dimensional figures, describe a sequence that exhibits the similarity between them.	SE: 315–316, 317–318, 327–329, 330	SE: 319–320, 331–332, 332A–332B
■ CC.8.G.5	Use informal arguments to establish facts about the angle sum and exterior angle of triangles, about the angles created when parallel lines are cut by a transversal, and the angle-angle criterion for similarity of triangles.	SE: 347–350, 353–355, 356, 358, 361–362	SE: 351–352, 359–360, 367–368

Understand and apply the Pythagorean Theorem.

Standard	Descriptor	Taught	Reinforced
■ CC.8.G.6	Explain a proof of the Pythagorean Theorem and its converse.	SE: 375–376, 381–383, 384	SE: 380, 385–386
■ CC.8.G.7	Apply the Pythagorean Theorem to determine unknown side lengths in right triangles in real-world and mathematical problems in two and three dimensions.	SE: 376–378	SE: 379–380, 386A–386B
■ CC.8.G.8	Apply the Pythagorean Theorem to find the distance between two points in a coordinate system.	SE: 387–390	SE: 391–392

Solve real-world and mathematical problems involving volume of cylinders, cones, and spheres.

Standard	Descriptor	Taught	Reinforced
■ CC.8.G.9	Know the formulas for the volumes of cones, cylinders, and spheres and use them to solve real-world and mathematical problems.	SE: 399–401, 402, 405–407, 408, 411–413, 414	SE: 403–404, 409–410, 415–416

8.SP STATISTICS AND PROBABILITY

Investigate patterns of association in bivariate data.

Standard	Descriptor	Taught	Reinforced
■ CC.8.SP.1	Construct and interpret scatter plots for bivariate measurement data to investigate patterns of association between two quantities. Describe patterns such as clustering, outliers, positive or negative association, linear association, and nonlinear association.	SE: 142–143, 144, 433–435, 436, 439–440, 442	SE: 145–146, 437–438, 443–444
■ CC.8.SP.2	Know that straight lines are widely used to model relationships between two quantitative variables. For scatter plots that suggest a linear association, informally fit a straight line, and informally assess the model fit by judging the closeness of the data points to the line.	SE: 139–140, 144, 439–440, 442	SE: 145–146, 443–444, 444A–444B

■ MAJOR CLUSTERS   ■ SUPPORTING CLUSTERS   ■ ADDITIONAL CLUSTERS

Standard	Descriptor	Taught	Reinforced
■ CC.8.SP.3	Use the equation of a linear model to solve problems in the context of bivariate measurement data, interpreting the slope and intercept.	SE: 140–141, 144, 440–442	SE: 145–146, 443–444, 444A–444B
■ CC.8.SP.4	Understand that patterns of association can also be seen in bivariate categorical data by displaying frequencies and relative frequencies in a two-way table. Construct and interpret a two-way table summarizing data on two categorical variables collected from the same subjects. Use relative frequencies calculated for rows or columns to describe possible association between the two variables.	SE: 451–453, 454, 457–461, 462	SE: 455–456, 463–464

Standard	Descriptor	Citations
MP MATHEMATICAL PRACTICES STANDARDS		*The mathematical practices standards are integrated throughout the book. See, for example, the citations below.*
CC.MP.1	**Make sense of problems and persevere in solving them.** Mathematically proficient students start by explaining to themselves the meaning of a problem and looking for entry points to its solution. They analyze givens, constraints, relationships, and goals. They make conjectures about the form and meaning of the solution and plan a solution pathway rather than simply jumping into a solution attempt. They consider analogous problems, and try special cases and simpler forms of the original problem in order to gain insight into its solution. They monitor and evaluate their progress and change course if necessary. Older students might, depending on the context of the problem, transform algebraic expressions or change the viewing window on their graphing calculator to get the information they need. Mathematically proficient students can explain correspondences between equations, verbal descriptions, tables, and graphs or draw diagrams of important features and relationships, graph data, and search for regularity or trends. Younger students might rely on using concrete objects or pictures to help conceptualize and solve a problem. Mathematically proficient students check their answers to problems using a different method, and they continually ask themselves, "Does this make sense?" They can understand the approaches of others to solving complex problems and identify correspondences between different approaches.	SE: 14, 120, 178, 202, 211, 219, 242, 254–255, 308, 380, 392, 415, 455–456
CC.MP.2	**Reason abstractly and quantitatively.** Mathematically proficient students make sense of quantities and their relationships in problem situations. They bring two complementary abilities to bear on problems involving quantitative relationships: the ability to decontextualize—to abstract a given situation and represent it symbolically and manipulate the representing symbols as if they have a life of their own, without necessarily attending to their referents—and the ability to contextualize, to pause as needed during the manipulation process in order to probe into the referents for the symbols involved. Quantitative reasoning entails habits of creating a coherent representation of the problem at hand; considering the units involved; attending to the meaning of quantities, not just how to compute them; and knowing and flexibly using different properties of operations and objects.	SE: 14, 38, 82, 88, 103, 111, 153–154, 198–202, 214, 254–255, 354–355, 375–376

Standard	Descriptor	Citations
CC.MP.3	**Construct viable arguments and critique the reasoning of others.** Mathematically proficient students understand and use stated assumptions, definitions, and previously established results in constructing arguments. They make conjectures and build a logical progression of statements to explore the truth of their conjectures. They are able to analyze situations by breaking them into cases, and can recognize and use counterexamples. They justify their conclusions, communicate them to others, and respond to the arguments of others. They reason inductively about data, making plausible arguments that take into account the context from which the data arose. Mathematically proficient students are also able to compare the effectiveness of two plausible arguments, distinguish correct logic or reasoning from that which is flawed, and—if there is a flaw in an argument—explain what it is. Elementary students can construct arguments using concrete referents such as objects, drawings, diagrams, and actions. Such arguments can make sense and be correct, even though they are not generalized or made formal until later grades. Later, students learn to determine domains to which an argument applies. Students at all grades can listen or read the arguments of others, decide whether they make sense, and ask useful questions to clarify or improve the arguments.	SE: 20, 100, 146, 208, 258, 302, 352, 410, 444
CC.MP.4	**Model with mathematics.** Mathematically proficient students can apply the mathematics they know to solve problems arising in everyday life, society, and the workplace. In early grades, this might be as simple as writing an addition equation to describe a situation. In middle grades, a student might apply proportional reasoning to plan a school event or analyze a problem in the community. By high school, a student might use geometry to solve a design problem or use a function to describe how one quantity of interest depends on another. Mathematically proficient students who can apply what they know are comfortable making assumptions and approximations to simplify a complicated situation, realizing that these may need revision later. They are able to identify important quantities in a practical situation and map their relationships using such tools as diagrams, two-way tables, graphs, flowcharts and formulas. They can analyze those relationships mathematically to draw conclusions. They routinely interpret their mathematical results in the context of the situation and reflect on whether the results make sense, possibly improving the model if it has not served its purpose.	SE: 73, 129–130, 204–205, 254–255, 363–364, 413, 457–461

Standard	Descriptor	Citations
CC.MP.5	**Use appropriate tools strategically.** Mathematically proficient students consider the available tools when solving a mathematical problem. These tools might include pencil and paper, concrete models, a ruler, a protractor, a calculator, a spreadsheet, a computer algebra system, a statistical package, or dynamic geometry software. Proficient students are sufficiently familiar with tools appropriate for their grade or course to make sound decisions about when each of these tools might be helpful, recognizing both the insight to be gained and their limitations. For example, mathematically proficient high school students analyze graphs of functions and solutions generated using a graphing calculator. They detect possible errors by strategically using estimation and other mathematical knowledge. When making mathematical models, they know that technology can enable them to visualize the results of varying assumptions, explore consequences, and compare predictions with data. Mathematically proficient students at various grade levels are able to identify relevant external mathematical resources, such as digital content located on a website, and use them to pose or solve problems. They are able to use technological tools to explore and deepen their understanding of concepts.	SE: 22, 53, 197, 227–231, 285, 315, 347–348, 353, 375, 399
CC.MP.6	**Attend to precision.** Mathematically proficient students try to communicate precisely to others. They try to use clear definitions in discussion with others and in their own reasoning. They state the meaning of the symbols they choose, including using the equal sign consistently and appropriately. They are careful about specifying units of measure, and labeling axes to clarify the correspondence with quantities in a problem. They calculate accurately and efficiently, express numerical answers with a degree of precision appropriate for the problem context. In the elementary grades, students give carefully formulated explanations to each other. By the time they reach high school they have learned to examine claims and make explicit use of definitions.	SE: 56, 106, 143, 173–178, 214, 234, 250, 352, 404, 437

Standard	Descriptor	Citations
CC.MP.7	**Look for and make use of structure.** Mathematically proficient students look closely to discern a pattern or structure. Young students, for example, might notice that three and seven more is the same amount as seven and three more, or they may sort a collection of shapes according to how many sides the shapes have. Later, students will see 7×8 equals the well remembered $7 \times 5 + 7 \times 3$, in preparation for learning about the distributive property. In the expression $x^2 + 9x + 14$, older students can see the 14 as 2×7 and the 9 as $2 + 7$. They recognize the significance of an existing line in a geometric figure and can use the strategy of drawing an auxiliary line for solving problems. They also can step back for an overview and shift perspective. They can see complicated things, such as some algebraic expressions, as single objects or as being composed of several objects. For example, they can see $5 - 3(x - y)^2$ as 5 minus a positive number times a square and use that to realize that its value cannot be more than 5 for any real numbers x and y.	SE: 10–11, 33–35, 45, 133–135, 153–154, 208, 297–300, 381, 434, 439–441
CC.MP.8	**Look for and express regularity in repeated reasoning.** Mathematically proficient students notice if calculations are repeated, and look both for general methods and for shortcuts. Upper elementary students might notice when dividing 25 by 11 that they are repeating the same calculations over and over again, and conclude they have a repeating decimal. By paying attention to the calculation of slope as they repeatedly check whether points are on the line through (1, 2) with slope 3, middle school students might abstract the equation $\frac{(y - 2)}{(x - 1)} = 3$. Noticing the regularity in the way terms cancel when expanding $(x - 1)(x + 1)$, $(x - 1)(x^2 + x + 1)$, and $(x - 1)(x^3 + x^2 + x + 1)$ might lead them to the general formula for the sum of a geometric series. As they work to solve a problem, mathematically proficient students maintain oversight of the process, while attending to the details. They continually evaluate the reasonableness of their intermediate results.	SE: 8, 33–35, 45, 107, 197, 235, 243, 251, 297–300, 388, 440

Succeeding with HMH Go Math

Actively participate in your learning with your write-in Student Edition. Explore concepts, take notes, answer questions, and complete your homework right in your textbook!

Explore Activities help you develop a deeper understanding of math concepts.

Essential Questions ensure that you know exactly what you are learning.

Scan QR codes with your smart phone or device to watch **Math On the Spot** tutorial videos for every example in the book!

Your Turn exercises check your understanding of new concepts.

Play strategy **Games and Activities** with classmates to practice using the concepts you have learned.

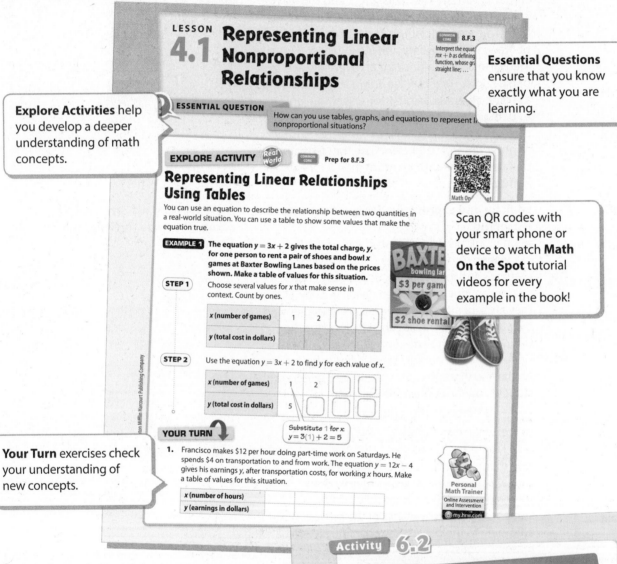

LESSON 4.1 Representing Linear Nonproportional Relationships

COMMON CORE 8.F.3
Interpret the equation mx + b as defining function, whose graph straight line; ...

ESSENTIAL QUESTION

How can you use tables, graphs, and equations to represent linear nonproportional situations?

EXPLORE ACTIVITY (Real World)   COMMON CORE Prep for 8.F.3

Representing Linear Relationships Using Tables

You can use an equation to describe the relationship between two quantities in a real-world situation. You can use a table to show some values that make the equation true.

EXAMPLE 1 The equation $y = 3x + 2$ gives the total charge, y, for one person to rent a pair of shoes and bowl x games at Baxter Bowling Lanes based on the prices shown. Make a table of values for this situation.

STEP 1 Choose several values for x that make sense in context. Count by ones.

x (number of games)	1	2		
y (total cost in dollars)				

STEP 2 Use the equation $y = 3x + 2$ to find y for each value of x.

x (number of games)	1	2		
y (total cost in dollars)	5			

Substitute 1 for x
$y = 3(1) + 2 = 5$

YOUR TURN

1. Francisco makes $12 per hour doing part-time work on Saturdays. He spends $4 on transportation to and from work. The equation $y = 12x - 4$ gives his earnings y, after transportation costs, for working x hours. Make a table of values for this situation.

x (number of hours)				
y (earnings in dollars)				

Personal Math Trainer
Online Assessment and Intervention
my.hrw.com

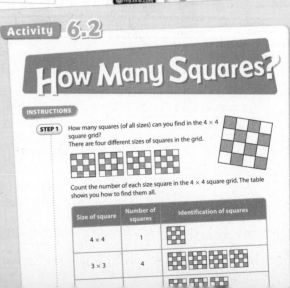

Activity 6.2

How Many Squares?

INSTRUCTIONS

STEP 1 How many squares (of all sizes) can you find in the 4 × 4 square grid?
There are four different sizes of squares in the grid.

Count the number of each size square in the 4 × 4 square grid. The table shows you how to find them all.

Size of square	Number of squares	Identification of squares
4 × 4	1	
3 × 3	4	

Are YOU Ready?

Complete these exercises to review skills you will need for this module.

Personal Math Trainer
Online Assessment and Intervention
my.hrw.com

Evaluate Expressions

EXAMPLE Evaluate $3x - 5$ for $x = -2$.

$3x - 5 = 3(-2) - 5$ Substitute the given value of x for x.

$= -6 - 5$ Multiply.

$= -11$ Subtract.

Evaluate each expression for the given value of x.

1. $2x + 3$ for $x = 3$ _____
2. $-4x + 7$ for $x = -1$ _____
3. $1.5x - 2.5$ for $x = 3$ _____
4. $0.4x + 6.1$ for $x = -5$ _____
5. $\frac{2}{3}x - 12$ for $x = 18$ _____
6. $-\frac{5}{8}x + 10$ for $x = -8$ _____

Connect Words and Equations

EXAMPLE Erik's earnings equal 9 dollars per hour.   Define the variables used in the situation.

$e = $ earnings; $h = $ hours   Identify the operation involved. "Per" indicates multiplication.

multiplication

$e = 9 \times h$ Write the equation.

Define the variables for each situation. Then write an equation.

7. Jana's age plus 5 equals her sister's age.

8. Andrew's class has 3 more students than Lauren's class.

9. The bank is 50 feet shorter than the firehouse.

10. The pencils were divided into 6 groups of 2.

150 Unit 2

Reading Start-Up

Visualize Vocabulary

Use the ✔ words to complete the graphic organizer. You will put one word in each oval.

Types of Quadrilaterals

A quadrilateral in which all sides are congruent and opposite sides are parallel.

A quadrilateral in which opposite sides are parallel and congruent.

A quadrilateral in which at least two sides are parallel.

Vocabulary

Review Words
coordinate plane (plano cartesiano)
✔ parallelogram (paralelogramo)
quadrilateral (cuadrilátero)
✔ rhombus (rombo)
✔ trapezoid (trapecio)

Preview Words
center of rotation (centro de rotación)
congruent (congruente)
image (imagen)
line of reflection (línea de reflexión)
preimage (imagen original)
reflection (reflexión)
rotation (rotación)
transformation (transformación)
translation (traslación)

Understand Vocabulary

Match the term on the left to the correct expression on the right.

1. transformation   A. A function that describes a change in the position, size, or shape of a figure.

2. reflection   B. A function that slides a figure along a straight line.

3. translation   C. A transformation that flips a figure across a line.

Active Reading

Booklet Before beginning the module, create a booklet to help you learn the concepts in this module. Write the main idea of each lesson on each page of the booklet. As you study each lesson, write important details that support the main idea, such as vocabulary and formulas. Refer to your finished booklet as you work on assignments and study for tests.

MODULE QUIZ

Ready to Go On?

Personal Math Trainer
Online Assessment and Intervention
my.hrw.com

6.1 Identifying and Representing Functions

Determine whether each relationship is a function.

1.
x	y
2	0
5	1
8	2
	3

2.
Input, x	Output, y
−1	6
3	5
6	5

3. $(2, 5), (7, 2), (-3, 4), (2, 9), (1, 1)$

6.2 Describing Functions

Determine whether each situation is linear or nonlinear, and proportional or nonproportional.

4. Joanna is paid $14 per hour.

5. Alberto started out bench pressing 50 pounds. He then added 5 pounds every week.

6.3 Comparing Functions

6. Which function is changing more quickly? Explain.

Function 1

Function 2	
Input, x	Output, y
2	11
3	6.5
4	2

6.4 Analyzing Graphs

7. Describe a graph that shows Sam running at a constant rate.

? ESSENTIAL QUESTION

8. How can you use functions to solve real-world problems?

Module 6 179

Unit 5 Performance Tasks

1. **CAREERS IN MATH** Hydrologist A hydrologist needs to estimate the mass of water in an underground aquifer, which is roughly cylindrical in shape. The diameter of the aquifer is 65 meters, and its depth is 8 meters. One cubic meter of water has a mass of about 1000 kilograms.

   a. The aquifer is completely filled with water. What is the total mass of the water in the aquifer? Explain how you found your answer. Use 3.14 for π and round your answer to the nearest kilogram.

   b. Another cylindrical aquifer has a diameter of 70 meters and a depth of 9 meters. The mass of the water in it is 27×10^7 kilograms. Is the aquifer totally filled with water? Explain your reasoning.

2. From his home, Myles walked his dog north 5 blocks, east 2 blocks, and then stopped at a drinking fountain. He then walked north 3 more blocks and east 4 more blocks. It started to rain so he cut through a field and walked straight home.

   a. Draw a diagram of his path.

   b. How many blocks did Myles walk in all? How much longer was his walk before it started to rain than his walk home?

© Houghton Mifflin Harcourt Publishing Company

CC11

GO DIGITAL

my.hrw.com

Enhance Your Learning!

Interactive Student Editions provide additional multimedia resources to enhance your learning. You can enter in answers, watch videos, explore concepts with virtual manipulatives, and get homework help!

 Real-World Videos show you how specific math topics can be used in all kinds of situations.

 Math On the Spot video tutorials provide step-by-step instruction of the math concepts covered in each example.

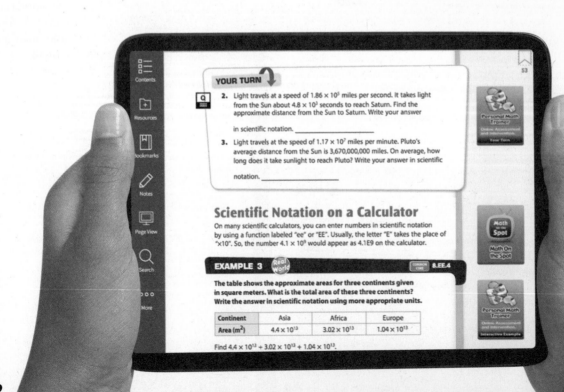

YOUR TURN

2. Light travels at a speed of 1.86×10^5 miles per second. It takes light from the Sun about 4.8×10^3 seconds to reach Saturn. Find the approximate distance from the Sun to Saturn. Write your answer in scientific notation. _____

3. Light travels at the speed of 1.17×10^7 miles per minute. Pluto's average distance from the Sun is 3,670,000,000 miles. On average, how long does it take sunlight to reach Pluto? Write your answer in scientific notation. _____

Scientific Notation on a Calculator

On many scientific calculators, you can enter numbers in scientific notation by using a function labeled "ee" or "EE". Usually, the letter "E" takes the place of "×10". So, the number 4.1×10^9 would appear as 4.1E9 on the calculator.

EXAMPLE 3 Real World   COMMON CORE **8.EE.4**

The table shows the approximate areas for three continents given in square meters. What is the total area of these three continents? Write the answer in scientific notation using more appropriate units.

Continent	Asia	Africa	Europe
Area (m²)	4.4×10^{13}	3.02×10^{13}	1.04×10^{13}

Find $4.4 \times 10^{13} + 3.02 \times 10^{13} + 1.04 \times 10^{13}$.

CC12

© Houghton Mifflin Harcourt Publishing Company • Image Credits: (smartphone) ©Scanrail/Fotolia.

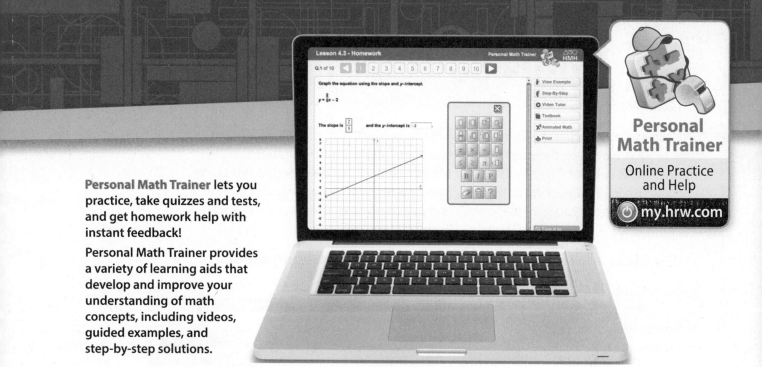

Personal Math Trainer lets you practice, take quizzes and tests, and get homework help with instant feedback!

Personal Math Trainer provides a variety of learning aids that develop and improve your understanding of math concepts, including videos, guided examples, and step-by-step solutions.

Personal Math Trainer
Online Practice and Help
my.hrw.com

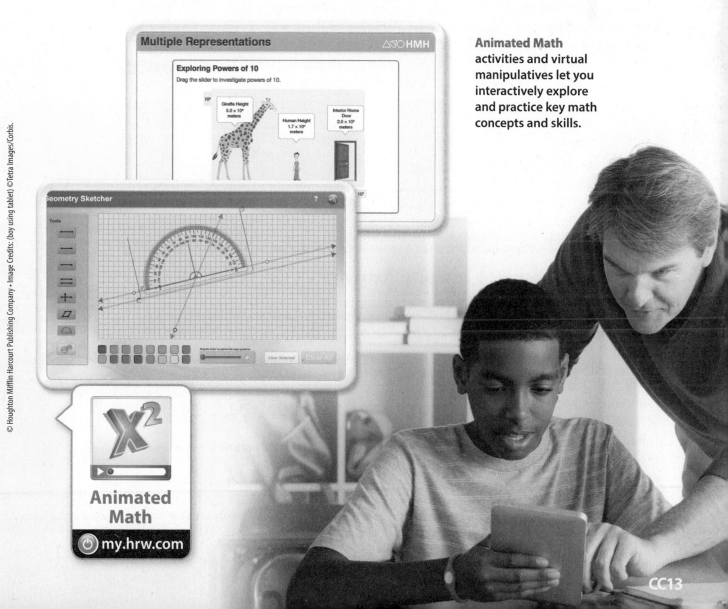

Animated Math activities and virtual manipulatives let you interactively explore and practice key math concepts and skills.

Animated Math
my.hrw.com

Standards for Mathematical Practice

The topics described in the Standards for Mathematical Content will vary from year to year. However, the *way* in which you learn, study, and think about mathematics will not. The Standards for Mathematical Practice describe skills that you will use in all of your math courses. These pages show some features of your book that will help you gain these skills and use them to master this year's topics.

MP.1 Make sense of problems and persevere in solving them.

Mathematically proficient students start by explaining to themselves the meaning of a problem… They analyze givens, constraints, relationships, and goals. They make conjectures about the form… of the solution and plan a solution pathway…

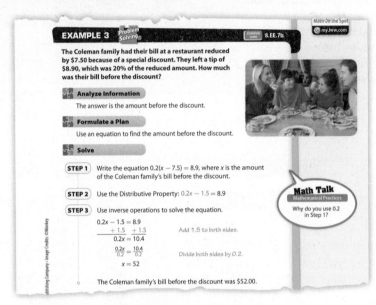

EXAMPLE 3 Problem Solving   COMMON CORE 8.EE.7b   Math On the Spot my.hrw.com

The Coleman family had their bill at a restaurant reduced by $7.50 because of a special discount. They left a tip of $8.90, which was 20% of the reduced amount. How much was their bill before the discount?

Analyze Information

The answer is the amount before the discount.

Formulate a Plan

Use an equation to find the amount before the discount.

Solve

STEP 1 Write the equation $0.2(x - 7.5) = 8.9$, where x is the amount of the Coleman family's bill before the discount.

STEP 2 Use the Distributive Property: $0.2x - 1.5 = 8.9$

STEP 3 Use inverse operations to solve the equation.

$$0.2x - 1.5 = 8.9$$
$$\underline{+ 1.5 \quad + 1.5} \qquad \text{Add 1.5 to both sides.}$$
$$0.2x = 10.4$$
$$\frac{0.2x}{0.2} = \frac{10.4}{0.2} \qquad \text{Divide both sides by 0.2.}$$
$$x = 52$$

The Coleman family's bill before the discount was $52.00.

Math Talk Mathematical Practices — Why do you use 0.2 in Step 1?

Problem-solving examples and exercises lead students through problem solving steps.

MP.2 Reason abstractly and quantitatively.

Mathematically proficient students… bring two complementary abilities to bear on problems…: the ability to decontextualize— to abstract a given situation and represent it symbolically… and the ability to contextualize, to pause… in order to probe into the referents for the symbols involved.

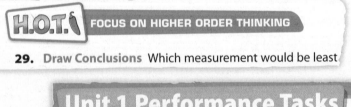

H.O.T. FOCUS ON HIGHER ORDER THINKING

29. **Draw Conclusions** Which measurement would be least

Unit 1 Performance Tasks

1. **CAREERS IN MATH** Astronomer An astro

Focus on Higher Order Thinking exercises in every lesson and **Performance Tasks** in every unit require you to use logical reasoning, represent situations symbolically, use mathematical models to solve problems, and state your answers in terms of a problem context.

MP.3   Construct viable arguments and critique the reasoning of others.

Mathematically proficient students... justify their conclusions, [and]... distinguish correct... reasoning from that which is flawed.

Reflect

2.   **Make a Conjecture**   Use your results from parts **E**, **H**, and
a conjecture about translations.

? **ESSENTIAL QUESTION CHECK-IN**

Essential Question Check-in and **Reflect** in every lesson ask you to evaluate statements, explain relationships, apply mathematical principles, make conjectures, construct arguments, and justify your reasoning.

MP.4   Model with mathematics.

Mathematically proficient students can apply... mathematics... to... problems... in everyday life, society, and the workplace.

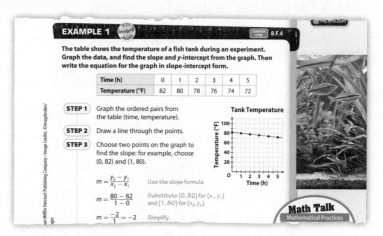

Real-world examples and **mathematical modeling** apply mathematics to other disciplines and real-world contexts such as science and business.

MP.5   Use appropriate tools strategically.

Mathematically proficient students consider the available tools when solving a... problem... [and] are... able to use technological tools to explore and deepen their understanding...

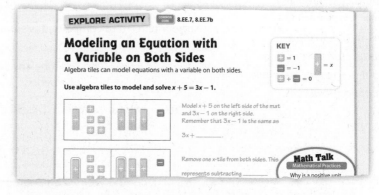

Exploration Activities in lessons use concrete and technological tools, such as manipulatives or graphing calculators, to explore mathematical concepts.

MP.6 Attend to precision.

Mathematically proficient students... communicate precisely... with others and in their own reasoning... [They] give carefully formulated explanations...

19. Communicate Mathematical Ideas Explain how you can fir height of a cylinder if you know the diameter and the volum an example with your explana

Key Vocabulary

slope *(pendiente)*
A measure of the steepness of a line on a graph; the rise divided by the run.

Precision refers not only to the correctness of calculations but also to the proper use of mathematical language and symbols. **Communicate Mathematical Ideas** exercises and **Key Vocabulary** highlighted for each module and unit help you learn and use the language of math to communicate mathematics precisely.

MP.7 Look for and make use of structure.

Mathematically proficient students... look closely to discern a pattern or structure... They can also step back for an overview and shift perspectives.

Follow the steps to informally prove the Triangle Sum Theorem. You should draw each step on your own paper. The figures below are provided for you to check your work.

A Draw a triangle and label the angles as $\angle 1$, $\angle 2$, and $\angle 3$ as shown.

B Draw line a through the base of the triangle.

C The Parallel Postulate states that through a point not on a line ℓ, there is exactly one line parallel to line ℓ. Draw line b parallel to line a, through the vertex opposite the base of the triangle.

D Extend each of the non-base sides of the triangle to form transversal s and transversal t. Transversals s and t intersect parallel lines a and b.

E Label the angles formed by line b and the transversals as $\angle 4$ and $\angle 5$.

F Because $\angle 4$ and _____ are alternate interior

Throughout the lessons, you will observe regularity in mathematical structures in order to make generalizations and make connections between related problems. For example, you can apply your knowledge of geometric theorems to determine when an auxiliary line would be helpful.

MP.8 Look for and express regularity in repeated reasoning.

Mathematically proficient students... look both for general methods and for shortcuts... [and] maintain oversight of the process, while attending to the details.

Use your pattern to complete this equation: $(7^2)^4 = 7^{\boxed{}}$.

B Describe any patterns you see. Use your pattern to of 1 pencil.

20. Look for a Pattern Describe the pattern in the equation. The equation.

$$0.3x + 0.03x + 0.003x + 0.0003x + \ldots = 3$$

You will look for repeated calculations and mathematical patterns in examples and exercises. Recognizing patterns can help you make generalizations and obtain a better understanding of the underlying mathematics.

COMMON CORE

GRADE 7 PART 1

Review Test

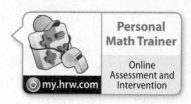

Personal
Math Trainer

Online
Assessment and
Intervention

my.hrw.com

Selected Response

1. Evaluate $a + b$ for $a = 34$ and $b = -6$.

 (A) 28   (C) -28

 (B) 40   (D) -40

2. A triangle has sides with lengths of $5x - 7$, $3x - 4$, and $2x - 6$. What is the perimeter of the triangle?

 (A) $10x - 17$ (C) $4x - 9$

 (B) $6x - 17$ (D) $-7x$

3. Which of the following ratios does *not* form a proportion?

 (A) $\frac{28}{49} \overset{?}{=} \frac{4}{7}$ (C) $\frac{4}{7} \overset{?}{=} \frac{16}{35}$

 (B) $\frac{4}{7} \overset{?}{=} \frac{16}{28}$ (D) $\frac{4}{7} \overset{?}{=} \frac{20}{35}$

4. For a sale, a store decreases its prices on all items by 25%. An item that cost $120 before the sale now costs $120 − 0.25($120). What is another expression for the sale price?

 (A) $120 − 25   (C) 0.25($120)

 (B) 0.75($120)   (D) $120 − 75

5. Write an equation that models the situation and find its solution.

It's going to be Lindsay's birthday soon, and her friends Mary, Mikhail, Anne, Kim, Makoto, and Isabel have contributed equal amounts of money to buy her a present. They have $36.00 to spend between them. Determine how much each contributed.

 (A) $6x = \$36.00$;   (C) $6x = \$36.00$;
    $x = \$108.00$ $x = \$216.00$

 (B) $7x = \$36.00$;   (D) $6x = \$36.00$
    $x = \$5.14$ $x = \$6.00$

6. Solve $4(a + 4) - 2 = 34$.

 (A) $a = -5$ (C) $a = 5$

 (B) $a = 8$ (D) $a = -8$

7. Four sisters bought a present for their father. They received a 10% discount on the original price of the gift. After the discount was taken, each sister paid $9.00. What was the original price of the gift?

 (A) $40.00   (C) $16.00

 (B) $36.00   (D) $32.73

8. Justin is redoing his bathroom floor with tiles measuring 6 in. by 13 in. The floor has an area of 8,500 in². What is the least number of tiles he will need?

 (A) 448 tiles   (C) 109 tiles

 (B) 108.97 tiles   (D) 108 tiles

9. One winter day, the temperature ranged from a high of 20 °F to a low of −25 °F. By how many degrees did the temperature change?

 (A) -5 °F   (C) -15 °F

 (B) 55 °F   (D) 45 °F

10. Terry drove 310 miles in 5 hours at a constant speed. How long would it take him to drive 403 miles at the same speed?

 (A) 3 hours   (C) 7 hours

 (B) 6.5 hours   (D) 62 hours

11. 128 is 74% of what number? If necessary, round your answer to the nearest hundredth.

 (A) 0.58   (C) 1.73

 (B) 94.72   (D) 172.97

12. Tell whether the data show a direct variation. If so, identify the constant of variation.

Number of Baskets	Cost
5	$15
7	$21
9	$27
13	$39
15	$45

Ⓐ direct variation; $k = \frac{1}{3}$

Ⓑ not a direct variation

Ⓒ direct variation; $k = 3$

Ⓓ direct variation; $k = 10$

13. The graph shows the distance Jamie walks over time. Does she walk at a constant or variable speed? How fast is Jamie walking?

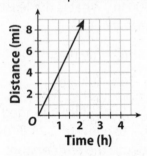

Ⓐ variable speed; 8 mi/h

Ⓑ constant speed; 4 mi/h

Ⓒ constant speed; 2 mi/h

Ⓓ constant speed; 8 mi/h

14. Darryl is reading a book at the rate of 4.5 pages per minute. What ordered pair on a graph of his reading rate would represent the number of minutes it would take him to read 90 pages?

Ⓐ (20, 90)

Ⓑ (4.5, 20)

Ⓒ (90, 4.5)

Ⓓ (4.5, 90)

Mini-Tasks

15. The water level in a plastic pool changed by −8 gallons each hour due to a small hole in the bottom. After 6 hours, the pool contained 132 gallons. How much water was in the pool originally?

_____

16. The ratio of adults to children attending a new exhibit at the museum was found to be 8:5. Based on this ratio, if 390 people attended one day, how many would be children?

_____

Performance Task

17. The graph shows the relationship between the total cost and the number of pounds of rice purchased.

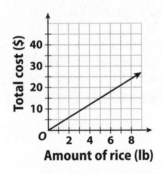

Part A: What does (6, 18) represent?

_____

Part B: Which point represents the unit price?

_____

Part C: How many pounds would you have to buy for the total to be $12? Explain how to find the answer.

_____

_____

COMMON CORE

GRADE 7 PART 2

Review Test

Personal Math Trainer

Online Assessment and Intervention

my.hrw.com

Selected Response

1. What are the actual dimensions of the Check-out Area?

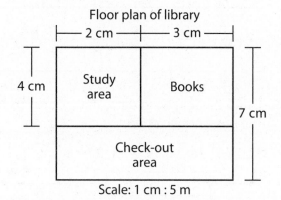

Floor plan of library

|← 2 cm →|← 3 cm →|

Study area

Books

4 cm

7 cm

Check-out area

Scale: 1 cm : 5 m

Ⓐ 25 m × 15 m Ⓒ 15 m × 35 m

Ⓑ 15 m × 20 m Ⓓ 2 m × 4 m

2. For a history fair, a school is building a circular wooden stage that will stand 2 feet off the ground. Find the area of the stage if the radius of the stage is 19 feet. Use 3.14 for π.

Ⓐ 1,133.54 ft² Ⓒ 2,267.08 ft²

Ⓑ 119.32 ft² Ⓓ 4534.16 ft²

3. Find the area of the circle to the nearest tenth. Use 3.14 for π.

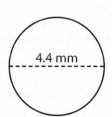

4.4 mm

Ⓐ 47.7 mm² Ⓒ 60.8 mm²

Ⓑ 15.2 mm² Ⓓ 13.8 mm²

4. What is the solution of the inequality $-0.4x - 1.2 > 0.8$?

Ⓐ $x < -5$ Ⓒ $x < -0.8$

Ⓑ $x < -1$ Ⓓ $x > 5$

5. Find m∠LMN.

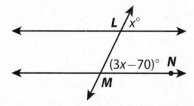

L $x°$

$(3x-70)°$ N

M

Ⓐ m∠LMN = 40° Ⓒ m∠LMN = 35°

Ⓑ m∠LMN = 45° Ⓓ m∠LMN = 50°

6. Ralph is an electrician. He charges an initial fee of $32, plus $33 per hour. If Ralph earned $197 on a job, how long did the job take?

Ⓐ 5.1 hours Ⓒ 5 hours

Ⓑ 132 hours Ⓓ 4 hours

7. Find the volume of the cylinder. Use 3.14 for π. Round your answer to the nearest tenth.

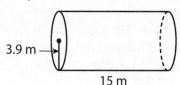

3.9 m

15 m

Ⓐ 183.7 m³ Ⓒ 2,865.6 m³

Ⓑ 716.4 m³ Ⓓ 2,755.4 m³

8. Which is the least valid way to simulate how many boys and girls are in a random sample of 20 students from a school population that is half boys and half girls?

Ⓐ Flip a coin 20 times, assigning one outcome to boys and the other to girls.

Ⓑ Drop 20 coins at once and count the number of each outcome.

Ⓒ Count how many boys and girls are in your math class and use a proportion.

Ⓓ Have a calculator generate 20 random integers and count the number of even and odd integers.

© Houghton Mifflin Harcourt Publishing Company

9. Roberto plays on the school baseball team. In the last 9 games, Roberto was at bat 32 times and got 11 hits. What is the experimental probability that Roberto will get a hit during his next time at bat? Express your answer as a fraction in simplest form.

Ⓐ $\frac{32}{11}$ Ⓒ $\frac{21}{32}$

Ⓑ $\frac{11}{32}$ Ⓓ $\frac{11}{21}$

10. A coin-operated machine sells plastic rings. It contains 14 pink rings, 10 green rings, 9 purple rings, and 13 black rings. Sarah puts a coin into the machine. Find the theoretical probability she gets a pink ring. Express your answer as a decimal. If necessary, round your answer to the nearest thousandth.

Ⓐ 3.286   Ⓒ 4.6

Ⓑ 0.304   Ⓓ 0.217

11. A manufacturer inspects a sample of 400 personal video players and finds that 399 of them have no defects. The manufacturer sent a shipment of 2000 video players to a distributor. Predict the number of players in the shipment that are likely to have no defects.

Ⓐ 5   Ⓒ 399

Ⓑ 1995   Ⓓ 1950

12. An experiment consists of rolling two fair number cubes. What is the probability that the sum of the two numbers will be 8? Express your answer as a fraction in simplest form.

Ⓐ $\frac{5}{36}$ Ⓒ $\frac{36}{5}$

Ⓑ $\frac{1}{9}$ Ⓓ $\frac{31}{36}$

Mini-Tasks

13. A map of Australia has a scale of 1 cm : 110 km. If the distance between Darwin and Alice Springs is 1444 kilometers, how far apart are they on the map, to the nearest tenth of a centimeter?

_____

14. The student council president wants to find out the opinion of the students on the issue of school lunch options. The president sends out a survey to a random sample of students in the school. What type of sample is this? Explain.

_____

_____

_____

_____

15. Using the following data, state the errors in the box-and-whisker plot.

33, 27, 6, 34, 31, 59, 26, 1, 30

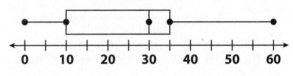

_____

_____

Performance Task

16. The number of goals scored by a hockey team in each of its first 10 games is 2, 4, 0, 3, 4, 1, 3, 1, 1, and 5.

a. Find the mean number of goals scored.

_____

b. Find the mean absolute deviation (MAD) of the number of goals scored.

_____

c. A second team in the same division scores a mean of 4.5 goals in its first 10 games, with the same MAD as the team above. Compare the difference in the teams' mean number of goals with the MAD in the number of goals scored.

_____

COMMON CORE

GRADE 8 PART 1

Benchmark Test

Personal Math Trainer

Online Assessment and Intervention

my.hrw.com

Selected Response

1. Multiply. Write the product as one power.
   $a^8 \cdot a^5$

   (A) a^{13} (C) a^{40}

   (B) a^3 (D) Cannot combine

2. Simplify $(6^{-4})^6$.

   (A) -24^6 (C) 6^2

   (B) $\frac{1}{6^{24}}$ (D) $\frac{1}{6^{10}}$

3. A square mosaic is made of small glass squares. If there are 196 small squares in the mosaic, how many are along an edge?

   (A) 98 squares   (C) 14 squares

   (B) 49 squares   (D) 16 squares

4. Simplify $2\sqrt{-19 + 44}$.

   (A) 13.3   (C) 10

   (B) 44   (D) 27

5. A passenger plane travels at about 7.97×10^2 feet per second. The plane takes 1.11×10^4 seconds to reach its destination.

   About how far must the plane travel to reach its destination? Write your answer in scientific notation.

   (A) 8.85×10^8 feet   (C) 8.85×10^6 feet

   (B) 9.08×10^6 feet   (D) 9.08×10^8 feet

6. Approximate $\sqrt{158}$ to the nearest hundredth.

   (A) 12.57   (C) 16.57

   (B) 16.62   (D) 8.52

7. Write a rule for the linear function.

x	y
−3	12
−2	10
3	0
5	−4

   (A) $y = -2x - 6$ (C) $y = \frac{1}{2}x + 6$

   (B) $y = -2x + 6$ (D) $y = \frac{1}{2}x - 6$

8. A remote-control airplane descends at a rate of 2 feet per second. After 3 seconds it is 67 feet above the ground. Write the equation in point-slope form that models the situation. Then, find the height of the plane after 8 seconds.

   (A) $y - 67 = -2(x - 3)$; 57 feet

   (B) $y - 67 = -3(x - 2)$; 49 feet

   (C) $y - 3 = -2(x - 67)$; 121 feet

   (D) $y - 2 = 67(x - 3)$; 337 feet

9. A bicyclist heads east at 19 km/h. After she has traveled 24.2 kilometers, another cyclist sets out in the same direction going 30 km/h. About how long will it take the second cyclist to catch up to the first cyclist?

   (A) It will take the second cyclist 3.2 hours to catch up to the first cyclist.

   (B) It will take the second cyclist 3.7 hours to catch up to the first cyclist.

   (C) It will take the second cyclist 2.2 hours to catch up to the first cyclist.

   (D) It will take the second cyclist 1.7 hours to catch up to the first cyclist.

© Houghton Mifflin Harcourt Publishing Company

10. What is the equation of the graph in slope-intercept form?

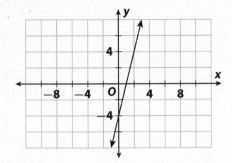

Ⓐ $y = -4x - 4$ 　Ⓒ $y = -5x - 4$

Ⓑ $y = 4x - 4$ 　Ⓓ $y = 5x - 4$

11. Solve $-2z + 3 + 7z = -12$.

Ⓐ $z = -3$ 　Ⓒ $z = 1$

Ⓑ $z = -15$ 　Ⓓ $z = -1.8$

12. Which equation has only one solution?

Ⓐ $c + 2 = c + 2$ 　Ⓒ $c + 2 = c - 2$

Ⓑ $c = -c + 2$ 　Ⓓ $c - c = 2$

13. Which ordered pair is a solution of the system of equations?

$y = 3x + 1$
$y = 5x - 1$

Ⓐ $(2, 3)$ 　Ⓒ $(1, 2)$

Ⓑ $(0, 1)$ 　Ⓓ $(1, 4)$

14. Which of these functions is *not* linear?

Ⓐ $y = x^2 - x$ 　Ⓒ $y = \frac{x}{3}$

Ⓑ $y = 1 - x$ 　Ⓓ $y = \frac{2}{3}x - 2x$

15. Which function has the greatest rate of change?

Ⓐ $y = -5x$

Ⓑ $\{(-1, -2), (1, 2), (3, 6), (5, 10), (7, 14)\}$

Ⓒ A fitness club charges a $200 membership fee plus monthly fees of $25.

Ⓓ $y = 3x - 16$

Mini-Tasks

16. The graph below shows an airplane's speed over a period of time. Describe the events.

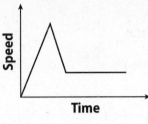

_____

_____

_____

_____

17. Identify $\sqrt{\frac{169}{64}}$ as *rational* or *irrational*. Explain your reasoning.

_____

Performance Task

18. Ashley reads 2 pages/minute for 10 minutes, takes a 10 minute break, and then reads at the same rate for 10 more minutes. Adam reads at the same rate the entire time. The equation for the number of pages he reads is $y = 1.2x$. How are these functions similar? How are they different?

_____

_____

_____

_____

_____

_____

_____

Selected Response

1. In the gift shop of the History of Flight museum, Elisa bought a kit to make a model of a jet airplane. The actual plane is 21 feet long with a wingspan of 17.5 feet. If the finished model will be 12 inches long, what will the wingspan be?

(A) 30.6 in.

(C) 14.4 in.

(B) 10 in.

(D) 5 in.

2. Find the angle measures in the isosceles triangle.

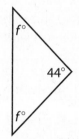

(A) $f = 18°$

(C) $f = 68°$

(B) $f = 118°$

(D) $f = 11.7°$

3. Which ordered pair is a solution of the system of equations?
$y = 3x - 1$
$y = 5x + 1$

(A) (4, 1)

(C) (−4, −1)

(B) (1, 4)

(D) (−1, −4)

4. Melanie is making a piece of jewelry that is in the shape of a right triangle. The two shorter sides of the piece of jewelry are 9 mm and 12 mm. Find the perimeter of the piece of jewelry.

(A) 32 mm

(C) 30 mm

(B) 36 mm

(D) 34 mm

5. Find the distance, to the nearest tenth, from $T(4, -2)$ to $U(-2, 3)$.

(A) −1.0 units

(C) 0.0 units

(B) 3.4 units

(D) 7.8 units

6. Which of the following is *not* a congruence transformation?

(A) A reflection over the *x*-axis.

(B) A dilation with scale factor 0.5.

(C) A translation 1 unit left.

(D) A dilation with scale factor 1.

7. Harry and Selma start driving from the same location. Harry drives 42 miles north while Selma drives 144 miles east. How far apart are Harry and Selma when they stop?

(A) 1,764 miles

(C) 22,500 miles

(B) 150 miles

(D) 20,736 miles

8. Which triangle with side lengths given below is a right triangle?

(A) 10, 15, 20

(C) 9, 40, 41

(B) 10, 24, 25

(D) 16, 20, 25

9. Angles *B* and *F* are corresponding angles formed by a transversal intersecting two parallel lines. Angle *B* has a measure of 44°. What is the measure of Angle *F*?

(A) 44°

(C) 90°

(B) 46°

(D) 136°

10. Which transformation below preserves similarity between the preimage and image, but does not preserve congruence?

(A) reflections

(C) translations

(B) rotations

(D) dilations

© Houghton Mifflin Harcourt Publishing Company

11. An artist is creating a large conical sculpture for a park. The cone has a height of 16 m and a diameter of 25 m. Find the volume of the sculpture to the nearest hundredth.

Ⓐ 833.33 m³   Ⓒ 2,616.67 m³

Ⓑ 7,850 m³   Ⓓ 209.33 m³

12. A cylindrical barrel has a radius of 7.6 ft and a height of 10.8 ft. Tripling which dimension(s) will triple the volume of the barrel?

Ⓐ height

Ⓑ radius

Ⓒ both height and radius

Ⓓ neither height nor radius

13. Which linear equation approximates the best fit to the data?

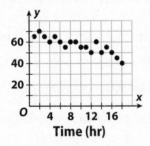

Time (hr)

Ⓐ $y = -2x + 65$ Ⓒ $y = -x + 68$

Ⓑ $y = -5x + 100$ Ⓓ $y = -0.5x + 55$

Mini-Tasks

14. On Monday, a work group eats at Ava's café, where a lunch special is $8 and a dessert is $2. The total is $108. On Friday, the group eats at Bo's café, where a lunch special is $6 and a dessert is $3. The total is $90. Each time, the group orders the same number of lunches and the same number of desserts. How many lunches and desserts are ordered?

_____

15. Dilate the figure by a scale factor of 0.5 with the origin as the center of dilation.

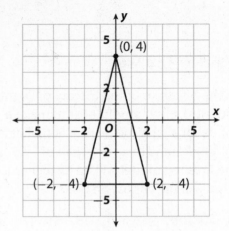

Performance Task

16. In a drought, many trees on a plot of land died. The table shows how many oak trees and pine trees survived or died.

Survived/ Died	Survived	Died	Total
Oak	60	20	80
Pine	72	48	120
Total	0	68	200

a. Create a two-way relative frequency table using decimals.

b. As a percent, what was the joint relative frequency of pine trees that died?

_____

c. Compare the conditional relative frequencies, in percent form, that a tree survived given that it was an oak and that it survived given that it was a pine.

_____

UNIT 1

Real Numbers, Exponents, and Scientific Notation

MODULE 1

Real Numbers

COMMON CORE 8.NS.1, 8.NS.2, 8.EE.2

MODULE 2

Exponents and Scientific Notation

COMMON CORE 8.EE.1, 8.EE.3, 8.EE.4

CAREERS IN MATH

Astronomer An astronomer is a scientist who studies and tries to interpret the universe beyond Earth. Astronomers use math to calculate distances to celestial objects and to create mathematical models to help them understand the dynamics of systems from stars and planets to black holes. If you are interested in a career as an astronomer, you should study the following mathematical subjects:

- Algebra
- Geometry
- Trigonometry
- Calculus

Research other careers that require creating mathematical models to understand physical phenomena.

Unit 1 Performance Task

At the end of the unit, check out how **astronomers** use math.

Use the puzzle to preview key vocabulary from this unit. Unscramble the circled letters to answer the riddle at the bottom of the page.

1. **TCREEFP SEAQUR**

2. **NOLRATAI RUNMEB**

3. **PERTIANEG MALCEDI**

4. **LAER SEBMNUR**

5. **NIISICFTCE OITANTON**

1. Has integers as its square roots. (Lesson 1.1)
2. Any number that can be written as a ratio of two integers. (Lesson 1.1)
3. A decimal in which one or more digits repeat infinitely. (Lesson 1.1)
4. The set of rational and irrational numbers. (Lesson 1.2)
5. A method of writing very large or very small numbers by using powers of 10. (Lesson 2.2)

Q: What keeps a square from moving?

A: _____ _____!

Real Numbers

ESSENTIAL QUESTION

How can you use real numbers to solve real-world problems?

Real-World Video

Living creatures can be classified into groups. The sea otter belongs to the kingdom Animalia and class Mammalia. Numbers can also be classified into groups such as rational numbers and integers.

my.hrw.com

GO DIGITAL

my.hrw.com

my.hrw.com

Go digital with your write-in student edition, accessible on any device.

Math On the Spot

Scan with your smart phone to jump directly to the online edition, video tutor, and more.

Animated Math

Interactively explore key concepts to see how math works.

Personal Math Trainer

Get immediate feedback and help as you work through practice sets.

Are YOU Ready?

Complete these exercises to review skills you will need for this module.

Find the Square of a Number

EXAMPLE   Find the square of $\frac{2}{3}$.

$\frac{2}{3} \times \frac{2}{3} = \frac{2 \times 2}{3 \times 3}$ Multiply the number by itself.

$= \frac{4}{9}$ Simplify.

Find the square of each number.

1. 7 _____

2. 21 _____

3. −3 _____

4. $\frac{4}{5}$ _____

5. 2.7 _____

6. $-\frac{1}{4}$ _____

7. −5.7 _____

8. $1\frac{2}{5}$ _____

Exponents

EXAMPLE $5^3 = 5 \times 5 \times 5$ Use the base, 5, as a factor 3 times.

$= 25 \times 5$ Multiply from left to right.

$= 125$

Simplify each exponential expression.

9. 9^2 _____

10. 2^4 _____

11. $\left(\frac{1}{3}\right)^2$ _____

12. $(-7)^2$ _____

13. 4^3 _____

14. $(-1)^5$ _____

15. 4.5^2 _____

16. 10^5 _____

Write a Mixed Number as an Improper Fraction

EXAMPLE $2\frac{2}{5} = 2 + \frac{2}{5}$ Write the mixed number as a sum of a whole number and a fraction.

$= \frac{10}{5} + \frac{2}{5}$ Write the whole number as an equivalent fraction with the same denominator as the fraction in the mixed number.

$= \frac{12}{5}$ Add the numerators.

Write each mixed number as an improper fraction.

17. $3\frac{1}{3}$ _____

18. $1\frac{5}{8}$ _____

19. $2\frac{3}{7}$ _____

20. $5\frac{5}{6}$ _____

Reading Start-Up

Visualize Vocabulary

Use the ✔ words to complete the graphic. You can put more than one word in each section of the triangle.

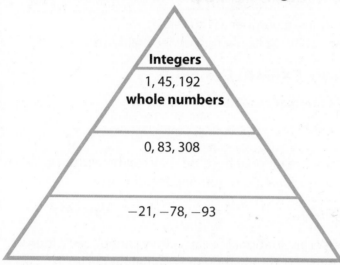

Integers

1, 45, 192
whole numbers

0, 83, 308

−21, −78, −93

Review Words
- integers *(enteros)*
- ✔ negative numbers *(números negativos)*
- ✔ positive numbers *(números positivos)*
- ✔ whole number *(número entero)*

Preview Words
- cube root *(raíz cúbica)*
- irrational numbers *(número irracional)*
- perfect cube *(cubo perfecto)*
- perfect square *(cuadrado perfecto)*
- principal square root *(raíz cuadrada principal)*
- rational number *(número racional)*
- real numbers *(número real)*
- repeating decimal *(decimal periódico)*
- square root *(raíz cuadrada)*
- terminating decimal *(decimal finito)*

Understand Vocabulary

Complete the sentences using the preview words.

1. One of the two equal factors of a number is a _____.

2. A _____ has integers as its square roots.

3. The _____ is the nonnegative square root of a number.

Active Reading

Layered Book Before beginning the lessons in this module, create a layered book to help you learn the concepts in this module. Label the flaps "Rational Numbers," "Irrational Numbers," "Square Roots," and "Real Numbers." As you study each lesson, write important ideas such as vocabulary, models, and sample problems under the appropriate flap.

Unpacking the Standards

Understanding the standards and the vocabulary terms in the standards will help you know exactly what you are expected to learn in this module.

COMMON CORE **8.NS.1**

Know that numbers that are not rational are called irrational. Understand informally that every number has a decimal expansion; for rational numbers show that the decimal expansion repeats eventually, and convert a decimal expansion which repeats eventually into a rational number.

Key Vocabulary

rational number *(número racional)*
A number that can be expressed as a ratio of two integers.

irrational number *(número irracional)*
A number that cannot be expressed as a ratio of two integers or as a repeating or terminating decimal.

What It Means to You

You will recognize a number as rational or irrational by looking at its fraction or decimal form.

UNPACKING EXAMPLE 8.NS.1

Classify each number as rational or irrational.

$$0.\overline{3} = \frac{1}{3} \qquad\qquad 0.25 = \frac{1}{4}$$

These numbers are rational because they can be written as ratios of integers or as repeating or terminating decimals.

$$\pi \approx 3.141592654\ldots \qquad\qquad \sqrt{5} \approx 2.236067977\ldots$$

These numbers are irrational because they cannot be written as ratios of integers or as repeating or terminating decimals.

COMMON CORE **8.NS.2**

Use rational approximations of irrational numbers to compare the size of irrational numbers, locate them approximately on a number line diagram, and estimate the value of expressions (e.g., π^2).

Visit **my.hrw.com** to see all the **Common Core Standards** unpacked.

my.hrw.com

What It Means to You

You will learn to estimate the values of irrational numbers.

UNPACKING EXAMPLE 8.NS.2

Estimate the value of $\sqrt{8}$.

8 is not a perfect square. Find the two perfect squares closest to 8.

8 is between the perfect squares 4 and 9.
So $\sqrt{8}$ is between $\sqrt{4}$ and $\sqrt{9}$.
   $\sqrt{8}$ is between 2 and 3.

8 is close to 9, so $\sqrt{8}$ is close to 3.
$2.8^2 = 7.84 \qquad 2.85^2 = 8.1225 \qquad 2.9^2 = 8.41$
$\sqrt{8}$ is between 2.8 and 2.9, but closer to 2.8.
A good estimate for $\sqrt{8}$ is 2.8.

LESSON 1.1 Rational and Irrational Numbers

COMMON CORE 8.NS.1
Know that numbers that are not rational are called irrational. Understand informally that every number has a decimal expansion; ... *Also 8.NS.2, 8.EE.2*

 ESSENTIAL QUESTION

How do you rewrite rational numbers and decimals, take square roots and cube roots, and approximate irrational numbers?

EXPLORE ACTIVITY COMMON CORE 8.NS.1

Expressing Rational Numbers as Decimals

Math On the Spot
⊙ my.hrw.com

A **rational number** is any number that can be written as a ratio in the form $\frac{a}{b}$, where a and b are integers and b is not 0. Examples of rational numbers are 6 and 0.5.

6 can be written as $\frac{6}{1}$.   0.5 can be written as $\frac{1}{2}$.

Every rational number can be written as a terminating decimal or a repeating decimal. A **terminating decimal**, such as 0.5, has a finite number of digits. A **repeating decimal** has a block of one or more digits that repeats indefinitely.

EXAMPLE 1 Write each fraction as a decimal.

A $\frac{1}{4}$

The fraction bar is a division symbol.
Divide the numerator by the denominator: $1 \div 4$.

Divide until the remainder is zero, adding zeros after the decimal point in the dividend as needed.

The rational number $\frac{1}{4}$ can be written as a terminating decimal. $\frac{1}{4} = \boxed{}$

$$4\overline{)1.00}$$
$$-\boxed{}$$
$$\overline{20}$$
$$-\boxed{}$$
$$\overline{0}$$

B $\frac{1}{3}$

Divide the numerator by the denominator: $1 \div 3$.

Divide until the remainder is zero or until the digits in the quotient begin to repeat.

Add zeros after the decimal point in the dividend as needed.

The rational number $\frac{1}{3}$ can be written as a repeating decimal, with a bar over the repeating digit(s). $\frac{1}{3} = \boxed{}$

$$3\overline{)1.000}$$
$$-\boxed{}$$
$$\overline{10}$$
$$-\boxed{}$$
$$\overline{10}$$
$$-\boxed{}$$
$$\overline{1}$$

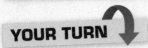

YOUR TURN

Write each fraction as a decimal.

1. $\frac{5}{11}$ _____

2. $\frac{1}{8}$ _____

3. $2\frac{1}{3}$ _____

Math On the Spot

⏻ my.hrw.com

Expressing Decimals as Rational Numbers

You can express terminating and repeating decimals as rational numbers.

EXAMPLE 2

COMMON CORE **8.NS.1**

Write each decimal as a fraction in simplest form.

A 0.825

The decimal 0.825 means "825 thousandths." Write this as a fraction.

$\frac{825}{1000}$ *To write "825 thousandths", put 825 over 1000.*

Then simplify the fraction.

$\frac{825 \div 25}{1000 \div 25} = \frac{33}{40}$ *Divide both the numerator and the denominator by 25.*

$0.825 = \frac{33}{40}$

B $0.\overline{37}$

Let $x = 0.\overline{37}$. The number $0.\overline{37}$ has 2 repeating digits, so multiply each side of the equation $x = 0.\overline{37}$ by 10^2, or 100.

$x = 0.\overline{37}$

$(100)x = 100(0.\overline{37})$

$100x = 37.\overline{37}$ *100 times $0.\overline{37}$ is $37.\overline{37}$.*

Because $x = 0.\overline{37}$, you can subtract x from one side and $0.\overline{37}$ from the other.

$100x = 37.\overline{37}$

$\underline{-x \quad\quad -0.\overline{37}}$

$99x = 37$ *$37.\overline{37}$ minus $0.\overline{37}$ is 37.*

Now solve the equation for x. Simplify if necessary.

$\frac{99x}{99} = \frac{37}{99}$ *Divide both sides of the equation by 99.*

$x = \frac{37}{99}$

YOUR TURN

Write each decimal as a fraction in simplest form.

4. 0.12 _____

5. $0.\overline{57}$ _____

6. 1.4 _____

Finding Square Roots and Cube Roots

The **square root** of a positive number p is x if $x^2 = p$. There are two square roots for every positive number. For example, the square roots of 36 are 6 and -6 because $6^2 = 36$ and $(-6)^2 = 36$. The square roots of $\frac{1}{25}$ are $\frac{1}{5}$ and $-\frac{1}{5}$. You can write the square roots of $\frac{1}{25}$ as $\pm\frac{1}{5}$. The symbol $\sqrt{}$ indicates the positive, or **principal square root**.

A number that is a **perfect square** has square roots that are integers. The number 81 is a perfect square because its square roots are 9 and -9.

The **cube root** of a positive number p is x if $x^3 = p$. There is one cube root for every positive number. For example, the cube root of 8 is 2 because $2^3 = 8$. The cube root of $\frac{1}{27}$ is $\frac{1}{3}$ because $\left(\frac{1}{3}\right)^3 = \frac{1}{27}$. The symbol $\sqrt[3]{}$ indicates the cube root.

A number that is a **perfect cube** has a cube root that is an integer. The number 125 is a perfect cube because its cube root is 5.

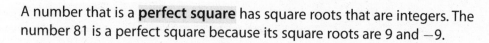

EXAMPLE 3 COMMON CORE 8.EE.2

Solve each equation for x.

A $x^2 = 121$

$x^2 = 121$ *Solve for x by taking the square root of both sides.*

$x = \pm\sqrt{121}$ *Apply the definition of square root.*

$x = \pm 11$ *Think: What numbers squared equal 121?*

The solutions are 11 and -11.

B $x^2 = \frac{16}{169}$

$x^2 = \frac{16}{169}$ *Solve for x by taking the square root of both sides.*

$x = \pm\sqrt{\frac{16}{169}}$ *Apply the definition of square root.*

$x = \pm\frac{4}{13}$ *Think: What numbers squared equal $\frac{16}{169}$?*

The solutions are $\frac{4}{13}$ and $-\frac{4}{13}$.

Math Talk

Mathematical Practices

Can you square an integer and get a negative number? What does this indicate about whether negative numbers have square roots?

C $729 = x^3$

$\sqrt[3]{729} = \sqrt[3]{x^3}$ Solve for x by taking the cube root of both sides.

$\sqrt[3]{729} = x$ Apply the definition of cube root.

$9 = x$ Think: What number cubed equals 729?

The solution is 9.

D $x^3 = \dfrac{8}{125}$

$\sqrt[3]{x^3} = \sqrt[3]{\dfrac{8}{125}}$ Solve for x by taking the cube root of both sides.

$x = \sqrt[3]{\dfrac{8}{125}}$ Apply the definition of cube root.

$x = \dfrac{2}{5}$ Think: What number cubed equals $\dfrac{8}{125}$?

The solution is $\dfrac{2}{5}$.

YOUR TURN

Solve each equation for x.

7. $x^2 = 196$ _____

8. $x^2 = \dfrac{9}{256}$ _____

9. $x^3 = 512$ _____

10. $x^3 = \dfrac{64}{343}$ _____

EXPLORE ACTIVITY 2   **COMMON CORE**   8.NS.2, 8.EE.2

Estimating Irrational Numbers

Irrational numbers are numbers that are not rational. In other words, they cannot be written in the form $\dfrac{a}{b}$, where a and b are integers and b is not 0. Square roots of perfect squares are rational numbers. Square roots of numbers that are not perfect squares are irrational. The number $\sqrt{3}$ is irrational because 3 is not a perfect square of any rational number.

Estimate the value of $\sqrt{2}$.

A   Since 2 is not a perfect square, $\sqrt{2}$ is irrational.

B   To estimate $\sqrt{2}$, first find two consecutive perfect squares that 2 is between. Complete the inequality by writing these perfect squares in the boxes.

$\boxed{} < 2 < \boxed{}$

C   Now take the square root of each number.

$\sqrt{\boxed{}} < \sqrt{2} < \sqrt{\boxed{}}$

D   Simplify the square roots of perfect squares.

$\boxed{} < \sqrt{2} < \boxed{}$

$\sqrt{2}$ is between _____ and _____.

E Estimate that $\sqrt{2} \approx 1.5$.

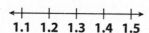

F To find a better estimate, first choose some numbers between 1 and 2 and square them. For example, choose 1.3, 1.4, and 1.5.

$1.3^2 =$ _____ $1.4^2 =$ _____ $1.5^2 =$ _____

Is $\sqrt{2}$ between 1.3 and 1.4? How do you know?

_____

_____

Is $\sqrt{2}$ between 1.4 and 1.5? How do you know?

_____

_____

$\sqrt{2}$ is between _____ and _____, so $\sqrt{2} \approx$ _____.

G Locate and label this value on the number line.

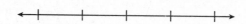

Reflect

11. How could you find an even better estimate of $\sqrt{2}$?

_____

_____

12. Find a better estimate of $\sqrt{2}$. Draw a number line and locate and label your estimate.

$\sqrt{2}$ is between _____ and _____, so $\sqrt{2} \approx$ _____.

13. Estimate the value of $\sqrt{7}$ to two decimal places. Draw a number line and locate and label your estimate.

$\sqrt{7}$ is between _____ and _____, so $\sqrt{7} \approx$ _____.

Write each fraction or mixed number as a decimal. (Explore Activity Example 1)

1. $\frac{2}{5}$ _____

2. $\frac{8}{9}$ _____

3. $3\frac{3}{4}$ _____

4. $\frac{7}{10}$ _____

5. $2\frac{3}{8}$ _____

6. $\frac{5}{6}$ _____

Write each decimal as a fraction or mixed number in simplest form. (Example 2)

7. 0.675 _____

8. 5.6 _____

9. 0.44 _____

10. $0.\overline{4}$

$10x = \boxed{}$

$-x \quad -\boxed{}$

$\boxed{}\, x = \boxed{}$

$x = $ _____

11. $0.\overline{26}$

$100x = \boxed{}$

$-x \quad -\boxed{}$

$\boxed{}\, x = \boxed{}$

$x = $ _____

12. $0.\overline{325}$

$1000x = \boxed{}$

$-x \quad -\boxed{}$

$\boxed{}\, x = \boxed{}$

$x = $ _____

Solve each equation for x. (Example 3)

13. $x^2 = 144$

$x = \pm\sqrt{\boxed{}} = \pm\boxed{}$

14. $x^2 = \frac{25}{289}$

$x = \pm\sqrt{\dfrac{\boxed{}}{\boxed{}}} = \pm\dfrac{\boxed{}}{\boxed{}}$

15. $x^3 = 216$

$x = \sqrt[3]{\boxed{}} = \boxed{}$

Approximate each irrational number to two decimal places without a calculator.
(Explore Activity 2)

16. $\sqrt{5} \approx \boxed{}$

17. $\sqrt{3} \approx \boxed{}$

18. $\sqrt{10} \approx \boxed{}$

? ESSENTIAL QUESTION CHECK-IN

19. What is the difference between rational and irrational numbers?

_____

_____

1.1 Independent Practice

COMMON CORE 8.NS.1, 8.NS.2, 8.EE.2

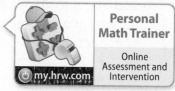

Personal Math Trainer

Online Assessment and Intervention

my.hrw.com

20. A $\frac{7}{16}$-inch-long bolt is used in a machine. What is the length of the bolt written as a decimal?

_____

21. The weight of an object on the moon is $\frac{1}{6}$ its weight on Earth. Write $\frac{1}{6}$ as a decimal.

_____

22. The distance to the nearest gas station is $2\frac{4}{5}$ kilometers. What is this distance written as a decimal?

_____

23. A baseball pitcher has pitched $98\frac{2}{3}$ innings. What is the number of innings written as a decimal?

_____

24. A heartbeat takes 0.8 second. How many seconds is this written as a fraction?

_____

25. There are 26.2 miles in a marathon. Write the number of miles using a fraction.

_____

26. The average score on a biology test was $72.\overline{1}$. Write the average score using a fraction.

_____

27. The metal in a penny is worth about 0.505 cent. How many cents is this written as a fraction?

_____

28. **Multistep** An artist wants to frame a square painting with an area of 400 square inches. She wants to know the length of the wood trim that is needed to go around the painting.

a. If x is the length of one side of the painting, what equation can you set up to find the length of a side? _____

b. Solve the equation you wrote in part a. How many solutions does the equation have?

_____

_____

c. Do all of the solutions that you found in part b make sense in the context of the problem? Explain.

_____

_____

_____

d. What is the length of the wood trim needed to go around the painting?

_____

29. Analyze Relationships To find $\sqrt{15}$, Beau found $3^2 = 9$ and $4^2 = 16$. He said that since 15 is between 9 and 16, $\sqrt{15}$ must be between 3 and 4. He thinks a good estimate for $\sqrt{15}$ is $\frac{3+4}{2} = 3.5$. Is Beau's estimate high, low, or correct? Explain.

_____

_____

_____

30. Justify Reasoning What is a good estimate for the solution to the equation $x^3 = 95$? How did you come up with your estimate?

_____

_____

_____

31. The volume of a sphere is 36π ft^3. What is the radius of the sphere? Use the formula $V = \frac{4}{3}\pi r^3$ to find your answer.

_____

 **FOCUS ON HIGHER ORDER THINKING**

32. Draw Conclusions Can you find the cube root of a negative number? If so, is it positive or negative? Explain your reasoning.

_____

_____

_____

33. Make a Conjecture Evaluate and compare the following expressions.

$$\sqrt{\frac{4}{25}} \text{ and } \frac{\sqrt{4}}{\sqrt{25}} \qquad \sqrt{\frac{16}{81}} \text{ and } \frac{\sqrt{16}}{\sqrt{81}} \qquad \sqrt{\frac{36}{49}} \text{ and } \frac{\sqrt{36}}{\sqrt{49}}$$

Use your results to make a conjecture about a division rule for square roots. Since division is multiplication by the reciprocal, make a conjecture about a multiplication rule for square roots.

_____

_____

34. Persevere in Problem Solving The difference between the solutions to the equation $x^2 = a$ is 30. What is a? Show that your answer is correct.

_____

_____

Work Area

LESSON
1.2 Sets of Real Numbers

COMMON CORE **8.NS.1**
Know that numbers that are not rational are called irrational. . . .

? **ESSENTIAL QUESTION**

How can you describe relationships between sets of real numbers?

EXPLORE ACTIVITY COMMON CORE **8.NS.1**

Classifying Real Numbers

Biologists classify animals based on shared characteristics. A cardinal is an animal, a vertebrate, a bird, and a passerine.

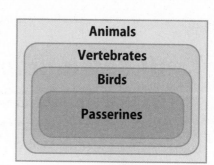

Animals
Vertebrates
Birds
Passerines

You know that the set of rational numbers consists of whole numbers, integers, decimals, and fractions. The set of **real numbers** consists of the set of rational numbers and the set of irrational numbers.

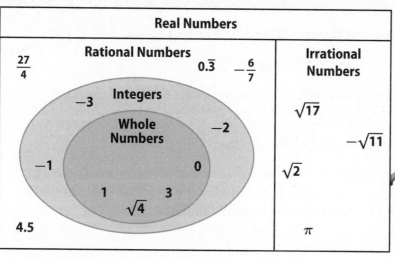

Real Numbers

Rational Numbers $\frac{27}{4}$ $0.\overline{3}$ $-\frac{6}{7}$

Integers -3
Whole Numbers
-1 0 -2
1 3
$\sqrt{4}$
4.5

Irrational Numbers
$\sqrt{17}$
$-\sqrt{11}$
$\sqrt{2}$
π

Passerines, such as the cardinal, are also called "perching birds."

EXAMPLE 1 **Write all the names that apply to each number.**

A $\sqrt{5}$
The number 5 under the square root symbol is a whole number that is not a perfect square.
_____
_____

B -17.84
-17.84 is a terminating decimal.
_____
_____

C $\frac{\sqrt{81}}{9}$
$\frac{\sqrt{81}}{9} = \frac{9}{9} = 1$
_____
_____
_____
_____

X²
Animated Math
my.hrw.com

YOUR TURN

Write all names that apply to each number.

1. A baseball pitcher has pitched $12\frac{2}{3}$ innings.

   _____

2. The length of the side of a square that has an

   area of 10 square yards. _____

Personal Math Trainer

Online Assessment and Intervention

my.hrw.com

Math On the Spot

my.hrw.com

Understanding Sets and Subsets of Real Numbers

By understanding which sets are subsets of types of numbers, you can verify whether statements about the relationships between sets are true or false.

EXAMPLE 2

COMMON CORE 8.NS.1

Tell whether the given statement is true or false. Explain your choice.

A All irrational numbers are real numbers.

True. Every irrational number is included in the set of real numbers. Irrational numbers are a subset of real numbers.

B No rational numbers are whole numbers.

False. A whole number can be written as a fraction with a denominator of 1, so every whole number is included in the set of rational numbers. Whole numbers are a subset of rational numbers.

Math Talk
Mathematical Practices

Give an example of a rational number that is a whole number. Show that the number is both whole and rational.

YOUR TURN

Tell whether the given statement is true or false. Explain your choice.

3. All rational numbers are integers.

   _____

   _____

   _____

4. Some irrational numbers are integers.

   _____

   _____

Personal Math Trainer

Online Assessment and Intervention

my.hrw.com

Identifying Sets for Real-World Situations

Real numbers can be used to represent real-world quantities. Highways have posted speed limit signs that are represented by natural numbers such as 55 mph. Integers appear on thermometers. Rational numbers are used in many daily activities, including cooking. For example, ingredients in a recipe are often given in fractional amounts such as $\frac{2}{3}$ cup flour.

EXAMPLE 3   COMMON CORE 8.NS.1

Identify the set of numbers that best describes each situation. Explain your choice.

A the number of people wearing glasses in a room

The set of whole numbers best describes the situation. The number of people wearing glasses may be 0 or a counting number.

B the circumference of a flying disk has a diameter of 8, 9, 10, 11, or 14 inches

The set of irrational numbers best describes the situation. Each circumference would be a product of π and the diameter, and any multiple of π is irrational.

YOUR TURN

Identify the set of numbers that best describes the situation. Explain your choice.

5. the amount of water in a glass as it evaporates

_____

_____

_____

6. the number of seconds remaining when a song is playing, displayed as a negative number

_____

_____

_____

Personal Math Trainer

Online Assessment and Intervention

my.hrw.com

Write all names that apply to each number. (Explore Activity Example 1)

1. $\frac{7}{8}$

_____

2. $\sqrt{36}$

_____

3. $\sqrt{24}$

_____

4. 0.75

_____

5. 0

_____

6. $-\sqrt{100}$

_____

7. $5.\overline{45}$

_____

8. $-\frac{18}{6}$

_____

Tell whether the given statement is true or false. Explain your choice.
(Example 2)

9. All whole numbers are rational numbers.

_____

_____

10. No irrational numbers are whole numbers.

_____

Identify the set of numbers that best describes each situation. Explain your choice. (Example 3)

11. the change in the value of an account when given to the nearest dollar

_____

_____

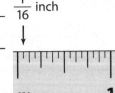

$\frac{1}{16}$ inch

12. the markings on a standard ruler

_____

IN.   1

? ESSENTIAL QUESTION CHECK-IN

13. What are some ways to describe the relationships between sets of numbers?

_____

_____

1.2 Independent Practice

 COMMON CORE **8.NS.1**

Personal Math Trainer

Online Assessment and Intervention

my.hrw.com

Write all names that apply to each number. Then place the numbers in the correct location on the Venn diagram.

14. $\sqrt{9}$ _____

15. 257 _____

16. $\sqrt{50}$ _____

17. $8\frac{1}{2}$ _____

18. 16.6 _____

19. $\sqrt{16}$ _____

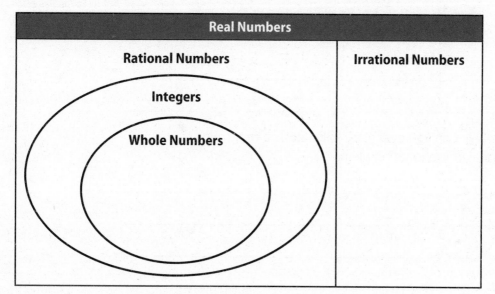

Identify the set of numbers that best describes each situation. Explain your choice.

20. the height of an airplane as it descends to an airport runway

_____

21. the score with respect to par of several golfers: 2, −3, 5, 0, −1

_____

_____

22. **Critique Reasoning** Ronald states that the number $\frac{1}{11}$ is not rational because, when converted into a decimal, it does not terminate. Nathaniel says it is rational because it is a fraction. Which boy is correct? Explain.

_____

_____

23. Critique Reasoning The circumference of a circular region is shown. What type of number best describes the diameter of the circle? Explain your answer. _____

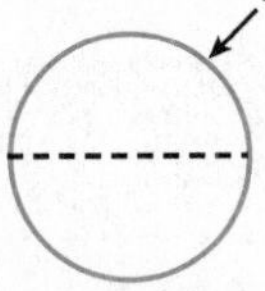

π mi

24. Critical Thinking A number is not an integer. What type of number can it be?

_____

25. A grocery store has a shelf with half-gallon containers of milk. What type of number best represents the total number of gallons?

_____

Work Area

26. Explain the Error Katie said, "Negative numbers are integers." What was her error?

_____

_____

27. Justify Reasoning Can you ever use a calculator to determine if a number is rational or irrational? Explain.

_____

_____

_____

_____

_____

_____

_____

28. Draw Conclusions The decimal $0.\overline{3}$ represents $\frac{1}{3}$. What type of number best describes $0.\overline{9}$, which is $3 \cdot 0.\overline{3}$? Explain.

_____

29. Communicate Mathematical Ideas Irrational numbers can never be precisely represented in decimal form. Why is this?

_____

_____

_____

_____

Ordering Real Numbers

COMMON CORE 8.NS.2
Use rational approximations of irrational numbers to compare the size of irrational numbers, locate them approximately on a number line diagram, and estimate the value of expressions (e.g., π^2).

? **ESSENTIAL QUESTION**

How do you order a set of real numbers?

EXPLORE ACTIVITY **COMMON CORE** 8.NS.2

Comparing Irrational Numbers

Between any two real numbers is another real number. To compare and order real numbers, you can approximate irrational numbers as decimals.

Math On the Spot
my.hrw.com

EXAMPLE 1 Compare $\sqrt{3} + 5$ ◯ $3 + \sqrt{5}$. Write $<$, $>$, or $=$.

STEP 1   Use perfect squares to estimate square roots.

Approximate $\sqrt{3}$. $\sqrt{3}$ is between $\sqrt{1}$ and $\sqrt{4}$, or between ____ and ____.

Approximate $\sqrt{5}$. $\sqrt{5}$ is between $\sqrt{4}$ and $\sqrt{9}$, or between ____ and ____.

STEP 2   Use your estimations to simplify the expressions.

$\sqrt{3} + 5$ is between ☐ $+ 5$ and ☐ $+ 5$, or between ____ and ____.

$3 + \sqrt{5}$ is between $3 +$ ☐ and $3 +$ ☐, or between ____ and ____.

So, $\sqrt{3} + 5$ ◯ $3 + \sqrt{5}$.

Reflect

1. If $7 + \sqrt{5}$ is equal to $\sqrt{5}$ plus a number, what do you know about the number? Why?

   _____

2. What are the closest two integers that $\sqrt{300}$ is between?

   _____

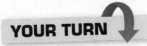 **YOUR TURN**

Compare. Write $<$, $>$, or $=$.

3. $\sqrt{2} + 4$ ◯ $2 + \sqrt{4}$ 4. $\sqrt{12} + 6$ ◯ $12 + \sqrt{6}$

Personal Math Trainer

Online Assessment and Intervention

my.hrw.com

My Notes

Ordering Real Numbers

You can compare and order real numbers and list them from least to greatest.

EXAMPLE 2

COMMON CORE 8.NS.2

Order $\sqrt{22}$, $\pi + 1$, and $4\frac{1}{2}$ from least to greatest.

STEP 1 First approximate $\sqrt{22}$.

$\sqrt{22}$ is between 4 and 5. Since you don't know where it falls between 4 and 5, you need to find a better estimate for $\sqrt{22}$ so you can compare it to $4\frac{1}{2}$.

Since 22 is closer to 25 than 16, use squares of numbers between 4.5 and 5 to find a better estimate of $\sqrt{22}$.

$4.5^2 = 20.25$ $4.6^2 = 21.16$ $4.7^2 = 22.09$ $4.8^2 = 23.04$

Since $4.7^2 = 22.09$, an approximate value for $\sqrt{22}$ is 4.7.

An approximate value of π is 3.14. So an approximate value of $\pi + 1$ is 4.14.

STEP 2 Plot $\sqrt{22}$, $\pi + 1$, and $4\frac{1}{2}$ on a number line.

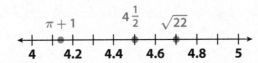

Read the numbers from left to right to place them in order from least to greatest.

From least to greatest, the numbers are $\pi + 1$, $4\frac{1}{2}$, and $\sqrt{22}$.

YOUR TURN

Order the numbers from least to greatest. Then graph them on the number line.

5. $\sqrt{5}$, 2.5, $\sqrt{3}$ _____

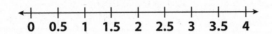

6. π^2, 10, $\sqrt{75}$ _____

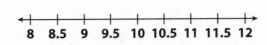

Math Talk

Mathematical Practices

If real numbers a, b, and c are in order from least to greatest, what is the order of their opposites from least to greatest? Explain.

Ordering Real Numbers in a Real-World Context

Calculations and estimations in the real world may differ. It can be important to know not only which are the most accurate but which give the greatest or least values, depending upon the context.

EXAMPLE 3   8.NS.2

Four people have found the distance in kilometers across a canyon using different methods. Their results are given in the table. Order the distances from greatest to least.

Distance Across Quarry Canyon (km)			
Juana	**Lee Ann**	**Ryne**	**Jackson**
$\sqrt{28}$	$\frac{23}{4}$	$5.\overline{5}$	$5\frac{1}{2}$

STEP 1   Write each value as a decimal.

$\sqrt{28}$ is between 5.2 and 5.3. Since $5.3^2 = 28.09$, an approximate value for $\sqrt{28}$ is 5.3.

$\frac{23}{4} = 5.75$

$5.\overline{5}$ is 5.555…, so $5.\overline{5}$ to the nearest hundredth is 5.56.

$5\frac{1}{2} = 5.5$

STEP 2   Plot $\sqrt{28}$, $\frac{23}{4}$, $5.\overline{5}$, and $5\frac{1}{2}$ on a number line.

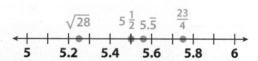

From greatest to least, the distances are:

$\frac{23}{4}$ km, $5.\overline{5}$ km, $5\frac{1}{2}$ km, $\sqrt{28}$ km.

YOUR TURN

7. Four people have found the distance in miles across a crater using different methods. Their results are given below.

Jonathan: $\frac{10}{3}$, Elaine: $3.\overline{45}$, José: $3\frac{1}{2}$, Lashonda: $\sqrt{10}$

Order the distances from greatest to least.

_____

Personal Math Trainer

Online Assessment and Intervention

⟳ my.hrw.com

Compare. Write <, >, or =. (Explore Activity Example 1)

1. $\sqrt{3} + 2 \bigcirc \sqrt{3} + 3$

2. $\sqrt{11} + 15 \bigcirc \sqrt{8} + 15$

3. $\sqrt{6} + 5 \bigcirc 6 + \sqrt{5}$

4. $\sqrt{9} + 3 \bigcirc 9 + \sqrt{3}$

5. $\sqrt{17} - 3 \bigcirc -2 + \sqrt{5}$

6. $10 - \sqrt{8} \bigcirc 12 - \sqrt{2}$

7. $\sqrt{7} + 2 \bigcirc \sqrt{10} - 1$

8. $\sqrt{17} + 3 \bigcirc 3 + \sqrt{11}$

9. Order $\sqrt{3}$, 2π, and 1.5 from least to greatest. Then graph them on the number line. (Example 2)

$\sqrt{3}$ is between _____ and _____, so $\sqrt{3} \approx$ _____.

$\pi \approx 3.14$, so $2\pi \approx$ _____.

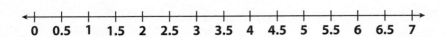

From least to greatest, the numbers are _____, _____,

_____.

10. Four people have found the perimeter of a forest using different methods. Their results are given in the table. Order their calculations from greatest to least. (Example 3)

_____

_____

Forest Perimeter (km)			
Leon	Mika	Jason	Ashley
$\sqrt{17} - 2$	$1 + \dfrac{\pi}{2}$	$\dfrac{12}{5}$	2.5

? ESSENTIAL QUESTION CHECK-IN

11. Explain how to order a set of real numbers.

_____

_____

_____

_____

_____

1.3 Independent Practice

COMMON CORE 8.NS.2

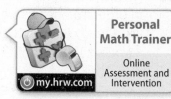

Personal Math Trainer

Online Assessment and Intervention

my.hrw.com

Order the numbers from least to greatest.

12. $\sqrt{7}, 2, \dfrac{\sqrt{8}}{2}$

_____

13. $\sqrt{10}, \pi, 3.5$

_____

14. $\sqrt{220}, -10, \sqrt{100}, 11.5$

_____

15. $\sqrt{8}, -3.75, 3, \dfrac{9}{4}$

_____

16. Your sister is considering two different shapes for her garden. One is a square with side lengths of 3.5 meters, and the other is a circle with a diameter of 4 meters.

  a. Find the area of the square. _____

  b. Find the area of the circle. _____

  c. Compare your answers from parts **a** and **b**. Which garden would give your sister the most space to plant?

  _____

  _____

17. Winnie measured the length of her father's ranch four times and got four different distances. Her measurements are shown in the table.

  a. To estimate the actual length, Winnie first approximated each distance to the nearest hundredth. Then she averaged the four numbers. Using a calculator, find Winnie's estimate.

  _____

  _____

Distance Across Father's Ranch (km)			
1	2	3	4
$\sqrt{60}$	$\dfrac{58}{8}$	$7.\overline{3}$	$7\dfrac{3}{5}$

  b. Winnie's father estimated the distance across his ranch to be $\sqrt{56}$ km. How does this distance compare to Winnie's estimate?

  _____

Give an example of each type of number.

18. a real number between $\sqrt{13}$ and $\sqrt{14}$ _____

19. an irrational number between 5 and 7 _____

20. A teacher asks his students to write the numbers shown in order from least to greatest. Paul thinks the numbers are already in order. Sandra thinks the order should be reversed. Who is right?

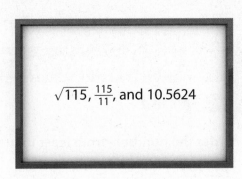

$\sqrt{115}$, $\frac{115}{11}$, and 10.5624

_____

_____

_____

21. Math History There is a famous irrational number called Euler's number, symbolized with an *e*. Like π, its decimal form never ends or repeats. The first few digits of *e* are 2.7182818284.

    a. Between which two square roots of integers could you find this number?

    _____

    b. Between which two square roots of integers can you find π?

    _____

 **FOCUS ON HIGHER ORDER THINKING**

22. Analyze Relationships There are several approximations used for π, including 3.14 and $\frac{22}{7}$. π is approximately 3.14159265358979…

    a. Label π and the two approximations on the number line.

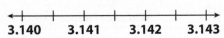

    3.140   3.141   3.142   3.143

    b. Which of the two approximations is a better estimate for π? Explain.

    _____

    c. Find a whole number *x* so that the ratio $\frac{x}{113}$ is a better estimate for π

    than the two given approximations. _____

23. Communicate Mathematical Ideas What is the fewest number of distinct points that must be graphed on a number line, in order to represent natural numbers, whole numbers, integers, rational numbers, irrational numbers, and real numbers? Explain.

_____

_____

_____

24. Critique Reasoning Jill says that $12.\overline{6}$ is less than 12.63. Explain her error.

_____

Work Area

Root-O!

INSTRUCTIONS

Playing the Game

STEP 1   Choose one person to be the caller. The caller can be a teacher, or students can take turns being caller. The caller gets a set of caller cards. All the other players get a game card and some counters. The center is a free space. Players should cover the center square before play begins.

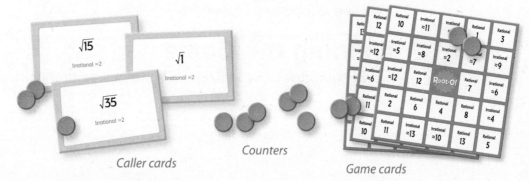

Caller cards   *Counters*   *Game cards*

STEP 2   The caller randomly draws a caller card and reads aloud the square-root expression to the players.

STEP 3   Players write down the expression on a piece of scratch paper and determine the classification (rational or irrational) and the equivalent or approximate integer value. If the same classification and value appear on a square of his/her game card, the player covers that square with a counter.

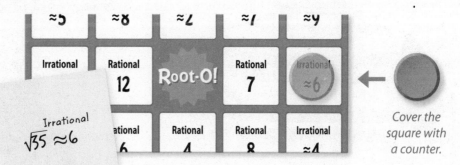

Cover the square with a counter.

STEP 4 Caller will then draw another caller card to continue the game.

STEP 5 Continue the game in this way until a player covers five squares in a row horizontally, vertically, or diagonally, and calls out "Root-O!"

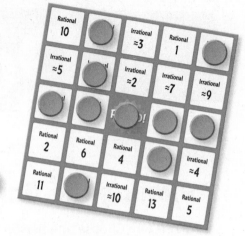

STEP 6 The prospective winning player will then check with the caller to verify that the squares covered on his/her game card correspond to cards that have been called. If there is a discrepancy, the player's game card is corrected and the game continues.

Winning the Game

A player who covers five squares in a horizontal, vertical, or diagonal row wins.

Ready to Go On?

1.1 Rational and Irrational Numbers

Write each fraction as a decimal or each decimal as a fraction.

1. $\frac{7}{20}$ _____

2. $1.\overline{27}$ _____

3. $1\frac{7}{8}$ _____

Solve each equation for x.

4. $x^2 = 81$ _____

5. $x^3 = 343$ _____

6. $x^2 = \frac{1}{100}$ _____

7. A square patio has an area of 200 square feet. How long is each side of the patio to the nearest 0.05? _____

1.2 Sets of Real Numbers

Write all names that apply to each number.

8. $\frac{121}{\sqrt{121}}$ _____

9. $\frac{\pi}{2}$ _____

10. Tell whether the statement "All integers are rational numbers" is true or false. Explain your choice.

_____

_____

1.3 Ordering Real Numbers

Compare. Write $<$, $>$, or $=$.

11. $\sqrt{8} + 3$ ◯ $8 + \sqrt{3}$

12. $\sqrt{5} + 11$ ◯ $5 + \sqrt{11}$

Order the numbers from least to greatest.

13. $\sqrt{99}$, π^2, $9.\overline{8}$ _____

14. $\sqrt{\frac{1}{25}}$, $\frac{1}{4}$, $0.\overline{2}$ _____

? ESSENTIAL QUESTION

15. How are real numbers used to describe real-world situations?

_____

_____

MODULE 1 MIXED REVIEW

Assessment Readiness

COMMON CORE

Personal Math Trainer

Online Assessment and Intervention

my.hrw.com

Selected Response

1. The square root of a number is 9. What is the other square root?

Ⓐ −9　　　　Ⓒ 3

Ⓑ −3　　　　Ⓓ 81

2. A square acre of land is 4,840 square yards. Between which two integers is the length of one side?

Ⓐ between 24 and 25 yards

Ⓑ between 69 and 70 yards

Ⓒ between 242 and 243 yards

Ⓓ between 695 and 696 yards

3. Which of the following is an integer but not a whole number?

Ⓐ −9.6　　　　Ⓒ 0

Ⓑ −4　　　　Ⓓ 3.7

4. Which statement is false?

Ⓐ No integers are irrational numbers.

Ⓑ All whole numbers are integers.

Ⓒ No real numbers are irrational numbers.

Ⓓ All integers greater than 0 are whole numbers.

5. Which set of numbers best describes the displayed weights on a digital scale that shows each weight to the nearest half pound?

Ⓐ whole numbers

Ⓑ rational numbers

Ⓒ real numbers

Ⓓ integers

6. Which of the following is not true?

Ⓐ $\pi^2 < 2\pi + 4$　　　Ⓒ $\sqrt{27} + 3 > \frac{17}{2}$

Ⓑ $3\pi > 9$　　　Ⓓ $5 - \sqrt{24} < 1$

7. Which number is between $\sqrt{21}$ and $\frac{3\pi}{2}$?

Ⓐ $\frac{14}{3}$　　　Ⓒ 5

Ⓑ $2\sqrt{6}$　　　Ⓓ $\pi + 1$

8. What number is shown on the graph?

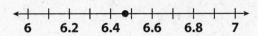

Ⓐ $\pi + 3$　　　Ⓒ $\sqrt{20} + 2$

Ⓑ $\sqrt{4} + 2.5$　　　Ⓓ $6.\overline{14}$

9. Which is in order from least to greatest?

Ⓐ $3.3, \frac{10}{3}, \pi, \frac{11}{4}$　　　Ⓒ $\pi, \frac{10}{3}, \frac{11}{4}, 3.3$

Ⓑ $\frac{10}{3}, 3.3, \frac{11}{4}, \pi$　　　Ⓓ $\frac{11}{4}, \pi, 3.3, \frac{10}{3}$

Mini-Task

10. The volume of a cube is given by $V = x^3$, where x is the length of an edge of the cube. The area of a square is given by $A = x^2$, where x is the length of a side of the square. A given cube has a volume of 1728 cubic inches.

a. Find the length of an edge.

_____

b. Find the area of one side of the cube.

_____

c. Find the surface area of the cube.

_____

d. What is the surface area in square feet?

_____

Exponents and Scientific Notation

ESSENTIAL QUESTION

How can you use scientific notation to solve real-world problems?

Real-World Video

The distance from Earth to other planets, moons, and stars is a very great number of kilometers. To make it easier to write very large and very small numbers, we use scientific notation.

my.hrw.com

GO DIGITAL
my.hrw.com

my.hrw.com

Go digital with your write-in student edition, accessible on any device.

Math On the Spot

Scan with your smart phone to jump directly to the online edition, video tutor, and more.

Animated Math

Interactively explore key concepts to see how math works.

Personal Math Trainer

Get immediate feedback and help as you work through practice sets.

Are YOU Ready?

Complete these exercises to review skills you will need for this module.

Exponents

EXAMPLE $10^4 = 10 \times 10 \times 10 \times 10$ Write the exponential expression
                          $= 10,000$ as a product.
                                                                              Simplify.

Write each exponential expression as a decimal.

1. 10^2 _____   **2.** 10^3 _____   **3.** 10^5 _____   **4.** 10^7 _____

Multiply and Divide by Powers of 10

EXAMPLE $0.0478 \times 10^5 = 0.0478 \times 100,000$ Identify the number of zeros
                              $= 4,780$ in the power of 10.
                                                                                 When multiplying, move the
                                                                                 decimal point to the *right* the
                                                                                 same number of places as
                                                                                 the number of zeros.

$37.9 \div 10^4 = 37.9 \div 10,000$ Identify the number of zeros in
                    $= 0.00379$ the power of 10.
                                                              When dividing, move the decimal
                                                              point to the *left* the same number
                                                              of places as the number of zeros.

Find each product or quotient.

5. 45.3×10^3 **6.** $7.08 \div 10^2$ **7.** 0.00235×10^6 **8.** $3,600 \div 10^4$

_____   _____   _____   _____

9. 0.5×10^2 **10.** $67.7 \div 10^5$ **11.** 0.0057×10^4 **12.** $195 \div 10^6$

_____   _____   _____   _____

Reading Start-Up

© Houghton Mifflin Harcourt Publishing Company

Visualize Vocabulary

Use the ✔ words to complete the Venn diagram. You can put more than one word in each section of the diagram.

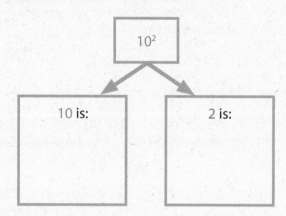

10^2

10 is:

2 is:

Understand Vocabulary

Complete the sentences using the preview words.

1. A number produced by raising a base to an exponent

   is a _____.

2. _____ is a method of writing very large or very small numbers by using powers of 10.

3. A _____ is any number that can be expressed as a ratio of two integers.

Active Reading

Two-Panel Flip Chart Create a two-panel flip chart to help you understand the concepts in this module. Label one flap "Positive Powers of 10" and the other flap "Negative Powers of 10." As you study each lesson, write important ideas under the appropriate flap. Include sample problems that will help you remember the concepts later when you look back at your notes.

Unpacking the Standards

Understanding the standards and the vocabulary terms in the standards will help you know exactly what you are expected to learn in this module.

COMMON CORE **8.EE.1**

Know and apply the properties of integer exponents to generate equivalent numerical expressions.

Key Vocabulary

integer *(entero)*
The set of whole numbers and their opposites

exponent *(exponente)*
The number that indicates how many times the base is used as a factor.

What It Means to You

You will use the properties of integer exponents to find equivalent expressions.

UNPACKING EXAMPLE 8.EE.1

Evaluate two different ways.

$$\frac{8^3}{8^5} \qquad \frac{8^3}{8^5} = \frac{8 \cdot 8 \cdot 8}{8 \cdot 8 \cdot 8 \cdot 8 \cdot 8} = \frac{1}{8 \cdot 8} = \frac{1}{64}$$

$$\frac{8^3}{8^5} = 8^{(3-5)} = 8^{-2} = \frac{1}{8^2} = \frac{1}{8 \cdot 8} = \frac{1}{64}$$

$$(3^2)^4 \qquad (3^2)^4 = (3^2)(3^2)(3^2)(3^2) = 3^{2+2+2+2} = 3^8 = 6,561$$

$$(3^2)^4 = 3^{(2 \cdot 4)} = 3^8 = 6,561$$

COMMON CORE **8.EE.3**

Use numbers expressed in the form of a single digit times an integer power of 10 to estimate very large or very small quantities, and to express how many times as much one is than the other.

Key Vocabulary

scientific notation *(notación científica)*
A method of writing very large or very small numbers by using powers of 10.

What It Means to You

You will convert very large numbers to scientific notation.

UNPACKING EXAMPLE 8.EE.3

There are about 55,000,000,000 cells in an average-sized adult. Write this number in scientific notation.

Move the decimal point to the left until you have a number that is greater than or equal to 1 and less than 10.

5.5 0 0 0 0 0 0 0 0 0   *Move the decimal point 10 places to the left.*

5.5   *Remove the extra zeros.*

You would have to multiply 5.5 by 10^{10} to get 55,000,000,000.

$$55,000,000,000 = 5.5 \times 10^{10}$$

Visit **my.hrw.com** to see all the **Common Core Standards** unpacked.

my.hrw.com

COMMON CORE **8.EE.1**

Know and apply the properties of integer exponents to generate equivalent numerical expressions.

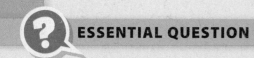

? **ESSENTIAL QUESTION**

How can you develop and use the properties of integer exponents?

EXPLORE ACTIVITY 1 COMMON CORE **8.EE.1**

Using Patterns of Integer Exponents

The table below shows powers of 5, 4, and 3.

$5^4 = 625$	$5^3 = 125$	$5^2 = 25$	$5^1 = 5$	$5^0 = \boxed{}$	$5^{-1} = \boxed{}$	$5^{-2} = \boxed{}$
$4^4 = 256$	$4^3 = 64$	$4^2 = 16$	$4^1 = 4$	$4^0 = \boxed{}$	$4^{-1} = \boxed{}$	$4^{-2} = \boxed{}$
$3^4 = 81$	$3^3 = 27$	$3^2 = 9$	$3^1 = 3$	$3^0 = \boxed{}$	$3^{-1} = \boxed{}$	$3^{-2} = \boxed{}$

A What pattern do you see in the powers of 5?

_____

_____

B What pattern do you see in the powers of 4?

_____

_____

C What pattern do you see in the powers of 3?

_____

_____

D Complete the table for the values of $5^0, 5^{-1}, 5^{-2}$.

E Complete the table for the values of $4^0, 4^{-1}, 4^{-2}$.

F Complete the table for the values of $3^0, 3^{-1}, 3^{-2}$.

Reflect

1. **Make a Conjecture** Write a general rule for the value of a^0. _____

2. **Make a Conjecture** Write a general rule for the value of a^{-n}. _____

Exploring Properties of Integer Exponents

A Complete the following equations.

$3 \cdot 3 \cdot 3 \cdot 3 \cdot 3 = 3^{\boxed{}}$

$(3 \cdot 3 \cdot 3 \cdot 3) \cdot 3 = 3^{\boxed{}} \cdot 3^{\boxed{}} = 3^{\boxed{}}$

$(3 \cdot 3 \cdot 3) \cdot (3 \cdot 3) = 3^{\boxed{}} \cdot 3^{\boxed{}} = 3^{\boxed{}}$

What pattern do you see when multiplying two powers with the same base?

_____

_____

Use your pattern to complete this equation: $5^2 \cdot 5^5 = 5^{\boxed{}}$.

B Complete the following equation:

$\dfrac{4^5}{4^3} = \dfrac{4 \cdot 4 \cdot 4 \cdot 4 \cdot 4}{4 \cdot 4 \cdot 4} = \dfrac{\overset{1}{\cancel{4}} \cdot \overset{1}{\cancel{4}} \cdot \overset{1}{\cancel{4}} \cdot 4 \cdot 4}{\underset{1}{\cancel{4}} \cdot \underset{1}{\cancel{4}} \cdot \underset{1}{\cancel{4}}} = 4 \cdot 4 = 4^{\boxed{}}$

What pattern do you see when dividing two powers with the same base?

_____

_____

_____

Use your pattern to complete this equation: $\dfrac{6^8}{6^3} = 6^{\boxed{}}$.

C Complete the following equations:

$(5^3)^2 = (5 \cdot 5 \cdot 5)^{\boxed{}} = (5 \cdot 5 \cdot 5) \cdot (5 \cdot 5 \cdot 5) = 5^{\boxed{}}$

What pattern do you see when raising a power to a power?

_____

_____

Use your pattern to complete this equation: $(7^2)^4 = 7^{\boxed{}}$.

> **Math Talk**
> *Mathematical Practices*
>
> Do the patterns you found in parts A–C apply if the exponents are negative? If so, give an example of each.

Reflect

Let *m* and *n* be integers.

3. **Make a Conjecture** Write a general rule for the value of $a^m \cdot a^n$. _____

4. **Make a Conjecture** Write a general rule for the value of $\frac{a^m}{a^n}$, $a \neq 0$. _____

5. **Make a Conjecture** Write a general rule for the value of $(a^m)^n$. _____

Applying Properties of Integer Exponents

You can use the general rules you found in the Explore Activities to simplify more complicated expressions.

Math On the Spot

my.hrw.com

My Notes

EXAMPLE 1 COMMON CORE **8.EE.1**

Simplify each expression.

A $(5 - 2)^5 \cdot 3^{-8} + (5 + 2)^0$

$(3)^5 \cdot 3^{-8} + (7)^0$ Simplify within parentheses.

$3^{5 + (-8)} + 1$ Use properties of exponents.

$3^{-3} + 1$ Simplify.

$\frac{1}{27} + 1 = 1\frac{1}{27}$ Apply the rule for negative exponents and add.

B $\dfrac{\left[(3 + 1)^2\right]^3}{(7 - 3)^2}$

$\dfrac{(4^2)^3}{4^2}$ Simplify within parentheses.

$\dfrac{4^6}{4^2}$ Use properties of exponents.

4^{6-2} Use properties of exponents.

$4^4 = 256$ Simplify.

YOUR TURN

Simplify each expression.

6. $\dfrac{\left[(6 - 1)^2\right]^2}{(3 + 2)^3}$

7. $(2^2)^3 - (10 - 6)^3 \cdot 4^{-5}$

_____   _____

Personal Math Trainer

Online Assessment and Intervention

my.hrw.com

© Houghton Mifflin Harcourt Publishing Company

Lesson 2.1 **35**

Guided Practice

Find the value of each power. (Explore Activity 1)

1. $8^{-1} =$ _____

2. $6^{-2} =$ _____

3. $256^0 =$ _____

4. $10^2 =$ _____

5. $5^4 =$ _____

6. $2^{-5} =$ _____

7. $4^{-5} =$ _____

8. $89^0 =$ _____

9. $11^{-3} =$ _____

Use properties of exponents to write an equivalent expression. (Explore Activity 2)

10. $4 \cdot 4 \cdot 4 = 4^{\boxed{}}$

11. $(2 \cdot 2) \cdot (2 \cdot 2 \cdot 2) = 2^{\boxed{}} \cdot 2^{\boxed{}} = 2^{\boxed{}}$

12. $\dfrac{6^7}{6^5} = \dfrac{6 \cdot 6 \cdot 6 \cdot 6 \cdot 6 \cdot 6 \cdot 6}{6 \cdot 6 \cdot 6 \cdot 6 \cdot 6} = \boxed{}^{\boxed{}}$

13. $\dfrac{8^{12}}{8^9} = 8^{\boxed{} - \boxed{}} = \boxed{}$

14. $5^{10} \cdot 5 \cdot 5 = 5^{\boxed{}}$

15. $7^8 \cdot 7^5 = \boxed{}^{\boxed{}}$

16. $(6^2)^4 = (6 \cdot 6)^{\boxed{}}$

$= (6 \cdot 6) \cdot (6 \cdot 6) \cdot \left(\boxed{} \cdot \boxed{} \right) \cdot \underline{}$

$= \boxed{}^{\boxed{}}$

17. $(3^3)^3 = (3 \cdot 3 \cdot 3)^3$

$= (3 \cdot 3 \cdot 3) \cdot \left(\boxed{} \cdot \boxed{} \cdot \boxed{} \right) \underline{}$

$= \boxed{}^{\boxed{}}$

Simplify each expression. (Example 1)

18. $(10 - 6)^3 \cdot 4^2 + (10 + 2)^2$ _____

19. $\dfrac{(12 - 5)^7}{\left[(3 + 4)^2 \right]^2}$ _____

? ESSENTIAL QUESTION CHECK-IN

20. Summarize the rules for multiplying powers with the same base, dividing powers with the same base, and raising a power to a power.

_____

_____

_____

_____

2.1 Independent Practice

 COMMON CORE 8.EE.1

Personal Math Trainer

Online Assessment and Intervention

my.hrw.com

21. Explain why the exponents cannot be added in the product $12^3 \cdot 11^3$.

_____

22. List three ways to express 3^5 as a product of powers.

_____

23. **Astronomy** The distance from Earth to the moon is about 22^4 miles. The distance from Earth to Neptune is about 22^7 miles. Which distance is the greater distance and about how many times greater is it?

_____

24. **Critique Reasoning** A student claims that $8^3 \cdot 8^{-5}$ is greater than 1. Explain whether the student is correct or not.

_____

_____

Find the missing exponent.

25. $\left(b^2\right)^{\boxed{}} = b^{-6}$

26. $x^{\boxed{}} \cdot x^6 = x^9$

27. $\dfrac{y^{25}}{y^{\boxed{}}} = y^6$

28. **Communicate Mathematical Ideas** Why do you subtract exponents when dividing powers with the same base?

_____

_____

_____

29. **Astronomy** The mass of the Sun is about 2×10^{27} metric tons, or 2×10^{30} kilograms. How many kilograms are in one metric ton?

_____

30. **Represent Real-World Problems** In computer technology, a kilobyte is 2^{10} bytes in size. A gigabyte is 2^{30} bytes in size. The size of a terabyte is the product of the size of a kilobyte and the size of a gigabyte. What is the size of a terabyte?

_____

31. Write equivalent expressions for $x^7 \cdot x^{-2}$ and $\frac{x^7}{x^2}$. What do you notice? Explain how your results relate to the properties of integer exponents.

_____

_____

_____

_____

A toy store is creating a large window display of different colored cubes stacked in a triangle shape. The table shows the number of cubes in each row of the triangle, starting with the top row.

Row	1	2	3	4
Number of cubes in each row	3	3^2	3^3	3^4

32. Look for a Pattern Describe any pattern you see in the table.

_____

33. Using exponents, how many cubes will be in Row 6? How many times as many cubes will be in Row 6 than in Row 3?

_____

34. Justify Reasoning If there are 6 rows in the triangle, what is the total number of cubes in the triangle? Explain how you found your answer.

_____

 FOCUS ON HIGHER ORDER THINKING

35. Critique Reasoning A student simplified the expression $\frac{6^2}{36^2}$ as $\frac{1}{3}$. Do you agree with this student? Explain why or why not.

_____

36. Draw Conclusions Evaluate $-a^n$ when $a = 3$ and $n = 2, 3, 4,$ and 5. Now evaluate $(-a)^n$ when $a = 3$ and $n = 2, 3, 4,$ and 5. Based on this sample, does it appear that $-a^n = (-a)^n$? If not, state the relationships, if any, between $-a^n$ and $(-a)^n$.

_____

_____

_____

_____

37. Persevere in Problem Solving A number to the 12th power divided by the same number to the 9th power equals 125. What is the number?

_____

Work Area

Zero and Negative Exponents

COMMON CORE 8.EE.1
Know and apply the properties of integer exponents to generate equivalent numerical expressions.

? ESSENTIAL QUESTION

 How can you derive the definition of a zero exponent and the definition of a negative exponent?

EXPLORE ACTIVITY 1   **COMMON CORE** 8.EE.1

Definition of Zero Exponent

You can use the properties of exponents and the properties of division with x^a to show that $x^0 = 1$.

A Complete the statement: $\dfrac{x^a}{x^a} = x^{\boxed{} - \boxed{}} = x^{\boxed{}}$

B Anything divided by itself is _____, so $\dfrac{x^a}{x^a} = $ _____.

C If $\dfrac{x^a}{x^a} = x^{\boxed{}}$ from Part A and $\dfrac{x^a}{x^a} = $ _____ from Part B, then $x^0 = $ _____.

Reflect

1. **Justify Reasoning** What property did you use to complete Part A?

_____

EXPLORE ACTIVITY 2   **COMMON CORE** 8.EE.1

Definition of Negative Exponent

You can use the definition and properties of exponents with $\dfrac{x^3}{x^5}$ to show that $x^{-2} = \dfrac{1}{x^2}$.

A Complete the statement: $\dfrac{x^3}{x^5} = x^{\boxed{} - \boxed{}} = x^{\boxed{}}$

B Complete the statement: $\dfrac{x^3}{x^5} = \dfrac{x \cdot \boxed{} \cdot \boxed{}}{x \cdot x \cdot \boxed{} \cdot \boxed{} \cdot \boxed{} \cdot \boxed{}} = \dfrac{1}{\boxed{} \cdot \boxed{}} = \dfrac{1}{x^{\boxed{}}}$.

C If $\dfrac{x^3}{x^5} = x^{\boxed{}}$ from Part A and $\dfrac{x^3}{x^5} = \dfrac{1}{x^{\boxed{}}}$ from Part B, then $x^{-2} = \dfrac{1}{x^{\boxed{}}}$.

Reflect

2. **Critique Reasoning** As you saw in Steps A–C, it can be shown that $x^{-n} = \frac{1}{x^n}$ for any n by using $\frac{x^a}{x^b}$, where $b > a$. Why is it necessary that $b > a$?

_____

_____

_____

Practice

1. Use x^4 to show that $x^0 = 1$.

_____

2. Use $\frac{x^4}{x^7}$ to show that $x^{-3} = \frac{1}{x^3}$.

_____

3. Use x^6 to show that $x^0 = 1$.

_____

4. Use x^7 to show that $x^0 = 1$.

_____

5. Use $\frac{x^3}{x^9}$ to show that $x^{-6} = \frac{1}{x^6}$.

_____

6. Use $\frac{x^2}{x^5}$ to show that $x^{-3} = \frac{1}{x^3}$.

_____

Scientific Notation with Positive Powers of 10

COMMON CORE 8.EE.3

Use numbers expressed in the form of a single digit times an integer power of 10 to estimate very large or very small quantities, ...

 ESSENTIAL QUESTION

How can you use scientific notation to express very large quantities?

EXPLORE ACTIVITY COMMON CORE 8.EE.3

Using Scientific Notation

Scientific notation is a method of expressing very large and very small numbers as a product of a number greater than or equal to 1 and less than 10, and a power of 10.

The weights of various sea creatures are shown in the table. Write the weight of the blue whale in scientific notation.

Sea Creature	Blue whale	Gray whale	Whale shark
Weight (lb)	250,000	68,000	41,200

A Move the decimal point in 250,000 to the left as many places as necessary to find a number that is greater than or equal to 1 and less than 10.

What number did you find? _____

B Divide 250,000 by your answer to **A**. Write your answer as a power of 10.

_____

C Combine your answers to **A** and **B** to represent 250,000.

$$250,000 = \boxed{} \times 10^{\boxed{}}$$

Repeat steps **A** through **C** to write the weight of the whale shark in scientific notation.

$$41,200 = \boxed{} \times 10^{\boxed{}}$$

Reflect

1. How many places to the left did you move the decimal point to write 41,200 in scientific notation? _____

2. What is the exponent on 10 when you write 41,200 in scientific notation?

_____

Writing a Number in Scientific Notation

To translate between standard notation and scientific notation, you can count the number of places the decimal point moves.

Writing Large Quantities in Scientific Notation

When the number is greater than or equal to 10, use a positive exponent.	$8\,4{,}0\,0\,0 = 8.4 \times 10^4$	The decimal point moves 4 places to the left.

EXAMPLE 1 · Real World

COMMON CORE 8.EE.3

The distance from Earth to the Sun is about 93,000,000 miles. Write this distance in scientific notation.

STEP 1 Move the decimal point in 93,000,000 to the left until you have a number that is greater than or equal to 1 and less than 10.

$9.3\,0\,0\,0\,0\,0\,0.$ Move the decimal point 7 places to the left.

9.3 Remove extra zeros.

STEP 2 Divide the original number by the result from Step 1.

$10{,}000{,}000$ Divide 93,000,000 by 9.3.

10^7 Write your answer as a power of 10.

STEP 3 Write the product of the results from Steps 1 and 2.

$93{,}000{,}000 = 9.3 \times 10^7$ miles   Write a product to represent 93,000,000 in scientific notation.

YOUR TURN

Write each number in scientific notation.

3. 6,400

4. 570,000,000,000

_____

5. A light-year is the distance that light travels in a year and is equivalent to 9,461,000,000,000 km. Write this distance in scientific notation.

_____

Writing a Number in Standard Notation

To translate between scientific notation and standard notation, move the decimal point the number of places indicated by the exponent in the power of 10. When the exponent is positive, move the decimal point to the right and add placeholder zeros as needed.

**Math On the Spot**
my.hrw.com

EXAMPLE 2

COMMON CORE | 8.EE.3

Write 3.5×10^6 in standard notation.

STEP 1 Use the exponent of the power of 10 to see how many places to move the decimal point.

6 places

STEP 2 Place the decimal point. Since you are going to write a number greater than 3.5, move the decimal point to the *right*. Add placeholder zeros if necessary.

3 5 0 0 0 0 0.

The number 3.5×10^6 written in standard notation is 3,500,000.

Reflect

6. Explain why the exponent in 3.5×10^6 is 6, while there are only 5 zeros in 3,500,000.

_____

_____

_____

7. What is the exponent on 10 when you write 5.3 in scientific notation?

_____

YOUR TURN

Write each number in standard notation.

8. 7.034×10^9 9. 2.36×10^5

_____   _____

10. The mass of one roosting colony of Monarch butterflies in Mexico was estimated at 5×10^6 grams. Write this mass in standard notation.

_____

Personal Math Trainer

Online Assessment and Intervention

my.hrw.com

© Houghton Mifflin Harcourt Publishing Company • Image Credits: ©Ingram Publishing/Alamy

My Notes

Write each number in scientific notation. (Explore Activity and Example 1)

1. 58,927
Hint: Move the decimal left 4 places.

_____

2. 1,304,000,000
Hint: Move the decimal left 9 places.

_____

3. 6,730,000

_____

4. 13,300

_____

5. An ordinary quarter contains about
97,700,000,000,000,000,000,000 atoms.

_____

6. The distance from Earth to the Moon is
about 384,000 kilometers.

_____

Write each number in standard notation. (Example 2)

7. 4×10^5
Hint: Move the decimal right 5 places.

_____

8. 1.8499×10^9
Hint: Move the decimal right 9 places.

_____

9. 6.41×10^3

_____

10. 8.456×10^7

_____

11. 8×10^5

_____

12. 9×10^{10}

_____

13. Diana calculated that she spent about 5.4×10^4 seconds doing her math
homework during October. Write this time in standard notation. (Example 2)

_____

14. The town recycled 7.6×10^6 cans this year. Write the number of cans in
standard notation. (Example 2)

_____

? **ESSENTIAL QUESTION CHECK-IN**

15. Describe how to write 3,482,000,000 in scientific notation.

_____

_____

_____

_____

2.2 Independent Practice

COMMON CORE 8.EE.3

Personal Math Trainer

Online Assessment and Intervention

my.hrw.com

Paleontology Use the table for problems 16–21. Write the estimated weight of each dinosaur in scientific notation.

Estimated Weight of Dinosaurs	
Name	**Pounds**
Argentinosaurus	220,000
Brachiosaurus	100,000
Apatosaurus	66,000
Diplodocus	50,000
Camarasaurus	40,000
Cetiosauriscus	19,850

16. *Apatosaurus* _____

17. *Argentinosaurus* _____

18. *Brachiosaurus* _____

19. *Camarasaurus* _____

20. *Cetiosauriscus* _____

21. *Diplodocus* _____

22. A single little brown bat can eat up to 1,000 mosquitoes in a single hour. Express in scientific notation how many mosquitoes a little brown bat might eat in 10.5 hours.

_____

23. **Multistep** Samuel can type nearly 40 words per minute. Use this information to find the number of hours it would take him to type 2.6×10^5 words.

_____

_____

24. **Entomology** A tropical species of mite named *Archegozetes longisetosus* is the record holder for the strongest insect in the world. It can lift up to 1.182×10^3 times its own weight.

a. If you were as strong as this insect, explain how you could find how many pounds you could lift.

_____

_____

_____

b. Complete the calculation to find how much you could lift, in pounds, if you were as strong as an *Archegozetes longisetosus* mite. Express your answer in both scientific notation and standard notation.

_____

_____

25. During a discussion in science class, Sharon learns that at birth an elephant weighs around 230 pounds. In four herds of elephants tracked by conservationists, about 20 calves were born during the summer. In scientific notation, express approximately how much the calves weighed all together.

_____

26. **Classifying Numbers** Which of the following numbers are written in scientific notation?

0.641×10^3 9.999×10^4

2×10^1 4.38×5^{10}

_____

27. Explain the Error Polly's parents' car weighs about 3500 pounds. Samantha, Esther, and Polly each wrote the weight of the car in scientific notation. Polly wrote 35.0×10^2, Samantha wrote 0.35×10^4, and Esther wrote 3.5×10^4.

a. Which of these girls, if any, is correct?

_____

b. Explain the mistakes of those who got the question wrong.

_____

_____

_____

28. Justify Reasoning If you were a biologist counting very large numbers of cells as part of your research, give several reasons why you might prefer to record your cell counts in scientific notation instead of standard notation.

_____

_____

_____

 FOCUS ON HIGHER ORDER THINKING

29. Draw Conclusions Which measurement would be least likely to be written in scientific notation: number of stars in a galaxy, number of grains of sand on a beach, speed of a car, or population of a country? Explain your reasoning.

_____

_____

30. Analyze Relationships Compare the two numbers to find which is greater. Explain how you can compare them without writing them in standard notation first.

$$4.5 \times 10^6 \qquad 2.1 \times 10^8$$

_____

_____

31. Communicate Mathematical Ideas To determine whether a number is written in scientific notation, what test can you apply to the first factor, and what test can you apply to the second factor?

_____

_____

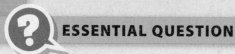

Comparing Very Large Numbers

COMMON CORE 8.EE.3

Use numbers expressed in the form of a single digit times an integer power of 10 to... express how many times as much one is than the other.

 ESSENTIAL QUESTION

How can you compare very large numbers in scientific notation?

EXPLORE ACTIVITY **COMMON CORE** 8.EE.3

Comparing Very Large Numbers

A Compare 8,000 and 200 using standard notation.

$\dfrac{8,000}{200} = \boxed{}$, so 8,000 is _____ times greater than 200.

B Compare 8,000 and 200 using scientific notation.

$8,000 = 8 \times 10^{\boxed{}}$ and $200 = 2 \times 10^{\boxed{}}$

First compare the powers of 10 in a ratio of greater to lesser:

$\dfrac{10^3}{10^2} = 10^{\boxed{}} = \boxed{}$

Then compare the corresponding multipliers: $\dfrac{\boxed{}}{2} = $ _____

So 8×10^3 is $10 \cdot$ _____ = _____ times greater than 2×10^2.

Reflect

1. When comparing two numbers in scientific notation, why would you compare the powers of 10 first to find which number is greater?

_____

_____

2. When comparing two numbers in scientific notation, if the powers of 10 are equal, how can you tell which number is greater?

_____

_____

Comparing Very Large Numbers in the Real World

Using scientific notation can help you compare very large numbers.

© Houghton Mifflin Harcourt Publishing Company

EXAMPLE

The average mass of a human is about 6×10^1 kilograms, and the average mass of an African elephant is about 6×10^3 kilograms. About how many times greater is the mass of an African elephant than the mass of a human?

$$\frac{10^3}{10^1} = 10^2 \qquad \text{Compare the powers of 10.}$$

$$\frac{6}{6} = 1 \qquad \text{Compare the multipliers.}$$

So, the mass of an African elephant is about 1×10^2, or 100 times greater than the mass of a human.

Practice

1. Complete the statements to express how many times greater 6×10^7 is than 3×10^7.

   $$\frac{\boxed{}}{10^7} = 10^{\boxed{}} = \underline{\hspace{1.5cm}}, \text{ and } \frac{\boxed{}}{3} = \underline{\hspace{1.5cm}}$$

   So, 6×10^7 is $1 \cdot \underline{\hspace{1.5cm}} = \underline{\hspace{1.5cm}}$ times greater than 3×10^7.

2. The average mouse has a mass of about 2×10^4 milligrams, and the average housefly has a mass of about 1×10^1 milligrams. About how many times greater is the mass of a mouse than the mass of a housefly? Explain.

   _____

   _____

Determine which quantity is greater, and determine about how many times greater.

3. Chile: about 2×10^7 people

   Argentina: about 4×10^7 people

   _____

4. African elephant mass: 6×10^3 kg

   Asian elephant mass: 5×10^3 kg

   _____

Scientific Notation with Negative Powers of 10

COMMON CORE **8.EE.3**

Use numbers expressed in the form of a single digit times an integer power of 10 to estimate very large or very small quantities, ...

? ESSENTIAL QUESTION

How can you use scientific notation to express very small quantities?

EXPLORE ACTIVITY Real World   COMMON CORE **8.EE.3**

Animated Math
my.hrw.com

Negative Powers of 10

You can use what you know about writing very large numbers in scientific notation to write very small numbers in scientific notation.

A typical human hair has a diameter of 0.000025 meter. Write this number in scientific notation.

A Notice how the decimal point moves in the list below. Complete the list.

$2.345 \times 10^0 = 2.345$ It moves one place to the right with each increasing power of 10.

$2.345 \times 10^1 = 23.45$

$2.345 \times 10^2 = 234.5$

$2.345 \times 10^{\boxed{}} = 2345.$

$2.345 \times 10^0 = 2.345$ It moves one place to the left with each decreasing power of 10.

$2.345 \times 10^{-1} = 0.2345$

$2.345 \times 10^{-2} = 0.02345$

$2.345 \times 10^{\boxed{}} = 0.002345$

B Move the decimal point in 0.000025 to the right as many places as necessary to find a number that is greater than or equal to 1 and less than 10. What number did you find? _____

C Divide 0.000025 by your answer to **B**. _____

Write your answer as a power of 10. _____

D Combine your answers to **B** and **C** to represent 0.000025 in

scientific notation. _____

Reflect

1. When you move the decimal point, how can you know whether you are increasing or decreasing the number?

_____

2. Explain how the two steps of moving the decimal and multiplying by a power of 10 leave the value of the original number unchanged.

_____

Writing a Number in Scientific Notation

To write a number less than 1 in scientific notation, move the decimal point right and use a negative exponent.

Writing Small Quantities in Scientific Notation

When the number is between 0 and 1, use a negative exponent.	$0.0783 = 7.83 \times 10^{-2}$	The decimal point moves 2 places to the right.

EXAMPLE 1

COMMON CORE 8.EE.3

The average size of an atom is about 0.00000003 centimeter across. Write the average size of an atom in scientific notation.

Move the decimal point as many places as necessary to find a number that is greater than or equal to 1 and less than 10.

STEP 1 Place the decimal point.   3.0

STEP 2 Count the number of places you moved the decimal point.   8

STEP 3 Multiply 3.0 times a power of 10. 3.0×10 $\boxed{-8}$

Since 0.00000003 is less than 1, you moved the decimal point to the right and the exponent on 10 is negative.

The average size of an atom in scientific notation is 3.0×10^{-8}.

Reflect

3. **Critical Thinking** When you write a number that is less than 1 in scientific notation, how does the power of 10 differ from when you write a number greater than 1 in scientific notation?

_____

YOUR TURN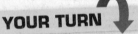

Write each number in scientific notation.

4. 0.0000829 _____

5. 0.000000302 _____

6. A typical red blood cell in human blood has a diameter of approximately 0.000007 meter. Write this diameter in scientific notation. _____

Math On the Spot
⏱ my.hrw.com

Personal Math Trainer
Online Assessment and Intervention
⏱ my.hrw.com

Writing a Number in Standard Notation

To translate between scientific notation and standard notation with very small numbers, you can move the decimal point the number of places indicated by the exponent on the power of 10. When the exponent is negative, move the decimal point to the left.

Math On the Spot

🕐 my.hrw.com

EXAMPLE 2 Real World

COMMON CORE 8.EE.3

Platelets are one component of human blood. A typical platelet has a diameter of approximately 2.33×10^{-6} meter. Write 2.33×10^{-6} in standard notation.

STEP 1 Use the exponent of the power of 10 to see how many places to move the decimal point.   6 places

STEP 2 Place the decimal point. Since you are going to write a number less than 2.33, move the decimal point to the *left*. Add placeholder zeros if necessary.   0.00000233

The number 2.33×10^{-6} in standard notation is 0.00000233.

Math Talk
Mathematical Practices

Describe the two factors that multiply together to form a number written in scientific notation.

Reflect

7. **Justify Reasoning** Explain whether 0.9×10^{-5} is written in scientific notation. If not, write the number correctly in scientific notation.

_____

_____

_____

8. Which number is larger, 2×10^{-3} or 3×10^{-2}? Explain.

_____

YOUR TURN

Write each number in standard notation.

9. 1.045×10^{-6}

10. 9.9×10^{-5}

_____   _____

11. Jeremy measured the length of an ant as 1×10^{-2} meter. Write this length in standard notation.

_____

Personal Math Trainer

Online Assessment and Intervention

🕐 my.hrw.com

© Houghton Mifflin Harcourt Publishing Company

Write each number in scientific notation. (Explore Activity and Example 1)

1. 0.000487
   Hint: Move the decimal right 4 places.

   _____

2. 0.000028
   Hint: Move the decimal right 5 places.

   _____

3. 0.000059

   _____

4. 0.0417

   _____

5. Picoplankton can be as small as 0.00002 centimeter.

   _____

6. The average mass of a grain of sand on a beach is about 0.000015 gram.

   _____

Write each number in standard notation. (Example 2)

7. 2×10^{-5}
   Hint: Move the decimal left 5 places.

   _____

8. 3.582×10^{-6}
   Hint: Move the decimal left 6 places.

   _____

9. 8.3×10^{-4}

   _____

10. 2.97×10^{-2}

    _____

11. 9.06×10^{-5}

    _____

12. 4×10^{-5}

    _____

13. The average length of a dust mite is approximately 0.0001 meter. Write this number in scientific notation. (Example 1)

    _____

14. The mass of a proton is about 1.7×10^{-24} gram. Write this number in standard notation. (Example 2)

    _____

? ESSENTIAL QUESTION CHECK-IN

15. Describe how to write 0.0000672 in scientific notation.

    _____

    _____

    _____

2.3 Independent Practice

COMMON CORE 8.EE.3

Personal Math Trainer

Online Assessment and Intervention

my.hrw.com

Use the table for problems 16–21. Write the diameter of the fibers in scientific notation.

Average Diameter of Natural Fibers	
Animal	**Fiber Diameter (cm)**
Vicuña	0.0008
Angora rabbit	0.0013
Alpaca	0.00277
Angora goat	0.0045
Llama	0.0035
Orb web spider	0.015

16. Alpaca

_____

17. Angora rabbit

_____

18. Llama

_____

19. Angora goat

_____

20. Orb web spider

_____

21. Vicuña

_____

22. Make a Conjecture Which measurement would be least likely to be written in scientific notation: the thickness of a dog hair, the radius of a period on this page, the ounces in a cup of milk? Explain your reasoning.

_____

_____

23. Multiple Representations Convert the length 7 centimeters to meters. Compare the numerical values when both numbers are written in scientific notation.

_____

_____

_____

_____

24. Draw Conclusions A graphing calculator displays 1.89×10^{12} as 1.89E12. How do you think it would display 1.89×10^{-12}? What does the E stand for?

_____

_____

25. Communicate Mathematical Ideas When a number is written in scientific notation, how can you tell right away whether or not it is greater than or equal to 1?

_____

_____

_____

26. The volume of a drop of a certain liquid is 0.000047 liter. Write the volume of the drop of liquid in scientific notation.

_____

27. Justify Reasoning If you were asked to express the weight in ounces of a ladybug in scientific notation, would the exponent of the 10 be positive or negative? Justify your response.

_____

_____

Physical Science The table shows the length of the radii of several very small or very large items. Complete the table.

	Item	Radius in Meters (Standard Notation)	Radius in Meters (Scientific Notation)
28.	The Moon	1,740,000	
29.	Atom of silver		1.25×10^{-10}
30.	Atlantic wolfish egg	0.0028	
31.	Jupiter		7.149×10^{7}
32.	Atom of aluminum	0.000000000182	
33.	Mars		3.397×10^{6}

34. List the items in the table in order from the smallest to the largest.

_____

_____

 **FOCUS ON HIGHER ORDER THINKING**

35. Analyze Relationships Write the following diameters from least to greatest.

1.5×10^{-2} m 1.2×10^{2} m 5.85×10^{-3} m 2.3×10^{-2} m 9.6×10^{-1} m

_____

_____

36. Critique Reasoning Jerod's friend Al had the following homework problem:

Express 5.6×10^{-7} in standard form.

Al wrote 56,000,000. How can Jerod explain Al's error and how to correct it?

_____

_____

_____

37. Make a Conjecture Two numbers are written in scientific notation. The number with a positive exponent is divided by the number with a negative exponent. Describe the result. Explain your answer.

_____

_____

_____

Work Area

Comparing Very Small Numbers

COMMON CORE **8.EE.3**
Use numbers expressed in the form of a single digit times an integer power of 10 to... express how many times as much one is than the other.

 ESSENTIAL QUESTION

How can you compare very small numbers in scientific notation?

EXPLORE ACTIVITY COMMON CORE **8.EE.3**

Comparing Very Small Numbers

A Compare 0.0000003 and 0.00009 using standard notation.

Multiply the fraction by a ratio equal to 1, and simplify.

$$\frac{0.00009}{0.0000003} = \frac{0.00009}{0.0000003} \cdot \frac{10^{\boxed{}}}{10^7} = \frac{\boxed{}}{3} = \boxed{}$$

So, 0.00009 is _____ times greater than 0.0000003.

B Compare 0.0000003 and 0.00009 using scientific notation.

$0.0000003 = 3 \times 10^{\boxed{}}$ and $0.00009 = 9 \times 10^{\boxed{}}$

First compare the powers of 10 in a ratio of greater to lesser:

$$\frac{10^{-5}}{10^{-7}} = 10^{\boxed{}} = \boxed{}$$

Then compare the corresponding multipliers: $\dfrac{\boxed{}}{3} = $ _____

So, 9×10^{-5} is $100 \cdot$ _____ = _____ times greater than 3×10^{-7}.

Reflect

1. Explain why 9×10^{-5} is greater than 3×10^{-7}.

_____

_____

2. Use both standard notation and scientific notation to explain why 1×10^{-1} is less than 1×10^{0}.

_____

_____

_____

Comparing Very Small Numbers in the Real World

Using scientific notation can help you compare very small numbers.

EXAMPLE

 COMMON CORE 8.EE.3

The thickness of a piece of paper is about 8×10^{-5} meter. The thickness of a human hair is about 2×10^{-5} meter. About how many times thicker is a piece of paper than a human hair?

$$\frac{10^{-5}}{10^{-5}} = 10^0 = 1 \qquad \text{Compare the powers of 10.}$$

$$\frac{8}{2} = 4 \qquad \text{Compare the multipliers.}$$

So, a piece of paper is about $1 \cdot 4 = 4$ times thicker than a human hair.

Practice

1. Complete the statements to express how many times greater 4×10^{-2} is than 2×10^{-4}.

$$\frac{\boxed{}}{10^{-4}} = 10^{\boxed{}} = \underline{\hspace{2cm}}, \text{ and } \frac{\boxed{}}{2} = \underline{\hspace{2cm}}$$

So, 4×10^{-2} is $100 \cdot \boxed{} = \boxed{}$ times greater than 2×10^{-4}.

2. The diameter of a human red blood cell is about 7×10^{-3} mm, and the diameter of a grain of salt is about 3×10^{-1} mm. Which is larger? About how many times larger? Explain.

_____

_____

3. The average mass of a golden hamster is about 100 grams. The average mass of an African elephant is about 6×10^3 kilograms. About how many times greater is the mass of the elephant than the mass of the hamster? Use scientific notation to explain.

_____

_____

4. The diameter of a cold virus cell is about 3×10^{-9} meter, and the diameter of a streptococcus bacterium cell is about 9×10^{-7} meter. Which is greater and about how many times greater?

_____

_____

Operations with Scientific Notation

COMMON CORE 8.EE.4

Perform operations ... in scientific notation. ... choose units of appropriate size for measurements .... Interpret scientific notation ... generated by technology.

? ESSENTIAL QUESTION

How do you add, subtract, multiply, and divide using scientific notation?

EXPLORE ACTIVITY COMMON CORE 8.EE.4

Adding and Subtracting with Scientific Notation

Numbers in scientific notation can be added and subtracted, either directly or by rewriting them in standard form.

EXAMPLE 1 The table below shows the population of the three largest countries in North America in 2011. Find the total population of these countries.

Country	United States	Canada	Mexico
Population	3.1×10^8	3.38×10^7	1.1×10^8

Method 1:

STEP 1 Write each population with the same power of 10.

United States: _____ $\times 10^8$

Canada: _____ $\times 10^8$

Mexico: _____ $\times 10^8$

STEP 2 Add the multipliers for each population.

$3.1 + \boxed{} + \boxed{} = \boxed{}$

STEP 3 Write the final answer in scientific notation: _____ $\times 10^8$.

Method 2:

STEP 1 Write each number in standard notation.

United States: _____

Canada: _____

Mexico: _____

STEP 2 Find the sum of the numbers in standard notation.

$310{,}000{,}000 + \boxed{} + \boxed{} = \boxed{}$

STEP 3 Write the final answer in scientific notation: _____ $\times 10^8$.

YOUR TURN

Personal Math Trainer
Online Assessment and Intervention

my.hrw.com

1. Using the population table above, how many more people live in Mexico than in Canada? Write your answer in scientific notation.

Math On the Spot
my.hrw.com

Multiplying and Dividing with Scientific Notation

Numbers in scientific notation can be multiplied and divided directly by using properties of exponents.

EXAMPLE 2 *Problem Solving* COMMON CORE 8.EE.4

When the Sun makes an orbit around the center of the Milky Way, it travels 2.025×10^{14} kilometers. The orbit takes 225 million years. At what rate does the Sun travel? Write your answer in scientific notation.

Analyze Information

The answer is the number of kilometers per year that the Sun travels around the Milky Way.

Formulate a Plan

Set up a division problem using Rate $= \frac{\text{Distance}}{\text{Time}}$ to represent the situation.

Solve

Math Talk
Mathematical Practices

Could you write 2.025×10^{14} in standard notation to do the division? Would this be a good way to solve the problem?

STEP 1 Substitute the values from the problem into the Rate formula.

Rate $= \frac{2.025 \times 10^{14} \text{ kilometers}}{225,000,000 \text{ years}}$

STEP 2 Write the expression for rate with years in scientific notation.

Rate $= \frac{2.025 \times 10^{14} \text{ kilometers}}{2.25 \times 10^{8} \text{ years}}$ 225 million $= 2.25 \times 10^{8}$

STEP 3 Find the quotient by dividing the decimals and using the laws of exponents.

$2.025 \div 2.25 = 0.9$ *Divide the multipliers.*

$\frac{10^{14}}{10^{8}} = 10^{14-8} = 10^{6}$ *Divide the powers of 10.*

STEP 4 Combine the answers to write the rate in scientific notation.

Rate $= 0.9 \times 10^{6} = 9.0 \times 10^{5}$ km per year

Justify and Evaluate

Check your answer using multiplication.

$900,000 \times 225,000,000 = 202,500,000,000,000$, or 2.025×10^{14}. The answer is correct.

YOUR TURN

2. Light travels at a speed of 1.86×10^5 miles per second. It takes light from the Sun about 4.8×10^3 seconds to reach Saturn. Find the approximate distance from the Sun to Saturn. Write your answer

in scientific notation. _____

3. Light travels at the speed of 1.17×10^7 miles per minute. Pluto's average distance from the Sun is 3,670,000,000 miles. On average, how long does it take sunlight to reach Pluto? Write your answer in scientific

notation. _____

Scientific Notation on a Calculator

On many scientific calculators, you can enter numbers in scientific notation by using a function labeled "ee" or "EE". Usually, the letter "E" takes the place of "×10". So, the number 4.1×10^9 would appear as 4.1E9 on the calculator.

Math On the Spot

my.hrw.com

EXAMPLE 3 *Real World*   COMMON CORE 8.EE.4

The table shows the approximate areas for three continents given in square meters. What is the total area of these three continents? Write the answer in scientific notation using more appropriate units.

Continent	Asia	Africa	Europe
Area (m²)	4.4×10^{13}	3.02×10^{13}	1.04×10^{13}

Find $4.4 \times 10^{13} + 3.02 \times 10^{13} + 1.04 \times 10^{13}$.

Enter 4.4E13 + 3.02E13 + 1.04E13 on your calculator.

Write the results from your calculator: 8.46E13.

Write this number in scientific notation: 8.46×10^{13} m².

Square kilometers is more appropriate: 8.46×10^7 km².

> Because 1 km = 1,000 m, 1 km² = 1,000² m², or 10⁶ m². Divide by 10⁶.

YOUR TURN

Write each number using calculator notation.

4. 7.5×10^5 **5.** 3×10^{-7} **6.** 2.7×10^{13}

_____   _____   _____

Write each number using scientific notation.

7. 4.5E−1   **8.** 5.6E12   **9.** 6.98E−8

_____   _____   _____

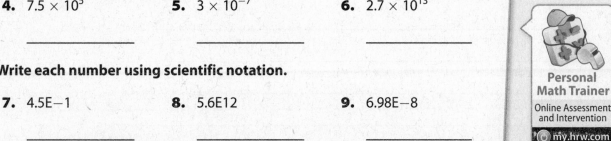

Add or subtract. Write your answer in scientific notation. (Explore Activity Example 1)

1. $4.2 \times 10^6 + 2.25 \times 10^5 + 2.8 \times 10^6$

$4.2 \times 10^6 + \boxed{} \times 10^{\boxed{}} + 2.8 \times 10^6$

$4.2 + \boxed{} + \boxed{}$

$\boxed{} \times 10^{\boxed{}}$

2. $8.5 \times 10^3 - 5.3 \times 10^3 - 1.0 \times 10^2$

$8.5 \times 10^3 - 5.3 \times 10^3 - \boxed{} \times 10^{\boxed{}}$

$\boxed{} - \boxed{} - \boxed{}$

$\boxed{} \times 10^{\boxed{}}$

3. $1.25 \times 10^2 + 0.50 \times 10^2 + 3.25 \times 10^2$

_____

4. $6.2 \times 10^5 - 2.6 \times 10^4 - 1.9 \times 10^2$

_____

Multiply or divide. Write your answer in scientific notation. (Example 2)

5. $\left(1.8 \times 10^9\right)\left(6.7 \times 10^{12}\right)$ _____

6. $\dfrac{3.46 \times 10^{17}}{2 \times 10^9}$ _____

7. $\left(5 \times 10^{12}\right)\left(3.38 \times 10^6\right)$ _____

8. $\dfrac{8.4 \times 10^{21}}{4.2 \times 10^{14}}$ _____

Write each number using calculator notation. (Example 3)

9. 3.6×10^{11}

_____

10. 7.25×10^{-5}

_____

11. 8×10^{-1}

_____

Write each number using scientific notation. (Example 3)

12. 7.6E−4

_____

13. 1.2E16

_____

14. 9E1

_____

? ESSENTIAL QUESTION CHECK-IN

15. How do you add, subtract, multiply, and divide numbers written in scientific notation?

_____

_____

_____

_____

_____

2.4 Independent Practice

 COMMON CORE   8.EE.4

Personal Math Trainer

Online Assessment and Intervention

my.hrw.com

16. An adult blue whale can eat 4.0×10^7 krill in a day. At that rate, how many krill can an adult blue whale eat in 3.65×10^2 days?

_____

17. A newborn baby has about 26,000,000,000 cells. An adult has about 4.94×10^{13} cells. How many times as many cells does an adult have than a newborn? Write your answer in scientific notation.

_____

Represent Real-World Problems The table shows the number of tons of waste generated and recovered (recycled) in 2010.

	Paper	**Glass**	**Plastics**
Tons generated	7.131×10^7	1.153×10^7	3.104×10^7
Tons recovered	4.457×10^7	0.313×10^7	0.255×10^7

18. What is the total amount of paper, glass, and plastic waste generated?

_____

19. What is the total amount of paper, glass, and plastic waste recovered?

_____

20. What is the total amount of paper, glass, and plastic waste *not* recovered?

_____

21. Which type of waste has the lowest recovery ratio?

_____

Social Studies The table shows the approximate populations of three countries.

Country	China	France	Australia
Population	1.3×10^9	6.48×10^7	2.15×10^7

22. How many more people live in France than in Australia?

_____

23. The area of Australia is 2.95×10^6 square miles. What is the approximate average number of people per square mile in Australia?

_____

_____

24. How many times greater is the population of China than the population of France? Write your answer in standard notation.

_____

25. Mia is 7.01568×10^6 minutes old. Convert her age to more appropriate units using years, months, and days. Assume each month to have 30.5 days.

_____

26. Courtney takes 2.4×10^4 steps during her a long-distance run. Each step covers an average of 810 mm. What total distance (in mm) did Courtney cover during her run? Write your answer in scientific notation. Then convert the distance to the more appropriate unit kilometers. Write that answer in standard form.

_____

27. **Social Studies** The U.S. public debt as of October 2010 was $\$9.06 \times 10^{12}$. What was the average U.S. public debt per American if the population in 2010 was 3.08×10^8 people?

_____

 FOCUS ON HIGHER ORDER THINKING

© Houghton Mifflin Harcourt Publishing Company

Work Area

28. **Communicate Mathematical Ideas** How is multiplying and dividing numbers in scientific notation different from adding and subtracting numbers in scientific notation?

_____

_____

_____

_____

_____

29. **Explain the Error** A student found the product of 8×10^6 and 5×10^9 to be 4×10^{15}. What is the error? What is the correct product?

_____

_____

30. **Communicate Mathematical Ideas** Describe a procedure that can be used to simplify $\dfrac{\left(4.87 \times 10^{12}\right) - \left(7 \times 10^{10}\right)}{\left(3 \times 10^7\right) + \left(6.1 \times 10^8\right)}$. Write the expression in scientific notation in simplified form.

_____

_____

_____

_____

_____

_____

Ready to Go On?

Personal Math Trainer
Online Assessment and Intervention
my.hrw.com

2.1 Integer Exponents

Find the value of each power.

1. 3^{-4} _____

2. 35^0 _____

3. 4^4 _____

Use the properties of exponents to write an equivalent expression.

4. $8^3 \cdot 8^7$ _____

5. $\dfrac{12^6}{12^2}$ _____

6. $(10^3)^5$ _____

2.2 Scientific Notation with Positive Powers of 10

Convert each number to scientific notation or standard notation.

7. 2,000 _____

8. 91,007,500 _____

9. 1.0395×10^9 _____

10. 4×10^2 _____

2.3 Scientific Notation with Negative Powers of 10

Convert each number to scientific notation or standard notation.

11. 0.02 _____

12. 0.000701 _____

13. 8.9×10^{-5} _____

14. 4.41×10^{-2} _____

2.4 Operations with Scientific Notation

Perform the operation. Write your answer in scientific notation.

15. $7 \times 10^6 - 5.3 \times 10^6$ _____

16. $3.4 \times 10^4 + 7.1 \times 10^5$ _____

17. $(2 \times 10^4)(5.4 \times 10^6)$ _____

18. $\dfrac{7.86 \times 10^9}{3 \times 10^4}$ _____

19. Neptune's average distance from the Sun is 4.503×10^9 km. Mercury's average distance from the Sun is 5.791×10^7 km. About how many times farther from the Sun is Neptune than Mercury? Write your answer in scientific notation.

_____

? ESSENTIAL QUESTION

20. How is scientific notation used in the real world?

_____

_____

_____

COMMON CORE
Assessment Readiness

Personal Math Trainer
Online Assessment and Intervention
my.hrw.com

Selected Response

1. Which of the following is equivalent to 6^{-3}?

  Ⓐ 216   Ⓒ $-\frac{1}{216}$

  Ⓑ $\frac{1}{216}$ Ⓓ -216

2. About 786,700,000 passengers traveled by plane in the United States in 2010. What is this number written in scientific notation?

  Ⓐ $7,867 \times 10^5$ passengers

  Ⓑ 7.867×10^2 passengers

  Ⓒ 7.867×10^8 passengers

  Ⓓ 7.867×10^9 passengers

3. In 2011, the population of Mali was about 1.584×10^7 people. What is this number written in standard notation?

  Ⓐ 1.584 people

  Ⓑ 1,584 people

  Ⓒ 15,840,000 people

  Ⓓ 158,400,000 people

4. The square root of a number is between 7 and 8. Which could be the number?

  Ⓐ 72   Ⓒ 51

  Ⓑ 83   Ⓓ 66

5. Each entry-level account executive in a large company makes an annual salary of $\$3.48 \times 10^4$. If there are 5.2×10^2 account executives in the company, how much do they make in all?

  Ⓐ $\$6.69 \times 10^1$

  Ⓑ $\$3.428 \times 10^4$

  Ⓒ $\$3.532 \times 10^4$

  Ⓓ $\$1.8096 \times 10^7$

6. Place the numbers in order from least to greatest.

  $0.24, 4 \times 10^{-2}, 0.042, 2 \times 10^{-4}, 0.004$

  Ⓐ $2 \times 10^{-4}, 4 \times 10^{-2}, 0.004, 0.042, 0.24$

  Ⓑ $0.004, 2 \times 10^{-4}, 0.042, 4 \times 10^{-2}, 0.24$

  Ⓒ $0.004, 2 \times 10^{-4}, 4 \times 10^{-2}, 0.042, 0.24$

  Ⓓ $2 \times 10^{-4}, 0.004, 4 \times 10^{-2}, 0.042, 0.24$

7. Guillermo is $5\frac{5}{6}$ feet tall. What is this number of feet written as a decimal?

  Ⓐ 5.7 feet   Ⓒ 5.83 feet

  Ⓑ $5.\overline{7}$ feet   Ⓓ $5.8\overline{3}$ feet

8. A human hair has a width of about 6.5×10^{-5} meter. What is this width written in standard notation?

  Ⓐ 0.00000065 meter

  Ⓑ 0.0000065 meter

  Ⓒ 0.000065 meter

  Ⓓ 0.00065 meter

Mini-Task

9. Consider the following numbers: 7000, 700, 70, 0.7, 0.07, 0.007

  a. Write the numbers in scientific notation.

  _____

  _____

  b. Look for a pattern in the given list and the list in scientific notation. Which numbers are missing from the lists?

  _____

  c. Make a conjecture about the missing numbers.

  _____

  _____

Study Guide Review

MODULE 1 Real Numbers

Key Vocabulary
cube root *(raiz cúbica)*
irrational number *(número irracional)*
perfect cube *(cubo perfecto)*
perfect square *(cuadrado perfecto)*
principal square root *(raíz cuadrada principal)*
rational number *(número racional)*
real number *(número real)*
repeating decimal *(decimal periódico)*
square root *(raíz cuadrada)*
terminating decimal *(decimal finito)*

? **ESSENTIAL QUESTION**

How can you use real numbers to solve real-world problems?

EXAMPLE 1

Write $0.\overline{81}$ as a fraction in simplest form.

$$x = 0.\overline{81}$$
$$100x = 81.\overline{81}$$
$$\underline{-x \quad -0.\overline{81}}$$
$$99x = 81$$
$$x = \frac{81}{99}$$
$$x = \frac{9}{11}$$

EXAMPLE 2

Solve each equation for x.

A $x^2 = 289$

$x = \pm\sqrt{289}$

$x = \pm 17$

The solutions are 17 and -17.

B $x^3 = 1,000$

$x = \sqrt[3]{1,000}$

$x = 10$

The solution is 10.

EXAMPLE 3

Write all names that apply to each number.

A $5.\overline{4}$
rational, real

$5.\overline{4}$ is a repeating decimal.

B $\frac{8}{4}$
whole, integer, rational, real

$\frac{8}{4} = 2$

C $\sqrt{13}$
irrational, real

13 is a whole number that is not a perfect square.

EXAMPLE 4

Order 6, 2π, and $\sqrt{38}$ from least to greatest.

2π is approximately equal to 2 × 3.14, or 6.28.

$\sqrt{38}$ is approximately 6.15 based on the following reasoning.

$$\sqrt{36} < \sqrt{38} < \sqrt{49} \qquad 6 < \sqrt{38} < 7 \qquad 6.1^2 = 37.21 \qquad 6.2^2 = 38.44$$

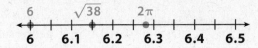

From least to greatest, the numbers are 6, $\sqrt{38}$, and 2π.

EXERCISES

Find the two square roots of each number. If the number is not a perfect square, approximate the values to the nearest 0.05.
(Lesson 1.1)

1. 16 _____

2. $\frac{4}{25}$ _____

3. 225 _____

4. $\frac{1}{49}$ _____

5. $\sqrt{10}$ _____

6. $\sqrt{18}$ _____

Write each decimal as a fraction in simplest form. (Lesson 1.1)

7. $0.\overline{5}$ _____

8. $0.\overline{63}$ _____

9. $0.2\overline{14}$ _____

Solve each equation for x. (Lesson 1.1)

10. $x^2 = 361$

11. $x^3 = 1{,}728$

12. $x^2 = \frac{49}{121}$

_____

_____

_____

Write all names that apply to each number. (Lesson 1.2)

13. $\frac{2}{3}$

14. $-\sqrt{100}$

_____

_____

15. $\frac{15}{5}$

16. $\sqrt{21}$

_____

_____

Compare. Write <, >, or =. (Lesson 1.3)

17. $\sqrt{7} + 5 \bigcirc 7 + \sqrt{5}$

18. $6 + \sqrt{8} \bigcirc \sqrt{6} + 8$

19. $\sqrt{4} - 2 \bigcirc 4 - \sqrt{2}$

Order the numbers from least to greatest. (Lesson 1.3)

20. $\sqrt{81}, \frac{72}{7}, 8.9$ _____

21. $\sqrt{7}, 2.55, \frac{7}{3}$ _____

Exponents and Scientific Notation

? ESSENTIAL QUESTION

How can you use scientific notation to solve real-world problems?

EXAMPLE 1

Write each measurement in scientific notation.

A The diameter of Earth at the equator is approximately 12,700 kilometers.

Move the decimal point in 12,700 four places to the left: 1.2 7 0 0.

$12{,}700 = 1.27 \times 10^4$

B The diameter of a human hair is approximately 0.00254 centimeters.

Move the decimal point in 0.00254 three places to the right: 0.0 0 2.5 4

$0.00254 = 2.54 \times 10^{-3}$

EXAMPLE 2

Find the quotient: $\dfrac{2.4 \times 10^7}{9.6 \times 10^3}$

Divide the multipliers: $2.4 \div 9.6 = 0.25$

Divide the powers of ten: $\dfrac{10^7}{10^3} = 10^{7-3} = 10^4$

Combine the answers and write the product in scientific notation.

$0.25 \times 10^4 = 0.25 \times (10 \times 10^3) = (0.25 \times 10) \times 10^3 = 2.5 \times 10^3$

EXERCISES

Write each number in scientific notation. (Lessons 2.2, 2.3)

1. 25,500,000 _____

2. 0.00734 _____

Write each number in standard notation. (Lessons 2.2, 2.3)

3. 5.23×10^4 _____

4. 1.33×10^{-5} _____

Simplify each expression. (Lessons 2.1, 2.4)

5. $(9 - 7)^3 \cdot 5^0 + (8 + 3)^2$ _____

6. $\dfrac{(4 + 2)^2}{[(9 - 3)^3]^2}$ _____

7. $3.2 \times 10^5 + 1.25 \times 10^4 + 2.9 \times 10^5$

_____

8. $(2{,}600)(3.24 \times 10^4)$

_____

Unit 1 Performance Tasks

1. **CAREERS IN MATH** **Astronomer** An astronomer is studying Proxima Centauri, which is the closest star to our Sun. Proxima Centauri is 39,900,000,000,000,000 meters away.

   a. Write this distance in scientific notation.

   _____

   b. Light travels at a speed of 3.0×10^8 m/s (meters per second). How can you use this information to calculate the time in seconds it takes for light from Proxima Centauri to reach Earth? How many seconds does it take? Write your answer in scientific notation.

   _____

   _____

   c. Knowing that 1 year $= 3.1536 \times 10^7$ seconds, how many years does it take for light to travel from Proxima Centauri to Earth? Write your answer in standard notation. Round your answer to two decimal places.

   _____

2. Cory is making a poster of common geometric shapes. He draws a square with a side of length 4^3 cm, an equilateral triangle with a height of $\sqrt{200}$ cm, a circle with a circumference of 8π cm, a rectangle with length $\frac{122}{5}$ cm, and a parallelogram with base 3.14 cm.

   a. Which of these numbers are irrational?

   _____

   b. Write the numbers in this problem in order from least to greatest. Approximate π as 3.14.

   _____

   c. Explain why 3.14 is rational, but π is not.

   _____

   _____

   _____

UNIT 1 MIXED REVIEW
Assessment Readiness
COMMON CORE

Personal Math Trainer
Online Assessment and Intervention
my.hrw.com

Selected Response

1. A square on a large calendar has an area of 4,220 square millimeters. Between which two integers is the length of one side of the square?

Ⓐ between 20 and 21 millimeters

Ⓑ between 64 and 65 millimeters

Ⓒ between 204 and 205 millimeters

Ⓓ between 649 and 650 millimeters

2. Which of the following numbers is rational but **not** an integer?

Ⓐ −9   Ⓒ 0

Ⓑ −4.3   Ⓓ 3

3. Which statement is false?

Ⓐ No integers are irrational numbers.

Ⓑ All whole numbers are integers.

Ⓒ All rational numbers are real numbers.

Ⓓ All integers are whole numbers.

4. In 2011, the population of Laos was about 6.586×10^6 people. What is this number written in standard notation?

Ⓐ 6,586 people

Ⓑ 658,600 people

Ⓒ 6,586,000 people

Ⓓ 65,860,000 people

5. Which of the following is **not** true?

Ⓐ $\sqrt{16} + 4 > \sqrt{4} + 5$

Ⓑ $4\pi > 12$

Ⓒ $\sqrt{18} + 2 < \frac{15}{2}$

Ⓓ $6 - \sqrt{35} < 0$

6. Which number is between $\sqrt{50}$ and $\frac{5\pi}{2}$?

Ⓐ $\frac{22}{3}$ Ⓒ 6

Ⓑ $2\sqrt{8}$ Ⓓ $\pi + 3$

7. Which number is indicated on the number line?

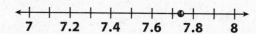

Ⓐ $\pi + 4$

Ⓑ $\frac{152}{20}$

Ⓒ $\sqrt{14} + 4$

Ⓓ $7.\overline{8}$

8. Which of the following is the number 5.03×10^{-5} written in standard form?

Ⓐ 503,000

Ⓑ 50,300,000

Ⓒ 0.00503

Ⓓ 0.0000503

9. In a recent year, about 20,700,000 passengers traveled by train in the United States. What is this number written in scientific notation?

Ⓐ 2.07×10^1 passengers

Ⓑ 2.07×10^4 passengers

Ⓒ 2.07×10^7 passengers

Ⓓ 2.07×10^8 passengers

10. A quarter weighs about 0.025 pounds. What is this weight written in scientific notation?

Ⓐ 2.5×10^{-2} pounds

Ⓑ 2.5×10^1 pounds

Ⓒ 2.5×10^{-1} pounds

Ⓓ 2.5×10^2 pounds

11. Which fraction is equivalent to $0.\overline{45}$?

    (A) $\frac{4}{9}$ (C) $\frac{4}{5}$

    (B) $\frac{5}{9}$ (D) $\frac{5}{11}$

12. What is the value of x if $x^2 = \frac{36}{81}$?

    (A) $\frac{2}{3}$ (C) $\frac{4}{9}$

    (B) $\pm\frac{2}{3}$ (D) $\pm\frac{4}{9}$

13. What is $\dfrac{[(9-2)^2]^4}{(4+3)^5}$ written in simplest form?

    (A) 7

    (B) 21

    (C) 49

    (D) 343

14. The total land area on Earth is about 6×10^7 square miles. The land area of Australia is about 3×10^6 square miles. About how many times larger is the land area on Earth than the land area of Australia?

    (A) 2

    (B) 10

    (C) 20

    (D) 60

15. What is the value of the expression $8.3 \times 10^4 - 2.5 \times 10^3 - 1.9 \times 10^4$ written in scientific notation?

    (A) 3.9×10^3

    (B) 3.9×10^4

    (C) 6.15×10^3

    (D) 6.15×10^4

16. What is the value of the expression $(2.3 \times 10^7)(1.4 \times 10^{-2})$ written in scientific notation?

    (A) 3.7×10^{-14}

    (B) 3.7×10^5

    (C) 0.322×10^6

    (D) 3.22×10^5

17. What is the value of $\sqrt[3]{64}$?

    (A) 2

    (B) 4

    (C) 8

    (D) 16

Mini-Task

18. Amanda says that a human fingernail has a thickness of about 4.2×10^{-4} meter. Justin says that a human fingernail has a thickness of about 0.42 millimeter.

    a. What is the width in meters written in standard notation?

    _____

    b. Do Justin's and Amanda's measurements agree? Explain.

    _____

    _____

    _____

    _____

    c. Explain why Justin's estimate of the thickness of a human fingernail is more appropriate than Amanda's estimate.

    _____

    _____

    _____

    _____

    _____

    _____

Proportional and Nonproportional Relationships and Functions

MODULE 3

Proportional Relationships

COMMON CORE 8.EE.5, 8.EE.6, 8.F.2, 8.F.4

MODULE 4

Nonproportional Relationships

COMMON CORE 8.EE.6, 8.F.2, 8.F.3, 8.F.4

MODULE 5

Writing Linear Equations

COMMON CORE 8.F.4, 8.SP.1, 8.SP.2, 8.SP.3

MODULE 6

Functions

COMMON CORE 8.EE.5, 8.F.1, 8.F.2, 8.F.3, 8.F.4, 8.F.5

CAREERS IN MATH

Cost Estimator A cost estimator determines the cost of a product or project, which helps businesses decide whether or not to manufacture a product or build a structure. Cost estimators analyze the costs of labor, materials, and use of equipment, among other things. Cost estimators use math when they assemble and analyze data. If you are interested in a career as a cost estimator, you should study these mathematical subjects:

- Algebra
- Trigonometry
- Calculus

Research other careers that require analyzing costs.

Unit 2 Performance Task

At the end of the unit, check out how **cost estimators** use math.

Vocabulary Preview

Use the puzzle to preview key vocabulary from this unit. Unscramble the circled letters within the found words to answer the riddle at the bottom of the page.

```
D  I  N  T  F  O  K  F  Z  Y  X  I  R  H  Ⓛ
T  I  Ⓞ  N  O  T  N  I  R  A  V  Z  B  I
U  U  R  Z  I  E  K  N  M  C  J  E  H  Z  N
Ⓟ  N  X  E  V  T  T  H  W  C  V  W  S  E  E
T  A  E  B  U  E  C  E  K  Q  O  P  D  U  A
U  I  V  Ⓡ  N  P  Ⓝ  M  K  Q  W  N  Z  R
Ⓞ  X  G  C  B  O  I  Q  U  M  Y  X  P  L  E
C  P  E  B  Ⓛ  K  B  T  J  F  H  L  A  K  Q
J  Ⓟ  V  S  L  Q  M  J  Ⓡ  G  H  R  U  N  U
T  E  F  N  I  Z  B  M  C  A  D  A  X  A  Ⓐ
T  T  O  S  V  D  T  H  W  B  T  D  B  E  T
K  O  O  I  I  E  Y  W  U  O  Q  E  P  K  I
P  G  T  G  L  S  O  J  Q  R  F  D  I  Q  Ⓞ
D  T  A  M  H  Q  T  S  T  A  J  Q  X  O  N
B  Ⓘ  V  A  R  I  A  T  E  D  A  Ⓣ  A  Y  N
```

- The *y*-coordinate of the point where the graph crosses the *y*-axis. (Lesson 4.2)
- A rule that assigns exactly one output to each input. (Lesson 6.1)
- The result after applying the function machine's rule. (Lesson 6.1)
- A rate in which the second quantity in the comparison is one unit. (Lesson 3.3)
- The ratio of change in rise to the corresponding change in run on a graph. (Lesson 3.2)
- A set of data that is made up of two paired variables. (Lesson 5.3)
- An equation whose solutions form a straight line on a coordinate plane. (Lesson 4.1)

© Houghton Mifflin Harcourt Publishing Company

Q: How much of the money earned does a professional sports team pay its star athlete?

A: An __ __ __ __ __ __ __ – __ __ __ __ __ __ __ __!

Proportional Relationships

ESSENTIAL QUESTION

How can you use proportional relationships to solve real-world problems?

Real-World Video

Speedboats can travel at fast rates while sailboats travel more slowly. If you graphed distance versus time for both types of boats, you could tell by the steepness of the graph which boat was faster.

my.hrw.com

GO DIGITAL

my.hrw.com

my.hrw.com

Go digital with your write-in student edition, accessible on any device.

Math On the Spot

Scan with your smart phone to jump directly to the online edition, video tutor, and more.

Animated Math

Interactively explore key concepts to see how math works.

Personal Math Trainer

Get immediate feedback and help as you work through practice sets.

Are YOU Ready?

Complete these exercises to review skills you will need for this module.

Personal Math Trainer

Online Assessment and Intervention

my.hrw.com

Write Fractions as Decimals

EXAMPLE $\dfrac{1.7}{2.5} = ?$

Multiply the numerator and the denominator by a power of 10 so that the denominator is a whole number.

$\dfrac{1.7 \times 10}{2.5 \times 10} = \dfrac{17}{25}$

Write the fraction as a division problem.
Write a decimal point and zeros in the dividend.
Place a decimal point in the quotient.
Divide as with whole numbers.

$$\begin{array}{r} 0.68 \\ 25\overline{)17.00} \\ -15\,0 \\ \hline 2\,00 \\ -2\,00 \\ \hline 0 \end{array}$$

Write each fraction as a decimal.

1. $\dfrac{3}{8}$ _____

2. $\dfrac{0.3}{0.4}$ _____

3. $\dfrac{0.13}{0.2}$ _____

4. $\dfrac{0.39}{0.75}$ _____

5. $\dfrac{4}{5}$ _____

6. $\dfrac{0.1}{2}$ _____

7. $\dfrac{3.5}{14}$ _____

8. $\dfrac{7}{14}$ _____

9. $\dfrac{0.3}{10}$ _____

Solve Proportions

EXAMPLE $\dfrac{5}{7} = \dfrac{x}{14}$

$\dfrac{5 \times 2}{7 \times 2} = \dfrac{x}{14}$ $7 \times 2 = 14$, so multiply the numerator and denominator by 2.

$\dfrac{10}{14} = \dfrac{x}{14}$ $5 \times 2 = 10$

$x = 10$

Solve each proportion for x.

10. $\dfrac{20}{18} = \dfrac{10}{x}$ _____

11. $\dfrac{x}{12} = \dfrac{30}{72}$ _____

12. $\dfrac{x}{4} = \dfrac{4}{16}$ _____

13. $\dfrac{11}{x} = \dfrac{132}{120}$ _____

14. $\dfrac{36}{48} = \dfrac{x}{4}$ _____

15. $\dfrac{x}{9} = \dfrac{21}{27}$ _____

16. $\dfrac{24}{16} = \dfrac{x}{2}$ _____

17. $\dfrac{30}{15} = \dfrac{6}{x}$ _____

18. $\dfrac{3}{x} = \dfrac{18}{36}$ _____

Reading Start-Up

Vocabulary

Review Words
- constant *(constante)*
- ✔ equivalent ratios *(razones equivalentes)*
- proportion *(proporción)*
- rate *(tasa)*
- ✔ ratios *(razón)*
- ✔ unit rates *(tasas unitarias)*

Preview Words
- constant of proportionality *(constante de proporcionalidad)*
- proportional relationship *(relación proporcional)*
- rate of change *(tasa de cambio)*
- slope *(pendiente)*

Visualize Vocabulary

Use the ✔ words to complete the diagram.

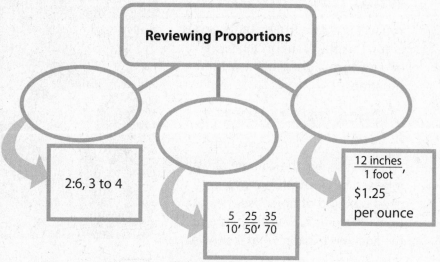

Reviewing Proportions

2:6, 3 to 4

$\dfrac{5}{10}, \dfrac{25}{50}, \dfrac{35}{70}$

$\dfrac{12 \text{ inches}}{1 \text{ foot}}$, $1.25 per ounce

Understand Vocabulary

Match the term on the left to the definition on the right.

1. unit rate

2. constant of proportionality

3. proportional relationship

A. A constant ratio of two variables related proportionally.

B. A rate in which the second quantity in the comparison is one unit.

C. A relationship between two quantities in which the ratio of one quantity to the other quantity is constant.

Active Reading

Key-Term Fold Before beginning the module, create a key-term fold to help you learn the vocabulary in this module. Write the highlighted vocabulary words on one side of the flap. Write the definition for each word on the other side of the flap. Use the key-term fold to quiz yourself on the definitions used in this module.

Unpacking the Standards

Understanding the standards and the vocabulary terms in the standards will help you know exactly what you are expected to learn in this module.

COMMON CORE 8.EE.5

Graph proportional relationships, interpreting the unit rate as the slope of the graph. Compare two different proportional relationships represented in different ways.

Key Vocabulary

proportional relationship
(relación proporcional)
A relationship between two quantities in which the ratio of one quantity to the other quantity is constant.

slope *(pendiente)*
A measure of the steepness of a line on a graph; the rise divided by the run.

unit rate *(tasa unitaria)*
A rate in which the second quantity in the comparison is one unit.

What It Means to You

You will use data from a table and a graph to apply your understanding of rates to analyzing real-world situations.

UNPACKING EXAMPLE 8.EE.5

The table shows the volume of water released by Hoover Dam over a certain period of time. Use the data to make a graph. Find the slope of the line and explain what it shows.

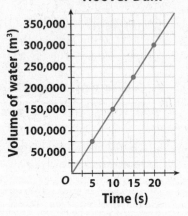

Water Released from Hoover Dam	
Time (s)	**Volume of water (ft³)**
5	75,000
10	150,000
15	225,000
20	300,000

Water Released from Hoover Dam

The slope of the line is 15,000. This means that for every second that passed, 15,000 ft³ of water was released from Hoover Dam.

Suppose another dam releases water over the same period of time at a rate of 180,000 ft³ per minute. How do the two rates compare?

180,000 ft³ per minute is equal to 3,000 ft³ per second. This rate is one fifth the rate released by the Hoover Dam over the same time period.

Visit **my.hrw.com** to see all the **Common Core Standards** unpacked.

⊙ my.hrw.com

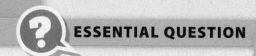
? ESSENTIAL QUESTION

How can you use tables, graphs, and equations to represent proportional situations?

EXPLORE ACTIVITY   COMMON CORE **Prep for 8.EE.6**

Representing Proportional Relationships with Tables

In 1870, the French writer Jules Verne published *20,000 Leagues Under the Sea*, one of the most popular science fiction novels ever written. One definition of a *league* is a unit of measure equaling 3 miles.

A Complete the table.

Distance (leagues)	1	2	6		20,000
Distance (miles)	3		36		

B What relationships do you see among the numbers in the table?

_____

_____

C For each column of the table, find the ratio of the distance in miles to the distance in leagues. Write each ratio in simplest form.

$\dfrac{3}{1} = \boxed{}$ $\dfrac{\boxed{}}{2} = \boxed{}$ $\dfrac{\boxed{}}{6} = \boxed{}$ $\dfrac{36}{\boxed{}} = \boxed{}$ $\dfrac{\boxed{}}{20,000} = \boxed{}$

D What do you notice about the ratios? _____

Reflect

1. If you know the distance between two points in leagues, how can you find the distance in miles? _____

2. If you know the distance between two points in miles, how can you find the distance in leagues? _____

© Houghton Mifflin Harcourt Publishing Company

Representing Proportional Relationships with Equations

The ratio of the distance in miles to the distance in leagues is constant. This relationship is said to be *proportional*. A **proportional relationship** is a relationship between two quantities in which the ratio of one quantity to the other quantity is constant.

A proportional relationship can be described by an equation of the form $y = kx$, where k is a number called the **constant of proportionality**.

Sometimes it is useful to use another form of the equation, $k = \frac{y}{x}$.

EXAMPLE 1

COMMON CORE 8.EE.6

Meghan earns $12 an hour at her part-time job. Show that the relationship between the amount she earned and the number of hours she worked is a proportional relationship. Then write an equation for the relationship.

STEP 1 Make a table relating amount earned to number of hours.

> For every hour Meghan works, she earns $12. So, for 8 hours of work, she earns $8 \times \$12 = \$96$.

Number of hours	1	2	4	8
Amount earned ($)	12	24	48	96

STEP 2 For each number of hours, write the relationship of the amount earned and the number of hours as a ratio in simplest form.

$\dfrac{\text{amount earned}}{\text{number of hours}}$ $\dfrac{12}{1} = \dfrac{12}{1}$ $\dfrac{24}{2} = \dfrac{12}{1}$ $\dfrac{48}{4} = \dfrac{12}{1}$ $\dfrac{96}{8} = \dfrac{12}{1}$

Since the ratios for the two quantities are all equal to $\frac{12}{1}$, the relationship is proportional.

STEP 3 Write an equation.

> First tell what the variables represent.

Let x represent the number of hours.
Let y represent the amount earned.

Use the ratio as the constant of proportionality in the equation $y = kx$.

The equation is $y = \frac{12}{1}x$ or $y = 12x$.

Math Talk
Mathematical Practices

Describe two real-world quantities with a proportional relationship that can be described by the equation $y = 25x$.

YOUR TURN

3. Fifteen bicycles are produced each hour at the Speedy Bike Works. Show that the relationship between the number of bikes produced and the number of hours is a proportional relationship. Then write an equation for the relationship. _____

© Houghton Mifflin Harcourt Publishing Company

Representing Proportional Relationships with Graphs

You can represent a proportional relationship with a graph. The graph will be a line that passes through the origin (0, 0). The graph shows the relationship between distance measured in miles to distance measured in leagues.

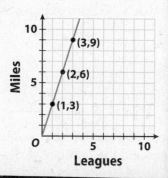

Math On the Spot

my.hrw.com

EXAMPLE 2 · Real World

COMMON CORE 8.EE.6

The graph shows the relationship between the weight of an object on the Moon and its weight on Earth. Write an equation for this relationship.

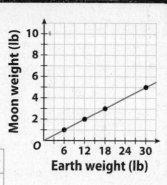

STEP 1 Use the points on the graph to make a table.

Earth weight (lb)	6	12	18	30
Moon weight (lb)	1	2	3	5

STEP 2 Find the constant of proportionality.

$\dfrac{\text{Moon weight}}{\text{Earth weight}}$ $\dfrac{1}{6} = \dfrac{1}{6}$ $\dfrac{2}{12} = \dfrac{1}{6}$ $\dfrac{3}{18} = \dfrac{1}{6}$ $\dfrac{5}{30} = \dfrac{1}{6}$

The constant of proportionality is $\dfrac{1}{6}$.

STEP 3 Write an equation.

Let x represent weight on Earth.

Let y represent weight on the Moon.

The equation is $y = \dfrac{1}{6}x$.   *Replace k with $\dfrac{1}{6}$ in $y = kx$.*

YOUR TURN

The graph shows the relationship between the amount of time that a backpacker hikes and the distance traveled.

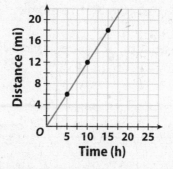

4. What does the point (5, 6) represent?

_____

5. What is the equation of the relationship?

_____

Personal Math Trainer

Online Assessment and Intervention

my.hrw.com

1. **Vocabulary** A proportional relationship is a relationship between two quantities in which the ratio of one quantity to the other quantity

   | is / is not | constant.

2. **Vocabulary** When writing an equation of a proportional relationship in the form $y = kx$, k represents the _____.

3. Write an equation that describes the proportional relationship between the number of days and the number of weeks in a given length of time. (Explore Activity and Example 1)

   a. Complete the table.

Time (weeks)	1	2	4		10
Time (days)	7			56	

   b. Let x represent _____.

   Let y represent _____.

   The equation that describes the relationship is _____.

Each table or graph represents a proportional relationship. Write an equation that describes the relationship. (Example 1 and Example 2)

4. **Physical Science** The relationship between the numbers of oxygen atoms and hydrogen atoms in water is shown below.

Oxygen atoms	2	5		120
Hydrogen atoms	4		34	

   _____

5.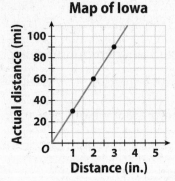

   Map of Iowa

   _____

? ESSENTIAL QUESTION CHECK-IN

6. If you know the equation of a proportional relationship, how can you draw the graph of the equation?

   _____

   _____

3.1 Independent Practice

 COMMON CORE 8.EE.6, 8.F.4

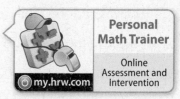
Personal Math Trainer

Online Assessment and Intervention

my.hrw.com

The table shows the relationship between temperatures measured on the Celsius and Fahrenheit scales.

Celsius temperature	0	10	20	30	40	50
Fahrenheit temperature	32	50	68	86	104	122

7. Is the relationship between the temperature scales proportional? Why or why not?

_____

_____

8. Describe the graph of the Celsius-Fahrenheit relationship.

_____

_____

9. **Analyze Relationships** Ralph opened a savings account with a deposit of $100. Every month after that, he deposited $20 more.

a. Why is the relationship described not proportional?

_____

_____

b. How could the situation be changed to make the situation proportional?

_____

_____

10. **Represent Real-World Problems** Describe a real-world situation that can be modeled by the equation $y = \frac{1}{20}x$. Be sure to describe what each variable represents.

_____

_____

Look for a Pattern **The variables x and y are related proportionally.**

11. When $x = 8$, $y = 20$. Find y when $x = 42$. _____

12. When $x = 12$, $y = 8$. Find x when $y = 12$. _____

13. The graph shows the relationship between the distance that a snail crawls and the time that it crawls.

Snail Crawling

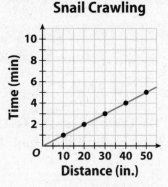

a. Use the points on the graph to make a table.

Distance (in.)					
Time (min)					

b. Write the equation for the relationship and tell what each variable represents.

_____

_____

c. How long does it take the snail to crawl 85 inches? _____

 **FOCUS ON HIGHER ORDER THINKING**

Work Area

14. Communicate Mathematical Ideas Explain why all of the graphs in this lesson show the first quadrant but omit the other three quadrants.

_____

_____

_____

_____

15. Analyze Relationships Complete the table.

Length of side of square	1	2	3	4	5
Perimeter of square					
Area of square					

a. Are the length of a side of a square and the perimeter of the square related proportionally? Why or why not?

_____

_____

b. Are the length of a side of a square and the area of the square related proportionally? Why or why not?

_____

_____

16. Make a Conjecture A table shows a proportional relationship where k is the constant of proportionality. The rows are then switched. How does the new constant of proportionality relate to the original one?

_____

Rate of Change and Slope

COMMON CORE 8.F.4

...Determine the rate of change...of the function from...two (x, y) values, including reading these from a table or from a graph....

? **ESSENTIAL QUESTION**

How do you find a rate of change or a slope?

EXPLORE ACTIVITY   COMMON CORE 8.F.4

Math On the Spot
my.hrw.com

Investigating Rates of Change

A **rate of change** is a ratio of the amount of change in the dependent variable, or *output*, to the amount of change in the independent variable, or *input*.

EXAMPLE 1 Eve keeps a record of the number of lawns she has mowed and the money she has earned. Tell whether the rates of change are constant or variable.

	Day 1	Day 2	Day 3	Day 4
Number of lawns	1	3	6	8
Amount earned ($)	15	45	90	120

STEP 1 Identify the input and output variables.

Input: _____ Output: _____

STEP 2 Find the rates of change.

Day 1 to Day 2: $\dfrac{\text{change in \$}}{\text{change in lawns}} = \dfrac{45 - 15}{3 - 1} = \dfrac{\square}{\square} = \square$

Day 2 to Day 3: $\dfrac{\text{change in \$}}{\text{change in lawns}} = \dfrac{\square - \square}{6 - 3} = \dfrac{\square}{\square} = \square$

Day 3 to Day 4: $\dfrac{\text{change in \$}}{\text{change in lawns}} = \dfrac{120 - \square}{\square - 6} = \dfrac{\square}{\square} = \square$

The rates of change are constant: $ _____ per lawn.

YOUR TURN

1. The table shows the approximate height of a football after it is kicked. Tell whether the rates of change are constant or variable.

Find the rates of change in ft/s: _____

The rates of change are   **constant / variable**.

Time (s)	Height (ft)
0	0
0.5	18
1.5	31
2	26

Personal Math Trainer
Online Assessment and Intervention
my.hrw.com

Using Graphs to Find Rates of Change

You can also use a graph to find rates of change.

The graph shows the distance Nathan bicycled over time. What is Nathan's rate of change?

A Find the rate of change from 1 hour to 2 hours.

$$\frac{\text{change in distance}}{\text{change in time}} = \frac{30 - \square}{2 - 1} = \frac{\square}{1} = \square \text{ miles per hour}$$

B Find the rate of change from 1 hour to 4 hours.

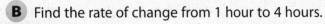

$$\frac{\text{change in distance}}{\text{change in time}} = \frac{60 - \square}{4 - \square} = \frac{\square}{\square} = \square \text{ miles per hour}$$

C Find the rate of change from 2 hours to 4 hours.

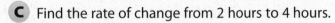

$$\frac{\text{change in distance}}{\text{change in time}} = \frac{60 - \square}{4 - \square} = \frac{\square}{\square} = \square \text{ miles per hour}$$

D Recall that the graph of a proportional relationship is a line through the origin. Explain whether the relationship between Nathan's time and distance is a proportional relationship.

_____

_____

Reflect

2. **Make a Conjecture** Does a proportional relationship have a constant rate of change?

_____

3. Does it matter what interval you use when you find the rate of change of a proportional relationship? Explain.

_____

_____

Calculating Slope *m*

When the rate of change of a relationship is constant, any segment of its graph has the same steepness. The constant rate of change is called the *slope* of the line.

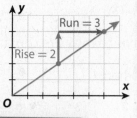

Slope Formula

The **slope** of a line is the ratio of the change in *y*-values (rise) for a segment of the graph to the corresponding change in *x*-values (run).

$$m = \frac{y_2 - y_1}{x_2 - x_1}$$

EXAMPLE 2

COMMON CORE 8.F.4

Find *m*, the slope of the line.

My Notes

STEP 1 Choose two points on the line.
$P_1(x_1, y_1) = (-3, 2)$ $P_2(x_2, y_2) = (-6, 4)$

STEP 2 Find the change in *y*-values (rise $= y_2 - y_1$) and the change in *x*-values (run $= x_2 - x_1$) as you move from one point to the other.

rise $= y_2 - y_1$ run $= x_2 - x_1$
   $= 4 - 2$ $= -6 - (-3)$
   $= 2$ $= -3$

If you move up or right, the change is positive. If you move down or left, the change is negative.

STEP 3 $m = \dfrac{\text{rise}}{\text{run}} = \dfrac{y_2 - y_1}{x_2 - x_1}$

$= \dfrac{2}{-3}$

$= -\dfrac{2}{3}$

YOUR TURN

4. The graph shows the rate at which water is leaking from a tank. The slope of the line gives the leaking rate in gallons per minute. Find the slope of the line.

Rise = _____   Run = _____

Slope = _____

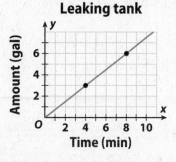

Leaking tank

Guided Practice

Tell whether the rates of change are constant or variable. (Explore Activity Example 1)

1. building measurements _____

Feet	3	12	27	75
Yards	1	4	9	25

2. computers sold _____

Week	2	4	9	20
Number Sold	6	12	25	60

3. distance an object falls _____

Distance (ft)	16	64	144	256
Time (s)	1	2	3	4

4. cost of sweaters _____

Number	2	4	7	9
Cost ($)	38	76	133	171

Erica walks to her friend Philip's house. The graph shows Erica's distance from home over time. (Explore Activity 2)

5. Find the rate of change from 1 minute to 2 minutes.

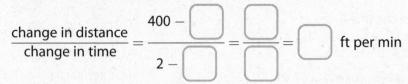

$$\frac{\text{change in distance}}{\text{change in time}} = \frac{400 - \boxed{}}{2 - \boxed{}} = \frac{\boxed{}}{\boxed{}} = \boxed{} \text{ ft per min}$$

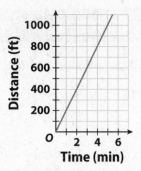

6. Find the rate of change from 1 minute to 4 minutes. _____

Find the slope of each line. (Example 2)

7.

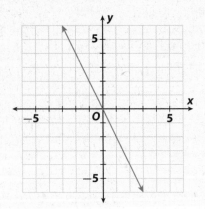

slope = _____

8.

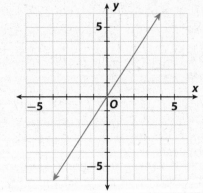

slope = _____

? ESSENTIAL QUESTION CHECK-IN

9. If you know two points on a line, how can you find the rate of change of the variables being graphed?

_____

_____

_____

3.2 Independent Practice

 8.F.4

10. Rectangle *EFGH* is graphed on a coordinate plane with vertices at $E(-3, 5)$, $F(6, 2)$, $G(4, -4)$, and $H(-5, -1)$.

   a. Find the slopes of each side.

   _____

   b. What do you notice about the slopes of opposite sides?

   _____

   c. What do you notice about the slopes of adjacent sides?

   _____

11. A bicyclist started riding at 8:00 A.M. The diagram below shows the distance the bicyclist had traveled at different times. What was the bicyclist's average rate of speed in miles per hour?

8:00 A.M. ← 4.5 miles → 8:18 A.M. ← 7.5 miles → 8:48 A.M.

_____

12. **Multistep** A line passes through $(6, 3)$, $(8, 4)$, and $(n, -2)$. Find the value of *n*.

_____

13. A large container holds 5 gallons of water. It begins leaking at a constant rate. After 10 minutes, the container has 3 gallons of water left.

   a. At what rate is the water leaking?

   _____

   b. After how many minutes will the container be empty?

   _____

14. **Critique Reasoning** Billy found the slope of the line through the points $(2, 5)$ and $(-2, -5)$ using the equation $\frac{2 - (-2)}{5 - (-5)} = \frac{2}{5}$. What mistake did he make?

_____

_____

15. Multiple Representations Graph parallelogram *ABCD* on a coordinate plane with vertices at *A*(3, 4), *B*(6, 1), *C*(0, −2), and *D*(−3, 1).

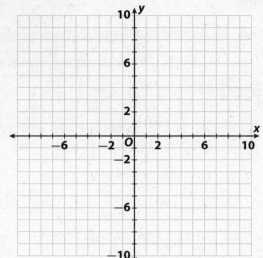

a. Find the slope of each side.

_____

_____

b. What do you notice about the slopes?

_____

_____

c. Draw another parallelogram on the coordinate plane. Do the slopes have the same characteristics?

_____

H.O.T. FOCUS ON HIGHER ORDER THINKING

Work Area

16. Communicate Mathematical Ideas Ben and Phoebe are finding the slope of a line. Ben chose two points on the line and used them to find the slope. Phoebe used two different points to find the slope. Did they get the same answer? Explain.

_____

_____

_____

17. Analyze Relationships Two lines pass through the origin. The lines have slopes that are opposites. Compare and contrast the lines.

_____

_____

_____

_____

18. Reason Abstractly What is the slope of the *x*-axis? Explain.

_____

_____

_____

Using Right Triangles to Explore Slope

COMMON CORE **8.EE.6**

Use similar triangles to explain why the slope *m* is the same between any two distinct points on a non-vertical line in the coordinate plane; . . .

? ESSENTIAL QUESTION

How can you show that the slope of a non-vertical line is constant between any two points on a line?

EXPLORE ACTIVITY COMMON CORE **8.EE.6**

Using Right Triangles to Find Slope

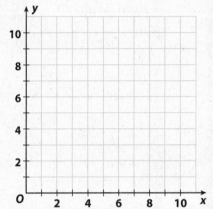

A Plot the points (0, 2) and (8, 6) on the grid. Draw a line through the points.

B Draw and label two different right triangles *A* and *B* with each hypotenuse on the line and a right-angle vertex at the intersection of two gridlines. Make sure that your triangles are the same shape but different sizes.

_____

C Use the triangles *A* and *B* that you drew to complete the table.

Triangle	Rise	Run	Rise/Run
A			
B			

D Are the ratios of *rise* to *run* of triangles *A* and *B* equivalent? Explain.

_____

_____

E Is the slope of the line constant between the points (0, 2) and (2, 3) and the points (2, 3) and (8, 6)? Explain.

_____

_____

Reflect

1. How does a slope of $\frac{3}{9}$ compare with a slope of $\frac{4}{12}$?

_____

1. Select any two pairs of points on the line graphed, draw corresponding right triangles indicating the rise and run for each pair, and show that the slope is the same between the two pairs of points.

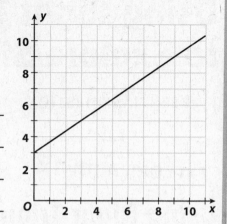

_____

_____

_____

2. The same line is used below to generate different triangles. Verify that the slope ratios are the same for all the triangles generated by points on this line.

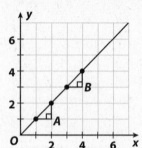 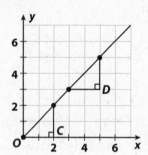 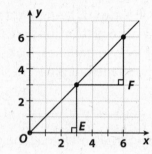

_____

_____

Use slope to determine whether the given points are all on the same line.

3. $(-6, -2)$, $(0, -5)$, $(2, -6)$

_____

_____

4. $(-10, -2)$, $(-5, 0)$, $(10, 6)$

_____

_____

5. A line passes through the point $(0, 0)$ and has a _rise_ over _run_ ratio of $\frac{4}{3}$. Give two other points that the line passes through.

_____

6. A wheelchair ramp is allowed a maximum of one inch of rise for every foot of run. Give the dimensions of three different wheelchair ramps that would meet this requirement.

_____

_____

Interpreting the Unit Rate as Slope

COMMON CORE 8.EE.5

Graph proportional relationships, interpreting the unit rate as the slope of the graph. Compare two different proportional relationships represented in different ways. *Also 8.F.2, 8.F.4*

? **ESSENTIAL QUESTION**

How do you interpret the unit rate as slope?

EXPLORE ACTIVITY **COMMON CORE** 8.EE.5, 8.F.4

Relating the Unit Rate to Slope

A rate is a comparison of two quantities that have different units, such as miles and hours. A **unit rate** is a rate in which the second quantity in the comparison is one unit.

A storm is raging on Misty Mountain. The graph shows the constant rate of change of the snow level on the mountain.

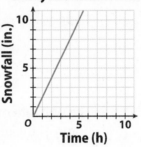

Misty Mountain Storm

A Find the slope of the graph using the points (1, 2) and (5, 10). Remember that the slope is the constant rate of change.

B Find the unit rate of snowfall in inches per hour. Explain your method.

_____

_____

C Compare the slope of the graph and the unit rate of change in the snow level. What do you notice?

_____

D Which unique point on this graph gives you the slope of the graph and the unit rate of change in the snow level? Explain how you found the point.

_____

_____

_____

_____

Graphing Proportional Relationships

You can use a table and a graph to find the unit rate and slope that describe a real-world proportional relationship. The constant of proportionality for a proportional relationship is the same as the slope.

EXAMPLE 1

COMMON CORE **8.EE.5**

Every 3 seconds, 4 cubic feet of water pass over a dam. Draw a graph of the situation. Find the unit rate of this proportional relationship.

STEP 1　Make a table.

Time (s)	3	6	9	12	15
Volume (ft³)	4	8	12	16	20

STEP 2　Draw a graph.

STEP 3　Find the slope.

$$\text{slope} = \frac{\text{rise}}{\text{run}} = \frac{8}{6}$$

$$= \frac{4}{3}$$

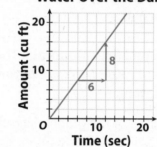

Water Over the Dam

The unit rate of water passing over the dam and the slope of the graph of the relationship are equal, $\frac{4}{3}$ cubic feet per second.

Math Talk
Mathematical Practices

In a proportional relationship, how are the constant of proportionality, the unit rate, and the slope of the graph of the relationship related?

Reflect

1. **What If?** Without referring to the graph, how do you know that the point $\left(1, \frac{4}{3}\right)$ is on the graph?

_____

_____

YOUR TURN

2. Tomas rides his bike at a steady rate of 2 miles every 10 minutes. Graph the situation. Find the unit rate of this proportional relationship.

_____

_____

_____

Tomas's Ride

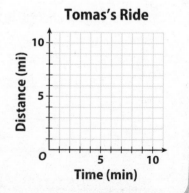

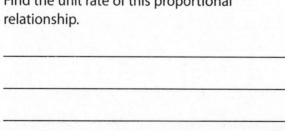

Using Slopes to Compare Unit Rates

You can compare proportional relationships presented in different ways.

Math On the Spot
my.hrw.com

EXAMPLE 2

COMMON CORE 8.EE.5, 8.F.2

The equation $y = 2.75x$ represents the rate, in barrels per hour, that oil is pumped from Well A. The graph represents the rate that oil is pumped from Well B. Which well pumped oil at a faster rate?

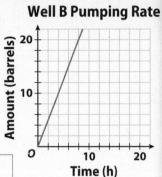

Well B Pumping Rate

STEP 1 Use the equation $y = 2.75x$ to make a table for Well A's pumping rate, in barrels per hour.

Time (h)	1	2	3	4
Quantity (barrels)	2.75	5.5	8.25	11

STEP 2 Use the table to find the slope of the graph of Well A.

$$\text{slope} = \text{unit rate} = \frac{5.5 - 2.75}{2 - 1} = \frac{2.75}{1} = \textbf{2.75 barrels/hour}$$

STEP 3 Use the graph to find the slope of the graph of Well B.

$$\text{slope} = \text{unit rate} = \frac{\text{rise}}{\text{run}} = \frac{10}{4} = \textbf{2.5 barrels/hour}$$

STEP 4 Compare the unit rates.

$2.75 > 2.5$, so Well A's rate, 2.75 barrels/hour, is faster.

Reflect

3. Describe the relationships among the slope of the graph of Well A's rate, the equation representing Well A's rate, and the constant of proportionality.

_____

_____

YOUR TURN

4. The equation $y = 375x$ represents the relationship between x, the time that a plane flies in hours, and y, the distance the plane flies in miles for Plane A. The table represents the relationship for Plane B. Find the slope of the graph for each plane and the plane's rate of speed. Determine which plane is flying at a faster rate of speed.

Time (h)	1	2	3	4
Distance (mi)	425	850	1275	1700

_____

Personal Math Trainer

Online Assessment and Intervention

my.hrw.com

Guided Practice

Give the slope of the graph and the unit rate. (Explore Activity and Example 1)

1. Jorge: 5 miles every 6 hours

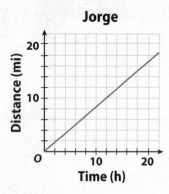

Jorge

_____

2. Akiko

Time (h)	4	8	12	16
Distance (mi)	5	10	15	20

Akiko

_____

3. The equation $y = 0.5x$ represents the distance Henry hikes, in miles, over time, in hours. The graph represents the rate that Clark hikes. Determine which hiker is faster. Explain. (Example 2)

_____

_____

_____

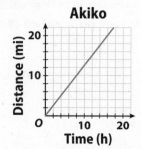

Clark

Write an equation relating the variables in each table. (Example 2)

4.
Time (x)	1	2	4	6
Distance (y)	15	30	60	90

_____

5.
Time (x)	16	32	48	64
Distance (y)	6	12	18	24

_____

? ESSENTIAL QUESTION CHECK-IN

6. Describe methods you can use to show a proportional relationship between two variables, *x* and *y*. For each method, explain how you can find the unit rate and the slope.

_____

_____

_____

_____

_____

3.3 Independent Practice

  8.EE.5, 8.F.2, 8.F.4

Personal
Math Trainer

Online
Assessment and
Intervention

my.hrw.com

7. A Canadian goose migrated at a steady rate of 3 miles every 4 minutes.

a. Fill in the table to describe the relationship.

Time (min)	4	8			20
Distance (mi)			9	12	

b. Graph the relationship.

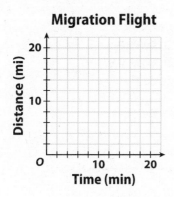

Migration Flight

c. Find the slope of the graph and describe what it means in the context of this problem.

_____

_____

_____

_____

8. Vocabulary A unit rate is a rate in which the

| first quantity / second quantity | in the comparison is one unit.

9. The table and the graph represent the rate at which two machines are bottling milk in gallons per second.

Machine 1

Time (s)	1	2	3	4
Amount (gal)	0.6	1.2	1.8	2.4

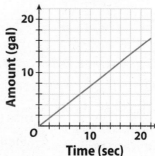

Machine 2

a. Determine the slope and unit rate of each machine.

_____

_____

b. Determine which machine is working at a faster rate.

_____

10. **Cycling** The equation $y = \frac{1}{9}x$ represents the distance y, in kilometers, that Patrick traveled in x minutes while training for the cycling portion of a triathlon. The table shows the distance y Jennifer traveled in x minutes in her training. Who has the faster training rate?

Time (min)	40	64	80	96
Distance (km)	5	8	10	12

_____

_____

_____

 FOCUS ON HIGHER ORDER THINKING

11. **Analyze Relationships** There is a proportional relationship between minutes and dollars per minute, shown on a graph of printing expenses. The graph passes through the point (1, 4.75). What is the slope of the graph? What is the unit rate? Explain.

_____

_____

_____

12. **Draw Conclusions** Two cars start at the same time and travel at different constant rates. A graph for Car A passes through the point (0.5, 27.5), and a graph for Car B passes through (4, 240). Both graphs show distance in miles and time in hours. Which car is traveling faster? Explain.

_____

_____

_____

_____

13. **Critical Thinking** The table shows the rate at which water is being pumped into a swimming pool.

Time (min)	2	5	7	12
Amount (gal)	36	90	126	216

Use the unit rate and the amount of water pumped after 12 minutes to find how much water will have been pumped into the pool after $13\frac{1}{2}$ minutes. Explain your reasoning.

_____

_____

_____

_____

Ready to Go On?

Personal Math Trainer
Online Assessment and Intervention
⏻ my.hrw.com

3.1 Representing Proportional Relationships

1. Find the constant of proportionality for the table of values.

x	2	3	4	5
y	3	4.5	6	7.5

_____

2. Phil is riding his bike. He rides 25 miles in 2 hours, 37.5 miles in 3 hours, and 50 miles in 4 hours. Find the constant of proportionality and write an equation to describe the situation.

_____

3.2 Rate of Change and Slope

Find the slope of each line.

3.

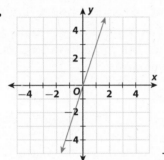

_____

4.

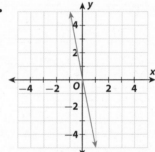

_____

3.3 Interpreting the Unit Rate as Slope

5. The distance Train A travels is represented by $d = 70t$, where d is the distance in kilometers and t is the time in hours. The distance Train B travels at various times is shown in the table. What is the unit rate of each train? Which train is going faster?

Time (hours)	Distance (km)
2	150
4	300
5	375

_____

? ESSENTIAL QUESTION

6. What is the relationship among proportional relationships, lines, rates of change, and slope?

_____

_____

COMMON CORE Assessment Readiness

Personal Math Trainer

Online Assessment and Intervention

my.hrw.com

Selected Response

1. Which of the following is equivalent to 5^{-1}?

Ⓐ 4

Ⓒ $-\frac{1}{5}$

Ⓑ $\frac{1}{5}$

Ⓓ -5

2. Prasert earns $9 an hour. Which table represents this proportional relationship?

Ⓐ
Hours	4	6	8
Earnings ($)	36	54	72

Ⓑ
Hours	4	6	8
Earnings ($)	36	45	54

Ⓒ
Hours	2	3	4
Earnings ($)	9	18	27

Ⓓ
Hours	2	3	4
Earnings ($)	18	27	54

3. A factory produces widgets at a constant rate. After 4 hours, 3,120 widgets have been produced. At what rate are the widgets being produced?

Ⓐ 630 widgets per hour

Ⓑ 708 widgets per hour

Ⓒ 780 widgets per hour

Ⓓ 1,365 widgets per hour

4. A full lake begins dropping at a constant rate. After 4 weeks it has dropped 3 feet. What is the unit rate of change in the lake's level compared to its full level?

Ⓐ 0.75 feet per week

Ⓑ 1.33 feet per week

Ⓒ −0.75 feet per week

Ⓓ −1.33 feet per week

5. What is the slope of the line below?

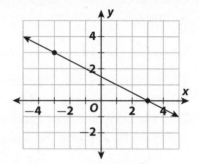

Ⓐ −2

Ⓒ $\frac{1}{2}$

Ⓑ $-\frac{1}{2}$

Ⓓ 2

6. Jim earns $41.25 in 5 hours. Susan earns $30.00 in 4 hours. Pierre's hourly rate is less than Jim's, but more than Susan's. What is his hourly rate?

Ⓐ $6.50

Ⓒ $7.35

Ⓑ $7.75

Ⓓ $8.25

Mini-Task

7. Joelle can read 3 pages in 4 minutes, 4.5 pages in 6 minutes, and 6 pages in 8 minutes.

a. Make a table of the data.

Minutes			
Pages			

b. Use the values in the table to find the unit rate.

_____

c. Graph the relationship between minutes and pages read.

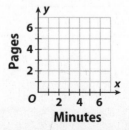

Nonproportional Relationships

ESSENTIAL QUESTION

How can you use non-proportional relationships to solve real-world problems?

Real-World Video

The distance a car can travel on a tank of gas or a full battery charge in an electric car depends on factors such as fuel capacity and the car's efficiency. This is described by a nonproportional relationship.

© my.hrw.com

GO DIGITAL
my.hrw.com

my.hrw.com	**Math On the Spot**	**Animated Math**	**Personal Math Trainer**
Go digital with your write-in student edition, accessible on any device.	Scan with your smart phone to jump directly to the online edition, video tutor, and more.	Interactively explore key concepts to see how math works.	Get immediate feedback and help as you work through practice sets.

Are YOU Ready?

Complete these exercises to review skills you will need for this module.

Integer Operations

EXAMPLE	$-7 - (-4) = -7 + 4$	To subtract an integer, add its opposite.
	$\|-7\| - \|4\|$	The signs are different, so find the difference of the absolute values.
	$7 - 4$, or 3	
	$= -3$	Use the sign of the number with the greater absolute value.

Find each difference.

1. $3 - (-5)$ _____

2. $-4 - 5$ _____

3. $6 - 10$ _____

4. $-5 - (-3)$ _____

5. $8 - (-8)$ _____

6. $9 - 5$ _____

7. $-3 - 9$ _____

8. $0 - (-6)$ _____

9. $12 - (-9)$ _____

10. $-6 - (-4)$ _____

11. $-7 - 10$ _____

12. $5 - 14$ _____

Graph Ordered Pairs (First Quadrant)

EXAMPLE	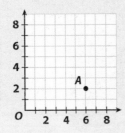	To graph a point at (6, 2), start at the origin.
		Move 6 units right.
		Then move 2 units up.
		Graph point A(6, 2).

Graph each point on the coordinate grid.

13. B (0, 5)

14. C (8, 0)

15. D (5, 7)

16. E (2, 3)

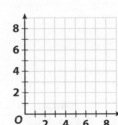

© Houghton Mifflin Harcourt Publishing Company

Reading Start-Up

Vocabulary

Review Words

ordered pair *(par ordenado)*

proportional relationship *(relación proporcional)*

✔ rate of change *(tasa de cambio)*

✔ slope *(pendiente)*

✔ x-coordinate *(coordenada x)*

✔ y-coordinate *(coordenada y)*

Preview Words

linear equation *(ecuación lineal)*

slope-intercept form of an equation *(forma de pendiente-intersección)*

y-intercept *(intersección con el eje y)*

Visualize Vocabulary

Use the ✔ words to complete the diagram. You can put more than one word in each box.

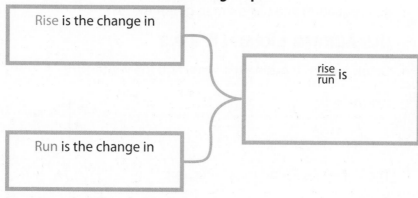

Reviewing Slope

Rise is the change in

Run is the change in

$\frac{rise}{run}$ is

Understand Vocabulary

Complete the sentences using the preview words.

1. The y-coordinate of the point where a graph of a line crosses the

   y-axis is the _____.

2. A _____ is an equation whose solutions form

   a straight line on a coordinate plane.

3. A linear equation written in the form $y = mx + b$ is the

   _____.

Active Reading

Booklet Before beginning the module, create a booklet to help you learn the concepts. Write the main idea of each lesson on each page of the booklet. As you study each lesson, write important details that support the main idea, such as vocabulary and formulas. Refer to your finished booklet as you work on assignments and study for tests.

MODULE 4

Unpacking the Standards

Understanding the standards and the vocabulary terms in the standards will help you know exactly what you are expected to learn in this module.

COMMON CORE **8.F.3**

Interpret the equation $y = mx + b$ as defining a linear function whose graph is a straight line.

Key Vocabulary

slope *(pendiente)*
A measure of the steepness of a line on a graph; the rise divided by the run.

y-intercept *(intersección con el eje y)*
The *y*-coordinate of the point where the graph of a line crosses the *y*-axis.

What It Means to You

You will identify the slope and the *y*-intercept of a line by looking at its equation and use them to graph the line.

UNPACKING EXAMPLE 8.F.3

Graph $y = 3x - 2$ using the slope and the *y*-intercept.

$y = mx + b$

slope   y-intercept

The slope *m* is 3, and the *y*-intercept is -2.

Plot the point $(0, -2)$. Use the slope $3 = \frac{3}{1}$ to find another point by moving *up* 3 and to the *right* 1. Draw the line through the points.

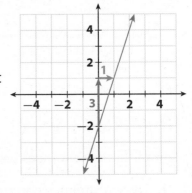

COMMON CORE **8.F.3**

Give examples of functions that are not linear.

Key Vocabulary

function *(función)*
An input-output relationship that has exactly one output for each input.

linear function *(función lineal)*
A function whose graph is a straight line.

What It Means to You

You will distinguish linear relationships from nonlinear relationships by looking at graphs.

UNPACKING EXAMPLE 8.F.3

Which relationship is linear and which is nonlinear?

$P = 4s$

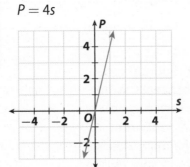

$A = s^2$

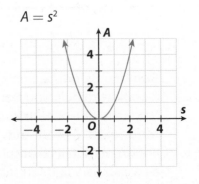

$P = 4s$ is linear because its graph is a line.

$A = s^2$ is not linear because its graph is not a line.

© Houghton Mifflin Harcourt Publishing Company

Representing Linear Nonproportional Relationships

COMMON CORE 8.F.3

Interpret the equation $y = mx + b$ as defining a linear function, whose graph is a straight line; ...

? ESSENTIAL QUESTION

How can you use tables, graphs, and equations to represent linear nonproportional situations?

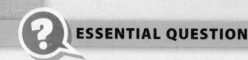 **EXPLORE ACTIVITY** COMMON CORE Prep for 8.F.3

Representing Linear Relationships Using Tables

You can use an equation to describe the relationship between two quantities in a real-world situation. You can use a table to show some values that make the equation true.

EXAMPLE 1 **The equation $y = 3x + 2$ gives the total charge, y, for one person to rent a pair of shoes and bowl x games at Baxter Bowling Lanes based on the prices shown. Make a table of values for this situation.**

STEP 1 Choose several values for x that make sense in context. Count by ones.

x (number of games)	1	2		
y (total cost in dollars)				

STEP 2 Use the equation $y = 3x + 2$ to find y for each value of x.

x (number of games)	1	2		
y (total cost in dollars)	5			

Substitute 1 for x:
$y = 3(1) + 2 = 5$

YOUR TURN

1. Francisco makes $12 per hour doing part-time work on Saturdays. He spends $4 on transportation to and from work. The equation $y = 12x - 4$ gives his earnings y, after transportation costs, for working x hours. Make a table of values for this situation.

x (number of hours)				
y (earnings in dollars)				

Personal Math Trainer

Online Assessment and Intervention

my.hrw.com

Examining Linear Relationships

Recall that a proportional relationship is a relationship between two quantities in which the ratio of one quantity to the other quantity is constant. The graph of a proportional relationship is a line through the origin. Relationships can have a constant rate of change but not be proportional.

The entrance fee for Mountain World theme park is $20. Visitors purchase additional $2 tickets for rides, games, and food. The equation $y = 2x + 20$ gives the total cost, y, to visit the park, including purchasing x tickets.

STEP 1 Complete the table.

x (number of tickets)	0	2	4	6	8
y (total cost in dollars)	20				

STEP 2 Plot the ordered pairs from the table. Describe the shape of the graph.

_____

Theme Park Costs

STEP 3 Find the rate of change between each point and the next. Is the rate constant?

_____

STEP 4 Calculate $\frac{y}{x}$ for the values in the table. Explain why the relationship between number of tickets and total cost is not proportional.

_____

_____

_____

Reflect

2. **Analyze Relationships** Would it make sense to add more points to the graph from $x = 0$ to $x = 10$? Would it make sense to connect the points with a line? Explain.

_____

_____

_____

_____

Representing Linear Relationships Using Graphs

A **linear equation** is an equation whose solutions are ordered pairs that form a line when graphed on a coordinate plane. Linear equations can be written in the form $y = mx + b$. When $b \neq 0$, the relationship between x and y is *nonproportional*.

Math On the Spot
my.hrw.com

EXAMPLE 2

COMMON CORE 8.F.3

The diameter of a Douglas fir tree is currently 10 inches when measured at chest height. Over the next 50 years, the diameter is expected to increase by an average growth rate of $\frac{2}{5}$ inch per year. The equation $y = \frac{2}{5}x + 10$ gives y, the diameter of the tree in inches, after x years. Draw a graph of the equation. Describe the relationship.

STEP 1 Make a table. Choose several values for x that make sense in context. To make calculations easier, choose multiples of 5.

x (years)	0	10	20	30	50
y (diameter in inches)	10	14	18	22	30

STEP 2 Plot the ordered pairs from the table. Then draw a line connecting the points to represent all the possible solutions.

STEP 3 The relationship is linear but nonproportional. The graph is a line but it does not go through the origin.

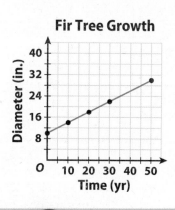

Fir Tree Growth

YOUR TURN

3. Make a table and graph the solutions of the equation $y = -2x + 1$.

x	−1	0	1	2
y				

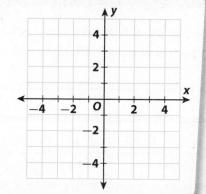

Personal Math Trainer

Online Assessment and Intervention

my.hrw.com

© Houghton Mifflin Harcourt Publishing Company • Image Credits: ©Don Mason/Corbis

Make a table of values for each equation. (Explore Activity Example 1)

1. $y = 2x + 5$

x	−2	−1	0	1	2
y					

2. $y = \frac{3}{8}x - 5$

x	−8	0	8		
y					

Explain why each relationship is not proportional. (Explore Activity 2)

3.

x	0	2	4	6	8
y	3	7	11	15	19

First calculate $\frac{y}{x}$ for the values in the table.

_____

_____

_____

_____

4.

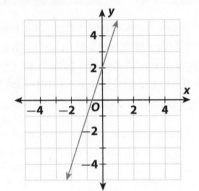

_____

_____

Complete the table for the equation. Then use the table to graph the equation. (Example 2)

5. $y = x - 1$

x	−2	−1	0	1	2
y					

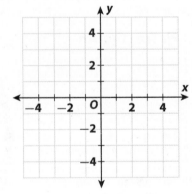

? ESSENTIAL QUESTION CHECK-IN

6. How can you choose values for x when making a table of values representing a real world situation?

_____

_____

_____

4.1 Independent Practice

COMMON CORE 8.F.3

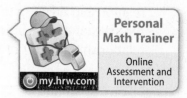

Personal Math Trainer

Online Assessment and Intervention

my.hrw.com

State whether the graph of each linear relationship is a solid line or a set of unconnected points. Explain your reasoning.

7. The relationship between the number of $4 lunches you buy with a $100 school lunch card and the money remaining on the card

_____

_____

_____

_____

8. The relationship between time and the distance remaining on a 3-mile walk for someone walking at a steady rate of 2 miles per hour

_____

_____

_____

_____

9. Analyze Relationships Simone paid $12 for an initial year's subscription to a magazine. The renewal rate is $8 per year. This situation can be represented by the equation $y = 8x + 12$, where x represents the number of years the subscription is renewed and y represents the total cost.

a. Make a table of values for this situation.

b. Draw a graph to represent the situation. Include a title and axis labels.

c. Explain why this relationship is not proportional.

_____

_____

_____

_____

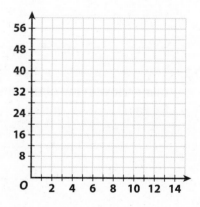

d. Does it make sense to connect the points on the graph with a solid line? Explain.

_____

_____

_____

10. Analyze Relationships A proportional relationship is a linear relationship because the rate of change is constant (and equal to the constant of proportionality). What is required of a proportional relationship that is *not* required of a general linear relationship?

_____

_____

11. Communicate Mathematical Ideas Explain how you can identify a linear non-proportional relationship from a table, a graph, and an equation.

_____

_____

_____

 **FOCUS ON HIGHER ORDER THINKING**

Work Area

12. Critique Reasoning George observes that for every increase of 1 in the value of *x*, there is an increase of 60 in the corresponding value of *y*. He claims that the relationship represented by the table is proportional. Critique George's reasoning.

x	1	2	3	4	5
y	90	150	210	270	330

_____

_____

_____

_____

_____

13. Make a Conjecture Two parallel lines are graphed on a coordinate plane. How many of the lines could represent proportional relationships? Explain.

_____

_____

_____

_____

_____

Determining Slope and *y*-intercept

...; derive the equation $y = mx$ for a line through the origin and the equation $y = mx + b$ for a line intercepting the vertical axis at *b*. Also 8.F.4

? ESSENTIAL QUESTION

How can you determine the slope and the *y*-intercept of a line?

EXPLORE ACTIVITY 1   COMMON CORE 8.EE.6

Investigating Slope and *y*-intercept

The graph of every nonvertical line crosses the *y*-axis. The **y-intercept** is the *y*-coordinate of the point where the graph intersects the *y*-axis. The *x*-coordinate of this point is always 0.

The graph represents the linear equation $y = -\frac{2}{3}x + 4$.

STEP 1   Find the slope of the line using the points (0, 4) and (−3, 6).

$$m = \frac{6 - \boxed{}}{\boxed{} - 0} = \frac{\boxed{}}{\boxed{}} = \boxed{}$$

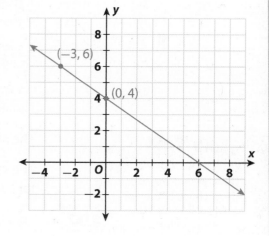

STEP 2   The line also contains the point (6, 0). What is the slope using (0, 4) and (6, 0)? Using (−3, 6) and (6, 0). What do you notice?

_____

STEP 3   Compare your answers in Steps 1 and 2 with the equation of the graphed line.

_____

_____

STEP 4   Find the value of *y* when *x* = 0 using the equation $y = -\frac{2}{3}x + 4$. Describe the point on the graph that corresponds to this solution.

_____

STEP 5   Compare your answer in Step 4 with the equation of the line.

_____

_____

Determining Rate of Change and Initial Value

The linear equation shown is written in the **slope-intercept form of an equation**. Its graph is a line with **slope m** and **y-intercept b**.

$$y = mx + b$$
slope y-intercept

A linear relationship has a constant rate of change. You can find the **rate of change m** and the **initial value b** for a linear situation from a table of values.

EXAMPLE 1

COMMON CORE   8.F.4

A phone salesperson is paid a minimum weekly salary and a commission for each phone sold, as shown in the table. Confirm that the relationship is linear and give the constant rate of change and the initial value.

STEP 1 Confirm that the rate of change is constant.

$$\frac{\text{change in income}}{\text{change in phones sold}} = \frac{630-480}{20-10} = \frac{150}{10} = 15$$

$$\frac{\text{change in income}}{\text{change in phones sold}} = \frac{780-630}{30-20} = \frac{150}{10} = 15$$

$$\frac{\text{change in income}}{\text{change in phones sold}} = \frac{930-780}{40-30} = \frac{150}{10} = 15$$

Number of Phones Sold	Weekly Income ($)
10	$480
20	$630
30	$780
40	$930

The rate of change is a constant, **15**.

The salesperson receives a $15 commission for each phone sold.

STEP 2 Find the initial value when the number of phones sold is 0.

−10 −10

Number of phones sold	0	10	20
Weekly income ($)	330	480	630

Work backward from $x = 10$ to $x = 0$ to find the initial value.

−150 −150

The initial value is $330. The salesperson receives a salary of $330 each week before commissions.

> **Math Talk**
> **Mathematical Practices**
> How do you use the rate of change to work backward to find the initial value?

YOUR TURN

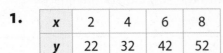
Find the slope and y-intercept of the line represented by each table.

1.

x	2	4	6	8
y	22	32	42	52

_____

2.

x	1	2	3	4
y	8	15	22	29

_____

Deriving the Slope-intercept Form of an Equation

In the following Explore Activity, you will derive the slope-intercept form of an equation.

STEP 1 Let L be a line with slope m and y-intercept b. Circle the point that must be on the line. Justify your choice.

$(b, 0)$ $(0, b)$ $(0, m)$ $(m, 0)$

_____

_____

STEP 2 Recall that slope is the ratio of change in y to change in x. Complete the equation for the slope m of the line using the y-intercept $(0, b)$ and another point (x, y) on the line.

$$m = \frac{y - \boxed{}}{\boxed{} - 0}$$

STEP 3 In an equation of a line, we often want y by itself on one side of the equation. Solve the equation from Step 2 for y.

$$m = \frac{y - b}{x} \qquad \text{Simplify the denominator.}$$

$$m \cdot \boxed{} = \frac{y - b}{x} \cdot \boxed{} \qquad \text{Multiply both sides of the equation by _____.}$$

$$m \boxed{} = y - b$$

$$mx + \boxed{} = y - b + \boxed{} \qquad \text{Add _____ to both sides of the equation.}$$

$$mx + \boxed{} = y$$

$$y = mx + \boxed{} \qquad \text{Write the equation with } y \text{ on the left side.}$$

Reflect

3. Critical Thinking Write the equation of a line with slope m that passes through the origin. Explain your reasoning.

_____

_____

_____

Find the slope and y-intercept of the line in each graph. (Explore Activity 1)

1.

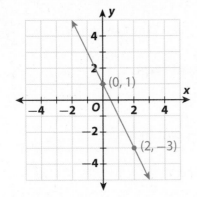

slope m = _____ y-intercept b = _____

2.

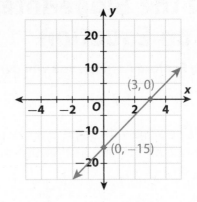

slope m = _____ y-intercept b = _____

3.

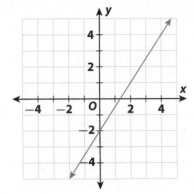

slope m = _____ y-intercept b = _____

4.

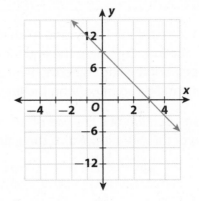

slope m = _____ y-intercept b = _____

Find the slope and y-intercept of the line represented by each table. (Example 1)

5.

x	0	2	4	6	8
y	1	7	13	19	25

slope m = _____ y-intercept b = _____

6.

x	0	5	10	15	20
y	140	120	100	80	60

slope m = _____ y-intercept b = _____

? **ESSENTIAL QUESTION CHECK-IN**

7. How can you determine the slope and the y-intercept of a line from a graph?

_____

_____

_____

4.2 Independent Practice

COMMON CORE **8.EE.6, 8.F.4**

Personal Math Trainer

Online Assessment and Intervention

my.hrw.com

8. Some carpet cleaning costs are shown in the table. The relationship is linear. Find and interpret the rate of change and the initial value for this situation.

Rooms cleaned	1	2	3	4
Cost ($)	125	175	225	275

_____

_____

_____

9. Make Predictions The total cost to pay for parking at a state park for the day and rent a paddleboat are shown.

a. Find the cost to park for a day and the hourly rate to rent a paddleboat.

_____

_____

b. What will Lin pay if she rents a paddleboat for 3.5 hours and splits the total cost with a friend? Explain.

_____

_____

Number of Hours	Cost ($)
1	$17
2	$29
3	$41
4	$53

10. Multi-Step Raymond's parents will pay for him to take sailboard lessons during the summer. He can take half-hour group lessons or half-hour private lessons. The relationship between cost and number of lessons is linear.

Lessons	1	2	3	4
Group ($)	55	85	115	145
Private ($)	75	125	175	225

a. Find the rate of change and the initial value for the group lessons.

_____

_____

b. Find the rate of change and the initial value for the private lessons.

_____

_____

c. Compare and contrast the rates of change and the initial values.

_____

_____

_____

Vocabulary **Explain why each relationship is not linear.**

11.

x	1	2	3	4
y	4.5	6.5	8.5	11.5

_____

_____

12.

x	3	5	7	9
y	140	126	110	92

_____

_____

13. Communicate Mathematical Ideas Describe the procedure you performed to derive the slope-intercept form of a linear equation.

_____

_____

_____

 **FOCUS ON HIGHER ORDER THINKING**

Work Area

14. Critique Reasoning Your teacher asked your class to describe a real-world situation in which a *y*-intercept is 100 and the slope is 5. Your partner gave the following description: *My younger brother originally had 100 small building blocks, but he has lost 5 of them every month since.*

a. What mistake did your partner make?

_____

_____

b. Describe a real-world situation that does match the situation.

_____

_____

15. Justify Reasoning John has a job parking cars. He earns a fixed weekly salary of $300 plus a fee of $5 for each car he parks. His potential earnings for a week are shown in the graph. At what point does John begin to earn more from fees than his fixed salary? Justify your answer.

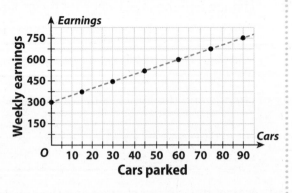

_____

_____

_____

Graphing Linear Nonproportional Relationships Using Slope and *y*-intercept

COMMON CORE 8.F.4
... Interpret the rate of change and initial value of a linear function in terms of the situation it models, and in terms of its graph.... *Also 8.F.3*

? ESSENTIAL QUESTION

How can you graph a line using the slope and *y*-intercept?

EXPLORE ACTIVITY **COMMON CORE** 8.F.3

Using Slope-intercept Form to Graph a Line

Recall that $y = mx + b$ is the slope-intercept form of the equation of a line. In this form, it is easy to see the slope m and the *y*-intercept b. So you can use this form to quickly graph a line by plotting the point $(0, b)$ and using the slope to find a second point.

EXAMPLE 1 **Graph each equation.**

A $y = \frac{2}{3}x - 1$

> **STEP 1** The *y*-intercept is $b = $ ____.
> Plot (0, ____).

> **STEP 2** Use the slope $m = $ ____ to find a second point. From (0, ____), count *up* ____ and *right* ____. The new point is (3, ____).

> **STEP 3** Draw a line through the points.

B $y = -\frac{5}{2}x + 3$

> **STEP 1** The *y*-intercept is $b = $ ____. Plot (0, ____).

> **STEP 2** Use the slope $m = $ ____ to find a second point. From (____, ____), count *down* ____ and _____ 2 to the new point (____, ____), OR from (____, ____), count *up* 5 and _____ 2 to the new point (____, ____).

> **STEP 3** Draw a line through the points.

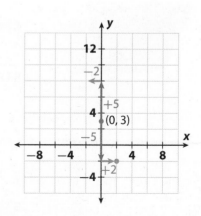

Reflect

1. **Draw Conclusions** How can you use the slope of a line to predict the way the line will be slanted? Explain.

_____

_____

YOUR TURN

Graph each equation.

2. $y = \frac{1}{2}x + 1$

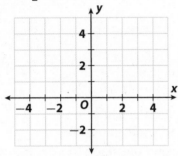

3. $y = -3x + 4$

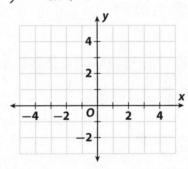

Personal Math Trainer
Online Assessment and Intervention
my.hrw.com

Math On the Spot
my.hrw.com

Analyzing a Graph

Many real-world situations can be represented by linear relationships. You can use graphs of linear relationships to visualize situations and solve problems.

EXAMPLE 2 Real World

COMMON CORE 8.F.4

Ken has a weekly goal of burning 2400 calories by taking brisk walks. The equation $y = -300x + 2400$ represents the number of calories y Ken has left to burn after x hours of walking which burns 300 calories per hour.

A Graph the equation $y = -300x + 2400$.

STEP 1 Write the slope as a fraction.

$$m = \frac{-300}{1} = \frac{-600}{2} = \frac{-900}{3}$$

Using the slope as $\frac{-900}{3}$ helps in drawing a more accurate graph.

STEP 2 Plot the point for the *y*-intercept: (0, 2400).

STEP 3 Use the slope to locate a second point.

From (0, 2400), count *down* 900 and *right* 3.

The new point is (3, 1500).

STEP 4 Draw a line through the two points.

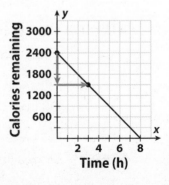

B After how many hours of walking will Ken have 600 calories left to burn? After how many hours will he reach his weekly goal?

STEP 1 Locate 600 calories on the *y*-axis. Read across and down to the *x*-axis.

Ken will have 600 calories left to burn after 6 hours.

STEP 2 Ken will reach his weekly goal when the number of calories left to burn is 0. Because every point on the *x*-axis has a *y*-value of 0, find the point where the line crosses the *x*-axis.

Ken will reach his goal after 8 hours of brisk walking.

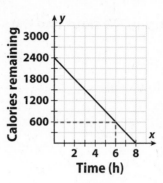

Math Talk
Mathematical Practices

What do the slope and the *y*-intercept of the line represent in this situation?

YOUR TURN

What If? Ken decides to modify his exercise plans from Example 2 by slowing the speed at which he walks. The equation for the modified plan is $y = -200x + 2400$.

4. Graph the equation.

5. How does the graph of the new equation compare with the graph in Example 2?

_____

_____

_____

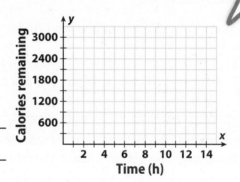

6. Will Ken have to exercise more or less to meet his goal? Explain.

_____

_____

_____

7. Suppose that Ken decides that instead of walking, he will jog, and that jogging burns 600 calories per hour. How do you think that this would change the graph?

_____

_____

_____

Personal Math Trainer

Online Assessment and Intervention

⟳ my.hrw.com

Graph each equation using the slope and the y-intercept. (Explore Activity Example 1)

1. $y = \frac{1}{2}x - 3$

slope = ____   y-intercept = ____

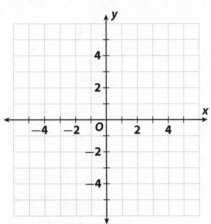

2. $y = -3x + 2$

slope = ____   y-intercept = ____

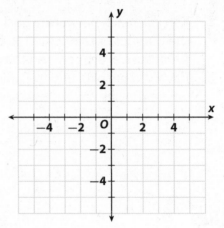

3. A friend gives you two baseball cards for your birthday. Afterward, you begin collecting them. You buy the same number of cards once each week. The equation $y = 4x + 2$ describes the number of cards, y, you have after x weeks. (Example 2)

a. Find and interpret the slope and the y-intercept of the line that represents this situation. Graph $y = 4x + 2$. Include axis labels.

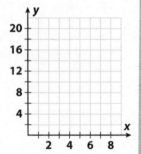

_____

_____

b. Discuss which points on the line do not make sense in this situation. Then plot three more points on the line that do make sense.

_____

_____

_____

? ESSENTIAL QUESTION CHECK-IN

4. Why might someone choose to use the y-intercept and the slope to graph a line?

_____

_____

_____

_____

Personal Math Trainer

Online Assessment and Intervention

my.hrw.com

4.3 Independent Practice

COMMON CORE 8.F.3, 8.F.4

5. Science A spring stretches in relation to the weight hanging from it according to the equation $y = 0.75x + 0.25$ where x is the weight in pounds and y is the length of the spring in inches.

a. Graph the equation. Include axis labels.

b. Interpret the slope and the y-intercept of the line.

_____

_____

_____

_____

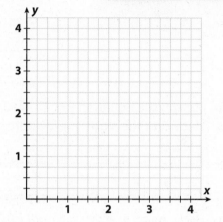

c. How long will the spring be if a 2-pound weight is hung on it? Will the length double if you double the weight? Explain

_____

Look for a Pattern **Identify the coordinates of four points on the line with each given slope and y-intercept.**

6. slope $= 5$, y-intercept $= -1$

_____

7. slope $= -1$, y-intercept $= 8$

_____

8. slope $= 0.2$, y-intercept $= 0.3$

_____

9. slope $= 1.5$, y-intercept $= -3$

_____

10. slope $= -\frac{1}{2}$, y-intercept $= 4$

_____

11. slope $= \frac{2}{3}$, y-intercept $= -5$

_____

12. A music school charges a registration fee in addition to a fee per lesson. Music lessons last 0.5 hour. The equation $y = 40x + 30$ represents the total cost y of x lessons. Find and interpret the slope and y-intercept of the line that represents this situation. Then find four points on the line.

_____

_____

13. A public pool charges a membership fee and a fee for each visit. The equation $y = 3x + 50$ represents the cost y for x visits.

   a. After locating the y-intercept on the coordinate plane shown, can you move up three gridlines and right one gridline to find a second point? Explain.

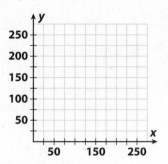

      _____

      _____

      _____

   b. Graph the equation $y = 3x + 50$. Include axis labels. Then interpret the slope and y-intercept.

      _____

      _____

   c. How many visits to the pool can a member get for $200?

      _____

 **FOCUS ON HIGHER ORDER THINKING**

14. Explain the Error A student says that the slope of the line for the equation $y = 20 - 15x$ is 20 and the y-intercept is 15. Find and correct the error.

_____

_____

_____

15. Critical Thinking Suppose you know the slope of a linear relationship and a point that its graph passes through. Can you graph the line even if the point provided does *not* represent the y-intercept? Explain.

_____

_____

_____

16. Make a Conjecture Graph the lines $y = 3x$, $y = 3x - 3$, and $y = 3x + 3$. What do you notice about the lines? Make a conjecture based on your observation.

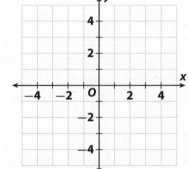

_____

_____

_____

Proportional and Nonproportional Situations

COMMON CORE 8.F.2

Compare properties of two functions each represented in a different way (algebraically, graphically, numerically in tables, or by verbal descriptions). *Also 8.F.3, 8.F.4*

? ESSENTIAL QUESTION

How can you distinguish between proportional and nonproportional situations?

EXPLORE ACTIVITY   COMMON CORE 8.F.3

Distinguish Between Proportional and Nonproportional Situations Using a Graph

Math On the Spot

⏻ my.hrw.com

If a relationship is nonlinear, it is nonproportional. If it is linear, it may be either proportional or nonproportional. When the graph of the linear relationship contains the origin, the relationship is proportional.

EXAMPLE 1 **The graph shows the sales tax charged based on the amount spent at a video game store in a particular city. Does the graph show a linear relationship? Is the relationship proportional or nonproportional?**

The graph shows a linear _____ relationship

because it is a _____ that contains the _____ .

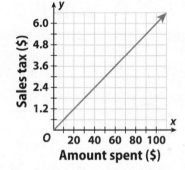

YOUR TURN

Determine if each of the following graphs represents a proportional or nonproportional relationship.

1.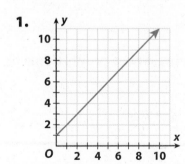

2.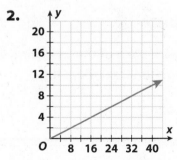

_____   _____

Personal Math Trainer

Online Assessment and Intervention

⏻ my.hrw.com

Distinguish Between Proportional and Nonproportional Situations Using an Equation

If an equation is not a linear equation, it represents a nonproportional relationship. A linear equation of the form $y = mx + b$ may represent either a proportional ($b = 0$) or nonproportional ($b \neq 0$) relationship.

EXAMPLE 2 Real World COMMON CORE 8.F.4

The number of years since Keith graduated from middle school can be represented by the equation $y = a - 14$, where y is the number of years and a is his age. Is the relationship between the number of years since Keith graduated and his age proportional or nonproportional?

$$y = a - 14$$

The equation is in the form $y = mx + b$, with a being used as the variable instead of x. The value of m is 1, and the value of b is -14. Since b is not 0, the relationship between the number of years since Keith graduated and his age is nonproportional.

Reflect

3. **Communicate Mathematical Ideas** In a proportional relationship, the ratio $\frac{y}{x}$ is constant. Show that this ratio is not constant for the equation $y = a - 14$.

_____

_____

4. **What If?** Suppose another equation represents Keith's age in months y given his age in years a. Is this relationship proportional? Explain.

_____

_____

YOUR TURN

Determine if each of the following equations represents a proportional or nonproportional relationship.

5. $d = 65t$

_____

6. $p = 0.1s + 2000$

_____

7. $n = 450 - 3p$

_____

8. $36 = 12d$

_____

Distinguish Between Proportional and Nonproportional Situations Using a Table

If there is not a constant rate of change in the data displayed in a table, then the table represents a nonlinear nonproportional relationship.

A linear relationship represented by a table is a proportional relationship when the quotient of each pair of numbers is constant. Otherwise, the linear relationship is nonproportional.

EXAMPLE 3 · Real World

COMMON CORE 8.F.4

The values in the table represent the numbers of U.S. dollars three tourists traded for Mexican pesos. The relationship is linear. Is the relationship proportional or nonproportional?

U.S. Dollars Traded	Mexican Pesos Received
130	1,690
255	3,315
505	6,565

$$\frac{1,690}{130} = \frac{169}{13} = 13$$

$$\frac{3,315}{255} = \frac{221}{17} = 13$$

Simplify the ratios to compare the pesos received to the dollars traded.

$$\frac{6,565}{505} = \frac{1313}{101} = 13$$

The ratio of pesos received to dollars traded is constant at 13 Mexican pesos per U.S. dollar. This is a proportional relationship.

Math Talk
Mathematical Practices

How could you confirm that the values in the table have a linear relationship?

YOUR TURN

Determine if the linear relationship represented by each table is a proportional or nonproportional relationship.

9.

x	y
2	30
8	90
14	150

10.

x	y
5	1
40	8
65	13

_____   _____

© Houghton Mifflin Harcourt Publishing Company • Image Credits: ©Jupiter Images/ Hemera Technologies/Getty Images

Comparing Proportional and Nonproportional Situations

You can use what you have learned about proportional and nonproportional relationships to compare similar real-world situations that are given using different representations.

EXAMPLE 4 Real World   COMMON CORE 8.F.2

A A laser tag league has the choice of two arenas for a tournament. In both cases, *x* is the number of hours and *y* is the total charge. Compare and contrast these two situations.

Arena A

$y = 225x$

Arena B

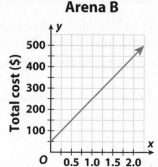

- **Arena A's** equation has the form $y = mx + b$, where $b = 0$. So, Arena A's charges are a proportional relationship. The hourly rate, $225, is greater than Arena B's, but there is no additional fee.

- **Arena B's** graph is a line that does not include the origin. So, Arena B's charges are a nonproportional relationship. Arena B has a $50 initial fee but its hourly rate, $200, is lower.

B Jessika is remodeling and has the choice of two painters. In both cases, *x* is the number of hours and *y* is the total charge. Compare and contrast these two situations.

Painter A

$y = \$45x$

Painter A's equation has the form $y = mx + b$, where $b = 0$. So, Painter A's charges are proportional. The hourly rate, $45, is greater than Painter B's, but there is no additional fee.

Painter B

x	0	1	2	3
y	20	55	90	125

Painter B's table is a nonproportional relationship because the ratio of *y* to *x* is not constant. Because the table contains the ordered pair (0, 20), Painter B charges an initial fee of $20, but the hourly rate, $35, is less than Painter A's.

YOUR TURN

11. Compare and contrast the following two situations.

Test-Prep Center A	Test-Prep Center B
The cost for Test-Prep Center A is given by $c = 20h$, where c is the cost in dollars and h is the number of hours you attend.	Test-Prep Center B charges $25 per hour to attend, but you have a $100 coupon that you can use to reduce the cost.

_____

_____

_____

_____

Personal Math Trainer

Online Assessment and Intervention

⏻ my.hrw.com

Guided Practice

Determine if each relationship is a proportional or nonproportional situation. Explain your reasoning.

(Explore Activity Example 1, Example 2, Example 4)

1.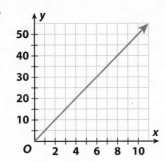

Look at the origin.

_____

_____

2.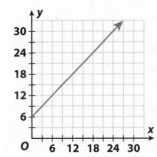

_____

_____

3. $q = 2p + \frac{1}{2}$

Compare the equation with $y = mx + b$.

_____

_____

_____

4. $v = \frac{1}{10}u$

_____

_____

_____

The tables represent linear relationships. Determine if each relationship is a proportional or nonproportional situation. (Example 3, Example 4)

5.

x	y
3	12
9	36
21	84

6.

x	y
22	4
46	8
58	10

Find the quotient of y and x.

_____   _____

_____   _____

_____   _____

7. The values in the table represent the numbers of households that watched three TV shows and the ratings of the shows. The relationship is linear. Describe the relationship in other ways. (Example 4)

Number of Households that Watched TV Show	TV Show Rating
15,000,000	12
20,000,000	16
25,000,000	20

_____

_____

_____

_____

? ESSENTIAL QUESTION CHECK-IN

8. How are using graphs, equations, and tables similar when distinguishing between proportional and nonproportional linear relationships?

_____

_____

_____

4.4 Independent Practice

 8.F.2, 8.F.3, 8.F.4

Personal Math Trainer

Online Assessment and Intervention

my.hrw.com

9. The graph shows the weight of a cross-country team's beverage cooler based on how much sports drink it contains.

a. Is the relationship proportional or nonproportional? Explain.

_____

_____

b. Identify and interpret the slope and the *y*-intercept.

_____

_____

In 10–11, tell if the relationship between a rider's height above the first floor and the time since the rider stepped on the elevator or escalator is proportional or nonproportional. Explain your reasoning.

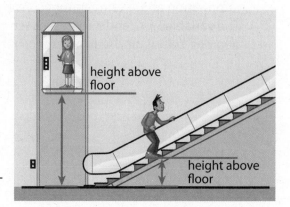

10. The elevator paused for 10 seconds after you stepped on before beginning to rise at a constant rate of 8 feet per second.

_____

_____

_____

11. Your height, *h*, in feet above the first floor on the escalator is given by $h = 0.75t$, where *t* is the time in seconds.

_____

12. **Analyze Relationships** Compare and contrast the two graphs.

Graph A

$y = \frac{1}{3}x$

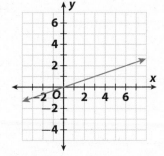

Graph B

$y = \sqrt{x}$

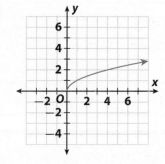

_____

_____

© Houghton Mifflin Harcourt Publishing Company

13. Represent Real-World Problems Describe a real-world situation where the relationship is linear and nonproportional.

_____

_____

Work Area

14. Mathematical Reasoning Suppose you know the slope of a linear relationship and one of the points that its graph passes through. How can you determine if the relationship is proportional or nonproportional?

_____

_____

_____

15. Multiple Representations An entrant at a science fair has included information about temperature conversion in various forms, as shown. The variables F, C, and K represent temperatures in degrees Fahrenheit, degrees Celsius, and kelvin, respectively.

Equation A $F = \frac{9}{5}C + 32$ Equation B $K = C + 273.15$	Table C	
	Degrees Celsius	kelvin
	8	281.15
	15	288.15
	36	309.15

a. Is the relationship between kelvins and degrees Celsius proportional? Justify your answer in two different ways.

_____

_____

_____

_____

b. Is the relationship between degrees Celsius and degrees Fahrenheit proportional? Why or why not?

_____

_____

_____

_____

Ready to Go On?

**Personal
Math Trainer**

Online Assessment
and Intervention

my.hrw.com

4.1 Representing Linear Nonproportional Relationships

1. Complete the table using
the equation $y = 3x + 2$.

x	−1	0	1	2	3
y					

4.2 Determining Slope and *y*-intercept

2. Find the slope and *y*-intercept
of the line in the graph.

_____

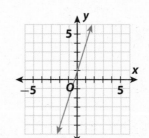

4.3 Graphing Linear Nonproportional Relationships

3. Graph the equation $y = 2x - 3$
using slope and *y*-intercept.

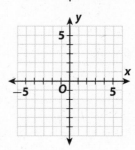

4.4 Proportional and Nonproportional Situations

4. Does the table represent a
proportional or a nonproportional
linear relationship?

x	1	2	3	4	5
y	4	8	12	16	20

_____

5. Does the graph in Exercise 2 represent a proportional
or a nonproportional linear relationship?   _____

6. Does the graph in Exercise 3 represent a proportional
or a nonproportional relationship?   _____

? ESSENTIAL QUESTION

7. How can you identify a linear nonproportional relationship from a
table, a graph, and an equation?

_____

_____

MODULE 4 MIXED REVIEW

Assessment Readiness

Personal
Math Trainer

Online
Assessment and
Intervention

my.hrw.com

Selected Response

1. The table below represents which equation?

x	−1	0	1	2
y	−10	−6	−2	2

(A) $y = -x - 10$ (C) $y = 4x - 6$

(B) $y = -6x$ (D) $y = -4x + 2$

2. The graph of which equation is shown below?

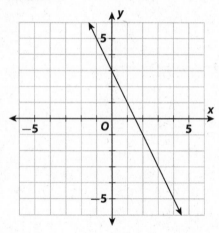

(A) $y = -2x + 3$ (C) $y = 2x + 3$

(B) $y = -2x + 1.5$ (D) $y = 2x + 1.5$

3. The table below represents a linear relationship.

x	2	3	4	5
y	4	7	10	13

What is the y-intercept?

(A) −4   (C) 2

(B) −2   (D) 3

4. Which equation represents a nonproportional relationship?

(A) $y = 3x + 0$ (C) $y = 3x + 5$

(B) $y = -3x$ (D) $y = \frac{1}{3}x$

5. The table shows a proportional relationship. What is the missing y-value?

x	4	10	12
y	6	15	?

(A) 16   (C) 18

(B) 20   (D) 24

6. What is 0.00000598 written in scientific notation?

(A) 5.98×10^{-6} (C) 59.8×10^{-6}

(B) 5.98×10^{-5} (D) 59.8×10^{-7}

Mini-Task

7. The graph shows a linear relationship.

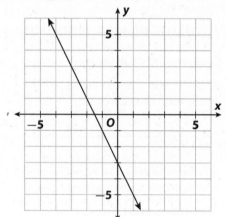

a. Is the relationship proportional or nonproportional?

_____

b. What is the slope of the line?

_____

c. What is the y-intercept of the line?

_____

d. What is the equation of the line?

_____

Writing Linear Equations

ESSENTIAL QUESTION

How can you use linear equations to solve real-world problems?

Real-World Video

Linear equations can be used to describe many situations related to shopping. If a store advertised four books for $32.00, you could write and solve a linear equation to find the price of each book.

my.hrw.com

© Houghton Mifflin Harcourt Publishing Company • Image Credits: ©Yellow Dog Productions/Getty Images

GO DIGITAL

my.hrw.com

my.hrw.com

Go digital with your write-in student edition, accessible on any device.

Math On the Spot

Scan with your smart phone to jump directly to the online edition, video tutor, and more.

Animated Math

Interactively explore key concepts to see how math works.

Personal Math Trainer

Get immediate feedback and help as you work through practice sets.

123

Are YOU Ready?

Complete these exercises to review skills you will need for this module.

Write Fractions as Decimals

EXAMPLE $\dfrac{0.5}{0.8} = ?$ Multiply the numerator and the denominator by a power of 10 so that the denominator is a whole number.

$\dfrac{0.5 \times 10}{0.8 \times 10} = \dfrac{5}{8}$

Write the fraction as a division problem.
Write a decimal point and zeros in the dividend.
Place a decimal point in the quotient.
Divide as with whole numbers.

$$
\begin{array}{r}
0.625 \\
8\overline{)5.000} \\
-48 \\
\hline
20 \\
-16 \\
\hline
40 \\
-40 \\
\hline
0
\end{array}
$$

Write each fraction as a decimal.

1. $\dfrac{3}{8}$ _____

2. $\dfrac{0.3}{0.4}$ _____

3. $\dfrac{0.13}{0.2}$ _____

4. $\dfrac{0.39}{0.75}$ _____

Inverse Operations

EXAMPLE
$$5n = 20$$
$$\dfrac{5n}{5} = \dfrac{20}{5}$$
$$n = 4$$

n is multiplied by 5.
To solve the equation, use the inverse operation, division.

$$k + 7 = 9$$
$$k + 7 - 7 = 9 - 7$$
$$k = 2$$

7 is added to k.
To solve the equation, use the inverse operation, subtraction.

Solve each equation using the inverse operation.

5. $7p = 28$ _____

6. $h - 13 = 5$ _____

7. $\dfrac{y}{3} = -6$ _____

8. $b + 9 = 21$ _____

9. $c - 8 = -8$ _____

10. $3n = -12$ _____

11. $-16 = m + 7$ _____

12. $\dfrac{t}{-5} = -5$ _____

Reading Start-Up

Visualize Vocabulary

Use the ✔ words to complete the diagram. You can put more than one word in each bubble.

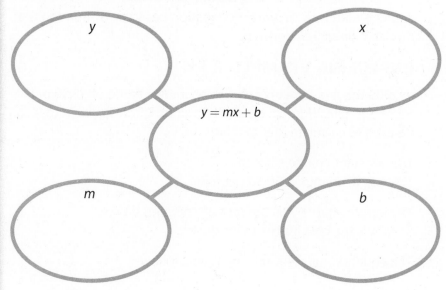

Understand Vocabulary

Complete the sentences using the preview words.

1. A set of data that is made up of two paired variables

   is _____.

2. When the rate of change varies from point to point, the relationship

   is a _____.

Vocabulary

Review Words
- ✔ linear equation (*ecuación lineal*)
- ordered pair (*par ordenado*)
- proportional relationship (*relación proporcional*)
- rate of change (*tasa de cambio*)
- ✔ slope (*pendiente*)
- ✔ slope-intercept form of an equation (*forma de pendiente-intersección*)
- ✔ x-coordinate (*coordenada x*)
- ✔ y-coordinate (*coordenada y*)
- ✔ y-intercept (*intersección con el eje y*)

Preview Words
- bivariate data (*datos bivariados*)
- nonlinear relationship (*relación no lineal*)

Active Reading

Tri-Fold Before beginning the module, create a tri-fold to help you learn the concepts and vocabulary in this module. Fold the paper into three sections. Label the columns "What I Know," "What I Need to Know," and "What I Learned." Complete the first two columns before you read. After studying the module, complete the third column.

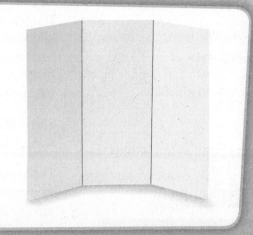

Unpacking the Standards

Understanding the standards and the vocabulary terms in the standards will help you know exactly what you are expected to learn in this module.

© Houghton Mifflin Harcourt Publishing Company

COMMON CORE 8.F.4

Construct a function to model a linear relationship between two quantities. Determine the rate of change and initial value of the function from a description of a relationship … Interpret the rate of change and initial value of a linear function in terms of the situation it models, and in terms of its graph or a table of values.

Key Vocabulary

rate of change *(tasa de cambio)*
A ratio that compares the amount of change in a dependent variable to the amount of change in an independent variable.

What It Means to You

You will learn how to write an equation based on a situation that models a linear relationship.

UNPACKING EXAMPLE 8.F.4

In 2006 the fare for a taxicab was an initial charge of $2.50 plus $0.30 per mile. Write an equation in slope-intercept form that can be used to calculate the total fare.

The constant charge is $2.50.
The rate of change is $0.30 per mile.

The input variable, x, is the number of miles driven.
So $0.3x$ is the cost for the miles driven.

The equation for the total fare, y, is as follows:

$$y = 0.3x + 2.5$$

COMMON CORE 8.SP.3

Use the equation of a linear model to solve problems in the context of bivariate measurement data, interpreting the slope and intercept.

Key Vocabulary

bivariate data *(datos bivariados)*
A set of data that is made up of two paired variables.

What It Means to You

You will see how to use a linear relationship between sets of data to make predictions.

UNPACKING EXAMPLE 8.SP.3

The graph shows the temperatures in degrees Celsius inside the earth at certain depths in kilometers. Use the graph to write an equation and find the temperature at a depth of 12 km.

The initial temperature is 20°C.
It increases at a rate of 10°C/km.

The equation is $t = 10d + 20$.
At a depth of 12 km, the temperature is 140°C.

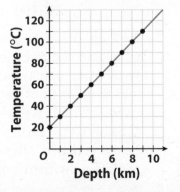

Temperature Inside Earth

Visit **my.hrw.com** to see all the **Common Core Standards** unpacked.

my.hrw.com

LESSON 5.1
Writing Linear Equations from Situations and Graphs

COMMON CORE 8.F.4

Construct a function to model a linear relationship between two quantities. Determine the rate of change and initial value.... Interpret the rate of change and initial value....

? ESSENTIAL QUESTION

How do you write an equation to model a linear relationship given a graph or a description?

EXPLORE ACTIVITY Real World   **COMMON CORE** 8.F.4

Writing an Equation in Slope-Intercept Form

Greta makes clay mugs and bowls as gifts at the Crafty Studio. She pays a membership fee of $15 a month and an equipment fee of $3.00 an hour to use the potter's wheel, table, and kiln. Write an equation in the form $y = mx + b$ that Greta can use to calculate her monthly costs.

A What is the input variable, x, for this situation?

_____

What is the output variable, y, for this situation?

_____

B During April, Greta does not use the equipment at all. What will be her number of hours (x) for April? _____

What will be her cost (y) for April? _____

What will be the y-intercept, b, in the equation? _____

C Greta spends 8 hours in May for a cost of $15 + 8($3) = _____.

In June, she spends 11 hours for a cost of _____.

From May to June, the change in x-values is _____.

From May to June, the change in y-values is _____.

What will be the slope, m, in the equation? _____

D Use the values for m and b to write an equation for Greta's costs in the form $y = mx + b$: _____

Math Talk
Mathematical Practices

What change could the studio make that would make a difference to the y-intercept of the equation?

Writing an Equation from a Graph

You can use information presented in a graph to write an equation in slope-intercept form.

EXAMPLE 1 COMMON CORE 8.F.4

A video club charges a one-time membership fee plus a rental fee for each DVD borrowed. Use the graph to write an equation in slope-intercept form to represent the amount spent, *y*, on *x* DVD rentals.

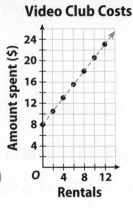

Video Club Costs

STEP 1 Choose two points on the graph, (x_1, y_1) and (x_2, y_2), to find the slope.

$m = \dfrac{y_2 - y_1}{x_2 - x_1}$ Find the change in y-values over the change in x-values.

$m = \dfrac{18 - 8}{8 - 0}$ Substitute (0, 8) for (x_1, y_1) and (8,18) for (x_2, y_2).

$m = \dfrac{10}{8} = 1.25$ Simplify.

STEP 2 Read the *y*-intercept from the graph.

The *y*-intercept is 8.

STEP 3 Use your slope and *y*-intercept values to write an equation in slope-intercept form.

$y = mx + b$ Slope-intercept form

$y = 1.25x + 8$ Substitute 1.25 for m and 8 for y.

Reflect

1. What does the value of the slope represent in this context?

_____

2. Describe the meaning of the *y*-intercept.

_____

YOUR TURN

3. The cash register subtracts $2.50 from a $25 Coffee Café gift card for every medium coffee the customer buys. Use the graph to write an equation in slope-intercept form to represent this situation.

_____

Amount on Gift Card

Writing an Equation from a Description

You can use information from a description of a linear relationship to find the slope and *y*-intercept and to write an equation.

Math On the Spot
⏻ my.hrw.com

EXAMPLE 2 COMMON CORE 8.F.4

The rent charged for space in an office building is a linear relationship related to the size of the space rented. Write an equation in slope-intercept form for the rent at West Main Street Office Rentals.

West Main St. Office Rentals 🏢
Offices for rent at convenient locations.

Monthly Rates:
600 square feet for **$750**
900 square feet for **$1150**

My Notes

STEP 1 Identify the input and output variables.

The input variable is the square footage of floor space.

The output variable is the monthly rent.

STEP 2 Write the information given in the problem as ordered pairs.

The rent for 600 square feet of floor space is $750: (600, 750)

The rent for 900 square feet of floor space is $1150: (900, 1150)

STEP 3 Find the slope.

$$m = \frac{y_2 - y_1}{x_2 - x_1} = \frac{1150 - 750}{900 - 600} = \frac{400}{300} = \frac{4}{3}$$

STEP 4 Find the *y*-intercept. Use the slope and one of the ordered pairs.

$y = mx + b$ Slope-intercept form

$750 = \frac{4}{3} \cdot 600 + b$ Substitute for *y*, *m*, and *x*.

$750 = 800 + b$ Multiply.

$-50 = b$ Subtract 800 from both sides.

STEP 5 Substitute the slope and *y*-intercept.

$y = mx + b$ Slope-intercept form

$y = \frac{4}{3}x - 50$ Substitute $\frac{4}{3}$ for *m* and −50 for *b*.

Reflect

4. Without graphing, tell whether the graph of this equation rises or falls from left to right. What does the sign of the slope mean in this context?

_____

_____

_____

YOUR TURN

5. Hari's weekly allowance varies depending on the number of chores he does. He received $16 in allowance the week he did 12 chores, and $14 in allowance the week he did 8 chores. Write an equation for his allowance in slope-intercept form. _____

Guided Practice

1. Li is making beaded necklaces. For each necklace, she uses 27 spacers, plus 5 beads per inch of necklace length. Write an equation to find how many beads Li needs for each necklace. (Explore Activity)

   a. input variable: _____

   b. output variable: _____

   c. equation: _____

2. Kate is planning a trip to the beach. She estimates her average speed to graph her expected progress on the trip. Write an equation in slope-intercept form that represents the situation. (Example 1)

   Choose two points on the graph to find the slope.

   $m = \dfrac{y_2 - y_1}{x_2 - x_1} =$ _____

   Read the *y*-intercept from the graph: $b =$ _____

   Use your slope and *y*-intercept values to write an equation in slope-intercept form. _____

   My Beach Trip

   Distance to beach (mi) — 100, 200, 300

   Driving time (h) — O 1 2 3 4 5 6

3. At 59 °F, crickets chirp at a rate of 76 times per minute, and at 65 °F, they chirp 100 times per minute. Write an equation in slope-intercept form that represents the situation. (Example 2)

   Input variable: _____   Output variable: _____

   $m = \dfrac{y_2 - y_1}{x_2 - x_1} =$ _____ Use the slope and one of the ordered

   pairs in $y = mx + b$ to find *b*. _____ = _____ · _____ + b; _____ = b

   Write an equation in slope-intercept form. _____

? ESSENTIAL QUESTION CHECK-IN

4. Explain what *m* and *b* in the equation $y = mx + b$ tell you about the graph of the line with that equation.

   _____

5.1 Independent Practice

COMMON CORE 8.F.4

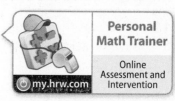

Personal Math Trainer

Online Assessment and Intervention

my.hrw.com

5. A dragonfly can beat its wings 30 times per second. Write an equation in slope-intercept form that shows the relationship between flying time in seconds and the number of times the dragonfly beats its wings.

_____

6. A balloon is released from the top of a platform that is 50 meters tall. The balloon rises at the rate of 4 meters per second. Write an equation in slope-intercept form that tells the height of the balloon above the ground after a given number of seconds.

_____

The graph shows a scuba diver's ascent over time.

7. Use the graph to find the slope of the line. Tell what the slope means in this context.

_____

_____

8. Identify the *y*-intercept. Tell what the *y*-intercept means in this context.

_____

Scuba Diver's Ascent

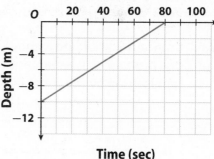

Time (sec)

9. Write an equation in slope-intercept form that represents the diver's depth over time.

_____

10. The formula for converting Celsius temperatures to Fahrenheit temperatures is a linear equation. Water freezes at 0 °C, or 32 °F, and it boils at 100 °C, or 212 °F. Find the slope and *y*-intercept for a graph that gives degrees Celsius on the horizontal axis and degrees Fahrenheit on the vertical axis. Then write an equation in slope-intercept form that converts degrees Celsius into degrees Fahrenheit.

_____

_____

11. The cost of renting a sailboat at a lake is $20 per hour plus $12 for lifejackets. Write an equation in slope-intercept form that can be used to calculate the total amount you would pay for using this sailboat.

_____

The graph shows the activity in a savings account.

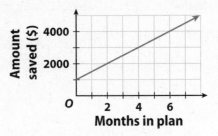

12. What was the amount of the initial deposit that started this savings account?

_____

13. Find the slope and *y*-intercept of the graphed line.

_____

14. Write an equation in slope-intercept form for the activity in this savings account.

_____

15. Explain the meaning of the slope in this graph.

_____

_____

 **FOCUS ON HIGHER ORDER THINKING**

16. **Communicate Mathematical Ideas** Explain how you decide which part of a problem will be represented by the variable *x*, and which part will be represented by the variable *y* in a graph of the situation.

_____

_____

_____

_____

17. **Represent Real-World Problems** Describe what would be true about the rate of change in a situation that could *not* be represented by a graphed line and an equation in the form $y = mx + b$.

_____

_____

_____

18. **Draw Conclusions** Must *m*, in the equation $y = mx + b$, always be a positive number? Explain.

_____

_____

_____

Writing Linear Equations from a Table

COMMON CORE 8.F.4

Construct a function to model a linear relationship between two quantities. Determine the rate of change and initial value.... Interpret the rate of change and initial value....

? ESSENTIAL QUESTION

How do you write an equation to model a linear relationship given a table?

EXPLORE ACTIVITY **COMMON CORE 8.F.4**

Graphing from a Table to Write an Equation

You can use information from a table to draw a graph of a linear relationship and to write an equation for the graphed line.

EXAMPLE 1 The table shows the temperature of a fish tank during an experiment. Graph the data, and find the slope and *y*-intercept from the graph. Then write the equation for the graph in slope-intercept form.

Time (h)	0	1	2	3	4	5
Temperature (°F)	82	80	78	76	74	72

STEP 1 Graph the ordered pairs from the table (time, temperature).

STEP 2 Draw a line through the points.

STEP 3 Choose two points on the graph to find the slope: for example, choose (0, 82) and (1, 80).

$$m = \frac{y_2 - y_1}{x_2 - x_1} = \frac{\boxed{} - \boxed{}}{\boxed{} - \boxed{}} = \underline{\hspace{2cm}}$$

Tank Temperature

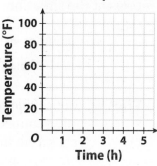

STEP 4 Read the *y*-intercept from the graph.

$b = \underline{\hspace{2cm}}$

STEP 5 Use these slope and *y*-intercept values to write an equation in slope-intercept form.

$y = mx + b$

$y = \boxed{} x + \boxed{}$

YOUR TURN

1. The table shows the volume of water released by Hoover Dam over a certain period of time. Graph the data, and find the slope and *y*-intercept from the graph. Then write the equation for the graph in slope-intercept form.

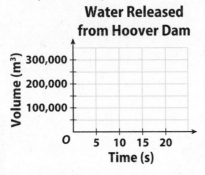

Water Released from Hoover Dam

Time (s)	Volume of water (m³)
5	75,000
10	150,000
15	225,000
20	300,000

Personal Math Trainer

Online Assessment and Intervention

my.hrw.com

Math On the Spot

my.hrw.com

Animated Math

my.hrw.com

Writing an Equation from a Table

The information from a table can also help you to write the equation that represents a given situation without drawing the graph.

EXAMPLE 2 **Real World**

COMMON CORE **8.F.4**

Elizabeth's cell phone plan lets her choose how many minutes are included each month. The table shows the plan's monthly cost *y* for a given number of included minutes *x*. Write an equation in slope-intercept form to represent the situation.

Minutes included, *x*	100	200	300	400	500
Cost of plan ($), *y*	14	20	26	32	38

STEP 1 Notice that the change in cost is the same for each increase of 100 minutes. So, the relationship is linear. Choose any two ordered pairs from the table to find the slope.

$$m = \frac{y_2 - y_1}{x_2 - x_1} = \frac{(20 - 14)}{(200 - 100)} = \frac{6}{100} = 0.06$$

STEP 2 Find the *y*-intercept. Use the slope and any point from the table.

$y = mx + b$	Slope-intercept form
$14 = 0.06 \cdot 100 + b$	Substitute for *y*, *m*, and *x*.
$14 = 6 + b$	Multiply.
$8 = b$	Subtract 6 from both sides.

STEP 3 Substitute the slope and *y*-intercept.

$y = mx + b$	Slope-intercept form
$y = 0.06x + 8$	Substitute 0.06 for *m* and 8 for *b*.

Reflect

2. What is the base price for the cell phone plan, regardless of how many minutes are included? What is the cost per minute? Explain.

_____

_____

_____

_____

_____

3. **What If?** Elizabeth's cell phone company changes the cost of her plan as shown below. Write an equation in slope-intercept form to represent the situation. How did the plan change?

Minutes included, x	100	200	300	400	500
Cost of plan ($), y	30	35	40	45	50

_____

_____

Math Talk
Mathematical Practices

Explain the meaning of the slope and y-intercept of the equation.

YOUR TURN

4. A salesperson receives a weekly salary plus a commission for each computer sold. The table shows the total pay, p, and the number of computers sold, n. Write an equation in slope-intercept form to represent this situation.

Number of computers sold, n	4	6	8	10	12
Total pay ($), p	550	700	850	1000	1150

_____

5. To rent a van, a moving company charges $40.00 plus $0.50 per mile. The table shows the total cost, c, and the number of miles driven, d. Write an equation in slope-intercept form to represent this situation.

Number of miles driven, d	10	20	30	40	50
Total cost ($), c	45	50	55	60	65

_____

Personal Math Trainer

Online Assessment and Intervention

⊕ my.hrw.com

1. Jaime purchased a $20 bus pass. Each time he rides the bus, a certain amount is deducted from the pass. The table shows the amount, *y*, left on his pass after *x* rides. Graph the data, and find the slope and *y*-intercept from the graph or from the table. Then write the equation for the graph in slope-intercept form. (Explore Activity Example 1)

Number of rides, *x*	0	4	8	12	16
Amount left on pass ($), *y*	20	15	10	5	0

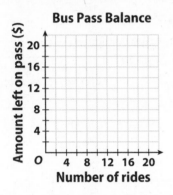

Bus Pass Balance

_____

The table shows the temperature (*y*) at different altitudes (*x*). This is a linear relationship. (Example 2)

Altitude (ft), *x*	0	2,000	4,000	6,000	8,000	10,000	12,000
Temperature (°F), *y*	59	51	43	35	27	19	11

2. Find the slope for this relationship.

_____

3. Find the *y*-intercept for this relationship.

_____

4. Write an equation in slope-intercept form that represents this relationship.

_____

5. Use your equation to determine the temperature at an altitude of 5000 feet.

_____

? **ESSENTIAL QUESTION CHECK-IN**

6. Describe how you can use the information in a table showing a linear relationship to find the slope and *y*-intercept for the equation.

_____

_____

_____

Name _____ Class _____ Date _____

5.2 Independent Practice

 8.F.4

Personal Math Trainer

Online Assessment and Intervention

my.hrw.com

7. The table shows the costs of a large cheese pizza with toppings at a local pizzeria. Graph the data, and find the slope and *y*-intercept from the graph. Then write the equation for the graph in slope-intercept form.

Number of toppings, *t*	0	1	2	3	4	5
Total cost ($), *C*	8	10	12	14	16	18

Cost of Large Pizza

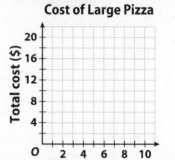

_____

8. The table shows how much an air-conditioning repair company charges for different numbers of hours of work. Graph the data, and find the slope and *y*-intercept from the graph. Then write the equation for the graph in slope-intercept form.

Number of hours (h), *t*	0	1	2	3	4	5
Amount charged ($), *A*	50	100	150	200	250	300

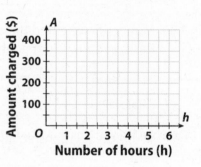

_____

9. A friend gave Ms. Morris a gift card for a local car wash. The table shows the linear relationship of how the value left on the card relates to the number of car washes.

Number of car washes, *x*	0	8	12
Amount left on card ($), *y*	30	18	12

a. Write an equation that shows the number of dollars left on the card.

_____

b. Explain the meaning of the negative slope in this situation.

_____

_____

c. What is the maximum value of *x* that makes sense in this context? Explain.

_____

The tables show linear relationships between *x* and *y*. Write an equation in slope-intercept form for each relationship.

10.

x	−2	−1	0	2
y	−1	0	1	3

11.

x	−4	1	0	6
y	14	4	6	−6

_____   _____

© Houghton Mifflin Harcourt Publishing Company

Lesson 5.2 **137**

12. **Finance** Desiree starts a savings account with $125.00. Every month, she deposits $53.50.

a. Complete the table to model the situation.

Month, x					
Amount in Savings ($), y					

b. Write an equation in slope-intercept form that shows how much money Desiree has in her savings account after x months.

_____

c. Use the equation to find how much money Desiree will have in savings after 11 months.

_____

13. Monty documented the amount of rain his farm received on a monthly basis, as shown in the table.

Month, x	1	2	3	4	5
Rainfall (in.), y	5	3	4.5	1	7

a. Is the relationship linear? Why or why not?

_____

_____

b. Can an equation be written to describe the amount of rain? Explain.

_____

 **FOCUS ON HIGHER ORDER THINKING**

14. **Analyze Relationships** If you have a table that shows a linear relationship, when can you read the value for b, in $y = mx + b$, directly from the table without drawing a graph or doing any calculations? Explain.

_____

_____

15. **What If?** Jaíme graphed linear data given in the form (cost, number). The y-intercept was 0. Jayla graphed the same data given in the form (number, cost). What was the y-intercept of her graph? Explain.

_____

_____

_____

Work Area

Linear Relationships and Bivariate Data

COMMON CORE 8.SP.1

Construct and interpret scatter plots for bivariate measurement data.... Describe patterns such as... linear association, and nonlinear association. *Also 8.SP.2, 8.SP.3*

? **ESSENTIAL QUESTION**

How can you contrast linear and nonlinear sets of bivariate data?

EXPLORE ACTIVITY   COMMON CORE 8.SP.2

Finding the Equation of a Linear Relationship

Math On the Spot
my.hrw.com

You can use the points on a graph of a linear relationship to write an equation for the relationship. The equation of a linear relationship is $y = mx + b$, where m is the rate of change, or slope, and b is the value of y when x is 0.

EXAMPLE 1 **A handrail runs alongside a stairway. As the horizontal distance from the bottom of the stairway changes, the height of the handrail changes. Show that the relationship is linear, and then find the equation for the relationship.**

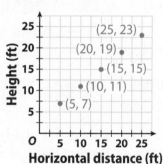

STEP 1 Show that the relationship is linear.

All of the points (5, 7), (10, 11), (15, 15), (20, 19), and (25, 23) lie on the same _____, so the relationship is _____. Draw a line through the points on the graph.

STEP 2 Write the equation of the linear relationship.

Choose two points to find the slope: (5, 7) and (25, 23).

$$m = \dfrac{23 - \boxed{}}{\boxed{} - 5}$$

$$= \dfrac{\boxed{}}{\boxed{}}, \text{ or } \underline{}$$

Choose a point and use the slope to substitute values for x, y, and m.

$$y = mx + b$$

$$\boxed{} = \boxed{}(5) + b$$

$$\boxed{} = \boxed{} + b$$

$$\boxed{} = b$$

The equation of the linear relationship is $y = \boxed{} x + \boxed{}$.

YOUR TURN

Find the equation of each linear relationship.

1.

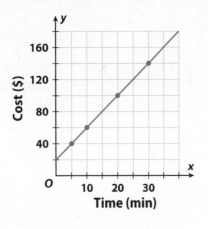

2.

Hours (x)	Number of units (y)
2	480
15	3,600
24	5,760
30	7,200
48	11,520
55	13,200

_____   _____

Math On the Spot

my.hrw.com

Making Predictions

You can use an equation of a linear relationship to predict a value between data points that you already know.

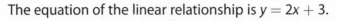

EXAMPLE 2

COMMON CORE 8.SP.3

The graph shows the cost for taxi rides of different distances. Predict the cost of a taxi ride that covers a distance of 6.5 miles.

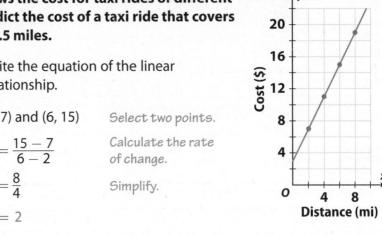

STEP 1 Write the equation of the linear relationship.

$(2, 7)$ and $(6, 15)$ Select two points.

$m = \dfrac{15 - 7}{6 - 2}$ Calculate the rate of change.

$= \dfrac{8}{4}$ Simplify.

$= 2$

$y = mx + b$

$15 = 2(6) + b$ Fill in values for x, y, and m.

$15 = 12 + b$ Simplify.

$3 = b$ Solve for b.

The equation of the linear relationship is $y = 2x + 3$.

You can check your equation using another point on the graph. Try $(8, 19)$. Substituting gives $19 = 2(8) + 3$. The right side simplifies to 19, so $19 = 19$. ✓

STEP 2 Use your equation from Step 1 to predict the cost of a 6.5-mile taxi ride.

$y = 2x + 3$

$y = 2(6.5) + 3$ Substitute $x = 6.5$.

               Solve for y.

$y = 16$

A taxi ride that covers a distance of 6.5 miles will cost $16.

Reflect

3. **What If?** Suppose a regulation changes the cost of the taxi ride to $1.80 per mile, plus a fee of $4.30. How does the price of the 6.5 mile ride compare to the original price?

_____

_____

4. How can you use a graph of a linear relationship to predict an unknown value of y for a given value of x within the region of the graph?

_____

_____

_____

5. How can you use a table of linear data to predict a value?

_____

_____

_____

YOUR TURN

Paulina's income from a job that pays her a fixed amount per hour is shown in the graph. Use the graph to find the predicted value.

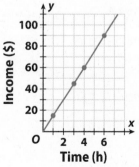

6. Income earned for working 2 hours

_____

7. Income earned for working 3.25 hours

_____

8. Total income earned for working for five 8-hour days all at the standard rate _____

Personal Math Trainer

Online Assessment and Intervention

🔵 my.hrw.com

Contrasting Linear and Nonlinear Data

Bivariate data is a set of data that is made up of two paired variables. If the relationship between the variables is linear, then the rate of change (slope) is constant. If the graph shows a **nonlinear relationship**, then the rate of change varies between pairs of points.

Andrew has two options in which to invest $200. Option A earns simple interest of 5%, while Option B earns interest of 5% compounded annually. The table shows the amount of the investment for both options over 20 years. Graph the data and describe the differences between the two graphs.

	Option A	Option B
Year, x	Total ($)	Total ($)
0	200.00	200.00
5	250.00	255.26
10	300.00	325.78
15	350.00	415.79
20	400.00	530.66

STEP 1 Graph the data from the table for Options A and B on the same coordinate grid.

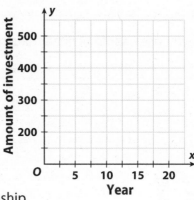

STEP 2 Find the rate of change between pairs of points for Option A and classify the relationship.

Option A	Rate of Change
(0, 200) and (5, 250)	$m = \dfrac{250 - 200}{5 - 0} = $ _____
(5, 250) and (10, 300)	
(10, 300) and (15, 350)	

The rate of change between the data values is _____ , so

the graph of Option A shows a _____ relationship.

STEP 3 Find the rate of change between pairs of points for Option B and classify the relationship.

Option B	Rate of Change
(0, 200) and (5, 255.26)	$m = \dfrac{252.26 - 200}{5 - 0} \approx$ _____
(5, 255.26) and (10, 325.78)	
(10, 325.78) and (15, 415.79)	

The rate of change between the data values is _____,

so the graph of Option B shows a _____ relationship.

Reflect

9. Why are the graphs drawn as lines or curves and not discrete points?

_____

_____

_____

_____

10. Can you determine by viewing the graph if the data have a linear or nonlinear relationship? Explain.

_____

_____

_____

_____

11. Draw Conclusions Find the differences in the account balances to the nearest dollar at 5 year intervals for Option B. How does the length of time that money is in an account affect the advantage that compound interest has over simple interest?

_____

_____

_____

Use the following graphs to find the equation of the linear relationship. (Explore Activity Example 1)

1.

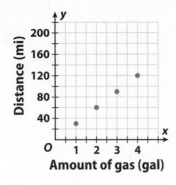

_____

2.

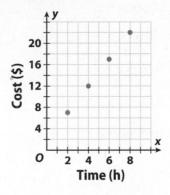

_____

3. The graph shows the relationship between the number of hours a kayak is rented and the total cost of the rental. Write an equation of the relationship. Then use the equation to predict the cost of a rental that lasts 5.5 hours. (Example 2)

_____

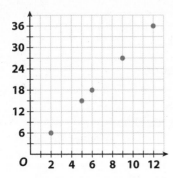

Does each of the following graphs represent a linear relationship? Why or why not? (Explore Activity 2)

4.

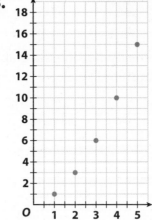

_____

_____

5.

_____

_____

? ESSENTIAL QUESTION CHECK-IN

6. How can you tell if a set of bivariate data shows a linear relationship?

_____

_____

5.3 Independent Practice

COMMON CORE 8.SP.1, 8.SP.2, 8.SP.3

Personal Math Trainer

Online Assessment and Intervention

my.hrw.com

Does each of the following tables represent a linear relationship? Why or why not?

7.

Number of boxes	Weight (kg)
3	15
9	45
21	105

8.

Day	Height (cm)
5	30
8	76.8
14	235.2

_____

_____

_____

_____

Explain whether or not you think each relationship is linear.

9. the cost of equal-priced DVDs and the number purchased

_____

10. the height of a person and the person's age

_____

11. the area of a square quilt and its side length

_____

_____

12. the number of miles to the next service station and the number of kilometers

_____

_____

13. **Multistep** The Mars Rover travels 0.75 feet in 6 seconds. Add the point to the graph. Then determine whether the relationship between distance and time is linear, and if so, predict the distance that the Mars Rover would travel in 1 minute.

_____

_____

_____

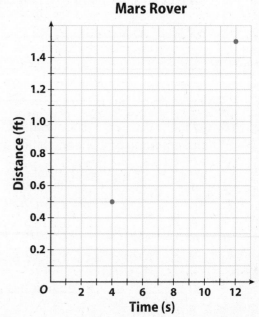

Mars Rover

14. Make a Conjecture Zefram analyzed a linear relationship, found that the slope-intercept equation was $y = 3.5x + 16$, and made a prediction for the value of y for a given value of x. He realized that he made an error calculating the y-intercept and that it was actually 12. Can he just subtract 4 from his prediction if he knows that the slope is correct? Explain.

_____

_____

 **FOCUS ON HIGHER ORDER THINKING**

15. Communicate Mathematical Ideas The table shows a linear relationship. How can you predict the value of y when $x = 6$ without finding the equation of the relationship?

x	y
4	38
8	76
12	114

_____

_____

_____

16. Critique Reasoning Louis says that if the differences between the values of x are constant between all the points on a graph, then the relationship is linear. Do you agree? Explain.

_____

_____

_____

17. Make a Conjecture Suppose you know the slope of a linear relationship and one of the points that its graph passes through. How could you predict another point that falls on the graph of the line?

_____

_____

_____

18. Explain the Error Thomas used (7, 17.5) and (18, 45) from a graph to find the equation of a linear relationship as shown. What was his mistake?

$$m = \frac{45 - 7}{18 - 17.5} = \frac{38}{0.5} = 79$$

$$y = 79x + b$$

$$45 = 79 \cdot 18 + b$$

$$45 = 1422 + b, \text{ so } b = -1377$$

The equation is $y = 79x - 1377$.

_____

Ready to Go On?

Personal Math Trainer

Online Assessment and Intervention

my.hrw.com

5.1 Writing Linear Equations from Situations and Graphs

Write the equation of each line in slope-intercept form.

1.

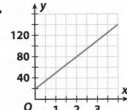

_____

2.

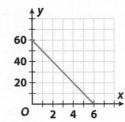

_____

5.2 Writing Linear Equations from a Table

Write the equation of each linear relationship in slope-intercept form.

3.

x	0	100	200	300
y	1.5	36.5	71.5	106.5

_____

4.

x	25	35	45	55
y	94	88	82	76

_____

5.3 Linear Relationships and Bivariate Data

Write the equation of the line that connects each set of data points.

5.

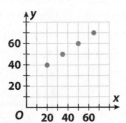

_____

6.

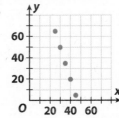

_____

? ESSENTIAL QUESTION

7. Write a real-world situation that can be represented by a linear relationship.

_____

_____

COMMON CORE

MODULE 5 MIXED REVIEW
Assessment Readiness

Personal Math Trainer

Online Assessment and Intervention

my.hrw.com

Selected Response

1. An hourglass is turned over with the top part filled with sand. After 3 minutes, there are 855 mL of sand in the top half. After 10 minutes, there are 750 mL of sand in the top half. Which equation represents this situation?

Ⓐ $y = 285x$

Ⓑ $y = -10.5x + 900$

Ⓒ $y = -15x + 900$

Ⓓ $y = 75x$

2. Which graph shows a linear relationship?

Ⓐ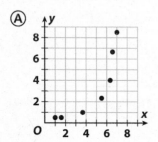

Ⓑ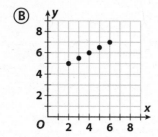

Ⓒ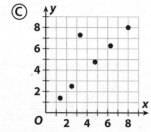

Ⓓ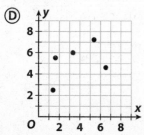

3. What are the slope and y-intercept of the relationship shown in the table?

x	10,000	20,000	30,000
y	2,500	3,000	3,500

Ⓐ slope = 0.05, y-intercept = 1,500

Ⓑ slope = 0.5, y-intercept = 1,500

Ⓒ slope = 0.05, y-intercept = 2,000

Ⓓ slope = 0.5, y-intercept = 2,000

4. Which is the sum of $3.15 \times 10^7 + 9.3 \times 10^6$? Write your answer in scientific notation.

Ⓐ 4.08×10^7

Ⓑ 4.08×10^6

Ⓒ 0.408×10^8

Ⓓ 40.8×10^6

Mini-Task

5. Franklin's faucet was leaking, so he put a bucket underneath to catch the water. After a while, Franklin started keeping track of how much water was in the bucket. His data is in the table below.

Hours	2	3	4	5
Quarts	5	6.5	8	9.5

a. Is the relationship linear or nonlinear?

_____

b. Write the equation for the relationship.

_____

c. Predict how much water will be in the bucket after 14 hours if Franklin doesn't stop the leak.

_____

Functions

? **ESSENTIAL QUESTION**

How can you use functions to solve real-world problems?

 my.hrw.com

Real-World Video

Computerized machines can assist doctors in surgeries such as laser vision correction. Each action the surgeon takes results in one end action by the machine. In math, functions also have a one-in-one-out relationship.

GO DIGITAL
my.hrw.com

my.hrw.com
Go digital with your write-in student edition, accessible on any device.

Math On the Spot
Scan with your smart phone to jump directly to the online edition, video tutor, and more.

Animated Math
Interactively explore key concepts to see how math works.

Personal Math Trainer
Get immediate feedback and help as you work through practice sets.

Are YOU Ready?

Complete these exercises to review skills you will need for this module.

Evaluate Expressions

EXAMPLE Evaluate $3x - 5$ for $x = -2$.

$3x - 5 = 3(-2) - 5$ Substitute the given value of x for x.

$= -6 - 5$ Multiply.

$= -11$ Subtract.

Evaluate each expression for the given value of x.

1. $2x + 3$ for $x = 3$ _____

2. $-4x + 7$ for $x = -1$ _____

3. $1.5x - 2.5$ for $x = 3$ _____

4. $0.4x + 6.1$ for $x = -5$ _____

5. $\frac{2}{3}x - 12$ for $x = 18$ _____

6. $-\frac{5}{8}x + 10$ for $x = -8$ _____

Connect Words and Equations

EXAMPLE Erik's earnings equal 9 dollars per hour.

e = earnings; h = hours   Define the variables used in the situation.

multiplication   Identify the operation involved. "Per" indicates multiplication.

$e = 9 \times h$ Write the equation.

Define the variables for each situation. Then write an equation.

7. Jana's age plus 5 equals her sister's age.

_____

8. Andrew's class has 3 more students than Lauren's class.

_____

9. The bank is 50 feet shorter than the firehouse.

_____

10. The pencils were divided into 6 groups of 2.

_____

© Houghton Mifflin Harcourt Publishing Company

Reading Start-Up

Visualize Vocabulary

Use the ✔ words to complete the diagram. You can put more than one word in each section of the diagram.

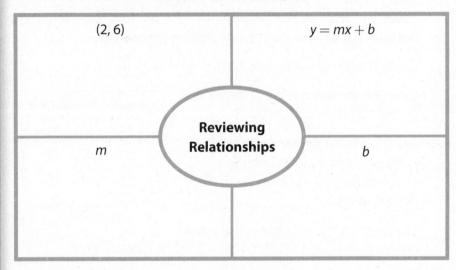

(2, 6)	$y = mx + b$
m	*b*

Reviewing Relationships

Understand Vocabulary

Complete the sentences using the preview words.

1. A rule that assigns exactly one output to each input

   is a _____.

2. The value that is put into a function is the _____.

3. The result after applying the function machine's rule is

   the _____.

© Houghton Mifflin Harcourt Publishing Company

Vocabulary

Review Words

- ✔ bivariate data *(datos bivariados)*
- ✔ linear equation *(ecuación lineal)*
- nonlinear relationship *(relación no lineal)*
- ✔ ordered pair *(par ordenado)*
- proporational relationship *(relación proporcional)*
- ✔ slope *(pendiente)*
- ✔ x-coordinate *(coordenada x)*
- ✔ y-coordinate *(coordenada y)*
- ✔ y-intercept *(intersección con el eje y)*

Preview Words

- function *(función)*
- input *(valor de entrada)*
- linear function *(función lineal)*
- output *(valor de salida)*

Active Reading

Double-Door Fold Create a double-door fold to help you understand the concepts in this module. Label one flap "Proportional Functions" and the other flap "Non-proportional Functions." As you study each lesson, write important ideas under the appropriate flap. Include any sample problems that will help you remember the concepts when you look back at your notes.

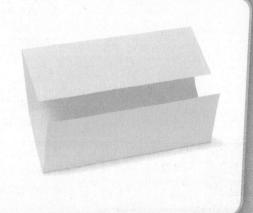

MODULE 6

Unpacking the Standards

Understanding the standards and the vocabulary terms in the standards will help you know exactly what you are expected to learn in this module.

8.F.1

Understand that a function is a rule that assigns to each input exactly one output. The graph of a function is the set of ordered pairs consisting of an input and the corresponding output.

Key Vocabulary

function *(función)*
An input-output relationship that has exactly one output for each input.

What It Means to You

You will identify sets of ordered pairs that are functions. A function is a rule that assigns exactly one output to each input.

UNPACKING EXAMPLE 8.F.1

Does the following table of inputs and outputs represent a function?

Yes, it is a function because each number in the input column is assigned to only one number in the output column.

Input	Output
14	110
20	130
22	120
30	110

The graph of the function is the set of ordered pairs (14, 110), (20, 130), (22, 120), and (30, 110).

8.F.2

Compare properties of two functions each represented in a different way (algebraically, graphically, numerically in tables, or by verbal descriptions).

What It Means to You

You will learn to identify and compare functions expressed as equations and tables.

UNPACKING EXAMPLE 8.F.2

A spider descends a 20-foot drainpipe at a rate of 2.5 feet per minute. Another spider descends a drainpipe as shown in the table. Find and compare the rates of change and initial values of the linear functions in terms of the situations they model.

Spider #1: $f(x) = -2.5x + 20$

Spider #2:

Time (min)	0	1	2
Height (ft)	32	29	26

For Spider #1, the rate of change is -2.5, and the initial value is 20. For Spider #2, the rate of change is -3, and the initial value is 32.

Spider #2 started at 32 feet, which is 12 feet higher than Spider #1. Spider #1 is descending at 2.5 feet per minute, which is 0.5 foot per minute slower than Spider #2.

Visit **my.hrw.com** to see all the **Common Core Standards** unpacked.

my.hrw.com

LESSON 6.1 Identifying and Representing Functions

COMMON CORE 8.F.1

Understand that a function is a rule that assigns to each input exactly one output. The graph of a function is the set of ordered pairs consisting of an input and the corresponding output.

 ESSENTIAL QUESTION

How can you identify and represent functions?

EXPLORE ACTIVITY COMMON CORE 8.F.1

Understanding Relationships

Carlos needs to buy some new pencils from the school supply store at his school. Carlos asks his classmates if they know how much pencils cost. Angela says she bought 2 pencils for $0.50. Paige bought 3 pencils for $0.75, and Spencer bought 4 pencils for $1.00.

Carlos thinks about the rule for the price of a pencil as a machine. When he puts the number of pencils he wants to buy into the machine, the machine applies a rule and tells him the total cost of that number of pencils.

Input    Output

	Number of Pencils	Rule	Total Cost
i.	2	?	
ii.	3	?	
iii.	4	?	
iv.	x		
v.	12		

A Use the prices in the problem to fill in total cost in rows **i–iii** of the table.

B Describe any patterns you see. Use your pattern to determine the cost of 1 pencil.

_____

_____

_____

C Use the pattern you identified to write the rule applied by the machine. Write the rule as an algebraic expression and fill in rule column row **iv** of the table.

D Carlos wants to buy 12 pencils. Use your rule to fill in row **v** of the table to show how much Carlos will pay for 12 pencils.

Reflect

1. How did you decide what operation to use in your rule?

_____

_____

2. **What If?** Carlos decides to buy erasers in a package. There are 6 pencil-top erasers in 2 packages of erasers.

   a. Write a rule in words for the number of packages Carlos needs to buy to get *x* erasers. Then write the rule as an algebraic expression.

   _____

   _____

   b. How many packages does Carlos need to buy to get 18 erasers?

   _____

Math On the Spot
my.hrw.com

Identifying Functions from Mapping Diagrams

A **function** assigns exactly one output to each input. The value that is put into a function is the **input**. The result is the **output**.

A mapping diagram can be used to represent a relationship between input values and output values. A mapping diagram represents a function if each input value is paired with only one output value.

EXAMPLE 1 8.F.1

Determine whether each relationship is a function.

A
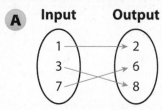

Since each input value is paired with only one output value, the relationship is a function.

© Houghton Mifflin Harcourt Publishing Company

Determine whether each relationship is a function.

B

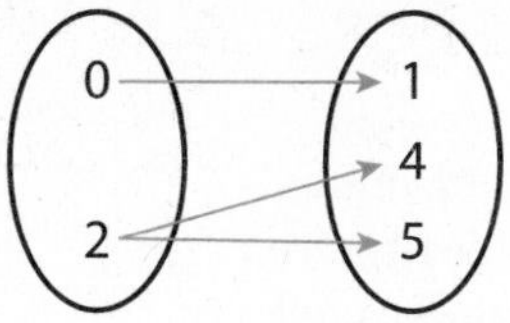

Since 2 is paired with more than one output value (both 4 and 5), the relationship is not a function.

Reflect

3. Is it possible for a function to have more than one input value but only one output value? Provide an illustration to support your answer.

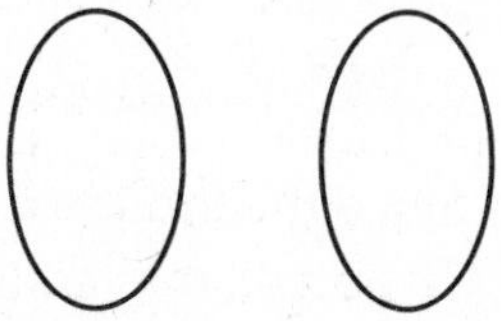

____

YOUR TURN

Determine whether each relationship is a function. Explain.

4.

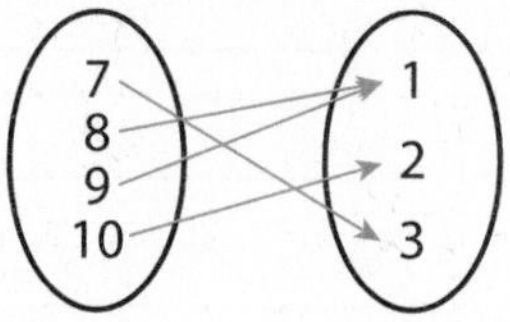

____

____

____

5.

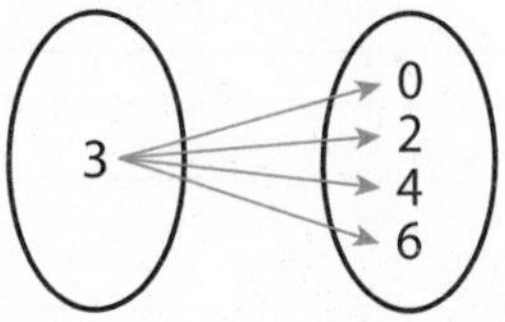

____

____

____

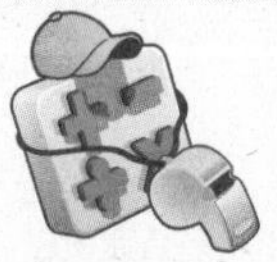

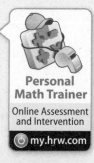

Personal Math Trainer

Online Assessment and Intervention

my.hrw.com

Math Talk

Mathematical Practices

What is always true about a mapping diagram that represents a function?

Identifying Functions from Tables

Relationships between input values and output values can also be represented using tables. The values in the first column are the input values. The values in the second column are the output values. The relationship represents a function if each input value is paired with only one output value.

Math On the Spot

my.hrw.com

EXAMPLE 2

COMMON CORE 8.F.1

My Notes

Determine whether each relationship is a function.

A

Input	Output
5	7
10	6
15	15
20	2
25	15

Since 15 is a repeated output value, one output value is paired with two input values. If this occurs in a relationship, the relationship can still be a function.

Since each input value is paired with only one output value, the relationship is a function.

Determine whether each relationship is a function.

B

Input	Output
1	10
5	8
4	6
1	4
7	2

Since 1 is a repeated input value, one input value is paired with two output values. Look back at the rule for functions. Is this relationship a function?

Since the input value 1 is paired with more than one output value (both 10 and 4), the relationship is not a function.

Reflect

6. What is always true about the numbers in the first column of a table that represents a function? Why must this be true?

_____

_____

_____

_____

_____

YOUR TURN

Determine whether each relationship is a function. Explain

7.

Input	Output
53	53
24	24
32	32
17	17
45	45

8.

Input	Output
14	52
8	21
27	16
36	25
8	34

_____   _____

_____   _____

_____   _____

_____   _____

Personal Math Trainer

Online Assessment and Intervention

my.hrw.com

Identifying Functions from Graphs

Graphs can be used to display relationships between two sets of numbers. Each point on a graph represents an ordered pair. The first coordinate in each ordered pair is the input value. The second coordinate is the output value. The graph represents a function if each input value is paired with only one output value.

Math On the Spot
my.hrw.com

EXAMPLE 3 COMMON CORE 8.F.1

The graph shows the relationship between the number of hours students spent studying for an exam and the exam grades. Is the relationship represented by the graph a function?

The input values are the number of hours spent studying by each student. The output values are the exam grades. The points represent the following ordered pairs:

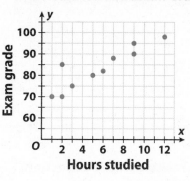

Hours Studied and Exam Grade

| (1, 70) | (2, 70) | (2, 85) | (3, 75) | (5, 80) |
| (6, 82) | (7, 88) | (9, 90) | (9, 95) | (12, 98) |

Notice that 2 is paired with both 70 and 85, and 9 is paired with both 90 and 95. Therefore, since these input values are paired with more than one output value, the relationship is not a function.

Reflect

9. Many real-world relationships are functions. For example, the amount of money made at a car wash is a function of the number of cars washed. Give another example of a real-world function.

_____

_____

YOUR TURN

10. The graph shows the relationship between the heights and weights of the members of a basketball team. Is the relationship represented by the graph a function? Explain.

_____

_____

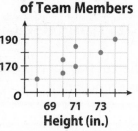

Heights and Weights of Team Members

Personal Math Trainer
Online Assessment and Intervention
my.hrw.com

Complete each table. In the row with x as the input, write a rule as an algebraic expression for the output. Then complete the last row of the table using the rule. (Explore Activity)

1.

Input	Output
Tickets	Cost ($)
2	40
5	100
7	140
x	
10	

2.

Input	Output
Minutes	Pages
2	1
10	5
20	10
x	
30	

3.

Input	Output
Muffins	Cost ($)
1	2.25
3	6.75
6	13.50
x	
12	

Determine whether each relationship is a function. (Examples 1 and 2)

4.

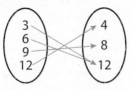

_____

_____

_____

5.

Input	Output
3	20
4	25
5	30
4	35
6	40

_____

_____

_____

6. The graph shows the relationship between the weights of 5 packages and the shipping charge for each package. Is the relationship represented by the graph a function? Explain.

_____

_____

Weights and Shipping Costs

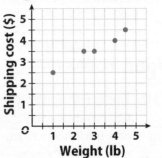

? **ESSENTIAL QUESTION CHECK-IN**

7. What are four different ways of representing functions? How can you tell if a relationship is a function?

_____

_____

6.1 Independent Practice

COMMON CORE 8.F.1

Personal Math Trainer

Online Assessment and Intervention

my.hrw.com

Determine whether each relationship represented by the ordered pairs is a function. Explain.

8. (2, 2), (3, 1), (5, 7), (8, 0), (9, 1)

_____

_____

_____

9. (0, 4), (5, 1), (2, 8), (6, 3), (5, 9)

_____

_____

_____

10. Draw Conclusions Joaquin receives $0.40 per pound for 1 to 99 pounds of aluminum cans he recycles. He receives $0.50 per pound if he recycles more than 100 pounds. Is the amount of money Joaquin receives a function of the weight of the cans he recycles? Explain your reasoning.

_____

_____

11. A biologist tracked the growth of a strain of bacteria, as shown in the graph.

a. Explain why the relationship represented by the graph is a function.

_____

_____

_____

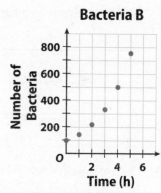

Bacteria B

b. What If? Suppose there was the same number of bacteria for two consecutive hours. Would the graph still represent a function? Explain.

_____

12. Multiple Representations Give an example of a function in everyday life, and represent it as a graph, a table, and a set of ordered pairs. Describe how you know it is a function.

_____

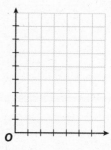

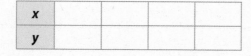

x			
y			

The graph shows the relationship between the weights of six wedges of cheese and the price of each wedge.

Cost of Cheese

13. Is the relationship represented by the graph a function? Justify your reasoning. Use the words "input" and "output" in your explanation, and connect them to the context represented by the graph.

_____

_____

14. **Analyze Relationships** Suppose the weights and prices of additional wedges of cheese were plotted on the graph. Might that change your answer to question 13? Explain your reasoning.

_____

_____

_____

_____

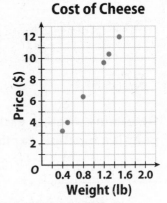

H.O.T. FOCUS ON HIGHER ORDER THINKING

Work Area

15. **Justify Reasoning** A mapping diagram represents a relationship that contains three different input values and four different output values. Is the relationship a function? Explain your reasoning.

_____

_____

_____

_____

16. **Communicate Mathematical Ideas** An onion farmer is hiring workers to help harvest the onions. He knows that the number of days it will take to harvest the onions is a function of the number of workers he hires. Explain the use of the word "function" in this context.

_____

_____

_____

_____

_____

6.2 Describing Functions

COMMON CORE 8.F.3

Interpret the equation $y = mx + b$ as defining a linear function, whose graph is a straight line; give examples of functions that are not linear. *Also 8.F.1.1*

? **ESSENTIAL QUESTION**

What are some characteristics that you can use to describe functions?

EXPLORE ACTIVITY   **COMMON CORE** 8.F.1

Investigating a Constant Rate of Change

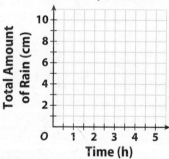

The U.S. Department of Agriculture defines heavy rain as rain that falls at a rate of 1.5 centimeters per hour.

A The table shows the total amount of rain that falls in various amounts of time during a heavy rain. Complete the table.

Time (h)	0	1	2	3	4	5
Total Amount of Rain (cm)	0	1.5				

B Plot the ordered pairs from the table on the coordinate plane at the right.

C How much rain falls in 3.5 hours? _____

D Plot the point corresponding to 3.5 hours of heavy rain.

E What do you notice about all of the points you plotted?

_____

F Is the total amount of rain that falls a function of the number of hours that rain has been falling? Why or why not?

_____

_____

Heavy Rainfall

(graph: vertical axis "Total Amount of Rain (cm)" marked 2, 4, 6, 8, 10; horizontal axis "Time (h)" marked 1, 2, 3, 4, 5, origin O)

Reflect

1. Suppose you continued to plot points for times between those in the table, such as 1.2 hours or 4.5 hours. What can you say about the locations of these points?

_____

_____

Graphing Linear Functions

The relationship you investigated in the previous activity can be represented by the equation $y = 1.5x$, where x is the time and y is the total amount of rain. The graph of the relationship is a line, so the equation is a **linear equation**. Since there is exactly one value of y for each value of x, the relationship is a function. It is a **linear function** because its graph is a nonvertical line.

EXAMPLE 1

COMMON CORE 8.F.3

The temperature at dawn was 8 °F and increased steadily 2 °F every hour. The equation $y = 2x + 8$ gives the temperature y after x hours. State whether the relationship between the time and the temperature is proportional or nonproportional. Then graph the function.

Math Talk

Mathematical Practices

Carrie said that for a function to be a linear function, the relationship it represents must be proportional. Do you agree or disagree? Explain.

STEP 1 Compare the equation with the general linear equation $y = mx + b$. $y = 2x + 8$ is in the form $y = mx + b$, with $m = 2$ and $b = 8$. Therefore, the equation is a linear equation. Since $b \neq 0$, the relationship is nonproportional.

STEP 2 Choose several values for the input x. Substitute these values for x in the equation to find the output y.

x	$2x + 8$	y	(x, y)
0	2(0) + 8	8	(0, 8)
2	2(2) + 8	12	(2, 12)
4	2(4) + 8	16	(4, 16)
6	2(6) + 8	20	(6, 20)

STEP 3 Graph the ordered pairs. Then draw a line through the points to represent the solutions of the function.

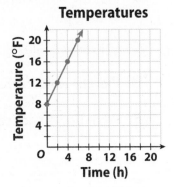

Temperatures

YOUR TURN

2. State whether the relationship between x and y in $y = 0.5x$ is proportional or nonproportional. Then graph the function.

_____

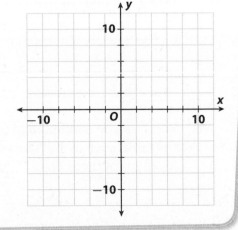

© Houghton Mifflin Harcourt Publishing Company

Determining Whether a Function is Linear

The linear equation in Example 1 has the form $y = mx + b$, where m and b are real numbers. Every equation in the form $y = mx + b$ is a linear equation. The linear equations represent linear functions. Equations that cannot be written in this form are not linear equations, and therefore are not linear functions.

Math On the Spot

⏻ my.hrw.com

EXAMPLE 2

COMMON CORE 8.F.3

A square tile has a side length of x inches. The equation $y = x^2$ gives the area of the tile in square inches. Determine whether the relationship between x and y is linear and, if so, if it is proportional.

STEP 1 Choose several values for the input x. Substitute these values for x in the equation to find the output y.

STEP 2 Graph the ordered pairs.

x	x^2	y	(x, y)
1	1^2	1	(1, 1)
2	2^2	4	(2, 4)
3	3^2	9	(3, 9)
4	4^2	16	(4, 16)

STEP 3 Identify the shape of the graph. The points suggest a curve, not a line. Draw a curve through the points to represent the solutions of the function.

STEP 4 Describe the relationship between x and y.

The graph is not a line so the relationship is not linear.

Only a linear relationship can be proportional, so the relationship is not proportional.

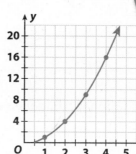

Animated Math

⏻ my.hrw.com

Math Talk
Mathematical Practices

How can you use the numbers in the table to decide whether or not the relationship between x and y is linear?

YOUR TURN

3. A soda machine makes $\frac{2}{3}$ gallon of soda every minute. The total amount y that the machine makes in x minutes is given by the equation $y = \frac{2}{3}x$. Determine whether the relationship between x and y is linear and, if so, if it is proportional.

Time (min), x	0	3		9
Amount (gal), y			4	

Making Soda

Amount (gal) vs. Time (min)

Personal Math Trainer

Online Assessment and Intervention

⏻ my.hrw.com

© Houghton Mifflin Harcourt Publishing Company

Plot the ordered pairs from the table. Then graph the function represented by the ordered pairs and tell whether the function is linear or nonlinear. (Examples 1 and 2)

1. $y = 5 - 2x$

Input, x	−1	1	3	5
Output, y				

2. $y = 2 - x^2$

Input, x	−2	−1	0	1	2
Output, y					

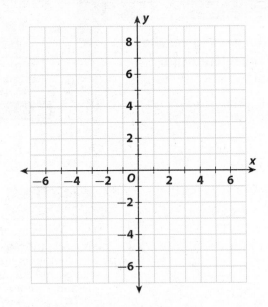

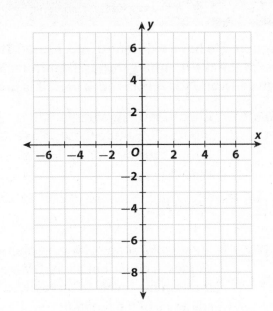

Explain whether each equation is a linear equation. (Example 2)

3. $y = x^2 - 1$

_____

_____

_____

_____

4. $y = 1 - x$

_____

_____

_____

_____

? **ESSENTIAL QUESTION CHECK-IN**

5. Explain how you can use a table of values, an equation, and a graph to determine whether a function represents a proportional relationship.

_____

_____

_____

6.2 Independent Practice

COMMON CORE 8.F.1, 8.F.3

Personal
Math Trainer

Online
Assessment and
Intervention

my.hrw.com

6. State whether the relationship between x and y in $y = 4x - 5$ is proportional or nonproportional. Then graph the function.

_____

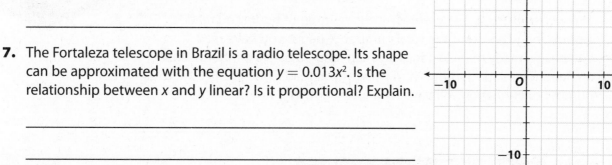

7. The Fortaleza telescope in Brazil is a radio telescope. Its shape can be approximated with the equation $y = 0.013x^2$. Is the relationship between x and y linear? Is it proportional? Explain.

_____

_____

8. Kiley spent $20 on rides and snacks at the state fair. If x is the amount she spent on rides, and y is the amount she spent on snacks, the total amount she spent can be represented by the equation $x + y = 20$. Is the relationship between x and y linear? Is it proportional? Explain.

_____

_____

_____

9. Represent Real-World Problems The drill team is buying new uniforms. The table shows y, the total cost in dollars, and x, the number of uniforms purchased.

Number of uniforms, x	1	3	5	9
Total cost ($), y	60	180	300	540

a. Use the data to draw a graph. Is the relationship between x and y linear? Explain.

_____

b. Use your graph to predict the cost of purchasing 12 uniforms.

_____

Drill Team Uniforms

10. Marta, a whale calf in an aquarium, is fed a special milk formula. Her handler uses a graph to track the number of gallons of formula y the calf drinks in x hours. Is the relationship between x and y linear? Is it proportional? Explain.

_____

_____

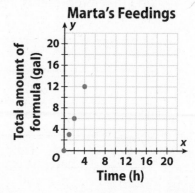

Marta's Feedings

11. Critique Reasoning A student claims that the equation $y = 7$ is not a linear equation because it does not have the form $y = mx + b$. Do you agree or disagree? Why?

_____

_____

_____

12. Make a Prediction Let x represent the number of hours you read a book and y represent the total number of pages you have read. You have already read 70 pages and can read 30 pages per hour. Write an equation relating x hours and y pages you read. Then predict the total number of pages you will have read after another 3 hours.

_____

 **FOCUS ON HIGHER ORDER THINKING**

13. Draw Conclusions Rebecca draws a graph of a real-world relationship that turns out to be a set of unconnected points. Can the relationship be linear? Can it be proportional? Explain your reasoning.

_____

_____

_____

14. Communicate Mathematical Ideas Write a real-world problem involving a proportional relationship. Explain how you know the relationship is proportional.

_____

_____

_____

_____

15. Justify Reasoning Show that the equation $y + 3 = 3(2x + 1)$ is linear and that it represents a proportional relationship between x and y.

_____

_____

_____

_____

Work Area

Creating Nonlinear Functions

COMMON CORE 8.F.3
...give examples of functions that are not linear.

? ESSENTIAL QUESTION

How can you create functions that are not linear?

EXPLORE ACTIVITY   COMMON CORE 8.F.3

Creating Functions That Are Not Linear

A A linear function can be written in the form $y = mx + b$. If a function cannot be written in the form $y = mx + b$, it is not linear. Use this information to write a function that is *not* linear.

_____

B A table of values for a linear function shows a constant difference in corresponding output values when there is a constant difference in the input values. Use this information to create a table of values for a function that is *not* linear.

x				
f(x)				

C A graph of a linear function consists of points that all lie along a line. Use this information to create a graph of a function that is *not* linear.

_____

D The perimeter P of a square with side length x is given by the linear function $P = 4x$. Create a nonlinear function based on a geometry formula that you know. HINT: What do you know about the area A of a square with side length x?

_____

_____

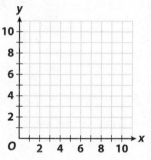

Reflect

1. Explain why the values in your table in Part B are nonlinear. Explain why the graph you created in Part C is not linear.

_____

_____

Marco has read 7 books for a summer reading club. He plans to read 2 books each week for the rest of the summer. The table shows the total number of books he will read over time.

Week, x	0	1	2	3	4
Total books read, f(x)	7	9	11	13	15

1. Create a table to show the reading plan for another book club member whose plan is represented with a nonlinear function.

Week, x	0	1	2	3	4
Total books read, f(x)					

2. Explain how you know the second book club member's plan is not linear.

_____

_____

For each linear situation described, give an adapted description that is not linear.

3. An art museum charges $6.50 per ticket.

_____

4. A hat collector gets 2 new hats each month.

_____

5. A game club gives members 200 points for beginning membership and 50 points for each game purchased.

_____

_____

Determine whether the graph is linear or nonlinear. Then write a situation for the graph.

6.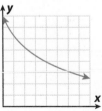

_____

_____

_____

7.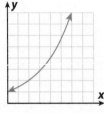

_____

_____

_____

8.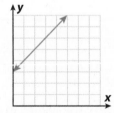

_____

_____

_____

How Many Squares?

STEP 1 How many squares (of all sizes) can you find in the 4 × 4 square grid?

There are four different sizes of squares in the grid.

    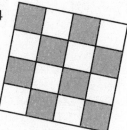

Count the number of each size square in the 4 × 4 square grid. The table shows you how to find them all.

Size of square	Number of squares	Identification of squares
4 × 4	1	
3 × 3	4	
2 × 2	9	
1 × 1	16	
Total	30	

The total number of squares in the 4 × 4 square grid is:

$f(4) = 1 + 4 + 9 + 16 = 30$

Notice the pattern. All the terms in $f(4)$ are perfect squares:

$f(4) = 1^2 + 2^2 + 3^2 + 4^2$

STEP 2 Draw a 5 × 5 square grid. Find the total number of different-sized squares in the grid to complete the table. Look for a pattern.

Size of square	5×5	4×4	3×3	2×2	1×1
Identification of squares					
Number of squares					

The total number of squares in the 5 × 5 square grid is:

$f(5) = 1 + 4 + \boxed{} + \boxed{} + \boxed{} = \boxed{}$

STEP 3 Repeat with a 6 × 6 grid and a 7 × 7 grid. Verify the pattern.

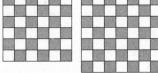

$f(6) = $ _____

$f(7) = $ _____

STEP 4 Use the pattern to write a function for the total number $f(n)$ of different-sized squares in an $n \times n$ grid.

$f(n) = 1^2 + 2^2 + \boxed{}^2 + \cdots + \boxed{}$

STEP 5 The function for the total number $f(n)$ of different-sized squares in an $n \times n$ grid can also be written $f(n) = \dfrac{n(n + 1)(2n + 1)}{6}$. Verify that this function works for 5 × 5, 6 × 6, and 7 × 7 square grids.

$$f(5) = \frac{\boxed{}\left(\boxed{} + 1\right)\left(2 \times \boxed{} + 1\right)}{6} = \boxed{}$$

$$f(6) = \frac{\boxed{}\left(\boxed{} + 1\right)\left(2 \times \boxed{} + 1\right)}{6} = \boxed{}$$

$$f(7) = \frac{\boxed{}\left(\boxed{} + 1\right)\left(2 \times \boxed{} + 1\right)}{6} = \boxed{}$$

_____

_____

COMMON CORE **8.F.2**

Compare properties of two functions each represented in a different way (algebraically, graphically, numerically in tables, or by verbal descriptions). *Also 8.EE.5, 8.F.4*

? ESSENTIAL QUESTION

How can you use tables, graphs, and equations to compare functions?

EXPLORE ACTIVITY COMMON CORE **8.F.2, 8.F.4**

Comparing a Table and an Equation

You can compare functions by writing them both as equations.

EXAMPLE 1 **Josh and Maggie buy MP3 files from different music services. The monthly cost, y dollars, for x songs is linear. The cost of Josh's service is $y = 0.50x + 10$. The cost of Maggie's service is shown below.**

Monthly Cost of MP3s at Maggie's Music Service					
Songs, x	5	10	15	20	25
Cost ($), y	4.95	9.90	14.85	19.80	24.75

A Write an equation to represent the monthly cost of Maggie's service.

STEP 1 Choose any two ordered pairs from the table to find the slope: for example, (5, 4.95) and (10, 9.90).

$$m = \frac{y_2 - y_1}{x_2 - x_1} = \frac{\boxed{} - 4.95}{10 - \boxed{}} = \frac{\boxed{}}{\boxed{}} = \underline{}$$

STEP 2 Find the y-intercept. Use the slope and any point.

Begin with slope-intercept form. $y = mx + b$

Substitute for y, m, and x. $4.95 = \boxed{} \cdot \boxed{} + b$

$$\boxed{} = b$$

STEP 3 Write the equation in slope-intercept form.

$y = \boxed{}x + \boxed{}$, or $y = \boxed{}x$

B Which service is cheaper when 30 songs are downloaded?

Josh's service: Maggie's service:

$y = 0.50x + 10$ $y = 0.99x$

$y = 0.50 \cdot \boxed{} + 10 = \boxed{}$ $y = 0.99 \cdot \boxed{} = \boxed{}$

_____ service is cheaper for 30 songs.

YOUR TURN

1. Quentin is choosing between buying books at the bookstore or buying online versions of the books for his tablet. The cost, y dollars, of ordering books online for x books is $y = 6.95x + 1.50$. The cost of buying the books at the bookstore is shown in the table. Which method of buying books is more expensive if Quentin wants to buy 6 books?

Cost of Books at the Bookstore					
Books, x	1	2	3	4	5
Cost ($), y	7.50	15.00	22.50	30.00	37.50

_____

EXPLORE ACTIVITY 2   COMMON CORE 8.F.2, 8.EE.5

Comparing a Table and a Graph

The table and graph show how many words Morgan and Brian typed correctly on a typing test. For both students, the relationship between words typed correctly and time is linear.

Morgan's Typing Test					
Time (min)	2	4	6	8	10
Words	30	60	90	120	150

Brian's Typing Test

(graph: Words vs. Time (min), straight line through origin)

A Find Morgan's unit rate.

_____

B Find Brian's unit rate.

_____

C Which student types more correct words per minute?

_____

Reflect

2. Katie types 17 correct words per minute. Explain how a graph of Katie's test results would compare to Morgan's and Brian's.

_____

_____

 **COMMON CORE** 8.F.2, 8.F.4

Comparing a Graph and a Description

Jamal wants to buy a new game system that costs $200. He does not have enough money to buy it today, so he compares layaway plans at different stores.

The plan at Store A is shown on the graph.

Store B requires an initial payment of $60 and weekly payments of $20 until the balance is paid in full.

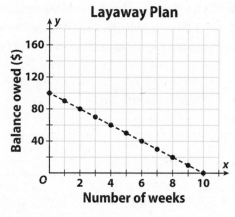

Layaway Plan

A Write an equation in slope-intercept form for Store A's layaway plan. Let x represent number of weeks and y represent balance owed.

_____

B Write an equation in slope-intercept form for Store B's layaway plan. Let x represent number of weeks and y represent balance owed.

_____

C Sketch a graph of the plan at Store B on the same grid as Store A.

D How can you use the graphs to tell which plan requires the greater down payment? How can you use the equations?

_____

_____

_____

E How can you use the graphs to tell which plan requires the greater weekly payment?

_____

_____

_____

F Which plan allows Jamal to pay for the game system faster? Explain.

_____

_____

Doctors have two methods of calculating maximum heart rate. With the first method, maximum heart rate, y, in beats per minute is $y = 220 - x$, where x is the person's age. Maximum heart rate with the second method is shown in the table. (Explore Activity Example 1)

Age, x	20	30	40	50	60
Heart rate (bpm), y	194	187	180	173	166

1. Which method gives the greater maximum heart rate for a 70-year-old?

_____

2. Are heart rate and age proportional or nonproportional for each method?

_____

Aisha runs a tutoring business. With Plan 1, students may choose to pay $15 per hour. With Plan 2, they may follow the plan shown on the graph. (Explore Activity 2 and 3)

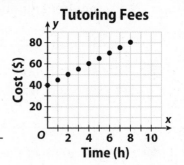

Tutoring Fees

3. Describe the plan shown on the graph.

_____

4. Sketch a graph showing the $15 per hour option.

5. What does the intersection of the two graphs mean?

_____

6. Which plan is cheaper for 10 hours of tutoring?

_____

7. Are cost and time proportional or nonproportional for each plan?

_____

_____

? ESSENTIAL QUESTION CHECK-IN

8. When using tables, graphs, and equations to compare functions, why do you find the equations for tables and graphs?

_____

_____

6.3 Independent Practice

COMMON CORE 8.EE.5, 8.F.2, 8.F.4

Personal Math Trainer

Online Assessment and Intervention

The table and graph show the miles driven and gas used for two scooters.

Scooter A

Distance (mi), x	Gas used (gal), y
150	2
300	4
450	6
600	8
750	10

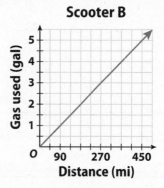

Scooter B

9. Which scooter uses fewer gallons of gas when 1350 miles are driven?

_____

10. Are gas used and miles proportional or nonproportional for each scooter?

_____

A cell phone company offers two texting plans to its customers. The monthly cost, y dollars, of one plan is $y = 0.10x + 5$, where x is the number of texts. The cost of the other plan is shown in the table.

Number of texts, x	100	200	300	400	500
Cost ($), y	20	25	30	35	40

11. Which plan is cheaper for under 200 texts? _____

12. The graph of the first plan does not pass through the origin. What does this indicate?

_____

_____

13. Brianna wants to buy a digital camera for a photography class. One store offers the camera for $50 down and a payment plan of $20 per month. The payment plan for a second store is described by $y = 15x + 80$, where y is the total cost in dollars and x is the number of months. Which camera is cheaper when the camera is paid off in 12 months? Explain.

_____

_____

14. The French club and soccer team are washing cars to earn money. The amount earned, y dollars, for washing x cars is a linear function. Which group makes the most money per car? Explain.

French Club	
Number of cars, x	**Amount earned ($), y**
2	10
4	20
6	30
8	40
10	50

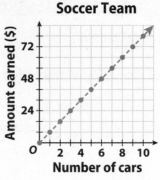

Soccer Team

_____

_____

_____

H.O.T. **FOCUS ON HIGHER ORDER THINKING**

Work Area

15. **Draw Conclusions** Gym A charges $60 a month plus $5 per visit. The monthly cost at Gym B is represented by $y = 5x + 40$, where x is the number of visits per month. What conclusion can you draw about the monthly costs of the gyms?

_____

_____

_____

16. **Justify Reasoning** Why will the value of y for the function $y = 5x + 1$ always be greater than that for the function $y = 4x + 2$ when $x > 1$?

_____

_____

_____

17. **Analyze Relationships** The equations of two functions are $y = -21x + 9$ and $y = -24x + 8$. Which function is changing more quickly? Explain.

_____

_____

_____

_____

Rate of Change and Initial Value

COMMON CORE **8.F.4**
... Determine the rate of change and initial value of the function from a description of a relationship or from two (x, y) values, including reading these from a table or from a graph. ...

 ESSENTIAL QUESTION

How can you interpret the rate of change and initial value of a linear function in terms of the situation it models?

EXPLORE ACTIVITY COMMON CORE 8.F.4

Determining Rate of Change and Initial Value

A pitcher with a maximum capacity of 4 cups contains 1 cup of apple juice concentrate. A faucet is turned on, filling the pitcher at a rate of $\frac{1}{4}$ cup per second. The amount A of liquid in the pitcher (in cups) is a function $A(t)$ of the time t (in seconds) that the water is running.

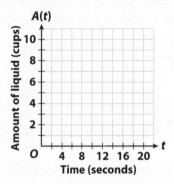

A The y-intercept, _____, is the initial amount in cups in the pitcher at time 0. Plot the point that corresponds to the y-intercept.

B The slope is the rate of change: _____ cup per second, or 1 cup every _____ seconds. So, the rise is _____ and the run is _____.

C Use the rise and run to move from the first point to a second point on the line, and plot a second point.

_____

D Connect the points and extend the line to the maximum value of the function, where $A(t) =$ _____ cups.

Reflect

1. How do you know what the maximum value of the function is in Part D?

_____

_____

The increase in pressure _P_ (in pounds per square inch, or psi) is a linear function of the depth _d_ (in feet) to which a scuba diver descends. This function, _P(d)_ = 0.445_d_ + 14.7, is graphed.

1. What is the initial value, and what does it represent?

_____

_____

2. What is the rate of change, and what does it represent?

_____

_____

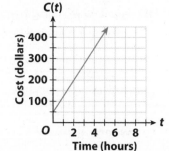

The cost of catering for a scholarship presentation dinner is $300 plus $10 per student. The cost _C_ is a function of the number _n_ of students.

3. Write the linear function _C(n)_.

_____

4. What are the initial value and rate of change, and what do they represent?

_____

_____

_____

_____

The cost for a plumber to make a repair is $50 for the service call plus $75 per hour.

5. Write the linear function _C(t)_.

_____

6. Identify the initial value, the rate of change, and their meanings.

_____

_____

_____

6.4 Analyzing Graphs

COMMON CORE 8.F.5

Describe qualitatively the functional relationship between two quantities by analyzing a graph … . Sketch a graph that exhibits the qualitative features of a function that has been described verbally.

? **ESSENTIAL QUESTION**

How can you describe a relationship given a graph and sketch a graph given a description?

EXPLORE ACTIVITY 1 *Real World*   COMMON CORE 8.F.5

Interpreting Graphs

A roller coaster park is open from May to October each year. The graph shows the number of park visitors over its season.

Park Visitors

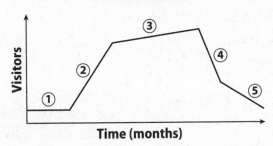

A Segment 1 shows that attendance during the opening weeks of the park's season stayed constant. Describe what Segment 2 shows.

_____

B Based on the time frame, give a possible explanation for the change in attendance represented by Segment 2.

_____

C Which segments of the graph show decreasing attendance? Give a possible explanation.

_____

_____

Reflect

1. Explain how the slope of each segment of the graph is related to whether attendance increases or decreases.

_____

_____

Matching Graphs to Situations

Grace, Jet, and Mike are studying 100 words for a spelling bee.

- Grace started by learning how to spell many words each day, but then learned fewer and fewer words each day.
- Jet learned how to spell the same number of words each day.
- Mike started by learning how to spell only a few words each day, but then learned a greater number of words each day.

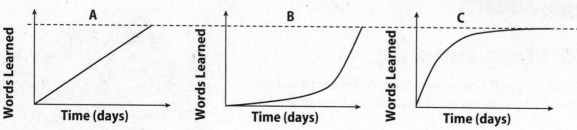

_____   _____   _____

A Describe the progress represented by Graph A.

_____

_____

Math Talk

Mathematical Practices

Tell whether each graph is linear or nonlinear and proportional or nonproportional.

B Describe the progress represented by Graph B.

_____

_____

_____

C Describe the progress represented by Graph C.

_____

_____

_____

D Determine which graph represents each student's study progress and write the students' names under the appropriate graphs.

Reflect

2. What would it mean if one of the graphs slanted downward?

_____

Sketching a Graph for a Situation

Mrs. Sutton provides free math tutoring to her students every day after school. No one comes to tutoring sessions during the first week of school. Over the next two weeks, use of the tutoring service gradually increases.

A Sketch a graph showing the number of students who use the tutoring service over the first three weeks of school.

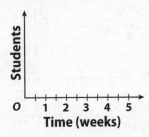

B Mrs. Sutton's students are told that they will have a math test at the end of the fifth week of school. How do you think this will affect the number of students who come to tutoring?

_____

_____

C Considering your answer to **B**, sketch a graph showing the number of students who might use the tutoring service over the first six weeks of school.

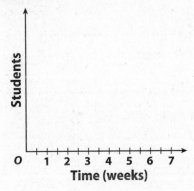

Reflect

3. If Mrs. Sutton offers bonus credit to students who come to tutoring, how might this affect the number of students?

_____

4. How would your answer to Question 3 affect the graph?

_____

_____

In a lab environment, colonies of bacteria follow a predictable pattern of growth. The graph shows this growth over time. (Explore Activity 1)

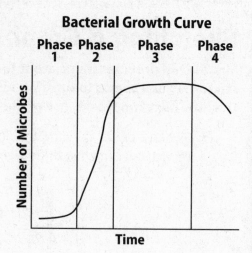

Bacterial Growth Curve

1. What is happening to the population during Phase 2?

_____

_____

2. What is happening to the population during Phase 4?

_____

_____

The graphs give the speeds of three people who are riding snowmobiles. Tell which graph corresponds to each situation. (Explore Activity 2)

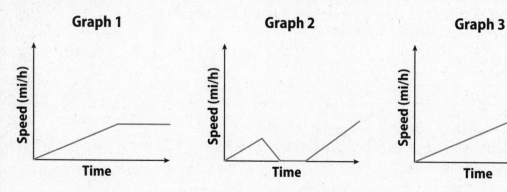

Graph 1   **Graph 2**   **Graph 3**

3. Chip begins his ride slowly but then stops to talk with some friends. After a few minutes, he continues his ride, gradually increasing his speed.

_____

4. Linda steadily increases her speed through most of her ride. Then she slows down as she nears some trees.

_____

5. Paulo stood at the top of a diving board. He walked to the end of the board, and then dove forward into the water. He plunged down below the surface, then swam straight forward while underwater. Finally, he swam forward and upward to the surface of the water. Draw a graph to represent Paulo's elevation at different distances from the edge of the pool.
(Explore Activity 3)

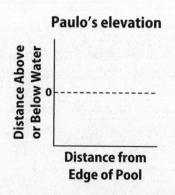

Paulo's elevation

6.4 Independent Practice

 COMMON CORE 8.F.5

Tell which graph corresponds to each situation below.

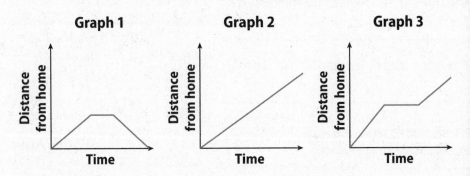

Graph 1 Graph 2 Graph 3

6. Arnold started from home and walked to a friend's house. He stayed with his friend for a while and then walked to another friend's house farther from home.

_____

7. Francisco started from home and walked to the store. After shopping, he walked back home.

_____

8. Celia walks to the library at a steady pace without stopping.

_____

Regina rented a motor scooter. The graph shows how far away she is from the rental site after each half hour of riding.

9. **Represent Real-World Problems** Use the graph to describe Regina's trip. You can start the description like this: "Regina left the rental shop and rode for an hour…"

_____

_____

_____

_____

Distance from Rental Site

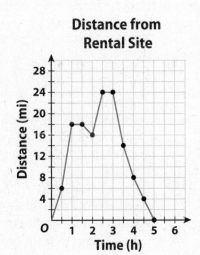

10. **Analyze Relationships** Determine during which half hour Regina covered the greatest distance.

_____

© Houghton Mifflin Harcourt Publishing Company • Image Credits: ©Adobe Image Library/Getty Images

The data in the table shows the speed of a ride at an amusement park at different times one afternoon.

Time	3:20	3:21	3:22	3:23	3:24	3:25
Speed (mi/h)	0	14	41	62	8	0

11. Sketch a graph that shows the speed of the ride over time.

12. Between which times is the ride's speed increasing the fastest?

_____

13. Between which times is the ride's speed decreasing the fastest?

_____

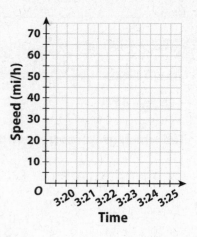

H.O.T. FOCUS ON HIGHER ORDER THINKING

A woodland area on an island contains a population of foxes. The graph describes the changes in the population over time.

14. **Justify Reasoning** What is happening to the fox population before time *t*? Explain your reasoning.

_____

_____

_____

_____

Fox Population

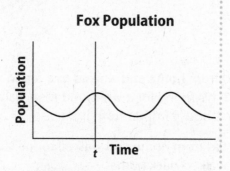

15. **What If?** Suppose at time *t*, a conservation organization moves a large group of foxes to the island. Sketch a graph to show how this action might affect the population on the island after time *t*.

16. **Make a Prediction** At some point after time *t*, a forest fire destroys part of the woodland area on the island. Describe how your graph from problem 15 might change.

_____

_____

_____

Fox Population

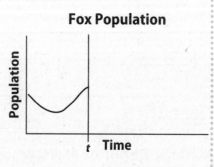

Work Area

Ready to Go On?

Personal Math Trainer

Online Assessment and Intervention

my.hrw.com

6.1 Identifying and Representing Functions

Determine whether each relationship is a function.

1.

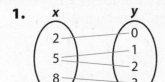

x	y
2	0
5	1
8	2
	3

_____

2.

Input, x	Output, y
−1	6
3	5
6	5

_____

3. (2, 5), (7, 2), (−3, 4), (2, 9), (1, 1)

_____

6.2 Describing Functions

Determine whether each situation is linear or nonlinear, and proportional or nonproportional.

4. Joanna is paid $14 per hour.

_____

5. Alberto started out bench pressing 50 pounds. He then added 5 pounds every week.

_____

6.3 Comparing Functions

6. Which function is changing more quickly? Explain.

_____

_____

_____

Function 1

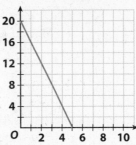

Function 2	
Input, x	**Output, y**
2	11
3	6.5
4	2

6.4 Analyzing Graphs

7. Describe a graph that shows Sam running at a constant rate.

_____

ESSENTIAL QUESTION

8. How can you use functions to solve real-world problems?

_____

MODULE 6 MIXED REVIEW

Assessment Readiness

COMMON CORE

Personal Math Trainer

Online Assessment and Intervention

my.hrw.com

Selected Response

1. Which table shows a proportional function?

Ⓐ
x	0	5	10
y	3	15	30

Ⓑ
x	0	5	10
y	10	20	30

Ⓒ
x	0	5	10
y	0	50	100

Ⓓ
x	0	5	10
y	10	5	0

2. What is the slope and y-intercept of the function shown in the table?

x	1	4	7
y	6	12	18

Ⓐ $m = -2; b = -4$

Ⓑ $m = -2; b = 4$

Ⓒ $m = 2; b = 4$

Ⓓ $m = 4; b = 2$

3. The table below shows some input and output values of a function.

Input	4	5	6	7
Output	14	17.5		24.5

What is the missing output value?

Ⓐ 20

Ⓑ 21

Ⓒ 22

Ⓓ 23

4. Tom walked to school at a steady pace, met his sister, and they walked home at a steady pace. Describe this graph.

Ⓐ V-shaped

Ⓑ upside down V-shaped

Ⓒ Straight line sloping up

Ⓓ Straight line sloping down

Mini-Task

5. Linear functions can be used to find the price of a building based on its floor area. Below are two of these functions.

$y = 40x + 15,000$

Floor Area (ft²)	400	700	1,000
Price ($1,000s)	32	56	80

a. Find and compare the slopes.

_____

_____

_____

b. Find and compare the y-intercepts.

_____

_____

_____

c. Describe each function as proportional or nonproportional.

_____

_____

_____

© Houghton Mifflin Harcourt Publishing Company

MODULE 3 ▸ Proportional Relationships

? ESSENTIAL QUESTION

How can you use proportional relationships to solve real-world problems?

EXAMPLE 1

Write an equation that represents the proportional relationship shown in the graph.

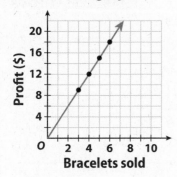

Use the points on the graph to make a table.

Bracelets sold	3	4	5	6
Profit ($)	9	12	15	18

Let *x* represent the number of bracelets sold.

Let *y* represent the profit.

The equation is $y = 3x$.

EXAMPLE 2

Find the slope of the line.

$slope = \dfrac{rise}{run}$

$= \dfrac{3}{-4}$

$= -\dfrac{3}{4}$

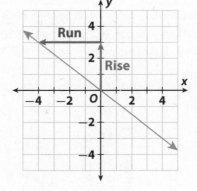

1. The table represents a proportional relationship. Write an equation that describes the relationship. Then graph the relationship represented by the data. (Lessons 3.1, 3.3, 3.4)

Time (*x*)	6	8	10	12
Distance (*y*)	3	4	5	6

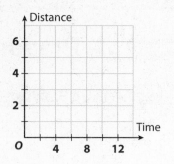

_____

Find the slope and the unit rate represented on each graph. (Lesson 3.2)

2.

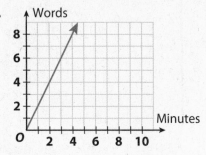

3.

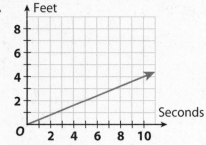

_____

MODULE **4** # Nonproportional Relationships

? **ESSENTIAL QUESTION**

How can you use nonproportional relationships to solve real-world problems?

Key Vocabulary

linear equation
(*ecuación lineal*)
slope-intercept form of an
equation (*forma de
pendiente-intersección*)
y-intercept
(*intersección con el eje* y)

EXAMPLE 1

Jai is saving to buy his mother a birthday gift. Each week, he saves $5. He started with $25. The equation $y = 5x + 25$ gives the total Jai has saved, *y*, after *x* weeks. Draw a graph of the equation. Then describe the relationship.

Use the equation to make a table. Then, graph the ordered pairs from the table, and draw a line through the points.

x (weeks)	0	1	2	3	4
y (savings in dollars)	25	30	35	40	45

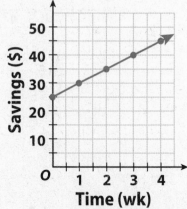

The relationship is linear but nonproportional.

EXAMPLE 2

Graph $y = -\frac{1}{2}x - 2$.

The slope is $\frac{-1}{2}$, or $-\frac{1}{2}$.

The y-intercept is -2.

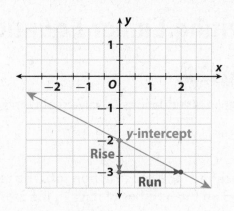

EXERCISES

Complete each table. Explain whether the relationship between x and y is proportional or nonproportional and whether it is linear. (Lesson 4.1)

1. $y = 10x - 4$

x	0	2		6
y	−4		36	

2. $y = -\frac{3}{2}x$

x	0		2	
y		−1.5		−4.5

_____

_____

3. Find the slope and y-intercept for the linear relationship shown in the table. Graph the line. Is the relationship proportional or nonproportional? (Lessons 4.2, 4.4)

x	−4	−1	0	1
y	−4	2	4	6

slope _____

y-intercept _____

The relationship is _____.

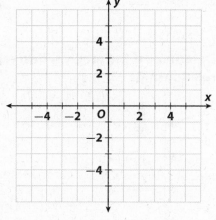

4. Tom's Taxis charges a fixed rate of $4 per ride plus $0.50 per mile. Carla's Cabs does not charge a fixed rate but charges $1.00 per mile. (Lesson 4.3)

a. Write an equation that represents the cost of Tom's Taxis. _____

b. Write an equation that represents the cost of Carla's cabs. _____

c. Steve calculated that for the distance he needs to travel, Tom's Taxis will charge the same amount as Carla's Cabs. Graph both equations. How far is Steve going to travel and how much will he pay?

_____

_____

Writing Linear Equations

Key Vocabulary
bivariate data (datos
   bivariados)
nonlinear relationship
   (relación no lineal)

? ESSENTIAL QUESTION

How can you use linear equations to solve real-world problems?

EXAMPLE 1

**Jose is renting a backhoe for a construction job. The rental charge
for a month is based on the number of days in the month and a
set charge per month. In September, which has 30 days, Jose paid
$700. In August, which has 31 days, he paid $715. Write an equation
in slope-intercept form that represents this situation.**

$(x_1, y_1), (x_2, y_2) \rightarrow (30, 700), (31, 715)$ Write the information given as ordered pairs.

$m = \dfrac{y_2 - y_1}{x_2 - x_1} = \dfrac{715 - 700}{31 - 30} = 15$ Find the slope.

$y = mx + b$ Slope-intercept form

$715 = 15(31) + b$ Substitute for y, m, and x to find b.

$250 = b$ Solve for b.

$y = 15x + 250$ Write the equation.

EXAMPLE 2

**Determine if the graph shown represents a linear or nonlinear
relationship.**

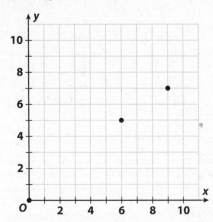

Points	Rate of Change
(0, 0) and (6, 5)	$m = \dfrac{5 - 0}{6 - 0} = \dfrac{5}{6}$
(6, 5) and (9, 7)	$m = \dfrac{7 - 5}{9 - 6} = \dfrac{2}{3}$
(0, 0) and (9, 7)	$m = \dfrac{7 - 0}{9 - 0} = \dfrac{7}{9}$

The rates of change are not constant. The graph represents a nonlinear relationship.

EXERCISES

1. Ms. Thompson is grading math tests. She is giving everyone that took the test a 10-point bonus. Each correct answer is worth 5 points. Write an equation in slope-intercept form that represents the scores on the tests. (Lesson 5.1)

_____

The table shows a pay scale based on years of experience. (Lessons 5.1, 5.2)

Experience (years), x	0	2	4	6	8
Hourly pay ($), y	9	14	19	24	29

2. Find the slope for this relationship. _____

3. Find the y-intercept. _____

4. Write an equation in slope-intercept form that represents this relationship. _____

5. Graph the equation, and use it to predict the hourly pay of someone with 10 years of experience.

_____

_____

_____

_____

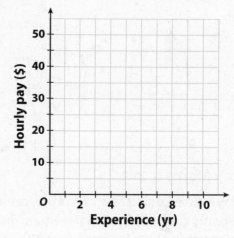

Does each of the following graphs represent a linear relationship? Why or why not? (Lesson 5.3)

6.

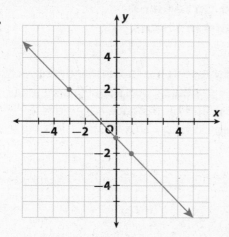

_____

_____

_____

7.

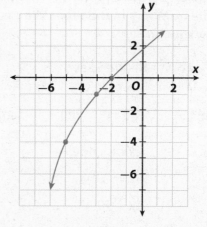

_____

_____

_____

Key Vocabulary
function *(función)*
input *(valor de entrada)*
linear function *(función lineal)*
output *(valor de salida)*

? ESSENTIAL QUESTION

How can you use functions to solve real-world problems?

EXAMPLE 1

Determine whether each relationship is a function.

A

Input	Output
3	10
4	4
5	2
4	0
6	5

The relationship is not a function, because an input, 4, is paired with 2 different outputs, 4 and 0.

B

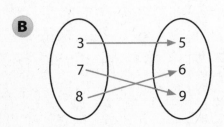

Since each input value is paired with only one output value, the relationship is a function.

EXAMPLE 2

Sally and Louis are on a long-distance bike ride. Sally bikes at a steady rate of 18 miles per hour. The distance *y* that Sally covers in *x* hours is given by the equation $y = 18x$. Louis's speed can be found by using the numbers in the table. Who will travel farther in 4 hours and by how much?

Louis's Biking Speed			
Time (h), *x*	3	5	7
Distance (mi), *y*	60	100	140

Each distance in the table is 20 times each number of hours. Louis's speed is 20 miles per hour, and his distance covered is represented by $y = 20x$.

Sally's ride:

$y = 18x$

$y = 18(4)$

$y = 72$

Louis's ride:

$y = 20x$

$y = 20(4)$

$y = 80$

Sally will ride 72 miles in 4 hours. Louis will ride 80 miles in 4 hours. Louis will go 8 miles farther.

EXERCISES

Determine whether each relationship is a function. (Lesson 6.1)

1.

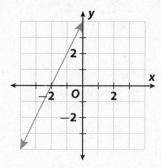

2.

Input	Output
−1	8
0	4
1	8
2	16

_____ _____

Tell whether the function is linear or nonlinear. (Lesson 6.2)

3. $y = 5x + \dfrac{1}{2}$ _____

4. $y = x^2 + 3$ _____

5. Elaine has a choice of two health club memberships. The first membership option is to pay $500 now and then pay $150 per month. The second option is shown in the table. Elaine plans to go to the club for 12 months. Which option is cheaper? Explain. (Lesson 6.3)

Months, x	1	2	3
Total paid ($), y	215	430	645

_____

_____

_____

6. Jenny rode her bike around her neighborhood. Use the graph to describe Jenny's bike ride. (Lesson 6.4)

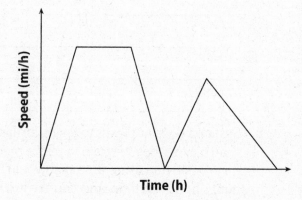

_____

_____

_____

_____

_____

_____

_____

1. **CAREERS IN MATH** | Cost Estimator To make MP3 players, a cost estimator determined it costs a company $1500 per week for overhead and $45 for each MP3 player made.

a. Define a variable to represent the number of players made. Then write an equation to represent the company's total cost *c*.

_____

b. One week, the company spends $5460 making MP3 players. How many players were made that week? Show your work.

_____

_____

c. If the company sells MP3 players for $120, how much profit would it make if it sold 80 players in one week? Explain how you found your answer.

_____

_____

2. A train from Portland, Oregon, to Los Angeles, California, travels at an average speed of 60 miles per hour and covers a distance of 963 miles. Susanna is taking the train from Portland to Los Angeles to see her aunt. She needs to arrive at her aunt's house by 8 p.m. It takes 30 minutes to get from the train station to her aunt's house.

a. By what time does the train need to leave Portland for Susanna to arrive by 8 p.m.? Explain how you got your answer. As part of your explanation, write a function that you used in your work.

_____

_____

_____

_____

b. Susanna does not want to leave Portland later than 10 p.m. or earlier than 6 a.m. Does the train in part **a** meet her requirements? If not, give a new departure time that would allow her to still get to her aunt's house on time, and find the arrival time of that train.

_____

_____

_____

UNIT 2 MIXED REVIEW
Assessment Readiness

COMMON CORE

Personal Math Trainer

Online Assessment and Intervention

my.hrw.com

Selected Response

1. Rickie earns $7 an hour babysitting. Which table represents this proportional relationship?

Ⓐ
Hours	4	6	8
Earnings ($)	28	42	56

Ⓑ
Hours	4	6	8
Earnings ($)	28	35	42

Ⓒ
Hours	2	3	4
Earnings ($)	7	14	21

Ⓓ
Hours	2	3	4
Earnings ($)	14	21	42

2. Which of the relationships below is a function?

Ⓐ (6, 3), (5, 2), (6, 8), (0, 7)

Ⓑ (8, 2), (1, 7), (−1, 2), (1, 9)

Ⓒ (4, 3), (3, 0), (−1, 3), (2, 7)

Ⓓ (7, 1), (0, 0), (6, 2), (0, 4)

3. Which set best describes the numbers used on the scale for a standard thermometer?

Ⓐ whole numbers

Ⓑ rational numbers

Ⓒ real numbers

Ⓓ integers

4. Which term refers to slope?

Ⓐ rate of change   Ⓒ y-intercept

Ⓑ equation   Ⓓ coordinate

5. The graph of which equation is shown below?

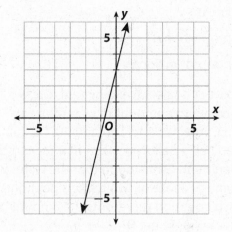

Ⓐ $y = 4x + 3$

Ⓑ $y = -4x - 0.75$

Ⓒ $y = -4x + 3$

Ⓓ $y = 4x - 0.75$

6. Which equation represents a nonproportional relationship?

Ⓐ $y = 5x$

Ⓑ $y = -5x$

Ⓒ $y = 5x + 3$

Ⓓ $y = -\frac{1}{5}x$

7. Which number is 7.0362×10^{-4} written in standard notation?

Ⓐ 0.000070362

Ⓑ 0.00070362

Ⓒ 7.0362

Ⓓ 7036.2

8. Which term does not correctly describe the relationship shown in the table?

x	0	2	4
y	0	70	140

- Ⓐ function
- Ⓑ linear
- Ⓒ proportional
- Ⓓ nonproportional

9. As part of a science experiment, Greta measured the amount of water flowing from Container A to Container B. Container B had half a gallon of water in it to start the experiment. Greta found that the water was flowing at a rate of two gallons per hour. Which equation represents the amount of water in Container B?

- Ⓐ $y = 2x$
- Ⓑ $y = 0.5x$
- Ⓒ $y = 2x + 0.5$
- Ⓓ $y = 0.5x + 2$

10. Carl and Jeannine both work at appliance stores. Carl earns a weekly salary of $600 plus $40 for each appliance he sells. The equation $p = 50n + 550$ represents the amount of money Jeannine earns in a week, p ($), as a function of the number of appliances she sells, n. Which of the following statements is true?

- Ⓐ Carl has a greater salary and a greater rate per appliance sold.
- Ⓑ Jeannine has a greater salary and a greater rate per appliance sold.
- Ⓒ Carl will earn more than Jeannine if they each sell 10 appliances in a given week.
- Ⓓ Both Carl and Jeannine earn the same amount if they each sell 5 appliances in a given week.

Mini-Task

11. The table below represents a linear relationship.

x	2	3	4	5
y	14	17	20	23

a. Find the slope for this relationship.

_____

b. Find the y-intercept. Explain how you found it.

_____

_____

_____

_____

c. Write an equation in slope-intercept form that represents this relationship.

_____

 Estimate your answer before solving the problem. Use your estimate to check the reasonableness of your answer.

12. Jacy has a choice of cell phone plans. Plan A is to pay $260 for the phone and then pay $70 per month for service. Plan B is to get the phone for free and pay $82 per month for service.

a. Write an equation to represent the total cost, c, of Plan A for m months.

_____

b. Write an equation to represent the total cost, c, of Plan B for m months.

_____

c. If Jacy plans to keep the phone for 24 months, which plan is cheaper? Explain.

_____

_____

_____

© Houghton Mifflin Harcourt Publishing Company

Solving Equations and Systems of Equations

MODULE 7

Solving Linear Equations

COMMON CORE 8.EE.7, 8.EE.7a, 8.EE.7b

MODULE 8

Solving Systems of Linear Equations

COMMON CORE 8.EE.8, 8.EE.8a, 8.EE.8b, 8.EE.8c

CAREERS IN MATH

Hydraulic Engineer A hydraulic engineer specializes in the behavior of fluids, mainly water. A hydraulic engineer applies the mathematics of fluid dynamics to the collection, transport, measurement, and regulation of water and other fluids.

If you are interested in a career in hydraulic engineering, you should study the following mathematical subjects:
- Algebra
- Geometry
- Trigonometry
- Probability and Statistics
- Calculus

Research other careers that require the understanding of the mathematics of fluid dynamics.

Unit 3 Performance Task

At the end of the unit, check out how **hydraulic engineers** use math.

Use the puzzle to preview key vocabulary from this unit. Unscramble the circled letters to answer the riddle at the bottom of the page.

1. FIACALRONT INFEOCIECTF

2. LCMADEI CINETFOEFIC

3. UQAOTENI

4. ROPWE

5. TNUSITBUOSIT DOHMTE

1. A number that is multiplied by the variable in an algebraic expression, where the number is a fraction. (Lesson 7.2)

2. A number that is multiplied by the variable in an algebraic expression, where the number is a decimal. (Lesson 7.2)

3. A mathematical statement that two expressions are equal. (Lesson 7.1)

4. A number that is formed by repeated multiplication of the same factor. Multiply by this to remove decimals from an unsolved equation. (Lesson 7.2)

5. A process used to solve systems of linear equations by solving an equation for one variable and then substituting the resulting expression for that variable into the other equation. (Lesson 8.2)

Q: What is the best time to divide a half dollar between two people?

A: at a ___ __ ___ __ __ __ __ ___ ___ __ ___ __!

Solving Linear Equations

ESSENTIAL QUESTION

How can you use equations with the variable on both sides to solve real-world problems?

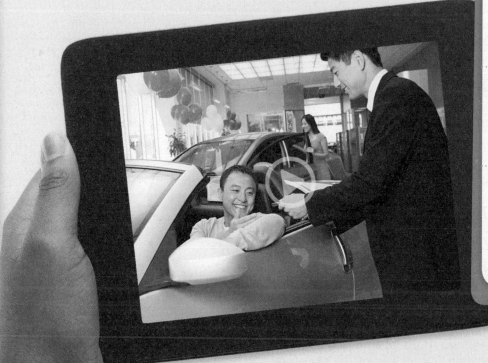

Real-World Video

Some employees earn commission plus their salary when they make a sale. There may be options about their pay structure. They can find the best option by solving an equation with the variable on both sides.

my.hrw.com

GO DIGITAL

my.hrw.com

my.hrw.com

Go digital with your write-in student edition, accessible on any device.

Math On the Spot

Scan with your smart phone to jump directly to the online edition, video tutor, and more.

Animated Math

Interactively explore key concepts to see how math works.

Personal Math Trainer

Get immediate feedback and help as you work through practice sets.

Are YOU Ready?

Complete these exercises to review skills you will need for this module.

Find Common Denominators

EXAMPLE Find the LCD of 3, 5, and 10.

3: 3, 6, 9, 12, 15, 18, 21, 24, 27, 30,...

5: 5, 10, 15, 20, 25, 30, 35,...

10: 10, 20, 30, 40, 50,...

List the multiples of each number. Choose the least multiple the lists have in common.
LCD(3, 5, 10) = 30

Find the LCD.

1. 8, 12 _____ **2.** 9, 12 _____ **3.** 15, 20 _____ **4.** 8, 10 _____

Multiply Decimals by Powers of 10

EXAMPLE 3.719×100

$3.719 \times 100 = 371.9$

Count the zeros in 100: 2 zeros
Move the decimal point 2 places to the right.

Find the product.

5. 0.683×100 **6.** $9.15 \times 1,000$ **7.** 0.005×100 **8.** $1,000 \times 1,000$

_____ _____ _____ _____

Connect Words and Equations

EXAMPLE Two times a number decreased by 5 is −6.

Two times x decreased by 5 is −6.

$2x - 5$ is −6

$2x - 5 = -6$

Represent the unknown with a variable.

Times means multiplication.
Decreased by means subtraction.

Place the equal sign.

Write an algebraic equation for the sentence.

9. The difference between three times a number and 7 is 14. _____

10. The quotient of five times a number and 7 is no more than 10. _____

11. 14 less than 3 times a number is 5 more than half of the number. _____

Reading Start-Up

© Houghton Mifflin Harcourt Publishing Company

Visualize Vocabulary

Use the ✔ words to complete the bubble map. You may put more than one word in each oval.

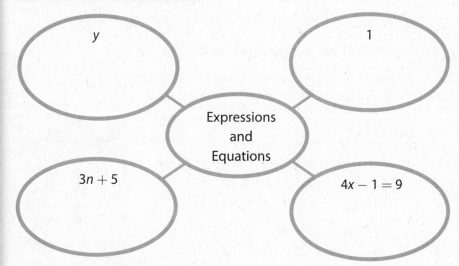

- y
- 1
- Expressions and Equations
- 3n + 5
- 4x − 1 = 9

Understand Vocabulary

Complete the sentences using the review words.

1. A value of the variable that makes an equation true is a _____.

2. The set of all whole numbers and their opposites are _____.

3. An _____ is an expression that contains at least one variable.

Active Reading

Layered Book Before beginning the module, create a layered book to help you learn the concepts in this module. At the top of the first flap, write the title of the book, "Solving Linear Equations." Then label each flap with one of the lesson titles in this module. As you study each lesson, write important ideas, such as vocabulary and formulas, under the appropriate flap.

Vocabulary

Review Words
- ✔ algebraic expression (*expresión algebraica*)
- coefficient (*coeficiente*)
- common denominator (*denominador común*)
- ✔ constant (*constante*)
- ✔ equation (*ecuación*)
- integers (*entero*)
- least common multiple (*mínimo común múltiplo*)
- operations (*operaciones*)
- solution (*solución*)
- ✔ variable (*variable*)

Unpacking the Standards

Understanding the standards and the vocabulary terms in the standards will help you know exactly what you are expected to learn in this module.

© Houghton Mifflin Harcourt Publishing Company · Image Credits: ©SW Productions/Getty Images

 8.EE.7a

Give examples of linear equations in one variable with one solution, infinitely many solutions, or no solutions. Show which of these possibilities is the case by successively transforming the given equation into simpler forms, until an equivalent equation of the form $x = a$, $a = a$, or $a = b$ results (where a and b are different numbers).

Key Vocabulary

linear equation in one variable
(ecuación lineal en una variable)
An equation that can be written in the form $ax = b$ where a and b are constants and $a \neq 0$.

What It Means to You

You will identify the number of solutions an equation has.

UNPACKING EXAMPLE 8.EE.7a

Your gym charges $50 per month. Find the number of months for which your costs will equal the cost of membership at each gym shown.

A: $40 per month plus $100 one-time fee
$50x = 40x + 100 \rightarrow x = 10$
Equal in 10 months → one solution

B: $50 per month plus $25 one-time fee
$50x = 50x + 25 \rightarrow 0 = 25$
Never equal → no solution

C: $40 per month plus $10 monthly garage fee
$50x = 40x + 10x \rightarrow x = x$
Equal for any number of months → infinitely many solutions

 8.EE.7b

Solve linear equations with rational number coefficients, including equations whose solutions require expanding expressions using the distributive property and collecting like terms.

Key Vocabulary

solution *(solución)*
In an equation, the value for the variable that makes the equation true.

Visit **my.hrw.com** to see all the **Common Core Standards** unpacked.

my.hrw.com

What It Means to You

You can write and solve an equation that has a variable on both sides of the equal sign.

UNPACKING EXAMPLE 8.EE.7b

Yellow Taxi has no pickup fee but charges $0.25 per mile. AAA Taxi charges $3 for pickup and $0.15 per mile. Find the number of miles for which the cost of the two taxis is the same.

$$0.25x = 3 + 0.15x$$
$$100(0.25x) = 100(3) + 100(0.15x)$$
$$25x = 300 + 15x$$
$$10x = 300$$
$$x = 30$$

The cost is the same for 30 miles.

Equations with the Variable on Both Sides

COMMON CORE **8.EE.7**

Solve linear equations in one variable. *Also 8.EE.7b*

 ESSENTIAL QUESTION

How can you represent and solve equations with the variable on both sides?

EXPLORE ACTIVITY COMMON CORE **8.EE.7, 8.EE.7b**

Modeling an Equation with a Variable on Both Sides

Algebra tiles can model equations with a variable on both sides.

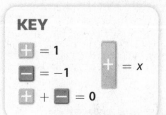

KEY

Use algebra tiles to model and solve $x + 5 = 3x - 1$.

Model $x + 5$ on the left side of the mat and $3x - 1$ on the right side.
Remember that $3x - 1$ is the same as

$3x + $ _____.

Remove one x-tile from both sides. This

represents subtracting _____ from both sides of the equation.

 **Math Talk**
Mathematical Practices
Why is a positive unit tile added to both sides in the third step?

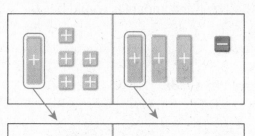

Place one +1-tile on both sides. This

represents adding _____ to both sides of the equation. Remove zero pairs.

Separate each side into 2 equal groups.

One x-tile is equivalent to _____ +1-tiles.

The solution is _____ = _____.

Reflect

1. How can you check the solution to $x + 5 = 3x - 1$ using algebra tiles?

_____

_____

Solving an Equation with the Variable on Both Sides

Equations with the variable on both sides can be used to compare costs of real-world situations. To solve these equations, use inverse operations to get the variable terms on one side of the equation.

EXAMPLE 1   Real World

COMMON CORE   8.EE.7, 8.EE.7b

Andy's Rental Car charges an initial fee of $20 plus an additional $30 per day to rent a car. Buddy's Rental Car charges an initial fee of $36 plus an additional $28 per day. For what number of days is the total cost charged by the companies the same?

STEP 1   Write an expression representing the total cost of renting a car from Andy's Rental Car.

Initial fee   +   Cost for x days
20   + $30x$

STEP 2   Write an expression representing the total cost of renting a car from Buddy's Rental Car.

Initial fee   +   Cost for x days
36   + $28x$

STEP 3   Write an equation that can be solved to find the number of days for which the total cost charged by the companies would be the same.

Total cost at Andy's   =   Total cost at Buddy's
$$20 + 30x = 36 + 28x$$

STEP 4   Solve the equation for x.

$$
\begin{aligned}
20 + 30x &= 36 + 28x & &\text{Write the equation.}\\
-28x\quad & \qquad -28x & &\text{Subtract } 28x \text{ from both sides.}\\
\hline
20 + 2x &= 36\\
-20\quad & \qquad -20 & &\text{Subtract 20 from both sides.}\\
\hline
2x &= 16\\
\frac{2x}{2} &= \frac{16}{2} & &\text{Divide both sides by 2.}\\
x &= 8
\end{aligned}
$$

The total cost is the same if the rental is for 8 days.

Math Talk
Mathematical Practices

When is it more economical to rent from Andy's Rental Car? When is it more economical to rent from Buddy's?

2. A water tank holds 256 gallons but is leaking at a rate of 3 gallons per week. A second water tank holds 384 gallons but is leaking at a rate of 5 gallons per week. After how many weeks will the amount of water in the two tanks be the same?

_____

Personal Math Trainer

Online Assessment and Intervention

⏱ my.hrw.com

Writing a Real-World Situation from an Equation

As shown in Example 1, an equation with the variable on both sides can be used to represent a real-world situation. You can reverse this process by writing a real-world situation for a given equation.

Math On the Spot

⏱ my.hrw.com

EXAMPLE 2 _Real World_   COMMON CORE 8.EE.7

My Notes

Write a real-world situation that could be modeled by the equation $150 + 25x = 55x$.

STEP 1 The left side of the equation consists of a constant plus a variable term. It could represent the total cost for doing a job where there is an initial fee plus an hourly charge.

STEP 2 The right side of the equation consists of a variable term. It could represent the cost for doing the same job based on an hourly charge only.

STEP 3 The equation $150 + 25x = 55x$ could be represented by this situation: A handyman charges $150 plus $25 per hour for house painting. A painter charges $55 per hour. How many hours would a job have to take for the handyman's fee and the painter's fee to be the same?

YOUR TURN

3. Write a real-world situation that could be modeled by the equation $30x = 48 + 22x$.

_____

_____

_____

_____

Personal Math Trainer

Online Assessment and Intervention

⏱ my.hrw.com

Use algebra tiles to model and solve each equation. (Explore Activity)

1. $x + 4 = -x - 4$ _____

2. $2 - 3x = -x - 8$ _____

3. At Silver Gym, membership is $25 per month, and personal training sessions are $30 each. At Fit Factor, membership is $65 per month, and personal training sessions are $20 each. In one month, how many personal training sessions would Sarah have to buy to make the total cost at the two gyms equal? (Example 1)

_____

4. Write a real-world situation that could be modeled by the equation $120 + 25x = 45x$. (Example 2)

_____

_____

_____

_____

5. Write a real-world situation that could be modeled by the equation $100 - 6x = 160 - 10x$. (Example 2)

_____

_____

_____

_____

_____

ESSENTIAL QUESTION CHECK-IN

6. How can you solve an equation with the variable on both sides?

_____

_____

_____

_____

7.1 Independent Practice

COMMON CORE **8.EE.7, 8.EE.7b**

Personal Math Trainer

Online Assessment and Intervention

Derrick's Dog Sitting

$12 plus $5 per hour

7. Derrick's Dog Sitting and Darlene's Dog Sitting are competing for new business. The companies ran the ads shown.

   a. Write and solve an equation to find the number of hours for which the total cost will be the same for the two services.

   _____

   b. **Analyze Relationships** Which dog sitting service is more economical to use if you need 5 hours of service? Explain.

   _____

   _____

Darlene's Dog Sitting

$18 plus $3 per hour

8. Country Carpets charges $22 per square yard for carpeting, and an additional installation fee of $100. City Carpets charges $25 per square yard for the same carpeting, and an additional installation fee of $70.

   a. Write and solve an equation to find the number of square yards of carpeting for which the total cost charged by the two companies will be the same.

   _____

   b. **Justify Reasoning** Mr. Shu wants to hire one of the two carpet companies to install carpeting in his basement. Is he more likely to hire Country Carpets or City Carpets? Explain your reasoning.

   _____

   _____

   _____

   _____

Write an equation to represent each relationship. Then solve the equation.

9. Two less than 3 times a number is the same as the number plus 10.

_____

10. A number increased by 4 is the same as 19 minus 2 times the number.

_____

11. Twenty less than 8 times a number is the same as 15 more than the number.

_____

12. The charges for an international call made using the calling card for two phone companies are shown in the table.

Phone Company	Charges
Company A	35¢ plus 3¢ per minute
Company B	45¢ plus 2¢ per minute

a. What is the length of a phone call that would cost the same no matter which company is used?

_____

b. **Analyze Relationships** When is it better to use the card from Company B?

_____

_____

 **FOCUS ON HIGHER ORDER THINKING**

13. **Draw Conclusions** Liam is setting up folding chairs for a meeting. If he arranges the chairs in 9 rows of the same length, he has 3 chairs left over. If he arranges the chairs in 7 rows of that same length, he has 19 left over. How many chairs does Liam have?

_____

14. **Explain the Error** Rent-A-Tent rents party tents for a flat fee of $365 plus $125 a day. Capital Rentals rents party tents for a flat fee of $250 plus $175 a day. Delia wrote the following equation to find the number of days for which the total cost charged by the two companies would be the same:

$$365x + 125 = 250x + 175$$

Find and explain the error in Delia's work. Then write the correct equation.

_____

_____

_____

_____

15. **Persevere in Problem Solving** Lilliana is training for a marathon. She runs the same distance every day for a week. On Monday, Wednesday, and Friday, she runs 3 laps on a running trail and then runs 6 more miles. On Tuesday and Sunday, she runs 5 laps on the trail and then runs 2 more miles. On Saturday, she just runs laps. How many laps does Lilliana run on Saturday?

_____

Work Area

© Houghton Mifflin Harcourt Publishing Company

Equations with Rational Numbers

COMMON CORE **8.EE.7b**

Solve linear equations with rational number coefficients, ... *Also 8.EE.7*

ESSENTIAL QUESTION

How can you solve equations with rational number coefficients and constants?

EXPLORE ACTIVITY COMMON CORE **8.EE.7b, 8.EE.7**

Solving an Equation That Involves Fractions

To solve an equation with the variable on both sides that involves fractions, start by eliminating the fractions from the equation.

 Math On the Spot
my.hrw.com

EXAMPLE 1 Solve $\frac{7}{10}n + \frac{3}{2} = \frac{3}{5}n + 2$.

STEP 1 Determine the least common multiple of the denominators: _____

STEP 2 Multiply both sides of the equation by the LCM.

$$\boxed{}\left(\frac{7}{10}n + \frac{3}{2}\right) = \boxed{}\left(\frac{3}{5}n + 2\right)$$

$$\boxed{}\,\cancel{10}\left(\frac{7}{\cancel{10}_1}n\right) + \boxed{}\,\cancel{10}\left(\frac{3}{\cancel{2}_1}\right) = \boxed{}\,\cancel{10}\left(\frac{3}{\cancel{5}_1}n\right) + 10(2)$$

$$\boxed{}\,n + \boxed{} = \boxed{}\,n + \boxed{}$$

STEP 3 Use inverse operations to solve the equation.

$$7n + 15 = 6n + 20$$

Subtract 15 from both sides.

$$-\boxed{} \qquad -\boxed{}$$

$$\boxed{} = 6n + \boxed{}$$

$$-\boxed{} \qquad -\boxed{}$$

Subtract 6n from both sides.

$$n = \boxed{}$$

Reflect

1. What is the advantage of multiplying both sides of the equation by the least common multiple of the denominators in the first step?

_____

2. **What If?** What happens in the first step if you multiply both sides by a common multiple of the denominators that is not the LCM?

_____

_____

YOUR TURN

Solve.

3. $\frac{1}{7}k - 6 = \frac{3}{7}k + 4$ _____

4. $\frac{5}{6}y + 1 = -\frac{1}{2}y + \frac{1}{4}$ _____

Math On the Spot

⏻ my.hrw.com

Solving an Equation that Involves Decimals

Solving an equation with the variable on both sides that involves decimals is similar to solving an equation with fractions. But instead of first multiplying both sides by the LCM, multiply by a power of 10 to eliminate the decimals.

EXAMPLE 2

COMMON CORE 8.EE.7, 8.EE.7b

Javier walks from his house to the zoo at a constant rate. After walking 0.75 mile, he meets his brother, Raul, and they continue walking at the same constant rate. When they arrive at the zoo, Javier has walked for 0.5 hour and Raul has walked for 0.2 hour. What is the rate in miles per hour at which the brothers walked to the zoo?

STEP 1 Write an equation for the distance from the brothers' house to the zoo, using the fact that distance equals rate times time. Let r = the brothers' walking rate.

$$\underbrace{0.2r + 0.75}_{\text{distance to zoo}} = \underbrace{0.5r}_{\text{distance to zoo}}$$

STEP 2 Multiply both sides of the equation by $10^2 = 100$.

$$100(0.2r) + 100(0.75) = 100(0.5r)$$
$$20r + 75 = 50r$$

> Multiplying by 100 clears the equation of decimals. Multiplying by 10 does not: $10 \times 0.75 = 7.5$.

STEP 3 Use inverse operations to solve the equation.

$$
\begin{array}{rcl}
20r + 75 &=& 50r \\
-20r & & -20r \\
\hline
75 &=& 30r
\end{array}
$$

Write the equation.

Subtract $20r$ from both sides.

$$\frac{75}{30} = \frac{30r}{30}$$

Divide both sides by 30.

$$2.5 = r$$

So, the brothers' constant rate of speed was 2.5 miles per hour.

YOUR TURN

5. Logan has two aquariums. One aquarium contains 1.3 cubic feet of water and the other contains 1.9 cubic feet of water. The water in the larger aquarium weighs 37.44 pounds more than the water in the smaller aquarium. Write an equation with a variable on both sides to represent the situation. Then find the weight of 1 cubic foot of water.

_____

Writing a Real-World Situation from an Equation

Real-world situations can often be represented by equations involving fractions and decimals. Fractions and decimals can represent quantities such as weight, volume, capacity, time, and temperature. Decimals can also be used to represent dollars and cents.

Math On the Spot

my.hrw.com

EXAMPLE 3 COMMON CORE 8.EE.7

My Notes

Write a real-world situation that can be modeled by the equation $0.95x = 0.55x + 60$.

The left side of the equation consists of a variable term. It could represent the total cost for x items.

The right side of the equation consists of a variable term plus a constant. It could represent the total cost for x items plus a flat fee.

The equation $0.95x = 0.55x + 60$ could be represented by this situation: Toony Tunes charges $0.95 for each song you download. Up With Downloads charges $0.55 for each song but also charges an annual membership fee of $60. How many songs must a customer download in a year so that the cost will be the same at both websites?

YOUR TURN

6. Write a real-world problem that can be modeled by the equation $\frac{1}{3}x + 10 = \frac{3}{5}x$.

_____

_____

_____

_____

Personal Math Trainer

Online Assessment and Intervention

my.hrw.com

1. Sandy is upgrading her Internet service. Fast Internet charges $60 for installation and $50.45 per month. Quick Internet has free installation but charges $57.95 per month. (Example 2)

   a. Write an equation that can be used to find the number of months at which the Internet service would cost the same.

     _____

   b. Solve the equation.

     _____

Solve. (Explore Activity Example 1 and Example 2)

2. $\frac{3}{4}n - 18 = \frac{1}{4}n - 4$

   _____

3. $6 + \frac{4}{5}b = \frac{9}{10}b$

   _____

4. $\frac{2}{11}m + 16 = 4 + \frac{6}{11}m$

   _____

5. $2.25t + 5 = 13.5t + 14$

   _____

6. $3.6w = 1.6w + 24$

   _____

7. $-0.75p - 2 = 0.25p$

   _____

8. Write a real-world problem that can be modeled by the equation $1.25x = 0.75x + 50$. (Example 3)

   _____

   _____

   _____

   _____

   _____

   _____

ESSENTIAL QUESTION CHECK-IN

9. How does the method for solving equations with fractional or decimal coefficients and constants compare with the method for solving equations with integer coefficients and constants?

   _____

   _____

   _____

7.2 Independent Practice

COMMON CORE 8.EE.7, 8.EE.7b

Personal
Math Trainer

Online
Assessment and
Intervention

my.hrw.com

10. Members of the Wide Waters Club pay $105 per summer season, plus $9.50 each time they rent a boat. Nonmembers must pay $14.75 each time they rent a boat. How many times would a member and a non-member have to rent a boat in order to pay the same amount?

_____

11. Margo can purchase tile at a store for $0.79 per tile and rent a tile saw for $24. At another store she can borrow the tile saw for free if she buys tiles there for $1.19 per tile. How many tiles must she buy for the cost to be the same at both stores?

_____

12. The charges for two shuttle services are shown in the table. Find the number of miles for which the cost of both shuttles is the same.

	Pickup Charge ($)	Charge per Mile ($)
Easy Ride	10	0.10
Best	0	0.35

13. **Multistep** Rapid Rental Car charges a $40 rental fee, $15 for gas, and $0.25 per mile driven. For the same car, Capital Cars charges $45 for rental and gas and $0.35 per mile.

a. For how many miles is the rental cost at both companies the same?

_____

b. What is that cost?

_____

14. Write an equation with the solution $x = 20$. The equation should have the variable on both sides, a fractional coefficient on the left side, and a fraction anywhere on the right side.

_____

15. Write an equation with the solution $x = 25$. The equation should have the variable on both sides, a decimal coefficient on the left side, and a decimal anywhere on the right side. One of the decimals should be written in tenths, the other in hundredths.

_____

16. **Geometry** The perimeters of the rectangles shown are equal. What is the perimeter of each rectangle?

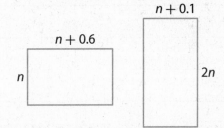

17. **Analyze Relationships** The formula $F = 1.8C + 32$ gives the temperature in degrees Fahrenheit (F) for a given temperature in degrees Celsius (C). There is one temperature for which the number of degrees Fahrenheit is equal to the number of degrees Celsius. Write an equation you can solve to find that temperature and then use it to find the temperature.

_____

18. Explain the Error Agustin solved an equation as shown. What error did Agustin make? What is the correct answer?

_____

_____

_____

_____

$$\frac{1}{3}x - 4 = \frac{3}{4}x + 1$$

$$12\left(\frac{1}{3}x\right) - 4 = 12\left(\frac{3}{4}x\right) + 1$$

$$4x - 4 = 9x + 1$$

$$-5 = 5x$$

$$x = -1$$

 FOCUS ON HIGHER ORDER THINKING

Work Area

19. Draw Conclusions Solve the equation $\frac{1}{2}x - 5 + \frac{2}{3}x = \frac{7}{6}x + 4$. Explain your results.

_____

_____

_____

_____

20. Look for a Pattern Describe the pattern in the equation. Then solve the equation.

$$0.3x + 0.03x + 0.003x + 0.0003x + \ldots = 3$$

_____

_____

_____

_____

21. Critique Reasoning Jared wanted to find three consecutive even integers whose sum was 4 times the first of those integers. He let k represent the first integer, then wrote and solved this equation: $k + (k + 1) + (k + 2) = 4k$. Did he get the correct answer? Explain.

_____

_____

_____

_____

_____

Equations with the Distributive Property

COMMON CORE 8.EE.7b
Solve linear equations with rational number coefficients, including equations whose solutions require expanding expressions using the distributive property and collecting like terms.

? ESSENTIAL QUESTION

How do you use the Distributive Property to solve equations?

EXPLORE ACTIVITY   COMMON CORE 8.EE.7b

Using the Distributive Property

The Distributive Property can be useful in solving equations.

Math On the Spot
my.hrw.com

EXAMPLE 1 Solve each equation.

A $3(x - 5) + 1 = 2 + x$

STEP 1 Use the Distributive Property.

Distribute 3 to the terms inside the parentheses.

$3x - \boxed{} + 1 = 2 + x$

Simplify.

$\boxed{} = 2 + x$

STEP 2 Use inverse operations to solve the equation.

Subtract _____ from both sides.

Add _____ to both sides.

Divide both sides by 2.

$$3x - 14 = 2 + x$$

$$\underline{- \boxed{} \qquad - \boxed{}}$$

$$2x - 14 = 2$$

$$+ \boxed{} = + \boxed{}$$

$$2x = 16$$

$$x = \boxed{}$$

B $5 - 7k = -4(k + 1) - 3$

STEP 1 Use the Distributive Property.

Distribute _____ to the terms inside the parentheses.

Simplify.

$5 - 7k = \boxed{} - 4 - 3$

$5 - 7k = \boxed{}$

STEP 2 Use inverse operations to solve the equation.

Add _____ to both sides.

$$5 - 7k = -4k - 7$$

$$\underline{+4k \qquad + \boxed{}}$$

$$5 - 3k = -7$$

Subtract _____ from both sides.

$$\underline{- \boxed{} \qquad - \boxed{}}$$

$$-3k = -12$$

Divide both sides by _____.

$$k = \boxed{}$$

YOUR TURN

Solve each equation.

1. $y - 5 = 3 - 9(y + 2)$ _____

2. $2(x - 7) - 10 = 12 - 4x$ _____

Math On the Spot

my.hrw.com

Using the Distributive Property on Both Sides

Some equations require the use of the Distributive Property on both sides.

EXAMPLE 2   COMMON CORE   **8.EE.7b**

Solve: $\frac{3}{4}(x - 13) = -2(9 + x)$

STEP 1   Eliminate the fraction.

$$\frac{3}{4}(x - 13) = -2(9 + x)$$

$$4 \times \frac{3}{4}(x - 13) = 4 \times [-2(9 + x)]$$ Multiply both sides by 4.

$$3(x - 13) = -8(9 + x)$$

Math Talk

Mathematical Practices

How can you eliminate fractions if there is a fraction being distributed on both sides of an equation?

STEP 2   Use the Distributive Property.

$$3x - 39 = -72 - 8x$$ Distribute 3 and −8 to the terms within the parentheses.

STEP 3   Use inverse operations to solve the equation.

$$3x - 39 = -72 - 8x$$

$$\underline{+8x \qquad\qquad +8x}$$ Add 8x to both sides.

$$11x - 39 = -72$$

$$\underline{+39 \quad +39}$$ Add 39 to both sides.

$$11x = -33$$

$$\frac{11x}{11} = \frac{-33}{11}$$ Divide both sides by 11.

$$x = -3$$

YOUR TURN

Solve each equation.

3. $-4(-5 - b) = \frac{1}{3}(b + 16)$ _____

4. $\frac{3}{5}(t + 18) = -3(2 - t)$ _____

Solving a Real-World Problem Using the Distributive Property

Solving a real-world problem may involve using the Distributive Property.

Math On the Spot

my.hrw.com

EXAMPLE 3 Problem Solving

COMMON CORE **8.EE.7b**

The Coleman family had their bill at a restaurant reduced by $7.50 because of a special discount. They left a tip of $8.90, which was 20% of the reduced amount. How much was their bill before the discount?

 Analyze Information

The answer is the amount before the discount.

 Formulate a Plan

Use an equation to find the amount before the discount.

 Solve

STEP 1 Write the equation $0.2(x - 7.5) = 8.9$, where x is the amount of the Coleman family's bill before the discount.

STEP 2 Use the Distributive Property: $0.2x - 1.5 = 8.9$

STEP 3 Use inverse operations to solve the equation.

$$0.2x - 1.5 = 8.9$$
$$\underline{+ 1.5 \quad + 1.5}$$
$$0.2x = 10.4 \qquad \text{Add 1.5 to both sides.}$$

$$\frac{0.2x}{0.2} = \frac{10.4}{0.2} \qquad \text{Divide both sides by 0.2.}$$

$$x = 52$$

The Coleman family's bill before the discount was $52.00.

Math Talk
Mathematical Practices

Why do you use 0.2 in Step 1?

 Justify and Evaluate

$52.00 - $7.50 = $44.50 and $0.2(\$44.50) = \$8.90$. This is the amount of the tip the Colemans left. The answer is reasonable.

YOUR TURN

5. The Smiths spend 8% of their budget on entertainment. Their total budget this year is $2,000 more than last year, and this year they plan to spend $3,840 on entertainment. What was their total budget last year? _____

Personal Math Trainer

Online Assessment and Intervention

my.hrw.com

Solve each equation.

1. $4(x + 8) - 4 = 34 - 2x$
(Explore Activity Ex. 1)

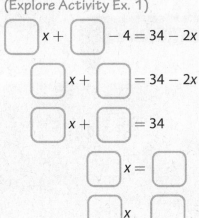

$$\boxed{}\, x + \boxed{} - 4 = 34 - 2x$$

$$\boxed{}\, x + \boxed{} = 34 - 2x$$

$$\boxed{}\, x + \boxed{} = 34$$

$$\boxed{}\, x = \boxed{}$$

$$\frac{\boxed{}\, x}{\boxed{}} = \frac{\boxed{}}{\boxed{}}$$

$$x = \boxed{}$$

2. $\frac{2}{3}(9 + x) = -5(4 - x)$ (Ex. 2)

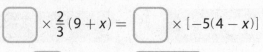

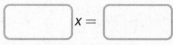

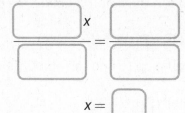

$$\boxed{} \times \frac{2}{3}(9 + x) = \boxed{} \times [-5(4 - x)]$$

$$\boxed{}(9 + x) = \boxed{}(4 - x)$$

$$\boxed{} + \boxed{}\, x = \boxed{} \bigcirc \boxed{}\, x$$

$$\boxed{}\, x = \boxed{}$$

$$\frac{\boxed{}\, x}{\boxed{}} = \frac{\boxed{}}{\boxed{}}$$

$$x = \boxed{}$$

3. $-3(x + 4) + 15 = 6 - 4x$
(Explore Activity Ex. 1)

_____

4. $10 + 4x = 5(x - 6) + 33$
(Explore Activity Ex. 1)

_____

5. $x - 9 = 8(2x + 3) - 18$
(Explore Activity Ex. 1)

_____

6. $-6(x - 1) - 7 = -7x + 2$
(Explore Activity Ex. 1)

_____

7. $\frac{1}{10}(x + 11) = -2(8 - x)$ (Ex. 2)

_____

8. $-(4 - x) = \frac{3}{4}(x - 6)$ (Ex. 2)

_____

9. $-8(8 - x) = \frac{4}{5}(x + 10)$ (Ex. 2)

_____

10. $\frac{1}{2}(16 - x) = -12(x + 7)$ (Ex. 2)

_____

11. Sandra saves 12% of her salary for retirement. This year her salary was $3,000 more than in the previous year, and she saved $4,200. What was her salary in the previous year? (Example 3)

Write an equation. _____

Sandra's salary in the previous year was _____.

? ESSENTIAL QUESTION CHECK-IN

12. When solving an equation using the Distributive Property, if the numbers being distributed are fractions, what is your first step? Why?

_____

7.3 Independent Practice

 8.EE.7b

Personal Math Trainer

Online Assessment and Intervention

my.hrw.com

13. Multistep Martina is currently 14 years older than her cousin Joey. In 5 years she will be 3 times as old as Joey. Use this information to answer the following questions.

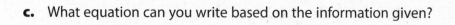

a. If you let *x* represent Joey's current age, what expression can you use to represent Martina's current age?

_____

b. Based on your answer to part a, what expression represents Joey's age in 5 years? What expression represents Martina's age in 5 years?

_____

c. What equation can you write based on the information given?

_____

d. What is Joey's current age? What is Martina's current age?

_____

14. As part of a school contest, Sarah and Luis are playing a math game. Sarah must pick a number between 1 and 50 and give Luis clues so he can write an equation to find her number. Sarah says, "If I subtract 5 from my number, multiply that quantity by 4, and then add 7 to the result, I get 35." What equation can Luis write based on Sarah's clues and what is Sarah's number?

_____

15. Critical Thinking When solving an equation using the Distributive Property that involves distributing fractions, usually the first step is to multiply by the LCD to eliminate the fractions in order to simplify computation. Is it necessary to do this to solve $\frac{1}{2}(4x + 6) = \frac{1}{3}(9x - 24)$? Why or why not?

_____

_____

_____

16. Solve the equation given in Exercise 15 with and without using the LCD of the fractions. Are your answers the same?

_____

17. Represent Real-World Problems A chemist mixed *x* milliliters of 25% acid solution with some 15% acid solution to produce 100 milliliters of a 19% acid solution. Use this information to fill in the missing information in the table and answer the questions that follow.

	ml of Solution	Percent Acid as a Decimal	ml of Acid
25% Solution	*x*		
15% Solution			
Mixture (19% Solution)	100		

a. What is the relationship between the milliliters of acid in the 25% solution, the milliliters of acid in the 15% solution, and the milliliters of acid in the mixture? _____

_____

_____

b. What equation can you use to solve for *x* based on your answer to part a? _____

c. How many milliliters of the 25% solution and the 15% solution did the chemist use in the mixture? _____

_____

© Houghton Mifflin Harcourt Publishing Company • Image Credits: ©D. Hurst/ Alamy Images

 **FOCUS ON HIGHER ORDER THINKING**

Work Area

18. Explain the Error Anne solved $5(2x) - 3 = 20x + 15$ for *x* by first distributing 5 on the left side of the equation. She got the answer $x = -3$. However, when she substituted -3 into the original equation for *x*, she saw that her answer was wrong. What did Anne do wrong, and

what is the correct answer? _____

_____

_____

19. Communicate Mathematical Ideas Explain a procedure that can be used to solve $5[3(x + 4) - 2(1 - x)] - x - 15 = 14x + 45$. Then solve the

equation. _____

_____

_____

_____

LESSON 7.4 Equations with Many Solutions or No Solution

 8.EE.7a

Give examples of linear equations ... with one solution, infinitely many solutions, or no solutions. Show which of these ... is the case by ... transforming the given equation into ... $x = a$, $a = a$, or $a = b$ ....

? ESSENTIAL QUESTION

How can you give examples of equations with a given number of solutions?

EXPLORE ACTIVITY **8.EE.7a**

Math On the Spot
⏻ my.hrw.com

Determining the Number of Solutions

So far, when you solved a linear equation in one variable, you found one value of x that makes the equation a true statement. When you simplify some equations, you may find that they do not have one solution.

EXAMPLE 1 Use the properties of equality to simplify each equation. Tell whether the final equation is a true statement.

A $4x - 3 = 2x + 13$

Add _____ to both sides.

Subtract _____ from both sides.

Divide both sides by _____.

The statement is true. There is one solution.

$$4x - 3 = 2x + 13$$
$$+ \boxed{} = + \boxed{}$$
$$\overline{4x = 2x + 16}$$
$$- \boxed{} \quad - \boxed{}$$
$$\overline{2x = 16}$$
$$\frac{2x}{\boxed{}} = \frac{16}{\boxed{}}$$
$$x = \boxed{}$$

B $4x - 5 = 2(2x - 1) - 3$

Apply the Distributive Property.

Simplify.

Subtract _____ from both sides.

The statement is true. There are many solutions.

$$4x - 5 = 2(2x - 1) - 3$$
$$4x - 5 = \boxed{} - \boxed{} - 3$$
$$4x - 5 = 4x - \boxed{}$$
$$\frac{- \boxed{}}{-5 =} \quad \frac{- \boxed{}}{-5}$$

 © Houghton Mifflin Harcourt Publishing Company

C $4x + 2 = 4x - 5$

Subtract _____ from both sides.

Subtract _____ from both sides.

The statement is false. There is no solution.

$$4x + 2 = 4x - 5$$

$$4x = 4x - 7$$

$$0 = -7$$

Reflect

Math Talk
Mathematical Practices

Why do you substitute values for x into the *original* equation?

1. What happens when you substitute any value for x in the original equation in part B? in the original equation in part C?

_____

_____

YOUR TURN

Use the properties of equality to simplify each equation. Tell whether the final equation is a true statement.

2. $2x + 1 = 5x - 8$ **3.** $3(4x + 3) - 2 = 12x + 7$ **4.** $3x - 9 = 5 + 3x$

_____   _____   _____

Personal
Math Trainer

Online Assessment
and Intervention

⏻ my.hrw.com

Math On the Spot
⏻ my.hrw.com

Writing Equations with a Given Number of Solutions

When you simplify an equation using the properties of equality, you will find one of three results.

Result	What does this mean?	How many solutions?
$x = a$	When the value of x is a, the equation is a true statement.	1
$a = a$	Any value of x makes the equation a true statement.	Infinitely many
$a = b$, where $a \neq b$	There is no value of x that makes the equation a true statement.	0

You can use these results to write a linear equation that has a given number of solutions.

EXAMPLE 2

Write a linear equation in one variable that has no solution.

You can use the strategy of working backward:

STEP 1 Start with a false statement such as $3 = 5$. Add the same variable term to both sides.

$3 + x = 5 + x$ *Add x to both sides.*

STEP 2 Next, add the same constant to both sides and combine like terms on each side of the equation.

$10 + x = 12 + x$ *Add 7 to both sides.*

STEP 3 Verify that your equation has no solutions by using properties of equality to simplify your equation.

$$10 + x = 12 + x$$
$$\underline{-x = -x}$$
$$10 = 12$$

> **Math Talk**
> Mathematical Practices
>
> What type of statement do you start with to write an equation with infinitely many solutions? Give an example.

Reflect

5. Explain why the result of the process above is an equation with no solution.

_____

_____

_____

_____

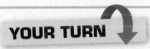

YOUR TURN

Tell whether each equation has one, zero, or infinitely many solutions.

6. $6 + 3x = x - 8$ _____

7. $8x + 4 = 4(2x + 1)$ _____

Complete each equation so that it has the indicated number of solutions.

8. No solution: $3x + 1 = 3x +$ _____

9. Infinitely many: $2x - 4 = 2x -$ _____

Personal
Math Trainer

Online Assessment
and Intervention

⏻ my.hrw.com

Use the properties of equality to simplify each equation. Tell whether the final equation is a true statement. (Explore Activity Example 1)

1. $3x - 2 = 25 - 6x$

$\underline{+\ 6x} \qquad \underline{\qquad +\ 6x}$

$\boxed{} - 2 = \boxed{}$

$\boxed{} = \boxed{}$

$\dfrac{\boxed{}x}{} = \dfrac{\boxed{}}{}$

$\dfrac{\boxed{}x}{\boxed{}} = \dfrac{\boxed{}}{\boxed{}}$

$x = \boxed{}$

The statement is $\boxed{}$.

2. $2x - 4 = 2(x - 1) + 3$

$2x - 4 = \boxed{} + 3$

$2x - 4 = 2x + \boxed{}$

$\dfrac{-\boxed{}}{} = \dfrac{-\boxed{}}{}$

$\boxed{} = \boxed{}$

The statement is $\boxed{}$.

3. How many solutions are there to the equation in Exercise 2? _____
(Explore Activity Example 1)

4. After simplifying an equation, Juana gets $6 = 6$. Explain what this means.
(Explore Activity Example 1)

_____

Write a linear equation in one variable that has infinitely many solutions. (Example 2)

5. Start with a _____ statement. $10 = \boxed{}$

Add the _____ to both sides. $10 + x = \boxed{}$

Add the _____ to both sides. $10 + x + 5 = \boxed{}$

Combine _____ terms. $\boxed{} = \boxed{}$

? **ESSENTIAL QUESTION CHECK-IN**

6. Give an example of an equation with an infinite number of solutions. Then make one change to the equation so that it has no solution.

_____

_____

7.4 Independent Practice

COMMON CORE 8.EE.7a

Personal Math Trainer

Online Assessment and Intervention

my.hrw.com

Tell whether each equation has one, zero, or infinitely many solutions.

7. $-(2x + 2) - 1 = -x - (x + 3)$

_____

8. $-2(z + 3) - z = -z - 4(z + 2)$

_____

Create an equation with the indicated number of solutions.

9. No solution:

$$3\left(x - \frac{4}{3}\right) = 3x + \boxed{}$$

10. Infinitely many solutions:

$$2(x - 1) + 6x = 4\left(\boxed{} - 1\right) + 2$$

11. One solution of $x = -1$:

$$5x - (x - 2) = 2x - \boxed{}$$

12. Infinitely many solutions:

$$-(x - 8) + 4x = 2\left(\boxed{}\right) + x$$

13. Persevere in Problem Solving The Dig It Project is designing two gardens that have the same perimeter. One garden is a trapezoid whose nonparallel sides are equal. The other is a quadrilateral. Two possible designs are shown at the right.

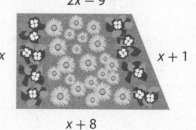

$2x - 2$

$x + 1$ $x + 1$

x

a. Based on these designs, is there more than one value for x? Explain how you know this.

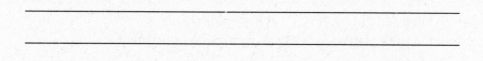

$2x - 9$

x $x + 1$

$x + 8$

b. Why does your answer to part a make sense in this context?

_____

_____

_____

c. Suppose the Dig It Project wants the perimeter of each garden to be 60 meters. What is the value of x in this case? How did you find this?

_____

_____

14. Critique Reasoning Lisa says that the indicated angles cannot have the same measure. Marita disagrees and says she can prove that they can have the same measure. Who do you agree with? Justify your answer.

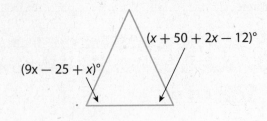

$(9x - 25 + x)°$

$(x + 50 + 2x - 12)°$

_____

_____

_____

_____

_____

15. Represent Real-World Problems Adele opens an account with $100 and deposits $35 a month. Kent opens an account with $50 and also deposits $35 a month. Will they have the same amount in their accounts at any point? If so, in how many months and how much will be in each account? Explain.

_____

_____

_____

 **FOCUS ON HIGHER ORDER THINKING**

Work Area

16. Communicate Mathematical Ideas Frank solved an equation and got the result $x = x$. Sarah solved the same equation and got $12 = 12$. Frank says that one of them is incorrect because you cannot get different results for the same equation. What would you say to Frank? If both results are indeed correct, explain how this happened.

_____

_____

_____

17. Critique Reasoning Matt said $2x - 7 = 2(x - 7)$ has infinitely many solutions. Is he correct? Justify Matt's answer or show how he is incorrect.

_____

_____

_____

Mathy Plants

INSTRUCTIONS

STEP 1   Solve each equation for the variable.

A _____ $3a + 17 = -25$

B _____ $2b - 25 + 5b = 7 - 32$

C _____ $2.7c - 4.5 = 3.6c - 9$

D _____ $\frac{5}{12}d + \frac{1}{6}d + \frac{1}{3}d + \frac{1}{12}d = 6$

E _____ $4e - 6e - 5 = 15$

F _____ $420 = 29f - 73$

G _____ $2(g + 6) = -20$

H _____ $2h + 7 = -3h + 52$

I _____ $96i + 245 = 53$

J _____ $3j + 7 = 46$

K _____ $\frac{1}{2}k = \frac{3}{4}k - \frac{1}{2}$

L _____ $30l + 240 = 50l - 160$

M _____ $4m + \frac{3}{8} = \frac{67}{8}$

N _____ $24 - 6n = 54$

O _____ $8.4o - 6.8 = 14.2 + 6.3o$

P _____ $4p - p + 8 = 2p + 5$

Q _____ $16 - 3q = 3q + 40$

R _____ $4 + \frac{1}{3}r = r - 8$

S _____ $\frac{2}{3}s - \frac{5}{6}s + \frac{1}{2} = -\frac{3}{2}$

T _____ $4 - 15 = 4t + 17$

U _____ $45 + 36u = 66 + 23u + 31$

V _____ $6v + 8 = -4 - 6v$

W _____ $4w + 3w - 6w = w + 15 + 2w - 3w$

X _____ $x + 2x + 3x + 4x + 5 = 75$

Y _____ $\dfrac{4 - y}{5} = \dfrac{2 - 2y}{8}$

Z _____ $- 11 = 25 - 4.5z$

STEP 2 Use the value of each variable to decode the answer to the riddle.

What happens to plants that live in a math classroom?

| −7 | 9 | −10 | −11 |

| −16 | 18 | 10 | 15 |

| 12 | −4 | 4 | −14 | 18 | −10 |

| 18 | 10 | 10 | −7 | 12 |

Ready to Go On?

7.1 Equations with the Variable on Both Sides

Solve.

1. $4a - 4 = 8 + a$ _____

2. $4x + 5 = x + 8$ _____

3. Hue is arranging chairs. She can form 6 rows of a given length with 3 chairs left over, or 8 rows of that same length if she gets 11 more chairs. Write and solve an equation to find how many chairs are in that row length.

_____

7.2 Equations with Rational Numbers

Solve.

4. $\frac{2}{3}n - \frac{2}{3} = \frac{n}{6} + \frac{4}{3}$ _____

5. $1.5d + 3.25 = 1 + 2.25d$ _____

6. Happy Paws charges $19.00 plus $1.50 per hour to keep a dog during the day. Woof Watchers charges $14.00 plus $2.75 per hour. Write and solve an equation to find for how many hours the total cost of the services is equal.

_____

7.3 Equations with the Distributive Property

Solve.

7. $14 + 5x = 3(-x + 3) - 11$ _____

8. $\frac{1}{4}(x - 7) = 1 + 3x$ _____

9. $-5(2x - 9) = 2(x - 8) - 11$ _____

10. $3(x + 5) = 2(3x + 12)$ _____

7.4 Equations with Many Solutions or No Solution

Tell whether each equation has one, zero, or infinitely many solutions.

11. $5(x - 3) + 6 = 5x - 9$ _____

12. $5(x - 3) + 6 = 5x - 10$ _____

13. $5(x - 3) + 6 = 4x + 3$ _____

MODULE 7 MIXED REVIEW

COMMON CORE

Assessment Readiness

Personal Math Trainer

Online Assessment and Intervention

my.hrw.com

Selected Response

1. Two cars are traveling in the same direction. The first car is going 40 mi/h, and the second car is going 55 mi/h. The first car left 3 hours before the second car. Which equation could you solve to find how many hours it will take for the second car to catch up to the first car?

(A) $55t + 3 = 40t$

(B) $55t + 165 = 40t$

(C) $40t + 3 = 55t$

(D) $40t + 120 = 55t$

2. Which linear equation is represented by the table?

x	−2	1	3	6
y	7	4	2	−1

(A) $y = -x + 5$ (C) $y = x + 3$

(B) $y = 2x - 1$ (D) $y = -3x + 11$

3. Shawn's Rentals charges $27.50 per hour to rent a surfboard and a wetsuit. Darla's Surf Shop charges $23.25 per hour to rent a surfboard plus $17 extra for a wetsuit. For what total number of hours are the charges for Shawn's Rentals the same as the charges for Darla's Surf Shop?

(A) 3   (C) 5

(B) 4   (D) 6

4. Which of the following is irrational?

(A) −8   (C) $\sqrt{11}$

(B) 4.63   (D) $\frac{1}{3}$

5. Greg and Jane left a 15% tip after dinner. The amount of the tip was $9. Greg's dinner cost $24. Which equation can you use to find x, the cost of Jane's dinner?

(A) $0.15x + 24 = 9$

(B) $0.15(x + 24) = 9$

(C) $15(x + 24) = 9$

(D) $0.15x = 24 + 9$

6. For the equation $3(2x - 5) = 6x + k$, which value of k will create an equation with infinitely many solutions?

(A) 15   (C) 5

(B) −5   (D) −15

7. Which of the following is equivalent to 2^{-4}?

(A) $\frac{1}{16}$ (C) −2

(B) $\frac{1}{8}$ (D) −16

Mini-Task

8. Use the figures below for parts *a* and *b*.

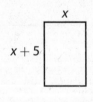
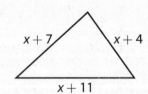

a. Both figures have the same perimeter. Solve for x.

_____

b. What is the perimeter of each figure?

_____

Solving Systems of Linear Equations

 ESSENTIAL QUESTION

How can you use systems of equations to solve real-world problems?

Real-World Video

The distance contestants in a race travel over time can be modeled by a system of equations. Solving such a system can tell you when one contestant will overtake another who has a head start, as in a boating race or marathon.

my.hrw.com

 GO DIGITAL
my.hrw.com

 my.hrw.com

Go digital with your write-in student edition, accessible on any device.

 Math On the Spot

Scan with your smart phone to jump directly to the online edition, video tutor, and more.

Animated Math

Interactively explore key concepts to see how math works.

 Personal Math Trainer

Get immediate feedback and help as you work through practice sets.

Are YOU Ready?

Complete these exercises to review skills you will need for this module.

Simplify Algebraic Expressions

EXAMPLE Simplify $5 - 4y + 2x - 6 + y$.
$-4y + y + 2x - 6 + 5$ Group like terms.
$-3y + 2x - 1$ Combine like terms.

Simplify.

1. $14x - 4x + 21$

2. $-y - 4x + 4y$

3. $5.5a - 1 + 21b + 3a$

4. $2y - 3x + 6x - y$

Graph Linear Equations

EXAMPLE Graph $y = -\frac{1}{3}x + 2$.
Step 1: Make a table of values.

x	$y = -\frac{1}{3}x + 2$	(x, y)
0	$y = -\frac{1}{3}(0) + 2 = 2$	$(0, 2)$
3	$y = -\frac{1}{3}(3) + 2 = 1$	$(3, 1)$

Step 2: Plot the points.
Step 3: Connect the points with a line.

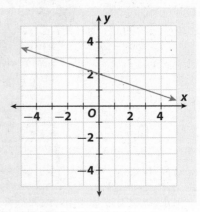

Graph each equation.

5. $y = 4x - 1$

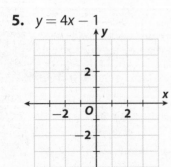

6. $y = \frac{1}{2}x + 1$

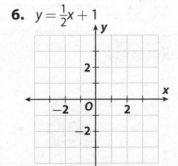

7. $y = -x$

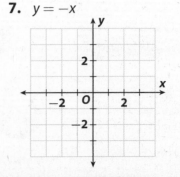

Reading Start-Up

Visualize Vocabulary

Use the ✔ words to complete the graphic.

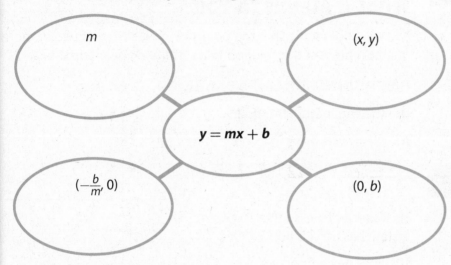

Review Words
 linear equation *(ecuación lineal)*
✔ ordered pair *(par ordenado)*
✔ slope *(pendiente)*
 slope-intercept form *(forma pendiente intersección)*
 x-axis *(eje x)*
✔ *x*-intercept *(intersección con el eje x)*
 y-axis *(eje y)*
✔ *y*-intercept *(intersección con el eje y)*

Preview Words
 solution of a system of equations *(solución de un sistema de ecuaciones)*
 system of equations *(sistema de ecuaciones)*

Understand Vocabulary

Complete the sentences using the preview words.

1. A _____ is any ordered pair that satisfies all the equations in a system.

2. A set of two or more equations that contain two or more variables is called a _____.

Active Reading

Four-Corner Fold Before beginning the module, create a four-corner fold to help you organize what you learn about solving systems of equations. Use the categories "Solving by Graphing," "Solving by Substitution," "Solving by Elimination," and "Solving by Multiplication." As you study this module, note similarities and differences among the four methods. You can use your four-corner fold later to study for tests and complete assignments.

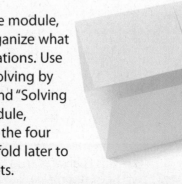

Unpacking the Standards

Understanding the standards and the vocabulary terms in the standards will help you know exactly what you are expected to learn in this module.

© Houghton Mifflin Harcourt Publishing Company

COMMON CORE 8.EE.8a

Understand that solutions to a system of two linear equations in two variables correspond to points of intersection of their graphs, because points of intersection satisfy both equations simultaneously.

COMMON CORE 8.EE.8b

Solve systems of two linear equations in two variables algebraically, and estimate solutions by graphing the equations. Solve simple cases by inspection.

Key Vocabulary

solution of a system of equations *(solución de un sistema de ecuaciones)* A set of values that make all equations in a system true.

system of equations *(sistema de ecuaciones)* A set of two or more equations that contain two or more variables.

 Visit **my.hrw.com** to see all the **Common Core Standards** unpacked.

my.hrw.com

What It Means to You

You will understand that the points of intersection of two or more graphs represent the solution to a system of linear equations.

UNPACKING EXAMPLE 8.EE.8a, 8.EE.8b

Use the elimination method.

A.

$$-x = -1 + y$$
$$\underline{x + y = 4}$$
$$y = y + 3$$

This is never true, so the system has no solution.

The lines never intersect.

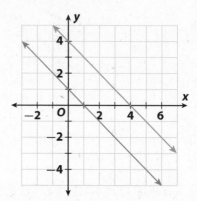

B.

$$2y + x = 1$$
$$y - 2 = x$$

Use the substitution method.

$$2y + (y - 2) = 1$$
$$3y - 2 = 1$$
$$y = 1$$
$$x = y - 2$$
$$x = 1 - 2$$
$$= -1$$

There is only one solution: $x = -1$, $y = 2$.

The lines intersect at a single point: $(-1, 2)$.

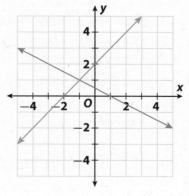

C.

$$3y - 6x = 3$$
$$y - 2x = 1$$

Use the multiplication method.

$$3y - 6x = 3$$
$$\underline{3y - 6x = 3}$$
$$0 = 0$$

This is always true. So the system has infinitely many solutions.

The graphs overlap completely. They are the same line.

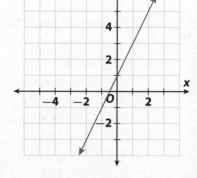

Solving Systems of Linear Equations by Graphing

COMMON CORE **8.EE.8a**

Understand that solutions to a system of two linear equations in two variables correspond to points of intersection of their graphs, because points of intersection satisfy both equations simultaneously. *Also 8.EE.8, 8.EE.8c*

? **ESSENTIAL QUESTION**

How can you solve a system of equations by graphing?

EXPLORE ACTIVITY COMMON CORE **8.EE.8a**

> Slope-intercept form is $y = mx + b$, where m is the slope and b is the y-intercept.

Investigating Systems of Equations

You have learned several ways to graph a linear equation in slope-intercept form. For example, you can use the slope and y-intercept or you can find two points that satisfy the equation and connect them with a line.

A Graph the pair of equations together: $\begin{cases} y = 3x - 2 \\ y = -2x + 3 \end{cases}$.

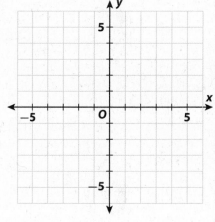

B Explain how to tell whether $(2, -1)$ is a solution of the equation $y = 3x - 2$ without using the graph.

_____

_____

C Explain how to tell whether $(2, -1)$ is a solution of the equation $y = -2x + 3$ without using the graph.

_____

_____

D Use the graph to explain whether $(2, -1)$ is a solution of each equation.

_____

_____

E Determine if the point of intersection is a solution of both equations.

Point of intersection: (⬜ , ⬜)

$y = 3x - 2$ ⬜ $= 3$ ⬜ $- 2$ $1 = $ ⬜

$y = -2x + 3$ ⬜ $= -2$ ⬜ $+ 3$ $1 = $ ⬜

The point of intersection **is / is not** the solution of both equations.

my.hrw.com

Solving Systems Graphically

An ordered pair (x, y) is a solution of an equation in two variables if substituting the x- and y-values into the equation results in a true statement. A **system of equations** is a set of equations that have the same variables. An ordered pair is a **solution of a system of equations** if it is a solution of every equation in the set.

Since the graph of an equation represents all ordered pairs that are solutions of the equation, if a point lies on the graphs of two equations, the point is a solution of both equations and is, therefore, a solution of the system.

My Notes

EXAMPLE 1

COMMON CORE 8.EE.8

Solve each system by graphing.

A $\begin{cases} y = -x + 4 \\ y = 3x \end{cases}$

STEP 1 Start by graphing each equation.

STEP 2 Find the point of intersection of the two lines. It appears to be (1, 3). Check by substitution to determine if it is a solution to both equations.

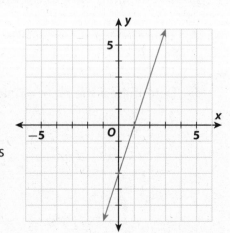

$y = -x + 4 \qquad y = 3x$

$3 \overset{?}{=} -(1) + 4 \qquad 3 \overset{?}{=} 3(1)$

$3 = 3 \checkmark \qquad\qquad 3 = 3 \checkmark$

The solution of the system is (1, 3).

B $\begin{cases} y = 3x - 3 \\ y = 3(x - 1) \end{cases}$

STEP 1 Start by graphing each equation.

STEP 2 Identify any ordered pairs that are solutions of both equations.

The graphs of the equations are the same line. So, every ordered pair that is a solution of one equation is also a solution of the other equation. The system has infinitely many solutions.

Reflect

1. A system of linear equations has infinitely many solutions. Does that mean any ordered pair in the coordinate plane is a solution?

   _____

   _____

2. Can you show algebraically that both equations in part B represent the same line? If so, explain how.

   _____

   _____

   _____

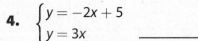

YOUR TURN

Solve each system by graphing. Check by substitution.

3. $\begin{cases} y = -x + 2 \\ y = -4x - 1 \end{cases}$ _____

   Check:

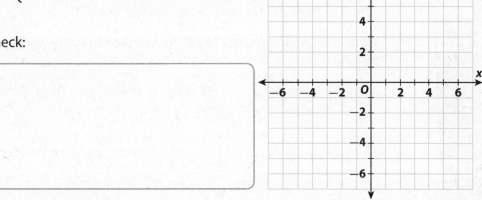

4. $\begin{cases} y = -2x + 5 \\ y = 3x \end{cases}$ _____

   Check:

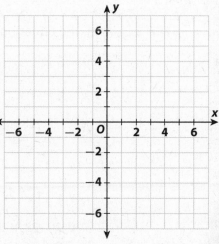

© Houghton Mifflin Harcourt Publishing Company

Personal Math Trainer

Online Assessment and Intervention

my.hrw.com

Solving Problems Using Systems of Equations

When using graphs to solve a system of equations, it is best to rewrite both equations in slope-intercept form for ease of graphing.

To write an equation in slope-intercept form starting from $ax + by = c$:

$$ax + by = c$$

$$by = c - ax \qquad \text{Subtract } ax \text{ from both sides.}$$

$$y = \frac{c}{b} - \frac{ax}{b} \qquad \text{Divide both sides by } b.$$

$$y = -\frac{a}{b}x + \frac{c}{b} \qquad \text{Rearrange the equation.}$$

EXAMPLE 2 　　　　　　　COMMON CORE　8.EE.8c, 8.EE.8

Keisha and her friends visit the concession stand at a football game. The stand charges $2 for a hot dog and $1 for a drink. The friends buy a total of 8 items for $11. Tell how many hot dogs and how many drinks they bought.

STEP 1　Let x represent the number of hot dogs they bought and let y represent the number of drinks they bought.

Write an equation representing the **number of items they purchased.**

Number of hot dogs	+	Number of drinks	=	Total items
x	+	y	=	8

Write an equation representing the **money spent on the items.**

Cost of 1 hot dog times number of hot dogs	+	Cost of 1 drink times number of drinks	=	Total cost
$2x$	+	$1y$	=	11

STEP 2　Write the equations in slope-intercept form. Then graph.

$$x + y = 8$$
$$y = 8 - x$$
$$y = -x + 8$$

$$2x + 1y = 11$$
$$1y = 11 - 2x$$
$$y = -2x + 11$$

Graph the equations $y = -x + 8$ and $y = -2x + 11$.

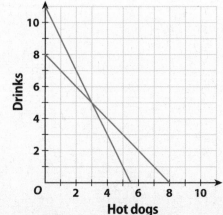

STEP 3 Use the graph to identify the solution of the system of equations. Check your answer by substituting the ordered pair into both equations.

Apparent solution: (3, 5)

Check:

$$x + y = 8 \qquad 2x + y = 11$$
$$3 + 5 \overset{?}{=} 8 \qquad 2(3) + 5 \overset{?}{=} 11$$
$$8 = 8 \checkmark \qquad 11 = 11 \checkmark$$

The point (3, 5) is a solution of both equations.

STEP 4 Interpret the solution in the original context.

Keisha and her friends bought 3 hot dogs and 5 drinks.

Reflect

5. **Conjecture** Why do you think the graph is limited to the first quadrant?

_____

_____

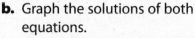

6. During school vacation, Marquis wants to go bowling and to play laser tag. He wants to play 6 total games but needs to figure out how many of each he can play if he spends exactly $20. Each game of bowling is $2 and each game of laser tag is $4.

   a. Let x represent the number of games Marquis bowls and let y represent the number of games of laser tag Marquis plays. Write a system of equations that describes the situation. Then write the equations in slope-intercept form.

   _____

   _____

   b. Graph the solutions of both equations.

   c. How many games of bowling and how many games of laser tag will Marquis play?

   _____

   _____

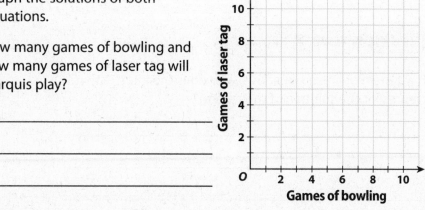

Personal Math Trainer

Online Assessment and Intervention

my.hrw.com

© Houghton Mifflin Harcourt Publishing Company

Solve each system by graphing. (Example 1)

1. $\begin{cases} y = 3x - 4 \\ y = x + 2 \end{cases}$ _____

2. $\begin{cases} x - 3y = 2 \\ -3x + 9y = -6 \end{cases}$ _____

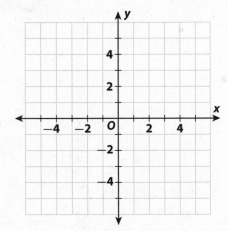

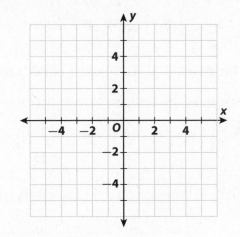

3. **Mrs. Morales wrote a test with 15 questions covering spelling and vocabulary. Spelling questions (x) are worth 5 points and vocabulary questions (y) are worth 10 points. The maximum number of points possible on the test is 100.** (Example 2)

   a. Write an equation in slope-intercept form to represent the number of questions on the test.

   _____

   b. Write an equation in slope-intercept form to represent the total number of points on the test.

   _____

   c. Graph the solutions of both equations.

   d. Use your graph to tell how many of each question type are on the test.

   _____

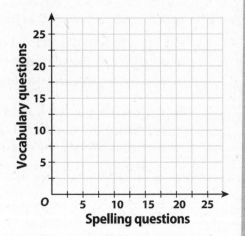

© Houghton Mifflin Harcourt Publishing Company

? ESSENTIAL QUESTION CHECK-IN

4. When you graph a system of linear equations, why does the intersection of the two lines represent the solution of the system?

_____

_____

8.1 Independent Practice

COMMON CORE 8.EE.8, 8.EE.8a, 8.EE.8c

Personal
Math Trainer

my.hrw.com

Online
Assessment and
Intervention

5. Vocabulary A _____ is a set of equations that have the same variables.

6. Eight friends started a business. They will wear either a baseball cap or a shirt imprinted with their logo while working. They want to spend exactly $36 on the shirts and caps. Shirts cost $6 each and caps cost $3 each.

a. Write a system of equations to describe the situation. Let x represent the number of shirts and let y represent the number of caps.

_____

_____

b. Graph the system. What is the solution and what does it represent?

Business Logo Wear

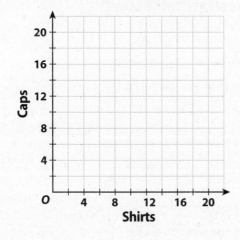

_____

_____

_____

_____

7. Multistep The table shows the cost for bowling at two bowling alleys.

	Shoe Rental Fee	Cost per Game
Bowl-o-Rama	$2.00	$2.50
Bowling Pinz	$4.00	$2.00

a. Write a system of equations, with one equation describing the cost to bowl at Bowl-o-Rama and the other describing the cost to bowl at Bowling Pinz. For each equation, let x represent the number of games played and let y represent the total cost.

_____

_____

b. Graph the system. What is the solution and what does it represent?

Cost of Bowling

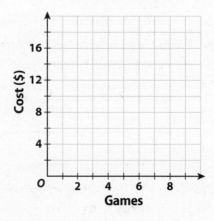

_____

_____

_____

_____

© Houghton Mifflin Harcourt Publishing Company

8. Multi-Step Jeremy runs 7 miles per week and increases his distance by 1 mile each week. Tony runs 3 miles per week and increases his distance by 2 miles each week. In how many weeks will Jeremy and Tony be running the same distance? What will that distance be?

_____

9. Critical Thinking Write a real-world situation that could be represented by the system of equations shown below.

$$\begin{cases} y = 4x + 10 \\ y = 3x + 15 \end{cases}$$

_____

_____

_____

 **FOCUS ON HIGHER ORDER THINKING**

Work Area

10. Multistep The table shows two options provided by a high-speed Internet provider.

	Setup Fee ($)	Cost per Month ($)
Option 1	50	30
Option 2	No setup fee	$40

a. In how many months will the total cost of both options be the same? What will that cost be?

_____

b. If you plan to cancel your Internet service after 9 months, which is the cheaper option? Explain.

_____

_____

_____

11. Draw Conclusions How many solutions does the system formed by $x - y = 3$ and $ay - ax + 3a = 0$ have for a nonzero number a? Explain.

_____

_____

_____

_____

LESSON 8.2 Solving Systems by Substitution

COMMON CORE 8.EE.8b
Solve systems of two linear equations in two variables algebraically, and estimate solutions by graphing the equations. ... *Also 8.EE.8c*

ESSENTIAL QUESTION

How do you use substitution to solve a system of linear equations?

EXPLORE ACTIVITY COMMON CORE 8.EE.8b

Math On the Spot

ⓞ my.hrw.com

Solving a Linear System by Substitution

The **substitution method** is used to solve systems of linear equations by solving an equation for one variable and then substituting the resulting expression for that variable into the other equation. The steps for this method are as follows:

1. Solve one of the equations for one of its variables.

2. Substitute the expression from Step 1 into the other equation and solve for the other variable.

3. Substitute the value from Step 2 into either original equation and solve to find the value of the variable in Step 1.

EXAMPLE 1 Solve the system of linear equations by substitution. Check your answer.

$$\begin{cases} -3x + y = 1 \\ 4x + y = 8 \end{cases}$$

STEP 1 Solve an equation for one variable.

Select one of the equations. $\qquad -3x + y = 1$

Solve for the variable y. $\qquad y = \boxed{}$

STEP 2 Substitute the expression for y in the other equation, and solve for x.

Substitute _____ for y. $\qquad 4x + \left(\boxed{}\right) = 8$

Combine like terms. $\qquad \boxed{} + 1 = 8$

Subtract _____ from each side. $\qquad 7x = \boxed{}$

Solve for x. $\qquad x = \boxed{}$

STEP 3 Substitute the value of x you found into one of the equations, and solve for the other variable, y.

$$-3x + y = 1$$

Substitute _____ for x. $\qquad -3\left(\boxed{}\right) + y = 1$

Simplify. $\qquad \boxed{} + y = 1$

Solve for y. $\qquad y = \boxed{}$

So (____ , ____) is the solution of the system.

STEP 4 Check the solution by graphing.

$$-3x + y = 1$$

x-intercept: $-3x + 0 = 1 \rightarrow x =$ ☐

y-intercept: $3(0) + y = 1 \rightarrow y =$ ☐

$$4x + y = 8$$

x-intercept: $4x + 0 = 8 \rightarrow x =$ ☐

y-intercept: $4(0) + y = 8 \rightarrow y =$ ☐

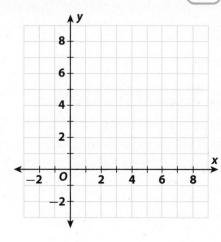

The graph confirms that the

solution is (____, ____).

Reflect

1. Is it more efficient to solve $-3x + y = 1$ for x? Why or why not?

_____

_____

2. Is there another way to solve the system?

_____

_____

3. What is another way to check your solution?

_____

_____

YOUR TURN

Solve each system of linear equations by substitution.

4. $\begin{cases} 3x + y = 11 \\ -2x + y = 1 \end{cases}$

5. $\begin{cases} 2x - 3y = -24 \\ x + 6y = 18 \end{cases}$

6. $\begin{cases} x - 2y = 5 \\ 3x - 5y = 8 \end{cases}$

_____   _____   _____

Personal Math Trainer

Online Assessment and Intervention

⏻ my.hrw.com

Using a Graph to Estimate the Solution of a System

You can use a graph to estimate the solution of a system of equations before solving the system algebraically.

Math On the Spot

my.hrw.com

EXAMPLE 2

COMMON CORE 8.EE.8b

Solve the system $\begin{cases} x - 4y = 4 \\ 2x - 3y = -3 \end{cases}$.

STEP 1 Sketch a graph of each equation by substituting values for x and generating values of y.

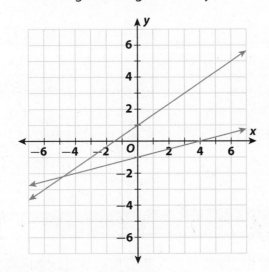

STEP 2 Find the intersection of the lines. The lines appear to intersect near $(-5, -2)$.

Math Talk
Mathematical Practices

In Step 2, how can you tell that $(-5, -2)$ is not the solution?

STEP 3 Solve the system algebraically.

Solve $x - 4y = 4$ for x.

$x - 4y = 4$
$\quad x = 4 + 4y$

Substitute to find y.

$2(4 + 4y) - 3y = -3$
$8 + 8y - 3y = -3$
$8 + 5y = -3$
$5y = -11$
$y = -\dfrac{11}{5}$

Substitute to find x.

$x = 4 + 4y$
$= 4 + 4\left(-\dfrac{11}{5}\right)$
$= \dfrac{20 - 44}{5}$
$= -\dfrac{24}{5}$

The solution is $\left(-\dfrac{24}{5}, -\dfrac{11}{5}\right)$.

STEP 4 Use the estimate you made using the graph to judge the reasonableness of your solution.

$-\dfrac{24}{5}$ is close to the estimate of -5, and $-\dfrac{11}{5}$ is close to the estimate of -2, so the solution seems reasonable.

7. Estimate the solution of the system $\begin{cases} x + y = 4 \\ 2x - y = 6 \end{cases}$ by sketching a graph of each linear function. Then solve the system algebraically. Use your estimate to judge the reasonableness of your solution.

The estimated solution is _____.

The algebraic solution is _____.

The solution is/is not reasonable because

_____

_____

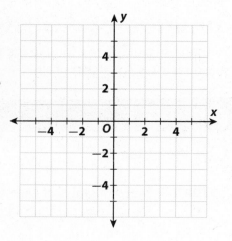

Math On the Spot

⏻ my.hrw.com

Solving Problems with Systems of Equations

EXAMPLE 3 🌎 Real World COMMON CORE 8.EE.8c

As part of Class Day, the eighth grade is doing a treasure hunt. Each team is given the following riddle and map. At what point is the treasure located?

There's pirate treasure to be found. So search on the island, all around. Draw a line through *A* and *B*. Then another through *C* and *D*. Dance a jig, "X" marks the spot. Where the lines intersect, that's the treasure's plot!

STEP 1 Give the coordinates of each point and find the slope of the line through each pair of points.

Math Talk

Mathematical Practices

Where do the lines appear to intersect? How is this related to the solution?

A: $(-2, -1)$	*C*: $(-1, 4)$
B: $(2, 5)$	*D*: $(1, -4)$

Slope: Slope:

$\dfrac{5 - (-1)}{2 - (-2)} = \dfrac{6}{4}$ $\dfrac{-4 - 4}{1 - (-1)} = \dfrac{-8}{2}$

$\qquad\qquad = \dfrac{3}{2}$ $\qquad\qquad\qquad = -4$

STEP 2 Write equations in slope-intercept form describing the line through points *A* and *B* and the line through points *C* and *D*.

Line through *A* and *B*:

Use the slope and a point to find *b*.

$5 = \left(\frac{3}{2}\right)2 + b$

$b = 2$

The equation is $y = \frac{3}{2}x + 2$.

Line through *C* and *D*:

Use the slope and a point to find *b*.

$4 = -4(-1) + b$

$b = 0$

The equation is $y = -4x$.

STEP 3 Solve the system algebraically.

Substitute $\frac{3}{2}x + 2$ for *y* in $y = -4x$ to find *x*.

$\frac{3}{2}x + 2 = -4x$

$\frac{11}{2}x = -2$

$x = -\frac{4}{11}$

Substitute to find *y*.

$y = -4\left(-\frac{4}{11}\right) = \frac{16}{11}$

The solution is $\left(-\frac{4}{11}, \frac{16}{11}\right)$.

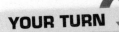

YOUR TURN

8. Ace Car Rental rents cars for *x* dollars per day plus *y* dollars for each mile driven. Carlos rented a car for 4 days, drove it 160 miles, and spent $120. Vanessa rented a car for 1 day, drove it 240 miles, and spent $80. Write equations to represent Carlos's expenses and Vanessa's expenses. Then solve the system and tell what each number represents.

_____

_____

_____

_____

_____

Personal Math Trainer

Online Assessment and Intervention

my.hrw.com

Solve each system of linear equations by substitution. (Explore Activity Example 1)

1. $\begin{cases} 3x - 2y = 9 \\ y = 2x - 7 \end{cases}$ _____

2. $\begin{cases} y = x - 4 \\ 2x + y = 5 \end{cases}$ _____

3. $\begin{cases} x + 4y = 6 \\ y = -x + 3 \end{cases}$ _____

4. $\begin{cases} x + 2y = 6 \\ x - y = 3 \end{cases}$ _____

Solve each system. Estimate the solution first. (Example 2)

5. $\begin{cases} 6x + y = 4 \\ x - 4y = 19 \end{cases}$

 Estimate _____

 Solution _____

6. $\begin{cases} x + 2y = 8 \\ 3x + 2y = 6 \end{cases}$

 Estimate _____

 Solution _____

7. $\begin{cases} 3x + y = 4 \\ 5x - y = 22 \end{cases}$

 Estimate _____

 Solution _____

8. $\begin{cases} 2x + 7y = 2 \\ x + y = -1 \end{cases}$

 Estimate _____

 Solution _____

9. Adult tickets to Space City amusement park cost x dollars. Children's tickets cost y dollars. The Henson family bought 3 adult and 1 child tickets for $163. The Garcia family bought 2 adult and 3 child tickets for $174. (Example 3)

 a. Write equations to represent the Hensons' cost and the Garcias' cost.

 Hensons' cost: _____   Garcias' cost: _____

 b. Solve the system.

 adult ticket price: _____   child ticket price: _____

? ESSENTIAL QUESTION CHECK-IN

10. How can you decide which variable to solve for first when you are solving a linear system by substitution?

 _____

 _____

 _____

8.2 Independent Practice

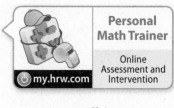

COMMON CORE 8.EE.8b, 8.EE.8c

11. Check for Reasonableness Zach solves the system $\begin{cases} x + y = -3 \\ x - y = 1 \end{cases}$ and finds the solution $(1, -2)$. Use a graph to explain whether Zach's solution is reasonable.

_____

_____

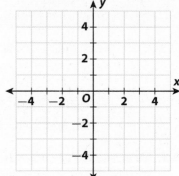

12. Represent Real-World Problems Angelo bought apples and bananas at the fruit stand. He bought 20 pieces of fruit and spent $11.50. Apples cost $0.50 and bananas cost $0.75 each.

   a. Write a system of equations to model the problem. (Hint: One equation will represent the number of pieces of fruit. A second equation will represent the money spent on the fruit.)

   _____

   b. Solve the system algebraically. Tell how many apples and bananas Angelo bought.

   _____

Apples $0.50
Bananas $0.75

13. Represent Real-World Problems A jar contains n nickels and d dimes. There is a total of 200 coins in the jar. The value of the coins is $14.00. How many nickels and how many dimes are in the jar?

_____

14. Multistep The graph shows a triangle formed by the x-axis, the line $3x - 2y = 0$, and the line $x + 2y = 10$. Follow these steps to find the area of the triangle.

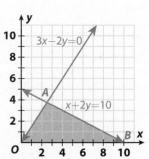

   a. Find the coordinates of point A by solving the system $\begin{cases} 3x - 2y = 0 \\ x + 2y = 10 \end{cases}$.

   Point A: _____

   b. Use the coordinates of point A to find the height of the triangle.

   height: _____

   c. What is the length of the base of the triangle?

   base: _____

   d. What is the area of the triangle? _____

15. Jed is graphing the design for a kite on a coordinate grid. The four vertices of the kite are at $A\left(-\frac{4}{3}, \frac{2}{3}\right)$, $B\left(\frac{14}{3}, -\frac{4}{3}\right)$, $C\left(\frac{14}{3}, -\frac{16}{3}\right)$, and $D\left(\frac{2}{3}, -\frac{16}{3}\right)$. One kite strut will connect points A and C. The other will connect points B and D. Find the point where the struts cross.

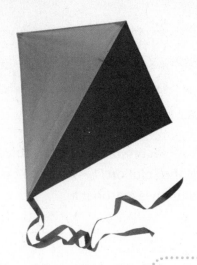

_____

16. Analyze Relationships Consider the system $\begin{cases} 6x - 3y = 15 \\ x + 3y = -8 \end{cases}$. Describe three different substitution methods that can be used to solve this system. Then solve the system.

_____

_____

_____

_____

_____

_____

17. Communicate Mathematical Ideas Explain the advantages, if any, that solving a system of linear equations by substitution has over solving the same system by graphing.

_____

_____

_____

_____

18. Persevere in Problem Solving Create a system of equations of the form $\begin{cases} Ax + By = C \\ Dx + Ey = F \end{cases}$ that has $(7, -2)$ as its solution. Explain how you found the system.

_____

_____

_____

_____

Work Area

? ESSENTIAL QUESTION

How do you solve a system of linear equations by adding or subtracting?

EXPLORE ACTIVITY COMMON CORE **8.EE.8b**

Math On the Spot

⏻ my.hrw.com

Solving a Linear System by Adding

The **elimination method** is another method used to solve a system of linear equations. In this method, one variable is *eliminated* by adding or subtracting the two equations of the system to obtain a single equation in one variable. The steps for this method are as follows:

1. Add or subtract the equations to eliminate one variable.

2. Solve the resulting equation for the other variable.

3. Substitute the value into either original equation to find the value of the eliminated variable.

EXAMPLE 1 Solve the system of equations by adding. Check your answer.

$$\begin{cases} 2x - 3y = 12 \\ x + 3y = 6 \end{cases}$$

STEP 1 Add the equations.

Write the equations so that like terms are aligned.

Notice that the terms −3y and _____ are opposites.

Add to eliminate the variable _____.

Simplify.

Divide each side by _____.

Simplify.

$$2x - 3y = 12$$
$$+ x + \boxed{} = 6$$
$$\overline{3x + \boxed{} = 18}$$
$$3x = 18$$
$$\frac{3x}{\boxed{}} = \frac{18}{\boxed{}}$$
$$x = \boxed{}$$

STEP 2 Substitute the solution into one of the original equations, and solve for y.

Use the second equation.

Substitute _____ for the variable x.

Subtract _____ from each side.

Divide each side by _____ and simplify.

$$x + 3y = 6$$
$$\boxed{} + 3y = 6$$
$$3y = \boxed{}$$
$$y = \boxed{}$$

STEP 3 Write the solution as an ordered pair: (____, ____)

STEP 4 Check the solution by graphing.

$$2x - 3y = 12$$

x-intercept: $2x - 3(0) = 12 \rightarrow x =$ ⬜

y-intercept: $2(0) - 3y = 12 \rightarrow y =$ ⬜

$$x + 3y = 6$$

x-intercept: $x + 3(0) = 6 \rightarrow x =$ ⬜

y-intercept: $0 + 3y = 6 \rightarrow y =$ ⬜

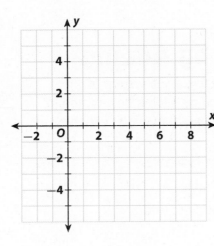

The graph confirms that the solution is (____, ____).

Reflect

1. Can this linear system be solved by subtracting one of the original equations from the other? Why or why not?

_____

_____

_____

2. What is another way to check your solution?

_____

_____

_____

 **YOUR TURN**

Solve each system of equations by adding. Check your answers.

3. $\begin{cases} x + y = -1 \\ x - y = 7 \end{cases}$

4. $\begin{cases} 2x + 2y = -2 \\ 3x - 2y = 12 \end{cases}$

5. $\begin{cases} 6x + 5y = 4 \\ -6x + 7y = 20 \end{cases}$

_____

_____

_____

Personal Math Trainer

Online Assessment and Intervention

my.hrw.com

Solving a Linear System by Subtracting

If both equations contain the same *x*- or *y*-term, you can solve by subtracting.

EXAMPLE 2   COMMON CORE 8.EE.8b

Solve the system of equations by subtracting. Check your answer.

$$\begin{cases} 3x + 3y = 6 \\ 3x - y = -6 \end{cases}$$

STEP 1 Subtract the equations.

$3x + 3y = 6$ *Write the equations so that like terms are aligned.*

$-(3x - y = -6)$ *Notice that both equations contain the term 3x.*

$0 + 4y = 12$ *Subtract to eliminate the variable x.*

$4y = 12$ *Simplify and solve for y.*

$y = 3$ *Divide each side by 4 and simplify.*

STEP 2 Substitute the solution into one of the original equations and solve for *x*.

$3x - y = -6$ *Use the second equation.*

$3x - 3 = -6$ *Substitute 3 for the variable y.*

$3x = -3$ *Add 3 to each side.*

$x = -1$ *Divide each side by 3 and simplify.*

STEP 3 Write the solution as an ordered pair: $(-1, 3)$

STEP 4 Check the solution by graphing.

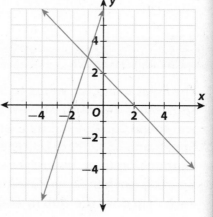

$3x + 3y = 6$	$3x - y = -6$
x-intercept: 2	*x*-intercept: -2
y-intercept: 2	*y*-intercept: 6

The point of intersection is $(-1, 3)$.

Reflect

6. What would happen if you added the original equations?

_____

_____

My Notes

7. How can you decide whether to add or subtract to eliminate a variable in a linear system? Explain your reasoning.

_____

_____

_____

_____

_____

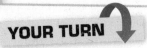

YOUR TURN

Solve each system of equations by subtracting. Check your answers.

8. $\begin{cases} 6x - 3y = 6 \\ 6x + 8y = -16 \end{cases}$

9. $\begin{cases} 4x + 3y = 19 \\ 6x + 3y = 33 \end{cases}$

10. $\begin{cases} 2x + 6y = 17 \\ 2x - 10y = 9 \end{cases}$

_____   _____   _____

Solving Problems with Systems of Equations

Many real-world situations can be modeled and solved with a system of equations.

EXAMPLE 3

COMMON CORE 8.EE.8c

The Polar Bear Club wants to buy snowshoes and camp stoves. The club will spend $554.50 to buy them at Top Sports and $602.00 to buy them at Outdoor Explorer, before taxes, but Top Sports is farther away. How many of each item does the club intend to buy?

	Snowshoes	Camp Stoves
Top Sports	$79.50 per pair	$39.25
Outdoor Explorer	$89.00 per pair	$39.25

STEP 1 Choose variables and write a system of equations.

Let x represent the number of pairs of snowshoes.

Let y represent the number of camp stoves.

Top Sports cost: $79.50x + 39.25y = 554.50$

Outdoor Explorer cost: $89.00x + 39.25y = 602.00$

STEP 2 Subtract the equations.

$$79.50x + 39.25y = 554.50$$

$$-(89.00x + 39.25y = 602.00)$$

Both equations contain the term 39.25y.

$$-9.50x + 0 \qquad = -47.50$$ *Subtract to eliminate the variable y.*

$$-9.50x = -47.50$$ *Simplify and solve for x.*

$$\frac{-9.50x}{-9.50} = \frac{-47.50}{-9.50}$$ *Divide each side by −9.50.*

$$x = 5$$ *Simplify.*

STEP 3 Substitute the solution into one of the original equations and solve for y.

$$79.50x + 39.25y = 554.50$$ *Use the first equation.*

$$79.50(5) + 39.25y = 554.50$$ *Substitute 5 for the variable x.*

$$397.50 + 39.25y = 554.50$$ *Multiply.*

$$39.25y = 157.00$$ *Subtract 397.50 from each side.*

$$\frac{39.25y}{39.25} = \frac{157.00}{39.25}$$ *Divide each side by 39.25.*

$$y = 4$$ *Simplify.*

STEP 4 Write the solution as an ordered pair: (5, 4)

The club intends to buy 5 pairs of snowshoes and 4 camp stoves.

YOUR TURN

11. At the county fair, the Baxter family bought 6 hot dogs and 4 juice drinks for $16.70. The Farley family bought 3 hot dogs and 4 juice drinks for $10.85. Find the price of a hot dog and the price of a juice drink.

_____

_____

Personal Math Trainer

Online Assessment and Intervention

my.hrw.com

1. Solve the system $\begin{cases} 4x + 3y = 1 \\ x - 3y = -11 \end{cases}$ by adding. (Explore Activity Example 1)

STEP 1 Add the equations.

$$4x + 3y = 1$$
$$+ \quad x - 3y = -11$$

Write the equations so that like terms are aligned.

$$5x + \boxed{} = \boxed{}$$

Add to eliminate the variable $\boxed{}$.

$$5x = \boxed{}$$

Simplify and solve for x.

$$x = \boxed{}$$

Divide both sides by $\boxed{}$ and simplify.

STEP 2 Substitute into one of the original equations and solve for y.

$$y = \boxed{} \qquad \text{So,} \boxed{} \text{ is the solution of the system.}$$

Solve each system of equations by adding or subtracting.
(Explore Activity Example 1, Example 2)

2. $\begin{cases} x + 2y = -2 \\ -3x + 2y = -10 \end{cases}$

3. $\begin{cases} 3x + y = 23 \\ 3x - 2y = 8 \end{cases}$

4. $\begin{cases} -4x - 5y = 7 \\ 3x + 5y = -14 \end{cases}$

_____

_____

_____

5. $\begin{cases} x - 2y = -19 \\ 5x + 2y = 1 \end{cases}$

6. $\begin{cases} 3x + 4y = 18 \\ -2x + 4y = 8 \end{cases}$

7. $\begin{cases} -5x + 7y = 11 \\ -5x + 3y = 19 \end{cases}$

_____

_____

_____

8. The Green River Freeway has a minimum and a maximum speed limit. Tony drove for 2 hours at the minimum speed limit and 3.5 hours at the maximum limit, a distance of 355 miles. Rae drove 2 hours at the minimum speed limit and 3 hours at the maximum limit, a distance of 320 miles. What are the two speed limits? (Example 3)

a. Write equations to represent Tony's distance and Rae's distance.

Tony: _____ Rae: _____

b. Solve the system.

minimum speed limit: _____ maximum speed limit: _____

© Houghton Mifflin Harcourt Publishing Company

? ESSENTIAL QUESTION CHECK-IN

9. Can you use addition or subtraction to solve any system? Explain.

_____

_____

8.3 Independent Practice

COMMON CORE **8.EE.8b, 8.EE.8c**

Personal Math Trainer

Online Assessment and Intervention

my.hrw.com

10. Represent Real-World Problems Marta bought new fish for her home aquarium. She bought 3 guppies and 2 platies for a total of $13.95. Hank also bought guppies and platies for his aquarium. He bought 3 guppies and 4 platies for a total of $18.33. Find the price of a guppy and the price of a platy.

_____

11. Represent Real-World Problems The rule for the number of fish in a home aquarium is 1 gallon of water for each inch of fish length. Marta's aquarium holds 13 gallons and Hank's aquarium holds 17 gallons. Based on the number of fish they bought in Exercise 10, how long is a guppy and how long is a platy?

_____

12. Line *m* passes through the points (6, 1) and (2, −3). Line *n* passes through the points (2, 3) and (5, −6). Find the point of intersection of these lines.

_____

13. Represent Real-World Problems Two cars got an oil change at the same auto shop. The shop charges customers for each quart of oil plus a flat fee for labor. The oil change for one car required 5 quarts of oil and cost $22.45. The oil change for the other car required 7 quarts of oil and cost $25.45. How much is the labor fee and how much is each quart of oil?

_____

14. Represent Real-World Problems A sales manager noticed that the number of units sold for two T-shirt styles, style A and style B, was the same during June and July. In June, total sales were $2779 for the two styles, with A selling for $15.95 per shirt and B selling for $22.95 per shirt. In July, total sales for the two styles were $2385.10, with A selling at the same price and B selling at a discount of 22% off the June price. How many T-shirts of each style were sold in June and July combined?

_____

15. Represent Real-World Problems Adult tickets to a basketball game cost $5. Student tickets cost $1. A total of $2,874 was collected on the sale of 1,246 tickets. How many of each type of ticket were sold?

_____

H.O.T. FOCUS ON HIGHER ORDER THINKING

16. **Communicate Mathematical Ideas** Is it possible to solve the system $\begin{cases} 3x - 2y = 10 \\ x + 2y = 6 \end{cases}$ by using substitution? If so, explain how. Which method, substitution or elimination, is more efficient? Why?

_____

_____

_____

_____

_____

_____

_____

17. Jenny used substitution to solve the system $\begin{cases} 2x + y = 8 \\ x - y = 1 \end{cases}$. Her solution is shown below.

Step 1 $y = -2x + 8$ Solve the first equation for y.

Step 2 $2x + (-2x + 8) = 8$ Substitute the value of y in an original equation.

Step 3 $2x - 2x + 8 = 8$ Use the Distributive Property.

Step 4 $8 = 8$ Simplify.

a. **Explain the Error** Explain the error Jenny made. Describe how to correct it.

_____

_____

_____

_____

b. **Communicate Mathematical Ideas** Would adding the equations have been a better method for solving the system? If so, explain why.

_____

_____

_____

_____

Solving Systems by Elimination with Multiplication

COMMON CORE 8.EE.8b
Solve systems of two linear equations in two variables algebraically, ... Also 8.EE.8c

? ESSENTIAL QUESTION

How do you solve a system of linear equations by multiplying?

EXPLORE ACTIVITY COMMON CORE 8.EE.8b

Solving a System by Multiplying and Adding

In some linear systems, neither variable can be eliminated by adding or subtracting the equations directly. In systems like these, you need to multiply one of the equations by a constant so that adding or subtracting the equations will eliminate one variable. The steps for this method are as follows:

1. Decide which variable to eliminate.
2. Multiply one equation by a constant so that adding or subtracting will eliminate that variable.
3. Solve the system using the elimination method.

EXAMPLE 1 Solve the system of equations by multiplying and adding.

$$\begin{cases} 2x + 10y = 2 \\ 3x - 5y = -17 \end{cases}$$

STEP 1

The coefficient of y in the first equation, 10, is 2 times the coefficient of y, 5, in the second equation. Also, the y-term in the first equation is being added, while the y-term in the second equation is being subtracted. To eliminate the _____, multiply the second equation by 2 and add this new equation to the first equation.

Multiply each term in the second equation by _____ to get opposite coefficients for the _____, and simplify.

Add the first equation to the new equation.

Add to eliminate the variable _____.

Simplify.

Divide each side by _____.

Simplify.

$\boxed{}(3x - 5y = -17)$

$\boxed{}x - \boxed{}y = -34$

$6x - 10y = -34$

$+\ 2x + \boxed{} = 2$

_____

$8x + \boxed{}y = -32$

$8x = -32$

$\dfrac{8x}{\boxed{}} = \dfrac{-32}{\boxed{}}$

$x = \boxed{}$

STEP 2 Substitute the solution into one of the original equations, and solve for *y*.

Use the first equation. $2x + 10y = 2$

Substitute _____ for the variable *x*. $2\left(\boxed{}\right) + 10y = 2$

Simplify. $\boxed{} + 10y = 2$

Add _____ to each side. $10y = \boxed{}$

Divide each side by _____, and simplify. $y = \boxed{}$

STEP 3 Write the solution as an ordered pair: (____ , ____).

STEP 4 Check your answer algebraically.

Substitute _____ for *x* and _____ for *y* in the original system.

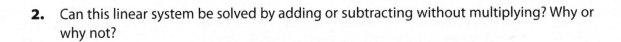

$$\begin{cases} 2x + 10y = 2 \rightarrow 2\left(\boxed{}\right) + 10\left(\boxed{}\right) = \boxed{} \checkmark \\ 3x - 5y = -17 \rightarrow 3\left(\boxed{}\right) - 5\left(\boxed{}\right) = \boxed{} \checkmark \end{cases}$$

The solution is correct.

Reflect

1. How can you solve this linear system by subtracting? Which is more efficient, adding or subtracting? Explain your reasoning.

_____

_____

2. Can this linear system be solved by adding or subtracting without multiplying? Why or why not?

_____

3. What would you need to multiply the second equation by to eliminate *x* by adding? Why might you choose to eliminate *y* instead of *x*?

_____

_____

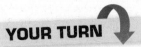 **YOUR TURN**

Solve each system of equations by multiplying and adding.

4. $\begin{cases} 5x + 2y = -10 \\ 3x + 6y = 66 \end{cases}$
5. $\begin{cases} 4x + 2y = 6 \\ 3x - y = -8 \end{cases}$
6. $\begin{cases} -6x + 9y = -12 \\ 2x + y = 0 \end{cases}$

_____   _____   _____

Personal Math Trainer

Online Assessment and Intervention

⏻ my.hrw.com

Solving a System by Multiplying and Subtracting

You can solve some systems of equations by multiplying one equation by a constant and then subtracting.

Math On the Spot
my.hrw.com

EXAMPLE 2

COMMON CORE 8.EE.8b

Solve the system of equations by multiplying and subtracting.

$$\begin{cases} 6x + 5y = 7 \\ 2x - 4y = -26 \end{cases}$$

STEP 1   Multiply the second equation by 3 and subtract this new equation from the first equation.

$3(2x - 4y) = -26$ Multiply each term in the second equation by 3 to get the same coefficients for the x-terms.

$6x - 12y = -78$ Simplify.

$$\begin{aligned} 6x + 5y &= 7 \\ -(6x - 12y &= -78) \end{aligned}$$ Subtract the new equation from the first equation.

$0x + 17y = 85$ Subtract to eliminate the variable x.

$17y = 85$ Simplify and solve for y.

$\dfrac{17y}{17} = \dfrac{85}{17}$ Divide each side by 17.

$y = 5$ Simplify.

STEP 2   Substitute the solution into one of the original equations and solve for x.

$6x + 5y = 7$ Use the first equation.

$6x + 5(5) = 7$ Substitute 5 for the variable y.

$6x + 25 = 7$ Simplify.

$6x = -18$ Subtract 25 from each side.

$x = -3$ Divide each side by 6 and simplify.

STEP 3   Write the solution as an ordered pair: $(-3, 5)$

STEP 4   Check your answer algebraically.
Substitute -3 for x and 5 for y in the original system.

$$\begin{cases} 6x + 5y = 7 \rightarrow 6(-3) + 5(5) = -18 + 25 = 7 \checkmark \\ 2x - 4y = -26 \rightarrow 2(-3) - 4(5) = -6 - 20 = -26 \checkmark \end{cases}$$

The solution is correct.

© Houghton Mifflin Harcourt Publishing Company

YOUR TURN

Solve each system of equations by multiplying and subtracting.

7. $\begin{cases} 3x - 7y = 2 \\ 6x - 9y = 9 \end{cases}$

8. $\begin{cases} -3x + y = 11 \\ 2x + 3y = -11 \end{cases}$

9. $\begin{cases} 9x + y = 9 \\ 3x - 2y = -11 \end{cases}$

_____   _____   _____

My Notes

Solving Problems with Systems of Equations

Many real-world situations can be modeled with a system of equations.

EXAMPLE 3 Problem Solving   COMMON CORE 8.EE.8c

The Simon family attended a concert and visited an art museum. Concert tickets were $24.75 for adults and $16.00 for children, for a total cost of $138.25. Museum tickets were $8.25 for adults and $4.50 for children, for a total cost of $42.75. How many adults and how many children are in the Simon family?

 Analyze Information

The answer is the number of adults and children.

 Formulate a Plan

Solve a system to find the number of adults and children.

Solve

STEP 1 Choose variables and write a system of equations. Let x represent the number of adults. Let y represent the number of children.

Concert cost: $24.75x + 16.00y = 138.25$
Museum cost: $8.25x + 4.50y = 42.75$

STEP 2 Multiply both equations by 100 to eliminate the decimals.

$100(24.75x + 16.00y = 138.25) \rightarrow 2{,}475x + 1{,}600y = 13{,}825$

$100(8.25x + 4.50y = 42.75) \rightarrow 825x + 450y = 4{,}275$

STEP 3 Multiply the second equation by 3 and subtract this new equation from the first equation.

$3(825x + 450y = 4,275)$ Multiply each term in the second equation by 3 to get the same coefficients for the x-terms.

$2,475x + 1,350y = 12,825$ Simplify.

$2,475x + 1,600y = 13,825$
$-(2,475x + 1,350y = 12,825)$ Subtract the new equation from the first equation.
_____

$0x + 250y = 1,000$ Subtract to eliminate the variable x.

$250y = 1,000$ Simplify and solve for y.

$\dfrac{250y}{250} = \dfrac{1,000}{250}$ Divide each side by 250.

$y = 4$ Simplify.

STEP 4 Substitute the solution into one of the original equations and solve for x.

$8.25x + 4.50y = 42.75$ Use the second equation.

$8.25x + 4.50(4) = 42.75$ Substitute 4 for the variable y.

$8.25x + 18 = 42.75$ Simplify.

$8.25x = 24.75$ Subtract 18 from each side.

$x = 3$ Divide each side by 8.25 and simplify.

STEP 5 Write the solution as an ordered pair: (3, 4).
There are 3 adults and 4 children in the family.

 Justify and Evaluate

Substituting $x = 3$ and $y = 4$ into the original equations results in true statements. The answer is correct.

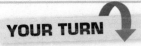

10. Contestants in the Run-and-Bike-a-thon run for a specified length of time, then bike for a specified length of time. Jason ran at an average speed of 5.2 mi/h and biked at an average speed of 20.6 mi/h, going a total of 14.2 miles. Seth ran at an average speed of 10.4 mi/h and biked at an average speed of 18.4 mi/h, going a total of 17 miles. For how long do contestants run and for how long do they bike?

_____

_____

Personal Math Trainer

Online Assessment and Intervention

my.hrw.com

1. Solve the system $\begin{cases} 3x - y = 8 \\ -2x + 4y = -12 \end{cases}$ by multiplying and adding. (Explore Activity Example 1)

STEP 1 Multiply the first equation by 4. Add to the second equation.

$4(3x - y = 8)$ *Multiply each term in the first equation by 4 to get opposite coefficients for the y-terms.*

$\boxed{}x - \boxed{}y = \boxed{}$ *Simplify.*

$+ \ (-2x) + \ 4y \ = -12$ *Add the second equation to the new equation.*

$10x = \boxed{}$ *Add to eliminate the variable* $\boxed{}$.

$x = \boxed{}$ *Divide both sides by* $\boxed{}$ *and simplify.*

STEP 2 Substitute into one of the original equations and solve for *y*.

$y = \boxed{}$ So, $\boxed{}$ is the solution of the system.

Solve each system of equations by multiplying first. (Explore Activity Example 1, Example 2)

2. $\begin{cases} x + 4y = 2 \\ 2x + 5y = 7 \end{cases}$ _____

3. $\begin{cases} 3x + y = -1 \\ 2x + 3y = 18 \end{cases}$ _____

4. $\begin{cases} 2x + 8y = 21 \\ 6x - 4y = 14 \end{cases}$ _____

5. $\begin{cases} 2x + y = 3 \\ -x + 3y = -12 \end{cases}$ _____

6. $\begin{cases} 6x + 5y = 19 \\ 2x + 3y = 5 \end{cases}$ _____

7. $\begin{cases} 2x + 5y = 16 \\ -4x + 3y = 20 \end{cases}$ _____

8. Bryce spent $5.26 on some apples priced at $0.64 each and some pears priced at $0.45 each. At another store he could have bought the same number of apples at $0.32 each and the same number of pears at $0.39 each, for a total cost of $3.62. How many apples and how many pears did Bryce buy? (Example 3)

   a. Write equations to represent Bryce's expenditures at each store.

   First store: _____   Second store: _____

   b. Solve the system.

   Number of apples: _____   Number of pears: _____

? **ESSENTIAL QUESTION CHECK-IN**

9. When solving a system by multiplying and then adding or subtracting, how do you decide whether to add or subtract?

   _____

   _____

8.4 Independent Practice

 COMMON CORE 8.EE.8b, 8.EE.8c

Personal Math Trainer

Online Assessment and Intervention

my.hrw.com

10. Explain the Error Gwen used elimination with multiplication to solve the system $\begin{cases} 2x + 6y = 3 \\ x - 3y = -1 \end{cases}$. Her work to find x is shown. Explain her error. Then solve the system.

$$2(x - 3y) = -1$$
$$2x - 6y = -1$$
$$\underline{+2x + 6y = 3}$$
$$4x + 0y = 2$$
$$x = \frac{1}{2}$$

_____

11. Represent Real-World Problems At Raging River Sports, polyester-fill sleeping bags sell for $79. Down-fill sleeping bags sell for $149. In one week the store sold 14 sleeping bags for $1,456.

Sleeping Bags

Nylon
Down-filled, 35°
$149

Flannel-lined
Polyester-filled, 40°
$79

a. Let x represent the number of polyester-fill bags sold and let y represent the number of down-fill bags sold. Write a system of equations you can solve to find the number of each type sold.

_____

b. Explain how you can solve the system for y by multiplying and subtracting.

_____

_____

c. Explain how you can solve the system for y using substitution.

_____

_____

_____

d. How many of each type of bag were sold?

_____

12. Twice a number plus twice a second number is 310. The difference between the numbers is 55. Find the numbers by writing and solving a system of equations. Explain how you solved the system.

_____

_____

_____

13. **Represent Real-World Problems** A farm stand sells apple pies and jars of applesauce. The table shows the number of apples needed to make a pie and a jar of applesauce. Yesterday, the farm picked 169 Granny Smith apples and 95 Red Delicious apples. How many pies and jars of applesauce can the farm make if every apple is used?

Type of apple	Granny Smith	Red Delicious
Needed for a pie	5	3
Needed for a jar of applesauce	4	2

_____

 FOCUS ON HIGHER ORDER THINKING

Work Area

14. **Make a Conjecture** Lena tried to solve a system of linear equations algebraically and in the process found the equation $5 = 9$. Lena thought something was wrong, so she graphed the equations and found that they were parallel lines. Explain what Lena's graph and equation could mean.

_____

_____

_____

_____

_____

15. Consider the system $\begin{cases} 2x + 3y = 6 \\ 3x + 7y = -1 \end{cases}$.

   a. **Communicate Mathematical Ideas** Describe how to solve the system by multiplying the first equation by a constant and subtracting. Why would this method be less than ideal?

   _____

   _____

   _____

   b. **Draw Conclusions** Is it possible to solve the system by multiplying both equations by integer constants? If so, explain how.

   _____

   _____

   _____

   c. Use your answer from part b to solve the system.

   _____

Solving Special Systems

COMMON CORE **8.EE.8b**
Solve systems of two linear equations in two variables algebraically, ... Solve simple cases by inspection. *Also 8.EE.8c*

ESSENTIAL QUESTION

How do you solve systems with no solution or infinitely many solutions?

EXPLORE ACTIVITY COMMON CORE 8.EE.8b

Solving Special Systems by Graphing

As with equations, some systems may have no solution or infinitely many solutions. One way to tell how many solutions a system has is by inspecting its graph.

Use the graph to solve each system of linear equations.

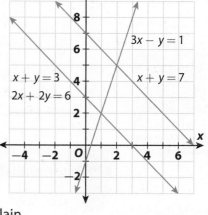

A $\begin{cases} x + y = 7 \\ 2x + 2y = 6 \end{cases}$

Is there a point of intersection? Explain.

_____

_____

Does this linear system have a solution? Use the graph to explain.

_____

_____

B $\begin{cases} 2x + 2y = 6 \\ x + y = 3 \end{cases}$

Is there a point of intersection? Explain.

_____

Does this linear system have a solution? Use the graph to explain.

_____

_____

Reflect

1. Use the graph to identify two lines that represent a linear system with exactly one solution. What are the equations of the lines? Explain your reasoning.

_____

2. If each equation in a system of two linear equations is represented by a different line when graphed, what is the greatest number of solutions the system can have? Explain your reasoning.

_____

_____

3. Identify the three possible numbers of solutions for a system of linear equations. Explain when each type of solution occurs.

_____

_____

_____

Math On the Spot

my.hrw.com

Solving Special Systems Algebraically

As with equations, if you solve a system of equations with no solution, you get a false statement, and if you solve a system with infinitely many solutions, you get a true statement.

EXAMPLE 1

COMMON CORE 8.EE.8b

My Notes

A Solve the system of linear equations by substitution.

$$\begin{cases} x - y = -2 \\ -x + y = \ 4 \end{cases}$$

STEP 1 Solve $x - y = -2$ for x:
$$x = y - 2$$

STEP 2 Substitute the resulting expression into the other equation and solve.

$-(y - 2) + y = 4$ *Substitute the expression for the variable x.*

$2 = 4$ *Simplify.*

STEP 3 Interpret the solution. The result is the false statement $2 = 4$, which means there is no solution.

STEP 4 Graph the equations to check your answer. The graphs do not intersect, so there is no solution.

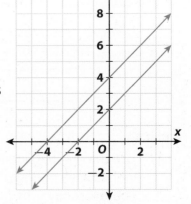

B Solve the system of linear equations by elimination.

$$\begin{cases} 2x + y = -2 \\ 4x + 2y = -4 \end{cases}$$

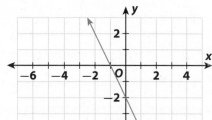

Math Talk
Mathematical Practices

What solution do you get when you solve the system in part B by substitution? Does this result change the number of solutions? Explain.

STEP 1 Multiply the first equation by -2.

$$-2(2x + y = -2) \rightarrow -4x + (-2y) = 4$$

STEP 2 Add the new equation from Step 1 to the original second equation.

$$\begin{array}{r} -4x + (-2y) = 4 \\ + \quad 4x + 2y = -4 \\ \hline 0x + 0y = 0 \\ 0 = 0 \end{array}$$

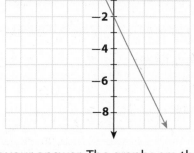

STEP 3 Interpret the solution. The result is the statement $0 = 0$, which is always true. This means that the system has infinitely many solutions.

STEP 4 Graph the equations to check your answer. The graphs are the same line, so there are infinitely many solutions.

Reflect

4. If x represents a variable and a and b represent constants so that $a \neq b$, interpret what each result means when solving a system of equations.

$x = a$ _____

$a = b$ _____

$a = a$ _____

5. In part B, can you tell without solving that the system has infinitely many solutions? If so, how?

_____

_____

_____

YOUR TURN

Solve each system. Tell how many solutions each system has.

6. $\begin{cases} 4x - 6y = 9 \\ -2x + 3y = 4 \end{cases}$

7. $\begin{cases} x + 2y = 6 \\ 2x - 3y = 26 \end{cases}$

8. $\begin{cases} 12x - 8y = -4 \\ -3x + 2y = 1 \end{cases}$

_____ _____ _____

_____ _____ _____

Personal Math Trainer

Online Assessment and Intervention

⏻ my.hrw.com

1. Use the graph to solve each system of linear equations. (Explore Activity)

   A. $\begin{cases} 4x - 2y = -6 \\ 2x - y = 4 \end{cases}$ **B.** $\begin{cases} 4x - 2y = -6 \\ x + y = 6 \end{cases}$ **C.** $\begin{cases} 2x - y = 4 \\ 6x - 3y = 12 \end{cases}$

STEP 1 Decide if the graphs of the equations in each system intersect, are parallel, or are the same line.

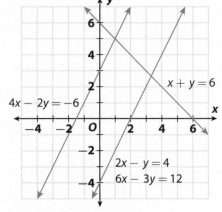

System A: The graphs _____ .

System B: The graphs _____ .

System C: The graphs _____ .

STEP 2 Decide how many points the graphs have in common.

Intersecting lines have _____ point(s) in common.

Parallel lines have _____ point(s) in common.

The same lines have _____ point(s) in common.

STEP 3 Solve each system.

System A has _____ points in common, so it has _____ solution.

System B has _____ point in common. That point is the solution, _____ .

System C has _____ points in common. _____ ordered pairs on the line will make both equations true.

Solve each system. Tell how many solutions each system has. (Example 1)

2. $\begin{cases} x - 3y = 4 \\ -5x + 15y = -20 \end{cases}$ **3.** $\begin{cases} 6x + 2y = -4 \\ 3x + y = 4 \end{cases}$ **4.** $\begin{cases} 6x - 2y = -10 \\ 3x + 4y = -25 \end{cases}$

_____   _____   _____

? ESSENTIAL QUESTION CHECK-IN

5. When you solve a system of equations algebraically, how can you tell whether the system has zero, one, or an infinite number of solutions?

_____

_____

_____

_____

8.5 Independent Practice

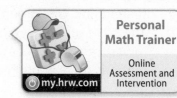

COMMON CORE 8.EE.8b, 8.EE.8c

Solve each system by graphing. Check your answer algebraically.

6. $\begin{cases} -2x + 6y = 12 \\ x - 3y = 3 \end{cases}$

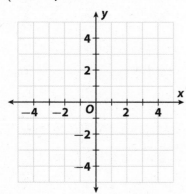

7. $\begin{cases} 15x + 5y = 5 \\ 3x + y = 1 \end{cases}$

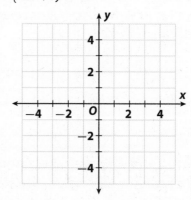

Solution: _____

Solution: _____

For Exs. 8–14, state the number of solutions for each system of linear equations.

8. a system whose graphs have the same slope but different y-intercepts

_____

9. a system whose graphs have the same y-intercepts but different slopes

_____

10. a system whose graphs have the same y-intercepts and the same slopes

_____

11. a system whose graphs have different y-intercepts and different slopes

_____

12. the system $\begin{cases} y = 2 \\ y = -3 \end{cases}$ _____

13. the system $\begin{cases} x = 2 \\ y = -3 \end{cases}$ _____

14. the system whose graphs were drawn using these tables of values:

Equation 1

x	0	1	2	3
y	1	3	5	7

Equation 2

x	0	1	2	3
y	3	5	7	9

_____

15. Draw Conclusions The graph of a linear system appears in a textbook. You can see that the lines do not intersect on the graph, but also they do not appear to be parallel. Can you conclude that the system has no solution? Explain.

_____

_____

16. **Represent Real-World Problems** Two school groups go to a roller skating rink. One group pays $243 for 36 admissions and 21 skate rentals. The other group pays $81 for 12 admissions and 7 skate rentals. Let x represent the cost of admission and let y represent the cost of a skate rental. Is there enough information to find values for x and y? Explain.

_____

17. **Represent Real-World Problems** Juan and Tory are practicing for a track meet. They start their practice runs at the same point, but Tory starts 1 minute after Juan. Both run at a speed of 704 feet per minute. Does Tory catch up to Juan? Explain.

_____

_____

_____

 FOCUS ON HIGHER ORDER THINKING

Work Area

18. **Justify Reasoning** A linear system with no solution consists of the equation $y = 4x - 3$ and a second equation of the form $y = mx + b$. What can you say about the values of m and b? Explain your reasoning.

_____

_____

_____

_____

19. **Justify Reasoning** A linear system with infinitely many solutions consists of the equation $3x + 5 = 8$ and a second equation of the form $Ax + By = C$. What can you say about the values of A, B, and C? Explain your reasoning.

_____

_____

_____

20. **Draw Conclusions** Both the points $(2, -2)$ and $(4, -4)$ are solutions of a system of linear equations. What conclusions can you make about the equations and their graphs?

_____

_____

Ready to Go On?

8.1 Solving Systems of Linear Equations by Graphing

Solve each system by graphing.

1. $\begin{cases} y = x - 1 \\ y = 2x - 3 \end{cases}$

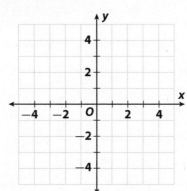

2. $\begin{cases} x + 2y = 1 \\ -x + y = 2 \end{cases}$

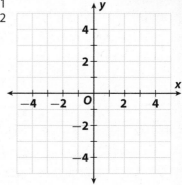

_____

_____

8.2 Solving Systems by Substitution

Solve each system of equations by substitution.

3. $\begin{cases} y = 2x \\ x + y = -9 \end{cases}$ _____

4. $\begin{cases} 3x - 2y = 11 \\ x + 2y = 9 \end{cases}$ _____

8.3 Solving Systems by Elimination

Solve each system of equations by adding or subtracting.

5. $\begin{cases} 3x + y = 9 \\ 2x + y = 5 \end{cases}$ _____

6. $\begin{cases} -x - 2y = 4 \\ 3x + 2y = 4 \end{cases}$ _____

8.4 Solving Systems by Elimination with Multiplication

Solve each system of equations by multiplying first.

7. $\begin{cases} x + 3y = -2 \\ 3x + 4y = -1 \end{cases}$ _____

8. $\begin{cases} 2x + 8y = 22 \\ 3x - 2y = 5 \end{cases}$ _____

8.5 Solving Special Systems

Solve each system. Tell how many solutions each system has.

9. $\begin{cases} -2x + 8y = 5 \\ x - 4y = -3 \end{cases}$ _____

10. $\begin{cases} 6x + 18y = -12 \\ x + 3y = -2 \end{cases}$ _____

 ESSENTIAL QUESTION

11. What are the possible solutions to a system of linear equations, and what do they represent graphically?

_____

_____

Selected Response

1. The graph of which equation is shown?

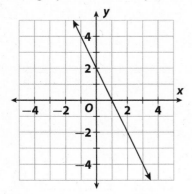

Ⓐ $y = -2x + 2$ Ⓒ $y = 2x + 2$

Ⓑ $y = -x + 2$ Ⓓ $y = 2x + 1$

2. Which best describes the solutions to the system $\begin{cases} x + y = -4 \\ -2x - 2y = 0 \end{cases}$?

Ⓐ one solution   Ⓒ infinitely many

Ⓑ no solution   Ⓓ $(0, 0)$

3. Which of the following represents 0.000056023 written in scientific notation?

Ⓐ 5.6023×10^5 Ⓒ 5.6023×10^{-4}

Ⓑ 5.6023×10^4 Ⓓ 5.6023×10^{-5}

4. Which is the solution to $\begin{cases} 2x - y = 1 \\ 4x + y = 11 \end{cases}$?

Ⓐ $(2, 3)$ Ⓒ $(-2, 3)$

Ⓑ $(3, 2)$ Ⓓ $(3, -2)$

5. Which expression can you substitute in the indicated equation to solve $\begin{cases} 3x - y = 5 \\ x + 2y = 4 \end{cases}$?

Ⓐ $2y - 4$ for x in $3x - y = 5$

Ⓑ $4 - x$ for y in $3x - y = 5$

Ⓒ $3x - 5$ for y in $3x - y = 5$

Ⓓ $3x - 5$ for y in $x + 2y = 4$

6. What is the solution to the system of linear equations shown on the graph?

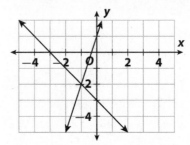

Ⓐ -1 Ⓒ $(-1, -2)$

Ⓑ -2 Ⓓ $(-2, -1)$

7. Which step could you use to start solving $\begin{cases} x - 6y = 8 \\ 2x - 5y = 3 \end{cases}$?

Ⓐ Add $2x - 5y = 3$ to $x - 6y = 8$.

Ⓑ Multiply $x - 6y = 8$ by 2 and add it to $2x - 5y = 3$.

Ⓒ Multiply $x - 6y = 8$ by 2 and subtract it from $2x - 5y = 3$.

Ⓓ Substitute $x = 6y - 8$ for x in $2x - 5y = 3$.

Mini-Task

8. A hot-air balloon begins rising from the ground at 4 meters per second at the same time a parachutist's chute opens at a height of 200 meters. The parachutist descends at 6 meters per second.

   a. Define the variables and write a system that represents the situation.

   _____

   _____

   b. Find the solution. What does it mean?

   _____

   _____

MODULE 7 Solving Linear Equations

? ESSENTIAL QUESTION

How can you use equations with variables on both sides to solve real-world problems?

EXAMPLE 1

A tutor gives students a choice of how to pay: a base rate of $20 plus $8 per hour, or a set rate of $13 per hour. Find the number of hours of tutoring for which the cost is the same for either choice.

Plan 1 cost: $20 + 8x$ Plan 2 cost: $13x$

$$20 + 8x = 13x \qquad \text{Write the equation.}$$
$$\underline{-8x \quad -8x} \qquad \text{Subtract } 8x \text{ from both sides.}$$
$$20 = 5x \qquad \text{Divide both sides by 5.}$$
$$x = 4$$

The cost is the same for 4 hours of tutoring.

EXAMPLE 2

Solve $-2.4(3x + 5) = 0.8(x + 3.5)$.

$$-2.4(3x + 5) = 0.8(x + 3.5)$$

$$10(-2.4)(3x + 5) = 10(0.8)(x + 3.5) \qquad \text{Multiply each side by 10 to clear some decimals.}$$

$$-24(3x + 5) = 8(x + 3.5)$$

$$-24(3x) - 24(5) = 8(x) + 8(3.5) \qquad \text{Apply the Distributive Property.}$$

$$-72x - 120 = 8x + 28$$

$$\underline{-8x \qquad\qquad -8x} \qquad \text{Subtract } 8x \text{ from both sides of the equation.}$$

$$-80x - 120 = 28$$

$$\underline{+120 \quad +120} \qquad \text{Add 120 to both sides of the equation.}$$

$$-80x = 148$$

$$\frac{-80x}{-80} = \frac{148}{-80} \qquad \text{Divide both sides of the equation by } -80.$$

$$x = -1.85$$

EXAMPLE 3

Solve 4(3x − 6) = 2(6x − 5).

$$4(3x - 6) = 2(6x - 5)$$

$12x - 24 = \quad 12x - 10$ Apply the Distributive Property.

$\underline{-12x \qquad\qquad -12x}$ Subtract 8x from both sides of the equation.

$-24 = -10$ The statement is false.

There is no value of x that makes a true statement. Therefore, this equation has no solution.

EXERCISES

Solve. (Lessons 7.1, 7.2, 7.3, 7.4)

1. $13.02 - 6y = 8y$ _____

2. $\frac{1}{5}x + 5 = 19 - \frac{1}{2}x$ _____

3. $7.3t + 22 = 2.1t - 22.2$ _____

4. $1.4 + \frac{2}{5}e = \frac{3}{15}e - 0.8$ _____

5. $5(x - 4) = 2(x + 5)$ _____

6. $-7(3 + t) = 4(2t + 6)$ _____

7. $\frac{3}{4}(x + 8) = \frac{1}{3}(x + 27)$ _____

8. $3(4x - 8) = \frac{1}{5}(35x + 30)$ _____

9. $-1.6(2y + 15) = -1.2(2y - 10)$

10. $9(4a - 2) = 12(3a + 8)$

_____

11. $6(x - \frac{1}{3}) = -2(x + 23)$

12. $8(p - 0.25) = 4(2p - 0.5)$

_____

13. Write a real-world situation that could be modeled by the equation $650 + 10m = 60m + 400$. (Lesson 7.1)

_____

_____

_____

_____

Solving Systems of Linear Equations

Key Vocabulary

solution of a system of equations *(solución de un sistema de ecuaciones)*

system of equations *(sistema de ecuaciones)*

? ESSENTIAL QUESTION

How can you use systems of equations to solve real-world problems?

EXAMPLE 1 Solve the system of equations by substitution.

$$\begin{cases} 3x + y = 7 \\ x + y = 3 \end{cases}$$

Step 1 Solve an equation for one variable.

$3x + y = 7$

$\qquad y = -3x + 7$

Step 2 Substitute the expression for y in the other equation and solve.

$\qquad x + y = 3$

$x + (-3x + 7) = 3$

$\qquad -2x + 7 = 3$

$\qquad\qquad -2x = -4$

$\qquad\qquad\quad x = 2$

Step 3 Substitute the value of x into one of the equations and solve for the other variable, y.

$x + y = 3$

$2 + y = 3$

$\qquad y = 1$

$(2, 1)$ is the solution of the system.

EXAMPLE 2 Solve the system of equations by elimination.

$$\begin{cases} x + y = 8 \\ 2x - 3y = 1 \end{cases}$$

Step 1 Multiply the first equation by 3 and add this new equation to the second equation.

$3(x + y = 8) = 3x + 3y = 24$

$3x + 3y = 24$

$\underline{2x - 3y = 1}$

$5x + 0y = 25$

$5x \qquad = 25$

$\quad x \qquad = 5$

Step 2 Substitute the solution into one of the original equations and solve for y.

$x + y = 8$

$5 + y = 8$

$\qquad y = 3$

$(5, 3)$ is the solution of the system.

EXERCISES

Solve each system of linear equations. (Lessons 8.1, 8.2, 8.3, 8.4, and 8.5)

14. $\begin{cases} x + y = -2 \\ 2x - y = 5 \end{cases}$

15. $\begin{cases} y = 2x + 1 \\ x + 2y = 17 \end{cases}$

16. $\begin{cases} y = -2x - 3 \\ 2x + y = 9 \end{cases}$

_____

17. $\begin{cases} y = 5 - x \\ 2x + 2y = 10 \end{cases}$

18. $\begin{cases} 2x - y = 26 \\ 3x - 2y = 42 \end{cases}$

19. $\begin{cases} 2x + 3y = 11 \\ 5x - 2y = 18 \end{cases}$

_____

20. Last week Andrew bought 3 pounds of zucchini and 2 pounds of tomatoes for $7.05 at a farm stand. This week he bought 4 pounds of zucchini and 3 pounds of tomatoes, at the same prices, for $9.83. What is the cost of 1 pound of zucchini and 1 pound of tomatoes at the farm stand?

_____

Unit 3 Performance Tasks

1. **CAREERS IN MATH** Hydraulic Engineer A hydraulic engineer is studying the pressure in a particular fluid. The pressure is equal to the atmospheric pressure 101 kN/m plus 8 kN/m for every meter below the surface, where kN/m is kilonewtons per meter, a unit of pressure.

a. Write an expression for the pressure at a depth of d_1 meters below the liquid surface.

_____

b. Write and solve an equation to find the depth at which the pressure is 200 kN/m.

_____

c. The hydraulic engineer alters the density of the fluid so that the pressure at depth d_2 below the surface is atmospheric pressure 101 kN/m plus 9 kN/m for every meter below the surface. Write an expression for the pressure at depth d_2.

_____

d. If the pressure at depth d_1 in the first fluid is equal to the pressure at depth d_2 in the second fluid, what is the relationship between d_1 and d_2? Explain how you found your answer.

_____

_____

_____

Selected Response

1. Ricardo and John start swimming from the same location. Ricardo starts 15 seconds before John and swims at a rate of 3 feet per second. John swims at a rate of 4 feet per second in the same direction as Ricardo. Which equation could you solve to find how long it will take John to catch up with Ricardo?

   (A) $4t + 3 = 3t$

   (B) $4t + 60 = 3t$

   (C) $3t + 3 = 4t$

   (D) $3t + 45 = 4t$

2. Gina and Rhonda work for different real estate agencies. Gina earns a monthly salary of $5,000 plus a 6% commission on her sales. Rhonda earns a monthly salary of $6,500 plus a 4% commission on her sales. How much must each sell to earn the same amount in a month?

   (A) $1,500   (C) $75,000

   (B) $15,000   (D) $750,000

3. What is the slope of the line?

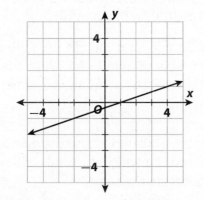

   (A) -3 (C) $\frac{1}{3}$

   (B) $-\frac{1}{3}$ (D) 3

4. What is the solution of the system of equations?
$$\begin{cases} y = 2x - 3 \\ 5x + y = 11 \end{cases}$$

   (A) $(2, 1)$

   (B) $(1, 2)$

   (C) $(3, -4)$

   (D) $(1, -1)$

5. Alana is having a party. She bought 3 rolls of streamers and 2 packages of balloons for $10.00. She realized she needed more supplies and went back to the store and bought 2 more rolls of streamers and 1 more package of balloons for $6.25. How much did each roll of streamers and each package of balloons cost?

   (A) streamers: $3.00, balloons: $2.00

   (B) streamers: $2.00, balloons: $1.00

   (C) streamers: $1.25, balloons: $2.50

   (D) streamers: $2.50, balloons: $1.25

6. The triangle and the rectangle have the same perimeter.

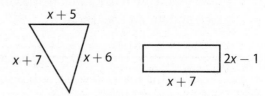

   Find the value of x.

   (A) 2

   (B) 10

   (C) 18

   (D) 24

7. What is the solution of the equation $8(3x + 4) = 2(12x - 8)$?

Ⓐ $x = -2$

Ⓑ $x = 2$

Ⓒ no solution

Ⓓ infinitely many solutions

8. A square wall tile has an area of 58,800 square millimeters. Between which two measurements is the length of one side?

Ⓐ between 24 and 25 millimeters

Ⓑ between 76 and 77 millimeters

Ⓒ between 242 and 243 millimeters

Ⓓ between 766 and 767 millimeters

Mini-Task

9. Lily and Alex went to a Mexican restaurant. Lily paid $9 for 2 tacos and 3 enchiladas, and Alex paid $12.50 for 3 tacos and 4 enchiladas.

a. Write a system of equations that represents this situation.

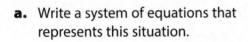

b. Use the system of equations to find how much the restaurant charges for a taco and for an enchilada.

c. Describe the method you used to solve the system of equations.

Hot Tip! Solutions of a system of two equations must make both equations true. Check solutions in both equations.

10. Use the system of equations to answer the questions below.

$$\begin{cases} 4x + 2y = -8 \\ 2x + y = 4 \end{cases}$$

a. Graph the equations on the grid.

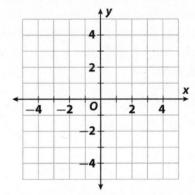

b. How many solutions does the system of equations have? Explain your answer.

11. Isaac wants to join a gym. He checked out the membership fees at two gyms.

Gym A charges a new member fee of $65 and $20 per month.

Gym B charges a new member fee of $25 and $35 per month, but Isaac will get a discount of 20% on the monthly fee.

a. Write an equation you can use to find the number of months for which the total costs at the gyms are the same.

b. Solve the equation to find the number of months for which the total costs of the gyms are the same.

Transformational Geometry

MODULE **9**

Transformations and Congruence

COMMON CORE 8.G.1, 8.G.2, 8.G.3

MODULE **10**

Transformations and Similarity

COMMON CORE 8.G.3, 8.G.4

© Houghton Mifflin Harcourt Publishing Company • Image Credits:
© Digital Vision/Getty Images

CAREERS IN MATH

Contractor A contractor is engaged in the construction, repair, and dismantling of structures such as buildings, bridges, and roads. Contractors use math when researching and implementing building codes, making measurements and scaling models, and in financial management.

If you are interested in a career as a contractor, you should study the following mathematical subjects:
- Business Math
- Geometry
- Algebra
- Trigonometry

Research other careers that require the use of business math and scaling.

Unit 4 Performance Task

At the end of the unit, check out how **contractors** use math.

Vocabulary Preview

Use the puzzle to preview key vocabulary from this unit. Unscramble the circled letters within found words to answer the riddle at the bottom of the page.

```
W T C F V A F I L I T U G N S
M U J L O C Z H B R S D E O W
F E Q V H B T E A N T P X I A
M Y J G B O G N P K G G B T Q
N X L H A A S E V Z R U B C W
L O X D M L A G R H H L R U A
G P I I A E M X K V A K X D K
B D E T N E M E G R A L N E A
W R I E C A N R E Y M A T R P
P O G L K E R O T A T I O N R
N Z Y E A C L R O V Z S P I U
U Y T J N T Q F N B X G G C J
O N E R Z I I P E I Y F A B W
I F V U C M S O G R P Q K B W
C Q T U I C C U N L N T L D Y
```

The input of a transformation. (Lesson 9.1)

A transformation that flips a figure across a line. (Lesson 9.2)

A transformation that slides a figure along a straight line. (Lesson 9.1)

A transformation that turns a figure around a given point. (Lesson 9.3)

The product of a figure made larger by dilation. (Lesson 10.1)

The product of a figure made smaller by dilation. (Lesson 10.1)

Scaled replicas that change the size but not the shape of a figure. (Lesson 10.1)

Q: What do you call an angle that's broken?

A: A __ __ __ __ __ __ __ __ __ __ __ __ __ __!

Transformations and Congruence

ESSENTIAL QUESTION

How can you use transformations and congruence to solve real-world problems?

Real-World Video

When a marching band lines up and marches across the field, they are modeling a translation. As they march, they maintain size and orientation. A translation is one type of transformation.

 my.hrw.com

GO DIGITAL

my.hrw.com

my.hrw.com

Go digital with your write-in student edition, accessible on any device.

Math On the Spot

Scan with your smart phone to jump directly to the online edition, video tutor, and more.

Animated Math

Interactively explore key concepts to see how math works.

Personal Math Trainer

Get immediate feedback and help as you work through practice sets.

Are YOU Ready?

Complete these exercises to review skills you will need for this module.

Integer Operations

EXAMPLE	$-3 - (-6) = -3 + 6$	To subtract an integer, add its opposite. The signs are different, so find the difference of the absolute values: $6 - 3 = 3$. Use the sign of the number with the greater absolute value.
	$= \lvert-3\rvert - \lvert6\rvert$	
	$= 3$	

Find each difference.

1. $5 - (-9)$

_____

2. $-6 - 8$

_____

3. $2 - 9$

_____

4. $-10 - (-6)$

_____

5. $3 - (-11)$

_____

6. $12 - 7$

_____

7. $-4 - 11$

_____

8. $0 - (-12)$

_____

Measure Angles

EXAMPLE

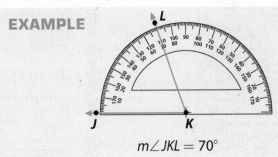

$m\angle JKL = 70°$

Place the center point of the protractor on the angle's vertex.

Align one ray with the base of the protractor.

Read the angle measure where the other ray intersects the semicircle.

Use a protractor to measure each angle.

9.

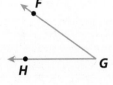

_____

10.

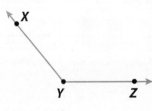

_____

11.

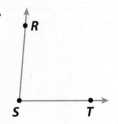

_____

Reading Start-Up

Visualize Vocabulary

Use the ✔ words to complete the graphic organizer. You will put one word in each oval.

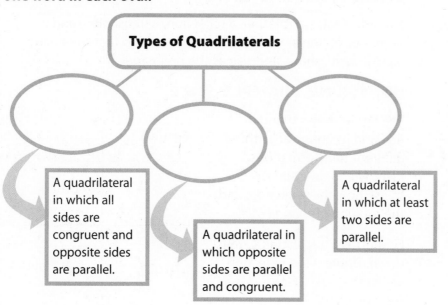

Types of Quadrilaterals

A quadrilateral in which all sides are congruent and opposite sides are parallel.

A quadrilateral in which opposite sides are parallel and congruent.

A quadrilateral in which at least two sides are parallel.

Vocabulary

Review Words

coordinate plane (*plano cartesiano*)

✔ parallelogram (*paralelogramo*)

quadrilateral (*cuadrilátero*)

✔ rhombus (*rombo*)

✔ trapezoid (*trapecio*)

Preview Words

center of rotation (*centro de rotación*)

congruent (*congruente*)

image (*imagen*)

line of reflection (*línea de reflexión*)

preimage (*imagen original*)

reflection (*reflexión*)

rotation (*rotación*)

transformation (*transformación*)

translation (*traslación*)

Understand Vocabulary

Match the term on the left to the correct expression on the right.

1. transformation
2. reflection
3. translation

A. A function that describes a change in the position, size, or shape of a figure.

B. A function that slides a figure along a straight line.

C. A transformation that flips a figure across a line.

Active Reading

Booklet Before beginning the module, create a booklet to help you learn the concepts in this module. Write the main idea of each lesson on each page of the booklet. As you study each lesson, write important details that support the main idea, such as vocabulary and formulas. Refer to your finished booklet as you work on assignments and study for tests.

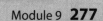

Unpacking the Standards

Understanding the standards and the vocabulary terms in the standards will help you know exactly what you are expected to learn in this module.

COMMON CORE 8.G.2

Understand that a two-dimensional figure is congruent to another if the second can be obtained from the first by a sequence of rotations, reflections, and translations; given two congruent figures, describe a sequence that exhibits the congruence between them.

What It Means to You

You will identify a rotation, a reflection, a translation, and a sequence of transformations, and understand that the image has the same shape and size as the preimage.

UNPACKING EXAMPLE 8.G.2

The figure shows triangle *ABC* and its image after three different transformations. Identify and describe the translation, the reflection, and the rotation of triangle *ABC*.

Figure 1 is a translation 4 units down. Figure 2 is a reflection across the *y*-axis. Figure 3 is a rotation of 180°.

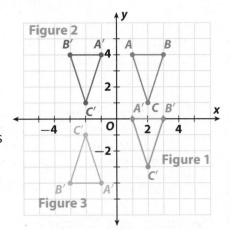

COMMON CORE 8.G.3

Describe the effect of dilations, translations, rotations, and reflections on two-dimensional figures using coordinates.

What It Means to You

You can use an algebraic representation to translate, reflect, or rotate a two-dimensional figure.

UNPACKING EXAMPLE 8.G.3

Rectangle *RSTU* with vertices $(-4, 1)$, $(-1, 1)$, $(-1, -3)$, and $(-4, -3)$ is reflected across the *y*-axis. Find the coordinates of the image.

The rule to reflect across the *y*-axis is to change the sign of the *x*-coordinate.

Coordinates	Reflect across the y-axis (−x, y)	Coordinates of image
$(-4, 1)$, $(-1, 1)$, $(-1, -3)$, $(-4, -3)$	$(-(-4), 1)$, $(-(-1), 1)$, $(-(-1), -3)$, $(-(-4), -3)$	$(4, 1)$, $(1, 1)$, $(1, -3)$, $(4, -3)$

The coordinates of the image are $(4, 1)$, $(1, 1)$, $(1, -3)$, and $(4, -3)$.

Visit **my.hrw.com** to see all the **Common Core Standards** unpacked.

⏻ my.hrw.com

Properties of Translations

COMMON CORE 8.G.1

Verify experimentally the properties of...translations. *Also 8.G.1a, 8.G.1b, 8.G.1c, 8.G.3*

? **ESSENTIAL QUESTION**

How do you describe the properties of translation and their effect on the congruence and orientation of figures?

EXPLORE ACTIVITY 1 COMMON CORE 8.G.1

Exploring Translations

You learned that a function is a rule that assigns exactly one output to each input. A **transformation** is a function that describes a change in the position, size, or shape of a figure. The input of a transformation is the **preimage**, and the output of a transformation is the **image**.

A **translation** is a transformation that slides a figure along a straight line.

The triangle shown on the grid is the preimage (input). The arrow shows the motion of a translation and how point A is translated to point A′.

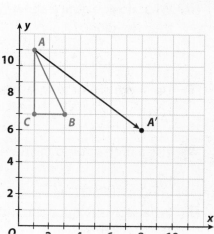

A Trace triangle *ABC* onto a piece of paper. Cut out your traced triangle.

B Slide your triangle along the arrow to model the translation that maps point *A* to point *A′*.

C The image of the translation is the triangle produced by the translation. Sketch the image of the translation.

D The vertices of the image are labeled using prime notation. For example, the image of *A* is *A′*. Label the images of points *B* and *C*.

E Describe the motion modeled by the translation.

Move _____ units right and _____ units down.

F Check that the motion you described in part **E** is the same motion that maps point *A* onto *A′*, point *B* onto *B′*, and point *C* onto *C′*.

Reflect

1. How is the orientation of the triangle affected by the translation?

_____

Properties of Translations

Use trapezoid *TRAP* to investigate the properties of translations.

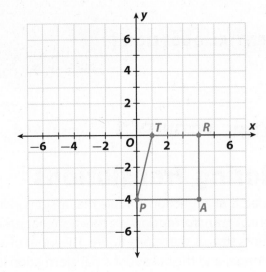

A   Trace the trapezoid onto a piece of paper. Cut out your traced trapezoid.

B   Place your trapezoid on top of the trapezoid in the figure. Then translate your trapezoid 5 units to the left and 3 units up. Sketch the image of the translation by tracing your trapezoid in this new location. Label the vertices of the image *T′, R′, A′,* and *P′.*

C   Use a ruler to measure the sides of trapezoid *TRAP* in centimeters.

     TR = _____   *RA* = _____   *AP* = _____   *TP* = _____

D   Use a ruler to measure the sides of trapezoid *T′R′A′P′* in centimeters.

     T′R′ = _____   *R′A′* = _____   *A′P′* = _____   *T′P′* = _____

E   What do you notice about the lengths of corresponding sides of the two figures?

_____

F   Use a protractor to measure the angles of trapezoid *TRAP.*

     m∠T = _____   *m∠R* = _____   *m∠A* = _____   *m∠P* = _____

G   Use a protractor to measure the angles of trapezoid *T′R′A′P′.*

     m∠T′ = _____   *m∠R′* = _____   *m∠A′* = _____   *m∠P′* = _____

H   What do you notice about the measures of corresponding angles of the two figures?

_____

I   Which sides of trapezoid *TRAP* are parallel? How do you know?

_____

     Which sides of trapezoid *T′R′A′P′* are parallel? _____

     What do you notice? _____

_____

Reflect

2. **Make a Conjecture** Use your results from parts **E**, **H**, and **I** to make a conjecture about translations.

_____

_____

3. Two figures that have the same size and shape are called *congruent*. What can you say about translations and congruence?

_____

Graphing Translations

To translate a figure in the coordinate plane, translate each of its vertices. Then connect the vertices to form the image.

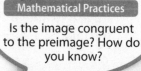
EXAMPLE 1

COMMON CORE 8.G.3

The figure shows triangle *XYZ*. Graph the image of the triangle after a translation of 4 units to the right and 1 unit up.

STEP 1 Translate point *X*.

Count right 4 units and up 1 unit and plot point *X'*.

STEP 2 Translate point *Y*.

Count right 4 units and up 1 unit and plot point *Y'*.

STEP 3 Translate point *Z*.

Count right 4 units and up 1 unit and plot point *Z'*.

STEP 4 Connect *X'*, *Y'*, and *Z'* to form triangle *X'Y'Z'*.

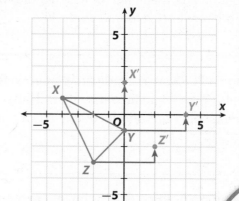

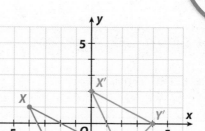

Each vertex is moved 4 units right and 1 unit up.

Math Talk
Mathematical Practices

Is the image congruent to the preimage? How do you know?

© Houghton Mifflin Harcourt Publishing Company

YOUR TURN

4. The figure shows parallelogram *ABCD*. Graph the image of the parallelogram after a translation of 5 units to the left and 2 units down.

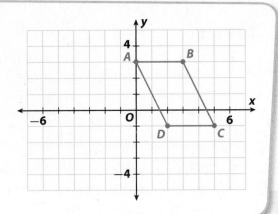

Guided Practice

1. **Vocabulary** A _____ is a change in the position, size, or shape of a figure.

2. **Vocabulary** When you perform a transformation of a figure on the coordinate plane, the input of the transformation is called

   the _____, and the output of the transformation is

   called the _____.

3. Joni translates a right triangle 2 units down and 4 units to the right. How does the orientation of the image of the triangle compare with the orientation of the preimage? (Explore Activity 1)

   _____

4. Rashid drew rectangle *PQRS* on a coordinate plane. He then translated the rectangle 3 units up and 3 units to the left and labeled the image *P'Q'R'S'*. How do rectangle *PQRS* and rectangle *P'Q'R'S'* compare? (Explore Activity 2)

   _____

5. The figure shows trapezoid *WXYZ*. Graph the image of the trapezoid after a translation of 4 units up and 2 units to the left. (Example 1)

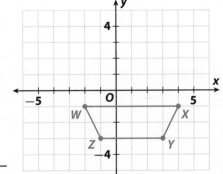

? ESSENTIAL QUESTION CHECK-IN

6. What are the properties of translations?

   _____

   _____

9.1 Independent Practice

COMMON CORE 8.G.1, 8.G.3

Personal Math Trainer

Online Assessment and Intervention

my.hrw.com

7. The figure shows triangle *DEF*.

   a. Graph the image of the triangle after the translation that maps point *D* to point *D'*.

   b. How would you describe the translation?

   _____

   _____

   c. How does the image of triangle *DEF* compare with the preimage?

   _____

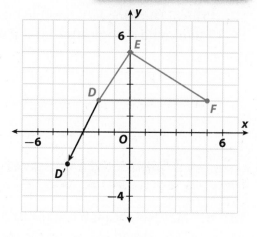

8. a. Graph quadrilateral *KLMN* with vertices *K*(−3, 2), *L*(2, 2), *M*(0, −3), and *N*(−4, 0) on the coordinate grid.

   b. On the same coordinate grid, graph the image of quadrilateral *KLMN* after a translation of 3 units to the right and 4 units up.

   c. Which side of the image is congruent to side $\overline{LM}$?

   _____

   Name three other pairs of congruent sides.

   _____

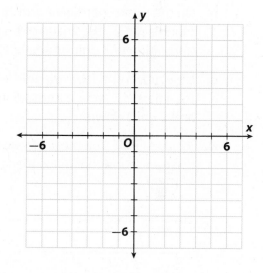

Draw the image of the figure after each translation.

9. 4 units left and 2 units down

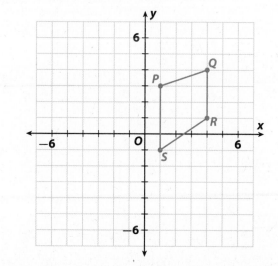

10. 5 units right and 3 units up

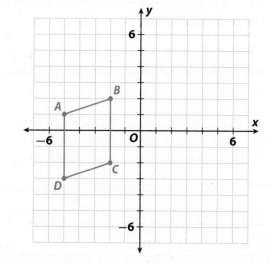

11. The figure shows the ascent of a hot air balloon. How would you describe the translation?

_____

_____

12. Critical Thinking Is it possible that the orientation of a figure could change after it is translated? Explain.

_____

_____

_____

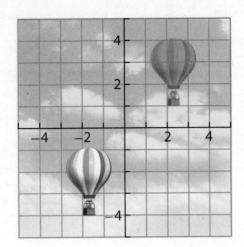

 **FOCUS ON HIGHER ORDER THINKING**

13. a. Multistep Graph triangle *XYZ* with vertices *X*(−2, −5), *Y*(2, −2), and *Z*(4, −4) on the coordinate grid.

  b. On the same coordinate grid, graph and label triangle *X′Y′Z′*, the image of triangle *XYZ* after a translation of 3 units to the left and 6 units up.

  c. Now graph and label triangle *X″Y″Z″*, the image of triangle *X′Y′Z′* after a translation of 1 unit to the left and 2 units down.

  d. Analyze Relationships How would you describe the translation that maps triangle *XYZ* onto triangle *X″Y″Z″*?

_____

_____

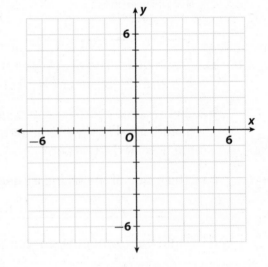

14. Critical Thinking The figure shows rectangle *P′Q′R′S′*, the image of rectangle *PQRS* after a translation of 5 units to the right and 7 units up. Graph and label the preimage *PQRS*.

15. Communicate Mathematical Ideas Explain why the image of a figure after a translation is congruent to its preimage.

_____

_____

_____

_____

_____

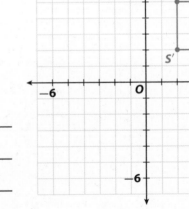

Properties of Reflections

COMMON CORE **8.G.1**
Verify experimentally the properties of ... reflections.... Also 8.G.1a, 8.G.1b, 8.G.1c, 8.G.3

? ESSENTIAL QUESTION

How do you describe the properties of reflection and their effect on the congruence and orientation of figures?

EXPLORE ACTIVITY 1 COMMON CORE **8.G.1**

Exploring Reflections

A **reflection** is a transformation that flips a figure across a line. The line is called the **line of reflection**. Each point and its image are the same distance from the line of reflection.

The triangle shown on the grid is the preimage. You will explore reflections across the x- and y-axes.

A Trace triangle *ABC* and the *x*- and *y*-axes onto a piece of paper.

B Fold your paper along the *x*-axis and trace the image of the triangle on the opposite side of the *x*-axis. Unfold your paper and label the vertices of the image *A′*, *B′*, and *C′*.

C What is the line of reflection for this transformation?

_____

D Find the perpendicular distance from each point to the line of reflection.

Point *A* _____   Point *B* _____   Point *C* _____

E Find the perpendicular distance from each point to the line of reflection.

Point *A′* _____   Point *B′* _____   Point *C′* _____

F What do you notice about the distances you found in **D** and **E**?

_____

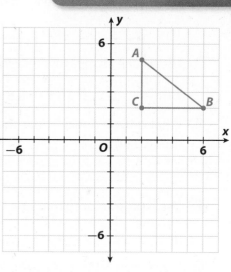

Reflect

1. Fold your paper from **A** along the *y*-axis and trace the image of triangle *ABC* on the opposite side. Label the vertices of the image *A″*, *B″*, and *C″*. What is the line of reflection for this transformation? _____

2. How does each image in your drawings compare with its preimage?

_____

Properties of Reflections

Use trapezoid *TRAP* to investigate the properties of reflections.

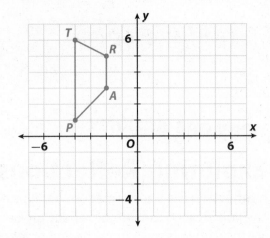

A Trace the trapezoid onto a piece of paper. Cut out your traced trapezoid.

B Place your trapezoid on top of the trapezoid in the figure. Then reflect your trapezoid across the *y*-axis. Sketch the image of the reflection by tracing your trapezoid in this new location. Label the vertices of the image *T′*, *R′*, *A′*, and *P′*.

C Use a ruler to measure the sides of trapezoid *TRAP* in centimeters.

TR = _____   RA = _____   AP = _____   TP = _____

D Use a ruler to measure the sides of trapezoid *T′R′A′P′* in centimeters.

T′R′ = _____   R′A′ = _____   A′P′ = _____   T′P′ = _____

E What do you notice about the lengths of corresponding sides of the two figures?

_____

F Use a protractor to measure the angles of trapezoid *TRAP*.

m∠T = _____   m∠R = _____   m∠A = _____   m∠P = _____

G Use a protractor to measure the angles of trapezoid *T′R′A′P′*.

m∠T′ = _____   m∠R′ = _____   m∠A′ = _____   m∠P′ = _____

H What do you notice about the measures of corresponding angles of the two figures?

_____

I Which sides of trapezoid *TRAP* are parallel? _____

Which sides of trapezoid *T′R′A′P′* are parallel? _____
What do you notice?

_____

_____

Reflect

3. **Make a Conjecture** Use your results from  **E** , **H** , and **I** to make a conjecture about reflections.

_____

_____

_____

Math Talk

Mathematical Practices

What can you say about reflections and congruence?

Graphing Reflections

To reflect a figure across a line of reflection, reflect each of its vertices. Then connect the vertices to form the image. Remember that each point and its image are the same distance from the line of reflection.

Math On the Spot

my.hrw.com

EXAMPLE 1

COMMON CORE 8.G.3

The figure shows triangle XYZ. Graph the image of the triangle after a reflection across the x-axis.

STEP 1 Reflect point X.

Point X is 3 units below the x-axis. Count 3 units above the x-axis and plot point X'.

STEP 2 Reflect point Y.

Point Y is 1 unit below the x-axis. Count 1 unit above the x-axis and plot point Y'.

STEP 3 Reflect point Z.

Point Z is 5 units below the x-axis. Count 5 units above the x-axis and plot point Z'.

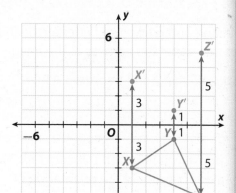

STEP 4 Connect X', Y', and Z' to form triangle X'Y'Z'.

Each vertex of the image is the same distance from the x-axis as the corresponding vertex in the original figure.

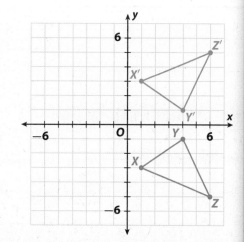

My Notes

© Houghton Mifflin Harcourt Publishing Company

Lesson 9.2 **287**

YOUR TURN

4. The figure shows pentagon *ABCDE*. Graph the image of the pentagon after a reflection across the *y*-axis.

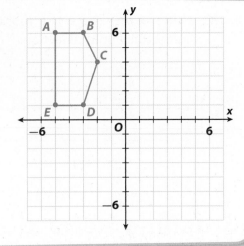

Guided Practice

1. **Vocabulary** A reflection is a transformation that flips a figure across

   a line called the _____.

2. The figure shows trapezoid *ABCD*. (Explore Activities 1 and 2 and Example 1)

   a. Graph the image of the trapezoid after a reflection across the *x*-axis. Label the vertices of the image.

   b. How do trapezoid *ABCD* and trapezoid *A'B'C'D'* compare?

   _____

   c. **What If?** Suppose you reflected trapezoid *ABCD* across the *y*-axis. How would the orientation of the image of the trapezoid compare with the orientation of the preimage?

   _____

   _____

   _____

   _____

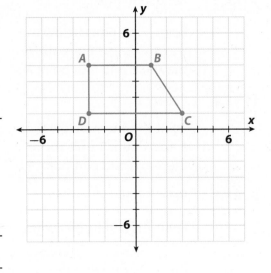

? ESSENTIAL QUESTION CHECK-IN

3. What are the properties of reflections?

   _____

   _____

9.2 Independent Practice

 8.G.1, 8.G.3

Personal Math Trainer

Online Assessment and Intervention

my.hrw.com

The graph shows four right triangles. Use the graph for Exercises 4–7.

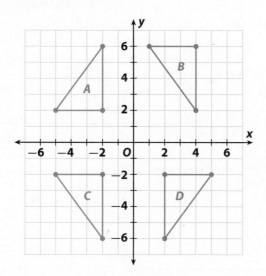

4. Which two triangles are reflections of each other across the *x*-axis?

_____

5. For which two triangles is the line of reflection the *y*-axis?

_____

6. Which triangle is a translation of triangle *C*? How would you describe the translation?

_____

_____

7. Which triangles are congruent? How do you know?

_____

_____

_____

_____

_____

8. a. Graph quadrilateral *WXYZ* with vertices *W*(−2, −2), *X*(3, 1), *Y*(5, −1), and *Z*(4, −6) on the coordinate grid.

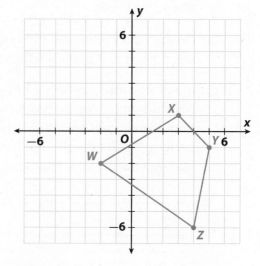

b. On the same coordinate grid, graph quadrilateral *W′X′Y′Z′*, the image of quadrilateral *WXYZ* after a reflection across the *x*-axis.

c. Which side of the image is congruent to side $\overline{YZ}$?

_____

Name three other pairs of congruent sides.

_____

_____

d. Which angle of the image is congruent to ∠*X*?

_____

Name three other pairs of congruent angles.

_____

_____

9. Critical Thinking Is it possible that the image of a point after a reflection could be the same point as the preimage? Explain.

_____

_____

10. a. Graph the image of the figure shown after a reflection across the *y*-axis.

b. On the same coordinate grid, graph the image of the figure you drew in part **a** after a reflection across the *x*-axis.

c. Make a Conjecture What other sequence of transformations would produce the same final image from the original preimage? Check your answer by performing the transformations. Then make a conjecture that generalizes your findings.

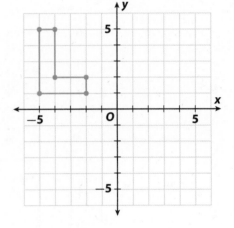

_____

_____

_____

_____

_____

11. a. Graph triangle *DEF* with vertices *D*(2, 6), *E*(5, 6), and *F*(5, 1) on the coordinate grid.

b. Next graph triangle *D′E′F′*, the image of triangle *DEF* after a reflection across the *y*-axis.

c. On the same coordinate grid, graph triangle *D″E″F″*, the image of triangle *D′E′F′* after a translation of 7 units down and 2 units to the right.

d. Analyze Relationships Find a different sequence of transformations that will transform triangle *DEF* to triangle *D″E″F″*.

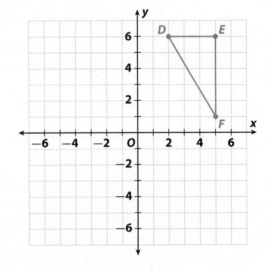

_____

_____

_____

_____

LESSON 9.3 Properties of Rotations

COMMON CORE 8.G.1

Verify experimentally the properties of rotations.... *Also 8.G.1a, 8.G.1b, 8.G.1c, 8.G.3*

? ESSENTIAL QUESTION

How do you describe the properties of rotation and their effect on the congruence and orientation of figures?

EXPLORE ACTIVITY 1 COMMON CORE **8.G.1**

Exploring Rotations

A **rotation** is a transformation that turns a figure around a given point called the **center of rotation**. The image has the same size and shape as the preimage.

The triangle shown on the grid is the preimage. You will use the origin as the center of rotation.

A Trace triangle *ABC* onto a piece of paper. Cut out your traced triangle.

B Rotate your triangle 90° counterclockwise about the origin. The side of the triangle that lies along the *x*-axis should now lie along the *y*-axis.

C Sketch the image of the rotation. Label the images of points *A*, *B*, and *C* as *A'*, *B'*, and *C'*.

D Describe the motion modeled by the rotation.

Rotate _____ degrees _____ about the origin.

E Check that the motion you described in **D** is the same motion that maps point *A* onto *A'*, point *B* onto *B'*, and point *C* onto *C'*.

Reflect

1. **Communicate Mathematical Ideas** How are the size and the orientation of the triangle affected by the rotation?

_____

_____

_____

2. Rotate triangle *ABC* 90° clockwise about the origin. Sketch the result on the coordinate grid above. Label the image vertices *A''*, *B''*, and *C''*.

© Houghton Mifflin Harcourt Publishing Company • Image Credits: ©IKO/Fotolia

Lesson 9.3 **291**

Properties of Rotations

Use trapezoid *TRAP* to investigate the properties of rotations.

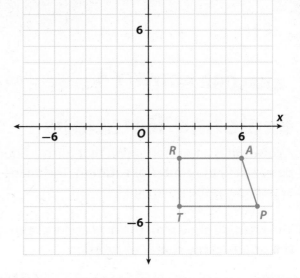

A Trace the trapezoid onto a piece of paper. Include the portion of the *x*- and *y*-axes bordering the third quadrant. Cut out your tracing.

B Place your trapezoid and axes on top of those in the figure. Then use the axes to help rotate your trapezoid 180° counterclockwise about the origin. Sketch the image of the rotation of your trapezoid in this new location. Label the vertices of the image *T′*, *R′*, *A′*, and *P′*.

C Use a ruler to measure the sides of trapezoid *TRAP* in centimeters.

TR = _____   RA = _____

AP = _____   TP = _____

D Use a ruler to measure the sides of trapezoid *T′R′A′P′* in centimeters.

T′R′ = _____   *R′A′* = _____

A′P′ = _____   *T′P′* = _____

E What do you notice about the lengths of corresponding sides of the two figures?

_____

F Use a protractor to measure the angles of trapezoid *TRAP*.

m∠T = _____   *m∠R* = _____   *m∠A* = _____   *m∠P* = _____

G Use a protractor to measure the angles of trapezoid *T′R′A′P′*.

m∠T′ = _____   *m∠R′* = _____   *m∠A′* = _____   *m∠P′* = _____

H What do you notice about the measures of corresponding angles of the two figures?

_____

I Which sides of trapezoid *TRAP* are parallel? _____

Which sides of trapezoid *T′R′A′P′* are parallel? _____

What do you notice? _____

_____

Reflect

3. Make a Conjecture Use your results from **E**, **H**, and **I** to make a conjecture about rotations.

_____

_____

4. Place your tracing back in its original position. Then perform a 180° _clockwise_ rotation about the origin. Compare the result with the result of the transformation in **B**.

_____

_____

Graphing Rotations

To rotate a figure in the coordinate plane, rotate each of its vertices. Then connect the vertices to form the image.

Math On the Spot
my.hrw.com

EXAMPLE 1

COMMON CORE 8.G.3

The figure shows triangle *ABC*. Graph the image of triangle *ABC* after a rotation of 90° clockwise.

STEP 1 Rotate the figure clockwise from the *y*-axis to the *x*-axis. Point *A* will still be at (0, 0).

Point *B* is 2 units to the left of the *y*-axis, so point *B'* is 2 units above the *x*-axis.

Point *C* is 2 units to the right of the *y*-axis, so point *C'* is 2 units below the *x*-axis.

STEP 2 Connect *A'*, *B'*, and *C'* to form the image triangle *A'B'C'*.

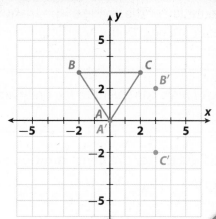

Math Talk
Mathematical Practices

How is the orientation of the triangle affected by the rotation?

Reflect

5. Is the image congruent to the preimage? How do you know?

_____

_____

_____

**Personal
Math Trainer**

Online Assessment
and Intervention

⏻ my.hrw.com

YOUR TURN

**Graph the image of quadrilateral *ABCD*
after each rotation.**

6. 180°

7. 270° clockwise

8. Find the coordinates of Point *C* after a 90°
counterclockwise rotation followed by a
180° rotation.

_____

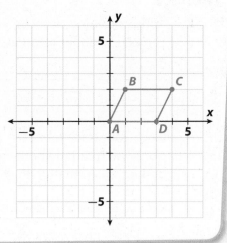

Guided Practice

1. Vocabulary A rotation is a transformation that turns a figure around a

given _____ called the center of rotation.

Siobhan rotates a right triangle 90° counterclockwise about the origin.

2. How does the orientation of the image of the triangle compare with the
orientation of the preimage? (Explore Activity 1)

_____

3. Is the image of the triangle congruent to the preimage? (Explore Activity 2)

_____

Draw the image of the figure after the given rotation about the origin. (Example 1)

4. 90° counterclockwise

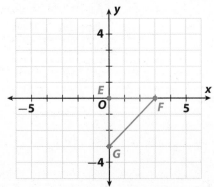

5. 180°

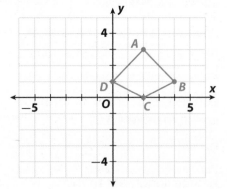

? **ESSENTIAL QUESTION CHECK-IN**

6. What are the properties of rotations?

_____

© Houghton Mifflin Harcourt Publishing Company

9.3 Independent Practice

 8.G.1, 8.G.3

Personal Math Trainer
Online Assessment and Intervention
my.hrw.com

7. The figure shows triangle *ABC* and a rotation of the triangle about the origin.

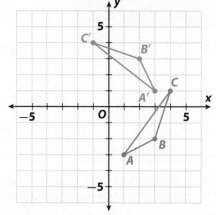

   a. How would you describe the rotation?

   _____

   _____

   b. What are the coordinates of the image?

   _____, _____, _____

8. The graph shows a figure and its image after a transformation.

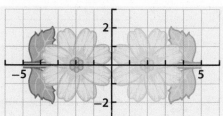

   a. How would you describe this as a rotation?

   _____

   _____

   b. Can you describe this as a transformation other than a rotation? Explain.

   _____

   _____

9. What type of rotation will preserve the orientation of the H-shaped figure in the grid?

   _____

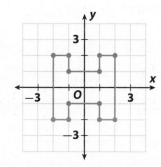

10. A point with coordinates $(-2, -3)$ is rotated 90° clockwise about the origin. What are the coordinates of its image?

   _____

Complete the table with rotations of 180° or 90°. Include the direction of rotation for rotations of 90°.

	Shape in quadrant	Image in quadrant	Rotation
11.	I	IV	
12.	III	I	
13.	IV	III	

Draw the image of the figure after the given rotation about the origin.

14. 180°

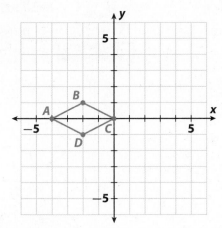

15. 270° counterclockwise

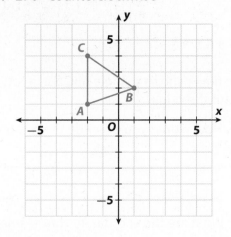

16. Is there a rotation for which the orientation of the image is always the same as that of the preimage? If so, what?

_____

17. Problem Solving Lucas is playing a game where he has to rotate a figure for it to fit in an open space. Every time he clicks a button, the figure rotates 90 degrees clockwise. How many times does he need to click the button so that each figure returns to its original orientation?

Figure A _____

Figure B _____

Figure C _____

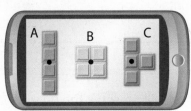

18. Make a Conjecture Triangle *ABC* is reflected across the *y*-axis to form the image *A'B'C'*. Triangle *A'B'C'* is then reflected across the *x*-axis to form the image *A"B"C"*. What type of rotation can be used to describe the relationship between triangle *A"B"C"* and triangle *ABC*?

_____

19. Communicate Mathematical Ideas Point *A* is on the *y*-axis. Describe all possible locations of image *A'* for rotations of 90°, 180°, and 270°. Include the origin as a possible location for *A*.

_____

_____

_____

_____

Algebraic Representations of Transformations

COMMON CORE 8.G.3
Describe the effect of . . . , translations, rotations, and reflections on two-dimensional figures using coordinates.

? ESSENTIAL QUESTION

How can you describe the effect of a translation, rotation, or reflection on coordinates using an algebraic representation?

EXPLORE ACTIVITY COMMON CORE 8.G.3

Algebraic Representations of Translations

The rules shown in the table describe how coordinates change when a figure is translated up, down, right, and left on the coordinate plane.

Math On the Spot
my.hrw.com

Translations	
Right a units	Add a to the x-coordinate: $(x, y) \rightarrow (x + a, y)$
Left a units	Subtract a from the x-coordinate: $(x, y) \rightarrow (x - a, y)$
Up b units	Add b to the y-coordinate: $(x, y) \rightarrow (x, y + b)$
Down b units	Subtract b from the y-coordinate: $(x, y) \rightarrow (x, y - b)$

EXAMPLE 1 Triangle XYZ has vertices X(0, 0), Y(2, 3), and Z(4, −1). Find the vertices of triangle X′Y′Z′ after a translation of 3 units to the right and 1 unit down. Then graph the triangle and its image.

Add 3 to the x-coordinate of each vertex, and subtract 1 from the y-coordinate of each vertex.

STEP 1 Apply the rule to find the vertices of the image.

Vertices of △XYZ	Rule: $(x + 3, y - 1)$	Vertices of △X′Y′Z′
X(0, 0)	(0 + 3, 0 − 1)	X′(___ , ___)
Y(2, 3)	(___ + 3, ___ − 1)	Y′(___ , ___)
Z(4, −1)	(4 + ___ , −1 − ___)	Z′(___ , ___)

STEP 2 Graph the image with triangle XYZ on the coordinate plane.

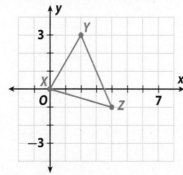

YOUR TURN

1. A rectangle has vertices at (0, −2), (0, 3), (3, −2), and (3, 3). What are the coordinates of the vertices of the image after the translation $(x, y) \rightarrow (x - 6, y - 3)$? Describe the translation.

_____

_____

Personal Math Trainer

Online Assessment and Intervention

⏻ my.hrw.com

Math On the Spot

⏻ my.hrw.com

Algebraic Representations of Reflections

The signs of the coordinates of a figure change when the figure is reflected across the x-axis and y-axis. The table shows the rules for changing the signs of the coordinates after a reflection.

Reflections	
Across the x-axis	Multiply each y-coordinate by −1: $(x, y) \rightarrow (x, -y)$
Across the y-axis	Multiply each x-coordinate by −1: $(x, y) \rightarrow (-x, y)$

My Notes

EXAMPLE 2

COMMON CORE 8.G.3

Rectangle *RSTU* has vertices R(−4, −1), S(−1, −1), T(−1, −3), and U(−4, −3). Find the vertices of rectangle *R'S'T'U'* after a reflection across the y-axis. Then graph the rectangle and its image.

STEP 1 Apply the rule to find the vertices of the image.

> Multiply the x-coordinate of each vertex by −1.

Vertices of *RSTU*	Rule: $(-1 \cdot x, y)$	Vertices of *R'S'T'U'*
R(−4, −1)	(−1 · (−4), − 1)	R'(4, −1)
S(−1, −1)	(−1 · (−1), − 1)	S'(1, −1)
T(−1, −3)	(−1 · (−1), − 3)	T'(1, −3)
U(−4, −3)	(−1 · (−4), − 3)	U'(4, −3)

STEP 2 Graph rectangle *RSTU* and its image.

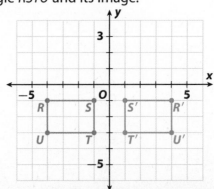

© Houghton Mifflin Harcourt Publishing Company

YOUR TURN

2. Triangle *ABC* has vertices *A*(−2, 6), *B*(0, 5), and *C*(3, −1). Find the vertices of triangle *A'B'C'* after a reflection across the *x*-axis.

Algebraic Representations of Rotations

When points are rotated about the origin, the coordinates of the image can be found using the rules shown in the table.

Rotations	
90° clockwise	Multiply each *x*-coordinate by −1; then switch the *x*- and *y*-coordinates: $(x, y) \rightarrow (y, -x)$
90° counterclockwise	Multiply each *y*-coordinate by −1; then switch the *x*- and *y*-coordinates: $(x, y) \rightarrow (-y, x)$
180°	Multiply both coordinates by −1: $(x, y) \rightarrow (-x, -y)$

EXAMPLE 3 COMMON CORE 8.G.3

Quadrilateral *ABCD* has vertices at *A*(−4, 2), *B*(−3, 4), *C*(2, 3), and *D*(0, 0). Find the vertices of quadrilateral *A'B'C'D'* after a 90° clockwise rotation. Then graph the quadrilateral and its image.

> Multiply the x-coordinate of each vertex by −1, and then switch the x- and y-coordinates.

STEP 1 Apply the rule to find the vertices of the image.

Vertices of *ABCD*	Rule: $(y, -x)$	Vertices of *A'B'C'D'*
A(−4, 2)	$(2, -1 \cdot (-4))$	*A'*(2, 4)
B(−3, 4)	$(4, -1 \cdot (-3))$	*B'*(4, 3)
C(2, 3)	$(3, -1 \cdot 2)$	*C'*(3, −2)
D(0, 0)	$(0, -1 \cdot 0)$	*D'*(0, 0)

STEP 2 Graph the quadrilateral and its image.

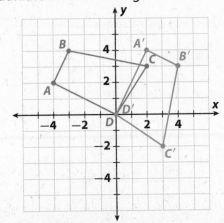

Reflect

3. **Communicate Mathematical Ideas** How would you find the vertices of an image if a figure were rotated 270° clockwise? Explain.

_____

_____

_____

YOUR TURN

4. A triangle has vertices at $J(-2, -4)$, $K(1, 5)$, and $L(2, 2)$. What are the coordinates of the vertices of the image after the triangle is rotated 90° counterclockwise?

_____

Guided Practice

1. Triangle _XYZ_ has vertices $X(-3, -2)$, $Y(-1, 0)$, and $Z(1, -6)$. Find the vertices of triangle $X'Y'Z'$ after a translation of 6 units to the right. Then graph the triangle and its image. (Explore Activity Example 1)

_____

2. Describe what happens to the _x_- and _y_-coordinates after a point is reflected across the _x_-axis. (Example 2)

_____

_____

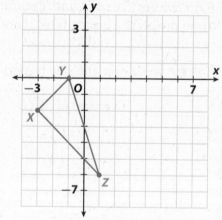

3. Use the rule $(x, y) \rightarrow (y, -x)$ to graph the image of the triangle at right. Then describe the transformation. (Example 3)

_____

❓ ESSENTIAL QUESTION CHECK-IN

4. How do the _x_- and _y_-coordinates change when a figure is translated right _a_ units and down _b_ units?

_____

_____

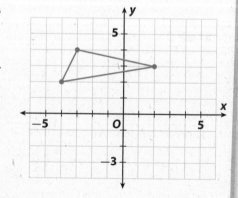

Personal
Math Trainer

Online
Assessment and
Intervention

my.hrw.com

9.4 Independent Practice

**Write an algebraic rule to describe each transformation.
Then describe the transformation.**

5.

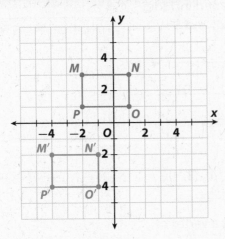

_____

6.

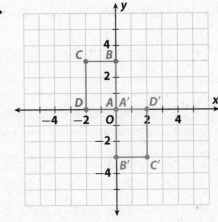

_____

7. Triangle *XYZ* has vertices *X*(6, −2.3), *Y*(7.5, 5), and *Z*(8, 4). When translated, *X'* has coordinates (2.8, −1.3). Write a rule to describe this transformation. Then find the coordinates of *Y'* and *Z'*.

_____

8. Point *L* has coordinates (3, −5). The coordinates of point *L'* after a reflection are (−3, −5). Without graphing, tell which axis point *L* was reflected across. Explain your answer.

_____

_____

9. Use the rule $(x, y) \rightarrow (x − 2, y − 4)$ to graph the image of the rectangle. Then describe the transformation.

_____

_____

10. Parallelogram *ABCD* has vertices *A*(−2, −5½), *B*(−4, −5½), *C*(−3, −2), and *D*(−1, −2). Find the vertices of parallelogram *A'B'C'D'* after a translation of 2½ units down.

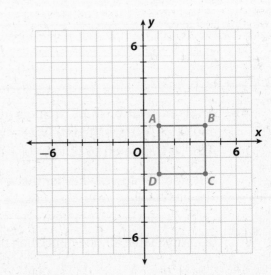

11. Alexandra drew the logo shown on half-inch graph paper. Write a rule that describes the translation Alexandra used to create the shadow on the letter A.

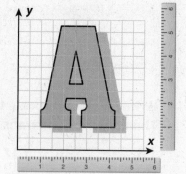

_____

12. Kite *KLMN* has vertices at *K*(1, 3), *L*(2, 4), *M*(3, 3), and *N*(2, 0). After the kite is rotated, *K'* has coordinates (−3, 1). Describe the rotation, and include a rule in your description. Then find the coordinates of *L'*, *M'*, and *N'*.

_____

_____

![H.O.T.] **FOCUS ON HIGHER ORDER THINKING**

13. Make a Conjecture Graph the triangle with vertices (−3, 4), (3, 4), and (−5, −5). Use the transformation (*y*, *x*) to graph its image.

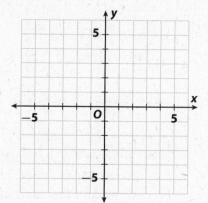

  a. Which vertex of the image has the same coordinates as a vertex of the original figure? Explain why this is true.

    _____

    _____

  b. What is the equation of a line through the origin and this point?

    _____

  c. Describe the transformation of the triangle.

    _____

14. Critical Thinking Mitchell says the point (0, 0) does not change when reflected across the *x*- or *y*-axis or when rotated about the origin. Do you agree with Mitchell? Explain why or why not.

_____

_____

_____

15. Analyze Relationships Triangle *ABC* with vertices *A*(−2, −2), *B*(−3, 1), and *C*(1, 1) is translated by $(x, y) \rightarrow (x − 1, y + 3)$. Then the image, triangle *A'B'C'*, is translated by $(x, y) \rightarrow (x + 4, y − 1)$, resulting in *A"B"C"*.

  a. Find the coordinates for the vertices of triangle *A"B"C"*.

    _____

  b. Write a rule for one translation that maps triangle *ABC* to triangle *A"B"C"*.

_____

Work Area

COMMON CORE **8.G.2**

Understand that a two-dimensional figure is congruent to another if the second can be obtained from the first by a sequence of rotations, reflections, and translations; given two congruent figures, describe a sequence that exhibits the congruence between them.

? ESSENTIAL QUESTION

What is the connection between transformations and figures that have the same shape and size?

EXPLORE ACTIVITY   COMMON CORE 8.G.2

Combining Transformations

Apply the indicated series of transformations to the triangle. Each transformation is applied to the image of the previous transformation, not the original figure. Label each image with the letter of the transformation applied.

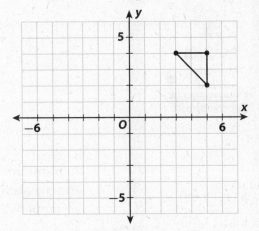

A Reflection across the x-axis

B $(x, y) \rightarrow (x - 3, y)$

C Reflection across the y-axis

D $(x, y) \rightarrow (x, y + 4)$

E Rotation 90° clockwise around the origin

F Compare the size and shape of the final image to that of the original figure.

_____

_____

Reflect

1. Which transformation(s) change the orientation of figures? Which do not?

_____

2. **Make a Conjecture** Two figures have the same size and shape. What does this indicate about the figures?

_____

_____

_____

Congruent Figures

Recall that segments and their images have the same length and angles and their images have the same measure under a translation, reflection, or rotation. Two figures are said to be **congruent** if one can be obtained from the other by a sequence of translations, reflections, and rotations. Congruent figures have the same size and shape.

When you are told that two figures are congruent, there must be a sequence of translations, reflections, and/or rotations that transforms one into the other.

EXAMPLE 1   COMMON CORE 8.G.2

A Identify a sequence of transformations that will transform figure *A* into figure *B*.

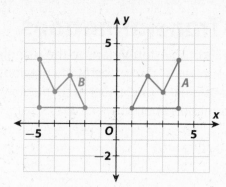

To transform figure *A* into figure *B*, you need to reflect it over the *y*-axis and translate one unit to the left. A sequence of transformations that will accomplish this is $(x, y) \rightarrow (-x, y)$ and $(x, y) \rightarrow (x - 1, y)$.

B Identify a sequence of transformations that will transform figure *B* into figure *C*.

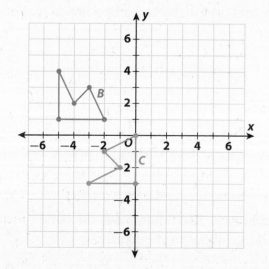

Math Talk

Mathematical Practices

How do you know that the sequence of transformations in Parts B and C must include a rotation?

Any sequence of transformations that changes figure *B* into figure *C* will need to include a rotation. A 90° counterclockwise rotation around the origin would result in the figure being oriented as figure *C*.

However, the rotated figure would be 2 units below and 1 unit to the left of where figure *C* is. You would need to translate the rotated figure up 2 units and right 1 unit.

The sequence of transformations is a 90° counterclockwise rotation about the origin, $(x, y) \rightarrow (-y, x)$, followed by $(x, y) \rightarrow (x + 1, y + 2)$.

C Identify a sequence of transformations that will transform figure *D* into figure *E*.

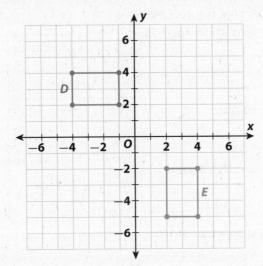

A sequence of transformations that changes figure *D* to figure *E* will need to include a rotation. A 90º clockwise rotation around the origin would result in the figure being oriented as figure *E*.

However, the rotated figure would be 6 units above where figure *E* is. You would need to translate the rotated figure down 6 units.

The sequence of transformations is a 90º clockwise rotation about the origin, $(x, y) \rightarrow (y, -x)$, followed by $(x, y) \rightarrow (x, y - 6)$.

YOUR TURN

3. Identify a sequence of transformations that will transform figure *A* into figure *B*.

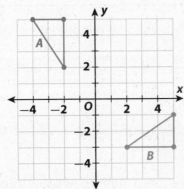

_____

_____

_____

Personal Math Trainer

Online Assessment and Intervention

my.hrw.com

1. Apply the indicated series of transformations to the rectangle. Each transformation is applied to the image of the previous transformation, not the original figure. Label each image with the letter of the transformation applied. (Explore Activity)

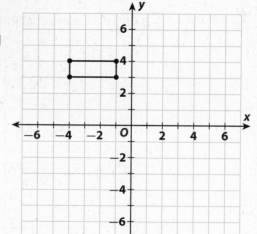

  a. Reflection across the *y*-axis

  b. Rotation 90° clockwise around the origin

  c. $(x, y) \rightarrow (x - 2, y)$

  d. Rotation 90° counterclockwise around the origin

  e. $(x, y) \rightarrow (x - 7, y - 2)$

Identify a sequence of transformations that will transform figure *A* into figure *C*. (Example 1)

2. What transformation is used to transform figure *A* into figure *B*?

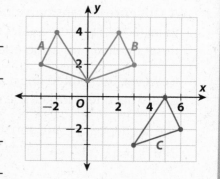

_____

_____

3. What transformation is used to transform figure *B* into figure *C*?

_____

_____

4. What sequence of transformations is used to transform figure *A* into figure *C*? Express the transformations algebraically.

_____

_____

5. **Vocabulary** What does it mean for two figures to be congruent?

_____

_____

© Houghton Mifflin Harcourt Publishing Company

? ESSENTIAL QUESTION CHECK-IN

6. After a sequence of translations, reflections, and rotations, what is true about the first figure and the final figure?

_____

_____

9.5 Independent Practice

COMMON CORE 8.G.2

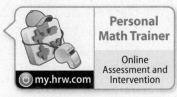

Personal Math Trainer

Online Assessment and Intervention

my.hrw.com

For each given figure A, graph figures B and C using the given sequence of transformations. State whether figures A and C have the same or different orientation.

7.

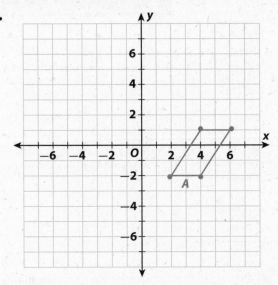

Figure B: a translation of 1 unit to the right and 3 units up

Figure C: a 90° clockwise rotation around the origin

_____

8.

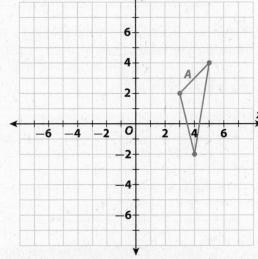

Figure B: a reflection across the y-axis

Figure C: a 180° rotation around the origin

_____

9.

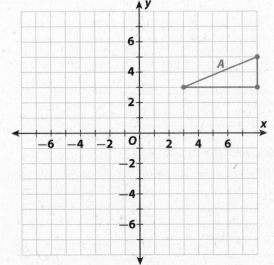

Figure B: a reflection across the y-axis

Figure C: a translation 2 units down

_____

10.

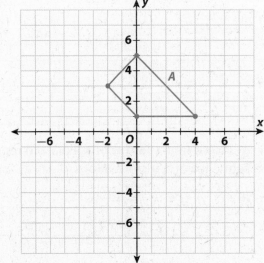

Figure B: a translation 2 units up

Figure C: a rotation of 180° around the origin

_____

11. Represent Real-World Problems A city planner wanted to place the new town library at site *A*. The mayor thought that it would be better at site *B*. What transformations were applied to the building at site *A* to relocate the building to site *B*? Did the mayor change the size or orientation of the library?

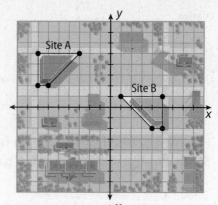

_____

_____

_____

12. Persevere in Problem Solving Find a sequence of three transformations that can be used to obtain figure *D* from figure *A*. Graph the figures *B* and *C* that are created by the transformations.

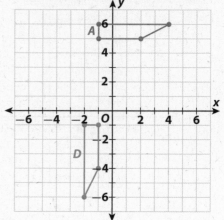

_____

_____

_____

_____

 **FOCUS ON HIGHER ORDER THINKING**

13. Counterexamples The Commutative Properties for Addition and Multiplication state that the order of two numbers being added or multiplied does not change the sum or product. Are translations and rotations commutative? If not, give a counterexample.

_____

_____

_____

_____

_____

14. Multiple Representations For each representation, describe a possible sequence of transformations.

a. $(x, y) \rightarrow (-x - 2, y + 1)$

_____

_____

b. $(x, y) \rightarrow (y, -x - 3)$

_____

_____

Work Area

Ready to Go On?

9.1–9.3 Properties of Translations, Reflections, and Rotations

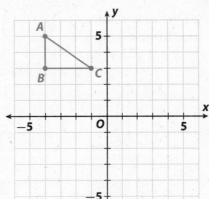

1. Graph the image of triangle *ABC* after a translation of 6 units to the right and 4 units down. Label the vertices of the image *A'*, *B'*, and *C'*.

2. On the same coordinate grid, graph the image of triangle *ABC* after a reflection across the *x*-axis. Label the vertices of the image *A"*, *B"*, and *C"*.

3. Graph the image of *HIJK* after it is rotated 180° about the origin. Label the vertices of the image *H'I'J'K'*.

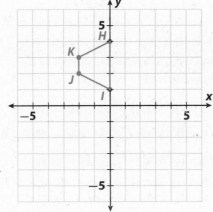

9.4 Algebraic Representations of Transformations

4. A triangle has vertices at (2, 3), (−2, 2), and (−3, 5). What are the coordinates of the vertices of the image after the translation $(x, y) \rightarrow (x + 4, y - 3)$?

_____

9.5 Congruent Figures

5. **Vocabulary** Translations, reflections, and rotations produce a figure

that is _____ to the original figure.

6. Use the coordinate grid for Exercise 3. Reflect *H'I'J'K'* over the *y*-axis, then rotate it 180° about the origin. Label the new figure *H"I"J"K"*.

? ESSENTIAL QUESTION

7. How can you use transformations to solve real-world problems?

_____

_____

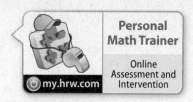
Selected Response

1. What would be the orientation of the figure L after a translation of 8 units to the right and 3 units up?

Ⓐ

Ⓒ

Ⓑ

Ⓓ

2. Figure A is reflected over the *y*-axis and then lowered 6 units. Which sequence describes these transformations?

Ⓐ $(x, y) \rightarrow (x, -y)$ and $(x, y) \rightarrow (x, y - 6)$

Ⓑ $(x, y) \rightarrow (-x, y)$ and $(x, y) \rightarrow (x, y - 6)$

Ⓒ $(x, y) \rightarrow (x, -y)$ and $(x, y) \rightarrow (x - 6, y)$

Ⓓ $(x, y) \rightarrow (-x, y)$ and $(x, y) \rightarrow (x - 6, y)$

3. What quadrant would the triangle be in after a rotation of 90° counterclockwise about the origin?

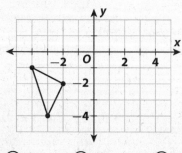

Ⓐ I   Ⓑ II   Ⓒ III   Ⓓ IV

4. Which rational number is greater than $-3\frac{1}{3}$ but less than $-\frac{4}{5}$?

Ⓐ -0.4 Ⓒ -0.19

Ⓑ $-\frac{9}{7}$ Ⓓ $-\frac{22}{5}$

5. Which of the following is **not** true of a trapezoid that has been reflected across the *x*-axis?

Ⓐ The new trapezoid is the same size as the original trapezoid.

Ⓑ The new trapezoid is the same shape as the original trapezoid.

Ⓒ The new trapezoid is in the same orientation as the original trapezoid.

Ⓓ The *x*-coordinates of the new trapezoid are the same as the *x*-coordinates of the original trapezoid.

6. A triangle with coordinates (6, 4), (2, −1), and (−3, 5) is translated 4 units left and rotated 180° about the origin. What are the coordinates of its image?

Ⓐ (2, 4), (−2, −1), (−7, 5)

Ⓑ (4, 6), (−1, 2), (5, −3)

Ⓒ (4, −2), (−1, 2), (5, 7)

Ⓓ (−2, −4), (2, 1), (7, −5)

Mini-Task

7. A rectangle with vertices (3, −2), (3, −4), (7, −2), (7, −4) is reflected across the *x*-axis and then rotated 90° counterclockwise.

a. In what quadrant does the image lie?

_____

b. What are the vertices of the image?

_____

c. What other transformations produce the same image?

_____

_____

Transformations and Similarity

 ESSENTIAL QUESTION

How can you use dilations and similarity to solve real-world problems?

 Real-World Video

To plan a mural, the artist first makes a smaller drawing showing what the mural will look like. Then the image is enlarged by a scale factor on the mural canvas. This enlargement is called a dilation.

my.hrw.com

GO DIGITAL
my.hrw.com

 my.hrw.com
Go digital with your write-in student edition, accessible on any device.

 Math On the Spot
Scan with your smart phone to jump directly to the online edition, video tutor, and more.

Animated Math
Interactively explore key concepts to see how math works.

 Personal Math Trainer
Get immediate feedback and help as you work through practice sets.

Are YOU Ready?

Complete these exercises to review skills you will need for this module.

Simplify Ratios

EXAMPLE $\frac{35}{21} = \frac{35 \div 7}{21 \div 7}$ To write a ratio in simplest form, find the greatest common factor of the numerator and denominator.

$= \frac{5}{3}$ Divide the numerator and denominator by the GCF.

Write each ratio in simplest form.

1. $\frac{6}{15}$ _____ **2.** $\frac{8}{20}$ _____ **3.** $\frac{30}{18}$ _____ **4.** $\frac{36}{30}$ _____

Multiply with Fractions and Decimals

EXAMPLE $2\frac{3}{5} \times 20$

$= \frac{13 \times 20}{5 \times 1}$ Write numbers as fractions and multiply.

$= \frac{13 \times \overset{4}{\cancel{20}}}{\underset{1}{\cancel{5}} \times 1}$ Simplify.

$= 52$

$\begin{array}{r} 6\,8 \\ \times 4.5 \\ \hline 3\,4\,0 \\ +2\,7\,2 \\ \hline 3\,0\,6.0 \end{array}$

Multiply as you would with whole numbers.

Place the decimal point in the answer based on the total number of decimal places in the two factors.

Multiply.

5. $60 \times \frac{25}{100}$ **6.** 3.5×40 **7.** 4.4×44 **8.** $24 \times \frac{8}{9}$

_____   _____   _____   _____

Graph Ordered Pairs (First Quadrant)

EXAMPLE

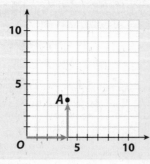

Graph the point A(4, 3.5).
Start at the origin.
Move 4 units right.
Then move 3.5 units up.
Graph point A(4, 3.5).

Graph each point on the coordinate grid above.

9. $B\,(9, 0)$ **10.** $C\,(2, 7)$ **11.** $D\,(0, 4.5)$ **12.** $E\,(6, 2.5)$

Reading Start-Up

Visualize Vocabulary

Use the ✔ words to complete the graphic organizer. You will put one word in each rectangle.

```
┌─────────────────┐        ┌─────────────────┐
│ The four regions │        │ The point where the │
│ on a coordinate  │        │ axes intersect to form │
│ plane.           │        │ the coordinate plane. │
└─────────────────┘        └─────────────────┘
            \                    /
             ┌──────────────────────┐
             │   Reviewing the      │
             │   Coordinate Plane   │
             └──────────────────────┘
            /                    \
┌─────────────────┐        ┌─────────────────┐
│ The horizontal   │        │ The vertical axis │
│ axis of a coordinate │    │ of a coordinate  │
│ plane.           │        │ plane.           │
└─────────────────┘        └─────────────────┘
```

Understand Vocabulary

Complete the sentences using the preview words.

1. A figure larger than the original, produced through dilation, is

   an _____.

2. A figure smaller than the original, produced through dilation, is

   a _____.

Active Reading

Key-Term Fold Before beginning the module, create a key-term fold to help you learn the vocabulary in this module. Write the highlighted vocabulary words on one side of the flap. Write the definition for each word on the other side of the flap. Use the key-term fold to quiz yourself on the definitions used in this module.

Vocabulary

Review Words

coordinate plane (*plano cartesiano*)

image (*imagen*)

✔ origin (*origen*)

preimage (*imagen original*)

✔ quadrants (*cuadrante*)

ratio (*razón*)

scale (*escala*)

✔ *x*-axis (*eje x*)

✔ *y*-axis (*eje y*)

Preview Words

center of dilation (*centro de dilatación*)

dilation (*dilatación*)

enlargement (*agrandamiento*)

reduction (*reducción*)

scale factor (*factor de escala*)

similar (*similar*)

Unpacking the Standards

Understanding the standards and the vocabulary terms in the standards will help you know exactly what you are expected to learn in this module.

COMMON CORE 8.G.3

Describe the effect of dilations, translations, rotations, and reflections on two-dimensional figures using coordinates.

What It Means to You

You will use an algebraic representation to describe a dilation.

UNPACKING EXAMPLE 8.G.3

The blue square *ABCD* is the preimage. Write two algebraic representations, one for the dilation to the green square and one for the dilation to the purple square.

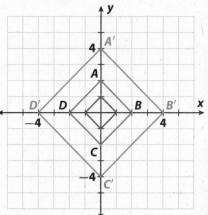

The coordinates of the vertices of the original image are multiplied by 2 for the green square.

Green square: $(x, y) \rightarrow (2x, 2y)$

The coordinates of the vertices of the original image are multiplied by $\frac{1}{2}$ for the purple square.

Purple square: $(x, y) \rightarrow \left(\frac{1}{2}x, \frac{1}{2}y\right)$

COMMON CORE 8.G.4

Understand that a two-dimensional figure is similar to another if the second can be obtained from the first by a sequence of rotations, reflections, translations, and dilations; given two similar two-dimensional figures, describe a sequence that exhibits the similarity between them.

What It Means to You

You will describe a sequence of transformations between two similar figures.

UNPACKING EXAMPLE 8.G.4

Identify a sequence of two transformations that will transform figure *A* into figure *B*.

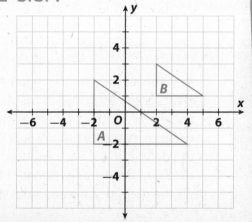

Dilate with center at the origin by a scale factor of $\frac{1}{2}$.

Then translate right 3 units and up 2 units.

Visit **my.hrw.com** to see all the **Common Core Standards** unpacked.

○ my.hrw.com

LESSON 10.1 Properties of Dilations

COMMON CORE 8.G.4

Understand that a two-dimensional figure is similar to another if the second can be obtained from the first by a sequence of ... dilations; ... *Also 8.G.3*

? ESSENTIAL QUESTION

How do you describe the properties of dilations?

EXPLORE ACTIVITY 1 COMMON CORE 8.G.4

Exploring Dilations

The missions that placed 12 astronauts on the moon were controlled at the Johnson Space Center in Houston. The toy models at the right are scaled-down replicas of the Saturn V rocket that powered the moon flights. Each replica is a transformation called a **dilation**. Unlike the other transformations you have studied—translations, rotations, and reflections—dilations change the size (but not the shape) of a figure.

Every dilation has a fixed point called the **center of dilation** located where the lines connecting corresponding parts of figures intersect.

Triangle R′S′T′ is a dilation of triangle RST. Point C is the center of dilation.

A Use a ruler to measure segments $\overline{CR}$, $\overline{CR'}$, $\overline{CS}$, $\overline{CS'}$, $\overline{CT}$, and $\overline{CT'}$ to the nearest millimeter. Record the measurements and ratios in the table.

CR′	CR	$\frac{CR'}{CR}$	CS′	CS	$\frac{CS'}{CS}$	CT′	CT	$\frac{CT'}{CT}$

B Write a conjecture based on the ratios in the table.

_____

C Measure and record the corresponding side lengths of the triangles.

R′S′	RS	$\frac{R'S'}{RS}$	S′T′	ST	$\frac{S'T'}{ST}$	R′T′	RT	$\frac{R'T'}{RT}$

D Write a conjecture based on the ratios in the table.

_____

E Measure the corresponding angles and describe your results.

_____

© Houghton Mifflin Harcourt Publishing Company

Lesson 10.1 **315**

Reflect

1. Two figures that have the same shape but different sizes are called *similar*. Are triangles *RST* and *R'S'T'* similar? Why or why not?

   _____

   _____

2. Compare the orientation of a figure with the orientation of its dilation.

   _____

EXPLORE ACTIVITY 2 COMMON CORE 8.G.3

Exploring Dilations on a Coordinate Plane

In this activity you will explore how the coordinates of a figure on a coordinate plane are affected by a dilation.

A Complete the table. Record the *x*- and *y*-coordinates of the points in the two figures and the ratios of the *x*-coordinates and the *y*-coordinates.

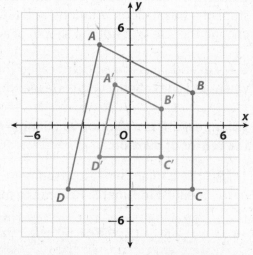

Vertex	*x*	*y*	Vertex	*x*	*y*	Ratio of *x*-coordinates (A'B'C'D' ÷ ABCD)	Ratio of *y*-coordinates (A'B'C'D' ÷ ABCD)
A'			A				
B'			B				
C'			C				
D'			D				

B Write a conjecture about the ratios of the coordinates of a dilation image to the coordinates of the original figure.

_____

_____

Reflect

3. In Explore Activity 1, triangle *R'S'T'* was larger than triangle *RST*. How is the relationship between quadrilateral *A'B'C'D'* and quadrilateral *ABCD* different?

_____

Math Talk
Mathematical Practices

How are dilations different from the other transformations you have learned about?

Math On the Spot
my.hrw.com

Finding a Scale Factor

As you have seen in the two activities, a dilation can produce a larger figure (an **enlargement**) or a smaller figure (a **reduction**). The **scale factor** describes how much the figure is enlarged or reduced. The scale factor is the ratio of a length of the image to the corresponding length on the original figure.

In Explore Activity 1, the side lengths of triangle *R'S'T'* were twice the length of those of triangle *RST*, so the scale factor was 2. In Explore Activity 2, the side lengths of quadrilateral *A'B'C'D'* were half those of quadrilateral *ABCD*, so the scale factor was 0.5.

EXAMPLE 1 Real World

COMMON CORE 8.G.4

An art supply store sells several sizes of drawing triangles. All are dilations of a single basic triangle. The basic triangle and one of its dilations are shown on the grid. Find the scale factor of the dilation.

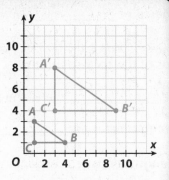

STEP 1 Use the coordinates to find the lengths of the sides of each triangle.

Triangle *ABC*: $AC = 2$ $CB = 3$

Triangle *A'B'C'*: $A'C' = 4$ $C'B' = 6$

Since the scale factor is the same for all corresponding sides, you can record just two pairs of side lengths. Use one pair as a check on the other.

Animated Math
my.hrw.com

STEP 2 Find the ratios of the corresponding sides.

$$\frac{A'C'}{AC} = \frac{4}{2} = 2 \qquad \frac{C'B'}{CB} = \frac{6}{3} = 2$$

The scale factor of the dilation is 2.

Reflect

4. Is the dilation an enlargement or a reduction? How can you tell?

_____

_____

YOUR TURN

5. Find the scale factor of
the dilation.

_____

_____

Math Talk

Mathematical Practices

Which scale factors lead
to enlargements? Which
scale factors lead to
reductions?

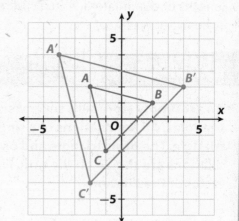

Guided Practice

Use triangles *ABC* and *A'B'C'* for 1–5. (Explore Activities 1 and 2, Example 1)

1. For each pair of corresponding vertices, find the ratio of the
x-coordinates and the ratio of the *y*-coordinates.

ratio of *x*-coordinates = _____

ratio of *y*-coordinates = _____

2. I know that triangle *A'B'C'* is a dilation of triangle *ABC*
because the ratios of the corresponding

x-coordinates are _____ and the ratios of the

corresponding *y*-coordinates are _____.

3. The ratio of the lengths of the corresponding sides of triangle *A'B'C'* and

triangle *ABC* equals _____.

4. The corresponding angles of triangle *ABC* and triangle *A'B'C'*

are _____.

5. The scale factor of the dilation is _____.

? ESSENTIAL QUESTION CHECK-IN

6. How can you find the scale factor of a dilation?

_____

_____

10.1 Independent Practice

COMMON CORE 8.G.3, 8.G.4

Personal Math Trainer

Online Assessment and Intervention

my.hrw.com

For 7–11, tell whether one figure is a dilation of the other or not. Explain your reasoning.

7. Quadrilateral *MNPQ* has side lengths of 15 mm, 24 mm, 21 mm, and 18 mm. Quadrilateral *M'N'P'Q'* has side lengths of 5 mm, 8 mm, 7 mm, and 4 mm.

_____

_____

_____

8. Triangle *RST* has angles measuring 38° and 75°. Triangle *R'S'T'* has angles measuring 67° and 38°. The sides are proportional.

_____

_____

_____

_____

9. Two triangles, Triangle 1 and Triangle 2, are similar.

_____

_____

_____

10. Quadrilateral *MNPQ* is the same shape but a different size than quadrilateral *M'N'P'Q*.

_____

_____

_____

_____

_____

11. On a coordinate plane, triangle *UVW* has coordinates *U*(20, −12), *V*(8, 6), and *W*(−24, −4). Triangle *U'V'W'* has coordinates *U'*(15, −9), *V'*(6, 4.5), and *W'*(−18, −3).

_____

_____

_____

_____

_____

_____

Complete the table by writing "same" or "changed" to compare the image with the original figure in the given transformation.

	Image Compared to Original Figure		
	Orientation	**Size**	**Shape**
12. Translation			
13. Reflection			
14. Rotation			
15. Dilation			

16. Describe the image of a dilation with a scale factor of 1.

_____

Identify the scale factor used in each dilation.

17.

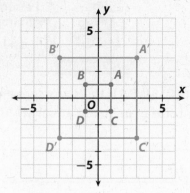

_____

18.

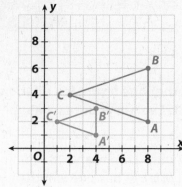

_____

Work Area

19. Critical Thinking Explain how you can find the center of dilation of a triangle and its dilation.

_____

_____

_____

20. Make a Conjecture

a. A square on the coordinate plane has vertices at $(-2, 2)$, $(2, 2)$, $(2, -2)$, and $(-2, -2)$. A dilation of the square has vertices at $(-4, 4)$, $(4, 4)$, $(4, -4)$, and $(-4, -4)$. Find the scale factor and the perimeter of each square.

_____

_____

b. A square on the coordinate plane has vertices at $(-3, 3)$, $(3, 3)$, $(3, -3)$, and $(-3, -3)$. A dilation of the square has vertices at $(-6, 6)$, $(6, 6)$, $(6, -6)$, and $(-6, -6)$. Find the scale factor and the perimeter of each square.

_____

_____

c. Make a conjecture about the relationship of the scale factor to the perimeter of a square and its image.

_____

_____

Algebraic Representations of Dilations

COMMON CORE **8.G.3**
Describe the effect of dilations, ... on two-dimensional figures using coordinates.

? **ESSENTIAL QUESTION**

How can you describe the effect of a dilation on coordinates using an algebraic representation?

EXPLORE ACTIVITY 1 COMMON CORE 8.G.3

Graphing Enlargements

When a dilation in the coordinate plane has the origin as the center of dilation, you can find points on the dilated image by multiplying the x- and y-coordinates of the original figure by the scale factor. For scale factor k, the algebraic representation of the dilation is $(x, y) \rightarrow (kx, ky)$. For enlargements, $k > 1$.

The figure shown on the grid is the preimage. The center of dilation is the origin.

A List the coordinates of the vertices of the preimage in the first column of the table.

Preimage (x, y)	Image (3x, 3y)
(2, 2)	(6, 6)

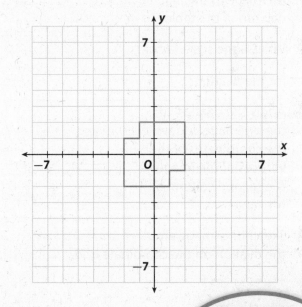

B What is the scale factor for the dilation? _____

C Apply the dilation to the preimage and write the coordinates of the vertices of the image in the second column of the table.

D Sketch the image after the dilation on the coordinate grid.

Math Talk
Mathematical Practices

What effect would the dilation $(x, y) \rightarrow (4x, 4y)$ have on the radius of a circle?

Reflect

1. How does the dilation affect the length of line segments?

_____

_____

2. How does the dilation affect angle measures?

_____

EXPLORE ACTIVITY 2   8.G.3

Graphing Reductions

For scale factors between 0 and 1, the image is smaller than the preimage. This is called a reduction.

The arrow shown is the preimage. The center of dilation is the origin.

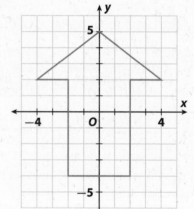

A List the coordinates of the vertices of the preimage in the first column of the table.

B What is the scale factor for the dilation? _____

C Apply the dilation to the preimage and write the coordinates of the vertices of the image in the second column of the table.

Preimage (x, y)	Image $\left(\frac{1}{2}x, \frac{1}{2}y\right)$

D Sketch the image after the dilation on the coordinate grid.

Reflect

3. How does the dilation affect the length of line segments?

_____

4. How would a dilation with scale factor 1 affect the preimage?

_____

Center of Dilation Outside the Image

The center of dilation can be inside *or* outside the original image and the dilated image. The center of dilation can be anywhere on the coordinate plane as long as the lines that connect each pair of corresponding vertices between the original and dilated image intersect at the center of dilation.

EXAMPLE 1   COMMON CORE 8.G.3

Graph the image of △ABC after a dilation with the origin as its center and a scale factor of 3. What are the vertices of the image?

STEP 1 Multiply each coordinate of the vertices of △ABC by 3 to find the vertices of the dilated image.

$$\triangle ABC\ (x, y) \rightarrow (3x, 3y)\ \triangle A'B'C'$$

$$A(1, 1) \rightarrow A'(1 \cdot 3, 1 \cdot 3) \rightarrow A'(3, 3)$$

$$B(3, 1) \rightarrow B'(3 \cdot 3, 1 \cdot 3) \rightarrow B'(9, 3)$$

$$C(1, 3) \rightarrow C'(1 \cdot 3, 3 \cdot 3) \rightarrow C'(3, 9)$$

The vertices of the dilated image are $A'(3, 3)$, $B'(9, 3)$, and $C'(3, 9)$.

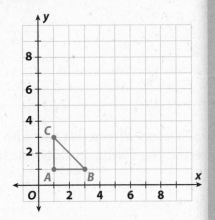

STEP 2 Graph the dilated image.

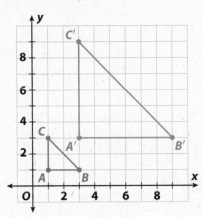

Math Talk
Mathematical Practices

Describe how you can check graphically that you have drawn the image triangle correctly.

YOUR TURN

5. Graph the image of △XYZ after a dilation with a scale factor of $\frac{1}{3}$ and the origin as its center. Then write an algebraic rule to describe the dilation.

_____

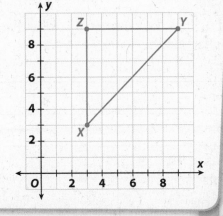

© Houghton Mifflin Harcourt Publishing Company

1. The grid shows a diamond-shaped preimage. Write the coordinates of the vertices of the preimage in the first column of the table. Then apply the dilation $(x, y) \rightarrow \left(\frac{3}{2}x, \frac{3}{2}y\right)$ and write the coordinates of the vertices of the image in the second column. Sketch the image of the figure after the dilation. (Explore Activities 1 and 2)

Preimage	Image
(2, 0)	(3, 0)

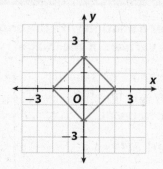

Graph the image of each figure after a dilation with the origin as its center and the given scale factor. Then write an algebraic rule to describe the dilation. (Example 1)

2. scale factor of 1.5

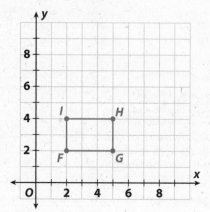

_____

3. scale factor of $\frac{1}{3}$

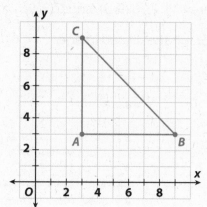

_____

? ESSENTIAL QUESTION CHECK-IN

4. A dilation of $(x, y) \rightarrow (kx, ky)$ when $0 < k < 1$ has what effect on the figure? What is the effect on the figure when $k > 1$?

_____

_____

_____

10.2 Independent Practice

COMMON CORE 8.G.3

Personal Math Trainer

Online Assessment and Intervention

my.hrw.com

5. The blue square is the preimage. Write two algebraic representations, one for the dilation to the green square and one for the dilation to the purple square.

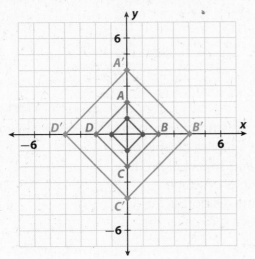

_____

_____

6. Critical Thinking A triangle has vertices $A(-5, -4)$, $B(2, 6)$, and $C(4, -3)$. The center of dilation is the origin and $(x, y) \rightarrow (3x, 3y)$. What are the vertices of the dilated image?

_____

_____

7. Critical Thinking $M'N'O'P'$ has vertices at $M'(3, 4)$, $N'(6, 4)$, $O'(6, 7)$, and $P'(3, 7)$. The center of dilation is the origin. $MNOP$ has vertices at $M(4.5, 6)$, $N(9, 6)$, $O'(9, 10.5)$, and $P'(4.5, 10.5)$. What is the algebraic representation of this dilation?

_____

8. Critical Thinking A dilation with center $(0,0)$ and scale factor k is applied to a polygon. What dilation can you apply to the image to return it to the original preimage?

_____

9. Represent Real-World Problems The blueprints for a new house are scaled so that $\frac{1}{4}$ inch equals 1 foot. The blueprint is the preimage and the house is the dilated image. The blueprints are plotted on a coordinate plane.

a. What is the scale factor in terms of inches to inches?

_____

b. One inch on the blueprint represents how many inches in the actual house? How many feet?

_____

c. Write the algebraic representation of the dilation from the blueprint to the house.

_____

d. A rectangular room has coordinates $Q(2, 2)$, $R(7, 2)$, $S(7, 5)$, and $T(2, 5)$ on the blueprint. The homeowner wants this room to be 25% larger. What are the coordinates of the new room?

_____

_____

e. What are the dimensions of the new room, in inches, on the blueprint? What will the dimensions of the new room be, in feet, in the new house?

_____

_____

_____

_____

10. Write the algebraic representation of the dilation shown.

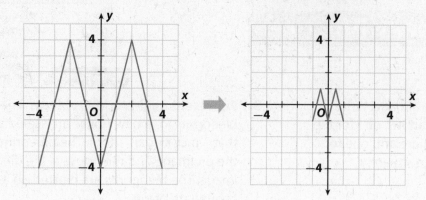

_____

Work Area

11. Critique Reasoning The set for a school play needs a replica of a historic building painted on a backdrop that is 20 feet long and 16 feet high. The actual building measures 400 feet long and 320 feet high. A stage crewmember writes $(x, y) \rightarrow \left(\frac{1}{12}x, \frac{1}{12}y \right)$ to represent the dilation. Is the crewmember's calculation correct if the painted replica is to cover the entire backdrop? Explain.

_____

_____

12. Communicate Mathematical Ideas Explain what each of these algebraic transformations does to a figure.

a. $(x, y) \rightarrow (y, -x)$ _____

b. $(x, y) \rightarrow (-x, -y)$ _____

c. $(x, y) \rightarrow (x, 2y)$ _____

_____

d. $(x, y) \rightarrow \left(\frac{2}{3}x, y \right)$ _____

_____

e. $(x, y) \rightarrow (0.5x, 1.5y)$ _____

_____

13. Communicate Mathematical Ideas Triangle _ABC_ has coordinates _A_(1, 5), _B_(−2, 1), and _C_(−2, 4). Sketch triangle _ABC_ and _A′B′C′_ for the dilation $(x, y) \rightarrow (-2x, -2y)$. What is the effect of a negative scale factor?

_____

_____

10.3 Similar Figures

COMMON CORE 8.G.4

Understand that a ... figure is similar to another if the second can be obtained ... by a sequence of rotations, reflections, translations, and dilations; given two similar ... figures, describe a sequence that exhibits the similarity between them.

? ESSENTIAL QUESTION

What is the connection between transformations and similar figures?

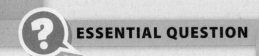 **EXPLORE ACTIVITY** COMMON CORE 8.G.4

Combining Transformations with Dilations

When creating an animation, figures need to be translated, reflected, rotated, and sometimes dilated. As an example of this, apply the indicated sequence of transformations to the rectangle. Each transformation is applied to the image of the previous transformation, not to the original figure. Label each image with the letter of the transformation applied.

A $(x, y) \rightarrow (x + 7, y - 2)$

B $(x, y) \rightarrow (x, -y)$

C rotation 90° clockwise around the origin

D $(x, y) \rightarrow (x + 5, y + 3)$

E $(x, y) \rightarrow (3x, 3y)$

F List the coordinates of the vertices of rectangle E.

_____

G Compare the following attributes of rectangle E to those of the original figure.

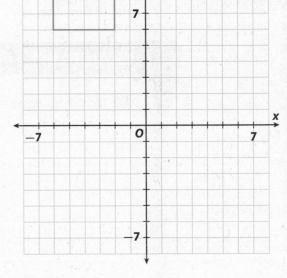

Shape	
Size	
Angle Measures	

Reflect

1. Which transformation represents the dilation? How can you tell?

_____

_____

2. A sequence of transformations containing a single dilation is applied to a figure. Are the original figure and its final image congruent? Explain.

_____

_____

Math On the Spot

my.hrw.com

Similar Figures

Two figures are **similar** if one can be obtained from the other by a sequence of translations, reflections, rotations, and dilations. Similar figures have the same shape but may be different sizes.

When you are told that two figures are similar, there must be a sequence of translations, reflections, rotations, and/or dilations that can transform one to the other.

EXAMPLE 1

COMMON CORE 8.G.4

A Identify a sequence of transformations that will transform figure *A* into figure *B*. Tell whether the figures are congruent. Tell whether they are similar.

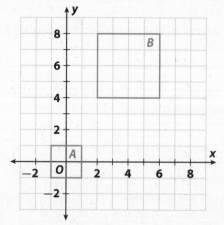

My Notes

Both figures are squares whose orientations are the same, so no reflection or rotation is needed. Figure *B* has sides twice as long as figure *A*, so a dilation with a scale factor of 2 is needed. Figure *B* is moved to the right and above figure *A*, so a translation is needed. A sequence of transformations that will accomplish this is a dilation by a scale factor of 2 centered at the origin followed by the translation $(x, y) \rightarrow (x + 4, y + 6)$. The figures are not congruent, but they are similar.

B Identify a sequence of transformations that will transform figure *C* into figure *D*. Include a reflection. Tell whether the figures are congruent. Tell whether they are similar.

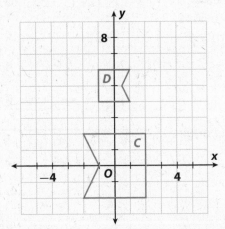

The orientation of figure *D* is reversed from that of figure *C*, so a reflection over the *y*-axis is needed. Figure *D* has sides that are half as long as figure *C*, so a dilation with a scale factor of $\frac{1}{2}$ is needed. Figure *D* is moved above figure *C*, so a translation is needed. A sequence of transformations that will accomplish this is a dilation by a scale factor of $\frac{1}{2}$ centered at the origin, followed by the reflection $(x, y) \rightarrow (-x, y)$, followed by the translation $(x, y) \rightarrow (x, y + 5)$. The figures are not congruent, but they are similar.

C Identify a sequence of transformations that will transform figure *C* into figure *D*. Include a rotation.

The orientation of figure *D* is reversed from that of figure *C*, so a rotation of 180º is needed. Figure *D* has sides that are half as long as figure *C*, so a dilation with a scale factor of $\frac{1}{2}$ is needed. Figure *D* is moved above figure *C*, so a translation is needed. A sequence of transformations that will accomplish this is a rotation of 180º about the origin, followed by a dilation by a scale factor of $\frac{1}{2}$ centered at the origin, followed by the translation $(x, y) \rightarrow (x, y + 5)$.

> **Math Talk**
> Mathematical Practices
>
> A figure and its image have different sizes and orientations. What do you know about the sequence of transformations that generated the image?

YOUR TURN

3. Look again at the Explore Activity. Start with the original figure. Create a new sequence of transformations that will yield figure *E*, the final image. Your transformations do not need to produce the images in the same order in which they originally appeared.

_____

_____

_____

Personal Math Trainer

Online Assessment and Intervention

my.hrw.com

1. Apply the indicated sequence of transformations to the square. Apply each transformation to the image of the previous transformation. Label each image with the letter of the transformation applied.
(Explore Activity)

A $(x, y) \rightarrow (-x, y)$

B Rotate the square 180° around the origin.

C $(x, y) \rightarrow (x - 5, y - 6)$

D $(x, y) \rightarrow \left(\frac{1}{2}x, \frac{1}{2}y\right)$

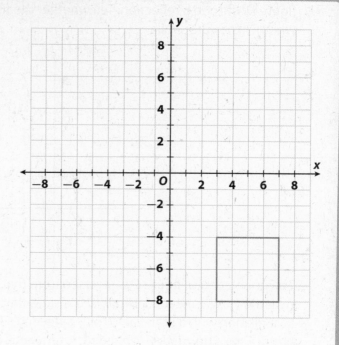

Identify a sequence of two transformations that will transform figure A into the given figure. (Example 1)

2. figure B

_____

_____

3. figure C

_____

_____

4. figure D

_____

_____

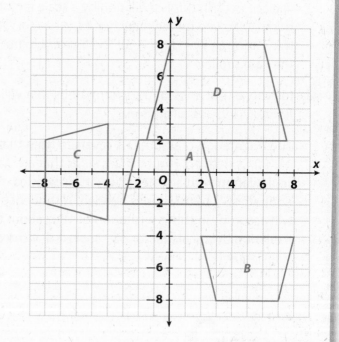

? ESSENTIAL QUESTION CHECK-IN

5. If two figures are similar but not congruent, what do you know about the sequence of transformations used to create one from the other?

_____

_____

10.3 Independent Practice

COMMON CORE 8.G.4

Personal Math Trainer

Online Assessment and Intervention

my.hrw.com

6. A designer creates a drawing of a triangular sign on centimeter grid paper for a new business. The drawing has sides measuring 6 cm, 8 cm, and 10 cm, and angles measuring 37°, 53°, and 90°. To create the actual sign shown, the drawing must be dilated using a scale factor of 40.

a. Find the lengths of the sides of the actual sign.

_____

b. Find the angle measures of the actual sign.

_____

c. The drawing has the hypotenuse on the bottom. The business owner would like it on the top. Describe two transformations that will do this.

_____

_____

d. The shorter leg of the drawing is currently on the left. The business owner wants it to remain on the left after the hypotenuse goes to the top. Which transformation in part c will accomplish this?

_____

In Exercises 7–10, the transformation of a figure into its image is described. Describe the transformations that will transform the image back into the original figure. Then write them algebraically.

7. The figure is reflected across the *x*-axis and dilated by a scale factor of 3.

_____

_____

8. The figure is dilated by a scale factor of 0.5 and translated 6 units left and 3 units up.

_____

_____

9. The figure is dilated by a scale factor of 5 and rotated 90° clockwise.

_____

_____

10. The figure is reflected across the *y*-axis and dilated by a scale factor of 4.

_____

_____

 **FOCUS ON HIGHER ORDER THINKING**

11. Draw Conclusions A figure undergoes a sequence of transformations that include dilations. The figure and its final image are congruent. Explain how this can happen.

_____

_____

12. Multistep As with geometric figures, graphs can be transformed through translations, reflections, rotations, and dilations. Describe how the graph of $y = x$ shown at the right is changed through each of the following transformations.

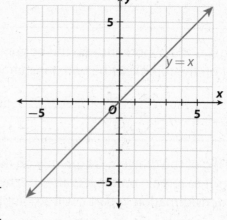

a. a dilation by a scale factor of 4

_____

_____

_____

_____

b. a translation down 3 units

_____

_____

c. a reflection across the *y*-axis

_____

_____

13. Justify Reasoning The graph of the line $y = x$ is dilated by a scale factor of 3 and then translated up 5 units. Is this the same as translating the graph up 5 units and then dilating by a scale factor of 3? Explain.

_____

_____

_____

Activity 10.3

Copy-Cat

INSTRUCTIONS

STEP 1 Use tape to secure the tracing paper onto the grid. Then trace the grid lines onto the tracing paper.

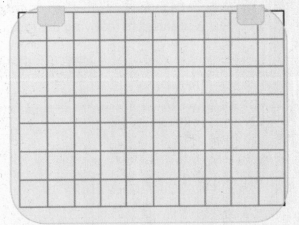

STEP 2 Remove the tracing paper from the grid paper and securely tape the tracing paper over the image that will be copied. Leave the tracing paper attached when you submit your work.

STEP 3 Create a blank grid on your large blank piece of paper or poster board. The blank grid should have the same number of squares as the grid on the tracing paper over the original image. The squares do not need to be the same size as those on the tracing paper.

STEP 4 Copy exactly the appearance of each square from the original image onto the corresponding square of the blank grid on the large piece of paper or poster board.

Be careful not to focus on the overall picture, only focus on one square at a time. It may help to do the squares in random order so that the squares are receiving the focus instead of the overall image.

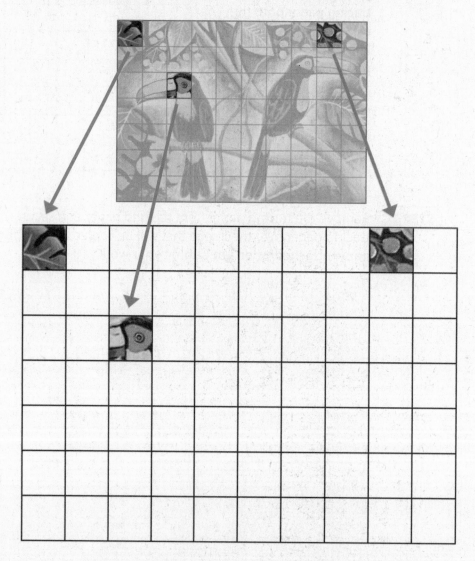

STEP 5 When you have copied all of the squares, the drawing on your finished grid should look like a dilation or copy of the original image.

Ready to Go On?

10.1 Properties of Dilations

Determine whether one figure is a dilation of the other. Justify your answer.

1. Triangle *XYZ* has angles measuring 54° and 29°. Triangle *X'Y'Z'* has angles measuring 29° and 92°.

_____

2. Quadrilateral *DEFG* has sides measuring 16 m, 28 m, 24 m, and 20 m. Quadrilateral *D'E'F'G'* has sides measuring 20 m, 35 m, 30 m, and 25 m.

_____

_____

10.2 Algebraic Representations of Dilations

Dilate each figure with the origin as the center of dilation.

3. $(x, y) \rightarrow (0.8x, 0.8y)$

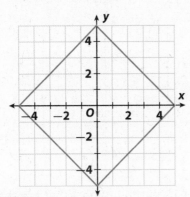

4. $(x, y) \rightarrow (2.5x, 2.5y)$

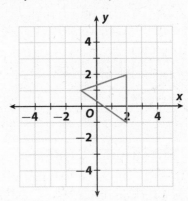

10.3 Similar Figures

5. Describe what happens to a figure when the given sequence of transformations is applied to it: $(x, y) \rightarrow (-x, y)$; $(x, y) \rightarrow (0.5x, 0.5y)$; $(x, y) \rightarrow (x - 2, y + 2)$

_____

_____

? ESSENTIAL QUESTION

6. How can you use dilations to solve real-world problems?

_____

Selected Response

1. A rectangle has vertices (6, 4), (2, 4), (6, −2), and (2, −2). What are the coordinates of the vertices of the image after a dilation with the origin as its center and a scale factor of 1.5?

   Ⓐ (9, 6), (3, 6), (9, −3), (3, −3)

   Ⓑ (3, 2), (1, 2), (3, −1), (1, −1)

   Ⓒ (12, 8), (4, 8), (12, −4), (4, −4)

   Ⓓ (15, 10), (5, 10), (15, −5), (5, −5)

2. Which represents the dilation shown where the black figure is the preimage?

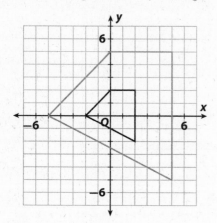

   Ⓐ $(x, y) \rightarrow (1.5x, 1.5y)$

   Ⓑ $(x, y) \rightarrow (2.5x, 2.5y)$

   Ⓒ $(x, y) \rightarrow (3x, 3y)$

   Ⓓ $(x, y) \rightarrow (6x, 6y)$

3. Identify the sequence of transformations that will reflect a figure over the x-axis and then dilate it by a scale factor of 3.

   Ⓐ $(x, y) \rightarrow (−x, y); (x, y) \rightarrow (3x, 3y)$

   Ⓑ $(x, y) \rightarrow (−x, y); (x, y) \rightarrow (x, 3y)$

   Ⓒ $(x, y) \rightarrow (x, −y); (x, y) \rightarrow (3x, y)$

   Ⓓ $(x, y) \rightarrow (x, −y); (x, y) \rightarrow (3x, 3y)$

4. Solve $−a + 7 = 2a − 8$.

   Ⓐ $a = −3$ Ⓒ $a = 5$

   Ⓑ $a = −\frac{1}{3}$ Ⓓ $a = 15$

5. Which equation does **not** represent a line with an x-intercept of 3?

   Ⓐ $y = −2x + 6$ Ⓒ $y = \frac{2}{3}x − 2$

   Ⓑ $y = −\frac{1}{3}x + 1$ Ⓓ $y = 3x − 1$

Mini-Task

6. The square is dilated under the dilation $(x, y) \rightarrow (0.25x, 0.25y)$.

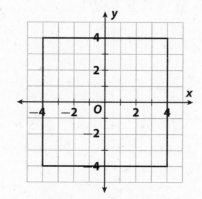

   a. Graph the image. What are the coordinates?

   _____

   b. What is the length of a side of the image?

   _____

   c. What are the perimeter and area of the preimage?

   _____

   d. What are the perimeter and area of the image?

   _____

MODULE 9 **Transformations and Congruence**

? ESSENTIAL QUESTION

How can you use transformations and congruence to solve real-world problems?

EXAMPLE

Translate triangle *XYZ* left 4 units and down 2 units. Graph the image and label the vertices.

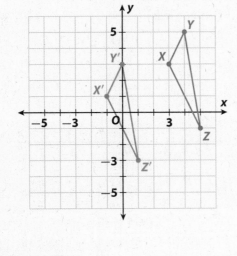

Translate the vertices by subtracting 4 from each *x*-coordinate and 2 from each *y*-coordinate. The new vertices are $X'(-1, 1)$, $Y'(0, 3)$, and $Z'(1, -3)$.

Connect the vertices to draw triangle *X'Y'Z'*.

EXERCISES

Perform the transformation shown. (Lessons 9.1, 9.2, 9.3)

1. Reflection over the *x*-axis

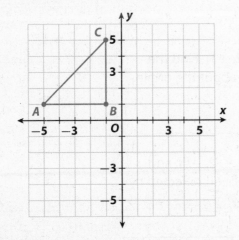

2. Translation 5 units right

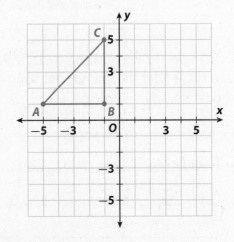

3. Rotation 90° counterclockwise about the origin

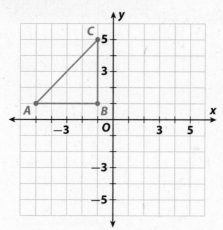

4. Translation 4 units right and 4 units down

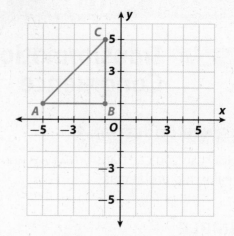

5. Quadrilateral *ABCD* with vertices *A*(4, 4), *B*(5, 1), *C*(5, −1) and *D*(4, −2) is translated left 2 units and down 3 units. Graph the preimage and the image. (Lesson 9.4)

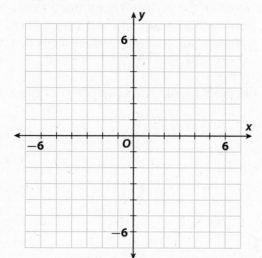

6. Triangle *ABC* with vertices *A*(1, 2), *B*(1, 4), and *C*(3, 3) is translated by $(x, y) \rightarrow (x - 4, y)$, and the result is reflected by $(x, y) \rightarrow (x, -y)$. Graph the preimage and the image. (Lesson 9.5)

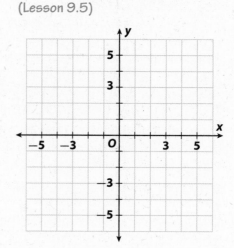

7. Triangle *RST* has vertices at (−8, 2), (−4, 0), and (−12, 8). Find the vertices after the triangle has been reflected over the *y*-axis. (Lesson 9.4)

_____

8. Triangle *XYZ* has vertices at (3, 7), (9, 14), and (12, −1). Find the vertices after the triangle has been rotated 180° about the origin. (Lesson 9.4)

_____

9. Triangle *MNP* has its vertices located at (−1, −4), (−2, −5), and (−3, −3). Find the vertices after the triangle has been reflected by $(x, y) \rightarrow (x, -y)$ and translated by $(x, y) \rightarrow (x + 6, y)$. (Lesson 9.5)

_____

Transformations and Similarity

Key Vocabulary

center of dilation (*centro de dilatación*)

dilation (*dilatación*)

enlargement (*agrandamiento*)

reduction (*reducción*)

scale factor (*factor de escala*)

similar (*semejantes*)

? **ESSENTIAL QUESTION**

How can you use dilations, similarity, and proportionality to solve real-world problems?

EXAMPLE

Dilate triangle *ABC* with the origin as the center of dilation and scale factor $\frac{1}{2}$. Graph the dilated image.

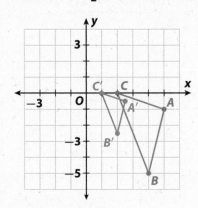

Multiply each coordinate of the vertices of *ABC* by $\frac{1}{2}$ to find the vertices of the dilated image.

$$A(5, -1) \rightarrow A'\left(5 \cdot \frac{1}{2}, -1 \cdot \frac{1}{2}\right) \rightarrow A'\left(2\frac{1}{2}, -\frac{1}{2}\right)$$

$$B(4, -5) \rightarrow B'\left(4 \cdot \frac{1}{2}, -5 \cdot \frac{1}{2}\right) \rightarrow B'\left(2, -2\frac{1}{2}\right)$$

$$C(2, 0) \rightarrow C'\left(2 \cdot \frac{1}{2}, 0 \cdot \frac{1}{2}\right) \rightarrow C'(1, 0)$$

EXERCISES

1. For each pair of corresponding vertices, find the ratio of the *x*-coordinates and the ratio of the *y*-coordinates. (Lesson 10.1)

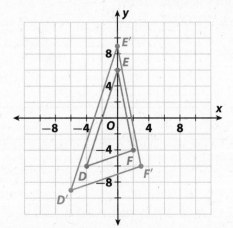

Ratio of *x*-coordinates: _____

Ratio of *y*-coordinates: _____

What is the scale factor of the dilation? _____

2. Rectangle *WXYZ* has vertices at $(-2, -1)$, $(-2, 1)$, $(2, -1)$, and $(2, 1)$. It is first dilated by $(x, y) \rightarrow (2x, 2y)$, and then translated by $(x, y) \rightarrow (x, y + 3)$. (Lesson 10.3)

a. What are the vertices of the image? _____

b. Are the preimage and image congruent? Are they similar? Explain.

_____

_____

Dilate each figure with the origin as the center of the dilation. List the vertices of the dilated figure then graph the figure. (Lesson 10.2)

3. $(x, y) \rightarrow \left(\frac{1}{4}x, \frac{1}{4}y\right)$

_____

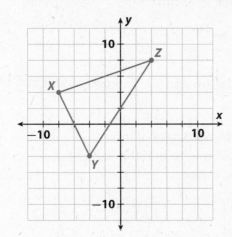

4. $(x, y) \rightarrow (2x, 2y)$

_____

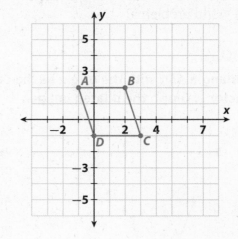

Unit 4 Performance Tasks

1. **CAREERS IN MATH** **Contractor** Fernando is expanding his dog's play yard. The original yard has a fence represented by rectangle *LMNO* on the coordinate plane. Fernando hires a contractor to construct a new fence that should enclose 6 times as much area as the current fence. The shape of the fence must remain the same. The contractor constructs the fence shown by rectangle *L'M'N'O'*.

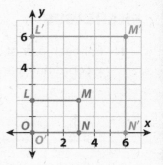

a. Did the contractor increase the area by the amount Fernando wanted? Explain.

_____

_____

b. Does the new fence maintain the shape of the old fence? How do you know?

_____

_____

2. A sail for a sailboat is represented by a triangle on the coordinate plane with vertices (0, 0), (5, 0), and (5, 4). The triangle is dilated by a scale factor of 1.5 with the origin as the center of dilation. Find the coordinates of the dilated triangle. Are the triangles similar? Explain.

_____

© Houghton Mifflin Harcourt Publishing Company

UNIT 4 MIXED REVIEW

Assessment Readiness

Personal
Math Trainer

Online
Assessment and
Intervention

my.hrw.com

Selected Response

1. What would be the orientation of the figure below after a reflection over the *x*-axis?

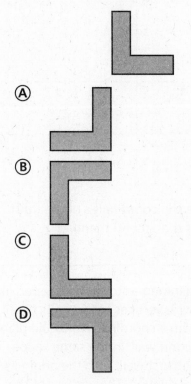

Ⓐ

Ⓑ

Ⓒ

Ⓓ

2. A triangle with coordinates (4, 2), (0, −3), and (−5, 3) is translated 5 units right and rotated 180° about the origin. What are the coordinates of its image?

Ⓐ (9, 2), (−1, −2), (5, −7)

Ⓑ (−10, 3), (−1, 2), (−5, −3)

Ⓒ (2, −1), (−3, −5), (3, −10)

Ⓓ (−9, −2), (−5, 3), (0, −3)

3. Quadrilateral *LMNP* has sides measuring 16, 28, 12, and 32. Which could be the side lengths of a dilation of *LMNP*?

Ⓐ 24, 40, 18, 90

Ⓑ 32, 60, 24, 65

Ⓒ 20, 35, 15, 40

Ⓓ 40, 70, 30, 75

4. The table below represents which equation?

x	−1	0	1	2
y	1	−2	−5	−8

Ⓐ $y = x + 2$

Ⓑ $y = -x$

Ⓒ $y = 3x + 6$

Ⓓ $y = -3x - 2$

5. Which of the following is **not** true of a trapezoid that has been translated 8 units down?

Ⓐ The new trapezoid is the same size as the original trapezoid.

Ⓑ The new trapezoid is the same shape as the original trapezoid.

Ⓒ The new trapezoid is in the same orientation as the original trapezoid.

Ⓓ The *y*-coordinates of the new trapezoid are the same as the *y*-coordinates of the original trapezoid.

6. Which represents a reduction?

Ⓐ $(x, y) \rightarrow (0.9x, 0.9y)$

Ⓑ $(x, y) \rightarrow (1.4x, 1.4y)$

Ⓒ $(x, y) \rightarrow (0.7x, 0.3y)$

Ⓓ $(x, y) \rightarrow (2.5x, 2.5y)$

7. Which is the solution for $4(x + 1) = 2(3x - 2)$?

Ⓐ $x = -4$

Ⓑ $x = -1$

Ⓒ $x = 0$

Ⓓ $x = 4$

8. A rectangle has vertices (8, 6), (4, 6), (8, −4), and (4, −4). What are the coordinates after dilating from the origin by a scale factor of 1.5?

Ⓐ (9, 6), (3, 6), (9, −3), (3, −3)

Ⓑ (10, 8), (5, 8), (10, −5), (5, −5)

Ⓒ (16, 12), (8, 12), (16, −8), (8, −8)

Ⓓ (12, 9), (6, 9), (12, −6), (6, −6)

Make sure you look at all answer choices before making your decision. Try substituting each answer choice into the problem if you are unsure of the answer.

9. Two apples plus four bananas cost $2.00. An apple costs twice as much as a banana. Using the equations $2a + 4b = 2.00$ and $a = 2b$, where a is the cost of one apple and b is the cost of one banana, what are a and b?

Ⓐ $a = \$0.25; b = \$0.25$

Ⓑ $a = \$0.25; b = \$0.50$

Ⓒ $a = \$0.50; b = \$0.25$

Ⓓ $a = \$0.50; b = \$0.50$

10. Which statement is false?

Ⓐ No integers are irrational numbers.

Ⓑ All whole numbers are integers.

Ⓒ No real numbers are rational numbers.

Ⓓ All integers greater than or equal to 0 are whole numbers.

11. Consider the system of equations $3x + 4y = 2$ and $2x − 4y = 8$. Which is its solution?

Ⓐ $x = −1, y = −2$

Ⓑ $x = 1, y = 2$

Ⓒ $x = −2, y = 1$

Ⓓ $x = 2, y = −1$

12. A triangle with vertices (−2, −3), (−4, 0), and (0, 0) is congruent to a second triangle located in quadrant I with two of its vertices at (3, 2) and (1, 5).

a. Graph the two triangles on the same coordinate grid.

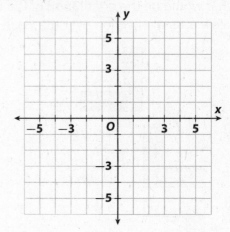

b. What are the coordinates of the third vertex of the second triangle?

_____

13. Tamiko is planning a stone wall shaped like a triangle, with vertices at (−1, −2), (2, 2), and (−2, 2) on a coordinate grid. She plans to add a second wall, in the same shape, enclosing the first wall, with the origin as the center of dilation. The vertices of the second wall are (−3, −6), (6, 6), and (−6, 6).

a. What scale factor did Tamiko use for the second wall?

_____

b. Are the two walls similar? Explain.

_____

_____

_____

_____

Measurement Geometry

MODULE 11

Angle Relationships in Parallel Lines and Triangles

COMMON CORE 8.G.5

MODULE 12

The Pythagorean Theorem

COMMON CORE 8.G.6, 8.G.7, 8.G.8

MODULE 13

Volume

COMMON CORE 8.G.9

CAREERS IN MATH

Hydrologist A hydrologist is a scientist who studies and solves water-related issues. A hydrologist might work to prevent or clean up polluted water sources, locate water supplies for urban or rural needs, or control flooding and erosion. A hydrologist uses math to assess water resources and mathematical models to understand water systems, as well as statistics to analyze phenomena such as rainfall patterns. If you are interested in a career as a hydrologist, you should study the following mathematical subjects:

- Algebra
- Trigonometry
- Calculus
- Statistics

Research other careers that require creating and using mathematical models to understand physical phenomena.

Unit 5 Performance Task

At the end of the unit, check out how **hydrologists** use math.

Vocabulary Preview

Use the puzzle to preview key vocabulary from this unit. Unscramble the circled letters to answer the riddle at the bottom of the page.

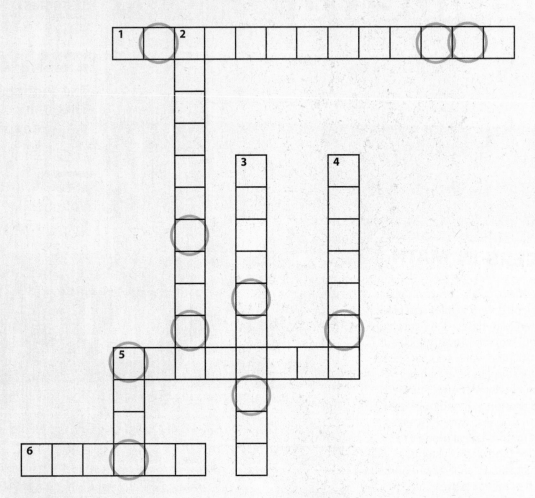

Across

1. The angle formed by two sides of a triangle (2 words) (Lesson 11.2)

5. A three-dimensional figure that has two congruent circular bases. (Lesson 13.1)

6. A three-dimensional figure with all points the same distance from the center. (Lesson 13.3)

Down

2. The line that intersects two or more lines. (Lesson 11.1)

3. The side opposite the right angle in a right triangle. (Lesson 12.1)

4. Figures with the same shape but not necessarily the same size. (Lesson 11.3)

5. A three-dimensional figure that has one vertex and one circular base. (Lesson 13.2)

Q: What do you call an angle that is adorable?

A: __ _____ _____!

Angle Relationships in Parallel Lines and Triangles

? ESSENTIAL QUESTION

How can you use angle relationships in parallel lines and triangles to solve real-world problems?

Real-World Video

Many cities are designed on a grid with parallel streets. If another street runs across the parallel lines, it is a transversal. Special relationships exist between parallel lines and transversals.

my.hrw.com

GO DIGITAL

my.hrw.com

my.hrw.com

Go digital with your write-in student edition, accessible on any device.

Math On the Spot

Scan with your smart phone to jump directly to the online edition, video tutor, and more.

Animated Math

Interactively explore key concepts to see how math works.

Personal Math Trainer

Get immediate feedback and help as you work through practice sets.

Are YOU Ready?

Complete these exercises to review skills you will need for this module.

Solve Two-Step Equations

EXAMPLE		
	$7x + 9 = 30$	Write the equation.
	$7x + 9 - 9 = 30 - 9$	Subtract 9 from both sides.
	$7x = 21$	Simplify.
	$\dfrac{7x}{7} = \dfrac{21}{7}$	Divide both sides by 7.
	$x = 3$	Simplify.

Solve for x.

1. $6x + 10 = 46$ **2.** $7x - 6 = 36$ **3.** $3x + 26 = 59$ **4.** $2x + 5 = -25$

_____ _____ _____ _____

5. $6x - 7 = 41$ **6.** $\dfrac{1}{2}x + 9 = 30$ **7.** $\dfrac{1}{3}x - 7 = 15$ **8.** $0.5x - 0.6 = 8.4$

_____ _____ _____ _____

Name Angles

EXAMPLE

Use three points of an angle, including the vertex, to name the angle. Write the vertex between the other two points: $\angle JKL$ or $\angle LKJ$. You can also use just the vertex letter to name the angle if there is no danger of confusing the angle with another. This is also $\angle K$.

Give two names for the angle formed by the dashed rays.

9. _____ **10.** _____ **11.** _____

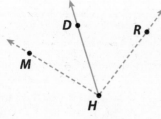

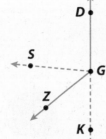

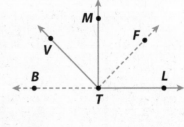

Reading Start-Up

Visualize Vocabulary

Use the ✔ words to complete the graphic. You can put more than one word in each section of the triangle.

Reviewing Angles

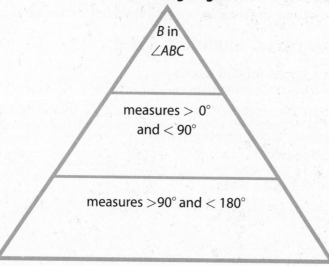

B in
∠*ABC*

measures > 0°
and < 90°

measures >90° and < 180°

Understand Vocabulary

Complete the sentences using preview words.

1. A line that intersects two or more lines is a _____.

2. Figures with the same shape but not necessarily the same size
   are _____.

3. An _____ is an angle formed by one side of
   the triangle and the extension of an adjacent side.

Active Reading

Pyramid Before beginning the module, create a pyramid to help you organize what you learn. Label each side with one of the lesson titles from this module. As you study each lesson, write important ideas like vocabulary, properties, and formulas on the appropriate side.

Unpacking the Standards

Understanding the standards and the vocabulary terms in the standards will help you know exactly what you are expected to learn in this module.

8.G.5

Use informal arguments to establish facts about the angle sum and exterior angle of triangles, about the angles created when parallel lines are cut by a transversal, and the angle-angle criterion for similarity of triangles.

Key Vocabulary

transversal *(transversal)*
   A line that intersects two or more lines.

What It Means to You

You will learn about the special angle relationships formed when parallel lines are intersected by a third line called a transversal.

UNPACKING EXAMPLE 8.G.5

Which angles formed by the transversal and the parallel lines seem to be congruent?

It appears that the angles below are congruent.

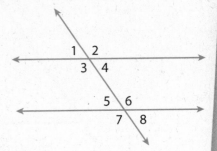

$\angle 1 \cong \angle 4 \cong \angle 5 \cong \angle 8$

$\angle 2 \cong \angle 3 \cong \angle 6 \cong \angle 7$

8.G.5

Use informal arguments to establish facts about the angle sum and exterior angle of triangles, about the angles created when parallel lines are cut by a transversal, and the angle-angle criterion for similarity of triangles.

What It Means to You

You will use the angle-angle criterion to determine similarity of two triangles.

UNPACKING EXAMPLE 8.G.5

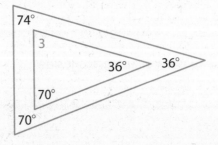

Explain whether the triangles are similar.

Two angles in the large triangle are congruent to two angles in the smaller triangle, so the third pair of angles must also be congruent, which makes the triangles similar.

$70° + 36° + m\angle 3 = 180°$

$m\angle 3 = 74°$

Visit **my.hrw.com** to see all the **Common Core Standards** unpacked.

my.hrw.com

346 Unit 5

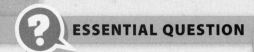

LESSON
11.1 Parallel Lines Cut by a Transversal

COMMON CORE **8.G.5**

Use informal arguments to establish facts about... the angles created when parallel lines are cut by a transversal....

? **ESSENTIAL QUESTION**

What can you conclude about the angles formed by parallel lines that are cut by a transversal?

EXPLORE ACTIVITY 1 COMMON CORE **8.G.5**

Parallel Lines and Transversals

A **transversal** is a line that intersects two lines in the same plane at two different points. Transversal *t* and lines *a* and *b* form eight angles.

Angle Pairs Formed by a Transversal	
Term	**Example**
Corresponding angles lie on the same side of the transversal *t*, on the same side of lines *a* and *b*.	∠1 and ∠5
Alternate interior angles are nonadjacent angles that lie on opposite sides of the transversal *t*, between lines *a* and *b*.	∠3 and ∠6
Alternate exterior angles lie on opposite sides of the transversal *t*, outside lines *a* and *b*.	∠1 and ∠8
Same-side interior angles lie on the same side of the transversal *t*, between lines *a* and *b*.	∠3 and ∠5

Use geometry software to explore the angles formed when a transversal intersects parallel lines.

A Construct a line and label two points on the line *A* and *B*.

B Create point *C* not on $\overleftrightarrow{AB}$. Then construct a line parallel to $\overleftrightarrow{AB}$ through point *C*. Create another point on this line and label it *D*.

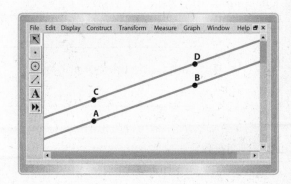

C Create two points outside the two parallel lines and label them *E* and *F*. Construct transversal $\overleftrightarrow{EF}$. Label the points of intersection *G* and *H*.

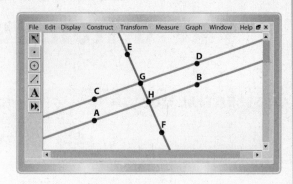

D Measure the angles formed by the parallel lines and the transversal. Write the angle measures in the table below.

E Drag point *E* or point *F* to a different position. Record the new angle measures in the table.

Angle	∠CGE	∠DGE	∠CGH	∠DGH	∠AHG	∠BHG	∠AHF	∠BHF
Measure								
Measure								

Reflect

Make a Conjecture **Identify the pairs of angles in the diagram. Then make a conjecture about their angle measures. Drag a point in the diagram to confirm your conjecture.**

1. corresponding angles

_____

_____

_____

2. alternate interior angles

_____

_____

3. alternate exterior angles

_____

_____

4. same-side interior angles

_____

_____

Justifying Angle Relationships

You can use tracing paper to informally justify your conclusions from the first Explore Activity.

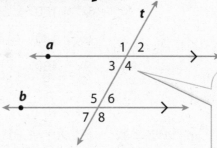

Lines *a* and *b* are parallel. (The black arrows on the diagram indicate parallel lines.)

> Recall that vertical angles are the opposite angles formed by two intersecting lines. $\angle 1$ and $\angle 4$ are vertical angles.

A Trace the diagram onto tracing paper.

B Position the tracing paper over the original diagram so that $\angle 1$ on the tracing is over $\angle 5$ on the original diagram. Compare the two angles. Do they appear to be congruent?

_____

_____

C Use the tracing paper to compare all eight angles in the diagram to each other. List all of the congruent angle pairs.

_____

_____

_____

Math Talk
Mathematical Practices

What do you notice about the special angle pairs formed by the transversal?

Finding Unknown Angle Measures

You can find any unknown angle measure when two parallel lines are cut by a transversal if you are given at least one other angle measure.

Math On the Spot
my.hrw.com

EXAMPLE 1 | COMMON CORE 8.G.5

A Find m$\angle 2$ when m$\angle 7 = 125°$.

$\angle 2$ is congruent to $\angle 7$ because they are alternate exterior angles.

Therefore, m$\angle 2 = 125°$.

B Find m$\angle VWZ$.

$\angle VWZ$ is supplementary to $\angle YVW$ because they are same-side interior angles.
m$\angle VWZ$ + m$\angle YVW = 180°$

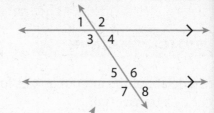

Animated Math
my.hrw.com

From the previous page, $m\angle VWZ + m\angle YVW = 180°$, $m\angle VWZ = 3x°$, and $m\angle YVW = 6x°$.

$$m\angle VWZ + m\angle YVW = 180°$$

$$3x° + 6x° = 180°$$ Replace $m\angle VWZ$ with $3x°$ and $m\angle YVW$ with $6x°$.

$$9x = 180$$ Combine like terms.

$$\frac{9x}{9} = \frac{180}{9}$$ Divide both sides by 9.

$$x = 20$$ Simplify.

$$m\angle VWZ = 3x° = (3 \cdot 20)° = 60°$$

Personal Math Trainer

Online Assessment and Intervention

⏻ my.hrw.com

YOUR TURN

Find each angle measure.

5. $m\angle GDE =$ _____

6. $m\angle BEF =$ _____

7. $m\angle CDG =$ _____

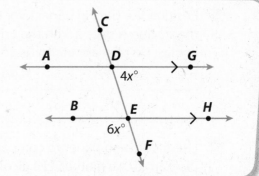

Guided Practice

Use the figure for Exercises 1–4. (Explore Activity 1 and Example 1)

1. $\angle UVY$ and _____ are a pair of corresponding angles.

2. $\angle WVY$ and $\angle VWT$ are _____ angles.

3. Find $m\angle SVW.$ _____

4. Find $m\angle VWT.$ _____

5. Vocabulary When two parallel lines are cut by a transversal,

_____ angles are supplementary. (Explore Activity 1)

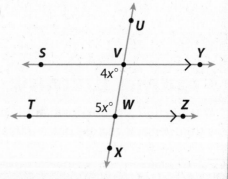

? ESSENTIAL QUESTION CHECK-IN

6. What can you conclude about the interior angles formed when two parallel lines are cut by a transversal?

_____

_____

11.1 Independent Practice

COMMON CORE 8.G.5

Personal Math Trainer

Online Assessment and Intervention

my.hrw.com

Vocabulary Use the figure for Exercises 7–10.

7. Name all pairs of corresponding angles.

_____

8. Name both pairs of alternate exterior angles.

_____

9. Name the relationship between ∠3 and ∠6.

_____

10. Name the relationship between ∠4 and ∠6.

_____

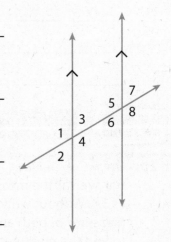

Find each angle measure.

11. m∠AGE when m∠FHD = 30° _____

12. m∠AGH when m∠CHF = 150° _____

13. m∠CHF when m∠BGE = 110° _____

14. m∠CHG when m∠HGA = 120° _____

15. m∠BGH = _____

16. m∠GHD = _____

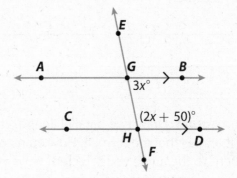

17. The Cross Country Bike Trail follows a straight line where it crosses 350th and 360th Streets. The two streets are parallel to each other. What is the measure of the larger angle formed at the intersection of the bike trail and 360th Street? Explain.

_____

_____

_____

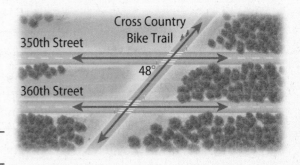

18. **Critical Thinking** How many different angles would be formed by a transversal intersecting three parallel lines? How many different angle measures would there be?

_____

_____

19. Communicate Mathematical Ideas In the diagram at the right, suppose m∠6 = 125°. Explain how to find the measures of each of the other seven numbered angles.

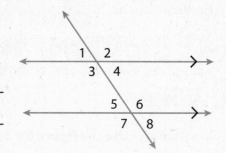

_____

_____

_____

_____

_____

_____

20. Draw Conclusions In a diagram showing two parallel lines cut by a transversal, the measures of two same-side interior angles are both given as $3x°$. Without writing and solving an equation, can you determine the measures of both angles? Explain. Then write and solve an equation to find the measures.

_____

_____

_____

21. Make a Conjecture Draw two parallel lines and a transversal. Choose one of the eight angles that are formed. How many of the other seven angles are congruent to the angle you selected? How many of the other seven angles are supplementary to your angle? Will your answer change if you select a different angle?

_____

22. Critique Reasoning In the diagram at the right, ∠2, ∠3, ∠5, and ∠8 are all congruent, and ∠1, ∠4, ∠6, and ∠7 are all congruent. Aiden says that this is enough information to conclude that the diagram shows two parallel lines cut by a transversal. Is he correct? Justify your answer.

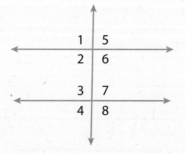

_____

_____

_____

_____

_____

Work Area

Angle Theorems for Triangles

COMMON CORE 8.G.5

Use informal arguments to establish facts about the angle sum and exterior angle of triangles.... *Also 8.EE.7, 8.EE.7b*

ESSENTIAL QUESTION

What can you conclude about the measures of the angles of a triangle?

EXPLORE ACTIVITY 1 COMMON CORE 8.G.5

Sum of the Angle Measures in a Triangle

There is a special relationship between the measures of the interior angles of a triangle.

A Draw a triangle and cut it out. Label the angles *A, B,* and *C.*

B Tear off each "corner" of the triangle. Each corner includes the vertex of one angle of the triangle.

C Arrange the vertices of the triangle around a point so that none of your corners overlap and there are no gaps between them.

D What do you notice about how the angles fit together around a point?

_____

E What is the measure of a straight angle? _____

F Describe the relationship among the measures of the angles of △*ABC.*

_____

The Triangle Sum Theorem states that for △*ABC,* m∠*A* + m∠*B* + m∠*C* = _____.

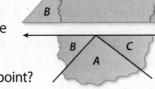

Reflect

1. Justify Reasoning Can a triangle have two right angles? Explain.

_____

_____

_____

2. Analyze Relationships Describe the relationship between the two acute angles in a right triangle. Explain your reasoning.

_____

_____

_____

Justifying the Triangle Sum Theorem

You can use your knowledge of parallel lines intersected by a transversal to informally justify the Triangle Sum Theorem.

Follow the steps to informally prove the Triangle Sum Theorem. You should draw each step on your own paper. The figures below are provided for you to check your work.

A Draw a triangle and label the angles as ∠1, ∠2, and ∠3 as shown.

B Draw line *a* through the base of the triangle.

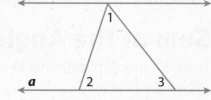

C The Parallel Postulate states that through a point not on a line ℓ, there is exactly one line parallel to line ℓ. Draw line *b* parallel to line *a,* through the vertex opposite the base of the triangle.

D Extend each of the non-base sides of the triangle to form transversal *s* and transversal *t*. Transversals *s* and *t* intersect parallel lines *a* and *b*.

E Label the angles formed by line *b* and the transversals as ∠4 and ∠5.

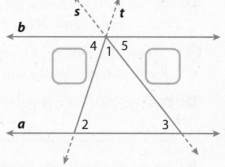

F Because ∠4 and _____ are alternate interior angles, they are _____.

Label ∠4 with the number of the angle to which it is congruent.

G Because ∠5 and _____ are alternate interior angles, they are _____.

Label ∠5 with the number of the angle to which it is congruent.

H The three angles that lie along line *b* at the vertex of the triangle are ∠1, ∠4, and ∠5. Notice that these three angles lie along a line.

So, $m\angle 1 + m\angle 4 + m\angle 5 =$ _____.

Because angles 2 and 4 are congruent and angles 3 and 5 are congruent, you can substitute $m\angle 2$ for $m\angle 4$ and $m\angle 3$ for $m\angle 5$ in the equation above.

So, $m\angle 1 + m\angle 2 + m\angle 3 =$ _____.

This shows that the sum of the angle measures in a triangle is

always _____.

Reflect

3. Analyze Relationships How can you use the fact that m∠4 + m∠1 + m∠5 = 180° to show that m∠2 + m∠1 + m∠3 = 180°?

_____

_____

_____

Finding Missing Angle Measures in Triangles

If you know the measures of two angles in a triangle, you can use the Triangle Sum Theorem to find the measure of the third angle.

EXAMPLE 1

COMMON CORE   8.EE.7

Find the missing angle measure.

My Notes

STEP 1 Write the Triangle Sum Theorem for this triangle.

m∠D + m∠E + m∠F = 180°

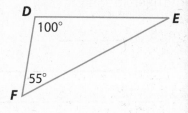

STEP 2 Substitute the given angle measures.

55° + m∠E + 100° = 180°

STEP 3 Solve the equation for m∠E.

$$55° + m\angle E + 100° = 180°$$

$$155° + m\angle E = 180°$$

$$\underline{-155°} \qquad \underline{-155°}$$

Subtract 155° from both sides. Simplify.

$$m\angle E = \quad 25°$$

So, m∠E = 25°.

YOUR TURN

Find the missing angle measure.

4.

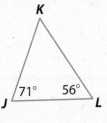

m∠K = _____

5.

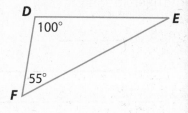

m∠R = _____

© Houghton Mifflin Harcourt Publishing Company

Exterior Angles and Remote Interior Angles

An **interior angle** of a triangle is formed by two sides of the triangle. An **exterior angle** is formed by one side of the triangle and the extension of an adjacent side. Each exterior angle has two remote interior angles. A **remote interior angle** is an interior angle that is not adjacent to the exterior angle.

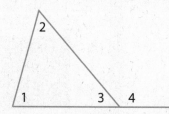

- ∠1, ∠2, and ∠3 are interior angles.
- ∠4 is an exterior angle.
- ∠1 and ∠2 are remote interior angles to ∠4.

There is a special relationship between the measure of an exterior angle and the measures of its remote interior angles.

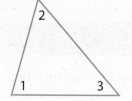

A Extend the base of the triangle and label the exterior angle as ∠4.

B The Triangle Sum Theorem states:

m∠1 + m∠2 + m∠3 = _____ .

C ∠3 and ∠4 form a _____ ,

so m∠3 + m∠4 = _____ .

D Use the equations in **B** and **C** to complete the following equation:

m∠1 + m∠2 + _____ = _____ + m∠4

E Use properties of equality to simplify the equation in **D** :

_____

The Exterior Angle Theorem states that the measure of an _____ angle

is equal to the sum of its _____ angles.

Reflect

6. Sketch a triangle and draw all of its exterior angles. How many exterior angles does a triangle have at each vertex?

_____

7. How many total exterior angles does a triangle have?

_____

Using the Exterior Angle Theorem

You can use the Exterior Angle Theorem to find the measures of the interior angles of a triangle.

EXAMPLE 2

COMMON CORE 8.EE.7b

Find m∠A and m∠B.

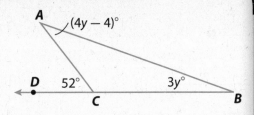

STEP 1 Write the Exterior Angle Theorem as it applies to this triangle.

$$m\angle A + m\angle B = m\angle ACD$$

STEP 2 Substitute the given angle measures.

$$(4y - 4)° + 3y° = 52°$$

STEP 3 Solve the equation for y.

$$(4y - 4)° + 3y° = 52°$$

$4y° - 4° + 3y° = 52°$		Remove parentheses.
$7y° - 4° = 52°$		Simplify.
$+4° \qquad +4°$		Add 4° to both sides.
$7y° = 56°$		Simplify.
$\dfrac{7y°}{7} = \dfrac{56°}{7}$		Divide both sides by 7.
$y = 8$		Simplify.

STEP 4 Use the value of y to find m∠A and m∠B.

$$m\angle A = 4y - 4 \qquad\qquad m\angle B = 3y$$
$$= 4(8) - 4 \qquad\qquad\quad = 3(8)$$
$$= 32 - 4 \qquad\qquad\qquad = 24$$
$$= 28$$

So, m∠A = 28° and m∠B = 24°.

> **Math Talk**
> Mathematical Practices
>
> Describe two ways to find m∠ACB.

YOUR TURN

8. Find m∠M and m∠N.

m∠M = _____

m∠N = _____

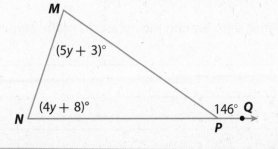

© Houghton Mifflin Harcourt Publishing Company

Find each missing angle measure. (Explore Activity 1 and Example 1)

1.

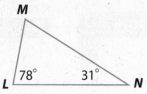

$m\angle M =$ _____

2.

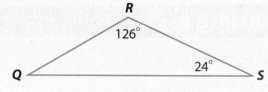

$m\angle Q =$ _____

Use the Triangle Sum Theorem to find the measure of each angle in degrees. (Explore Activity 2 and Example 1)

3.

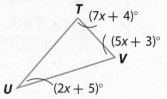

$m\angle T =$ _____, $m\angle U =$ _____,

$m\angle V =$ _____

4.

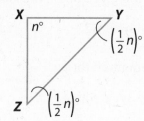

$m\angle X =$ _____, $m\angle Y =$ _____,

$m\angle Z =$ _____

Use the Exterior Angle Theorem to find the measure of each angle in degrees. (Explore Activity 3 and Example 2)

5.

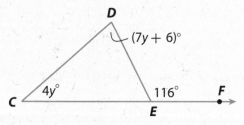

$m\angle C =$ _____, $m\angle D =$ _____,

$m\angle DEC =$ _____

6.

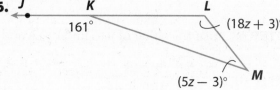

$m\angle L =$ _____, $m\angle M =$ _____,

$m\angle LKM =$ _____

? ESSENTIAL QUESTION CHECK-IN

7. Describe the relationships among the measures of the angles of a triangle.

_____

_____

_____

11.2 Independent Practice

COMMON CORE 8.EE.7, 8.EE.7b, 8.G.5

Find the measure of each angle.

8.

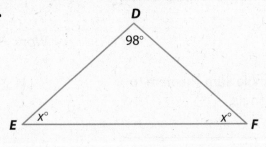

m∠E = _____

m∠F = _____

9.

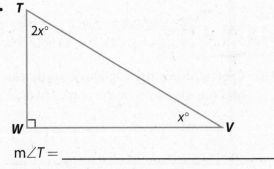

m∠T = _____

m∠V = _____

10.

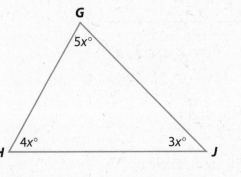

m∠G = _____

m∠H = _____

m∠J = _____

11.

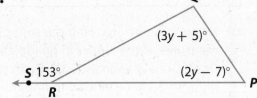

m∠Q = _____

m∠P = _____

m∠QRP = _____

12.

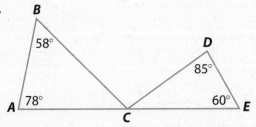

m∠ACB = _____

m∠BCD = _____

m∠DCE = _____

13.

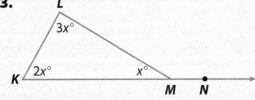

m∠K = _____

m∠L = _____

m∠KML = _____

m∠LMN = _____

14. Multistep The second angle in a triangle is five times as large as the first. The third angle is two-thirds as large as the first. Find the angle measures. _____

15. Analyze Relationships Can a triangle have two obtuse angles? Explain.

_____

_____

_____

_____

16. Critical Thinking Explain how you can use the Triangle Sum Theorem to find the measures of the angles of an equilateral triangle.

_____

_____

_____

_____

Work Area

17. a. Draw Conclusions Find the sum of the measures of the angles in quadrilateral *ABCD*. (Hint: Draw diagonal $\overline{AC}$. How can you use the figures you have formed to find the sum?)

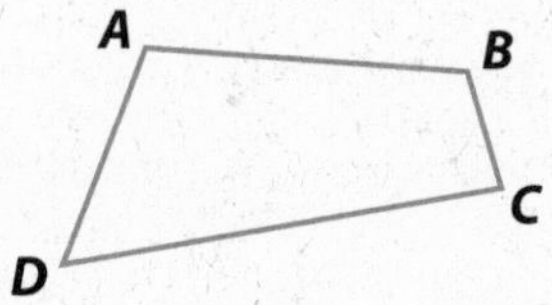

Sum = _____

b. Make a Conjecture Write a "Quadrilateral Sum Theorem." Explain why you think it is true.

_____

_____

_____

_____

_____

18. Communicate Mathematical Ideas Describe two ways that an exterior angle of a triangle is related to one or more of the interior angles.

_____

_____

_____

_____

LESSON 11.3 Angle-Angle Similarity

COMMON CORE 8.G.5

Use informal arguments to establish facts about ... the angle-angle criterion for similarity of triangles. *Also 8.EE.6, 8.EE.7*

? ESSENTIAL QUESTION

How can you determine when two triangles are similar?

EXPLORE ACTIVITY 1 **8.G.5**

Discovering Angle-Angle Similarity

Similar figures have the same shape but may have different sizes. Two triangles are **similar** if their corresponding angles are congruent and the lengths of their corresponding sides are proportional.

A Use your protractor and a straightedge to draw a triangle. Make one angle measure 45° and another angle measure 60°.

B Compare your triangle to those drawn by your classmates. How are the triangles the same?

_____

How are they different?

_____

C Use the Triangle Sum Theorem to find the measure of the third angle of your triangle.

_____

Reflect

1. If two angles in one triangle are congruent to two angles in another triangle, what do you know about the third pair of angles?

_____

2. Make a Conjecture Are two pairs of congruent angles enough information to conclude that two triangles are similar? Explain.

_____

_____

_____

© Houghton Mifflin Harcourt Publishing Company

Using the AA Similarity Postulate

Angle-Angle (AA) Similarity Postulate

If two angles of one triangle are congruent to two angles of another triangle, then the triangles are similar.

EXAMPLE 1

COMMON CORE 8.G.5

Explain whether the triangles are similar.

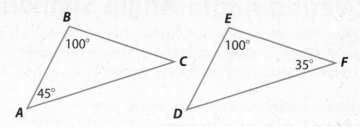

The figure shows only one pair of congruent angles. Find the measure of the third angle in each triangle.

$$45° + 100° + m\angle C = 180° \qquad 100° + 35° + m\angle D = 180°$$

$$145° + m\angle C = 180° \qquad 135° + m\angle D = 180°$$

$$145° + m\angle C - 145° = 180° - 145° \qquad 135° + m\angle D - 135° = 180° - 135°$$

$$m\angle C = 35° \qquad m\angle D = 45°$$

Because two angles in one triangle are congruent to two angles in the other triangle, the triangles are similar.

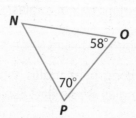

Math Talk

Mathematical Practices

Are all right triangles similar? Why or why not?

YOUR TURN

3. **Explain whether the triangles are similar.**

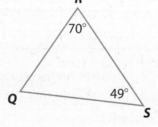

_____

_____

_____

Finding Missing Measures in Similar Triangles

Because corresponding angles are congruent and corresponding sides are proportional in similar triangles, you can use similar triangles to solve real-world problems.

Math On the Spot
my.hrw.com

EXAMPLE 2 Real World

COMMON CORE 8.EE.7

While playing tennis, Matt is 12 meters from the net, which is 0.9 meter high. He needs to hit the ball so that it just clears the net and lands 6 meters beyond the base of the net. At what height should Matt hit the tennis ball?

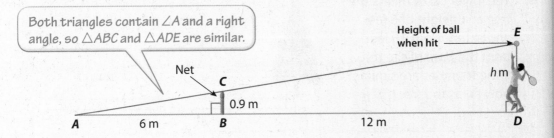

Both triangles contain ∠A and a right angle, so △ABC and △ADE are similar.

Net

Height of ball when hit

E

h m

C

0.9 m

A   6 m   B   12 m   D

In similar triangles, corresponding side lengths are proportional.

$$\frac{AD}{AB} = \frac{DE}{BC} \longrightarrow \frac{6+12}{6} = \frac{h}{0.9}$$ Substitute the lengths from the figure.

$$0.9 \times \frac{18}{6} = \frac{h}{0.9} \times 0.9$$ Use properties of equality to get h by itself.

$$0.9 \times 3 = h$$ Simplify.

$$2.7 = h$$ Multiply.

Matt should hit the ball at a height of 2.7 meters.

Reflect

4. **What If?** Suppose you set up a proportion so that each ratio compares parts of one triangle, as shown below.

height of △ABC ⟶ $\frac{BC}{AB} = \frac{DE}{AD}$ ⟵ height of △ADE
base of △ABC ⟶   ⟵ base of △ADE

Show that this proportion leads to the same value for h as in Example 2.

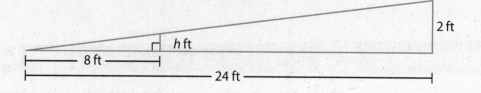

YOUR TURN

5. Rosie is building a wheelchair ramp that is 24 feet long and 2 feet high. She needs to install a vertical support piece 8 feet from the end of the ramp. What is the length of the support piece in inches?

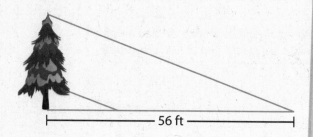

_2 ft_

_h ft_

_8 ft_

_24 ft_

_____

6. The lower cable meets the tree at a height of 6 feet and extends out 16 feet from the base of the tree. If the triangles are similar, how tall is the tree?

_56 ft_

_____

EXPLORE ACTIVITY 2 COMMON CORE 8.EE.6

Using Similar Triangles to Explain Slope

You can use similar triangles to show that the slope of a line is constant.

A Draw a line ℓ that is not a horizontal line. Label four points on the line as A, B, C, and D.

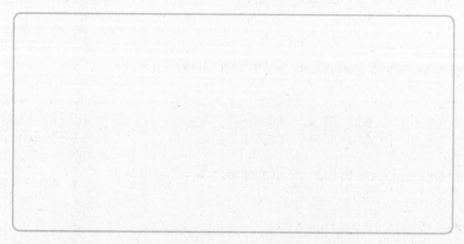

You need to show that the slope between points A and B is the same as the slope between points C and D.

B Draw the rise and run for the slope between points A and B. Label the intersection as point E. Draw the rise and run for the slope between points C and D. Label the intersection as point F.

C Write expressions for the slope between A and B and between C and D.

Slope between A and B: $\dfrac{BE}{\boxed{}}$ Slope between C and D: $\dfrac{\boxed{}}{CF}$

D Extend $\overleftrightarrow{AE}$ and $\overleftrightarrow{CF}$ across your drawing. $\overleftrightarrow{AE}$ and $\overleftrightarrow{CF}$ are both horizontal lines, so they are parallel.

Line ℓ is a _____ that intersects parallel lines.

E Complete the following statements:

$\angle BAE$ and _____ are corresponding angles and are _____.

$\angle BEA$ and _____ are right angles and are _____.

F By Angle–Angle Similarity, $\triangle ABE$ and _____ are similar triangles.

G Use the fact that the lengths of corresponding sides of similar triangles are proportional to complete the following ratios: $\dfrac{BE}{DF} = \dfrac{\boxed{}}{CF}$

H Recall that you can also write the proportion so that the ratios compare parts of the same triangle: $\dfrac{\boxed{}}{AE} = \dfrac{DF}{\boxed{}}$.

I The proportion you wrote in step **H** shows that the ratios you wrote in **C** are equal. So, the slope of line ℓ is constant.

Reflect

7. **What If?** Suppose that you label two other points on line ℓ as G and H. Would the slope between these two points be different than the slope you found in the Explore Activity? Explain.

_____

_____

_____

1. Explain whether the triangles are similar. Label the angle measures in the figure. (Explore Activity 1 and Example 1)

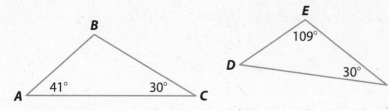

△ABC has angle measures _____ and △DEF has angle

measures _____. Because _____ in one

triangle are congruent to _____ in the other triangle, the

triangles are _____.

2. A flagpole casts a shadow 23.5 feet long. At the same time of day, Mrs. Gilbert, who is 5.5 feet tall, casts a shadow that is 7.5 feet long. How tall in feet is the flagpole? Round your answer to the nearest tenth. (Example 2)

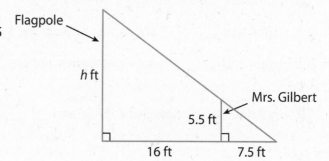

$$\frac{5.5}{\boxed{}} = \frac{h}{\boxed{}}$$

$h =$ _____ feet

3. Two transversals intersect two parallel lines as shown. Explain whether △ABC and △DEC are similar. (Example 1)

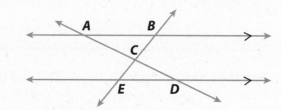

∠BAC and ∠EDC are _____ since they are _____.

∠ABC and ∠DEC are _____ since they are _____.

By _____, △ABC and △DEC are _____.

? ESSENTIAL QUESTION CHECK-IN

4. How can you determine when two triangles are similar?

_____

_____

_____

11.3 Independent Practice

 COMMON CORE 8.EE.6, 8.EE.7, 8.G.5

Use the diagrams for Exercises 5–7.

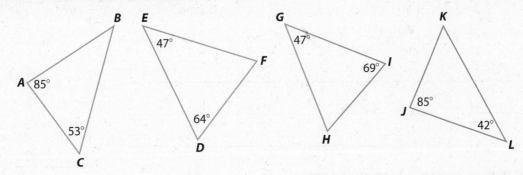

5. Find the missing angle measures in the triangles.

_____

6. Which triangles are similar?

_____

7. **Analyze Relationships** Determine which angles are congruent to the angles in △ABC.

_____

8. **Multistep** A tree casts a shadow that is 20 feet long. Frank is 6 feet tall, and while standing next to the tree he casts a shadow that is 4 feet long.

a. How tall is the tree? _____

b. How much taller is the tree than Frank? _____

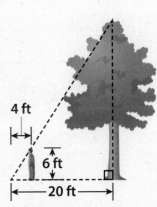

9. **Represent Real-World Problems** Sheila is climbing on a ladder that is attached against the side of a jungle gym wall. She is 5 feet off the ground and 3 feet from the base of the ladder, which is 15 feet from the wall. Draw a diagram to help you solve the problem. How high up the wall is the top of the ladder?

_____

10. **Justify Reasoning** Are two equilateral triangles always similar? Explain.

_____

_____

_____

11. Critique Reasoning Ryan calculated the missing measure in the diagram shown. What was his mistake?

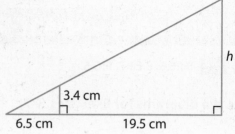

$$\frac{3.4}{6.5} = \frac{h}{19.5}$$

$$19.5 \times \frac{3.4}{6.5} = \frac{h}{19.5} \times 19.5$$

$$\frac{66.3}{6.5} = h$$

$$10.2 \text{ cm} = h$$

_____

_____

_____

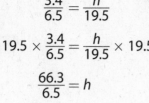 **FOCUS ON HIGHER ORDER THINKING**

Work Area

12. Communicate Mathematical Ideas For a pair of triangular earrings, how can you tell if they are similar? How can you tell if they are congruent?

_____

_____

_____

_____

13. Critical Thinking When does it make sense to use similar triangles to measure the height and length of objects in real life?

_____

_____

_____

14. Justify Reasoning Two right triangles on a coordinate plane are similar but not congruent. Each of the legs of both triangles are extended by 1 unit, creating two new right triangles. Are the resulting triangles similar? Explain using an example.

_____

_____

_____

_____

_____

_____

Similar Triangles and Slope

COMMON CORE **8.EE.6**

Use similar triangles to explain why the slope *m* is the same between any two distinct points on a non-vertical line in the coordinate plane; ...

 ESSENTIAL QUESTION

How can you apply the concept of similar triangles to prove that the slope of a line is constant between any two points on the line?

EXPLORE ACTIVITY COMMON CORE **8.EE.6**

Using Similar Triangles to Prove a Constant Slope

The R-value of insulation gives the material's resistance to heat flow. The graph shows the proportional relationship between the R-value and the thickness of fiberglass insulation.

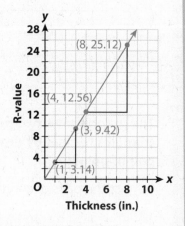

A The graph shows four points on the line and the triangles resulting from sketching the rise and run from one point to the next. Viewing the graph of R-value as a transversal to the rise and run segments, are the two pairs of corresponding angles along the transversal congruent? Explain.

_____

_____

_____

B What is the relationship between the two resulting triangles? Explain your answer.

_____

C Use the relationship from Part B to state the relationship between corresponding sides of the resulting triangles.

_____

D Use the properties of similar triangles to explain why the slope, or rise-to-run ratio, is constant between any two points on the line.

_____

_____

_____

E Use any two points to find the unit rate for this proportional relationship. Show your work.

_____

Reflect

1. **Communicate Mathematical Ideas** How can you use properties of similar triangles to show that the unit rate of a real-world proportional relationship is the same as the slope of its graph?

_____

_____

_____

_____

2. **Critical Thinking** What can you say about the *y*-value of the point (1, *y*) on the graph of a proportional relationship?

_____

Practice

The graph shows two pairs of points on a line and similar right triangles formed by drawing the rise and run segments for each pair of points.

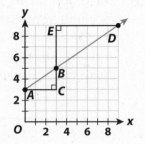

1. List the pairs of congruent angles and the similar triangles.

_____

_____

2. Use proportional corresponding side lengths to show that the slope of $\overline{AB}$ is equal to the slope of $\overline{BD}$.

_____

Use the graph at right for Exercises 3–8.

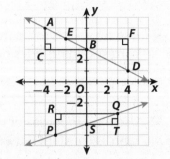

3. Name the pairs of congruent angles and similar triangles from the line containing *A* and *D*.

_____

_____

4. Name the pairs of congruent angles and similar triangles from the line containing *P* and *Q*.

_____

Complete each ratio.

5. $\dfrac{AC}{CB} = \dfrac{\boxed{}}{FE}$

6. $\dfrac{AB}{\boxed{}} = \dfrac{CB}{FE}$

7. $\dfrac{\boxed{}}{RP} = \dfrac{ST}{TQ}$

8. $\dfrac{PQ}{QS} = \dfrac{PR}{\boxed{}}$

Ready to Go On?

Personal
Math Trainer

Online Assessment
and Intervention

my.hrw.com

11.1 Parallel Lines Cut by a Transversal

In the figure, line $p \parallel$ line q. Find the measure of each angle if $m\angle 8 = 115°$.

1. $m\angle 7 = $ _____

2. $m\angle 6 = $ _____

3. $m\angle 1 = $ _____

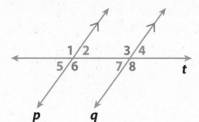

11.2 Angle Theorems for Triangles

Find the measure of each angle.

4. $m\angle A = $ _____

5. $m\angle B = $ _____

6. $m\angle BCA = $ _____

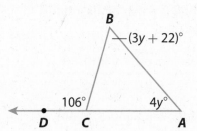

11.3 Angle-Angle Similarity

Triangle *FEG* is similar to triangle *IHJ*. Find the missing values.

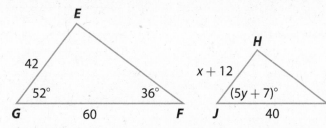

7. $x = $ _____

8. $y = $ _____

9. $m\angle H = $ _____

? ESSENTIAL QUESTION

10. How can you use similar triangles to solve real-world problems?

_____

_____

Selected Response

Use the figure for Exercises 1 and 2.

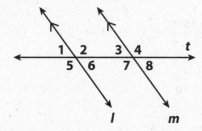

1. Which angle pair is a pair of alternate exterior angles?

(A) $\angle 5$ and $\angle 6$ (C) $\angle 5$ and $\angle 4$

(B) $\angle 6$ and $\angle 7$ (D) $\angle 5$ and $\angle 2$

2. Which of the following angles is **not** congruent to $\angle 3$?

(A) $\angle 1$ (C) $\angle 6$

(B) $\angle 2$ (D) $\angle 8$

3. The measures, in degrees, of the three angles of a triangle are given by $2x + 1$, $3x - 3$, and $9x$. What is the measure of the smallest angle?

(A) $13°$ (C) $36°$

(B) $27°$ (D) $117°$

4. Which is a possible measure of $\angle DCA$ in the triangle below?

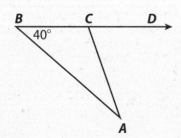

(A) $36°$ (C) $40°$

(B) $38°$ (D) $70°$

5. Kaylee wrote in her dinosaur report that the Jurassic period was 1.75×10^8 years ago. What is this number written in standard form?

(A) 1,750,000

(B) 17,500,000

(C) 175,000,000

(D) 17,500,000,000

6. Given that y is proportional to x, what linear equation can you write if y is 16 when x is 20?

(A) $y = 20x$ (C) $y = \frac{4}{5}x$

(B) $y = \frac{5}{4}x$ (D) $y = 0.6x$

Mini-Task

7. Two transversals intersect two parallel lines as shown.

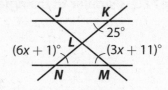

a. What is the value of x?

_____

b. What is the measure of $\angle LMN$?

_____

c. What is the measure of $\angle KLM$?

_____

d. Which two triangles are similar? How do you know?

_____

_____

_____

The Pythagorean Theorem

ESSENTIAL QUESTION

How can you use the Pythagorean Theorem to solve real-world problems?

Real-World Video

The sizes of televisions are usually described by the length of the diagonal of the screen. To find this length of the diagonal of a rectangle, you can use the Pythagorean Theorem.

my.hrw.com

GO DIGITAL
my.hrw.com

my.hrw.com
Go digital with your write-in student edition, accessible on any device.

Math On the Spot
Scan with your smart phone to jump directly to the online edition, video tutor, and more.

Animated Math
Interactively explore key concepts to see how math works.

Personal Math Trainer
Get immediate feedback and help as you work through practice sets.

Are YOU Ready?

Complete these exercises to review skills you will need for this module.

Personal Math Trainer

Online Assessment and Intervention

© my.hrw.com

Find the Square of a Number

> **EXAMPLE** Find the square of 2.7.
>
> $$\begin{array}{r} 2.7 \\ \times\ 2.7 \\ \hline 189 \\ 54\ \ \\ \hline 7.29 \end{array}$$
>
> Multiply the number by itself.
>
> So, $2.7^2 = 7.29$.

Find the square of each number.

1. 5 _____   **2.** 16 _____   **3.** −11 _____   **4.** $\frac{2}{7}$ _____

Order of Operations

> **EXAMPLE** $\sqrt{(5-2)^2 + (8-4)^2}$ First, operate within parentheses.
>
> $\sqrt{(3)^2 + (4)^2}$ Next, simplify exponents.
>
> $\sqrt{9 + 16}$ Then add and subtract left to right.
>
> $\sqrt{25}$ Finally, take the square root.
>
> 5

Evaluate each expression.

5. $\sqrt{(6+2)^2 + (3+3)^2}$ _____   **6.** $\sqrt{(9-4)^2 + (5+7)^2}$ _____

7. $\sqrt{(10-6)^2 + (15-12)^2}$ _____   **8.** $\sqrt{(6+9)^2 + (10-2)^2}$ _____

Simplify Numerical Expressions

> **EXAMPLE** $\frac{1}{2}(2.5)^2(4) = \frac{1}{2}(6.25)(4)$ Simplify the exponent.
>
> $= 12.5$ Multiply from left to right.

Simplify each expression.

9. $5(8)(10)$ _____   **10.** $\frac{1}{2}(6)(12)$ _____   **11.** $\frac{1}{3}(3)(12)$ _____

12. $\frac{1}{2}(8)^2(4)$ _____   **13.** $\frac{1}{4}(10)^2(15)$ _____   **14.** $\frac{1}{3}(9)^2(6)$ _____

Reading Start-Up

Vocabulary

Review Words
✔ acute angles (*ángulos agudos*)
✔ angles (*ángulos*)
  area (*área*)
  ordered pair (*par ordenado*)
✔ right angle (*ángulo recto*)
✔ right triangle (*triángulo recto*)
  square root (*raíz cuadrada*)
  x-coordinate (*coordenada x*)
  y-coordinate (*coordenada y*)

Preview Words
  hypotenuse (*hipotenusa*)
  legs (*catetos*)
  theorem (*teorema*)
  vertex (*vértice*)

Visualize Vocabulary

Use the ✔ words to complete the graphic.

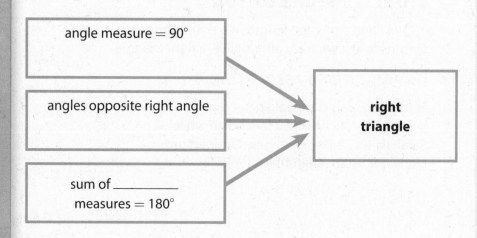

| angle measure = 90° |
| angles opposite right angle |
| sum of _____ measures = 180° |

→ **right triangle**

Understand Vocabulary

Match the term on the left to the correct expression on the right.

1. hypotenuse

2. theorem

3. legs

A. An idea that has been demonstrated as true.

B. The two sides that form the right angle of a right triangle.

C. The side opposite the right angle in a right triangle.

Active Reading

Booklet Before beginning the module, create a booklet to help you learn about the Pythagorean Theorem. Write the main idea of each lesson on each page of the booklet. As you study each lesson, write important details that support the main idea, such as vocabulary and formulas. Refer to your finished booklet as you work on assignments and study for tests.

Unpacking the Standards

Understanding the standards and the vocabulary terms in the standards will help you know exactly what you are expected to learn in this module.

© Houghton Mifflin Harcourt Publishing Company

 8.G.7

Apply the Pythagorean Theorem to determine unknown side lengths in right triangles in real-world and mathematical problems in two and three dimensions.

Key Vocabulary

Pythagorean Theorem
(Teorema de Pitágoras)
In a right triangle, the square of the length of the hypotenuse is equal to the sum of the squares of the lengths of the legs.

What It Means to You

You will find a missing length in a right triangle, or use side lengths to see whether a triangle is a right triangle.

UNPACKING EXAMPLE 8.G.7

Mark and Sarah start walking at the same point, but Mark walks 50 feet north while Sarah walks 75 feet east. How far apart are Mark and Sarah when they stop?

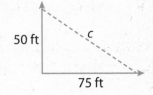

$$a^2 + b^2 = c^2 \qquad \text{Pythagorean Theorem}$$
$$50^2 + 75^2 = c^2 \qquad \text{Substitute.}$$
$$2500 + 5625 = c^2$$
$$8125 = c^2$$
$$90.1 \approx c$$

Mark and Sarah are approximately 90.1 feet apart.

8.G.8

Apply the Pythagorean Theorem to find the distance between two points in a coordinate system.

Key Vocabulary

coordinate plane
(plano cartesiano)
A plane formed by the intersection of a horizontal number line called the x-axis and a vertical number line called the y-axis.

What It Means to You

You can use the Pythagorean Theorem to find the distance between two points.

UNPACKING EXAMPLE 8.G.8

Find the distance between points A and B.

$$(AC)^2 + (BC)^2 = (AB)^2$$
$$(4 - 1)^2 + (6 - 2)^2 = (AB)^2$$
$$3^2 + 4^2 = (AB)^2$$
$$9 + 16 = (AB)^2$$
$$25 = (AB)^2$$
$$5 = AB$$

The distance is 5 units.

Visit **my.hrw.com** to see all the **Common Core Standards** unpacked.

my.hrw.com

The Pythagorean Theorem

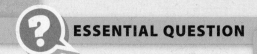
COMMON CORE 8.G.7

Apply the Pythagorean Theorem to determine unknown side lengths in right triangles in real-world and mathematical problems in two and three dimensions.
Also 8.G.6

 ESSENTIAL QUESTION

How can you prove the Pythagorean Theorem and use it to solve problems?

EXPLORE ACTIVITY COMMON CORE 8.G.6

Proving the Pythagorean Theorem

In a right triangle, the two sides that form the right angle are the **legs**. The side opposite the right angle is the **hypotenuse**.

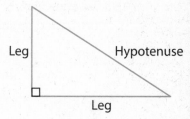

The Pythagorean Theorem

In a right triangle, the sum of the squares of the lengths of the legs is equal to the square of the length of the hypotenuse.

If a and b are legs and c is the hypotenuse, $a^2 + b^2 = c^2$.

A Draw a right triangle on a piece of paper and cut it out. Make one leg shorter than the other.

B Trace your triangle onto another piece of paper four times, arranging them as shown. For each triangle, label the shorter leg a, the longer leg b, and the hypotenuse c.

C What is the area of the unshaded square?

_____

Label the unshaded square with its area.

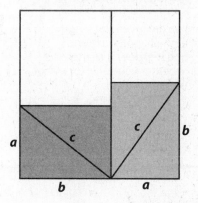

D Trace your original triangle onto a piece of paper four times again, arranging them as shown. Draw a line outlining a larger square that is the same size as the figure you made in **B**.

E What is the area of the unshaded square at the top right of the figure in **D**? at the top left?

_____

Label the unshaded squares with their areas.

F What is the total area of the unshaded regions in **D**?

_____

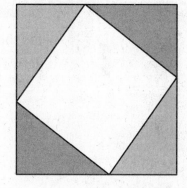

Reflect

1. Explain whether the figures in Ⓑ and Ⓓ have the same area.

   _____

2. Explain whether the unshaded regions of the figures in Ⓑ and Ⓓ have the same area.

   _____

   _____

   _____

3. **Analyze Relationships** Write an equation relating the area of the unshaded region in step Ⓑ to the unshaded region in Ⓓ.

   _____

Math On the Spot

my.hrw.com

Animated Math

my.hrw.com

Using the Pythagorean Theorem

You can use the Pythagorean Theorem to find the length of a side of a right triangle when you know the lengths of the other two sides.

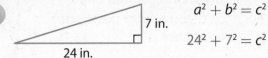

EXAMPLE 1

COMMON CORE 8.G.7

Find the length of the missing side.

Ⓐ

7 in.
24 in.

$$a^2 + b^2 = c^2$$
$$24^2 + 7^2 = c^2$$ Substitute into the formula.
$$576 + 49 = c^2$$ Simplify.
$$625 = c^2$$ Add.
$$25 = c$$ Take the square root of both sides.

The length of the hypotenuse is 25 inches.

Math Talk

Mathematical Practices

If you are given the length of the hypotenuse and one leg, does it matter whether you solve for a or b? Explain.

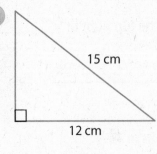

Ⓑ

15 cm
12 cm

$$a^2 + b^2 = c^2$$
$$a^2 + 12^2 = 15^2$$ Substitute into the formula.
$$a^2 + 144 = 225$$ Simplify.
$$a^2 = 81$$ Use properties of equality to get a^2 by itself.
$$a = 9$$ Take the square root of both sides.

The length of the leg is 9 centimeters.

YOUR TURN

Find the length of the missing side.

4.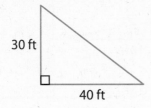

30 ft

40 ft

_____

5.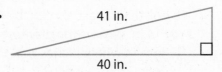

41 in.

40 in.

_____

Pythagorean Theorem in Three Dimensions

You can use the Pythagorean Theorem to solve problems in three dimensions.

Math On the Spot

⏻ my.hrw.com

EXAMPLE 2

COMMON CORE **8.G.7**

A box used for shipping narrow copper tubes measures 6 inches by 6 inches by 20 inches. What is the length of the longest tube that will fit in the box, given that the length of the tube must be a whole number of inches?

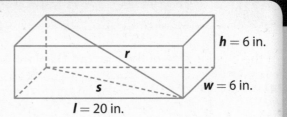

$h = 6$ in.

r

s

$w = 6$ in.

$l = 20$ in.

STEP 1　You want to find r, the length from a bottom corner to the opposite top corner. First, find s, the length of the diagonal across the bottom of the box.

$$w^2 + l^2 = s^2$$

$$6^2 + 20^2 = s^2 \qquad \text{Substitute into the formula.}$$

$$36 + 400 = s^2 \qquad \text{Simplify.}$$

$$436 = s^2 \qquad \text{Add.}$$

STEP 2　Use your expression for s to find r.

$$h^2 + s^2 = r^2$$

$$6^2 + 436 = r^2 \qquad \text{Substitute into the formula.}$$

$$472 = r^2 \qquad \text{Add.}$$

$$\sqrt{472} = r \qquad \text{Take the square root of both sides.}$$

$$21.7 \approx r \qquad \text{Use a calculator to round to the nearest tenth.}$$

The length of the longest tube that will fit in the box is 21 inches.

Math Talk

Mathematical Practices

Looking at Step 2, why did the calculations in Step 1 stop before taking the square root of both sides of the final equation?

© Houghton Mifflin Harcourt Publishing Company

6. Tina ordered a replacement part for her desk. It was shipped in a box that measures 4 in. by 4 in. by 14 in. What is the greatest length in whole inches that the part could have been?

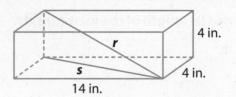

Guided Practice

1. Find the length of the missing side of the triangle. (Explore Activity 1 and Example 1)

$$a^2 + b^2 = c^2 \rightarrow 24^2 + \boxed{} = c^2 \rightarrow \boxed{} = c^2$$

The length of the hypotenuse is $\boxed{}$ feet.

10 ft

24 ft

2. Mr. Woo wants to ship a fishing rod that is 42 inches long to his son. He has a box with the dimensions shown. (Example 2)

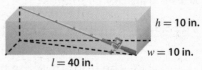

$h = 10$ in.
$w = 10$ in.
$l = 40$ in.

   a. Find the square of the length of the diagonal across the bottom of the box. _____

   b. Find the length from a bottom corner to the opposite top corner to the nearest tenth. Will the fishing rod fit? _____

? ESSENTIAL QUESTION CHECK-IN

3. State the Pythagorean Theorem and tell how you can use it to solve problems.

_____

_____

_____

_____

12.1 Independent Practice

COMMON CORE 8.G.6, 8.G.7

Personal Math Trainer

Online Assessment and Intervention

my.hrw.com

Find the length of the missing side of each triangle. Round your answers to the nearest tenth.

4.

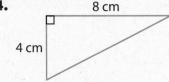

8 cm

4 cm

_____

5.

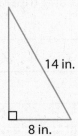

14 in.

8 in.

_____

6. The diagonal of a rectangular big-screen TV screen measures 152 cm. The length measures 132 cm. What is the height of the screen?   _____

7. Dylan has a square piece of metal that measures 10 inches on each side. He cuts the metal along the diagonal, forming two right triangles. What is the length of the hypotenuse of each right triangle to the nearest tenth of an inch?   _____

8. **Represent Real-World Problems** A painter has a 24-foot ladder that he is using to paint a house. For safety reasons, the ladder must be placed at least 8 feet from the base of the side of the house. To the nearest tenth of a foot, how high can the ladder safely reach?   _____

9. What is the longest flagpole (in whole feet) that could be

shipped in a box that measures 2 ft by 2 ft by 12 ft? _____

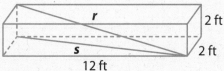

r

2 ft

s

12 ft

2 ft

10. **Sports** American football fields measure 100 yards long between the end zones, and are $53\frac{1}{3}$ yards wide. Is the length of the diagonal across this field more or less than 120 yards? Explain.

_____

11. **Justify Reasoning** A tree struck by lightning broke at a point 12 ft above the ground as shown. What was the height of the tree to the nearest tenth of a foot? Explain your reasoning.

12 ft

39 ft

_____

_____

Work Area

12. Multistep Main Street and Washington Avenue meet at a right angle. A large park begins at this corner. Joe's school lies at the opposite corner of the park. Usually Joe walks 1.2 miles along Main Street and then 0.9 miles up Washington Avenue to get to school. Today he walked in a straight path across the park and returned home along the same path. What is the difference in distance between the two round trips? Explain.

_____

_____

_____

13. Analyze Relationships An isosceles right triangle is a right triangle with congruent legs. If the length of each leg is represented by x, what algebraic expression can be used to represent the length of the hypotenuse? Explain your reasoning.

_____

_____

14. Persevere in Problem Solving A square hamburger is centered on a circular bun. Both the bun and the burger have an area of 16 square inches.

a. How far, to the nearest hundredth of an inch, does each corner of the burger stick out from the bun? Explain.

_____

_____

_____

_____

_____

b. How far does each bun stick out from the center of each side of the burger?

_____

c. Are the distances in part **a** and part **b** equal? If not, which sticks out more, the burger or the bun? Explain.

_____

_____

_____

LESSON
12.2
Converse of the Pythagorean Theorem

COMMON CORE 8.G.6

Explain a proof of the Pythagorean Theorem and its converse.

? **ESSENTIAL QUESTION**

How can you test the converse of the Pythagorean Theorem and use it to solve problems?

EXPLORE ACTIVITY COMMON CORE 8.G.6

Testing the Converse of the Pythagorean Theorem

The Pythagorean Theorem states that if a triangle is a right triangle, then $a^2 + b^2 = c^2$.

The *converse* of the Pythagorean Theorem states that if $a^2 + b^2 = c^2$, then the triangle is a right triangle.

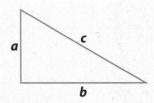

Decide whether the converse of the Pythagorean Theorem is true.

A Verify that the following sets of lengths make the equation $a^2 + b^2 = c^2$ true. Record your results in the table.

a	b	c	Is $a^2 + b^2 = c^2$ true?	Makes a right triangle?
3	4	5		
5	12	13		
7	24	25		
8	15	17		
20	21	29		

B For each set of lengths in the table, cut strips of grid paper with a width of one square and lengths that correspond to the values of *a*, *b*, and *c*.

C For each set of lengths, use the strips of grid paper to try to form a right triangle. An example using the first set of lengths is shown. Record your findings in the table.

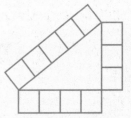

Reflect

1. **Draw Conclusions** Based on your observations, explain whether you think the converse of the Pythagorean Theorem is true.

_____

_____

Identifying a Right Triangle

The converse of the Pythagorean Theorem gives you a way to tell if a triangle is a right triangle when you know the side lengths.

EXAMPLE 1

 8.G.6

Tell whether each triangle with the given side lengths is a right triangle.

A 9 inches, 40 inches, and 41 inches

Let $a = 9$, $b = 40$, and $c = 41$.

$$a^2 + b^2 = c^2$$

$$9^2 + 40^2 \overset{?}{=} 41^2 \qquad \text{Substitute into the formula.}$$

$$81 + 1600 \overset{?}{=} 1681 \qquad \text{Simplify.}$$

$$1681 = 1681 \qquad \text{Add.}$$

Since $9^2 + 40^2 = 41^2$, the triangle is a right triangle by the converse of the Pythagorean Theorem.

B 8 meters, 10 meters, and 12 meters

Let $a = 8$, $b = 10$, and $c = 12$.

$$a^2 + b^2 = c^2$$

$$8^2 + 10^2 \overset{?}{=} 12^2 \qquad \text{Substitute into the formula.}$$

$$64 + 100 \overset{?}{=} 144 \qquad \text{Simplify.}$$

$$164 \neq 144 \qquad \text{Add.}$$

Since $8^2 + 10^2 \neq 12^2$, the triangle is not a right triangle by the converse of the Pythagorean Theorem.

YOUR TURN

Tell whether each triangle with the given side lengths is a right triangle.

2. 14 cm, 23 cm, and 25 cm

3. 16 in., 30 in., and 34 in.

4. 27 ft, 36 ft, 45 ft

5. 11 mm, 18 mm, 21 mm

Using the Converse of the Pythagorean Theorem

You can use the converse of the Pythagorean Theorem to solve real-world problems.

Math On the Spot
⏻ my.hrw.com

EXAMPLE 2   Real World   COMMON CORE 8.G.6

Katya is buying edging for a triangular flower garden she plans to build in her backyard. If the lengths of the three pieces of edging that she purchases are 13 feet, 10 feet, and 7 feet, will the flower garden be in the shape of a right triangle?

Use the converse of the Pythagorean Theorem. Remember to use the longest length for c.

Let $a = 7$, $b = 10$, and $c = 13$.

$$a^2 + b^2 = c^2$$

$$7^2 + 10^2 \overset{?}{=} 13^2 \qquad \text{Substitute into the formula.}$$

$$49 + 100 \overset{?}{=} 169 \qquad \text{Simplify.}$$

$$149 \neq 169 \qquad \text{Add.}$$

Since $7^2 + 10^2 \neq 13^2$, the garden will not be in the shape of a right triangle.

> ### Math Talk
> **Mathematical Practices**
>
> To what length, to the nearest tenth, can Katya trim the longest piece of edging to form a right triangle?

YOUR TURN

6. A blueprint for a new triangular playground shows that the sides measure 480 ft, 140 ft, and 500 ft. Is the playground in the shape of a right triangle? Explain.

   _____

   _____

7. A triangular piece of glass has sides that measure 18 in., 19 in., and 25 in. Is the piece of glass in the shape of a right triangle? Explain.

   _____

8. A corner of a fenced yard forms a right angle. Can you place a 12 foot long board across the corner to form a right triangle for which the leg lengths are whole numbers? Explain.

   _____

   _____

Personal Math Trainer

Online Assessment and Intervention

⏻ my.hrw.com

© Houghton Mifflin Harcourt Publishing Company

1. Lashandra used grid paper to construct the triangle shown. (Explore Activity)

   a. What are the lengths of the sides of Lashandra's triangle?

   _____units, _____units, _____units

   b. Use the converse of the Pythagorean Theorem to determine whether the triangle is a right triangle.

   $$a^2 + b^2 = c^2$$

   $$\boxed{}^2 + \boxed{}^2 \overset{?}{=} \boxed{}^2$$

   $$\boxed{} + \boxed{} \overset{?}{=} \boxed{}$$

   $$\boxed{} \overset{?}{=} \boxed{}$$

   The triangle that Lashandra constructed | is / is not | a right triangle.

2. A triangle has side lengths 9 cm, 12 cm, and 16 cm. Tell whether the triangle is a right triangle. (Example 1)

   Let $a =$ _____, $b =$ _____, and $c =$ _____.

   $$a^2 + b^2 = c^2$$

   $$\boxed{}^2 + \boxed{}^2 \overset{?}{=} \boxed{}^2$$

   $$\boxed{} + \boxed{} \overset{?}{=} \boxed{}$$

   $$\boxed{} \overset{?}{=} \boxed{}$$

   By the converse of the Pythagorean Theorem, the triangle | is / is not | a right triangle.

3. The marketing team at a new electronics company is designing a logo that contains a circle and a triangle. On one design, the triangle's side lengths are 2.5 in., 6 in., and 6.5 in. Is the triangle a right triangle? Explain. (Example 2)

   _____

? ESSENTIAL QUESTION CHECK-IN

4. How can you use the converse of the Pythagorean Theorem to tell if a triangle is a right triangle?

   _____

   _____

12.2 Independent Practice

COMMON CORE 8.G.6

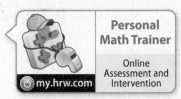

Personal Math Trainer

Online Assessment and Intervention

my.hrw.com

Tell whether each triangle with the given side lengths is a right triangle.

5. 11 cm, 60 cm, 61 cm

_____

6. 5 ft, 12 ft, 15 ft

_____

7. 9 in., 15 in., 17 in.

_____

8. 15 m, 36 m, 39 m

_____

9. 20 mm, 30 mm, 40 mm

_____

10. 20 cm, 48 cm, 52 cm

_____

11. 18.5 ft, 6 ft, 17.5 ft

_____

12. 2 mi, 1.5 mi, 2.5 mi

_____

13. 35 in., 45 in., 55 in.

_____

14. 25 cm, 14 cm, 23 cm

_____

15. The emblem on a college banner consists of the face of a tiger inside a triangle. The lengths of the sides of the triangle are 13 cm, 14 cm, and 15 cm. Is the triangle a right triangle? Explain.

_____

16. Kerry has a large triangular piece of fabric that she wants to attach to the ceiling in her bedroom. The sides of the piece of fabric measure 4.8 ft, 6.4 ft, and 8 ft. Is the fabric in the shape of a right triangle? Explain.

_____

17. A mosaic consists of triangular tiles. The smallest tiles have side lengths 6 cm, 10 cm, and 12 cm. Are these tiles in the shape of right triangles? Explain.

_____

18. **History** In ancient Egypt, surveyors made right angles by stretching a rope with evenly spaced knots as shown. Explain why the rope forms a right angle.

_____

_____

19. Justify Reasoning Yoshi has two identical triangular boards as shown. Can he use these two boards to form a rectangle? Explain.

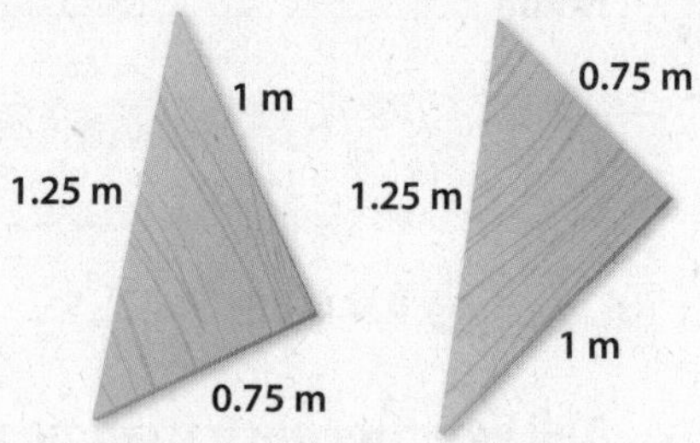

_____

_____

20. Critique Reasoning Shoshanna says that a triangle with side lengths 17 m, 8 m, and 15 m is not a right triangle because $17^2 + 8^2 = 353$, $15^2 = 225$, and $353 \neq 225$. Is she correct? Explain.

_____

_____

![H.O.T.] **FOCUS ON HIGHER ORDER THINKING**

21. Make a Conjecture Diondre says that he can take any right triangle and make a new right triangle just by doubling the side lengths. Is Diondre's conjecture true? Test his conjecture using three different right triangles.

_____

_____

_____

_____

22. Draw Conclusions A diagonal of a parallelogram measures 37 inches. The sides measure 35 inches and 1 foot. Is the parallelogram a rectangle? Explain your reasoning.

_____

_____

_____

_____

23. Represent Real-World Problems A soccer coach is marking the lines for a soccer field on a large recreation field. The dimensions of the field are to be 90 yards by 48 yards. Describe a procedure she could use to confirm that the sides of the field meet at right angles.

_____

_____

_____

_____

Work Area

Triple Concentration

INSTRUCTIONS

Playing the Game

STEP 1 Complete the Pythagorean Triples Worksheet to use as a reference for Pythagorean triples throughout the game.

Pythagorean Triples Worksheet (A)

Find the missing third number in each Pythagorean triple to complete the table. *HINT:* Multiples of Pythagorean triple are also Pythagorean triples.

$a^2 + b^2 = c^2$	a	b	c
$3^2 + 4^2 = \boxed{}^2$	3	4	
$6^2 + \boxed{}^2 = 10^2$	6		10
$\boxed{}^2 + 12^2 = 15^2$		12	15
$12^2 + 16^2 = \boxed{}^2$	12	16	
$5^2 + \boxed{}^2 = 13^2$	5		13
$\boxed{}^2 + 24^2 = 26^2$		24	26
$7^2 + 24^2 = \boxed{}^2$	7	24	
$8^2 + \boxed{}^2 = 17^2$	8		17

STEP 2 Arrange the 24 game cards randomly facedown in rows.

STEP 3 To start the game, each player turns over one card. The player whose card shows the largest number is Player 1, and will go first. Players observe the numbers showing, and then the cards are turned facedown again.

15

13

24

This is Player 1.

STEP 4   Players take turns moving clockwise.

When it is your turn, flip over any three cards, one at a time. Make sure that all players observe the cards. If the numbers shown form a Pythagorean triple, then pick up the cards, keep them, and take another turn. If they do not form a Pythagorean triple, then turn the cards facedown again in their original positions, and continue playing the game.

Is this a Pythagorean Triple?

STEP 5   Continue until all of the cards are removed.

 # Winning the Game

The player with the most triples at the end of the game wins.

Distance Between Two Points

COMMON CORE 8.G.8

Apply the Pythagorean Theorem to find the distance between two points in a coordinate system.

ESSENTIAL QUESTION

How can you use the Pythagorean Theorem to find the distance between two points on a coordinate plane?

EXPLORE ACTIVITY COMMON CORE 8.G.8

Pythagorean Theorem in the Coordinate Plane

Math On the Spot
🔴 my.hrw.com

EXAMPLE 1 The figure shows a right triangle. Approximate the length of the hypotenuse to the nearest tenth using a calculator.

STEP 1 Find the length of each leg.

The length of the vertical leg is _____ units.

The length of the horizontal leg is _____ units.

STEP 2 Let $a = 4$ and $b = 2$. Let c represent the length of the hypotenuse.

Use the Pythagorean Theorem to find c. $a^2 + b^2 = c^2$

Substitute into the formula. $\boxed{}^2 + \boxed{}^2 = c^2$

Simplify. $\boxed{} = c^2$

Take the square root of both sides. $\sqrt{\boxed{}} = c$

Use a calculator. Round to the nearest tenth. $\boxed{} \approx c$

STEP 3 Check for reasonableness by finding perfect squares close to 20.

$\sqrt{20}$ is between $\sqrt{16}$ and $\sqrt{25}$. $\sqrt{16} < \boxed{} < \sqrt{25}$

Simplify. $\boxed{} < \boxed{} < 5$

Because 4.5 is between _____ and _____ , the answer is reasonable.

The hypotenuse is about 4.5 units long.

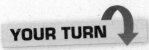
YOUR TURN

1. Approximate the length of the hypotenuse to the nearest tenth using a calculator.

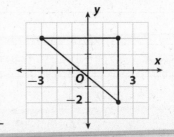

Personal Math Trainer
Online Assessment and Intervention
🔴 my.hrw.com

© Houghton Mifflin Harcourt Publishing Company

Finding the Distance Between Any Two Points

The Pythagorean Theorem can be used to find the distance between any two points (x_1, y_1) and (x_2, y_2) in the coordinate plane. The resulting expression is called the Distance Formula.

> **Distance Formula**
>
> In a coordinate plane, the distance d between two points (x_1, y_1) and (x_2, y_2) is
> $$d = \sqrt{(x_2 - x_1)^2 + (y_2 - y_1)^2}.$$

Use the Pythagorean Theorem to derive the Distance Formula.

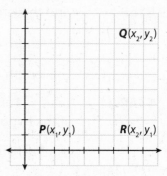

A To find the distance between points P and Q, draw segment $\overline{PQ}$ and label its length d. Then draw horizontal segment $\overline{PR}$ and vertical segment $\overline{QR}$. Label the lengths of these segments a and b. Triangle

PQR is a _____ triangle, with hypotenuse _____.

B Since $\overline{PR}$ is a horizontal segment, its length, a, is the difference

between its x-coordinates. Therefore, $a = x_2 -$ _____.

C Since $\overline{QR}$ is a vertical segment, its length, b, is the difference between

its y-coordinates. Therefore, $b = y_2 -$ _____.

D Use the Pythagorean Theorem to find d, the length of segment $\overline{PQ}$. Substitute the expressions from **B** and **C** for a and b.

$$d^2 = a^2 + b^2$$

$$d = \sqrt{a^2 + b^2}$$

$$d = \sqrt{\left(\boxed{} - \boxed{}\right)^2 + \left(\boxed{} - \boxed{}\right)^2}$$

> **Math Talk**
> Mathematical Practices
>
> What do $x_2 - x_1$ and $y_2 - y_1$ represent in terms of the Pythagorean Theorem?

Reflect

2. Why are the coordinates of point R the ordered pair (x_2, y_1)?

_____

_____

_____

Finding the Distance Between Two Points

The Pythagorean Theorem can be used to find the distance between two points in a real-world situation. You can do this by using a coordinate grid that overlays a diagram of the real-world situation.

Math On the Spot
my.hrw.com

EXAMPLE 2 Real World

COMMON CORE 8.G.8

Francesca wants to find the distance between her house on one side of a lake and the beach on the other side. She marks off a third point forming a right triangle, as shown. The distances in the diagram are measured in meters.

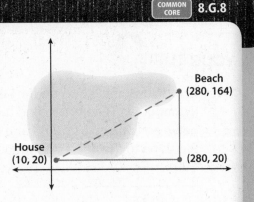

Use the Pythagorean Theorem to find the straight-line distance from Francesca's house to the beach.

STEP 1 Find the length of the horizontal leg.

The length of the horizontal leg is the absolute value of the difference between the x-coordinates of the points (280, 20) and (10, 20).

$$|280 - 10| = 270$$

The length of the horizontal leg is 270 meters.

STEP 2 Find the length of the vertical leg.

The length of the vertical leg is the absolute value of the difference between the y-coordinates of the points (280, 164) and (280, 20).

$$|164 - 20| = 144$$

The length of the vertical leg is 144 meters.

STEP 3 Let $a = 270$ and $b = 144$. Let c represent the length of the hypotenuse. Use the Pythagorean Theorem to find c.

$$a^2 + b^2 = c^2$$

$$270^2 + 144^2 = c^2 \qquad \text{Substitute into the formula.}$$

$$72{,}900 + 20{,}736 = c^2 \qquad \text{Simplify.}$$

$$93{,}636 = c^2 \qquad \text{Add.}$$

$$\sqrt{93{,}636} = c \qquad \text{Take the square root of both sides.}$$

$$306 = c \qquad \text{Simplify.}$$

The distance from Francesca's house to the beach is 306 meters.

> **Math Talk**
> Mathematical Practices
>
> Why is it necessary to take the absolute value of the coordinates when finding the length of a segment?

Reflect

3. Show how you could use the Distance Formula to find the distance from Francesca's house to the beach.

_____

_____

_____

YOUR TURN

4. Camp Sunshine is also on the lake. Use the Pythagorean Theorem to find the distance between Francesca's house and Camp Sunshine to the nearest tenth of a meter.

_____

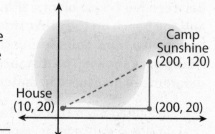

Camp Sunshine
(200, 120)

House
(10, 20)

(200, 20)

Guided Practice

1. Approximate the length of the hypotenuse of the right triangle to the nearest tenth using a calculator. (Explore Activity Example 1)

_____

2. Find the distance between the points (3, 7) and (15, 12) on the coordinate plane. (Explore Activity 2) _____

3. A plane leaves an airport and flies due north. Two minutes later, a second plane leaves the same airport flying due east. The flight plan shows the coordinates of the two planes 10 minutes later. The distances in the graph are measured in miles. Use the Pythagorean Theorem to find the distance shown between the two planes.

(Example 2) _____

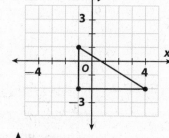

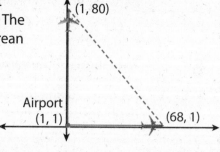

(1, 80)

Airport
(1, 1)

(68, 1)

❓ ESSENTIAL QUESTION CHECK-IN

4. Describe two ways to find the distance between two points on a coordinate plane.

_____

_____

_____

12.3 Independent Practice

COMMON CORE 8.G.8

Personal Math Trainer

my.hrw.com — Online Assessment and Intervention

5. A metal worker traced a triangular piece of sheet metal on a coordinate plane, as shown. The units represent inches. What is the length of the longest side of the metal triangle? Approximate the length to the nearest tenth of an inch using a calculator. Check that your answer is reasonable.

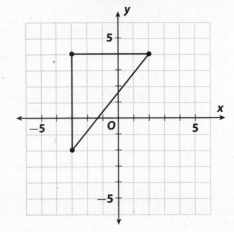

_____

6. When a coordinate grid is superimposed on a map of Harrisburg, the high school is located at (17, 21) and the town park is located at (28, 13). If each unit represents 1 mile, how many miles apart are the high school and the town park? Round your answer to the nearest tenth.

_____

7. The coordinates of the vertices of a rectangle are given by $R(-3, -4)$, $E(-3, 4)$, $C(4, 4)$, and $T(4, -4)$. Plot these points on the coordinate plane at the right and connect them to draw the rectangle. Then connect points E and T to form diagonal $\overline{ET}$.

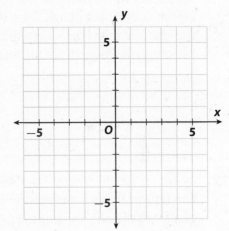

a. Use the Pythagorean Theorem to find the exact length of $\overline{ET}$.

_____

b. How can you use the Distance Formula to find the length of $\overline{ET}$? Show that the Distance Formula gives the same answer.

_____

_____

_____

_____

_____

8. **Multistep** The locations of three ships are represented on a coordinate grid by the following points: $P(-2, 5)$, $Q(-7, -5)$, and $R(2, -3)$. Which ships are farthest apart?

_____

9. Make a Conjecture Find as many points as you can that are 5 units from the origin. Make a conjecture about the shape formed if all the points 5 units from the origin were connected.

_____

_____

_____

10. Justify Reasoning The graph shows the location of a motion detector that has a maximum range of 34 feet. A peacock at point P displays its tail feathers. Will the motion detector sense this motion? Explain.

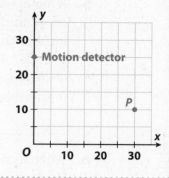

_____

_____

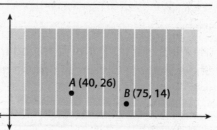
FOCUS ON HIGHER ORDER THINKING

Work Area

11. Persevere in Problem Solving One leg of an isosceles right triangle has endpoints (1, 1) and (6, 1). The other leg passes through the point (6, 2). Draw the triangle on the coordinate plane. Then show how you can use the Distance Formula to find the length of the hypotenuse. Round your answer to the nearest tenth.

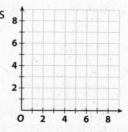

_____

_____

_____

12. Represent Real-World Problems
The figure shows a representation of a football field. The units represent yards. A sports analyst marks the locations of the football from where it was thrown (point A) and where it was caught (point B). Explain how you can use the Pythagorean Theorem to find the distance the ball was thrown. Then find the distance.

A (40, 26)

B (75, 14)

_____

_____

_____

_____

_____

Ready to Go On?

Personal Math Trainer
Online Assessment and Intervention
⏻ my.hrw.com

12.1 The Pythagorean Theorem

Find the length of the missing side.

1.

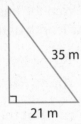

35 m

21 m

_____

2.

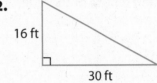

16 ft

30 ft

_____

12.2 Converse of the Pythagorean Theorem

Tell whether each triangle with the given side lengths is a right triangle.

3. 11, 60, 61 _____

4. 9, 37, 40 _____

5. 15, 35, 38 _____

6. 28, 45, 53 _____

7. Keelie has a triangular-shaped card. The lengths of its sides are 4.5 cm, 6 cm, and 7.5 cm. Is the card a right triangle?   _____

12.3 Distance Between Two Points

Find the distance between the given points. Round to the nearest tenth.

8. A and B _____

9. B and C _____

10. A and C _____

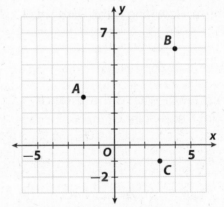

? ESSENTIAL QUESTION

11. How can you use the Pythagorean Theorem to solve real-world problems?

_____

_____

_____

COMMON CORE

MODULE 12 MIXED REVIEW
Assessment Readiness

Personal
Math Trainer

my.hrw.com

Online
Assessment and
Intervention

Selected Response

1. What is the missing length of the side?

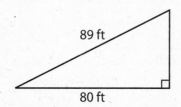

89 ft
80 ft

- Ⓐ 9 ft
- Ⓑ 30 ft
- Ⓒ 39 ft
- Ⓓ 120 ft

2. Which relation does **not** represent a function?

- Ⓐ (0, 8), (3, 8), (1, 6)
- Ⓑ (4, 2), (6, 1), (8, 9)
- Ⓒ (1, 20), (2, 23), (9, 26)
- Ⓓ (0, 3), (2, 3), (2, 0)

3. Two sides of a right triangle have lengths of 72 cm and 97 cm. The third side is **not** the hypotenuse. How long is the third side?

- Ⓐ 25 cm
- Ⓑ 45 cm
- Ⓒ 65 cm
- Ⓓ 121 cm

4. To the nearest tenth, what is the distance between point F and point G?

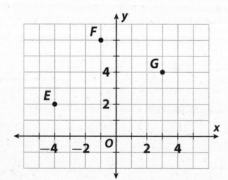

- Ⓐ 4.5 units
- Ⓑ 5.0 units
- Ⓒ 7.3 units
- Ⓓ 20 units

5. A flagpole is 53 feet tall. A rope is tied to the top of the flagpole and secured to the ground 28 feet from the base of the flagpole. What is the length of the rope?

- Ⓐ 25 feet
- Ⓑ 45 feet
- Ⓒ 53 feet
- Ⓓ 60 feet

6. Which set of lengths are **not** the side lengths of a right triangle?

- Ⓐ 36, 77, 85
- Ⓑ 20, 99, 101
- Ⓒ 27, 120, 123
- Ⓓ 24, 33, 42

7. A triangle has one right angle. What could the measures of the other two angles be?

- Ⓐ 25° and 65°
- Ⓑ 30° and 15°
- Ⓒ 55° and 125°
- Ⓓ 90° and 100°

Mini-Task

8. A fallen tree is shown on the coordinate grid below. Each unit represents 1 meter.

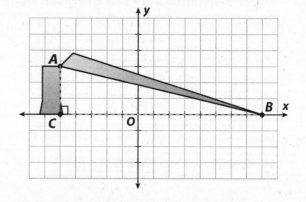

a. What is the distance from A to B?

_____

b. What was the height of the tree before it fell?

_____

Volume

? **ESSENTIAL QUESTION**

How can you use volume to solve real-world problems?

Real-World Video

Many foods are in the shape of cylinders, cones, and spheres. To find out how much of the food you are eating, you can use formulas for volume.

my.hrw.com

© Houghton Mifflin Harcourt Publishing Company

GO DIGITAL
my.hrw.com

my.hrw.com

Go digital with your write-in student edition, accessible on any device.

Math On the Spot

Scan with your smart phone to jump directly to the online edition, video tutor, and more.

Animated Math

Interactively explore key concepts to see how math works.

Personal Math Trainer

Get immediate feedback and help as you work through practice sets.

Are YOU Ready?

Complete these exercises to review skills you will need for this module.

Exponents

EXAMPLE $6^3 = 6 \times 6 \times 6$ Multiply the base (6) by itself the number of times indicated by the exponent (3).

$\qquad = 36 \times 6$ Find the product of the first two terms.

$\qquad = 216$ Find the product of all the terms.

Evaluate each exponential expression.

1. 11^2 _____ **2.** 2^5 _____ **3.** $\left(\dfrac{1}{5}\right)^3$ _____ **4.** $(0.3)^2$ _____

5. 2.1^3 _____ **6.** 0.1^3 _____ **7.** $\left(\dfrac{9.6}{3}\right)^2$ _____ **8.** 100^3 _____

Round Decimals

EXAMPLE Round 43.2685 to the underlined place.

$43.2685 \rightarrow 43.27$

The digit to be rounded: 6
The digit to its right is 8.
8 is *5 or greater,* so round *up.*
The rounded number is 43.27.

Round to the underlined place.

9. 2.3<u>7</u>4 _____ **10.** 12<u>6</u>.399 _____ **11.** 13.<u>9</u>577 _____ **12.** 42.6<u>9</u>0 _____

13. 134.<u>9</u>5 _____ **14.** 2.<u>0</u>486 _____ **15.** 63.6<u>3</u>52 _____ **16.** 98.<u>9</u>499 _____

Simplify Numerical Expressions

EXAMPLE $\dfrac{1}{3}(3.14)(4)^2(3) = \dfrac{1}{3}(3.14)(16)(3)$ Simplify the exponent.

$\qquad = 50.24$ Multiply from left to right.

Simplify each expression.

17. $3.14(5)^2(10)$ _____ **18.** $\dfrac{1}{3}(3.14)(3)^2(5)$ _____ **19.** $\dfrac{4}{3}(3.14)(3)^3$ _____

20. $\dfrac{4}{3}(3.14)(6)^3$ _____ **21.** $3.14(4)^2(9)$ _____ **22.** $\dfrac{1}{3}(3.14)(9)^2\left(\dfrac{2}{3}\right)$ _____

Reading Start-Up

© Houghton Mifflin Harcourt Publishing Company

Visualize Vocabulary

Use the ✔ words to complete the empty columns in the chart. You may use words more than once.

Shape	Distance Around	Attributes	Associated Review Words
circle		r, d	
square		90° corner, sides	
rectangle		90° corner, sides	

Understand Vocabulary

Complete the sentences using the preview words.

1. A three-dimensional figure that has one vertex and one circular base is a _____.

2. A three-dimensional figure with all points the same distance from the center is a _____.

3. A three-dimensional figure that has two congruent circular bases is a _____.

Vocabulary

Review Words

area *(área)*

base *(base, en numeración)*

✔ circumference *(circunferencia)*

✔ diameter *(diámetro)*

height *(altura)*

✔ length *(longitud)*

✔ perimeter *(perímetro)*

✔ radius *(radio)*

✔ right angle *(ángulo recto)*

✔ width *(ancho)*

Preview Words

cone *(cono)*

cylinder *(cilindro)*

sphere *(esfera)*

Active Reading

Three-Panel Flip Chart Before beginning the module, create a three-panel flip chart to help you organize what you learn. Label each flap with one of the lesson titles from this module. As you study each lesson, write important ideas like vocabulary, properties, and formulas under the appropriate flap.

COMMON CORE
Unpacking the Standards

Understanding the standards and the vocabulary terms in the standards will help you know exactly what you are expected to learn in this module.

COMMON CORE 8.G.9

Know the formulas for the volumes of cones, cylinders, and spheres and use them to solve real-world and mathematical problems.

Key Vocabulary

volume *(volumen)*
The number of cubic units needed to fill a given space.

cylinder *(cilindro)*
A three-dimensional figure with two parallel, congruent circular bases connected by a curved lateral surface.

What It Means to You

You will learn the formula for the volume of a cylinder.

UNPACKING EXAMPLE 8.G.9

The Asano Taiko Company of Japan built the world's largest drum in 2000. The drum's diameter is 4.8 meters, and its height is 4.95 meters. Estimate the volume of the drum.

$d = 4.8 \approx 5$ $V = (\pi r^2)h$ Volume of a cylinder

$h = 4.95 \approx 5$ $\approx (3)\,(2.5)^2 \cdot 5$ Use 3 for π.

$r = \dfrac{d}{2} \approx \dfrac{5}{2} = 2.5$ $= (3)\,(6.25)\,(5)$

                $= 18.75 \cdot 5$

                $= 93.75 \approx 94$

The volume of the drum is approximately 94 m³.

COMMON CORE 8.G.9

Know the formulas for the volumes of cones, cylinders, and spheres and use them to solve real-world and mathematical problems.

Key Vocabulary

cone *(cono)*
A three-dimensional figure with one vertex and one circular base.

sphere *(esfera)*
A three-dimensional figure with all points the same distance from the center.

What It Means to You

You will learn formulas for the volume of a cone and a sphere.

UNPACKING EXAMPLE 8.G.9

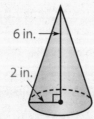

Find the volume of the cone. Use 3.14 for π.

$B = \pi(2^2) = 4\pi$ in²

$V = \dfrac{1}{3} \cdot 4\pi \cdot 6$ $V = \dfrac{1}{3}Bh$

$V = 8\pi$ Use 3.14 for π.

≈ 25.1 in³

The volume of the cone is approximately 25.1 in³.

The volume of a sphere with the same radius is
$V = \dfrac{4}{3}\pi r^3 \approx \dfrac{4}{3}(3)(2)^3 = 32$ in³.

© Houghton Mifflin Harcourt Publishing Company

COMMON CORE 8.G.9

Know the formulas for the volumes of...cylinders...and use them to solve real-world and mathematical problems.

? ESSENTIAL QUESTION

How do you find the volume of a cylinder?

EXPLORE ACTIVITY COMMON CORE 8.G.9

Modeling the Volume of a Cylinder

A **cylinder** is a three-dimensional figure that has two congruent circular bases that lie in parallel planes. The volume of any three-dimensional figure is the number of cubic units needed to fill the space taken up by the solid figure.

One cube represents one cubic unit of volume. You can develop the formula for the volume of a cylinder using an empty soup can or other cylindrical container. First, remove one of the bases.

A Arrange centimeter cubes in a single layer at the bottom of the cylinder. Fit as many cubes into the layer as possible. How many cubes are in this layer?

_____

B To find how many layers of cubes fit in the cylinder, make a stack of cubes along the inside of the cylinder. How many layers fit in the cylinder?

_____

C How can you use what you know to find the approximate number of cubes that would fit in the cylinder?

_____

_____

Reflect

1. Make a Conjecture Suppose you know the area of the base of a cylinder and the height of the cylinder. How can you find the cylinder's volume?

_____

2. Let the area of the base of a cylinder be B and the height of the cylinder be h. Write a formula for the cylinder's volume V. _____

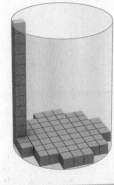

Finding the Volume of a Cylinder Using a Formula

Finding volumes of cylinders is similar to finding volumes of prisms. You find the volume V of both a prism and a cylinder by multiplying the height h by the area of the base B, so $V = Bh$.

The base of a cylinder is a circle, so for a cylinder, $B = \pi r^2$.

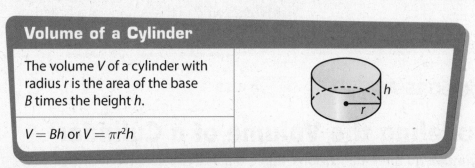

Volume of a Cylinder	
The volume V of a cylinder with radius r is the area of the base B times the height h.	
$V = Bh$ or $V = \pi r^2 h$	

EXAMPLE 1

COMMON CORE 8.G.9

Find the volume of each cylinder. Round your answers to the nearest tenth if necessary. Use 3.14 for π.

A

10 in.

3 in.

$V = \pi r^2 h$

$\approx 3.14 \cdot 3^2 \cdot 10$ Substitute.

$\approx 3.14 \cdot 9 \cdot 10$ Simplify.

≈ 282.6 Multiply.

The volume is about 282.6 in³.

B   6.4 cm   13 cm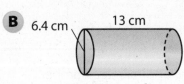

Since the diameter is 6.4 cm, the radius is 3.2 cm.

$V = \pi r^2 h$

$\approx 3.14 \cdot 3.2^2 \cdot 13$ Substitute.

$\approx 3.14 \cdot 10.24 \cdot 13$ Simplify.

≈ 418 Multiply.

> Recall that the diameter of a circle is twice the radius, so $2r = d$ and $r = \frac{d}{2}$.

The volume is about 418 cm³.

Reflect

3. **What If?** If you want a formula for the volume of a cylinder that involves the diameter d instead of the radius r, how can you rewrite it?

My Notes

YOUR TURN

Find the volume of each cylinder. Round your answers to the nearest tenth if necessary. Use 3.14 for π.

4.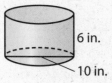

6 in.

10 in.

_____

5.

4 ft

12 ft

_____

Finding the Volume of a Cylinder in a Real-World Context

The Longhorn Band at the University of Texas at Austin has one of the world's largest bass drums, known as Big Bertha.

EXAMPLE 2 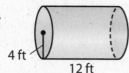   COMMON CORE 8.G.9

Big Bertha has a diameter of 8 feet and is 4.5 feet deep. Find the volume of the drum to the nearest tenth. Use 3.14 for π.

STEP 1   Find the radius of the drum.

$$r = \frac{d}{2} = \frac{8}{2} = 4 \text{ ft}$$

STEP 2   Find the volume of the drum.

$V = \pi r^2 h$

$\approx 3.14 \cdot 4^2 \cdot 4.5$ Substitute.

$\approx 3.14 \cdot 16 \cdot 4.5$ Simplify the exponent.

≈ 226.08 Multiply.

The volume of the drum is about 226.1 ft³.

The Univ. of Texas · Longhorn Band · Big Bertha

YOUR TURN

6. A drum company advertises a snare drum that is 4 inches high and 12 inches in diameter. Find the volume of the drum to the nearest tenth. Use 3.14 for π.

_____

© Houghton Mifflin Harcourt Publishing Company • Image Credits: ©Brian Bahr/Getty·Images

1. **Vocabulary** Describe the bases of a cylinder. (Explore Activity)

_____

2. Figure 1 shows a view from above of inch cubes on the bottom of a cylinder. Figure 2 shows the highest stack of cubes that will fit inside the cylinder. Estimate the volume of the cylinder. Explain your reasoning. (Explore Activity)

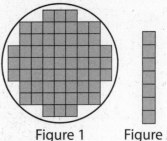

Figure 1   Figure 2

_____

_____

_____

3. Find the volume of the cylinder to the nearest tenth. Use 3.14 for π. (Example 1)

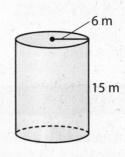

$V = \pi r^2 h$

$V = \pi \cdot \boxed{}^2 \cdot \boxed{}$

$\approx 3.14 \cdot \boxed{} \cdot \boxed{}$

$\approx \boxed{}$

6 m

15 m

The volume of the cylinder is approximately _____ m³.

4. A Japanese odaiko is a very large drum that is made by hollowing out a section of a tree trunk. A museum in Takayama City has three odaikos of similar size carved from a single tree trunk. The largest measures about 2.7 meters in both diameter and length, and weighs about 4.5 metric tons. Using the volume formula for a cylinder, approximate the volume of the drum to the nearest tenth. (Example 2)

The radius of the drum is about _____ m.

The volume of the drum is about _____ m³.

? ESSENTIAL QUESTION CHECK-IN

5. How do you find the volume of a cylinder? Describe which measurements of a cylinder you need to know.

_____

_____

_____

13.1 Independent Practice

COMMON CORE 8.G.9

Personal Math Trainer
Online Assessment and Intervention
my.hrw.com

Find the volume of each figure. Round your answers to the nearest tenth if necessary. Use 3.14 for π.

6.
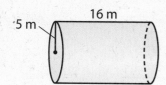
1.5 cm
11 cm

_____

7.
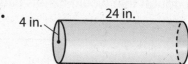
24 in.
4 in.

_____

8.
5 m
16 m

_____

9.
10 in.
12 in.
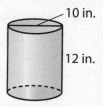

_____

10. A cylinder has a radius of 4 centimeters and a height of 40 centimeters.

_____

11. A cylinder has a radius of 8 meters and a height of 4 meters.

_____

Round your answer to the nearest tenth, if necessary. Use 3.14 for π.

12. The cylindrical Giant Ocean Tank at the New England Aquarium in Boston is 24 feet deep and has a radius of 18.8 feet. Find the volume of the tank.

_____

13. A standard-size bass drum has a diameter of 22 inches and is 18 inches deep. Find the volume of this drum.

_____

14. Grain is stored in cylindrical structures called silos. Find the volume of a silo with a diameter of 11.1 feet and a height of 20 feet.

_____

15. The Frank Erwin Center, or "The Drum," at the University of Texas in Austin can be approximated by a cylinder that is 120 meters in diameter and 30 meters in height. Find its volume.

_____

16. A barrel of crude oil contains about 5.61 cubic feet of oil. How many barrels of oil are contained in 1 mile (5280 feet) of a pipeline that has an inside diameter of 6 inches and is completely filled with oil? How much is "1 mile" of oil in this pipeline worth at a price of $100 per barrel?

_____

17. A pan for baking French bread is shaped like half a cylinder. It is 12 inches long and 3.5 inches in diameter. What is the volume of uncooked dough that would fill this pan?

_____

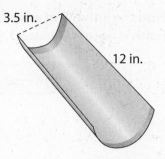

3.5 in.

12 in.

 **FOCUS ON HIGHER ORDER THINKING**

18. Explain the Error A student said the volume of a cylinder with a 3-inch diameter is two times the volume of a cylinder with the same height and a 1.5-inch radius. What is the error?

_____

_____

_____

Work Area

19. Communicate Mathematical Ideas Explain how you can find the height of a cylinder if you know the diameter and the volume. Include an example with your explanation.

_____

_____

_____

_____

_____

_____

20. Analyze Relationships Cylinder A has a radius of 6 centimeters. Cylinder B has the same height and a radius half as long as cylinder A. What fraction of the volume of cylinder A is the volume of cylinder B? Explain.

_____

_____

_____

_____

13.2 Volume of Cones

COMMON CORE 8.G.9

Know the formulas for the volumes of cones...and use them to solve real-world and mathematical problems.

? ESSENTIAL QUESTION

How do you find the volume of a cone?

EXPLORE ACTIVITY COMMON CORE 8.G.9

Modeling the Volume of a Cone

A **cone** is a three-dimensional figure that has one vertex and one circular base.

To explore the volume of a cone, Sandi does an experiment with a cone and a cylinder that have congruent bases and heights. She fills the cone with popcorn kernels and then pours the kernels into the cylinder. She repeats this until the cylinder is full.

Sandi finds that it takes 3 cones to fill the volume of the cylinder.

STEP 1 What is the formula for the volume V of a cylinder with base area B and height h? _____

STEP 2 What is the area of the base of the cone? _____

STEP 3 Sandi found that, when the bases and height are the same,

_____ times $V_{cone} = V_{cylinder}$.

STEP 4 How does the volume of the cone compare to the volume of the cylinder?

Volume of the cone: $V_{cone} = \dfrac{\boxed{}}{\boxed{}} \cdot V_{cylinder}$

Reflect

1. Use the conclusion from this experiment to write a formula for the volume of a cone in terms of the height and the radius. Explain.

_____

2. How do you think the formula for the volume of a cone is similar to the formula for the volume of a pyramid?

_____

Finding the Volume of a Cone Using a Formula

The formulas for the volume of a prism and the volume of a cylinder are the same: multiply the height h by the area of the base B, so $V = Bh$.

In the **Explore Activity**, you saw that the volume of a cone is one third the volume of a cylinder with the same base and height.

Volume of a Cone

The volume V of a cone with radius r is one third the area of the base B times the height h.

$$V = \frac{1}{3} Bh \text{ or } V = \frac{1}{3}\pi r^2 h$$

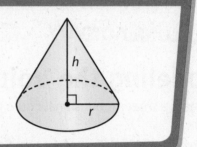

My Notes

EXAMPLE 1

COMMON CORE | 8.G.9

Find the volume of each cone. Round your answers to the nearest tenth. Use 3.14 for π.

A

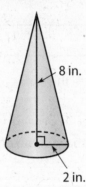

8 in.

2 in.

$V = \frac{1}{3}\pi r^2 h$

$\approx \frac{1}{3} \cdot 3.14 \cdot 2^2 \cdot 8$ Substitute.

$\approx \frac{1}{3} \cdot 3.14 \cdot 4 \cdot 8$ Simplify.

≈ 33.5 Multiply.

The volume is about 33.5 in³.

B Since the diameter is 8 ft, the radius is 4 ft.

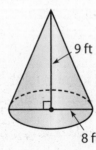

9 ft

8 ft

$V = \frac{1}{3}\pi r^2 h$

$\approx \frac{1}{3} \cdot 3.14 \cdot 4^2 \cdot 9$ Substitute.

$\approx \frac{1}{3} \cdot 3.14 \cdot 16 \cdot 9$ Simplify.

≈ 150.7 Multiply.

The volume is about 150.7 ft³.

Reflect

3. How can you rewrite the formula for the volume of a cone using the diameter d instead of the radius r? _____

YOUR TURN

Find the volume of each cone. Round your answers to the nearest tenth. Use 3.14 for π.

4.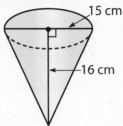
15 cm
16 cm

_____

5.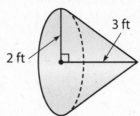
3 ft
2 ft

_____

Finding the Volume of a Volcano

The mountain created by a volcano is often cone–shaped.

 EXAMPLE 2 Real World   **COMMON CORE** 8.G.9

For her geography project, Karen built a clay model of a volcano in the shape of a cone. Her model has a diameter of 12 inches and a height of 8 inches. Find the volume of clay in her model to the nearest tenth. Use 3.14 for π.

STEP 1 Find the radius.

$r = \dfrac{12}{2} = 6$ in.

STEP 2 Find the volume of clay.

$V = \dfrac{1}{3}\pi r^2 h$

$\approx \dfrac{1}{3} \cdot 3.14 \cdot 6^2 \cdot 8$ Substitute.

$\approx \dfrac{1}{3} \cdot 3.14 \cdot 36 \cdot 8$ Simplify.

≈ 301.44 Multiply.

The volume of the clay is about 301.4 in³.

Math On the Spot

my.hrw.com

YOUR TURN

6. The cone of the volcano Parícutin in Mexico had a height of 410 meters and a diameter of 424 meters. Approximate the volume of the cone.

_____

1. The area of the base of a cylinder is 45 square inches and its height is 10 inches. A cone has the same area for its base and the same height. What is the volume of the cone? (Explore Activity)

$$V_{cylinder} = Bh = \boxed{} \cdot \boxed{} = \boxed{}$$

$$V_{cone} = \frac{1}{3} V_{cylinder}$$

$$= \frac{1}{3} \boxed{}$$

$$= \boxed{}$$

The volume of the cone is _____ in³.

2. A cone and a cylinder have congruent height and bases. The volume of the cone is 18 m³. What is the volume of the cylinder? Explain. (Explore Activity)

_____

_____

_____

_____

_____

Find the volume of each cone. Round your answer to the nearest tenth if necessary. Use 3.14 for π. (Example 1)

3.
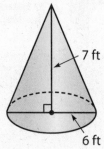
7 ft

6 ft

_____

4.
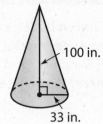
100 in.

33 in.

_____

5. Gretchen made a paper cone to hold a gift for a friend. The paper cone was 15 inches high and had a radius of 3 inches. Find the volume of the paper cone to the nearest tenth. Use 3.14 for π. (Example 2)

_____

6. A cone-shaped building is commonly used to store sand. What would be the volume of a cone-shaped building with a diameter of 50 meters and a height of 20 meters? Round your answer to the nearest tenth. Use 3.14 for π. (Example 2)

_____

? ESSENTIAL QUESTION CHECK-IN

7. How do you find the volume of a cone?

_____

_____

_____

13.2 Independent Practice

 8.G.9

Personal Math Trainer

my.hrw.com

Online Assessment and Intervention

Find the volume of each cone. Round your answers to the nearest tenth if necessary. Use 3.14 for π.

8.

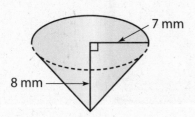

7 mm

8 mm

_____

9.

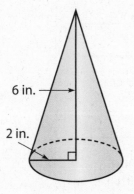

6 in.

2 in.

_____

10. A cone has a diameter of 6 centimeters and a height of 11.5 centimeters.

_____

11. A cone has a radius of 3 meters and a height of 10 meters.

_____

Round your answers to the nearest tenth if necessary. Use 3.14 for π.

12. Antonio is making mini waffle cones. Each waffle cone is 3 inches high and has a radius of $\frac{3}{4}$ inch. What is the volume of a waffle cone?

_____

13. A snack bar sells popcorn in cone-shaped containers. One container has a diameter of 8 inches and a height of 10 inches. How many cubic inches of popcorn does the container hold?

_____

14. A volcanic cone has a diameter of 300 meters and a height of 150 meters. What is the volume of the cone?

_____

15. **Multistep** Orange traffic cones come in a variety of sizes. Approximate the volume, in cubic inches, of a traffic cone that has a height of 2 feet and a diameter of 10 inches. Use 3.14 for π.

_____

Find the missing measure for each cone. Round your answers to the nearest tenth if necessary. Use 3.14 for π.

16. radius = _____

height = 6 in.

volume = 100.48 in³

17. diameter = 6 cm

height = _____

volume = 56.52 cm³

18. The diameter of a cone-shaped container is 4 inches, and its height is 6 inches. How much greater is the volume of a cylinder-shaped container with the same diameter and height? Round your answer to the nearest hundredth. Use 3.14 for π.

_____

19. Alex wants to know the volume of sand in an hourglass. When all the sand is in the bottom, he stands a ruler up beside the hourglass and estimates the height of the cone of sand.

    a. What else does he need to measure to find the volume of sand?

    _____

    _____

    b. Make a Conjecture If the volume of sand is increasing at a constant rate, is the height increasing at a constant rate? Explain.

    _____

    _____

    _____

20. Problem Solving The diameter of a cone is x cm, the height is 18 cm, and the volume is 301.44 cm³. What is x? Use 3.14 for π.

_____

21. Analyze Relationships A cone has a radius of 1 foot and a height of 2 feet. How many cones of liquid would it take to fill a cylinder with a diameter of 2 feet and a height of 2 feet? Explain.

_____

_____

_____

22. Critique Reasoning Herb knows that the volume of a cone is one third that of a cylinder with the same base and height. He reasons that a cone with the same height as a given cylinder but 3 times the radius should therefore have the same volume as the cylinder, since $\frac{1}{3} \cdot 3 = 1$. Is Herb correct? Explain.

_____

_____

_____

_____

_____

COMMON CORE **8.G.9**

Know the formulas for the volumes of...spheres and use them to solve real-world and mathematical problems.

? ESSENTIAL QUESTION

How do you find the volume of a sphere?

EXPLORE ACTIVITY COMMON CORE **8.G.9**

Modeling the Volume of a Sphere

A **sphere** is a three-dimensional figure with all points the same distance from the center. The **radius** of a sphere is the distance from the center to any point on the sphere.

You have seen that a cone fills $\frac{1}{3}$ of a cylinder of the same radius and height h. If you were to do a similar experiment with a sphere of the same radius, you would find that a sphere fills $\frac{2}{3}$ of the cylinder. The cylinder's height is equal to twice the radius of the sphere.

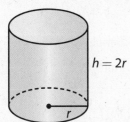 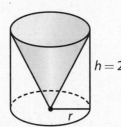 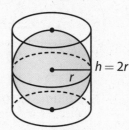

STEP 1 Write the formula $V = Bh$ for each shape. Use $B = \pi r^2$ and substitute the fractions you know for the cone and sphere.

Cylinder	Cone	Sphere
$V = \pi r^2 h$	$V = \frac{1}{3}\pi r^2 h$	$V = \frac{2}{3}\pi r^2 h$

STEP 2 Notice that a sphere always has a height equal to twice the radius. Substitute $2r$ for h.

$V = \frac{2}{3}\pi r^2(2r)$

STEP 3 Simplify this formula for the volume of a sphere.

$V = \boxed{}\pi r^3$

Reflect

1. **Analyze Relationships** A cone has a radius of r and a height of $2r$. A sphere has a radius of r. Compare the volume of the sphere and cone.

_____

_____

_____

Finding the Volume of a Sphere Using a Formula

The Explore Activity illustrates a formula for the volume of a sphere with radius *r*.

> ### Volume of a Sphere
>
> The volume *V* of a sphere is $\frac{4}{3}\pi$ times the cube of the radius *r*.
>
> $$V = \frac{4}{3}\pi r^3$$
>
>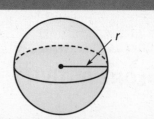

EXAMPLE 1

COMMON CORE   8.G.9

Find the volume of each sphere. Round your answers to the nearest tenth if necessary. Use 3.14 for π.

A

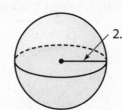

2.1 cm

$V = \frac{4}{3}\pi r^3$

$\approx \frac{4}{3} \cdot 3.14 \cdot 2.1^3$ Substitute.

$\approx \frac{4}{3} \cdot 3.14 \cdot 9.26$ Simplify.

≈ 38.8 Multiply.

The volume is about 38.8 cm³.

Math Talk

Mathematical Practices

If you know the diameter of a sphere, how would the formula for the volume of a sphere be written in terms of *d*?

B

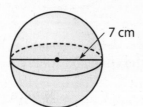

7 cm

Since the diameter is 7 cm, the radius is 3.5 cm.

$V = \frac{4}{3}\pi r^3$

$\approx \frac{4}{3} \cdot 3.14 \cdot 3.5^3$ Substitute.

$\approx \frac{4}{3} \cdot 3.14 \cdot 42.9$ Simplify.

≈ 179.6 Multiply.

The volume is about 179.6 cm³.

© Houghton Mifflin Harcourt Publishing Company

Personal Math Trainer

Online Assessment and Intervention

my.hrw.com

YOUR TURN

Find the volume of each sphere. Round your answers to the nearest tenth. Use 3.14 for π.

2. A sphere has a radius of 10 centimeters. _____

3. A sphere has a diameter of 3.4 meters. _____

Finding the Volume of a Sphere in a Real-World Context

Many sports, including golf and tennis, use a ball that is spherical in shape.

EXAMPLE 2

COMMON CORE 8.G.9

Soccer balls come in several different sizes. One soccer ball has a diameter of 22 centimeters. What is the volume of this soccer ball? Round your answer to the nearest tenth. Use 3.14 for π.

STEP 1 Find the radius.

$$r = \frac{d}{2} = 11 \text{ cm}$$

STEP 2 Find the volume of the soccer ball.

$$V = \frac{4}{3}\pi r^3$$

$$\approx \frac{4}{3} \cdot 3.14 \cdot 11^3 \qquad \text{Substitute.}$$

$$\approx \frac{4}{3} \cdot 3.14 \cdot 1331 \qquad \text{Simplify.}$$

$$\approx 5572.4533 \qquad \text{Multiply.}$$

The volume of the soccer ball is about 5572.5 cm³.

Reflect

4. What is the volume of the soccer ball in terms of π, to the nearest whole number multiple? Explain your answer.

_____

_____

5. **Analyze Relationships** The diameter of a basketball is about 1.1 times that of a soccer ball. The diameter of a tennis ball is about 0.3 times that of a soccer ball. How do the volumes of these balls compare to that of a soccer ball? Explain.

_____

_____

_____

YOUR TURN

6. Val measures the diameter of a ball as 12 inches. How many cubic inches of air does this ball hold, to the nearest tenth? Use 3.14 for π.

_____

1. **Vocabulary** A sphere is a three-dimensional figure with all points

   _____ from the center. (Explore Activity)

2. **Vocabulary** The _____ is the distance from the center
   of a sphere to a point on the sphere. (Explore Activity)

**Find the volume of each sphere. Round your answers to the nearest tenth
if necessary. Use 3.14 for π.** (Example 1)

3.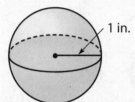
   1 in.

   _____

4.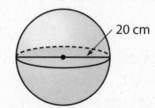
   20 cm

   _____

5. A sphere has a radius of 1.5 feet. _____

6. A sphere has a diameter of 2 yards. _____

7. A baseball has a diameter of 2.9 inches. Find the volume of the baseball. Round
   your answer to the nearest tenth if necessary. Use 3.14 for π. (Example 2) _____

8. A basketball has a radius of 4.7 inches. What is its volume to the nearest
   cubic inch. Use 3.14 for π. (Example 2) _____

9. A company is deciding whether to package a ball
   in a cubic box or a cylindrical box. In either case,
   the ball will touch the bottom, top, and sides.
   (Explore Activity)

   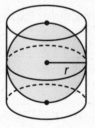
   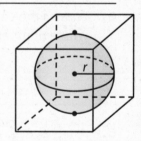

   a. What portion of the space inside the cylindrical
      box is empty? Explain.

      _____

   b. Find an expression for the volume of the cubic box. _____

   c. About what portion of the space inside the cubic box is empty? Explain.

      _____

      _____

? ESSENTIAL QUESTION CHECK-IN

10. Explain the steps you use to find the volume of a sphere.

    _____

13.3 Independent Practice

COMMON CORE 8.G.9

Personal Math Trainer

Online Assessment and Intervention

my.hrw.com

Find the volume of each sphere. Round your answers to the nearest tenth if necessary. Use 3.14 for π.

11. radius of 3.1 meters _____

12. diameter of 18 inches _____

13. $r = 6$ in. _____

14. $d = 36$ m _____

15.

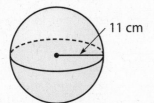

11 cm

_____

16.

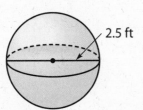

2.5 ft

_____

The eggs of birds and other animals come in many different shapes and sizes. Eggs often have a shape that is nearly spherical. When this is true, you can use the formula for a sphere to find their volume.

17. The green turtle lays eggs that are approximately spherical with an average diameter of 4.5 centimeters. Each turtle lays an average of 113 eggs at one time. Find the total volume of these eggs, to the nearest cubic centimeter.

_____

18. Hummingbirds lay eggs that are nearly spherical and about 1 centimeter in diameter. Find the volume of an egg. Round your answer to the nearest tenth.

_____

19. Fossilized spherical eggs of dinosaurs called titanosaurid sauropods were found in Patagonia. These eggs were 15 centimeters in diameter. Find the volume of an egg. Round your answer to the nearest tenth.

_____

20. **Persevere in Problem Solving** An ostrich egg has about the same volume as a sphere with a diameter of 5 inches. If the eggshell is about $\frac{1}{12}$ inch thick, find the volume of just the shell, not including the interior of the egg. Round your answer to the nearest tenth.

_____

21. **Multistep** Write the steps you would use to find a formula for the volume of the figure at right. Then write the formula.

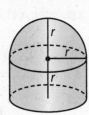

_____

_____

_____

_____

_____

_____

_____

_____

22. Critical Thinking Explain what happens to the volume of a sphere if you double the radius.

_____

23. Multistep A cylindrical can of tennis balls holds a stack of three balls so that they touch the can at the top, bottom, and sides. The radius of each ball is 1.25 inches. Find the volume inside the can that is not taken up by the three tennis balls.

_____

 **FOCUS ON HIGHER ORDER THINKING**

Work Area

24. Critique Reasoning A sphere has a radius of 4 inches, and a cube-shaped box has an edge length of 7.5 inches. J.D. says the box has a greater volume, so the sphere will fit in the box. Is he correct? Explain.

_____

_____

_____

25. Critical Thinking Which would hold the most water: a bowl in the shape of a hemisphere with radius r, a cylindrical glass with radius r and height r, or a cone-shaped drinking cup with radius r and height r? Explain.

_____

_____

_____

26. Analyze Relationships Hari has models of a sphere, a cylinder, and a cone. The sphere's diameter and the cylinder's height are the same, $2r$. The cylinder has radius r. The cone has diameter $2r$ and height $2r$. Compare the volumes of the cone and the sphere to the volume of the cylinder.

_____

_____

_____

27. A spherical helium balloon that is 8 feet in diameter can lift about 17 pounds. What does the diameter of a balloon need to be to lift a person who weighs 136 pounds? Explain.

_____

_____

Ready to Go On?

13.1 Volume of Cylinders

Find the volume of each cylinder. Round your answers to the nearest tenth if necessary. Use 3.14 for π.

1.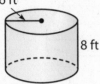

6 ft

8 ft

_____

2. A can of juice has a radius of 4 inches and a height of 7 inches. What is the volume of the can?

_____

13.2 Volume of Cones

Find the volume of each cone. Round your answers to the nearest tenth if necessary. Use 3.14 for π.

3.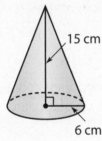

15 cm

6 cm _____

4.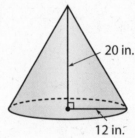

20 in.

12 in. _____

13.3 Volume of Spheres

Find the volume of each sphere. Round your answers to the nearest tenth if necessary. Use 3.14 for π.

5.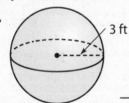

3 ft

_____

6.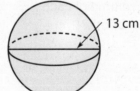

13 cm

_____

? ESSENTIAL QUESTION

7. What measurements do you need to know to find the volume of a cylinder? a cone? a sphere?

_____

_____

Selected Response

1. The bed of a pickup truck measures 4 feet by 8 feet. To the nearest inch, what is the length of the longest thin metal bar that will lie flat in the bed?

(A) 11 ft 3 in. (C) 8 ft 11 in.

(B) 10 ft 0 in. (D) 8 ft 9 in.

2. Using 3.14 for π, what is the volume of the cylinder below to the nearest tenth?

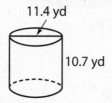

11.4 yd

10.7 yd

(A) 102 cubic yards

(B) 347.6 cubic yards

(C) 1,091.6 cubic yards

(D) 4,366.4 cubic yards

3. Rhett made mini waffle cones for a birthday party. Each waffle cone was 3.5 inches high and had a radius of 0.8 inches. What is the volume of each cone to the nearest hundredth?

(A) 1.70 cubic inches

(B) 2.24 cubic inches

(C) 2.34 cubic inches

(D) 8.79 cubic inches

4. What is the volume of a cone that has a height of 17 meters and a base with a radius of 6 meters? Use 3.14 for π and round to the nearest tenth.

(A) 204 cubic meters

(B) 640.6 cubic meters

(C) 2,562.2 cubic meters

(D) 10,249 cubic meters

5. Using 3.14 for π, what is the volume of the sphere to the nearest tenth?

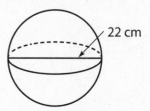

22 cm

(A) 4180 cubic centimeters

(B) 5572.5 cubic centimeters

(C) 33,434.7 cubic centimeters

(D) 44,579.6 cubic centimeters

Mini-Task

6. A diagram of a deodorant container is shown. It is made up of a cylinder and half of a sphere.

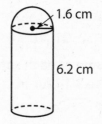

1.6 cm

6.2 cm

Use 3.14 for π and round answers to the nearest tenth.

a. What is the volume of the half sphere?

_____

b. What is the volume of the cylinder?

_____

c. What is the volume of the whole figure?

_____

MODULE 11 ## Angle Relationships in Parallel Lines and Triangles

Key Vocabulary

alternate exterior angles
(*ángulos alternos externos*)

alternate interior angles
(*ángulos alternos internos*)

corresponding angles
(*ángulos correspondientes (para líneas)*)

exterior angle (*ángulo externo*)

interior angle (*ángulos internos*)

remote interior angle
(*ángulo interno remoto*)

same-side interior angles
(*ángulos internos del mismo lado*)

similar (*semejantes*)

transversal (*transversal*)

? **ESSENTIAL QUESTION**

How can you solve real-world problems that involve angle relationships in parallel lines and triangles?

EXAMPLE 1

Find each angle measure when m∠6 = 81°.

A $m\angle 5 = 180° - 81° = 99°$

5 and 6 are supplementary angles.

B $m\angle 1 = 99°$

1 and 5 are corresponding angles.

C $m\angle 3 = 180° - 81° = 99°$

3 and 6 are same-side interior angles.

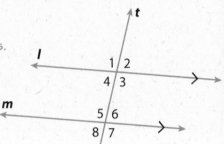

EXAMPLE 2

Are the triangles similar? Explain your answer.

$y = 180° - (67° + 35°)$

$y = 78°$

$x = 180° - (67° + 67°)$

$x = 46°$

The triangles are not similar, because they do not have 2 or more pairs of corresponding congruent angles.

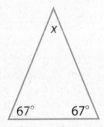

EXERCISES

1. If m∠GHA = 106°, find the measures of the given angles.
(Lesson 11.1)

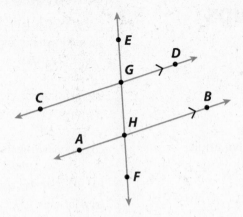

m∠EGC = _____

m∠EGD = _____

m∠BHF = _____

m∠HGD = _____

2. Find the measure of the missing angles. (Lesson 11.2)

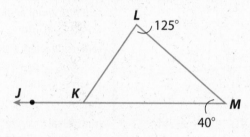

m∠JKL = _____

m∠LKM = _____

3. Is the larger triangle similar to the smaller triangle?
Explain your answer. (Lesson 11.3)

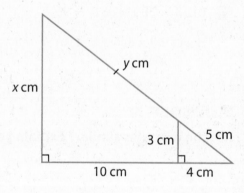

_____

_____

_____

4. Find the value of x and y in the figure. (Lesson 11.3)

_____

5. If m∠CJI = 132° and m∠EIH = 59°, find the measures of
the given angles. (Lesson 11.1)

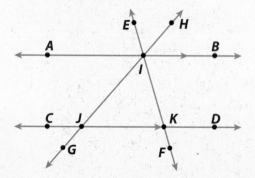

m∠IKJ = _____

m∠HIB = _____

m∠EIJ = _____

m∠AIK = _____

The Pythagorean Theorem

Key Vocabulary

hypotenuse *(hipotenusa)*

legs *(catetos)*

Pythagorean Theorem
(teorema de Pitágoras)

? **ESSENTIAL QUESTION**

How can you use the Pythagorean Theorem to solve real-world problems?

EXAMPLE 1

Find the missing side length.
Round your answer to the nearest tenth.

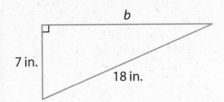

$a^2 + b^2 = c^2$

$7^2 + b^2 = 18^2$

$49 + b^2 = 324$

$b^2 = 275$

$b = \sqrt{275} \approx 16.6$

The length of the leg is about 16.6 inches.

EXAMPLE 2

Thomas drew a diagram to represent the location of his house, the school, and his friend Manuel's house. What is the distance from the school to Manuel's house? Round your answer to the nearest tenth.

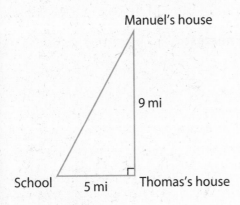

$a^2 + b^2 = c^2$

$5^2 + 9^2 = c^2$

$25 + 81 = c^2$

$c^2 = 106$

$c = \sqrt{106} \approx 10.3$

The distance from the school to Manuel's house is about 10.3 miles.

EXERCISES

Find the missing side lengths. Round your answers to the nearest hundredth. (Lesson 12.1)

1.

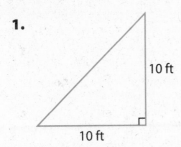

10 ft

10 ft

2.

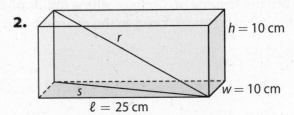

$h = 10$ cm

r

s

$w = 10$ cm

$\ell = 25$ cm

3. Hye Sun has a modern coffee table whose top is a triangle with the following side lengths: 8 feet, 3 feet, and 5 feet. Is Hye Sun's coffee table top a right triangle? (Lesson 12.2)

_____

4. Find the length of each side of triangle *ABC*. If necessary, round your answers to the nearest hundredth. (Lesson 12.3)

$\overline{AB}$ _____

$\overline{BC}$ _____

$\overline{AC}$ _____

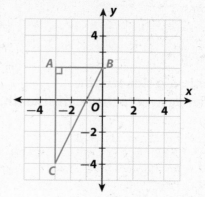

MODULE 13 **Volume**

Key Vocabulary
cone *(cono)*
cylinder *(cilindro)*
sphere *(esfera)*

(?) ESSENTIAL QUESTION

How can you solve real-world problems that involve volume?

EXAMPLE 1

Find the volume of the cistern. Round your answer to the nearest hundredth.

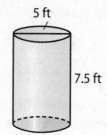

5 ft

7.5 ft

$V = \pi r^2 h$

$\approx 3.14 \cdot 2.5^2 \cdot 7.5$

$\approx 3.14 \cdot 6.25 \cdot 7.5$

≈ 147.19

The cistern has a volume of approximately 147.19 cubic feet.

EXAMPLE 2

Find the volume of a sphere with a radius of 3.7 cm. Write your answer in terms of π and to the nearest hundredth.

$V = \frac{4}{3}\pi r^3$ $V = \frac{4}{3}\pi r^3$

$\approx \frac{4}{3} \cdot \pi \cdot 3.7^3$ $\approx \frac{4}{3} \cdot 3.14 \cdot 3.7^3$

$\approx \frac{4}{3} \cdot \pi \cdot 50.653$ $\approx \frac{4}{3} \cdot 3.14 \cdot 50.653$

$\approx 67.54\pi$ ≈ 212.07

The volume of the sphere is approximately 67.54π cm³, or 212.07 cm³.

EXERCISES

Find the volume of each figure. Round your answers to the nearest hundredth. (Lessons 13.1, 13.2, 13.3)

1.

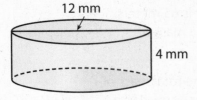

12 mm

4 mm

_____

2.

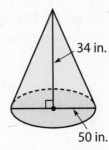

34 in.

50 in.

_____

3. Find the volume of a ball with a radius of 1.68 inches. _____

4.

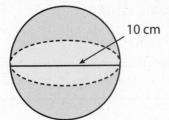

10 cm

_____

5.

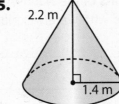

2.2 m

1.4 m

_____

6. A round above-ground swimming pool has a diameter of 15 ft and a height of 4.5 ft. What is the volume of the swimming pool? _____

7.

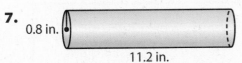

0.8 in.

11.2 in.

8.

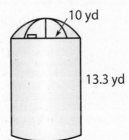

10 yd

13.3 yd

_____

9. A paper cup in the shape of a cone has a height of 4.7 inches and a diameter of 3.6 inches. What is the volume of the paper cup? _____

1. **CAREERS IN MATH** | Hydrologist A hydrologist needs to estimate the mass of water in an underground aquifer, which is roughly cylindrical in shape. The diameter of the aquifer is 65 meters, and its depth is 8 meters. One cubic meter of water has a mass of about 1000 kilograms.

   a. The aquifer is completely filled with water. What is the total mass of the water in the aquifer? Explain how you found your answer. Use 3.14 for π and round your answer to the nearest kilogram.

   _____

   _____

   _____

   b. Another cylindrical aquifer has a diameter of 70 meters and a depth of 9 meters. The mass of the water in it is 27×10^7 kilograms. Is the aquifer totally filled with water? Explain your reasoning.

   _____

   _____

   _____

2. From his home, Myles walked his dog north 5 blocks, east 2 blocks, and then stopped at a drinking fountain. He then walked north 3 more blocks and east 4 more blocks. It started to rain so he cut through a field and walked straight home.

   a. Draw a diagram of his path.

   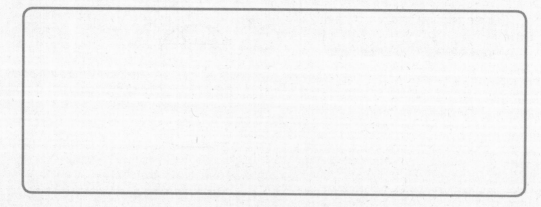

   b. How many blocks did Myles walk in all? How much longer was his walk before it started to rain than his walk home?

   _____

Assessment Readiness

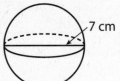

Selected Response

1. Which of the following angle pairs formed by a transversal that intersects two parallel lines are not congruent?

(A) alternate interior angles

(B) adjacent angles

(C) corresponding angles

(D) alternate exterior angles

2. The measures of the three angles of a triangle are given by $3x + 1$, $2x - 3$, and $9x$. What is the measure of the smallest angle?

(A) 13° (C) 29°

(B) 23° (D) 40°

3. Using 3.14 for π, what is the volume of the cylinder?

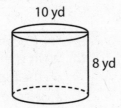

10 yd

8 yd

(A) 200 cubic yards

(B) 628 cubic yards

(C) 1256 cubic yards

(D) 2512 cubic yards

4. Which of the following is **not** true?

(A) $\sqrt{36} + 2 > \sqrt{16} + 5$

(B) $5\pi < 17$

(C) $\sqrt{10} + 1 < \frac{9}{2}$

(D) $5 - \sqrt{35} < 0$

5. A pole is 65 feet tall. A support wire is attached to the top of the pole and secured to the ground 33 feet from the base of the pole. Find the approximate length of the wire.

(A) 32 feet (C) 56 feet

(B) 73 feet (D) 60 feet

6. Using 3.14 for π, what is the volume of the sphere to the nearest tenth?

7 cm

(A) 205.1 cm³

(B) 1077 cm³

(C) 179.5 cm³

(D) 4308.1 cm³

7. Which set of lengths are **not** the side lengths of a right triangle?

(A) 28, 45, 53 (C) 36, 77, 85

(B) 13, 84, 85 (D) 16, 61, 65

8. Which statement describes the solution of a system of linear equations for two lines with different slopes and different y-intercepts?

(A) one nonzero solution

(B) infinitely many solutions

(C) no solution

(D) solution of 0

9. What is the side length of a cube that has a volume of 729 cubic inches?

(A) 7 inches (C) 9 inches

(B) 8 inches (D) 10 inches

10. What is the solution to the system of equations?

$$\begin{cases} x + 3y = 5 \\ 2x - y = -4 \end{cases}$$

(A) no solution

(B) infinitely many solutions

(C) (2, 1)

(D) (−1, 2)

Mini-Tasks

11. In the figure shown, m∠*AGE* = (5*x* − 7)°
and m∠*BGH* = (3*x* + 19)°.

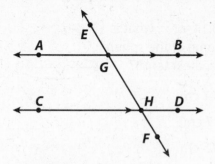

   a. Find the value of *x*. _____

   b. Find m∠*AGE*. _____

   c. Find m∠*GHD*. _____

12. Tom drew two right triangles as shown with
angle measures to the nearest whole unit.

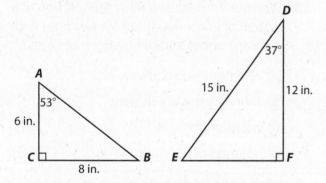

   a. Find the length of $\overline{AB}$ in triangle *ABC*.

   _____

   b. Find the length of $\overline{EF}$ in triangle *DEF*.

   _____

   c. Are the triangles similar? Explain your
answer.

   _____

   _____

   _____

   _____

 **Read graphs and diagrams
carefully. Look at the labels for
important information.**

13. In the diagram, the figure at the top of the
cone is a hemisphere.

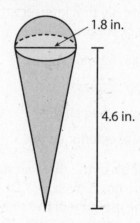

   a. What is the volume of the cone?
Round your answer to the nearest
hundredth.

   _____

   b. What is the volume of the hemisphere
on the top of the cone? Round your
answer to the nearest hundredth.

   _____

   c. What would be the radius of a sphere
with the same total volume as the figure?
Explain how you found your answer.

   _____

   _____

   _____

   _____

   _____

   _____

MODULE **14**

Scatter Plots

COMMON CORE — 8.SP.1, 8.SP.2, 8.SP.3

MODULE **15**

Two-Way Tables

COMMON CORE — 8.SP.4

CAREERS IN MATH

Psychologist A psychologist investigates the physical, mental, emotional, and social aspects of human behavior. Psychologists use math to evaluate and interpret data about human activities and the human mind. They create and use mathematical models to predict behavior of humans, both individually and in groups.

If you are interested in a career in psychology, you should study the following mathematical subjects:

- Algebra
- Trigonometry
- Probability and Statistics
- Calculus

Research other careers that require the analysis of data and use of mathematical models.

Unit 6 Performance Task

At the end of the unit, check out how **psychologists** use math.

© Houghton Mifflin Harcourt Publishing Company • Image Credits: ©Ron Levine/Getty Images

Vocabulary Preview

Use the puzzle to preview key vocabulary from this unit. Unscramble the circled letters within found words to answer the riddle at the bottom of the page.

```
E I F N R B W D F M O N J O V
N L E L H L D C C W O T R U R
O Y P T R (E) N D L I N E I T W
I Q V M M V I B T U D D B L F
T U D K A E B A B R S Q I I W
(A) R Q O S S L T S M N T B E C
I Y S Z Y U (M) P K D G U E R Q
C B T S P B T A B Q P B H R V
O U M O M G V C R W Q Z U E E
S W P R K V T U E G L M G Z S
S X L E T V U G Q C I J I G C
A D E O A B L W A D N N B U
G V J Q V C X A Y I V M A Z W
N L F W O M A T L T U Z B L M
(N) O I T A L O P R E T N I V G
```

A description of how sets of data are related. (Lesson 14.1)

A set of closely related data. (Lesson 14.1)

A data point that is very different from the rest of the data in the set. (Lesson 14.1)

A straight line that comes closest to the points on a scatter plot (2 words). (Lesson 14.2)

Using a trend line to predict a value between data points you already know. (Lesson 14.2)

A relative frequency found by dividing a row total or a column total by the grand total. (Lesson 15.2)

Q: Why doesn't Joe Average have any friends?

A: Because he's so ___ ___ ___ ___!

Scatter Plots

? ESSENTIAL QUESTION

How can you use scatter plots to solve real-world problems?

Real-World Video

An anthropologist measures dinosaur bones. To estimate a dinosaur's height based on the length of a bone, he can make a scatter plot comparing bone length and height of several dinosaurs.

⊙ my.hrw.com

GO DIGITAL

my.hrw.com

my.hrw.com

Go digital with your write-in student edition, accessible on any device.

Math On the Spot

Scan with your smart phone to jump directly to the online edition, video tutor, and more.

Animated Math

Interactively explore key concepts to see how math works.

Personal Math Trainer

Get immediate feedback and help as you work through practice sets.

Are YOU Ready?

Complete these exercises to review skills you will need for this module.

my.hrw.com

Personal Math Trainer

Online Assessment and Intervention

Evaluate Expressions

EXAMPLE Evaluate $4x + 3$ for $x = 5$.

$4x + 3 = 4(5) + 3$ Substitute the given value for x.

$= 20 + 3$ Multiply.

$= 23$ Add.

Evaluate each expression for the given value of x.

1. $6x - 5$ for $x = 4$

2. $-2x + 7$ for $x = 2$

3. $5x - 6$ for $x = 3$

_____

_____

_____

4. $0.5x + 8.4$ for $x = -1$

5. $\frac{3}{4}x - 9$ for $x = -20$

6. $1.4x + 3.5$ for $x = -4$

_____

_____

_____

Solve Two-Step Equations

EXAMPLE

$5x + 3 = -7$

$\underline{\quad -3 = -3\quad}$ Subtract 3 from both sides.

$5x = -10$

$\dfrac{5x}{5} = \dfrac{-10}{5}$ Divide both sides by 5.

$x = -2$

Solve for x.

7. $3x + 4 = 10$

8. $5x - 11 = 34$

9. $-2x + 5 = -9$

10. $8x + 13 = -11$

_____

_____

_____

_____

11. $4x - 7 = -27$

12. $\frac{1}{2}x + 16 = 39$

13. $\frac{2}{3}x - 16 = 12$

14. $0.5x - 1.5 = -6.5$

_____

_____

_____

_____

Reading Start-Up

Visualize Vocabulary

Use the ✔ words to complete the right column of the chart.

Reviewing Slope	
Mathematical Representation	**Review Word**
$y = mx + b$	
y	
m	
x	
b	

Understand Vocabulary

Match the term on the left to the correct expression on the right.

1. cluster

2. outlier

3. trend line

A. A data point that is very different from the rest of the data in a set

B. A straight line that comes closest to the points on a scatter plot.

C. A set of closely grouped data.

© Houghton Mifflin Harcourt Publishing Company

Active Reading

Two-Panel Flip Chart Create a two-panel flip chart, to help you understand the concepts in this module. Label each flap with the title of one of the lessons in the module. As you study each lesson, write important ideas under the appropriate flap. Include any sample problems or equations that will help you remember the concepts later when you look back at your notes.

Vocabulary

Review Words

bivariate data *(datos bivariados)*

data *(datos)*

✔ linear equation *(ecuación lineal)*

✔ slope *(pendiente)*

✔ slope-intercept form of an equation *(forma pendiente-intersección)*

✔ *x*-coordinate *(coordenada x)*

✔ *y*-coordinate *(coordenada y)*

✔ *y*-intercept *(intersección con el eje y)*

Preview Words

cluster *(agrupación)*

outlier *(valor extremo)*

scatter plot *(diagrama de dispersión)*

trend line *(línea de tendencia)*

COMMON
CORE

MODULE 14

Unpacking the Standards

Understanding the standards and the vocabulary terms in the standards will help you know exactly what you are expected to learn in this module.

COMMON
CORE **8.SP.1**

Construct and interpret scatter plots for bivariate measurement data to investigate patterns of association between two quantities. Describe patterns such as clustering, outliers, positive or negative association, linear association, and nonlinear association.

What It Means to You

You will describe how the data in a scatter plot are related.

UNPACKING EXAMPLE 8.SP.1

The scatter plot shows Bob's height at various ages. Describe the type(s) of association between Bob's age and his height. Explain.

As Bob gets older, his height increases roughly along a straight line on the graph, so the association is positive and basically linear.

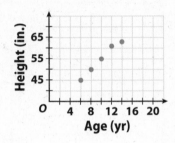

COMMON
CORE **8.SP.2**

Know that straight lines are widely used to model relationships between two quantitative variables. For scatter plots that suggest a linear association, informally fit a straight line, and informally assess the model fit by judging the closeness of the data points to the line.

What It Means to You

You will use a trend line to show the relationship between two quantities.

UNPACKING EXAMPLE 8.SP.2

Joyce is training for a 10K race. For each of her training runs, she recorded the distance she ran and the time she ran. She made a scatter plot of her data and drew a trend line. Use the trend line to predict how long it would take Joyce to run 4.5 miles.

Distance (mi)	Time (min)
4	38
2	25
1	7
2	16
3	26
5	55
2	20
4	45
3	31

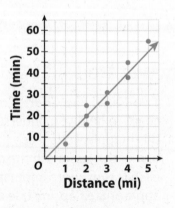

For a distance of 4.5 miles, the trend line shows a time of 45 minutes. So, it will take Joyce about 45 minutes to run 4.5 miles.

Visit **my.hrw.com** to see all the **Common Core Standards** unpacked.

my.hrw.com

Scatter Plots and Association

COMMON CORE **8.SP.1**

Construct and interpret scatter plots.... Describe patterns such as clustering, outliers, positive or negative association, linear association, and nonlinear association.

ESSENTIAL QUESTION

How can you construct and interpret scatter plots?

EXPLORE ACTIVITY 1  COMMON CORE **8.SP.1**

Making a Scatter Plot

Recall that a set of bivariate data involves two variables. Bivariate data are used to explore the relationship between two variables. You can graph bivariate data on a *scatter plot*. A **scatter plot** is a graph with points plotted to show the relationship between two sets of data.

The final question on a math test reads, "How many hours did you spend studying for this test?" The teacher records the number of hours each student studied and the grade the student received on the test.

Hours Spent Studying	Test Grade
0	75
0.5	80
1	80
1	85
1.5	85
1.5	95
2	90
3	100
4	90

A Make a prediction about the relationship between the number of hours spent studying and test grades.

_____

_____

_____

B Make a scatter plot. Graph hours spent studying as the independent variable and test grades as the dependent variable.

Reflect

1. What trend do you see in the data?

_____

_____

2. **Justify Reasoning** Do you think the grade associated with studying for 10 hours would follow this trend?

_____

_____

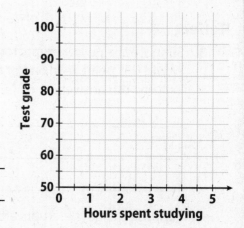

Interpreting Clusters and Outliers

A **cluster** is a set of closely grouped data. Data may cluster around a point or along a line. An **outlier** is a data point that is very different from the rest of the data in the set.

A scientist gathers information about the eruptions of Old Faithful, a geyser in Yellowstone National Park. She uses the data to create a scatter plot. The data show the length of time between eruptions (interval) and how long the eruption lasts (duration).

A Describe any clusters you see in the scatter plot.

_____

_____

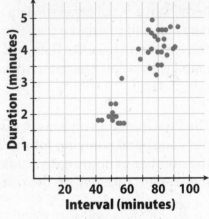

B What do the clusters tell you about eruptions of Old Faithful?

_____

_____

C Describe any outliers you see in the scatter plot.

_____

_____

Math Talk
Mathematical Practices

If the point (20, 1) appeared on the scatter plot, would it be an outlier? Explain.

Reflect

3. Suppose the geyser erupts for 2.2 minutes after a 75-minute interval. Would this point lie in one of the clusters? Would it be an outlier? Explain your answer.

_____

_____

_____

4. Suppose the geyser erupts after an 80-minute interval. Give a range of possible duration times for which the point on the scatter plot would not be considered an outlier. Explain your reasoning.

_____

_____

Determining Association

Association describes how sets of data are related. A *positive* association means that both data sets increase together. A *negative* association means that as one data set increases, the other decreases. *No* association means that there is no relationship between the two data sets.

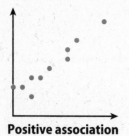
Positive association

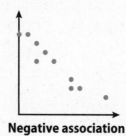
Negative association

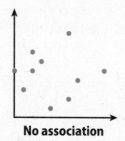
No association

Data that show a positive or negative association and lie basically along a line exhibit a *linear* association. Data that show a positive or negative association but do not lie basically along a line exhibit a *nonlinear* association.

EXAMPLE 1

 COMMON CORE 8.SP.1

Susan asked 20 people if they would buy a new product she developed at each of several prices. The scatter plot shows how many of the 20 said "yes" at a given price. Describe the association between price and the number of buyers.

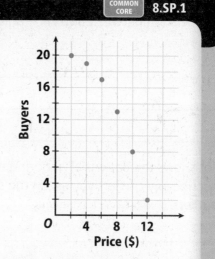

As price increases, the number of buyers decreases. So, there is a negative association. Because the data points do not lie along a line, the association is nonlinear.

Reflect

5. **What If?** Based on the association shown in the scatter plot, what might happen if Susan increased the price to $14?

_____

YOUR TURN

6. The plot shows the reading level and height for 16 students in a district. Describe the association and give a possible reason for it.

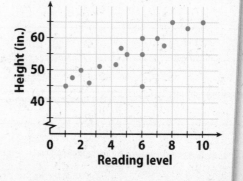

_____

_____

_____

© Houghton Mifflin Harcourt Publishing Company

Bob recorded his height at different ages. The table below shows his data.

Age (years)	6	8	10	12	14
Height (inches)	45	50	55	61	63

1. Make a scatter plot of Bob's data. (Explore Activity 1)

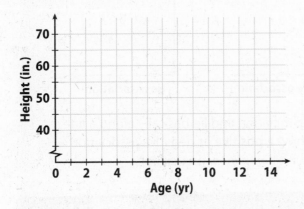

2. Describe the association between Bob's age and his height. Explain the association. (Example 1)

_____

_____

_____

3. The scatter plot shows the basketball shooting results for 14 players. Describe any clusters you see in the scatter plot. Identify any outliers. (Explore Activity 2)

_____

_____

_____

Basketball Shooting

ESSENTIAL QUESTION CHECK-IN

4. Explain how you can make a scatter plot from a set of bivariate data.

_____

_____

_____

_____

14.1 Independent Practice

COMMON CORE 8.SP.1

Personal Math Trainer

Online Assessment and Intervention

my.hrw.com

Sports Use the scatter plot for 5–8.

Olympic Men's Long Jump Winning Distances

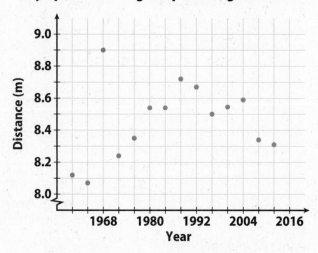

5. Describe the association between the year and the distance jumped for the years 1960 to 1988.

_____

_____

_____

6. Describe the association between the year and the distance jumped for the years after 1988.

_____

_____

_____

_____

7. For the entire scatter plot, is the association between the year and the distance jumped linear or nonlinear?

_____

_____

_____

_____

8. Identify the outlier and interpret its meaning.

_____

_____

_____

_____

9. Communicate Mathematical Ideas Compare a scatter plot that shows no association to one that shows negative association.

_____

_____

_____

_____

_____

_____

For 10–11, describe a set of real-world bivariate data that the given scatter plot could represent. Define the variable represented on each axis.

10.

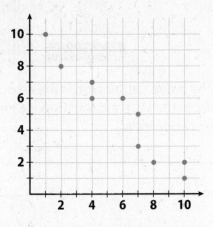

_____

_____

_____

11.

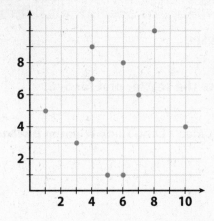

_____

_____

_____

H.O.T. **FOCUS ON HIGHER ORDER THINKING**

12. **Multiple Representations** Describe what you might see in a table of bivariate data that would lead you to conclude that the scatter plot of the data would show a cluster.

_____

_____

13. **Justify Reasoning** Is it possible for a scatter plot to have a positive or negative association that is not linear? Explain.

_____

_____

_____

14. **Critical Thinking** To try to increase profits, a theater owner increases the price of a ticket by $25 every month. Describe what a scatter plot might look like if x represents the number of months and y represents the profits. Explain your reasoning.

_____

_____

_____

_____

_____

Work Area

Trend Lines and Predictions

COMMON CORE 8.SP.3

Use the equation of a linear model to solve problems in the context of bivariate measurement data, interpreting the slope and intercept. *Also 8.SP.1, 8.SP.2*

? ESSENTIAL QUESTION

How can you use a trend line to make a prediction from a scatter plot?

EXPLORE ACTIVITY 1 **COMMON CORE 8.SP.2, 8.SP.1**

Drawing a Trend Line

When a scatter plot shows a linear association, you can use a line to model the relationship between the variables. A **trend line** is a straight line that comes closest to the points on a scatter plot.

Joyce is training for a 10K race. For some of her training runs, she records the distance she ran and how many minutes she ran.

A Make a scatter plot of Joyce's running data.

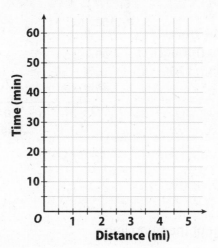

Distance (mi)	Time (min)
4	38
2	25
1	7
2	16
3	26
5	55
2	20
4	45
3	31

B To draw a trend line, use a straight edge to draw a line that has about the same number of points above and below it. Ignore any outliers.

C Use your trend line to predict how long it would take Joyce to run 4.5 miles.

_____

Reflect

1. How well does your trend line fit the data? Explain.

_____

_____

2. Do you think you can use a scatter plot that shows no association to make a prediction? Explain your answer.

_____

_____

Finding the Equation of a Trend Line

You can use two points on a trend line to write an equation in slope-intercept form for the trend line.

EXAMPLE 1

COMMON CORE 8.SP.3

The scatter plot and trend line show the relationship between the number of chapters and the total number of pages for several books. Write an equation for the trend line.

Math Talk
Mathematical Practices
Why are (5, 50) and (17, 170) the best points to use to draw the trend line?

STEP 1 Find the slope of the trend line. The line passes through points (5, 50) and (17, 170).

$m = \dfrac{y_2 - y_1}{x_2 - x_1}$ *Use the slope formula.*

$m = \dfrac{170 - 50}{17 - 5}$ *Substitute (5, 50) for (x_1, y_1) and (17, 170) for (x_2, y_2).*

$m = \dfrac{120}{12} = 10$ *Simplify.*

STEP 2 Find the *y*-intercept of the trend line.

$y = mx + b$ *Slope-intercept form*

$50 = 10 \cdot 5 + b$ *Substitute 50 for y, 10 for m, and 5 for x.*

$50 = 50 + b$ *Simplify.*

$50 - 50 = 50 - 50 + b$ *Subtract 50 from both sides.*

$0 = b$ *Simplify.*

STEP 3 Use your slope and *y*-intercept values to write the equation.

$y = mx + b$ *Slope-intercept form*

$y = 10x + 0$ *Substitute 10 for m and 0 for y.*

The equation for the trend line is $y = 10x$.

Reflect

3. What type(s) of association does the scatter plot show?

_____

4. What is the meaning of the slope in this situation?

_____

5. What is the meaning of the *y*-intercept in this situation?

_____

 YOUR TURN

6. The scatter plot and trend line show the relationship between the number of rainy days in a month and the number of umbrellas sold each month. Write an equation for the trend line.

_____

_____

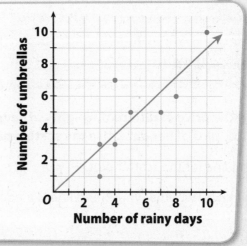

Personal
Math Trainer

Online Assessment
and Intervention

⏻ my.hrw.com

 EXPLORE ACTIVITY 2 · Real World · COMMON CORE · **8.SP.3**

Making Predictions

When you use a trend line or its equation to predict a value between data points that you already know, you *interpolate* the predicted value. When you make a prediction that is outside the data that you know, you *extrapolate* the predicted value.

Use the equation of the trend line in Example 1 to predict how many pages would be in a book with 26 chapters.

Is this prediction an example of interpolation or extrapolation? _____

$y =$ ⬚ Write the equation for your trend line.

$y =$ ⬚ Substitute the number of chapters for *x*.

$y =$ ⬚ Simplify.

I predict that a book with 26 chapters will have _____ pages.

© Houghton Mifflin Harcourt Publishing Company

Reflect

7. **Make a Prediction** Predict how many pages would be in a book with 14 chapters. Is this prediction an example of interpolation or extrapolation?

_____

8. Do you think that extrapolation or interpolation is more accurate? Explain.

_____

_____

_____

Guided Practice

Angela recorded the price of different weights of several bulk grains. She made a scatter plot of her data. Use the scatter plot for 1–4.

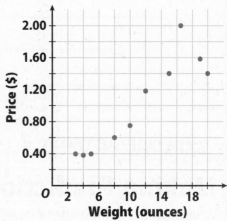

1. Draw a trend line for the scatter plot. (Explore Activity 1)

2. How do you know whether your trend line is a good fit for the data? (Explore Activity 1)

_____

_____

_____

3. Write an equation for your trend line. (Example 1) _____

4. Use the equation for your trend line to interpolate the price of 7 ounces and extrapolate the price of 50 ounces.

(Explore Activity 2) _____

? ESSENTIAL QUESTION CHECK-IN

5. A trend line passes through two points on a scatter plot. How can you use the trend line to make a prediction between or outside the given data points?

_____

_____

_____

Name_____ Class_____ Date_____

14.2 Independent Practice

COMMON CORE 8.SP.1, 8.SP.2, 8.SP.3

Use the data in the table for Exercises 6–10.

Apparent Temperature Due to Wind at 15 °F						
Wind speed (mi/h)	10	20	.30	40	50	60
Wind chill (°F)	2.7	−2.3	−5.5	−7.9	−9.8	−11.4

6. Make a scatter plot of the data and draw a trend line.

7. What type of association does the trend line show?

_____

8. Write an equation for your trend line. _____

9. **Make a Prediction** Use the trend line to predict the wind chill at these wind speeds.

a. 36 mi/h _____   **b.** 100 mi/h _____

10. What is the meaning of the slope of the line?

_____

_____

Apparent Temperature Due to Wind at 15 °F

[graph: Wind chill (°F) on vertical axis from −12 to 4; Wind speed (mi/h) on horizontal axis marked 20, 40, 60, 80]

Use the data in the table for Exercises 11–14.

Apparent Temperature Due to Humidity at a Room Temperature of 72 °F						
Humidity (%)	0	20	40	60	80	100
Apparent temperature (°F)	64	67	70	72	74	76

11. Make a scatter plot of the data and draw a trend line.

12. Write an equation for your trend line.

_____

13. **Make a Prediction** Use the trend line to predict the apparent

temperature at 70% humidity. _____

14. What is the meaning of the y-intercept of the line?

_____

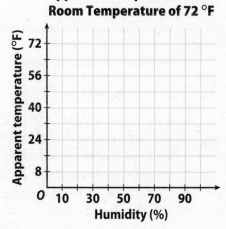

Apparent Temperature at a Room Temperature of 72 °F

[graph: Apparent temperature (°F) on vertical axis marked 8, 24, 40, 56, 72; Humidity (%) on horizontal axis marked 10, 30, 50, 70, 90]

15. Communicate Mathematical Ideas Is it possible to draw a trend line on a scatter plot that shows no association? Explain.

_____

_____

_____

16. Critique Reasoning Sam drew a trend line that had about the same number of data points above it as below it, but did not pass through any data points. He then picked two data points to write the equation for the line. Is this a correct way to write the equation? Explain.

_____

_____

_____

_____

17. Marlene wanted to find a relationship between the areas and populations of counties in Texas. She plotted x (area in square miles) and y (population) for two counties on a scatter plot:

Kent County (903, 808)   Edwards County (2118, 2002)

She concluded that the population of Texas counties is approximately equal to their area in square miles and drew a trend line through her points.

a. Critique Reasoning Do you agree with Marlene's method of creating a scatter plot and a trend line? Explain why or why not.

_____

_____

_____

b. Counterexamples Harris County has an area of 1778 square miles and a population of about 4.3 million people. Dallas County has an area of 908 square miles and a population of about 2.5 million people. What does this data show about Marlene's conjecture that the population of Texas counties is approximately equal to their area?

_____

_____

_____

_____

Prime Predictions

Recall that a prime number is a number that is divisible by only 1 and itself. There are infinitely many prime numbers, but there is no formula to find them.

$2 3 5 7 11$

In this activity, you will find prime numbers and attempt to predict prime numbers.

INSTRUCTIONS

STEP 1 Use a Sieve of Eratosthenes to find all prime numbers less than 50.

How to Create a Sieve of Eratosthenes
- Make a list of whole numbers in order from 1 to 50 in boxes of grid paper.
- Cross off 1 because it is not prime.
- The next number, 2, is prime. Circle it. Cross off all multiples of 2 because they are not prime.
- Circle the next number on the list that is not crossed off, 3. It is prime. Cross off all multiples of 3 because they are not prime.
- Continue with the prime number 5 and its multiples.
- Repeat this process until all of the numbers are circled or crossed off. The circled numbers will all be prime numbers.

A partially completed Sieve of Eratosthenes is shown.

1	2	3	4	5	6	7	8	9	10
11	12	13	14	15	16	17	18	19	20
21	22	23	24	25	26	27	28	29	30
31	32	33	34	35	36	37	38	39	40

STEP 2 Create a scatter plot of the first 15 prime numbers.

Prime number, x	2	3	5												
Position in sequence, y	1	2	3	4	5	6	7	8	9	10	11	12	13	14	15

✸ *Use the prime numbers as the x-coordinates and their positions as the y-coordinates.*

STEP 3 Estimate a trend line for your scatter plot.

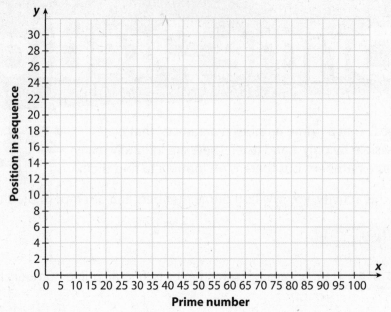

STEP 4 Use your trend line to estimate the remaining prime numbers less than 100.

Prime number														
Position in sequence	16	17	18	19	20	21	22	23	24	25	26	27	28	29	30

STEP 5 Use the Sieve of Eratosthenes to find the actual remaining prime numbers less than 100. How do your estimates compare to the actual prime numbers?

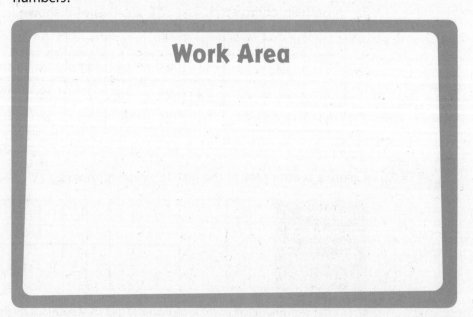

Work Area

Ready to Go On?

14.1 Scatter Plots and Association

An auto store is having a sale on motor oil. The chart shows the price per quart as the number of quarts purchased increases. Use the data for Exs. 1–2.

Number of quarts	1	2	3	4	5	6
Price per quart ($)	2	1.50	1.25	1.10	1	0.95

1. Use the given data to make a scatter plot.

2. Describe the association you see between the number of quarts purchased and the price per quart. Explain.

   _____

   _____

   _____

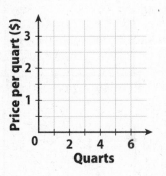

14.2 Trend Lines and Predictions

The scatter plot below shows data comparing wind speed and wind chill for an air temperature of 20°F. Use the scatter plot for Exs. 3–5.

3. Draw a trend line for the scatter plot.

4. Write an equation for your trend line.

   _____

5. Use your equation to predict the wind chill to the nearest degree for a wind speed of 60 mi/h.

   _____

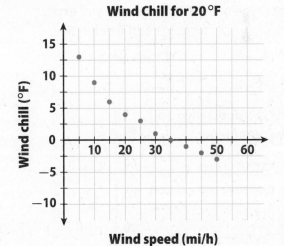

Wind Chill for 20°F

ESSENTIAL QUESTION

6. How can you use scatter plots to solve real-world problems?

   _____

   _____

MODULE 14 MIXED REVIEW

Assessment Readiness

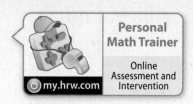

Personal
Math Trainer

Online
Assessment and
Intervention

my.hrw.com

Selected Response

1. Which scatter plot could have a trend line whose equation is $y = 3x + 10$?

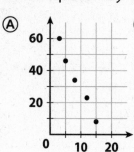

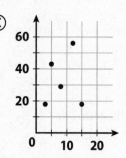

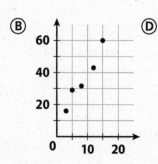

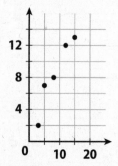

2. What type of association would you expect between a person's age and hair length?

Ⓐ linear   Ⓒ none

Ⓑ negative   Ⓓ positive

3. Which is **not** shown on the scatter plot?

Ⓐ cluster

Ⓑ negative association

Ⓒ outlier

Ⓓ positive association

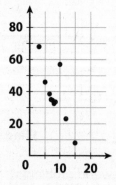

4. A restaurant claims to have served 352,000,000 hamburgers. What is this number in scientific notation?

Ⓐ 3.52×10^6 Ⓒ 35.2×10^7

Ⓑ 3.52×10^8 Ⓓ 352×10^6

5. Which equation describes the relationship between x and y in the table?

x	−8	−4	0	4	8
y	2	1	0	−1	−2

Ⓐ $y = -4x$ Ⓒ $y = 4x$

Ⓑ $y = -\frac{1}{4}x$ Ⓓ $y = \frac{1}{4}x$

Mini-Task

6. Use the data in the table.

Temp (°F)	97	94	87	92	100	90
Pool visitors	370	315	205	135	365	240

a. Make a scatterplot of the data.

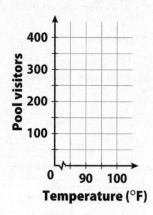

b. Which data point is an outlier?

_____

c. Predict the number of visitors on a day when the high temperature is 102 °F.

_____

Two-Way Tables

 ESSENTIAL QUESTION

How can you use two-way frequency tables to solve real-world problems?

Real-World Video

Two-way tables can help identify and compare probabilities for non-numerical data, such as the probability that girls will like one of two sports teams more than boys will.

 my.hrw.com

GO DIGITAL
my.hrw.com

my.hrw.com

Go digital with your write-in student edition, accessible on any device.

Math On the Spot

Scan with your smart phone to jump directly to the online edition, video tutor, and more.

Animated Math

Interactively explore key concepts to see how math works.

Personal Math Trainer

Get immediate feedback and help as you work through practice sets.

Are YOU Ready?

Complete these exercises to review skills you will need for this module.

Personal Math Trainer

my.hrw.com

Online Assessment and Intervention

Simplify Fractions

EXAMPLE Simplify $\frac{18}{30}$.

$$\frac{1, 2, 3, 6, 9, 18}{1, 2, 3, 5, 6, 10, 30}$$

$$\frac{18 \div 6}{30 \div 6} = \frac{3}{5}$$

List all the factors of the numerator and denominator.

Find the greatest common factor (GCF). Divide the numerator and denominator by the GCF.

Write each fraction in simplest form.

1. $\frac{25}{30}$ _____

2. $\frac{27}{36}$ _____

3. $\frac{14}{16}$ _____

4. $\frac{15}{45}$ _____

5. $\frac{27}{63}$ _____

6. $\frac{45}{75}$ _____

7. $\frac{8}{27}$ _____

8. $\frac{16}{28}$ _____

Fractions, Decimals, Percents

EXAMPLE Write $\frac{13}{20}$ as a decimal and a percent.

$$
\begin{array}{r}
0.65 \\
20\overline{)13.00} \\
12\,0 \\
\hline
100 \\
-100 \\
\hline
0
\end{array}
$$

$0.65 = 65\%$

Write the fraction as a division problem. Write a decimal point and zeros in the dividend.

Place a decimal point in the quotient.

Write the decimal as a percent.

Write each fraction as a decimal and a percent.

9. $\frac{7}{8}$ _____

10. $\frac{4}{5}$ _____

11. $\frac{5}{4}$ _____

12. $\frac{3}{10}$ _____

13. $\frac{19}{20}$ _____

14. $\frac{7}{25}$ _____

Find the Percent of a Number

EXAMPLE 6.5% of 24 = ?

$6.5\% = 0.065$

$$
\begin{array}{r}
24 \\
\times\ 0.065 \\
\hline
1.56
\end{array}
$$

Write the percent as a decimal.

Multiply.

Find each percent of a number.

15. 4% of 40 _____

16. 7% of 300 _____

17. 4.3% of 1,200 _____

18. 2.9% of 780 _____

19. 1.6% of 75.20 _____

20. 3.56% of 3,200 _____

Reading Start-Up

© Houghton Mifflin Harcourt Publishing Company

Visualize Vocabulary

Use the ✔ words to complete the chart.

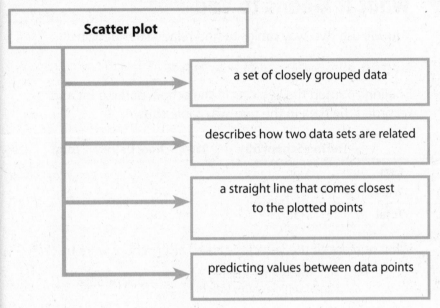

Scatter plot

→ a set of closely grouped data

→ describes how two data sets are related

→ a straight line that comes closest to the plotted points

→ predicting values between data points

Understand Vocabulary

Complete the sentences using preview words.

1. The _____ is the number of times an event occurs.

2. A _____ shows the frequencies of data that is categorized two ways.

3. _____ is the ratio of the number of times an event occurs to the total number of events.

Vocabulary

Review Words

✔ association *(asociación)*

✔ cluster *(grupo)*

data *(datos)*

✔ interpolation *(interpolación)*

extrapolation *(extrapolación)*

outlier *(parte aislada)*

scatter plot *(gráfico de dispersión)*

✔ trend line *(la línea de tendencia)*

Preview Words

conditional relative frequency *(frecuencia relativa condicional)*

frequency *(frecuencia)*

joint relative frequency *(frecuencia relativa conjunta)*

marginal relative frequency *(frecuencia relativa marginal)*

relative frequency *(frecuencia relativa)*

two-way table *(tabla de doble entrada)*

two-way relative frequency table *(tabla de frecuencia relativa de doble entrada)*

Active Reading

Tri-Fold Before beginning the module, create a tri-fold to help you learn the concepts and vocabulary in this module. Fold the paper into three sections. Label the columns "What I Know," "What I Want to Know," and "What I Learned." Complete the first two columns before you read. After studying the module, complete the third column.

Unpacking the Standards

Understanding the standards and the vocabulary terms in the standards will help you know exactly what you are expected to learn in this module.

 8.SP.4

Understand that patterns of association can also be seen in bivariate categorical data by displaying frequencies and relative frequencies in a two-way table. Construct and interpret a two-way table summarizing data on two categorical variables collected from the same subjects. …

Key Vocabulary

two-way table *(tabla de doble entrada)* A table that displays two-variable data by organizing it into rows and columns.

What It Means to You

You will use two-way tables to find relative frequencies.

UNPACKING EXAMPLE 8.SP.4

Soojinn counted the vehicles in the school parking lot and recorded the data in the two-way table shown.

	During School Day	**After School Day**	**Total**
Cars	36	14	50
Trucks	19	6	25
Total	55	20	75

What percent of the vehicles parked after school were trucks?

$$\frac{\text{trucks after school}}{\text{total vehicles after school}} = \frac{6}{20} = 0.3, \text{ or } 30\%$$

30% of the vehicles in the school parking lot after school were trucks.

 8.SP.4

… Use relative frequencies calculated for rows or columns to describe possible association between the two variables.

Key Vocabulary

conditional relative frequency *(frecuencia relativa condicional)* The ratio of a joint relative frequency to a related marginal relative frequency in a two-way table.

What It Means to You

You will use two-way tables to find conditional relative frequencies.

UNPACKING EXAMPLE 8.SP.4

Soojinn determined the gender of the driver for each of the 55 vehicles parked in the school parking lot during the day.

	Male	**Female**	**Total**
Cars	8	25	33
Trucks	15	7	22
Total	23	32	55

What is the conditional relative frequency that a driver is female given that the vehicle is a car?

$$\frac{\text{female car drivers}}{\text{total cars}} = \frac{25}{33} \approx 0.758, \text{ or about } 76\%$$

There is a 76% likelihood that a driver is female given that the vehicle is a car.

Visit **my.hrw.com** to see all the **Common Core Standards** unpacked.

my.hrw.com

Two-Way Frequency Tables

COMMON CORE 8.SP.4

Understand that patterns ... can be seen in bivariate categorical data by displaying frequencies in a two-way table. Construct and interpret a two-way table .... Use relative frequencies ... to describe possible association ....

 ESSENTIAL QUESTION

How can you construct and interpret two-way frequency tables?

EXPLORE ACTIVITY COMMON CORE 8.SP.4

Making a Two-Way Table

The **frequency** is the number of times an event occurs. A **two-way table** shows the frequencies of data that is categorized two ways. The rows indicate one categorization and the columns indicate another.

A poll of 120 town residents found that 40% own a bike. Of those who own a bike, 75% shop at the farmer's market. Of those who do not own a bike, 25% shop at the farmer's market.

	Farmer's Market	No Farmer's Market	TOTAL
Bike			
No Bike			
TOTAL			

A Start in the bottom right cell of the table. Enter the total number of people polled.

B **Fill in the right column.** 40% of 120 people polled own a bike.

The remaining people polled do not own a bike.

C **Fill in the top row.** 75% of those who own a bike also shop at the market.

The remaining bike owners do not shop at the market.

D **Fill in the second row.** 25% of those who do not own a bike shop at the market.

The remaining people without bikes do not shop at the market.

E **Fill in the last row.** In each column, add the numbers in the first two rows to find the total number of people who shop at the farmer's market and who do not shop at the farmer's market.

Reflect

1. How can you check that your table is completed correctly?

_____

_____

Math On the Spot

my.hrw.com

Animated Math

my.hrw.com

Deciding Whether There Is an Association

Relative frequency is the ratio of the number of times an event occurs to the total number of events. In the Explore Activity, the relative frequency of bike owners who shop at the farmer's market is $\frac{36}{120} = 0.30 = 30\%$. You can use relative frequencies to decide if there is an association between two variables or events.

EXAMPLE 1   COMMON CORE 8.SP.4

Determine whether there is an association between the events.

A One hundred teens were polled about whether they are required to do chores and whether they have a curfew. Is there an association between having a curfew and having to do chores?

	Curfew	No Curfew	TOTAL
Chores	16	4	20
No Chores	16	64	80
TOTAL	32	68	100

> **Math Talk**
> **Mathematical Practices**
> What is the difference between frequency and relative frequency?

STEP 1 Find the relative frequency of having to do chores.

Total who have to do chores → $\frac{20}{100} = 0.20 = 20\%$
Total number of teens polled →

STEP 2 Find the relative frequency of having to do chores among those who have a curfew.

Number with a curfew who have chores → $\frac{16}{32} = 0.50 = 50\%$
Total number with a curfew →

STEP 3 **Compare the relative frequencies.** Students who have a curfew are more likely to have to do chores than the general population. There is an association. The relative frequencies show that students who have a curfew are more likely to have to do chores than the general population of teens polled in the survey.

B Data from 200 flights were collected. The flights were categorized as domestic or international and late or not late. Is there an association between international flights and a flight being late?

	Late	Not Late	TOTAL
Domestic	30	120	150
International	10	40	50
TOTAL	40	160	200

STEP 1 **Find the relative frequency of a flight being late.**

Total flights that are late → $\frac{40}{200} = 0.20 = 20\%$
Total number of flights →

STEP 2 **Find the relative frequency of a flight being late among international flights.**

Number of international flights that are late → $\frac{10}{50} = 0.20 = 20\%$
Total number of international flights →

STEP 3 **Compare the relative frequencies.** International flights are no more likely to be late than flights in general. There is no association. The relative frequencies show that international flights are just as likely to be late as any other flight.

YOUR TURN

2. Data from 200 middle school and high school students were collected. Students were asked whether or not they had visited at least one national park. Is there an association between being a high school student and visiting a national park? Explain.

	Have Visited a National Park	Have NOT Visited a National Park	TOTAL
Middle School	25	55	80
High School	80	40	120
TOTAL	105	95	200

_____

_____

_____

_____

_____

_____

Personal Math Trainer
Online Assessment and Intervention
my.hrw.com

1. In a survey of 50 students, 60% said that they have a cat. Of the students who have a cat, 70% also have a dog. Of the students who do not have a cat, 75% have a dog. Complete the two-way table. (Explore Activity)

	Dog	No Dog	TOTAL
Cat			
No Cat			
TOTAL			

   a. Enter the total number of students surveyed in the bottom right cell of the table.

   b. Fill in right column.

   c. Fill in top row.

   d. Fill in second row.

   e. Fill in last row.

2. The results of a survey at a school are shown. Is there an association between being a boy and being left-handed? Explain. (Example 1)

	Left-handed	Right-handed	TOTAL
Boys	14	126	140
Girls	10	90	100
TOTAL	24	216	240

   _____

   _____

   _____

? ESSENTIAL QUESTION CHECK-IN

3. Voters were polled to see whether they supported Smith or Jones. Can you construct a two-way table of the results? Why or why not?

   _____

   _____

   _____

15.1 Independent Practice

 8.SP.4

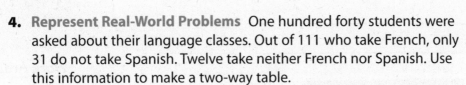

4. Represent Real-World Problems One hundred forty students were asked about their language classes. Out of 111 who take French, only 31 do not take Spanish. Twelve take neither French nor Spanish. Use this information to make a two-way table.

	Take French	Do NOT Take French	TOTAL
Take Spanish			
Do NOT Take Spanish			
TOTAL			

5. Represent Real-World Problems Seventh- and eighth-grade students were asked whether they preferred science or math.

a. Complete the two-way table.

	Prefer Science	Prefer Math	TOTAL
Seventh Grade		72	96
Eighth Grade	32		
TOTAL			176

b. Is there an association between being in eighth grade and preferring math? Explain.

_____

_____

_____

_____

6. Persevere in Problem Solving The table gives partial information on the number of men and women who play in the four sections of the Metro Orchestra.

a. Complete the table.

	Strings	Brass	Woodwinds	Percussion	TOTAL
Men	13	7		5	33
Women			10		
TOTAL	55			9	98

b. Is there an association between being a woman and playing strings? Explain.

_____

_____

_____

_____

 **FOCUS ON HIGHER ORDER THINKING**

7. Multi-Step The two-way table below shows the results of a survey of Florida teenagers who were asked whether they preferred surfing or snorkeling.

a. To the right of the number in each cell, write the relative frequency of the number compared to the total for the *row* the number is in. Round to the nearest percent.

	Prefer Surfing	**Prefer Snorkeling**	**TOTAL**
Ages 13–15	52 _____ ; _____	78 _____ ; _____	130 100%
Ages 16–18	52 _____ ; _____	28 _____ ; _____	80 _____
TOTAL	104 _____ ; _____	106 _____ ; _____	210 _____

b. Explain the meaning of the relative frequency you wrote beside 28.

_____

_____

_____

c. To the right of each number you wrote in part a, write the relative frequency of each number compared to the total for the *column* the number is in. Are the relative frequencies the same? Why or why not?

_____

_____

_____

d. Explain the meaning of the relative frequency you wrote beside 28.

_____

_____

_____

LESSON 15.2 Two-Way Relative Frequency Tables

COMMON CORE 8.SP.4

Understand that patterns ... can be seen in bivariate categorical data by displaying frequencies in a two-way table. Construct and interpret a two-way table ... . Use relative frequencies calculated for rows or columns to describe possible association ... .

? **ESSENTIAL QUESTION**

How can categorical data be organized and analyzed?

EXPLORE ACTIVITY 1   COMMON CORE 8.SP.4

Creating a Relative Frequency Table

The frequency table below shows the results of a survey that Maria took at her school. She asked 50 randomly selected students whether they preferred dogs, cats, or other pets. Convert this table to a *relative frequency* table that uses decimals as well as one that uses percents.

Preferred Pet	Dog	Cat	Other	TOTAL
Frequency	22	15	13	50

A Divide the numbers in the frequency table by the total to obtain relative frequencies as decimals. Record the results in the table below.

Preferred Pet	Dog	Cat	Other	TOTAL
Relative Frequency	$\frac{22}{50} = 0.44$			

B Write the decimals as percents in the table below.

Preferred Pet	Dog	Cat	Other	TOTAL
Relative Frequency	44%			

Reflect

1. How can you check that you have correctly converted frequencies to relative frequencies?

_____

_____

2. Explain why the number in the Total column of a relative frequency table is always 1 or 100%.

_____

_____

© Houghton Mifflin Harcourt Publishing Company

Lesson 15.2 **457**

Creating a Two-Way Frequency Table

In the previous Explore Activity, the categorical variable was pet preference, and the variable had three possible data values: dog, cat, and other. The frequency table listed the frequency for each value of that single variable. If you have two categorical variables whose values have been paired, you list the frequencies of the paired values in a **two-way frequency table.**

For her survey, Maria also recorded the gender of each student. The results are shown in the two-way frequency table below. Each entry is the frequency of students who prefer a certain pet *and* are a certain gender. For instance, 10 girls prefer dogs as pets. Complete the table.

Preferred Pet / Gender	Dog	Cat	Other	TOTAL
Girl	10	9	3	
Boy	12	6	10	
TOTAL				

A Find the total for each gender by adding the frequencies in each row.

B Find the total for each pet by adding the frequencies in each column.

C Find the grand total, which is the sum of the row totals as well as the sum of the column totals. Write this in the lower-right corner.

Reflect

3. Where have you seen the numbers in the Total row before?

_____

4. In terms of Maria's survey, what does the grand total represent?

_____

Creating a Two-Way Relative Frequency Table

You can obtain *relative* frequencies from a two-way frequency table:

- A **joint relative frequency** is found by dividing a frequency that is not in the Total row or the Total column by the grand total.
- A **marginal relative frequency** is found by dividing a row total or a column total by the grand total.

A **two-way relative frequency table** displays both joint relative frequencies and marginal relative frequencies.

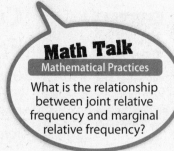

Math Talk

Mathematical Practices

What is the relationship between joint relative frequency and marginal relative frequency?

Create a two-way relative frequency table for Maria's data.

A Divide each number in the two-way frequency table from the previous Explore Activity by the grand total. Write the quotients as decimals.

Preferred Pet / Gender	Dog	Cat	Other	TOTAL
Girl	$\frac{10}{50} = 0.2$			
Boy				
TOTAL	$\frac{22}{50} = 0.44$			$\frac{50}{50} = 1$

B Check by adding the joint relative frequencies in a row or column to see if the sum equals that row's or column's marginal relative frequency.

Girl row: $0.2 +$ _____ $+$ _____ $=$ _____

Boy row: _____ $+$ _____ $+$ _____ $=$ _____

Dog column: $0.2 +$ _____ $=$ _____

Cat column: _____ $+$ _____ $=$ _____

Other column: _____ $+$ _____ $=$ _____

Reflect

5. A joint relative frequency in a two-way relative frequency table tells you what portion of the entire data set falls into the intersection of a particular value of one variable and a particular value of the other variable. What is the joint relative frequency of students surveyed who are boys and prefer cats as pets?

_____

6. A marginal relative frequency in a two-way relative frequency table tells you what portion of the entire data set represents a particular value of just one of the variables. What is the marginal relative frequency of students surveyed who are boys?

_____

Calculating Conditional Relative Frequencies

One other type of relative frequency that you can obtain from a two-way frequency table is a *conditional relative frequency*. A **conditional relative frequency** is found by dividing a frequency that is not in the Total row or the Total column by the frequency's row total or column total.

EXAMPLE 1   **8.SP.4**

From Maria's two-way frequency table you know that 22 students are girls and 15 students prefer cats. You also know that 9 students are girls who prefer cats. Use this to find each conditional relative frequency.

A Find the conditional relative frequency that a student surveyed prefers cats as pets, given that the student is a girl.

Divide the number of girls who prefer cats by the number of girls. Express your answer as a decimal and as a percent.

$\frac{9}{22}$ = 0.409, or 40.9%

B Find the conditional relative frequency that a student surveyed is a girl, given that the student prefers cats as pets.

Divide the number of girls who prefer cats by the number of students who prefer cats. Express your answer as a decimal and as a percent.

$\frac{9}{15}$ = 0.6, or 60%

Reflect

7. When calculating a conditional relative frequency, why do you divide by a row total or a column total and not by the grand total?

_____

_____

_____

_____

My Notes

YOUR TURN

8. You can obtain conditional relative frequencies from a two-way relative frequency table. Find the conditional relative frequency that a student prefers cats as pets, given that the student is a girl.

_____

Finding Possible Associations Between Variables

You can use conditional relative frequency to see if there is an association between two variables.

Math On the Spot

my.hrw.com

EXAMPLE 2 *Real World*

COMMON CORE 8.SP.4

Maria conducted her survey because she was interested in the question "Does gender influence what type of pet people prefer?" If there is no influence, then the distribution of gender within each subgroup of pet preference should roughly equal the distribution of gender within the whole group. Use the results of Maria's survey to investigate possible influences of gender on pet preference.

My Notes

STEP 1 Identify the percent of all students surveyed who are girls: 44%

STEP 2 Determine each conditional relative frequency.

Of the 22 students who prefer dogs as pets, 10 are girls.
Percent who are girls, given a preference for dogs as pets: 45%

Of the 15 students who prefer cats as pets, 9 are girls.
Percent who are girls, given a preference for cats as pets: 60%

Of the 13 students who prefer other pets. 3 are girls.
Percent who are girls, given a preference for other pets: 23%

STEP 3 Interpret the results by comparing each conditional relative frequency to the percent of all students surveyed who are girls.

The percent of girls among students who prefer dogs is close to 44%, so gender does not appear to influence preference for dogs.

The percent of girls among students who prefer cats is much greater than 44%, so girls are more likely than boys to prefer cats.

The percent of girls among students who prefer other pets is much less than 44%, so girls are less likely than boys to prefer other pets.

YOUR TURN

9. Suppose you analyzed the data by focusing on boys rather than girls. How would the percent in Step 1 change? How would the percents in Step 2 change? How would the conclusions in Step 3 change?

_____

_____

_____

Personal Math Trainer

Online Assessment and Intervention

my.hrw.com

1. In a class survey, students were asked to choose their favorite vacation destination. The results are displayed by gender in the two-way frequency table. (Explore Activities 1–3)

Preferred Pet / Gender	Seashore	Mountains	Other	TOTAL
Girl	7	3	2	
Boy	5	2	6	
TOTAL				

a. Find the total for each gender by adding the frequencies in each row. Write the row totals in the Total column.

b. Find the total for each preferred vacation spot by adding the frequencies in each column. Write the column totals in the Total row.

c. Write the grand total (the sum of the row totals and the column totals) in the lower-right corner of the table.

d. Create a two-way relative frequency table by dividing each number in the above table by the grand total. Write the quotients as decimals.

Preferred Pet / Gender	Seashore	Mountains	Other	TOTAL
Girl				
Boy				
TOTAL				

e. Use the table to find the joint relative frequency of students surveyed who are boys and who prefer vacationing in the mountains. _____

f. Use the table to find the marginal relative frequency of students surveyed who prefer vacationing at the seashore. _____

g. Find the conditional relative frequency that a student surveyed prefers vacationing in the mountains, given that the student is a girl. Interpret this result. (Examples 1–2)

_____

 ESSENTIAL QUESTION CHECK-IN

2. How can you use a two-way frequency table to learn more about its data?

_____

_____

15.2 Independent Practice

COMMON CORE 8.SP.4

Personal Math Trainer

Online Assessment and Intervention

my.hrw.com

Stefan surveyed 75 of his classmates about their participation in school activities as well as whether they have a part-time job. The results are shown in the two-way frequency table. Use the table for Exercises 3–6.

Job \ Activity	Clubs Only	Sports Only	Both	Neither	TOTAL
Yes		12		9	51
No	5		10		
TOTAL	15	18			75

3. **a.** Complete the table.

b. Explain how you found the correct data to enter in the table.

_____

_____

_____

_____

4. Create a two-way relative frequency table using decimals. Round to the nearest hundredth.

Job \ Activity	Clubs Only	Sports Only	Both	Neither	TOTAL
Yes					
No					
TOTAL					

5. Give each relative frequency as a percent.

a. the joint relative frequency of students surveyed who participate in school clubs only and have part-time jobs _____

b. the marginal frequency of students surveyed who do not have a part-time job _____

c. the conditional relative frequency that a student surveyed participates in both school clubs and sports, given that the student has a part-time job _____

6. Discuss possible influences of having a part-time job on participation in school activities. Support your response with an analysis of the data.

_____

_____

_____

_____

 **FOCUS ON HIGHER ORDER THINKING**

7. The head of quality control for a chair manufacturer collected data on the quality of two types of wood that the company grows on its tree farm. The table shows the acceptance and rejection data.

Accept/Reject Wood	Accepted	Rejected	TOTAL
White Oak	245	105	350
Redwood	140	110	250
TOTAL	385	215	600

a. Critique Reasoning To create a two-way relative frequency table for this data, the head of quality control divided each number in each row by the row total. Is this correct? Explain.

_____

_____

b. Draw Conclusions Are any of the data the head of quality control entered into the two-way relative frequency table correct? If so, which is and which isn't? Explain.

_____

_____

_____

_____

8. Analyze Relationships What is the difference between relative frequency and conditional relative frequency?

_____

_____

_____

Work Area

Ready to Go On?

Personal Math Trainer

Online Assessment and Intervention

ⓗ my.hrw.com

15.1 Two-Way Frequency Tables

Martin collected data from students about whether they played a musical instrument. The table shows his results. Use the table for Exercises 1–4.

	Instrument	No Instrument	TOTAL
Boys	42	70	112
Girls	48		88
Total	90	110	200

1. Of the students surveyed, how many played an instrument? _____

2. How many girls surveyed did NOT play an instrument? _____

3. What is the relative frequency of a student playing an instrument? Write the answer as a percent. _____

4. What is the relative frequency of playing an instrument among boys? Write the answer as a decimal. _____

15.2 Two-Way Relative Frequency Tables

Students were asked how they traveled to school. The two-way relative frequency table shows the results. Use the table for Exercises 5–7. Write answers as decimals rounded to the nearest hundredth.

	Method			
School	Car	Bus	Other	TOTAL
Middle School	0.18	0.14	0.10	0.42
High School	0.38	0.12	0.08	0.58
TOTAL	0.56	0.26	0.18	1.00

5. What is the joint relative frequency of high school students who ride the bus? _____

6. What is the marginal relative frequency of students surveyed who are in middle school? _____

7. What is the conditional relative frequency that a student rides the bus, given that the student is in middle school? _____

❓ ESSENTIAL QUESTION

8. How can you use two-way tables to solve real-world problems?

_____

_____

MODULE 15 MIXED REVIEW

Assessment Readiness

COMMON CORE

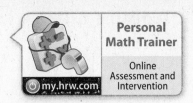

Personal Math Trainer

Online Assessment and Intervention

my.hrw.com

Selected Response

The table gives data on the length of time that teachers at Tenth Avenue School have taught. Use the table for Exercises 1–5.

	Fewer than 10 years	10 or more years	TOTAL
Male	9	6	15
Female	?	4	25
TOTAL	30	10	40

1. How many female teachers have taught for fewer than 10 years?

   Ⓐ 4   Ⓒ 21
   Ⓑ 9   Ⓓ 30

2. What is the relative frequency of teachers who have taught for 10 or more years?

   Ⓐ 10%   Ⓒ 30%
   Ⓑ 25%   Ⓓ 60%

3. What is the relative frequency of having taught for fewer than 10 years among male teachers?

   Ⓐ 0.09   Ⓒ 0.6
   Ⓑ 0.225   Ⓓ 1.50

4. What is the joint relative frequency of female teachers who have taught for more than 10 years?

   Ⓐ 4%   Ⓒ 16%
   Ⓑ 10%   Ⓓ 25%

5. What is the marginal relative frequency of teachers who are female?

   Ⓐ 0.16   Ⓒ 0.4
   Ⓑ 0.25   Ⓓ 0.625

6. A triangle has an exterior angle of $x°$. Which of the following represents the measure of the interior angle next to it?

   Ⓐ $(180 - x)°$ Ⓒ $(90 - x)°$
   Ⓑ $(x - 180)°$ Ⓓ $(x - 90)°$

7. What is the volume of a cone that has a diameter of 12 cm and a height of 4 cm? Use 3.14 for π and round to the nearest tenth.

   Ⓐ 25.12 cm³   Ⓒ 150.72 cm³
   Ⓑ 602.88 cm³   Ⓓ 1,808.64 cm³

Mini-Task

8. The table gives data on books read by members of the Summer Reading Club.

	Fewer than 25 books	25 or more books	TOTAL
Boys	7	21	28
Girls	9	27	36
TOTAL	16	48	64

   a. Find the relative frequency of a club member reading fewer than 25 books.

   _____

   b. Find the relative frequency of reading fewer than 25 books among girl club members.

   _____

   c. Is there an association between being a girl and reading fewer than 25 books? Explain.

   _____

   _____

   _____

   _____

Study Guide Review

MODULE 14 Scatter Plots

 Key Vocabulary
cluster *(agrupación)*
outlier *(valor extremo)*
scatter plot *(diagrama de dispersión)*
trend line *(línea de tendencia)*

? ESSENTIAL QUESTION

How can you use scatter plots to solve real-world problems?

EXAMPLE 1

As part of a research project, a researcher made a table of test scores and the number of hours of sleep a person got the night before the test. Make a scatter plot of the data. Does the data show a positive association, negative association, or no association?

Sleep (hours)	Test score
4	30
5	40
6	50
6	70
8	100
9	90
10	100

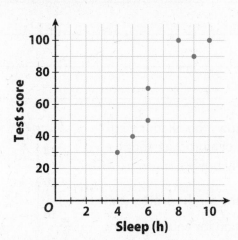

The data show a positive association. Generally, as the number of hours of sleep increases, so do the test scores.

EXAMPLE 2

Write an equation for a trend line of the data shown on the graph.

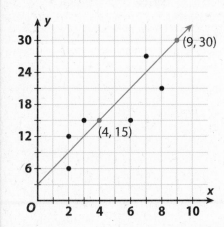

$m = \dfrac{30 - 15}{9 - 4} = 3$ Find the slope.

$15 = 3(4) + b$ Find the y-intercept.

$b = 3$

$y = 3x + 3$ Use the slope and y-intercept to write the equation.

EXERCISES

1. The table shows the income of 8 households, in thousands of dollars, and the number of televisions in each household. (Lesson 14.1)

Income ($1000)	20	20	30	30	40	60	70	90
Number of televisions	4	0	1	2	2	3	3	4

a. Make a scatter plot of the data.

b. Describe the association between income and number of televisions. Are any of the values outliers?

_____

_____

_____

_____

_____

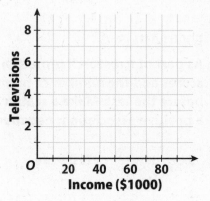

2. The scatter plot shows the relationship between the price of a product and the number of potential buyers. (Lesson 14.2)

a. Draw a trend line for the scatter plot.

b. Write an equation for your trend line.

_____

c. When the price of the product is $3.50, the number of potential buyers will be

about _____.

d. When the price of the product is $5.50, the number of potential buyers will be

about _____.

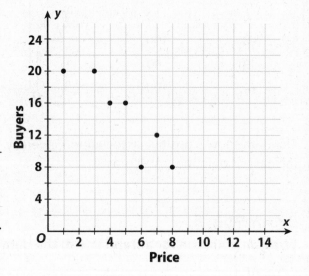

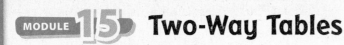

Two-Way Tables

Key Vocabulary

conditional relative frequency *(frecuencia relativa condicional)*

frequency *(frecuencia)*

joint relative frequency *(frecuencia relativa común)*

marginal relative frequency *(frecuencia relativa marginal)*

relative frequency *(frecuencia relativa)*

two-way frequency table *(tabla de frecuencia de doble entrada)*

two-way relative frequency table *(tabla de frecuencia relativa de doble entrada)*

two-way table *(tabla de doble entrada)*

ESSENTIAL QUESTION

How can you use two-way tables to solve real-world problems?

EXAMPLE

A movie theater kept a record of patrons who bought tickets for a particular movie for two different times. The results are shown in the two-way frequency table. Create a two-way relative frequency table of these data.

	5:00 P.M. Showing	8:00 P.M. Showing	Total
Adults	22	39	61
Children	40	25	65
Total	62	64	126

Step 1: Divide each entry by the total number of patrons. Round to the nearest hundredth.

	5:00 P.M. Showing	8:00 P.M. Showing	Total
Adults	$\frac{22}{126} \approx 0.17$	$\frac{39}{126} \approx 0.31$	$\frac{61}{126} \approx 0.48$
Children	$\frac{40}{126} \approx 0.32$	$\frac{25}{126} \approx 0.20$	$\frac{65}{126} \approx 0.52$
Total	$\frac{62}{126} \approx 0.49$	$\frac{64}{126} \approx 0.51$	$\frac{126}{126} \approx 1.00$

Step 2: Convert decimals to percents.

	5:00 P.M. Showing	8:00 P.M. Showing	Total
Adults	17%	31%	48%
Children	32%	20%	52%
Total	49%	51%	100%

EXERCISES

Use the tables in the Example to answer each question.

1. What is the joint relative frequency of patrons who are adults and attended the 8:00 P.M. showing? _____

2. What is the marginal relative frequency of patrons who went to the 8:00 P.M. showing? _____

3. What is the conditional relative frequency that a patron is an adult, given that the patron attends the 8:00 P.M. showing? _____

1. **CAREERS IN MATH** **Psychologist** A psychologist gave a test to 15 women of different ages to measure their short-term memory. The test score scale goes from 0 to 24, and a higher score means that the participant has a better short-term memory. The scatter plot shows the results of this study.

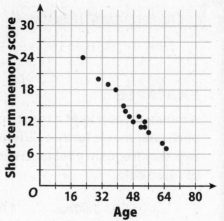

a. Describe the pattern in the data. Is there a positive or negative correlation?

_____

_____

b. Draw a line of best fit on the scatter plot and estimate its slope. Interpret the slope in the context of the problem.

_____

_____

c. In another test, a 70-year-old woman scored 8. Does your line of best fit predict a higher or lower score? What may have happened?

_____

_____

2. Kalila has developed two different varieties of tomatoes, called Big Red and Sweet Summer, which she grows in her garden. When she harvests the tomatoes, she measures the diameters of each variety. The results are shown in the table.

	Diameter ≤ 2 in.	Diameter > 2 in.
Big Red	36	45
Sweet Summer	28	39

a. Use the data to create a two-way frequency table.

	Diameter ≤ 2 in.	Diameter > 2 in.	Total
Big Red			
Sweet Summer			
Total			

b. What is the relative frequency of a tomato having a diameter that is greater than two inches? Round to the nearest percent. _____

c. What is the relative frequency of having a diameter that is greater than two inches among Big Red tomatoes? Round to the nearest percent. _____

d. Is there an association between Big Red tomatoes and diameters that are greater than two inches? Explain.

_____

_____

Selected Response

1. A local election conducted an exit poll of the age and gender of its voters. The results are shown in the two-way frequency table.

	18–62 years old	63 years and older	Total
Female	142	22	164
Male	126	15	141
Total	268	37	305

What percent of the voters were female and 18 to 62 years old?

Ⓐ 6.5%　　　Ⓒ 53%

Ⓑ 47%　　　Ⓓ 87%

2. What type of association is there between the speed of a car and the distance the car travels in a given time at that speed?

Ⓐ cluster

Ⓑ negative association

Ⓒ no association

Ⓓ positive association

3. Using 3.14 for π, what is the volume of the sphere to the nearest tenth?

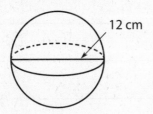

12 cm

Ⓐ 508.7 cubic centimeters

Ⓑ 678.2 cubic centimeters

Ⓒ 904.3 cubic centimeters

Ⓓ 2713 cubic centimeters

Hot Tip! Read graphs and diagrams carefully. Look at the labels for important information.

4. Which scatter plot could have a trend line given by the equation $y = -4x + 70$?

Ⓐ
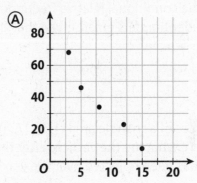

Ⓑ
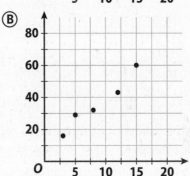

Ⓒ
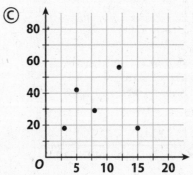

Ⓓ
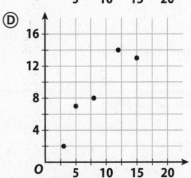

5. A group of middle school students were asked whether they prefer communicating with their friends by text message or email. The results are shown in the two-way frequency table.

	Text Message	Email	Total
Female	28	16	44
Male	31	18	49
Total	59	34	93

What is the conditional relative frequency that a student prefers email, given that the student is female?

Ⓐ 17%   Ⓒ 47%

Ⓑ 36%   Ⓓ 64%

6. The vertices of a triangle are (11, 9), (7, 4), and (1, 11). What are the vertices after the triangle has been reflected over the *y*-axis?

Ⓐ (9, 11), (4, 7), (11, 1)

Ⓑ (11, −9), (7, −4), (1, −11)

Ⓒ (9, 11), (4, 7), (11, 1)

Ⓓ (−11, 9), (−7, 4), (−1, 11)

7. Which of the following is **not** shown on the scatter plot below?

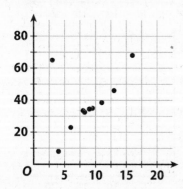

Ⓐ cluster

Ⓑ negative association

Ⓒ outlier

Ⓓ positive association

Mini-Task

8. A scatter plot and trend line of the weight of a Chihuahua puppy versus age is shown.

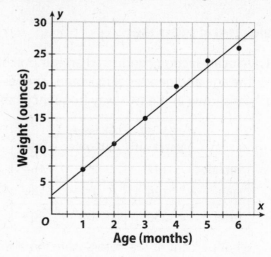

a. The trend line for these data is given by $y = 4x + 3$. What does the 3 represent in this context?

_____

_____

_____

b. If you use the trend line to predict the weight of the puppy after 60 months, the result is 243 ounces, or about 15 pounds. Is this a reasonable weight for the Chihuahua at 5 years old? Explain.

_____

_____

_____

_____

UNIT 1 **Selected Answers**

Selected Answers

MODULE 1

LESSON 1.1

Your Turn

1. $0.\overline{45}$ **2.** 0.125 **3.** $2.\overline{3}$ **4.** $\frac{3}{25}$ **5.** $\frac{19}{33}$

6. $1\frac{2}{5}$ **7.** $x = \pm 14$ **8.** $x = \pm\frac{3}{16}$

9. $x = 8$ **10.** $x = \frac{4}{7}$

Guided Practice

1. 0.4 **2.** $0.\overline{8}$ **3.** 3.75 **4.** 0.7

5. 2.375 **6.** $0.8\overline{3}$ **7.** $\frac{27}{40}$ **8.** $5\frac{3}{5}$ **9.** $\frac{11}{25}$

10. $4.\overline{4}; 0.\overline{4}; 9; 4; \frac{4}{9}$ **11.** $26.\overline{26}; 0.\overline{26};$
$99; 26; \frac{26}{99}$ **12.** $325.\overline{325}; 0.\overline{325}; 999;$
$325; \frac{325}{999}$ **13.** $144; \pm12$ **14.** $\frac{25}{289}; \pm\frac{5}{17}$
15. $216; 6$ **16.** 2.25 **17.** 1.75
18. 3.15

Independent Practice

21. $0.1\overline{6}$ **23.** $98.\overline{6}$ innings
25. $26\frac{1}{5}$ mi **27.** $\frac{101}{200}$ cent
29. His estimate is low because
15 is very close to 16, so $\sqrt{15}$ is
very close to $\sqrt{16}$, or 4. A better
estimate would be 3.8 or 3.9.
31. 3 feet
33. $\sqrt{\frac{4}{25}} = \frac{2}{5} = \frac{\sqrt{4}}{\sqrt{25}}; \sqrt{\frac{16}{81}} = \frac{4}{9} = \frac{\sqrt{16}}{\sqrt{81}};$
$\sqrt{\frac{36}{49}} = \frac{6}{7} = \frac{\sqrt{36}}{\sqrt{49}}; \frac{\sqrt{a}}{\sqrt{b}} = \sqrt{\frac{a}{b}};$
$\sqrt{a} \cdot \sqrt{b} = \sqrt{a \cdot b}$

LESSON 1.2

Your Turn

1. rational, real **2.** irrational,
real **3.** False. Every integer is
a rational number, but every
rational number is not an integer.
Rational numbers such as $\frac{3}{5}$ and
$-\frac{5}{2}$ are not integers. **4.** False. Real
numbers are either rational or
irrational numbers. Integers are
rational numbers, so no integers
are irrational numbers. **5.** Real
numbers; the amount can be any
number greater than 0. **6.** Real
numbers; the number of seconds
left can be any number less than 0.

Guided Practice

1. rational, real **2.** whole, integer,
rational, real **3.** irrational, real
4. rational, real **5.** whole, integer,
rational, real **6.** integer, rational,
real **7.** rational, real **8.** integer,
rational, real **9.** True. Whole
numbers are a subset of the set
of rational numbers and can
be written as a ratio of the
whole number to 1. **10.** True.
Whole numbers are rational
numbers. **11.** Integers; the
change can be a whole dollar
amount and can be positive,
negative, or zero. **12.** Rational
numbers; the ruler is marked
every $\frac{1}{16}$th inch.

Independent Practice

15. whole, integer, rational,
real **17.** rational, real **19.** whole,
integer, rational, real **21.** Integers;
the scores are counting numbers,
their opposites, and zero.
23. Whole; the diameter is $\frac{\pi}{\pi} =$
1 mile. **25.** rational number
27. Sample answer: If the
calculator shows a terminating
decimal, the number is rational.
Otherwise, you cannot tell
because you see only a few digits.

LESSON 1.3

Your Turn

3. $>$ **4.** $<$ **5.** $\sqrt{3}, \sqrt{5}, 2.5$

6. $\sqrt{75}, \pi^2, 10$

7. $3\frac{1}{2}$ mi, $3.\overline{45}$ mi, $\frac{10}{3}$ mi, $\sqrt{10}$ mi

Guided Practice

1. $<$ **2.** $>$ **3.** $<$ **4.** $<$ **5.** $>$
6. $<$ **7.** $>$ **8.** $>$ **9.** $1.7; 1.8; 1.75;$
$6.28; 1.5; \sqrt{3}; 2\pi$ **10.** $\left(1 + \frac{\pi}{2}\right)$ km,
2.5 km, $\frac{12}{5}$ km, $(\sqrt{17} - 2)$ km

Independent Practice

13. $\pi, \sqrt{10}, 3.5$ **15.** $-3.75, \frac{9}{4}, \sqrt{8}, 3$
17a. $\sqrt{60} \approx 7.7.5, \frac{58}{8} = 7.25,$
$7.\overline{3} \approx 7.33, 7\frac{3}{5} = 7.60,$ so the
average is 7.4825 km. **b.** They
are nearly identical. $\sqrt{56}$ is
approximately $7.4833\ldots$
19. Sample answer: $\sqrt{31}$
21a. between $\sqrt{7} \approx 2.65$ and
$\sqrt{8} \approx 2.83$ **b.** between $\sqrt{9} = 3$
and $\sqrt{10} \approx 3.16$ **23.** 2 points; A
rational number and an irrational
number cannot be represented
by the same point on the number
line.

MODULE 2

LESSON 2.1

Your Turn

6. 5 **7.** $63\frac{15}{16}$

Guided Practice

1. $\frac{1}{8}$ **2.** $\frac{1}{36}$ **3.** 1 **4.** 100 **5.** 625
6. $\frac{1}{32}$ **7.** $\frac{1}{1024}$ **8.** 1 **9.** $\frac{1}{1331}$ **10.** 4^3
11. $2^2 \cdot 2^3 = 2^5$ **12.** 6^2
13. $8^{12-9} = 8^3$ **14.** 5^{12} **15.** 7^{13}
16. $4; 6; 6; (6 \cdot 6); 6^8$ **17.** $3; 3; 3;$
$(3 \cdot 3 \cdot 3); 3^9$ **18.** 1168 **19.** 343

Independent Practice

21. The exponents cannot be
added because the bases are not
the same.
23. Earth to Neptune; 22^3, or
$10,648$, times greater. **25.** -3
27. 19 **29.** 10^3 kg, or 1000 kg
31. Both expressions equal x^5,
so $x^7 \cdot x^{-2} = \frac{x^7}{x^2}$. When multiplying
powers with the same base, you
add exponents; $7 + (-2) = 5$.
When dividing powers with

© Houghton Mifflin Harcourt Publishing Company

Selected Answers **SA1**

the same base, you subtract exponents; $7 - 2 = 5$. In cases like this, $x^n \cdot x^{-m} = \frac{x^n}{x^m}$.

33. 3^6; 3^3

35. No; $\frac{6^2}{36^2} = \frac{6 \cdot 6}{36 \cdot 36} = \frac{6 \cdot 6}{6 \cdot 6 \cdot 6 \cdot 6} = \frac{1}{6 \cdot 6} = \frac{1}{36}$

37. The number is 5.

LESSON 2.2

Your Turn

3. 6.4×10^3 **4.** 5.7×10^{11}
5. 9.461×10^{12} km **8.** 7,034,000,000
9. 236,000 **10.** 5,000,000 g

Guided Practice

1. 5.8927×10^4 **2.** 1.304×10^9
3. 6.73×10^6 **4.** 1.33×10^4
5. 9.77×10^{22} **6.** 3.84×10^5
7. 400,000 **8.** 1,849,900,00
9. 6,410 **10.** 84,560,00
11. 800,000 **12.** 90,000,000,000
13. 54,00 s **14.** 7,600,000 cans

Independent Practice

17. 2.2×10^5 lb **19.** 4×10^4 lb
21. 5×10^4 lb **23.** $108\frac{1}{3}$ hours or 108 hours and 20 minutes
25. 4.6×10^3 lb **27a.** None of the girls has the correct answer.
b. Polly and Samantha have the decimal in the wrong place; Esther miscounted the number of places the decimal moved. **29.** The speed of a car because it is likely to be less than 100. **31.** Is the first factor greater than 1 and less than 10? Is the second factor a power of 10?

LESSON 2.3

Your Turn

4. 8.29×10^{-5} **5.** 3.02×10^{-7}
6. 7×10^{-6} m **9.** 0.000001045
10. 0.000099 **11.** 0.01 m

Guided Practice

1. 4.87×10^{-4} **2.** 2.8×10^{-5}
3. 5.9×10^{-5} **4.** 4.17×10^{-2}
5. 2×10^{-5} **6.** 1.5×10^{-5}
7. 0.00002 **8.** 0.000003582
9. 0.00083 **10.** 0.0297
11. 0.0000906 **12.** 0.00004
13. 1×10^{-4}
14. 0.00000000000000000000000017

Independent Practice

17. 1.3×10^{-3} cm **19.** 4.5×10^{-3} cm **21.** 8×10^{-4} cm
23. 7 cm $= 0.07$ m, 7 cm $= 7 \times 10^0$ cm; 0.07 m $= 7 \times 10^{-2}$ m
The first factors are the same; the exponents differ by 2. **25.** If the exponent on 10 is nonnegative, the number is greater than or equal to 1. **27.** Negative, because a ladybug would weigh less than 1 ounce. **29.** 0.000000000125
31. 71,490,000 **33.** 3,397,000
35. 5.85×10^{-3} m, 1.5×10^{-2} m, 2.3×10^{-2} m, 9.6×10^{-1} m, 1.2×10^2 m **37.** The result will be greater than the number with the positive exponent because the divisor is less than 1.

LESSON 2.4

Your Turn

1. 7.62×10^7 more people
2. 8.928×10^8 miles
3. 3.14×10^2 minutes **4.** 7.5E5
5. 3E−7 **6.** 2.7E13 **7.** 4.5×10^{-1}
8. 5.6×10^{12} **9.** 6.98×10^{-8}

Guided Practice

1. 0.225; 6; 0.225; 2.8; 7.225×10^6
2. 0.10; 3; 8.5; 5.3; 0.10; 3.1×10^3
3. 5×10^2 **4.** 5.9381×10^5
5. 1.206×10^{22} **6.** 1.73×10^8
7. 1.69×10^{19} **8.** 2×10^7
9. 3.6E11 **10.** 7.25E−5 **11.** 8E−1
12. 7.6×10^{-4} **13.** 1.2×10^{16}
14. 9×10^1

Independent Practice

17. about 1.9×10^3 as many
19. 5.025×10^7 tons **21.** Plastics
23. about 7 people per square mile **25.** 13 years, 3 months, 22.5 days **27.** 2.94×10^4, or $29,400 per person. **29.** The student is off by a power of 10. The correct product is 40×10^{15}, or 4.0×10^{16}.

UNIT 2 Selected Answers

LESSON 3.1

Your Turn

3. $y = 15x$ **4.** 6 miles hiked in 5 hours **5.** $y = \frac{6}{5}x$

Guided Practice

1. is **2.** constant of proportionality **3a.** The pairs (weeks, days) are (2, 14), (4, 28), (8, 56), (10, 70). **b.** the time in weeks; the time in days; $y = 7x$ **4.** The pairs (oxygen atoms, hydrogen atoms) are (5, 10), (17, 34), (120, 240); $y = 2x$ **5.** $y = 30x$

Independent Practice

7. No; the ratios of the numbers in each column are not equal.
9a. Sample answer: The account had a balance of $100 to begin with. **b.** Sample answer: Have Ralph open the account with no money to begin with and then put $20 in every month. **11.** $y = 105$
13a. The pairs (distance, time) are (10, 1), (20, 2), (30, 3), (40, 4), (50, 5). **b.** $y = \frac{1}{10}x$, where y is the time in minutes and x is the distance in inches. **c.** 8.5 minutes **15.** For $S = 1$, $P = 4$ and $A = 1$; For $S = 2$, $P = 8$ and $A = 4$; For $S = 3$, $P = 12$ and $A = 9$; For $S = 4$, $P = 16$ and $A = 16$; For $S = 5$, $P = 20$ and $A = 25$. **a.** Yes. The ratio of the perimeter of a square to its side length is always 4. **b.** No. The ratio of the area of a square to its side length is not constant.

LESSON 3.2

Your Turn

1. 36, 13, −10; variable **4.** +3; +4; $\frac{3}{4}$

Guided Practice

1. constant **2.** variable
3. variable **4.** constant **5.** 200; 1; 200; 1; 200 **6.** 200 ft per min
7. −2 **8.** $\frac{3}{2}$

Independent Practice

11. 15 miles per hour
13a. 1 gallon every 5 minutes, or 0.2 gal/min **b.** 25 minutes
15.

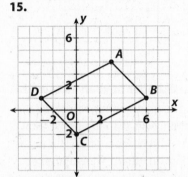

a. slope $\overline{AB} = -1$; slope $\overline{BC} = \frac{1}{2}$; slope $\overline{CD} = -1$; slope $\overline{DA} = \frac{1}{2}$
b. The slopes of the opposite sides are the same. **c.** Yes; opposite sides still have the same slope. **17.** Sample answer: One line has a positive slope and one has a negative slope. The lines are equally steep, but one slants upward left to right and the other slants downward left to right. The lines cross at the origin.

LESSON 3.3

Your Turn

2. His unit rate and the slope of a graph of the ride both equal $\frac{1}{5}$ mi/min.

Tomas's Ride

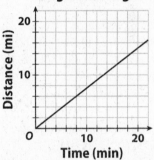

4. A: 375, 375 mi/h; B: 425, 425 mi/h; B is flying faster.

Guided Practice

1. slope = unit rate = $\frac{5}{6}$ mi/h
2. slope = unit rate = $\frac{5}{4}$ mi/h
3. Clark is faster. From the equation, Henry's rate is equal to 0.5, or $\frac{1}{2}$ mile per hour. Clark's rate is the slope of the line, which is $\frac{3}{2}$, or 1.5 miles per hour.
4. $y = 15x$ **5.** $y = \frac{3}{8}x$

Independent Practice

7a. The pairs (time, distance) are (4, 3), (8, 6), (12, 9), (16, 12), (20, 15).
b.

Migration Flight

(graph: Distance (mi) vs Time (min))

c. $\frac{3}{4}$; The unit rate of migration of the goose and the slope of the graph both equal $\frac{3}{4}$ mi/min.
9a. Machine 1: slope = unit rate = $\frac{0.6}{1}$ = 0.6 gal/s; Machine 2: slope = unit rate = $\frac{3}{4}$ = 0.75 gal/s
b. Machine 2 is working at a faster rate since 0.75 > 0.6. **11.** slope = unit rate = 4.75. If the graph of a proportional relationship passes through the point (1, r), then r equals the slope and the unit rate, which is $4.75/min. **13.** 243 gallons; Sample answer: The unit rate is $\frac{36}{2}$ = 18 gal/min. So, $1\frac{1}{2}$ min after 12 min, an additional $18 \times 1\frac{1}{2}$ = 27 gal will be pumped in. The total is 216 + 27 = 243 gal.

UNIT 2 Selected Answers *(cont'd)*

LESSON 4.1

Your Turn

1. Sample answer: (2, 20), (3, 32), (4, 44), (5, 56) **3.** (−1, 3), (0, 1), (1, −1), (2, −3)

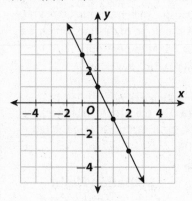

Guided Practice

1. (−2,1), (−1, 3), (0, 5), (1, 7), (2, 9) **2.** (−8, −8), (0, −5), (8, −2), (16, 1), (24, 4) **3.** Undefined, 3.5, 2.75, 2.5, 2.375; The ratio $\frac{y}{x}$ is not constant. **4.** The graph is a line, but it does not pass through the origin. **5.** (−2, −3), (−1, −2), (0, −1), (1, 0), (2, 1)

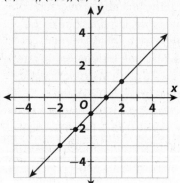

Independent Practice

7. Set of unconnected points; you cannot buy a fractional part of a lunch. **9a.** Sample answer: For (x, y) where x is number of years renewed and y is total cost in dollars: (0, 12), (1, 20), (2, 28), (3, 36), (4, 44)

b.

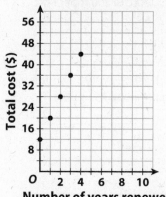

Magazine Subscription Costs

c. The graph does not include the origin. Also, the ratio of the total cost and number of years is not constant. **d.** No; the number of years must be a whole number, so total cost goes up in $8 increments. **11.** Sample answer: In a table, the ratios $\frac{y}{x}$ will not be equal; a graph will not pass through the origin; an equation will be in the form $y = mx + b$ where $b \neq 0$. **13.** At most one: A line representing a proportional relationship must pass through the origin. A line parallel to it cannot also pass through the origin.

LESSON 4.2

Your Turn

1. $m = 5$; $b = 12$ **2.** $m = 7$; $b = 1$

Guided Practice

1. −2; 1 **2.** 5; −15 **3.** $\frac{3}{2}$; −2 **4.** −3; 9 **5.** 3; 1 **6.** −4; 140

Independent Practice

9a. $5 to park; $12 per hour **b.** $23.50; (3.5 hours × $12 per hour + $5) ÷ 2 = $23.50 **11.** Rate of change is constant from 1 to 2 to 3, but not from 3 to 4. **13.** Express the slope m between a random point (x, y) on the line and the point (0, b) where the line crosses the y-axis. Then solve the equation for y.

15. After parking 61 cars; John earns a fixed weekly salary of $300 plus $5 for each car he parks. He earns the same in fees as his fixed salary for parking 300 ÷ 5 = 60 cars.

LESSON 4.3

Your Turn

2.

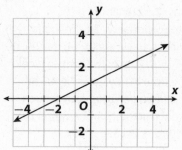

3.

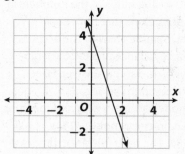

4.

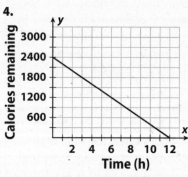

5. The new graph has the same y-intercept but a slope of −200 instead of −300. **6.** The calories left to burn will decrease more slowly with each hour of exercise, so it will take longer for Ken to meet his goal. **7.** The y-intercept would not change, but the slope would become −600, which is much steeper. The line would intersect the x-axis when x = 4 hours.

Guided Practice

1. $\frac{1}{2}$; −3

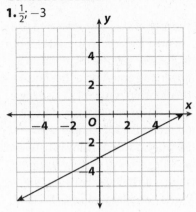

2. −3; 2

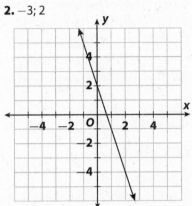

3a. Slope = 4; y-intercept = 2; you start with 2 cards and add 4 cards each week.

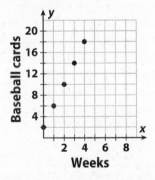

b. The points with coordinates that are not whole numbers; you will not buy part of a baseball card and you are buying only once a week.

Independent Practice

5a.

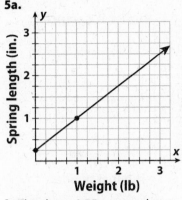

b. The slope, 0.75, means that the spring stretches by 0.75 inch with each additional pound of weight. The y-intercept, 0.25, is the unstretched length of the spring in inches. **c.** 1.75 inches; no; the length with a 4-pound weight is 3.25 in., not 3.5 in. **7.** (0, 8), (1, 7), (2, 6), (3, 5) **9.** (0, −3), (1, −1.5), (2, 0), (3, 1.5) **11.** (0, −5), (3, −3), (6, −1), (9, 1) **13a.** Yes; Since the horizontal and vertical gridlines each represent 25 units, moving up 3 gridlines and right 1 gridline represents a slope of $\frac{75}{25}$, or 3. **b.** m = 3 so $3 is the charge per visit; b = 50 so the membership fee is $50.

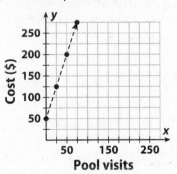

c. 50 visits **15.** Yes; plot the point and use the slope to find a second point. Then draw a line through the two points.

LESSON 4.4

Your Turn

1. nonproportional
2. proportional
5. proportional
6. nonproportional

7. nonproportional
8. nonproportional
9. nonproportional
10. proportional
11. Test-Prep Center A's charges are proportional, but B's are not. Center B offers a coupon for an initial credit, but its hourly rate, $25, is higher than Center A's hourly rate of $20. So, Center B will cost more in the long run.

Guided Practice

1. Proportional; the line includes the origin. **2.** Nonproportional; the line does not include the origin. **3.** Nonproportional; when the equation is written in the form y = mx + b, the value of b is not 0. **4.** Proportional; when the equation is written in the form y = mx + b, the value of b is 0. **5.** Proportional; the quotient of x and x is constant, 4, for every number pair. **6.** No; the quotient of y and x is not constant for every number pair. **7.** Sample answer: The rating is proportional to the number of households watching: the quotient of the rating and the number of households is always 0.0000008.

Independent Practice

9a. Nonproportional; the graph does not pass through the origin, so b ≠ 0. **b.** m = 0.5, b = 10; each cup of sports drink weighs a half pound. The empty cooler weighs 10 pounds. **11.** Proportional; this equation has the form y = mx + b where b = 0.

15a. No; from Equation B, the y-intercept is 273.15, not 0, so the graph does not include the origin. From Table C, the quotient of K and C is not constant.
b. No; Equation A is in the form y = mx + b, with F instead of y and C instead of x. The value of b is 32, not 0, so the relationship is not proportional.

MODULE 5

LESSON 5.1

Your Turn

3. $y = -2.5x + 25$ **5.** $y = 0.5x + 10$

Guided Practice

1a. the length of the necklace in inches **b.** the total number of beads in the necklace
c. $y = 5x + 27$ **2.** $\frac{0 - 300}{5 - 0} = \frac{-300}{5} = -60$; 300; $y = -60x + 300$
3. temperature; chirps per minute; $\frac{100 - 76}{65 - 59} = \frac{24}{6} = 4$; $100 = 4 \cdot 65 + b$; -160; $y = 4x - 160$

Independent Practice

5. $y = 30x$ **7.** $m = 0.125$; the diver ascends at a rate of 0.125 m/s
9. $y = 0.125x - 10$ **11.** $y = 20x + 12$ **13.** $m = 500$; $b = 1000$
15. The amount of money in the savings account increases by $500 each month. **17.** The rate of change would not be constant. Using different pairs of points in the slope formula would give different results.

LESSON 5.2

Your Turn

1. $m = 15,000$; $b = 0$; $y = 15,000x$

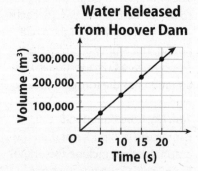

Water Released from Hoover Dam

4. $p = 75n + 250$ **5.** $c = 0.50d + 40$

Guided Practice

1. $m = -1.25$; $b = 20$; $y = -1.25x + 20$

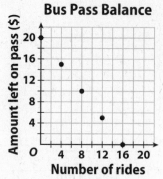

Bus Pass Balance

2. $m = \frac{51 - 59}{2000 - 0} = \frac{-8}{2000} = -0.004$
3. $b = 59$ **4.** $y = -0.004x + 59$
5. $y = -0.004(5000) + 59 = 39°F$

Independent Practice

7. $m = 2$; $b = 8$; $C = 2t + 8$
9a. $y = -1.5x + 30$ **b.** The number of dollars left decreases as the number of car washes increases. **c.** 20; after 20 washes there is no money left on the card.
11. $y = -2x + 6$ **13a.** No, the change between weeks is constant, but the change in the amount of rain is not constant.
b. No; there is no apparent pattern in the table. **15.** 0; Jaíme's graph contained (0, 0). Since Jayla's data were the same, but with x and y switched, her graph also contained (0, 0).

LESSON 5.3

Your Turn

1. $y = 4x + 20$ **2.** $y = 240x$
6. $30 **7.** $48.75 **8.** $600

Guided Practice

1. $y = 30x$ **2.** $y = 2.5x + 2$ **3.** $y = 20x + 30$; $140 **4.** Yes, because the graph has a constant rate of change. **5.** No, because the graph does not have a constant rate of change.

Independent Practice

7. Yes, because the rate of change is constant. **9.** Linear; the rate of change is the cost of a DVD, which is constant. **11.** Not linear;

the rate of change in the area of a square increases as the side length increases. **13.** The relationship is linear; the equation of the linear relationship is $y = 0.125x$, so the Mars Rover would travel 7.5 feet in 60 seconds. **15.** Sample answer: Because $x = 6$ lies halfway between $x = 4$ and $x = 8$, so the y-value should lie halfway between the corresponding y-values. **17.** Find the equation of the linear relationship using the slope and given point, and then insert any x-value to find a y-value on the graph of the line.

MODULE 6

LESSON 6.1

Your Turn

4. Function; each input value is paired with only one output value. **5.** Not a function; the input value is paired with more than one output value. **7.** Function; each input value is paired with only one output value. **8.** Not a function; the input value 8 is paired with more than one output value.
10. Not a function; input values are paired with more than one output values; (70, 164) and (70, 174)

Guided Practice

1. $20x$; 200 **2.** $\frac{x}{2}$; 15 **3.** $2.25x$; 27.00 **4.** Function; each input value is paired with only one output value **5.** Not a function; the input value 4 is paired with more than one output value.
6. Yes; each input value is paired with only one output value.

Independent Practice

9. Not a function; the input value 5 is paired with more than one output value. **11a.** There is only one number of bacteria for each number of hours, so each input is paired with only one output.

b. Yes. Each input value would still be paired with only one output value. **13.** Yes. Each input value (the weight) is paired with only one output value (the price). **15.** It does not represent a function. For the input values to be paired with all four output values, at least one of the input values would be paired with more than one output value.

LESSON 6.2

Your Turn

2. proportional

3. $(x, y) = (0, 0), (3, 2), (6, 4), (9, 6)$; linear; proportional

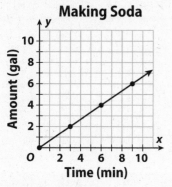

Making Soda

Guided Practice

1. $(-1, 7), (1, 3), (3, -1), (5, -5)$; linear

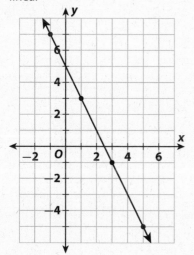

2. $(-2, -2), (-1, 1), (0, 2), (1, 1), (2, -2)$; nonlinear

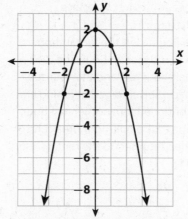

3. No; the equation cannot be written in the form $y = mx + b$, and the graph of the solutions is not a line. **4.** Yes; the equation can be written in the form $y = mx + b$, and the graph of the solutions is a line.

Independent Practice

7. No. The relationship is not linear because x is squared, so it will not be proportional. **9a.** Yes. The graph of the solutions lie in a line.

Drill Team Uniforms

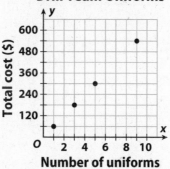

b. $720

11. Disagree; the equation can be written in the form $y = mx + b$ where m is 0, and the graph of the solutions is a horizontal line. **13.** The relationship is linear if the points all lie on the same line, and proportional if it is linear and a line through the points passes through the origin. **15.** Applying the Distr. Prop gives $y + 3 = 6x + 3$, or $y = 6x$. This is in the form $y = mx + b$ with $b = 0$, so it is linear and proportional.

LESSON 6.3

Your Turn

1. Buying at the bookstore is more expensive.

Guided Practice

1. The second method (159 bpm vs. 150 bpm) gives the greater heart rate. **2.** Heart rate and age are nonproportional for each method. **3.** Students pay a $40 fee and $5 per hour.
4.

Tutoring Fees

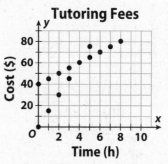

5. With both plans, it costs $60 for 4 hours of tutoring. **6.** Plan 2 ($90 vs. $150) is cheaper for 10 hours of tutoring. **7.** Cost and time are proportional for Plan 1 and nonproportional for Plan 2.

Independent Practice

9. Scooter B (15 gallons vs. 18 gallons) uses fewer gallons of gas. **11.** the first plan **13.** The camera at the second store; the cost at the first store is $290 and the cost at the second store is $260. **15.** Since the rate per visit is the same, the monthly cost of Gym A is always more than Gym B. **17.** $y = -24x + 8$ is changing more quickly because even though -24 is less than -21, the absolute value of -24 is greater than the absolute value of -21.

LESSON 6.4

Guided Practice

1. The graph is increasing quickly. This shows a period of rapid growth.

2. The number of bacteria is decreasing.

3. Graph 2 **4.** Graph 3

5.

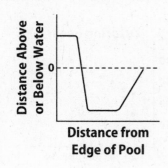

Independent Practice

7. Graph 1

9. Regina left the rental shop and rode for an hour. She took a half-hour rest and then started back. She changed her mind and continued for another half hour. She took a half-hour break and then returned to the rental shop.

11.

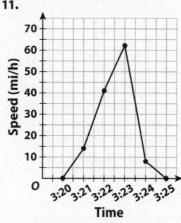

13. 3:23 to 3:24

15.

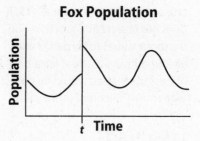

UNIT 3 Selected Answers

LESSON 7.1

Your Turn

2. 64 weeks

Guided Practice

1. $x = -4$ **2.** $x = 5$ **3.** 4 personal training sessions

Independent Practice

7a. $12 + 5x = 18 + 3x$; $x = 3$; 3 hours **b.** Darlene's Dog Sitting; the cost would be $33, as opposed to $37 at Derrick's Dog Sitting. **9.** $3x - 2 = x + 10$; $x = 6$ **11.** $8x - 20 = x + 15$; $x = 5$ **13.** $9x + 3 = 7x + 19$; $x = 8$; 75 chairs **15.** $3x + 6 = 5x + 2$; $x = 2$; 6 laps

LESSON 7.2

Your Turn

3. $k = -35$ **4.** $y = -\frac{9}{16}$
5. $1.9x = 1.3x + 37.44$; 62.4 lb

Guided Practice

1a. $60 + 50.45x = 57.95x$ **b.** $x = 8$; 8 months **2.** $n = 28$ **3.** $b = 60$
4. $m = 33$ **5.** $t = -0.8$ **6.** $w = 12$
7. $p = -2$

Independent Practice

11. 60 tiles **13a.** 100 mi
b. $80 **17.** $C = 1.8C + 32$;
$-40°F = -40°C$ **19.** When you attempt to solve the equation, you eliminate the variable from both sides of the equation, leaving a false statement such as $-30 = 24$. Since the statement is false, the equation must not have a solution. **21.** No; his equation gives 3, 4, and 5 as the integers. The correct equation is $k + (k + 2) + (k + 4) = 4k$, which gives $k = 6$ and the integers 6, 8, 10.

LESSON 7.3

Your Turn

1. $y = -1$ **2.** $x = 6$ **3.** $b = -4$
4. $t = 7$ **5.** $46,000

Guided Practice

1. 4; 32; 4; 28; 6; 28; 6; 6; 6; 6; 6; 6; $x = 1$ **2.** 3; 3; 2; -15; 18; 2; -60; $+$; 15; -13; -78; -13; -78; -13; -13; $x = 6$ **3.** $x = 3$ **4.** $x = 7$ **5.** $x = -1$
6. $x = 3$ **7.** $x = 9$ **8.** $x = -2$
9. $x = 10$ **10.** $x = -8$
11. $0.12(x + 3,000) = 4,200$; $32,000

Independent Practice

13. a. $x + 14$ **b.** Joey's age in 5 years: $x + 5$; Martina's age in 5 years: $x + 19$ **c.** $3(x + 5) = x + 19$ **d.** Joey: 2 years old; Martina: 16 years old
15. It is not necessary. In this case, distributing the fractions directly results in whole number coefficients and constants.
17. Table first row: 0.25, 0.25x; table second row: $100 - x$, 0.15, $0.15(100 - x)$; table third row: 0.19, 19 **a.** The milliliters of acid in the 25% solution plus the milliliters of acid in the 15% solution equals the milliliters of acid in the mixture. **b.** $0.25x + 0.15(100 - x) = 19$ **c.** The chemist used 40 ml of the 25% solution and 60 ml of the 15% solution.
19. Use the Distributive Property to distribute both 3 and 2 inside the square parentheses on the left side. Combine like terms inside the square parentheses. Then use the Distributive Property again to distribute 5. Combine like terms on the left side and use inverse operations to solve the equation. $x = 1$

LESSON 7.4

Your Turn

2. True **3.** True **4.** False
6. one solution
7. infinitely many solutions
8. Sample answer: 6; Any number except 1 will yield no solution. **9.** 4

Guided Practice

1. $9x$; 25; $+$ 2; $+$ 2; 9; 27; 9; 27; 9; 9; $x = 3$; true
2. $2x - 2$; 1; $2x$; $2x$; $-4 = 1$; false
3. none
4. Any value of x will result in a true statement; infinitely many solutions
5. true; same variable; same constant; like; 10; $10 + x$; $10 + x + 5$; $15 + x = 15 + x$

Independent Practice

7. $0 = 0$; infinitely many solutions
9. Sample answer: 5 **11.** $x + 1$
13. a. Yes; because the perimeters are equal, you get the equation $(2x - 2) + (x + 1) + x + (x + 1) = (2x - 9) + (x + 1) + (x + 8) + x$, or $5x = 5x$. Since $5x = 5x$ is a true statement, there are an infinite number of values for x.
b. The condition was that the two perimeters are to be equal. However, a specific number was not given, so there are an infinite number of possible perimeters.
c. 12; Sample answer: I used the trapezoid and wrote the equation $(2x - 2) + (x + 1) + x + (x + 1) = 60$. Solving this gives $x = 12$.
15. No; setting the expressions equal to each other and solving gives $100 + 35x = 50 + 35x$, or $100 = 50$, which is false.
17. Matt is incorrect. He applied the Distributive Property to the right side incorrectly. Correctly simplified, the equation is $0 = -7$, which is false, meaning no solution.

LESSON 8.1

Your Turn

3. $(-1, 3)$

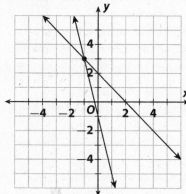

4. $(1, 3)$

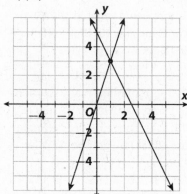

6a. $x + y = 6$ and $2x + 4y = 20$;
$y = -x + 8$ and $y = -0.5x + 5$

b.

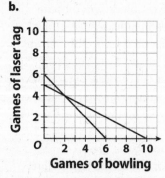

c. Marquis will bowl 2 games and play 4 games of laser tag.

Guided Practice

1. $(3, 5)$

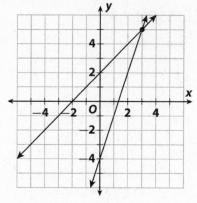

2. infinitely many solutions

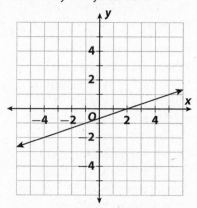

3a. $y = -x + 15$ **b.** $y = -0.5x + 10$

c.

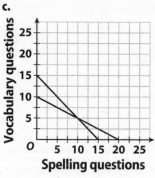

d. 10 spelling questions and 5 vocabulary questions

Independent Practice

5. system of equations

7a. $y = 2.50x + 2$; $y = 2x + 4$

b. The solution is $(4, 12)$. The cost at both alleys will be the same for 4 games bowled, $12.

Cost of Bowling

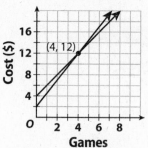

11. Infinitely many; Rearranging the left side of the 2nd equation and subtracting $3a$ from both sides gives $-ax + ay = -3a$. Dividing both sides by $-a$ gives $x - y = 3$. The equations describe the same line.

LESSON 8.2

Your Turn

4. $(2, 5)$ **5.** $(-6, 4)$ **6.** $(-9, -7)$

7.

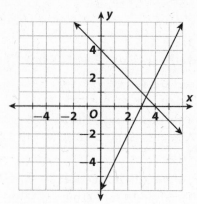

Estimate: $(3, 1)$
Solution: $\left(\frac{10}{3}, \frac{2}{3}\right)$
The solution is reasonable because $\frac{10}{3}$ is close to the estimate of 3 and $\frac{2}{3}$ is close to the estimate of 1.

8. Carlos: $4x + 160y = 120$
Vanessa: $x + 240y = 80$
$(20, 0.25)$; 20 represents the cost per day: $20; 0.25 represents the cost per mile: $0.25

Guided Practice

1. $(5, 3)$ **2.** $(3, -1)$ **3.** $(2, 1)$ **4.** $(4, 1)$
5. Estimate: $(2, -5)$;
Solution: $\left(\frac{7}{5}, -\frac{22}{5}\right)$

6. Estimate: $(-1, 5)$;
Solution: $\left(-1, \frac{9}{2}\right)$
7. Estimate: $(3, -6)$;
Solution: $\left(\frac{13}{4}, -\frac{23}{4}\right)$
8. Estimate: $(-1, 1)$;
Solution: $\left(-\frac{3}{4}, \frac{1}{2}\right)$
9. a. Henson's cost: $3x + y = 163$;
Garcia's cost: $2x + 3y = 174$
b. adult ticket price: $45; child ticket price: $28

Independent Practice
11.

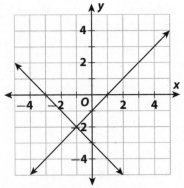

The graph shows that the x-coordinate of the solution is negative, so Zach's solution is not reasonable.
13. 120 nickels and 80 dimes
15. $\left(\frac{8}{3}, -\frac{10}{3}\right)$
17. The substitution method has the advantage of always giving an exact answer. Graphing produces an exact answer only if the solution is an ordered pair whose coordinates are integers.

LESSON 8.3

Your Turn
3. $(3, -4)$ **4.** $(2, -3)$ **5.** $(-1, 2)$
8. $(0, -2)$ **9.** $(7, -3)$ **10.** $\left(7, \frac{1}{2}\right)$
11. hot dog: $1.95; juice drink: $1.25

Guided Practice
1. Step 1: 0; -10; y; -10; -2; 5.
Step 2: 3; $(-2, 3)$ **2.** $(2, -2)$
3. $(6, 5)$ **4.** $(7, -7)$ **5.** $(-3, 8)$
6. $(2, 3)$ **7.** $(-5, -2)$
8. a. Tony: $2x + 3.5y = 355$;
Rae: $2x + 3y = 320$
b. Minimum speed limit: 55 mi/h; maximum speed limit: 70 mi/h

Independent Practice
11. Guppy: 3 inches; platy: 2 inches
13. Labor fee: $14.95; quart of oil: $1.50
15. 407 adult tickets; 839 student tickets
17. a. Jenny substituted her expression for y into the same equation she used to find y. She should substitute her expression into the other equation. **b.** Yes; adding the equations would have resulted in $3x = 9$, easily giving $x = 3$ after dividing each side by 3. Substitution requires many more steps.

LESSON 8.4

Your Turn
4. $(-8, 15)$ **5.** $(-1, 5)$ **6.** $\left(\frac{1}{2}, -1\right)$
7. $(3, 1)$ **8.** $(-4, -1)$
9. $\left(\frac{1}{3}, 6\right)$ **10.** Contestants run 0.75 hour and bike 0.5 hour.

Guided Practice
1. Step 1: 12; 4; 32; 20; y; 2; 10.
Step 2: -2; $(2, -2)$ **2.** $(6, -1)$
3. $(-3, 8)$ **4.** $\left(\frac{7}{2}, \frac{7}{4}\right)$ **5.** $(3, -3)$
6. $(4, -1)$ **7.** $(-2, 4)$
8. a. First store: $0.64x + 0.45y = 5.26$; second store: $0.32x + 0.39y = 3.62$ **b.** Number of apples: 4; number of pears: 6

Independent Practice
11. a. $\begin{cases} 79x + 149y = 1{,}456 \\ x + y = 14 \end{cases}$
b. Multiply the second equation by 79. Subtract the new equation from the first one and solve the resulting equation for y.
c. Solve the second equation for x. Substitute the expression for x in the first equation and solve the resulting equation for y.
d. 9 polyester-fill, 5 down-fill
13. 21 pies, 16 jars of applesauce
15. a. Multiply the first equation by 1.5 and subtract. This would be less than ideal because you would introduce decimals into the solution process. **b.** Yes; multiply the first equation by 3 and the

second equation by 2. Both x-term coefficients would be 6. Solve by eliminating the x-terms using subtraction. **c.** $(9, -4)$

LESSON 8.5

Your Turn
6. no solution **7.** $(10, -2)$; one solution **8.** infinitely many solutions

Guided Practice
1. Step 1: are parallel; intersect; are the same line Step 2: one; no; an infinite number of Step 3: no, no; 1, (1, 5); an infinite number of, All
2. infinitely many solutions **3.** no solution **4.** $(-3, -4)$; one solution

Independent Practice
7.

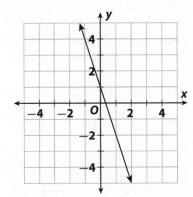

infinitely many solutions
9. one solution **11.** one solution
13. one solution
15. No; although the lines do not intersect on the graph, they intersect at a point that is not on the graph. To prove that a system has no solution, you must do so algebraically.
17. No; both Juan and Tory run at the same rate, so the lines representing the distances each has run are parallel. There is no solution to the system.
19. A, B, and C must all be the same multiple of 3, 5, and 8, respectively. The two equations represent a single line, so the coefficients and constants of one equation must be a multiple of the other.

LESSON 9.1

Your Turn

4.

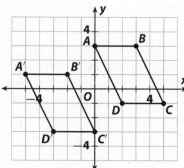

Guided Practice

1. transformation **2.** preimage; image **3.** The orientation will be the same. **4.** They are congruent.

5.

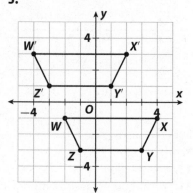

Independent Practice

7a.

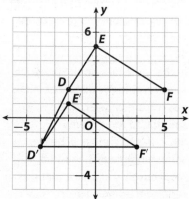

b. The translation moved the triangle 2 units to the left and 4 units down. **c.** They are congruent.

9.

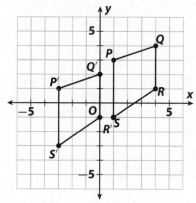

11. The hot air balloon was translated 4 units to the right and 5 units up.

13a.–c.

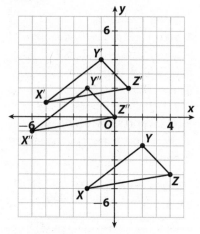

d. The original triangle was translated 4 units up and 4 units to the left.

LESSON 9.2

Your Turn

4.

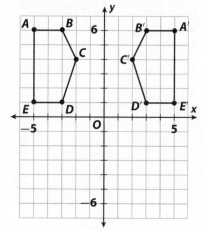

Guided Practice

1. line of reflection

2a.

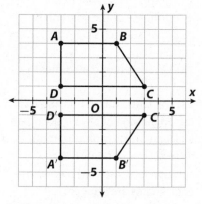

b. They are congruent. **c.** The orientation would be reversed horizontally: the figure from left to right in the preimage would match the figure from right to left in the image.

Independent Practice

5. *C* and *D* **7.** Sample answer: Since each triangle is either a reflection or translation of triangle *C*, they are all congruent. **9.** Yes; if the point lies on the line of reflection, then the image and the preimage will be the same point.

11a.–c.

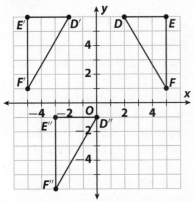

d. Sample answer: Translate triangle *DEF* 7 units down and 2 units to the left. Then reflect the image across the *y*-axis.

LESSON 9.3

Your Turn

6.–7.

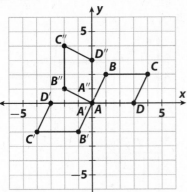

8. (2, −4)

Guided Practice

1. point **2.** The triangle is turned 90° to the left about vertex *E*.
3. Yes, the figures are congruent.
4.

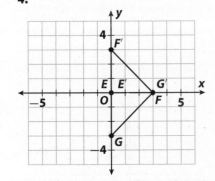

5.

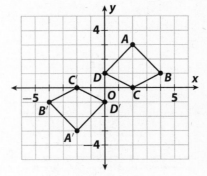

Independent Practice

7a. *ABC* was rotated 90° counterclockwise. **b.** *A'* (3, 1); *B'* (2, 3); *C'* (−1, 4) **9.** 180° rotation
11. 90° clockwise **13.** 90° clockwise

15.

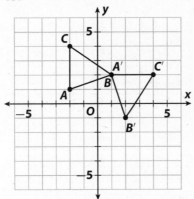

17. 2 times; 1 time; 4 times
19. Sample answer: If *A* is at the origin, then so is *A'* for any rotation about the origin. Otherwise, *A'* is on the *x*-axis for 90° and 270° rotations and on the *y*-axis for a 180° rotation.

LESSON 9.4

Your Turn

1. (−6, −5), (−6, 0), (−3, −5), and (−3, 0); the rectangle is translated 6 units to the left and 3 units down. **2.** *A'*(−2, −6), *B'*(0, −5), and *C'*(3, 1) **4.** *J'*(4, −2), *K'*(−5, 1), and *L'*(−2, 2)

Guided Practice

1. *X'*(3, −2), *Y'*(5, 0), and *Z'*(7, −6)

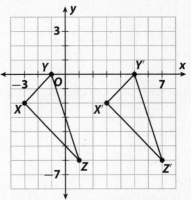

2. The *x*-coordinate remains the same, while the *y*-coordinate changes sign. **3.** The triangle is rotated 90° clockwise.

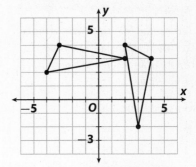

Independent Practice

5. (*x*, *y*) → (*x* + 5, *y* − 2); translation of 2 units to the left and 5 units down **7.** (*x*, *y*) → (*x* − 3.2, *y* + 1); *Y'*(4.3, 6), *Z'*(4.8, 5)
9. The rectangle is translated 2 units to the left and 4 units down.

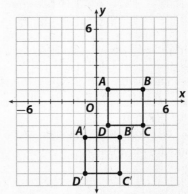

11. (*x*, *y*) → (*x* + 0.5, *y* − 0.25)
13a. (−5, −5); *x* and *y* are equal, so switching *x* and *y* has no effect on the coordinates. **b.** *y* = *x* **c.** The triangle is reflected across the line *y* = *x*.

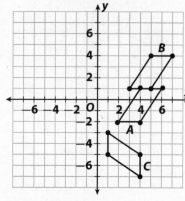

15a. *A"*(1, 0), *B"*(0, 3), and *C"*(4, 3)
b. $(x, y) \rightarrow (x + 3, y + 2)$

LESSON 9.5

Your Turn

3. Rotation 90° clockwise about the origin, translation 5 units down; $(x, y) \rightarrow (y, -x)$, $(x, y) \rightarrow (x, y - 5)$

Guided Practice

1.

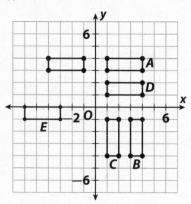

2. reflection across the *y*-axis
3. translation 3 units right and 4 units down
4. $(x, y) \rightarrow (-x, y)$, $(x, y) \rightarrow (x + 3, y - 4)$
5. The figures have the same size and the same shape.

Independent Practice

7.

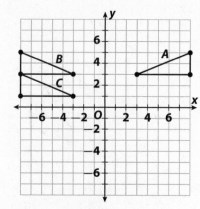

Different orientation
9.

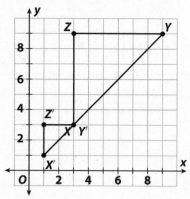

Different orientation
11. Sample answer: translation 2 units right and 4 units down, reflection across *y*-axis; size: no; orientation: yes
13. No; the point (1, 2) translated 2 units to the right becomes (3, 2), then rotated 90° clockwise about the origin, it becomes (2, −3). The point (1, 2) rotated 90° clockwise around the origin becomes (2, −1), then translated 2 units to the right, it becomes (4, −1), which is not the same.

MODULE 10

LESSON 10.1

Your Turn

5. The scale factor is 0.5.

Guided Practice

1. 2; 2 **2.** equal; equal **3.** 2
4. congruent **5.** 2

Independent Practice

7. No; the ratios of the lengths of the corresponding sides are not equal. **9.** Yes; a dilation produces an image similar to the original figure. **11.** Yes; each coordinate of triangle *U'V'W'* is $\frac{3}{4}$ times the corresponding coordinate of triangle *UVW*. **13.** changed; same; same **15.** same; changed; same
17. 3 **19.** Locate the corresponding vertices of the triangles, and draw lines connecting each pair. The lines will intersect at the center of dilation.

LESSON 10.2

Your Turn

5. $(x, y) \rightarrow \left(\frac{1}{3}x, \frac{1}{3}y\right)$

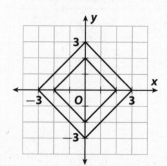

Guided Practice

1.

PreImage	Image
(2, 0)	(3, 0)
(0, 2)	(0, 3)
(−2, 0)	(−3, 0)
(0, −2)	(0, −3)

2.

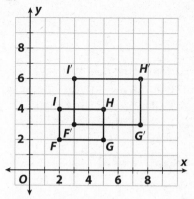

$(x, y) \rightarrow (1.5x, 1.5y)$

3.

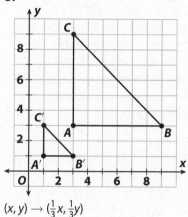

$(x, y) \rightarrow (\frac{1}{3}x, \frac{1}{3}y)$

Independent Practice

5. Green square: $(x, y) \rightarrow (2x, 2y)$; Purple square $(x, y) \rightarrow (\frac{1}{2}x, \frac{1}{2}y)$
7. $(x, y) \rightarrow (\frac{2}{3}x, \frac{2}{3}y)$ **9a.** The scale factor is 48. **b.** 48 inches or 4 feet **c.** $(x, y) \rightarrow (48x, 48y)$

d. $Q'(2.5, 2.5)$, $R'(8.75, 2.5)$, $S'(8.75, 6.25)$, and $T'(2.5, 6.25)$
e. Dimensions on blueprint: 6.25 in. by 3.75 in. Dimensions in house: 25 ft by 15 ft **11.** The crewmember's calculation is incorrect. The scale factor is $\frac{1}{20}$, not $\frac{1}{12}$. **13.** The figure is dilated by a factor of 2, but the orientation of the figure is rotated 180°.

LESSON 10.3

Your Turn

3. Sample answer: $(x, y) \rightarrow (x + 7, y - 12)$; rotation 90° counterclockwise about the origin; $(x, y) \rightarrow (x + 5, y + 3)$; $(x, y) \rightarrow (3x, 3y)$

Guided Practice

1.

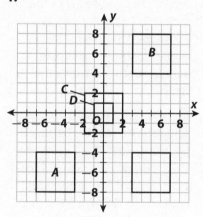

2. $(x, y) \rightarrow (x, -y)$; $(x, y) \rightarrow (x + 5, y - 6)$
3. $(x, y) \rightarrow (x, y + 6)$; rotate 90° counterclockwise
4. $(x, y) \rightarrow (1.5x, 1.5y)$; $(x, y) \rightarrow (x + 3, y + 5)$

Independent Practice

7. Dilate the image by a scale factor of $\frac{1}{3}$ and reflect it back across the x-axis; $(x, y) \rightarrow (\frac{1}{3}x, \frac{1}{3}y)$, $(x, y) \rightarrow (x, -y)$.
9. Rotate the image 90° counterclockwise and dilate it by a factor of $\frac{1}{5}$; $(x, y) \rightarrow (-y, x)$, $(x, y) \rightarrow (\frac{1}{5}x, \frac{1}{5}y)$.
11. There can be an even number of dilations in pairs where each has the opposite effect.
13. No; dilate first: $(0, 0) \rightarrow (0, 0) \rightarrow (0, 5)$ and $(1, 1) \rightarrow (3, 3) \rightarrow (3, 8)$, so $y = x + 5$; translate first: $(0, 0) \rightarrow (0, 5) \rightarrow (0, 15)$ and $(1, 1) \rightarrow (1, 6) \rightarrow (3, 18)$, so $y = x + 15$.

UNIT 5 Selected Answers

© Houghton Mifflin Harcourt Publishing Company

LESSON 11.1

Your Turn

5. 72° **6.** 108° **7.** 108°

Guided Practice

1. $\angle VWZ$ **2.** alternate interior
3. 80° **4.** 100° **5.** same-side interior

Independent Practice

7. $\angle 1$ and $\angle 5$, $\angle 2$ and $\angle 6$, $\angle 3$
and $\angle 7$, $\angle 4$ and $\angle 8$ **9.** alternate
interior angles **11.** 30°
13. 110° **15.** 78° **17.** 132°; the
48° angle is supplementary to
the larger angle because the two
angles are same-side interior
angles. **19.** $\angle 6$ and $\angle 2$ are corr.,
so m$\angle 2 = 125°$. $\angle 6$ and $\angle 3$ are alt.
int., so m$\angle 3 = 125°$. $\angle 3$ and $\angle 7$
are corr., so m$\angle 7 = 125°$. $\angle 6$ and
$\angle 4$ are same-side int., so m$\angle 4 =$
$180° - 125°$, or 55°. $\angle 4$ and $\angle 8$ are
corr., so m$\angle 8 = 55°$. $\angle 4$ and $\angle 5$
are alt. int., so m$\angle 5 = 55°$. $\angle 1$ and
$\angle 5$ are corr., so m$\angle 1 = 55°$.
21. 3 angles; 4 angles; no

LESSON 11.2

Your Turn

4. 53° **5.** 90° **8.** 78°; 68°

Guided Practice

1. 71° **2.** 30° **3.** 88°; 29°; 63°
4. 90°; 45°; 45° **5.** 40°; 76°; 64°
6. 129°; 32°; 19°

Independent Practice

9. 60°; 30° **11.** 98°; 55°; 27°
13. 60°; 90°; 30°; 150° **15.** No; the
measure of an obtuse angle is
greater than 90°. If a triangle had
two obtuse angles, the sum of
their measures would be greater
than 180°, the sum of the angle
measures of a triangle. **17a.**
360° **b.** The sum of the angle
measures of a quadrilateral is 360°.

Sample answer: Any quadrilateral
can be divided into two triangles,
so the sum of its angle measures is
$2 \times 180° = 360°$.

LESSON 11.3

Your Turn

3. The triangles are not similar
because only one angle is
congruent. The angle measures of
the triangles are 70°, 58°, and 52°
and 70°, 61°, and 49°. **5.** 8 inches
6. 21 ft

Guided Practice

1. 41°, 109°, and 30°; 41°, 109°,
and 30°; two angles; two angles;
similar **2.** 7.5; 23.5; 17.2
3. congruent; alternate interior
angles; congruent; alternate
interior angles; AA Similarity;
similar

Independent Practice

5. m$\angle B = 42°$, m$\angle F = 69°$, m$\angle H =$
64°, m$\angle K = 53°$ **7.** $\angle J \cong \angle A$,
$\angle L \cong \angle B$, and $\angle K \cong \angle C$ **9.** 25 feet
11. In the first line, Ryan should
have added 19.5 and 6.5 to get
a denominator of 26 for the
expression on the right side to get
the correct value of 13.6 cm for h.

MODULE 12

LESSON 12.1

Your Turn

4. 50 ft **5.** 9 in. **6.** $r = \sqrt{228}$, so
the greatest length is 15 in.

Guided Practice

1. 10^2, 676, 26 **2a.** 1700
2b. 41.2 in.; yes

Independent Practice

5. 11.5 in. **7.** 14.1 in. **9.** 12 feet
11. 52.8 ft; $12^2 + 39^2 = c^2$, so 144
$+ 1521 = c^2$, $1665 = c^2$, and $40.8 \approx$
c. Adding this to the height of the

bottom of the tree: $40.8 + 12 =$
52.8 ft. **13.** $\sqrt{x^2 + x^2}$ (or $\sqrt{2x^2}$ or
$x\sqrt{2}$); if $a = x$ and $b = x$, then
$x^2 + x^2 = c^2$. Thus, $c = \sqrt{x^2 + x^2}$.

LESSON 12.2

Your Turn

2. not a right triangle **3.** right
triangle **4.** right triangle **5.** not
a right triangle **6.** Yes; $140^2 +$
$480^2 = 250,000$; $500^2 = 250,000$;
$250,000 = 250,000$ **7.** No; $18^2 +$
$19^2 = 685$, $25^2 = 625$, $685 \neq$
625 **8.** No; there are no pairs of
whole numbers whose squares
add to $12^2 = 144$.

Guided Practice

1a. 6; 8, 10 **b.** 6, 8, 10; 36, 64, 100;
100, 100; is **2.** 9, 12, 16; 9, 12, 16;
81, 144, 256; 225, 256; is not
3. Yes; $2.5^2 + 6^2 = 42.25$, $6.5^2 =$
42.25, $42.25 = 42.25$

Independent Practice

5. right triangle **7.** not a right
triangle **9.** not a right triangle
11. right triangle **13.** not a right
triangle **15.** No; $13^2 + 14^2 = 365$,
$15^2 = 225$, and $365 \neq 225$.
17. No; $6^2 + 10^2 = 136$, $12^2 = 144$,
and $136 \neq 144$. **19.** Yes; since
$0.75^2 + 1^2 = 1.25^2$, the triangles
are right triangles. Adjoining them
at their hypotenuses will form a
rectangle with sides 1 m and
0.75 m. **21.** Yes **23.** The diagonals
should measure $\sqrt{90^2 + 48^2} = 102$
yards if the sides of the field meet
at right angles.

LESSON 12.3

Your Turn

1. 6.4 units **4.** approximately
214.7 meters

Guided Practice

1. 5.8 units **2.** 13 units
3. 103.6 miles

Independent Practice

7a. $ET = \sqrt{113}$ units **b.** Let $(x_1, y_1) = (-3, 4)$ and $(x_2, y_2) = (4, -4)$. Substitute the coordinates into the Distance Formula and then simplify. **9.** (5, 0), (4, 3), (3, 4), (0, 5), (−3, 4), (−4, 3), (−5, 0), (−4, −3), (−3, −4), (0, −5), (3, −4), (4, −3); The points would form a circle.

11.

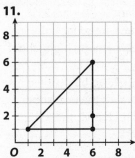

Let $(x_1, y_1) = (6, 6)$, and $(x_2, y_2) = (1, 1)$. Use the Distance Formula to show that hypotenuse $= \sqrt{50} \approx 7.1$.

LESSON 13.1

Your Turn

4. 471 in³ **5.** 602.9 ft³ **6.** 452.2 in³

Guided Practice

1. two congruent circles that lie in parallel planes **2.** Sample answer: 427 in³; there are 61 cubes on the bottom of the cylinder. The height is 7 cubes. $V = 61 \times 7 = 427$ in³
3. 6; 15; 36; 15; 1695.6; 1695.6
4. 1.35; 15.5

Independent Practice

7. 1205.8 in³ **9.** 942 in³ **11.** 803.8 m³
13. 6838.9 in³ **15.** 339,120 m³
17. 57.7 in³ **19.** Divide the diameter by 2 to find the radius. Substitute the volume and radius in $V = \pi r^2 h$ and solve for h.

LESSON 13.2

Your Turn

4. 942 cm³ **5.** 12.6 ft³ **6.** about 19,300,000 m³

Guided Practice

1. 45; 10; 450; 450; 150; 150 **2.** 54 m³; the volume of a cylinder is 3 times the volume of a cone with a congruent base and height.
3. 65.9 ft³ **4.** 113,982 in³ **5.** 141.3 in³
6. 13,083.3 m³

Independent Practice

9. 25.1 in³ **11.** 94.2 m³ **13.** 167.5 in³
15. 628 in³ **17.** 6 cm **19a.** either the diameter or the radius of the base **b.** No; the cone is tapered from top to bottom. An equal volume of sand has a smaller radius and a greater height as the sand rises. **21.** Since the radius and height of the cones and cylinder are the same, it will take 3 cones to equal the volume of the cylinder.

LESSON 13.3

Your Turn

2. 4186.7 cm³ **3.** 20.6 m³
6. 904.3 in³

Guided Practice

1. the same distance **2.** radius
3. 4.2 in³ **4.** 4,186.7 cm³ **5.** 14.1 ft³
6. 4.2 yd³ **7.** 12.8 in³ **8.** 435 in³
9a. $\frac{1}{3}$; the ball takes up $\frac{2}{3}$ of the space, so $\frac{1}{3}$ is empty. **b.** $(2r)^3 = 8r^3$
c. Almost $\frac{1}{2}$; the empty space is $8r^3 - \frac{4}{3}\pi r^3$, or about $3.81r^3$, and $\frac{3.81}{8} \approx 0.48$.

Independent Practice

11. 124.7 m³ **13.** 904.3 in³
15. 5572.5 cm³ **17.** 5389 cm³
19. 1766.3 cm³ **21.** Divide $V = \frac{4}{3}\pi r^3$ by 2 to find the volume of the hemisphere: $V = \frac{2}{3}\pi r^3$. Add the volume of the cylinder, $V = \pi r^2 h = \pi r^3$: $V = \frac{2}{3}\pi r^3 + \pi r^3 = \frac{5}{3}\pi r^3$.
23. 12.3 in³ **25.** The cylindrical glass; the cylinder has a volume of πr^3, the hemisphere's volume is $\frac{2}{3}\pi r^3$, and the cone's volume is $\frac{1}{3}\pi r^3$. **27.** About 16 feet; 136 is 8 times 17, so the volume must be 8 times as big. Because $2^3 = 8$, this means the radius, and thus the diameter, must be twice as big.

UNIT 6 Selected Answers

MODULE 14

LESSON 14.1

Your Turn

6. Positive and basically linear: older students would be taller and read at a higher level.

Guided Practice

1.
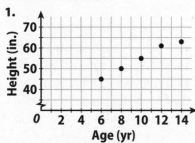

2. Positive and basically linear; the plot shows Bob's height increasing as he gets older. **3.** There is a cluster for 20–23 shots attempted and a lesser one for 7–14 shots attempted; (35, 18) is an outlier.

Independent Practice

5. A generally positive linear association: as the year increases, so does the winning distance. **7.** Nonlinear; the points generally rise up to 1988 and then fall from 1988 to 2012, so there is no overall linear pattern. **13.** Yes; for example, the points may appear to lie along a rising or falling curve, or may generally rise or fall, but not in a way that suggests a linear association.

LESSON 14.2

Your Turn

6. Sample answer: $y = \frac{9}{10}x$

Guided Practice

Answers for 1–4 may vary slightly.

1.
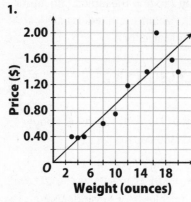

2. Most data points are close to the trend line, with about the same number of points above and below the line. **3.** $y = 0.09x$
4. $0.63; $4.50

Independent Practice

Answers for 6–14 may vary slightly.

7. negative; basically linear
9a. about $-6°$F **b.** about $-22°$F

11.

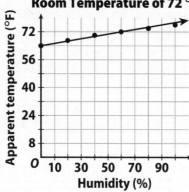

13. about 73°F **17a.** No; two data points are not enough to create a scatter plot or trendline. A random sample of many counties should be used. **b.** Marlene's conjecture is incorrect. Harris and Dallas counties are counterexamples to Marlene's original conclusion.

MODULE 15

LESSON 15.1

Your Turn

2. Yes; the relative frequency of visiting a park $= \frac{105}{200} = 0.525 = 52.5\%$; relative frequency of visiting a park among high school students $= \frac{80}{120} \approx 0.667 = 66.7\%$; $66.7\% > 52.5\%$, so being in high school improves the likelihood that a student has visited a national park.

Guided Practice

1.

	Dog	No Dog	TOTAL
Cat	21	9	30
No Cat	15	5	20
TOTAL	36	14	50

2. No; the relative frequency of being left-handed ($\frac{24}{240} = 10\%$) is the same as the relative frequency of being left-handed among boys ($\frac{14}{140} = 10\%$).

Independent Practice

5.a.

	Prefer Science	Prefer Math	TOTAL
Seventh Grade	24	72	96
Eighth Grade	32	48	80
TOTAL	56	120	176

b. No; the relative frequency of preferring math is $\frac{120}{176} \approx 68\%$, and the relative frequency of preferring math among eighth graders is $\frac{48}{80} = 60\%$, so eighth graders are slightly less likely to prefer math than the general population of students polled.

7.a.

	Prefer Surfing	Prefer Snorkeling	TOTAL
Ages 13–15	52 40%; 50%	78 60%; 74%	130 100%
Ages 16–18	52 65%; 50%	28 35%; 26%	80 100%
TOTAL	104 50%; 100%	106 50%; 100%	210 100%

b. It is the relative frequency of teenagers who are 16 to 18 years old and who prefer snorkeling to all 16- to 18-year-olds who were surveyed.

c. No; the total numbers in the last column (ages) are not the same as the total numbers in the last row (preferences), so the relative frequencies are different.

d. It is the relative frequency of teenagers who are 16 to 18 years old and who prefer snorkeling to all of those surveyed who prefer snorkeling.

LESSON 15. 2

Your Turn

8. $\frac{0.18}{0.44} \approx 0.409$, or 40.9%

9. Step1: 44% becomes 56%; Step 2: 45% becomes 55%, 60% becomes 40%, and 23% becomes 77%; Step 3: conclusions would not change.

Guided Practice

1. a-c. TOTAL row: 12, 5, 8, 25; TOTAL column: 12, 13, 25

d.

Gender \ Preferred Pet	Seashore	Mountains	Other	TOTAL
Girl	0.28	0.12	0.08	0.48
Boy	0.2	0.08	0.24	0.52
TOTAL	0.48	0.2	0.32	1.00

e. 0.08, or 8% **f.** 0.48, or 48%

g. 0.6, or 60%; girls are more likely than boys to prefer the mountains.

Independent Practice

3. a. first row: 10, 20; second row: 6, 3, 24; third row: 30, 12

b. Sample answer: I worked backward from the given data, using the fact that the sum of the entries in each row and each column must equal the total for that row or column.

5. a. 13% **b.** 32% **c.** about 40%

7. a. No; each data value should have been divided by the grand total, 600, not by the row total.

b. Yes, the data in the Total row and Total column are correct. These entries were created by dividing each entry by 600, the grand total, which results in the correct marginal relative frequency. The joint relative frequencies are incorrect.

Glossary/Glosario

ENGLISH	SPANISH	EXAMPLES
absolute value The distance of a number from zero on a number line; shown by | |.	**valor absoluto** Distancia a la que está un número de 0 en una recta numérica. El símbolo del valor absoluto es | |.	$\|-5\| = 5$
accuracy The closeness of a given measurement or value to the actual measurement or value.	**exactitud** Cercanía de una medida o un valor a la medida o el valor real.	
acute angle An angle that measures greater than 0° and less than 90°.	**ángulo agudo** Ángulo que mide mas de 0° y menos de 90°.	
acute triangle A triangle with all angles measuring less than 90°.	**triángulo acutángulo** Triángulo en el que todos los ángulos miden menos de 90°.	
Addition Property of Equality The property that states that if you add the same number to both sides of an equation, the new equation will have the same solution.	**Propiedad de igualdad de la suma** Propiedad que establece que puedes sumar el mismo número a ambos lados de una ecuación y la nueva ecuación tendrá la misma solución.	$14 - 6 = 8$ $\underline{+6 \quad +6}$ $14 = 14$
Addition Property of Opposites The property that states that the sum of a number and its opposite equals zero.	**Propiedad de la suma de los opuestos** Propiedad que establece que la suma de un número y su opuesto es cero.	$12 + (-12) = 0$
additive inverse The opposite of a number.	**inverso aditivo** El opuesto de un número.	The additive inverse of 5 is -5.
adjacent angles Angles in the same plane that have a common vertex and a common side.	**ángulos adyacentes** Ángulos en el mismo plano que comparten un vértice y un lado.	
algebraic expression An expression that contains at least one variable.	**expresión algebraica** Expresión que contiene al menos una variable.	$x + 8$ $4(m - b)$
algebraic inequality An inequality that contains at least one variable.	**desigualdad algebraica** Desigualdad que contiene al menos una variable.	$x + 3 > 10$ $5a > b + 3$

ENGLISH	SPANISH	EXAMPLES

alternate exterior angles For two lines intersected by a transversal, a pair of angles that lie on opposite sides of the transversal and outside the other two lines.

ángulos alternos externos Dadas dos rectas cortadas por una transversal, par de ángulos no adyacentes ubicados en los lados opuestos de la transversal y fuera de las otras dos rectas.

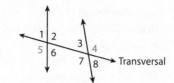

∠4 and ∠5 are alternate exterior angles.

alternate interior angles For two lines intersected by a transversal, a pair of nonadjacent angles that lie on opposite sides of the transversal and between the other two lines.

ángulos alternos internos Dadas dos rectas cortadas por una transversal, par de ángulos no adyacentes ubicados en los lados opuestos de la transversal y entre de las otras dos rectas.

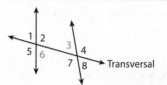

∠3 and ∠6 are alternate interior angles.

angle A figure formed by two rays with a common endpoint called the vertex.

ángulo Figura formada por dos rayos con un extremo común llamado vértice.

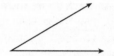

angle bisector A line, segment, or ray that divides an angle into two congruent angles.

bisectriz de un ángulo Línea, segmento o rayo que divide un ángulo en dos ángulos congruentes.

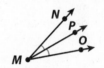

$\overrightarrow{MP}$ is an angle bisector.

arc An unbroken part of a circle.

arco Parte continua de un círculo.

area The number of square units needed to cover a given surface.

área El número de unidades cuadradas que se necesitan para cubrir una superficie dada.

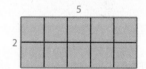

arithmetic sequence An ordered list of numbers in which the difference between consecutive terms is always the same.

sucesión aritmética Lista ordenada de números en la que la diferencia entre términos consecutivos es siempre la misma.

The sequence 2, 5, 8, 11, 14 … is an arithmetic sequence.

association A description of how data sets are related.

asociación Descripción de cómo se relaciona un conjunto de datos.

Associative Property (of Addition) The property that states that for all real numbers a, b, and c, the sum is always the same, regardless of their grouping.

Propiedad asociativa (de la suma) Propiedad que establece que para todos los números reales a, b y c, la suma siempre es la misma sin importar cómo se agrupen.

$a + b + c = (a + b) + c =$
$a + (b + c)$

Glossary/Glosario

ENGLISH	SPANISH	EXAMPLES
Associative Property (of Multiplication) The property that states that for all real numbers *a, b,* and *c,* their product is always the same, regardless of their grouping.	**Propiedad asociativa (de la multiplicación)** Propiedad que establece que para todos los números reales *a, b* y *c,* el producto siempre es el mismo, sin importar cómo se agrupen.	$a \cdot b \cdot c = (a \cdot b) \cdot c = a \cdot (b \cdot c)$
average The sum of a set of data divided by the number of items in the data set; also called *mean.*	**promedio** La suma de los elementos de un conjunto de datos dividida entre el número de elementos del conjunto. También se llama media.	Data set: 4, 6, 7, 8, 10 Average: $\dfrac{4+6+7+8+10}{5}$ $= \dfrac{35}{5} = 7$

B

back-to-back stem-and-leaf plot A stem-and-leaf plot that compares two sets of data by displaying one set of data to the left of the stem and the other to the right.	**diagrama doble de tallo y hojas** Diagrama de tallo y hojas que compara dos conjuntos de datos presentando uno de ellos a la izquierda del tallo y el otro a la derecha.	Data set A: 9, 12, 14, 16, 23, 27 Data set B: 6, 8, 10, 13, 15, 16, 21 Set A | | Set B 9 | 0 | 6 8 6 4 2 | 1 | 0 3 5 6 7 3 | 2 | 1 *Key:* |2| 1 means 21 7 |2| means 27
bar graph A graph that uses vertical or horizontal bars to display data.	**gráfica de barras** Gráfica en la que se usan barras verticales u horizontales para presentar datos.	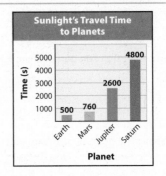
base When a number is raised to a power, the number that is used as a factor is the base.	**base** Cuando un número es elevado a una potencia, el número que se usa como factor es la base.	$3^5 = 3 \cdot 3 \cdot 3 \cdot 3 \cdot 3$; 3 is the base.
base (of a polygon or three-dimensional figure) A side of a polygon; a face of a three-dimensional figure by which the figure is measured or classified.	**base (de un polígono o figura tridimensional)** Lado de un polígono; cara de una figura tridimensional según la cual se mide o se clasifica la figura.	 Bases of a cylinder Bases of a prism Base of a cone Base of a pyramid

ENGLISH	SPANISH	EXAMPLES

biased question A question that leads people to give a certain answer.

pregunta tendenciosa pregunta que lleva a las personas a dar una respuesta determinada

---

biased sample A sample that does not fairly represent the population.

muestra no representativa Muestra que no representa adecuadamente la población.

---

binomial A polynomial with two terms.

binomio Polinomio con dos términos.

$x + y$
$2a^2 - 3$
$4m^3n^2 + 6mn^4$

---

bisect To divide into two congruent parts.

trazar una bisectriz Dividir en dos partes congruentes.

$\overrightarrow{JK}$ bisects $\angle LJM$.

---

bivariate data A set of data that is made of two paired variables.

datos bivariados Conjunto de datos compuesto de dos variables apareadas.

---

boundary line The set of points where the two sides of a two-variable linear inequality are equal.

línea de límite Conjunto de puntos donde los dos lados de una desigualdad lineal con dos variables son iguales.

---

box-and-whisker plot A graph that shows how data are distributed by using the median, quartiles, least value, and greatest value; also called a *box plot*.

gráfica de mediana y rango Gráfica para demostrar la distribución de datos utilizando la mediana, los cuartiles y los valores menos y más grande; también llamado gráfica de caja.

---

break (graph) A zigzag on a horizontal or vertical scale of a graph that indicates that some of the numbers on the scale have been omitted.

discontinuidad (gráfica) Zig-zag en la escala horizontal o vertical de una gráfica que indica la omisión de algunos de los números de la escala.

C

capacity The amount a container can hold when filled.

capacidad Cantidad que cabe en un recipiente cuando se llena.

A large milk container has a capacity of 1 gallon.

Celsius A metric scale for measuring temperature in which 0 °C is the freezing point of water and 100 °C is the boiling point of water; also called *centigrade*.

Celsius Escala métrica para medir la temperatura, en la que 0 °C es el punto de congelación del agua y 100 °C es el punto de ebullición. También se llama *centígrado*.

Glossary/Glosario

center (of a circle) The point inside a circle that is the same distance from all the points on the circle.

centro (de un círculo) Punto interior de un círculo que se encuentra a la misma distancia de todos los puntos de la circunferencia.

center of dilation The point of intersection of lines through each pair of corresponding vertices in a dilation.

centro de una dilatación Punto de intersección de las líneas que pasan a través de cada par de vértices correspondientes en una dilatación.

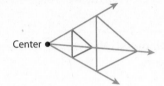

center of rotation The point about which a figure is rotated.

centro de una rotación Punto alrededor del cual se hace girar una figura.

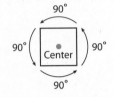

central angle An angle formed by two radii with its vertex at the center of a circle.

ángulo central de un círculo Ángulo formado por dos radios cuyo vértice se encuentra en el centro de un círculo.

chord A segment with its endpoints on a circle.

cuerda Segmento de recta cuyos extremos forman parte de un círculo.

circle The set of all points in a plane that are the same distance from a given point called the center.

círculo Conjunto de todos los puntos en un plano que se encuentran a la misma distancia de un punto dado llamado centro.

circle graph A graph that uses sectors of a circle to compare parts to the whole and parts to other parts.

gráfica circular Gráfica que usa secciones de un círculo para comparar partes con el todo y con otras partes.

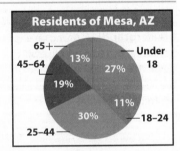

circuit A path in a graph that begins and ends at the same vertex.

circuito Una trayectoria en una gráfica que empieza y termina en el mismo vértice.

circumference The distance around a circle.

circunferencia Distancia alrededor de un círculo.

ENGLISH	SPANISH	EXAMPLES
clockwise A circular movement in the direction shown.	**en el sentido de las manecillas del reloj** Movimiento circular en la dirección que se indica.	
cluster A set of closely grouped data.	**agrupación** Conjunto de datos bien agrupados.	
clustering A condition that occurs when data points in a scatter plot are grouped more in one part of the graph than another.	**arracimando** Una condición que ocurre cuando los datos están apiñando en una parte de una diagrama de dispersión mas que en otras partes.	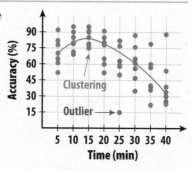
coefficient The number that is multiplied by the variable in an algebraic expression.	**coeficiente** Número que se multiplica por la variable en una expresión algebraica.	5 is the coefficient in 5*b*.
combination An arrangement of items or events in which order does not matter.	**combinación** Agrupación de objetos o sucesos en la que el orden no es importante.	For objects *A, B, C,* and *D,* there are 6 different combinations of 2 objects: *AB, AC, AD, BC, BD, CD.*
commission A fee paid to a person for making a sale.	**comisión** Pago que recibe una persona por realizar una venta.	
commission rate The fee paid to a person who makes a sale expressed as a percent of the selling price.	**tasa de comisión** Pago que recibe una persona por hacer una venta, expresado como un porcentaje del precio de venta.	A commission rate of 5% on a sale of $10,000 results in a commission of $500.
common denominator A denominator that is the same in two or more fractions.	**denominador común** Denominador que es común a dos o más fracciones.	The common denominator of $\frac{5}{8}$ and $\frac{2}{8}$ is 8.
common factor A number that is a factor of two or more numbers.	**factor común** Número que es factor de dos o más números.	8 is a common factor of 16 and 40.
common multiple A number that is a multiple of each of two or more numbers.	**múltiplo común** Número que es múltiplo de dos o más números.	15 is a common multiple of 3 and 5.
common ratio The ratio each term is multiplied by to produce the next term in a geometric sequence.	**razón común** Razón por la que se multiplica cada término para obtener el siguiente término de una sucesión geométrica.	In the geometric sequence 32, 16, 8, 4, 2, …, the common ratio is $\frac{1}{2}$.
Commutative Property (of Addition) The property that states that two or more numbers can be added in any order without changing the sum.	**Propiedad conmutativa (de la suma)** Propiedad que establece que sumar dos o más números en cualquier orden no altera la suma.	$8 + 20 = 20 + 8; a + b = b + a$

Glossary/Glosario

Commutative Property (of Multiplication) The property that states that two or more numbers can be multiplied in any order without changing the product.

Propiedad conmutativa (de la multiplicación) Propiedad que establece que multiplicar dos o más números en cualquier orden no altera el producto.

$6 \cdot 12 = 12 \cdot 6; a \cdot b = b \cdot a$

---

compatible numbers Numbers that are close to the given numbers that make estimation or mental calculation easier.

números compatibles Números que están cerca de los números dados y hacen más fácil la estimación o el cálculo mental.

To estimate $7,957 + 5,009$, use the compatible numbers 8,000 and 5,000: $8,000 + 5,000 = 13,000$

---

complement The set of all outcomes in the sample space that are not the event.

complemento La serie de resultados que no están en el suceso.

Experiment: rolling a number cube
Sample space: {1, 2, 3, 4, 5, 6}
Event: rolling a 1, 3, 4, or 6
Complement: rolling a 2 or 5

---

complementary angles Two angles whose measures add to 90°.

ángulos complementarios Dos ángulos cuyas medidas suman 90°.

The complement of a 53° angle is a 37° angle.

---

composite figure A figure made up of simple geometric shapes.

figura compuesta Figura formada por figuras geométricas simples.

---

composite number A number greater than 1 that has more than two whole-number factors.

número compuesto Número mayor que 1 que tiene más de dos factores que son números cabales.

4, 6, 8, and 9 are composite numbers.

---

compound interest Interest earned or paid on principal and previously earned or paid interest.

interés compuesto Interés que se gana o se paga sobre el capital y los intereses previamente ganados o pagados.

If $100 is put into an account with an interest rate of 5% compounded monthly, then after 2 years, the account will have $100 \left(1 + \frac{0.05}{12}\right)^{12 \cdot 2} =$ $110.49

---

conditional relative frequency The ratio of a joint relative frequency to a related marginal relative frequency in a two-way table.

frecuencia relativa condicional Razón de una frecuencia relativa conjunta a una frecuencia relativa marginal en una tabla de doble entrada.

---

cone A three-dimensional figure with one vertex and one circular base.

cono Figura tridimensional con un vértice y una base circular.

---

congruence transformation A transformation that results in an image that is the same shape and the same size as the original figure.

transformación de congruencia Una transformación que resulta en una imagen que tiene la misma forma y el mismo tamaño como la figura original.

ENGLISH	SPANISH	EXAMPLES
congruent Having the same size and shape; the symbol for congruent is ≅.	**congruentes** Que tienen la misma forma y el mismo tamaño expresado por ≅.	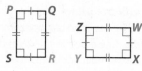 $PQRS \cong WXYZ$
congruent angles Angles that have the same measure.	**ángulos congruentes** Ángulos que tienen la misma medida.	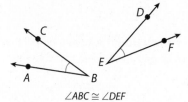 $\angle ABC \cong \angle DEF$
congruent figures See *congruent*.	**figuras congruentes** Vea *congruentes*.	
congruent segments Segments that have the same length.	**segmentos congruentes** Segmentos que tienen la misma longitud.	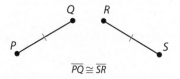 $\overline{PQ} \cong \overline{SR}$
conjecture A statement believed to be true.	**conjetura** Enunciado que se supone verdadero.	
constant A value that does not change.	**constante** Valor que no cambia.	$3, 0, \pi$
constant of variation The constant k in direct and inverse variation equations.	**constante de variación** La constante k en ecuaciones de variación directa e inversa.	$y = 5x$ ↑ Constant of variation
continuous graph A graph made up of connected lines or curves.	**gráfica continua** Gráfica compuesta por líneas rectas o curvas conectadas.	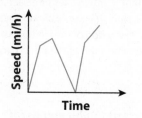
convenience sample A sample based on members of the population that are readily available.	**muestra de conveniencia** Una muestra basada en miembros de la población que están fácilmente disponibles.	
conversion factor A fraction whose numerator and denominator represent the same quantity but use different units; the fraction is equal to 1 because the numerator and denominator are equal.	**factor de conversión** Fracción cuyo numerador y denominador representan la misma cantidad pero con unidades distintas; la fracción es igual a 1 porque el numerador y el denominador son iguales.	$\frac{24 \text{ hours}}{1 \text{ day}}$ and $\frac{1 \text{ day}}{24 \text{ hours}}$
coordinate One of the numbers of an ordered pair that locate a point on a coordinate graph.	**coordenada** Uno de los números de un par ordenado que ubica un punto en una gráfica de coordenadas.	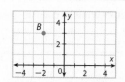 The coordinates of *B* are (−2, 3).

Glossary/Glosario

Glossary/Glosario

coordinate plane A plane formed by the intersection of a horizontal number line called the *x*-axis and a vertical number line called the *y*-axis.

plano cartesiano Plano formado por la intersección de una recta numérica horizontal llamada eje *x* y otra vertical llamada eje *y*.

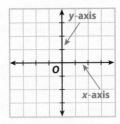

correlation The description of the relationship between two data sets.

correlación Descripción de la relación entre dos conjuntos de datos.

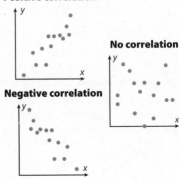

correspondence The relationship between two or more objects that are matched.

correspondencia La relación entre dos o más objetos que coinciden.

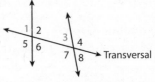

∠*A* and ∠*D* are corresponding angles.

$\overline{AB}$ and $\overline{DE}$ are corresponding sides.

corresponding angles (for lines) For two lines intersected by a transversal, a pair of angles that lie on the same side of the transversal and on the same sides of the other two lines.

ángulos correspondientes (en líneas) Dadas dos rectas cortadas por una transversal, el par de ángulos ubicados en el mismo lado de la transversal y en los mismos lados de las otras dos rectas.

∠1 and ∠3 are corresponding angles.

corresponding angles (of polygons) Angles in the same relative position in polygons with an equal number of sides.

ángulos correspondientes (en polígonos) Ángulos en la misma posición formaron cuando una tercera línea interseca dos líneas.

∠*A* and ∠*D* are corresponding angles.

corresponding sides Matching sides of two or more polygons.

lados correspondientes Lados que se ubican en la misma posición relativa en dos o más polígonos.

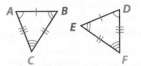

$\overline{AB}$ and $\overline{DE}$ are corresponding sides.

counterclockwise A circular movement in the direction shown.

en sentido contrario a las manecillas del reloj Movimiento circular en la dirección que se indica.

counterexample An example that proves that a conjecture or statement is false.

contraejemplo Ejemplo que demuestra que una conjetura o enunciado es falso.

cube (geometric figure) A rectangular prism with six congruent square faces.

cubo (figura geométrica) Prisma rectangular con seis caras cuadradas congruentes.

cube (in numeration) A number raised to the third power.

cubo (en numeración) Número elevado a la tercera potencia.

$2^3 = 2 \cdot 2 \cdot 2 = 8$
8 is the cube of 2.

cube root A number, written as $\sqrt[3]{x}$, whose cube is x.

raíz cúbica Número, expresado como $\sqrt[3]{x}$, cuyo cubo es x.

$\sqrt[3]{8} = \sqrt[3]{2 \cdot 2 \cdot 2} = 2$
2 is the cube root of 8.

cumulative frequency The sum of successive data items.

frecuencia acumulativa La suma de datos sucesivos.

customary system of measurement The measurement system often used in the United States.

sistema usual de medidas El sistema de medidas que se usa comúnmente en Estados Unidos.

inches, feet, miles, ounces, pounds, tons, cups, quarts, gallons

cylinder A three-dimensional figure with two parallel, congruent circular bases connected by a curved lateral surface.

cilindro Figura tridimensional con dos bases circulares paralelas y congruentes, unidas por una superficie lateral curva.

D

decagon A polygon with ten sides.

decágono Polígono de diez lados.

degree The unit of measure for angles or temperature.

grado Unidad de medida para ángulos y temperaturas.

degree of a polynomial The highest power of the variable in a polynomial.

grado de un polinomio La potencia más alta de la variable en un polinomio.

The polynomial $4x^5 - 6x^2 + 7$ has degree 5.

denominator The bottom number of a fraction that tells how many equal parts are in the whole.

denominador Número que está abajo en una fracción y que indica en cuántas partes iguales se divide el entero.

In the fraction $\frac{2}{5}$, 5 is the denominator.

Density Property The property that states that between any two real numbers there is always another real number.

Propiedad de densidad Propiedad según la cual entre dos números reales cualesquiera siempre hay otro número real.

Glossary/Glosario

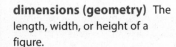

dependent events Events for which the outcome of one event affects the probability of the other.

sucesos dependientes Dos sucesos son dependientes si el resultado de uno afecta la probabilidad del otro.

A bag contains 3 red marbles and 2 blue marbles. Drawing a red marble and then drawing a blue marble without replacing the first marble is an example of dependent events.

---

dependent variable The output of a function; a variable whose value depends on the value of the input, or independent variable.

variable dependiente Salida de una función; variable cuyo valor depende del valor de la entrada, o variable independiente.

For $y = 2x + 1$, y is the dependent variable.
input: x output: y

---

diagonal A line segment that connects two nonadjacent vertices of a polygon.

diagonal Segmento de recta que une dos vértices no adyacentes de un polígono.

---

diameter A line segment that passes through the center of a circle and has endpoints on the circle, or the length of that segment.

diámetro Segmento de recta que pasa por el centro de un círculo y tiene sus extremos en la circunferencia, o bien la longitud de ese segmento.

---

dilation A transformation that enlarges or reduces a figure.

dilatación Transformación que agranda o reduce una figura.

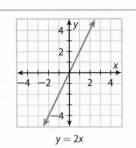

---

dimensions (geometry) The length, width, or height of a figure.

dimensiones (geometría) Longitud, ancho o altura de una figura.

---

dimensions (of a matrix) The number of horizontal rows and vertical columns in a matrix.

dimensiones (de una matriz) Número de filas y columnas que hay en una matriz.

---

direct variation A linear relationship between two variables, x and y, that can be written in the form $y = kx$, where k is a nonzero constant.

variación directa Relación lineal entre dos variables, x e y, que puede expresarse en la forma $y = kx$, donde k es una constante distinta de cero.

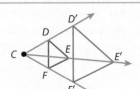

$y = 2x$

---

discount The amount by which the original price is reduced.

descuento Cantidad que se resta del precio original de un artículo.

---

discrete graph A graph made up of unconnected points.

gráfica discreta Gráfica compuesta de puntos no conectados.

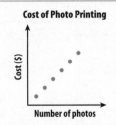

Cost of Photo Printing

Cost ($)

Number of photos

Glossary/Glosario

ENGLISH	SPANISH	EXAMPLES
disjoint events See *mutually exclusive*.	**sucesos disjuntos** Vea *mutuamente excluyentes*.	
Distributive Property For all real numbers a, b, and c, $a(b + c) = ab + ac$, and $a(b - c) = ab - ac$.	**Propiedad distributiva** Dados los números reales a, b, y c, $a(b + c) = ab + ac$, y $a(b - c) = ab - ac$.	$5 \cdot 21 = 5(20 + 1) =$ $(5 \cdot 20) + (5 \cdot 1)$
dividend The number to be divided in a division problem.	**dividendo** Número que se divide en un problema de división.	In $8 \div 4 = 2$, 8 is the dividend.
divisible Can be divided by a number without leaving a remainder.	**divisible** Que se puede dividir entre un número sin dejar residuo.	18 is divisible by 3.
Division Property of Equality The property that states that if you divide both sides of an equation by the same nonzero number, the new equation will have the same solution.	**Propiedad de igualdad de la división** Propiedad que establece que puedes dividir ambos lados de una ecuación entre el mismo número distinto de cero, y la nueva ecuación tendrá la misma solución.	
divisor The number you are dividing by in a division problem.	**divisor** El número entre el que se divide en un problema de división.	In $8 \div 4 = 2$, 4 is the divisor.
dodecahedron A polyhedron with 12 faces.	**dodecaedro** Poliedro de 12 caras.	
domain The set of all possible input values of a function.	**dominio** Conjunto de todos los posibles valores de entrada de una función.	The domain of the function $y = x^2 + 1$ is all real numbers.
double-bar graph A bar graph that compares two related sets of data.	**gráfica de doble barra** Gráfica de barras que compara dos conjuntos de datos relacionados.	

ENGLISH	SPANISH	EXAMPLES

double-line graph A line graph that shows how two related sets of data change over time.

gráfica de doble línea Gráfica lineal que muestra cómo cambian con el tiempo dos conjuntos de datos relacionados.

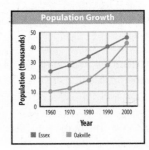

edge The line segment along which two faces of a polyhedron intersect.

arista Segmento de recta donde se intersecan dos caras de un poliedro.

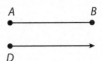

endpoint A point at the end of a line segment or ray.

extremo Un punto ubicado al final de un segmento de recta o rayo.

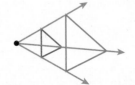

enlargement An increase in size of all dimensions in the same proportions.

agrandamiento Aumento de tamaño de todas las dimensiones en las mismas proporciones.

entries (of a matrix)
Individual entries in a matrix.

elementos (de una matriz)
Entradas individuales de una matriz.

equally likely Outcomes that have the same probability.

resultados igualmente probables Resultados que tienen la misma probabilidad de ocurrir.

When tossing a coin, the outcomes "heads" and "tails" are equally likely.

equation A mathematical sentence that shows that two expressions are equivalent.

ecuación Enunciado matemático que indica que dos expresiones son equivalentes.

$x + 4 = 7$
$6 + 1 = 10 - 3$

equilateral triangle A triangle with three congruent sides.

triángulo equilátero Triángulo con tres lados congruentes.

equivalent Having the same value.

equivalentes Que tienen el mismo valor.

equivalent expressions
Expressions that have the same value for all values of the variables.

expresiones equivalentes Las expresiones equivalentes tienen el mismo valor para todos los valores de las variables.

$4x + 5x$ and $9x$ are equivalent expressions.

equivalent fractions Fractions that name the same amount or part.

fracciones equivalentes Fracciones que representan la misma cantidad o parte.

$\frac{1}{2}$ and $\frac{2}{4}$ are equivalent fractions.

ENGLISH	SPANISH	EXAMPLES
equivalent ratios Ratios that name the same comparison.	**razones equivalentes** Razones que representan la misma comparación.	$\frac{1}{2}$ and $\frac{2}{4}$ are equivalent ratios.
estimate (n) An answer that is close to the exact answer and is found by rounding or other methods. **(v)** To find such an answer.	**estimación** Una solución aproximada a la respuesta exacta que se halla mediante el redondeo u otros métodos. **estimar** Hallar una solución aproximada a la respuesta exacta.	500 is an estimate for the sum $98 + 287 + 104$.
evaluate To find the value of a numerical or algebraic expression.	**evaluar** Hallar el valor de una expresión numérica o algebraica.	Evaluate $2x + 7$ for $x = 3$. $2x + 7$ $2(3) + 7$ $6 + 7$ 13
event An outcome or set of outcomes of an experiment or situation.	**suceso** Un resultado o una serie de resultados de un experimento o una situación.	When rolling a number cube, the event "an odd number" consists of the outcomes 1, 3, and 5.
expanded form A number written as the sum of the values of its digits.	**forma desarrollada** Número escrito como suma de los valores de sus dígitos.	236,536 written in expanded form is $200,000 + 30,000 + 6,000 + 500 + 30 + 6$.
experiment (probability) In probability, any activity based on chance (such as tossing a coin).	**experimento (probabilidad)** En probabilidad, cualquier actividad basada en la posibilidad, como lanzar una moneda.	Tossing a coin 10 times and noting the number of "heads"
experimental probability The ratio of the number of times an event occurs to the total number of trials, or times that the activity is performed.	**probabilidad experimental** Razón del número de veces que ocurre un suceso al número total de pruebas o al número de que se realiza el experimento.	Kendra attempted 27 free throws and made 16 of them. Her experimental probability of making a free throw is $\frac{\text{number made}}{\text{number attempted}} = \frac{16}{27} \approx 0.59$.
exponent The number that indicates how many times the base is used as a factor.	**exponente** Número que indica cuántas veces se usa la base como factor.	$2^3 = 2 \times 2 \times 2 = 8$; 3 is the exponent.
exponential decay An exponential function of the form $f(x) = a \cdot r^x$ in which $0 < r < 1$.	**decremento exponencial** Función exponencial del tipo $f(x) = a \cdot r^x$ en la cual $0 < r < 1$.	
exponential form A number written with a base and an exponent.	**forma exponencial** Se dice que un número está en forma exponencial cuando se escribe con una base y un exponente.	4^2 is the exponential form for $4 \cdot 4$.
exponential function A nonlinear function in which the variable is in the exponent.	**función exponencial** Función no lineal en la que la variable está en el exponente.	$f(x) = 4^x$
exponential growth An exponential function of the form $f(x) = a \cdot r^x$ in which $r > 1$.	**crecimiento exponencial** Función exponencial del tipo $f(x) = a \cdot r^x$ en la cual $r > 1$.	

© Houghton Mifflin Harcourt Publishing Company

Glossary/Glosario

expression A mathematical phrase that contains operations, numbers, and/or variables.

expresión Enunciado matemático que contiene operaciones, números y/o variables.

$6x + 1$

---

exterior angle (of a polygon) An angle formed by one side of a polygon and the extension of an adjacent side.

ángulo extreno de un polígono Ángulo formado por un lado de un polígono y la prolongación del lado adyacente.

face A flat surface of a polyhedron.

cara Superficie plana de un poliedro.

---

factor A number that is multiplied by another number to get a product.

factor Número que se multiplica por otro para hallar un producto.

7 is a factor of 21 since $7 \cdot 3 = 21$.

---

factorial The product of all whole numbers except zero that are less than or equal to a number.

factorial El producto de todos los números cabales, excepto cero, que son menores que o iguales a un número.

4 factorial $= 4! = 4 \cdot 3 \cdot 2 \cdot 1$

Fahrenheit A temperature scale in which 32 °F is the freezing point of water and 212 °F is the boiling point of water.

Fahrenheit Escala de temperatura en la que 32° F es el punto de congelación del agua y 212° F es el punto de ebullición.

---

fair When all outcomes of an experiment are equally likely, the experiment is said to be fair.

justo Se dice de un experimento donde todos los resultados posibles son igualmente probables.

When tossing a coin, heads and tails are equally likely, so it is a fair experiment.

Fibonacci sequence The infinite sequence of numbers (1, 1, 2, 3, 5, 8, 13,…); starting with the third term, each number is the sum of the two previous numbers; it is named after the thirteenth-century mathematician Leonardo Fibonacci.

sucesión de Fibonacci La sucesión infinita de números (1, 1, 2, 3, 5, 8, 13…); a partir del tercer término, cada número es la suma de los dos anteriores. Esta sucesión lleva el nombre de Leonardo Fibonacci, un matemático del siglo XIII.

1, 1, 2, 3, 5, 8, 13, . . .

---

first differences A sequence formed by subtracting each term of a sequence from the next term.

primeras diferencias Sucesión que se forma al restar cada término de una sucesión del término siguiente.

For the sequence 4, 7, 10, 13, 16, . . ., the first differences are all 3.

---

first quartile The median of the lower half of a set of data; also called *lower quartile*.

primer cuartil La mediana de la mitad inferior de un conjunto de datos. También se llama *cuartil inferior*.

ENGLISH	SPANISH	EXAMPLES

FOIL An acronym for the terms used when multiplying two binomials: the First, Outer, Inner, and Last terms.

FOIL Sigla en inglés de los términos que se usan al multiplicar dos binomios: los primeros, los externos, los internos y los últimos (First, Outer, Inner, Last).

$$(x + 2)(x - 3) = x^2 - 3x + 2x - 6$$
$$= x^2 - x - 6$$

---

formula A rule showing relationships among quantities.

fórmula Regla que muestra relaciones entre cantidades.

$A = \ell w$ is the formula for the area of a rectangle.

---

fractal A structure with repeating patterns containing shapes that are like the whole but are of different sizes throughout.

fractal Estructura con patrones repetidos que contiene figuras similares al patrón general pero de diferente tamaño.

---

fraction A number in the form $\frac{a}{b}$, where $b \neq 0$.

fracción Número escrito en la forma $\frac{a}{b}$, donde $b \neq 0$.

$\frac{2}{3}$

---

frequency The number of times the value appears in the data set.

frecuencia Cantidad de veces que aparece el valor en un conjunto de datos.

Data set: 5, 6, 6, 7, 8, 9
The data value 6 has a frequency of 2.

---

frequency table A table that lists items together according to the number of times, or frequency, that the items occur.

tabla de frecuencia Una tabla en la que se organizan los datos de acuerdo con el número de veces que aparece cada valor (o la frecuencia).

Data set: 1, 1, 2, 2, 3, 5, 5, 5
Frequency table:

Data	Frequency
1	2
2	2
3	1

---

function An input-output relationship that has exactly one output for each input.

función Regla que relaciona dos candidates de forma que a cada valor de entrada corresponde exactamente un valor de salida.

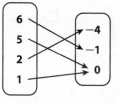

---

function notation The notation used to describe a function.

notación de función Notación que se usa para describir una función.

Equation: $y = 2x$
Function notation: $f(x) = 2x$

---

function table A table of ordered pairs that represent solutions of a function.

tabla de función Tabla de pares ordenados que representan soluciones de una función.

x	3	4	5	6
y	7	9	11	13

Fundamental Counting Principle If one event has m possible outcomes and a second event has n possible outcomes after the first event has occurred, then there are $m \cdot n$ total possible outcomes for the two events.

Principio fundamental de conteo Si un suceso tiene m resultados posibles y otro suceso tiene n resultados posibles después de ocurrido el primer suceso, entonces hay $m \cdot n$ resultados posibles en total para los dos sucesos.

There are 4 colors of shirts and 3 colors of pants. There are $4 \cdot 3 = 12$ possible outfits.

Glossary/Glosario

Glossary/Glosario

geometric probability A form of theoretical probability determined by a ratio of geometric measures such as lengths, areas, or volumes.

probabilidad geométrica Método para calcular probabilidades basado en una medida geométrica como la longitud o el área.

The probability of the pointer landing on red is $\frac{80}{360}$, or $\frac{2}{9}$.

geometric sequence An ordered list of numbers that has a common ratio between consecutive terms.

sucesión geométrica Lista ordenada de números que tiene una razón común entre términos consecutivos.

The sequence 2, 4, 8, 16 . . . is a geometric sequence.

graph of an equation A graph of the set of ordered pairs that are solutions of the equation.

gráfica de una ecuación Gráfica del conjunto de pares ordenados que son soluciones de la ecuación.

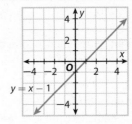

$y = x - 1$

great circle A circle on a sphere such that the plane containing the circle passes through the center of the sphere.

círculo máximo Círculo de una esfera tal que el plano que contiene el círculo pasa por el centro de la esfera.

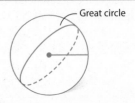

Great circle

greatest common factor (GCF) The largest common factor of two or more given numbers.

máximo común divisor (MCD) El mayor de los factores comunes compartidos por dos o más números dados.

The GCF of 27 and 45 is 9.

H

height In a pyramid or cone, the perpendicular distance from the base to the opposite vertex.

altura En una pirámide o cono, la distancia perpendicular desde la base al vértice opuesto.

In a triangle or quadrilateral, the perpendicular distance from the base to the opposite vertex or side.

En un triángulo o cuadrilátero, la distancia perpendicular desde la base de la figura al vértice o lado opuesto.

In a prism or cylinder, the perpendicular distance between the bases.

En un prisma o cilindro, la distancia perpendicular entre las bases.

hemisphere A half of a sphere.

hemisferio La mitad de una esfera.

---

heptagon A seven-sided polygon.

heptágono Polígono de siete lados.

---

hexagon A six-sided polygon.

hexágono Polígono de seis lados.

---

histogram A bar graph that shows the frequency of data within equal intervals.

histograma Gráfica de barras que muestra la frecuencia de los datos en intervalos iguales.

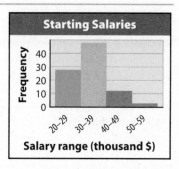

---

hypotenuse In a right triangle, the side opposite the right angle.

hipotenusa En un triángulo rectángulo, el lado opuesto al ángulo recto.

Identity Property Addition The property that states the sum of zero and any number is that number.

Propiedad de identidad de la suma Propiedad que establece que la suma de cero y cualquier número es ese número.

$4 + 0 = 4$
$-3 + 0 = -3$

Identity Property Multiplication The property that states that the product of 1 and any number is that number.

Propiedad de identidad de la multiplicación Propiedad que establece que el producto de 1 y cualquier número es ese número.

$4 \cdot 1 = 4$
$-3 \cdot 1 = -3$

---

image A figure resulting from a transformation.

imagen Figura que resulta de una transformación.

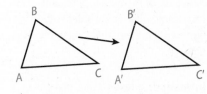

A'B'C' is the image of ABC.

---

improper fraction A fraction in which the numerator is greater than or equal to the denominator.

fracción impropia Fracción cuyo numerador es mayor que o igual al denominador.

$\frac{17}{5}, \frac{3}{3}$

ENGLISH	SPANISH	EXAMPLES
independent events Events for which the outcome of one event does not affect the probability of the other.	**sucesos independientes** Dos sucesos son independientes si el resultado de uno no afecta la probabilidad del otro.	A bag contains 3 red marbles and 2 blue marbles. Drawing a red marble, replacing it, and then drawing a blue marble is an example of independent events.
independent variable The input of a function; a variable whose value determines the value of the output, or dependent variable.	**variable independiente** Entrada de una función; variable cuyo valor determina el valor de la salida, o variable dependiente.	For $y = 2x + 1$, x is the independent variable. input: x output: y
indirect measurement The technique of using similar figures and proportions to find a measure.	**medición indirecta** La técnica de usar figuras semejantes y proporciones para hallar una medida.	
inductive reasoning Using a pattern to make a conclusion.	**razonamiento inductivo** Uso de un patrón para sacar una conclusión.	
inequality A mathematical sentence that shows the relationship between quantities that are not equivalent.	**desigualdad** Enunciado matemático que muestra una relación entre cantidades que no son equivalentes.	$5 < 8$ $5x + 2 \geq 12$
input The value substituted into an expression or function.	**valor de entrada** Valor que se usa para sustituir una variable en una expresión o función.	For the function $y = 6x$, the input 4 produces an output of 24.
inscribed angle An angle formed by two chords with its vertex on a circle.	**ángulo inscrito** Ángulo formado por dos cuerdas cuyo vértice está en un círculo.	
integers The set of whole numbers and their opposites.	**enteros** Conjunto de todos los números cabales y sus opuestos.	$\ldots -3, -2, -1, 0, 1, 2, 3, \ldots$
interest The amount of money charged for borrowing or using money.	**interés** Cantidad de dinero que se cobra por el préstamo o uso del dinero.	
interior angles Angles on the inner sides of two lines cut by a transversal.	**ángulos internos** Ángulos en los lados internos de dos líneas intersecadas por una transversal.	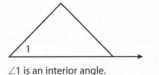 ∠1 is an interior angle.
interquartile range (IQR) The difference of the third (upper) and first (lower) quartiles in a data set, representing the middle half of the data.	**rango intercuartil (RIC)** Diferencia entre el tercer cuartil (superior) y el primer cuartil (inferior) de un conjunto de datos, que representa la mitad central de los datos.	 Interquartile range: $36 - 23 = 13$
intersecting lines Lines that cross at exactly one point.	**líneas secantes** Líneas que se cruzan en un solo punto.	

Glossary/Glosario

interval The space between marked values on a number line or the scale of a graph.

intervalo El espacio entre los valores marcados en una recta numérica o en la escala de una gráfica.

---

inverse operations Operations that undo each other: addition and subtraction, or multiplication and division.

operaciones inversas Operaciones que se cancelan mutuamente: suma y resta, o multiplicación y división.

Addition and subtraction are inverse operations:

$5 + 3 = 8; 8 - 3 = 5$

Multiplication and division are inverse operations:

$2 \cdot 3 = 6; 6 \div 3 = 2$

---

inverse variation A relationship in which one variable quantity increases as another variable quantity decreases; the product of the variables is a constant.

variación inversa Relación en la que una cantidad variable aumenta a medida que otra cantidad variable disminuye; el producto de las variables es una constante.

$xy = 7, y = \frac{7}{x}$

---

irrational number A number that cannot be expressed as a ratio of two integers or as a repeating or terminating decimal.

número irracional Número que no se puede expresar como una razón de dos enteros ni como un decimal periódico o finito.

$\sqrt{2}, \pi$

---

isolate the variable To get a variable alone on one side of an equation or inequality in order to solve the equation or inequality.

despejar la variable Dejar sola la variable en un lado de una ecuación o desigualdad para resolverla.

$$x + 7 = 22$$
$$\underline{-7 \quad -7}$$
$$x \quad = 15$$

$$\frac{12}{3} = \frac{3x}{3}$$
$$4 = x$$

---

isometric drawing A representation of a three-dimensional figure that is drawn on a grid of equilateral triangles.

dibujo isométrico Representación de una figura tridimensional que se dibuja sobre una cuadrícula de triángulos equiláteros.

---

isosceles triangle A triangle with at least two congruent sides.

triángulo isósceles Triángulo que tiene al menos dos lados congruentes.

---

joint relative frequency The ratio of the frequency in a particular category divided by the total number of data values.

frecuencia relativa conjunta La razón de la frecuencia en una determinada categoría dividida entre el número total de valores.

L

lateral area The sum of the areas of the lateral faces of a prism or pyramid, or the area of the lateral surface of a cylinder or cone.

área lateral Suma de las áreas de las caras laterales de un prisma o pirámide, o área de la superficie lateral de un cilindro o cono.

Lateral area = area of the 5 rectangular faces

Glossary/Glosario

lateral face In a prism or a pyramid, a face that is not a base.

cara lateral En un prisma o pirámide, una cara que no es la base.

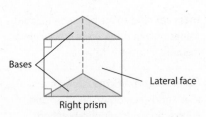

Bases

Lateral face

Right prism

lateral surface In a cylinder, the curved surface connecting the circular bases; in a cone, the curved surface that is not a base.

superficie lateral En un cilindro, superficie curva que une las bases circulares; en un cono, la superficie curva que no es la base.

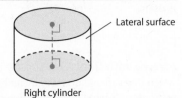

Lateral surface

Right cylinder

least common denominator (LCD) The least common multiple of two or more denominators.

mínimo común denominador (mcd) El mínimo común múltiplo más pequeño de dos o más denominadores.

The LCD of $\frac{3}{4}$ and $\frac{5}{6}$ is 12.

least common multiple (LCM) The smallest whole number, other than zero, that is a multiple of two or more given numbers.

mínimo común múltiplo (mcm) El menor de los números cabales, distinto de cero, que es múltiplo de dos o más números dados.

The LCM of 6 and 10 is 30.

legs In a right triangle, the sides that include the right angle; in an isosceles triangle, the pair of congruent sides.

catetos En un triángulo rectángulo, los lados adyacentes al ángulo recto. En un triángulo isósceles, el par de lados congruentes.

Leg

Leg

like fractions Fractions that have the same denominator.

fracciones semejantes Fracciones que tienen el mismo denominador.

$\frac{5}{12}$ and $\frac{7}{12}$ are like fractions.

like terms Terms that have the same variable raised to the same exponents.

términos semejantes Términos que contienen las mismas variables elevada a las mismas exponentes.

In the expression $3a^2 + 5b + 12a^2$, $3a^2$ and $12a^2$ are like terms.

line A straight path that has no thickness and extends forever.

línea Un trazo recto que no tiene grosor y se extiende infinitamente.

line graph A graph that uses line segments to show how data changes.

gráfica lineal Gráfica que muestra cómo cambian los datos mediante segmentos de recta.

line of best fit A straight line that comes closest to the points on a scatter plot.

línea de mejor ajuste La línea recta que más se aproxima a los puntos de un diagrama de dispersión.

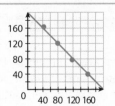

Glossary/Glosario

ENGLISH	SPANISH	EXAMPLES
line of reflection A line that a figure is flipped across to create a mirror image of the original figure.	**línea de reflexión** Línea sobre la cual se invierte una figura para crear una imagen reflejada de la figura original.	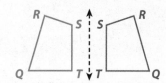
line of symmetry A line that divides a figure into two congruent reflected halves.	**eje de simetría** Línea que divide una figura en dos mitades reflejas.	
line plot A number line with marks or dots that show frequency.	**diagrama de acumulación** Recta numérica con marcas o puntos que indican la frecuencia.	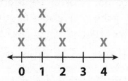 Number of Pets
line segment A part of a line consisting of two endpoints and all points between them.	**segmento de recta** Parte de una línea que consiste en dos extremos y todos los puntos entre éstos.	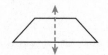
line symmetry A figure has line symmetry if one half is a mirror image of the other half.	**simetría axial** Una figura tiene simetría axial si una de sus mitades es la imagen reflejada de la otra.	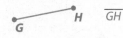
linear equation An equation whose solutions form a straight line on a coordinate plane.	**ecuación lineal** Ecuación cuyas soluciones forman una línea recta en un plano cartesiano.	$y = 2x + 1$
linear function A function whose graph is a straight line.	**función lineal** Función cuya gráfica es una línea recta.	$y = x - 1$ 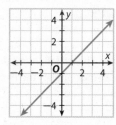
linear inequality A mathematical sentence using $<$, $>$, $\leq$, or $\geq$ whose graph is a region with a straight-line boundary.	**desigualdad lineal** Enunciado matemático en que se usan los símbolos $<$, $>$, $\leq$, o $\geq$ y cuya gráfica es una región con una línea de límite recta.	
literal equation An equation that contains two or more variables.	**ecuación literal** Ecuación que contiene dos o más variables.	$d = rt$ $A = bh$

Glossary/Glosario

major arc An arc that is more than half of a circle.

arco mayor Arco que es más de la mitad de un círculo.

$\widearc{ADC}$ is a major arc of the circle.

---

marginal relative frequency The sum of the joint relative frequencies in a row or column of a two-way table.

frecuencia relativa marginal La suma de las frecuencias relativas conjuntas en una fila o columna de una tabla de doble entrada.

---

matrix A rectangular arrangement of data enclosed in brackets.

matriz Arreglo rectangular de datos encerrado entre corchetes.

$$\begin{bmatrix} 1 & 0 & 3 \\ -2 & 2 & -5 \\ 7 & -6 & 3 \end{bmatrix}$$

---

mean The sum of a set of data divided by the number of items in the data set; also called *average*.

media La suma de todos los elementos de un conjunto de datos dividida entre el número de elementos del conjunto. También se llama promedio.

Data set: 4, 6, 7, 8, 10

Mean: $\frac{4+6+7+8+10}{5} = \frac{35}{5} = 7$

---

mean absolute deviation (MAD) The mean distance between each data value and the mean of the data set.

desviación absoluta media (DAM) Distancia media entre cada dato y la media del conjunto de datos.

---

measure of center A measure used to describe the middle of a data set; the mean, median, and mode are measures of center. Also called *measure of central tendency*.

medida de tendencia dominante Medida que describe la parte media de un conjunto de datos; la media, la mediana y la moda son medidas de tendencia dominante.

---

median The middle number, or the mean (average) of the two middle numbers, in an ordered set of data.

mediana El número intermedio o la media (el promedio) de los dos números intermedios en un conjunto ordenado de datos.

Data set: 4, 6, 7, 8, 10

Median: 7

---

metric system of measurement A decimal system of weights and measures that is used universally in science and commonly throughout the world.

sistema métrico de medición Sistema decimal de pesos y medidas empleado universalmente en las ciencias y de uso común en todo el mundo.

centimeters, meters, kilometers, grams, kilograms, milliliters, liters

---

midpoint The point that divides a line segment into two congruent line segments.

punto medio El punto que divide un segmento de recta en dos segmentos de recta congruentes.

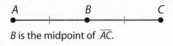

B is the midpoint of $\overline{AC}$.

---

minor arc An arc that is less than half of a circle.

arco menor Arco que es menor que la mitad de un círculo.

$\widearc{AC}$ is the minor arc of the circle.

mixed number A number made up of a whole number that is not zero and a fraction.

número mixto Número compuesto por un número cabal distinto de cero y una fracción.

$4\frac{1}{8}$

---

mode The number or numbers that occur most frequently in a set of data; when all numbers occur with the same frequency, we say there is no mode.

moda Número o números más frecuentes en un conjunto de datos; si todos los números aparecen con la misma frecuencia, no hay moda.

Data set: 3, 5, 8, 8, 10
Mode: 8

---

monomial A number or a product of numbers and variables with exponents that are whole numbers.

monomio Un número o un producto de números y variables con exponentes que son números cabales.

$3x^2y^4$

Multiplication Property of Equality The property that states that if you multiply both sides of an equation by the same number, the new equation will have the same solution.

Propiedad de igualdad de la multiplicación Propiedad que establece que puedes multiplicar ambos lados de una ecuación por el mismo número y la nueva ecuación tendrá la misma solución.

$3 \cdot 4 = 12$
$3 \cdot 4 \cdot 2 = 12 \cdot 2$
$\qquad 24 = 24$

Multiplication Property of Zero The property that states that for all real numbers a, $a \cdot 0 = 0$ and $0 \cdot a = 0$.

Propiedad de multiplicación del cero Propiedad que establece que para todos los números reales a, $a \cdot 0 = 0$ y $0 \cdot a = 0$.

---

multiplicative inverse A number times its multiplicative inverse is equal to 1; also called *reciprocal*.

inverso multiplicativo Un número multiplicado por su inverso multiplicativo es igual a 1. También se llama *recíproco*.

The multiplicative inverse of $\frac{4}{5}$ is $\frac{5}{4}$.

---

multiple The product of any number and a nonzero whole number is a multiple of that number.

múltiplo El producto de cualquier número y un número cabal distinto de cero es un múltiplo de ese número.

---

mutually exclusive Two events are mutually exclusive if they cannot occur in the same trial of an experiment.

mutuamente excluyentes Dos sucesos son mutuamente excluyentes cuando no pueden ocurrir en la misma prueba de un experimento.

When rolling a number cube once, rolling a 3 and rolling an even number are mutually exclusive events.

N

negative correlation Two data sets have a negative correlation if one set of data values increases while the other decreases.

correlación negativa Dos conjuntos de datos tienen correlación negativa si los valores de un conjunto aumentan a medida que los valores del otro conjunto disminuyen.

---

negative integer An integer less than zero.

entero negativo Entero menor que cero.

-2 is a negative integer.

ENGLISH	SPANISH	EXAMPLES

net An arrangement of two-dimensional figures that can be folded to form a polyhedron.

plantilla Arreglo de figuras bidimensionales que se doblan para formar un poliedro.

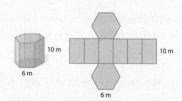

---

network A set of points and the line segments or arcs that connect the points.

red Conjunto de puntos y los segmentos de recta o arcos que los conectan.

---

no correlation Two data sets have no correlation when there is no relationship between their data values.

sin correlación Caso en que los valores de dos conjuntos no muestran ninguna relación.

---

nonlinear function A function whose graph is not a straight line.

función no lineal Función cuya gráfica no es una línea recta.

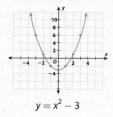

$y = x^2 - 3$

---

nonlinear relationship A relationship between two variables in which the data do not increase or decrease together at the same rate.

relación no lineal Relación entre dos variables en la cual los datos no aumentan o disminuyen al mismo tiempo a una tasa constante.

---

nonterminating decimal A decimal that never ends.

decimal infinito Decimal que nunca termina.

$0.\overline{3}$

---

numerator The top number of a fraction that tells how many parts of a whole are being considered.

numerador El número de arriba de una fracción; indica cuántas partes de un entero se consideran.

$\frac{4}{5}$ ← numerator

---

numerical expression An expression that contains only numbers and operations.

expresión numérica Expresión que incluye sólo números y operaciones.

$(2 \cdot 3) + 1$

---

obtuse angle An angle whose measure is greater than 90° but less than 180°.

ángulo obtuso Ángulo que mide más de 90° y menos de 180°.

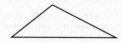

---

obtuse triangle A triangle containing one obtuse angle.

triángulo obtusángulo Triángulo que tiene un ángulo obtuso.

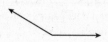

---

octagon An eight-sided polygon.

octágono Polígono de ocho lados.

odds A comparison of the number of ways an event can occur and the number of ways an event can *not* occur.

probabilidades Comparación del número de las maneras que puede ocurrir un suceso y el número de maneras que no puede ocurrir el suceso.

---

odds against The ratio of the number of unfavorable outcomes to the number of favorable outcomes.

probabilidades en contra Razón del número de resultados no favorables al número de resultados favorables.

The odds against rolling a 3 on a number cube are 5:1.

---

odds in favor The ratio of the number of favorable outcomes to the number of unfavorable outcomes.

probabilidades a favor Razón del número de resultados favorables al número de resultados no favorables.

The odds in favor of rolling a 3 on a number cube are 1:5.

---

opposites Two numbers that are an equal distance from zero on a number line; also called *additive inverse*.

opuestos Dos números que están a la misma distancia de cero en una recta numérica. También se llaman *inversos aditivos*.

5 and −5 are opposites.

---

order of operations A rule for evaluating expressions: First perform the operations in parentheses, then compute powers and roots, then perform all multiplication and division from left to right, and then perform all addition and subtraction from left to right.

orden de las operaciones Regla para evaluar expresiones: primero se hacen las operaciones entre paréntesis, luego se hallan las potencias y raíces, después todas las multiplicaciones y divisiones de izquierda a derecha, y por último, todas las sumas y restas de izquierda a derecha.

$4^2 + 8 \div 2$ Evaluate the power.
$16 + 8 \div 2$ Divide.
$16 + 4$ Add.
20

---

ordered pair A pair of numbers that can be used to locate a point on a coordinate plane.

par ordenado Par de números que sirven para ubicar un punto en un plano cartesiano.

The coordinates of B are (−2, 3).

---

origin The point where the *x*-axis and *y*-axis intersect on the coordinate plane; (0, 0).

origen Punto de intersección entre el eje *x* y el eje *y* en un plano cartesiano: (0, 0).

---

orthogonal views A drawing that shows the top, bottom, front, back, and side views of a three-dimensional object.

vista ortogonal Un dibujo que muestra la vista superior, inferior, frontal, posterior y lateral de un objeto de tres dimensiones.

---

outcome (probability) A possible result of a probability experiment.

resultado (en probabilidad) Posible resultado de un experimento de probabilidad.

When rolling a number cube, the possible outcomes are 1, 2, 3, 4, 5, and 6.

Glossary/Glosario

ENGLISH	SPANISH	EXAMPLES
outlier A value much greater or much less than the others in a data set.	**valor extremo** Un valor mucho mayor o menor que los demás valores de un conjunto de datos.	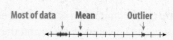
output The value that results from the substitution of a given input into an expression or function.	**valor de salida** Valor que resulta después de sustituir una variable por un valor de entrada determinado en una expresión o función.	For the function $y = 6x$, the input 4 produces an output of 24.

P

ENGLISH	SPANISH	EXAMPLES
parabola The graph of a quadratic function.	**parábola** Gráfica de una función cuadrática.	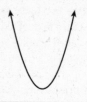
parallel lines Lines in a plane that do not intersect.	**líneas paralelas** Líneas que se encuentran en el mismo plano pero que nunca se intersecan.	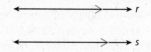
parallelogram A quadrilateral with two pairs of parallel sides.	**paralelogramo** Cuadrilátero con dos pares de lados paralelos.	
pentagon A five-sided polygon.	**pentágono** Polígono de cinco lados.	
percent A ratio comparing a number to 100.	**porcentaje** Razón que compara un número con el número 100.	$45\% = \frac{45}{100}$
percent change The amount stated as a percent that a number increases or decreases.	**porcentaje de cambio** Cantidad en que un número aumenta o disminuye, expresada como un porcentaje.	
percent decrease A percent change describing a decrease in a quantity.	**porcentaje de disminución** Porcentaje de cambio en que una cantidad disminuye.	An item that costs $8 is marked down to $6. The amount of the decrease is $2, and the percent decrease is $\frac{2}{8} = 0.25 = 25\%$.
percent increase A percent change describing an increase in a quantity.	**porcentaje de incremento** Porcentaje de cambio en que una cantidad aumenta.	The price of an item increases from $8 to $12. The amount of the increase is $4, and the percent increase is $\frac{4}{8} = 0.5 = 50\%$.
perfect cube A cube of a whole number.	**cubo perfecto** El cubo de un número cabal.	$2^3 = 8$, so 8 is a perfect cube.
perfect square A square of a whole number.	**cuadrado perfecto** El cuadrado de un número cabal.	$5^2 = 25$, so 25 is a perfect square.
perimeter The distance around a polygon.	**perímetro** Distancia alrededor de un polígono.	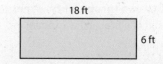 perimeter $= 18 + 6 + 18 + 6 = 48$ ft

Glossary/Glosario

ENGLISH	SPANISH	EXAMPLES
permutation An arrangement of items or events in which order is important.	**permutación** Arreglo de objetos o sucesos en el que el orden es importante.	For objects A, B, and C, there are 6 different permutations: ABC, ACB, BAC, BCA, CAB, CBA.
perpendicular bisector A line that intersects a segment at its midpoint and is perpendicular to the segment.	**mediatriz** Línea que cruza un segmento en su punto medio y es perpendicular al segmento.	
perpendicular lines Lines that intersect to form right angles.	**líneas perpendiculares** Líneas que al intersecarse forman ángulos rectos.	
pi (π) The ratio of the circumference of a circle to the length of its diameter; $\pi \approx 3.14$ or $\frac{22}{7}$.	**pi (π)** Razón de la circunferencia de un círculo a la longitud de su diámetro; $\pi \approx 3.14$ ó $\frac{22}{7}$.	
plane A flat surface that has no thickness and extends forever.	**plano** Superficie plana que no tiene ningún grueso y que se extiende por siempre.	
point An exact location that has no size.	**punto** Ubicación exacta que no tiene ningún tamaño.	$P \bullet$
point-slope form The equation of a line in the form of $y - y_1 = m(x - x_1)$, where m is the slope and (x_1, y_1) is a specific point on the line.	**forma de punto y pendiente** Ecuación lineal del tipo $y - y_1 = m(x - x_1)$, donde m es la pendiente y (x_1, y_1) es un punto específico de la línea.	$y - 3 = 2(x - 3)$
polygon A closed plane figure formed by three or more line segments that intersect only at their endpoints (vertices).	**polígono** Figura plana cerrada, formada por tres o más segmentos de recta que se intersecan sólo en sus extremos (vértices).	
polyhedron A three-dimensional figure in which all the surfaces or faces are polygons.	**poliedro** Figura tridimensional cuyas superficies o caras tiene forma de polígonos.	
polynomial One monomial or the sum or difference of monomials.	**polinomio** Un monomio o la suma o la diferencia de monomios.	$2x^2 + 3xy - 7y^2$
population The entire group of objects or individuals considered for a survey.	**población** Grupo completo de objetos o individuos que se desea estudiar.	In a survey about study habits of middle school students, the population is all middle school students.

Glossary/Glosario

positive correlation Two data sets have a positive correlation when their data values increase or decrease together.

correlación positiva Dos conjuntos de datos tienen una correlación positiva cuando los valores de ambos conjuntos aumentan o disminuyen al mismo tiempo.

---

positive integer An integer greater than zero.

entero positivo Entero mayor que cero.

2 is a positive integer.

---

power A number produced by raising a base to an exponent.

potencia Número que resulta al elevar una base a un exponente.

$2^3 = 8$, so 2 to the 3rd power is 8.

---

preimage The original figure in a transformation.

imagen original Figura original en una transformación.

---

prime factorization A number written as the product of its prime factors.

factorización prima Un número escrito como el producto de sus factores primos.

$10 = 2 \cdot 5$,
$24 = 2^3 \cdot 3$

---

prime number A whole number greater than 1 that has exactly two factors, itself and 1.

número primo Número cabal mayor que 1 que sólo es divisible entre 1 y él mismo.

5 is prime because its only factors are 5 and 1.

---

principal The initial amount of money borrowed or saved.

principal Cantidad inicial de dinero depositada o recibida en préstamo.

---

principal square root The nonnegative square root of a number.

raíz cuadrada principal Raíz cuadrada no negativa de un número.

$\sqrt{25} = 5$; the principal square root of 25 is 5.

---

prism A polyhedron that has two congruent, polygon-shaped bases and other faces that are all parallelograms.

prisma Poliedro con dos bases congruentes con forma de polígono y caras con forma de paralelogramo.

---

probability A number from 0 to 1 (or 0% to 100%) that describes how likely an event is to occur.

probabilidad Un número entre 0 y 1 (ó 0% y 100%) que describe qué tan probable es un suceso.

A bag contains 3 red marbles and 4 blue marbles. The probability of randomly choosing a red marble is $\frac{3}{7}$.

---

proper fraction A fraction in which the numerator is less than the denominator.

fracción propia Fracción en la que el numerador es menor que el denominador.

$\frac{3}{4}, \frac{1}{12}, \frac{7}{8}$

---

proportion An equation that states that two ratios are equivalent.

proporción Ecuación que establece que dos razones son equivalentes.

$\frac{2}{3} = \frac{4}{6}$

---

proportional relationship A relationship between two quantities in which the ratio of one quantity to the other quantity is constant.

relación proporcional Relación entre dos cantidades en que la razón de una cantidad a la otra es constante.

ENGLISH	SPANISH	EXAMPLES
protractor A tool for measuring angles.	**transportador** Instrumento para medir ángulos.	
pyramid A polyhedron with a polygon base and triangular sides that all meet at a common vertex.	**pirámide** Poliedro cuya base es un polígono; tiene caras triangulares que se juntan en un vértice común.	
Pythagorean Theorem In a right triangle, the square of the length of the hypotenuse is equal to the sum of the squares of the lengths of the legs.	**Teorema de Pitágoras** En un triángulo rectángulo, la suma de los cuadrados de los catetos es igual al cuadrado de la hipotenusa.	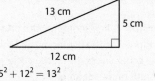 $5^2 + 12^2 = 13^2$ $25 + 144 = 169$
Pythagorean triple A set of three positive integers a, b, and c such that $a^2 + b^2 = c^2$.	**Tripleta de Pitágoras** Conjunto de tres números enteros positivos de cero a, b y c tal que $a^2 + b^2 = c^2$.	3, 4, 5 because $3^2 + 4^2 = 5^2$

quadrant The x- and y-axes divide the coordinate plane into four regions. Each region is called a quadrant.	**cuadrante** El eje x y el eje y dividen el plano cartesiano en cuatro regiones. Cada región recibe el nombre de cuadrante.	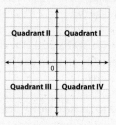
quadratic function A function of the form $y = ax^2 + bx + c$, where $a \neq 0$.	**función cuadrática** Función del tipo $y = ax^2 + bx + c$, donde $a \neq 0$.	$y = x^2 - 6x + 8$
quadrilateral A four-sided polygon.	**cuadrilátero** Polígono de cuatro lados.	
quarterly Four times a year.	**trimestral** Cuatro veces al año.	
quartile Three values, one of which is the median, that divide a data set into fourths.	**cuartil** Cada uno de tres valores, uno de los cuales es la mediana, que dividen en cuartos un conjunto de datos.	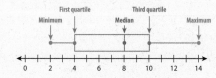
quotient The result when one number is divided by another.	**cociente** Resultado de dividir un número entre otro.	In $8 \div 4 = 2$, 2 is the quotient.

radical symbol The symbol $\sqrt{}$ used to represent the nonnegative square root of a number.

símbolo de radical El símbolo $\sqrt{}$ con que se representa la raíz cuadrada no negativa de un número.

---

radius A line segment with one endpoint at the center of the circle and the other endpoint on the circle, or the length of that segment.

radio Segmento de recta con un extremo en el centro de un círculo y el otro en la circunferencia, o bien se llama radio a la longitud de ese segmento.

---

random numbers In a set of random numbers, each number has an equal chance of appearing.

muestra aleatoria Muestra en la que cada individuo u objeto de la población tiene la misma posibilidad de ser elegido.

---

random sample A sample in which each individual or object in the entire population has an equal chance of being selected.

números aleatorios En un conjunto de números aleatorios, todos los números tienen la misma probabilidad de ser seleccionados.

---

range (in statistics) The difference between the greatest and least values in a data set.

rango (en estadística) Diferencia entre los valores máximo y mínimo de un conjunto de datos.

Data set: 3, 5, 7, 7, 12
Range: $12 - 3 = 9$

---

range (of a function) The set of all possible output values of a function.

rango (en una función) El conjunto de todos los valores posibles de una función.

The range of $y = |x|$ is $y \geq 0$.

---

rate A ratio that compares two quantities measured in different units.

tasa Una razón que compara dos cantidades medidas en diferentes unidades.

The speed limit is 55 miles per hour or 55 mi/h.

---

rate of change A ratio that compares the amount of change in a dependent variable to the amount of change in an independent variable.

tasa de cambio Razón que compara la cantidad de cambio de la variable dependiente con la cantidad de cambio de la variable independiente.

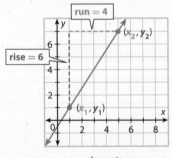

Rate of change $= \dfrac{\text{change in } y}{\text{change in } x} = \dfrac{6}{4} = \dfrac{3}{2}$

---

rate of interest The percent charged or earned on an amount of money; see *simple interest*.

tasa de interés Porcentaje que se cobra por una cantidad de dinero prestada o que se gana por una cantidad de dinero ahorrada; ver *interés simple*.

ENGLISH	SPANISH	EXAMPLES
ratio A comparison of two quantities by division.	**razón** Comparación de dos cantidades mediante una división.	12 to 25, 12:25, $\frac{12}{25}$
rational number Any number that can be expressed as a ratio of two integers.	**número racional** Número que se puede escribir como una razón de dos enteros.	6 can be expressed as $\frac{6}{1}$. 0.5 can be expressed as $\frac{1}{2}$.
ray A part of a line that starts at one endpoint and extends forever in one direction.	**rayo** Parte de una línea que comienza en un extremo y se extiende de manera infinitamente en una dirección.	 *D*
real number A rational or irrational number.	**número real** Número racional o irracional.	
reciprocal One of two numbers whose product is 1; also called *multiplicative inverse*.	**recíproco** Uno de dos números cuyo producto es igual a 1. También se llama *inverso multiplicativo*.	The reciprocal of $\frac{2}{3}$ is $\frac{3}{2}$.
rectangle A parallelogram with four right angles.	**rectángulo** Paralelogramo con cuatro ángulos rectos.	
rectangular prism A polyhedron whose bases are rectangles and whose other faces are parallelograms.	**prisma rectangular** Poliedro cuyas bases son rectángulos y cuyas caras tienen forma de paralelogramo.	
reduction A decrease in the size of all dimensions.	**reducción** Disminución de tamaño en todas las dimensiones de una figura.	
reflection A transformation of a figure that flips the figure across a line.	**reflexión** Transformación que ocurre cuando se invierte una figura sobre una línea.	
regular polygon A polygon with congruent sides and angles.	**polígono regular** Polígono con lados y ángulos congruentes.	
regular pyramid A pyramid whose base is a regular polygon and whose lateral faces are all congruent.	**pirámide regular** Pirámide que tiene un polígono regular como base y caras laterales congruentes.	
relation A set of ordered pairs.	**relación** Conjunto de pares ordenados.	(0, 5), (0, 4), (2, 3), (4, 0)
relative frequency The frequency of a specific data value divided by the total number of data values in the set.	**frecuencia relativa** La frecuencia de un valor dividido por el número total de los valores en el conjunto.	

Glossary/Glosario

relatively prime Two numbers are relatively prime if their greatest common factor (GCF) is 1.

primo relativo Dos números son primos relativos si su máximo común divisor (MCD) es 1.

8 and 15 are relatively prime.

---

remote interior angle An interior angle of a polygon that is not adjacent to the exterior angle.

ángulo interno remoto Ángulo interno de un polígono que no es adyacente al ángulo externo.

---

repeating decimal A decimal in which one or more digits repeat infinitely.

decimal periódico Decimal en el que uno o más dígitos se repiten infinitamente.

$0.757575... = 0.\overline{75}$

---

rhombus A parallelogram with all sides congruent.

rombo Paralelogramo en el que todos los lados son congruentes.

---

right angle An angle that measures 90°.

ángulo recto Ángulo que mide exactamente 90°.

---

right cone A cone in which a perpendicular line drawn from the base to the tip (vertex) passes through the center of the base.

cono regular Cono en el que una línea perpendicular trazada de la base a la punta (vértice) pasa por el centro de la base.

Right cone

---

right triangle A triangle containing a right angle.

triángulo rectángulo Triángulo que tiene un ángulo recto.

---

rise The vertical change when the slope of a line is expressed as the ratio $\frac{rise}{run}$, or "rise over run."

distancia vertical El cambio vertical cuando la pendiente de una línea se expresa como la razón $\frac{distancia\ vertical}{distancia\ horizontal}$, o "distancia vertical sobre distancia horizontal".

For the points $(3, -1)$ and $(6, 5)$, the rise is $5 - (-1) = 6$.

---

rotation A transformation in which a figure is turned around a point.

rotación Transformación que ocurre cuando una figura gira alrededor de un punto.

---

rotational symmetry A figure has rotational symmetry if it can be rotated less than 360° around a central point and coincide with the original figure.

simetría de rotación Ocurre cuando una figura gira menos de 360° alrededor de un punto central sin dejar de ser congruente con la figura original.

Glossary/Glosario

ENGLISH	SPANISH	EXAMPLES
run The horizontal change when the slope of a line is expressed as the ratio $\frac{rise}{run}$, or "rise over run."	**distancia horizontal** El cambio horizontal cuando la pendiente de una línea se expresa como la razón $\frac{distancia\ vertical}{distancia\ horizontal}$, o "distancia vertical sobre distancia horizontal".	For the points $(3, -1)$ and $(6, 5)$, the run is $6 - 3 = 3$.

sales tax A percent of the cost of an item that is charged by governments to raise money.	**impuesto sobre la venta** Porcentaje del costo de un artículo que los gobiernos cobran para recaudar fondos.	
same-side interior angles A pair of angles on the same side of a transversal and between two lines intersected by the transversal.	**ángulo internos del mismo lado** Dadas dos rectas cortadas por una transversal, par de ángulos ubicados en el mismo lado de la transversal y entre las dos rectas.	
sample A part of the population.	**muestra** Una parte de la población.	
sample space All possible outcomes of an experiment.	**espacio muestral** Conjunto de todos los resultados posibles de un experimento.	When rolling a number cube, the sample space is 1, 2, 3, 4, 5, 6.
scale The ratio between two sets of measurements.	**escala** La razón entre dos conjuntos de medidas.	1 cm : 5 mi
scale drawing A drawing that uses a scale to make an object smaller than (a reduction) or larger than (an enlargement) the real object.	**dibujo a escala** Dibujo en el que se usa una escala para que un objeto se vea menor (reducción) o mayor (agrandamiento) que el objeto real al que representa.	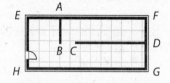 A blueprint is an example of a scale drawing.
scale factor The ratio used to enlarge or reduce similar figures.	**factor de escala** Razón empleada para agrandar o reducir figuras semejantes.	
scale model A proportional model of a three-dimensional object.	**modelo a escala** Modelo proporcional de un objeto tridimensional.	
scalene triangle A triangle with no congruent sides.	**triángulo escaleno** Triángulo que no tiene lados congruentes.	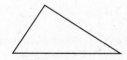
scatter plot A graph with points plotted to show a possible relationship between two sets of data.	**diagrama de dispersión** Gráfica de puntos que muestra una posible relación entre dos conjuntos de datos.	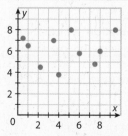

Glossary/Glosario

Glossary/Glosario

scientific notation A method of writing very large or very small numbers by using powers of 10.

notación científica Método que se usa para escribir números muy grandes o muy pequeños mediante potencias de 10.

$12{,}560{,}000{,}000{,}000 =$
1.256×10^{13}

---

second quartile The median of a set of data.

segundo cuartil Mediana de un conjunto de datos.

Data set: 4, 6, 7, 8, 10
Second quartile: 7

---

segment A part of a line between two endpoints.

segmento Parte de una línea entre dos extremos.

$\overline{GH}$

---

self-selected sample A sample in which members choose to be in the sample.

muestra auto-seleccionada Una muestra en la que los miembros eligen participar.

A store provides survey cards for customers who choose to fill them out.

---

sequence An ordered list of numbers.

sucesión Lista ordenada de números.

2, 4, 6, 8, 10, …

---

side A line bounding a geometric figure; one of the faces forming the outside of an object.

lado Línea que delimita las figuras geométricas; una de las caras que forman la parte exterior de un objeto.

---

similar Figures with the same shape but not necessarily the same size.

semejantes Figuras que tienen la misma forma, pero no necesariamente el mismo tamaño.

---

similarity transformation A transformation that results in an image that is the same shape, but not necessarily the same size, as the original figure.

transformación de semejanza Una transformación que resulta en una imagen que tiene la misma forma, pero no necesariamente el mismo tamaño como la figura original.

---

simple interest A fixed percent of the principal. It is found using the formula $I = Prt$, where P represents the principal, r the rate of interest, and t the time.

interés simple Un porcentaje fijo del capital. Se calcula con la fórmula $I = Cit$, donde C representa el capital, i, la tasa de interés y t, el tiempo.

$100 is put into an account with a simple interest rate of 5%. After 2 years, the account will have earned $I = 100 \cdot 0.05 \cdot 2 = \$10$.

---

simplest form A fraction in which the numerator and denominator have no common factors other than 1.

mínima expresión Una fracción está en su mínima expresión cuando el numerador y el denominador no tienen más factor común que 1.

Fraction: $\frac{8}{12}$

Simplest form: $\frac{2}{3}$

---

simplify To write a fraction or expression in simplest form.

simplificar Escribir una fracción o expresión numérica en su mínima expresión.

---

simulation A model of an experiment, often one that would be too difficult or too time-consuming to actually perform.

simulación Representación de un experimento, por lo general, de uno cuya realización sería demasiado difícil o llevaría mucho tiempo.

ENGLISH	SPANISH	EXAMPLES
slant height (of a regular pyramid) The distance from the vertex of a regular pyramid to the midpoint of an edge of the base.	**altura inclinada (de una pirámide)** Distancia desde el vértice de una pirámide hasta el punto medio de una arista de la base.	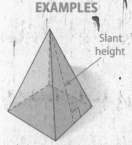 Slant height **Regular pyramid**
slant height (of a right cone) The distance from the vertex of a right cone to a point on the edge of the base.	**altura inclinada (de un cono recto)** Distancia desde el vértice de un cono recto hasta un punto en el borde de la base.	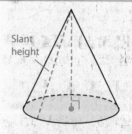 Slant height
slope A measure of the steepness of a line on a graph; the rise divided by the run.	**pendiente** Medida de la inclinación de una línea en una gráfica. Razón de la distancia vertical a la distancia horizontal.	$\text{Slope} = \frac{\text{rise}}{\text{run}} = \frac{3}{4}$ 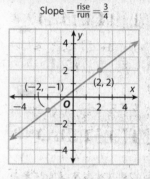
slope-intercept form A linear equation written in the form $y = mx + b$, where m represents slope and b represents the y-intercept.	**forma de pendiente-intersección** Ecuación lineal escrita en la forma $y = mx + b$, donde m es la pendiente y b es la intersección con el eje y.	$y = 6x - 3$
solution of an equation A value or values that make an equation true.	**solución de una ecuación** Valor o valores que hacen verdadera una ecuación.	Equation: $x + 2 = 6$ Solution: $x = 4$
solution of an inequality A value or values that make an inequality true.	**solución de una desigualdad** Valor o valores que hacen verdadera una desigualdad.	Inequality: $x + 3 \geq 10$ Solution: $x \geq 7$
solution of a system of equations A set of values that make all equations in a system true.	**solución de un sistema de ecuaciones** Conjunto de valores que hacen verdaderas todas las ecuaciones de un sistema.	System: $\begin{cases} x + y = -1 \\ -x + y = -3 \end{cases}$ Solution: $(1, -2)$
solution set The set of values that make a statement true.	**conjunto solución** Conjunto de valores que hacen verdadero un enunciado.	Inequality: $x + 3 \geq 5$ Solution set: $x \geq 2$ ←——+—+—+—+—+—+—+—+—+—+—→ $-4\ -3\ -2\ -1\ \ 0\ \ 1\ \ 2\ \ 3\ \ 4\ \ 5\ \ 6$
solve To find an answer or a solution.	**resolver** Hallar una respuesta o solución.	

Glossary/Glosario

ENGLISH	SPANISH	EXAMPLES

sphere A three-dimensional figure with all points the same distance from the center.

esfera Figura tridimensional en la que todos los puntos están a la misma distancia del centro.

---

square A rectangle with four congruent sides.

cuadrado Rectángulo con cuatro lados congruentes.

---

square (numeration) A number raised to the second power.

cuadrado (en numeración) Número elevado a la segunda potencia.

In 5^2, the number 5 is squared.

---

square root A number that is multiplied by itself to form a product is called a square root of that product.

raíz cuadrada El número que se multiplica por sí mismo para formar un producto se denomina la raíz cuadrada de ese producto.

A square root of 16 is 4, because $4^2 = 4 \cdot 4 = 16$.
Another square root of 16 is -4 because $(-4)^2 = (-4)(-4) = 16$.

---

stem-and-leaf plot A graph used to organize and display data so that the frequencies can be compared.

diagrama de tallo y hojas Gráfica que muestra y ordena los datos, y que sirve para comparar las frecuencias.

Stem	Leaves
3	2 3 4 4 7 9
4	0 1 5 7 7 7 8
5	1 2 2 3

Key: 3|2 means 3.2

---

straight angle An angle that measures 180°.

ángulo llano Ángulo que mide exactamente 180°.

---

substitute To replace a variable with a number or another expression in an algebraic expression.

sustituir Reemplazar una variable por un número u otra expresión en una expresión algebraica.

Substituting 3 for m in the expression $5m - 2$ gives $5(3) - 2 = 15 - 2 = 13$.

Subtraction Property of Equality The property that states that if you subtract the same number from both sides of an equation, the new equation will have the same solution.

Propiedad de igualdad de la resta Propiedad que establece que puedes restar el mismo número de ambos lados de una ecuación y la nueva ecuación tendrá la misma solución.

$$
\begin{array}{r}
14 - 6 = \ \ 8 \\
\underline{-6 = -6} \\
14 - 12 = \ \ 2
\end{array}
$$

---

supplementary angles Two angles whose measures have a sum of 180°.

ángulos suplementarios Dos ángulos cuyas medidas suman 180°.

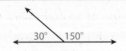

---

surface area The sum of the areas of the faces, or surfaces, of a three-dimensional figure.

área total Suma de las áreas de las caras, o superficies, de una figura tridimensional.

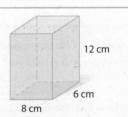

Surface area = $2(8)(12) + 2(8)(6) + 2(12)(6) = 432 \text{ cm}^2$

Glossary/Glosario

system of equations A set of two or more equations that contain two or more variables. | **sistema de ecuaciones** Conjunto de dos o más ecuaciones que contienen dos o más variables. | $\begin{cases} x+y=-1 \\ -x+y=-3 \end{cases}$

systematic sample A sample of a population that has been selected using a pattern. | **muestra sistemática** Muestra de una población, que ha sido elegida mediante un patrón. | To conduct a phone survey, every tenth name is chosen from the phone book.

term (in an expression) A part of an expression that is added or subtracted. | **término (en una expresión)** Las partes de una expresión que se suman o se restan. |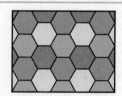

term (in a sequence) An element or number in a sequence. | **término (en una sucesión)** Elemento o número de una sucesión. | 5 is the third term in the sequence 1, 3, 5, 7, 9, …

terminating decimal A decimal number that ends, or terminates. | **decimal finito** Decimal con un número determinado de posiciones decimales. | 6.75

tessellation A repeating pattern of plane figures that completely cover a plane with no gaps or overlaps. | **teselado** Patrón repetido de figuras planas que cubren totalmente un plano sin superponerse ni dejar huecos. |

theoretical probability The ratio of the number of ways an event can occur to the number of equally likely outcomes. | **probabilidad teórica** Razón del número de las maneras que puede ocurrir un suceso al numero total de resultados igualmente probables. | When rolling a number cube, the theoretical probability of rolling a 4 is $\frac{1}{6}$.

third quartile The median of the upper half of a set of data; also called *upper quartile*. | **tercer cuartil** La mediana de la mitad superior de un conjunto de datos. También se llama *cuartil superior*. |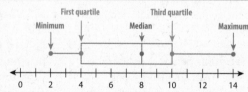

transformation A change in the size or position of a figure. | **transformación** Cambio en el tamaño o la posición de una figura. |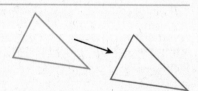

translation A movement (slide) of a figure along a straight line. | **traslación** Desplazamiento de una figura a lo largo de una línea recta. |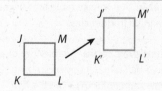

Glossary/Glosario **G39**

ENGLISH	SPANISH	EXAMPLES

transversal A line that intersects two or more lines.

transversal Línea que cruza dos o más líneas.

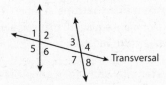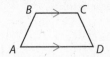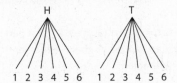

---

trapezoid A quadrilateral with at least one pair of parallel sides.

trapecio Cuadrilátero con al menos un par de lados paralelos.

---

tree diagram A branching diagram that shows all possible combinations or outcomes of an event.

diagrama de árbol Diagrama ramificado que muestra todas las posibles combinaciones o resultados de un suceso.

---

trend line A line on a scatter plot that helps show the correlation between data sets more clearly.

línea de tendencia Línea en un diagrama de dispersión que sirve para mostrar la correlación entre conjuntos de datos más claramente. *ver también* línea de mejor ajuste.

---

trial Each repetition or observation of an experiment.

prueba Una sola repetición u observación de un experimento.

When rolling a number cube, each roll is one trial.

Triangle Inequality Theorem The theorem that states that the sum of the lengths of any two sides of a triangle is greater than the length of the third side.

Teorema de desigualdad de triángulos El teorema dice que la suma de cualquier dos lados de un tríangulo es mayor que la longitud del lado tercero.

Can form a triangle · Cannot form a triangle

Triangle Sum Theorem The theorem that states that the measures of the angles in a triangle add up to 180°.

Teorema de la suma del triángulo Teorema que establece que las medidas de los ángulos de un triángulo suman 180°.

---

triangular prism A polyhedron whose bases are triangles and whose other faces are parallelograms.

prisma triangular Poliedro cuyas bases son triángulos y cuyas demás caras tienen forma de paralelogramo.

---

trinomial A polynomial with three terms.

trinomio Polinomio con tres términos.

$4x^2 + 3xy - 5y^2$

---

two-way relative frequency table A two-way table that displays relative frequencies.

tabla de frecuencia relativa de doble entrada Una tabla de doble entrada que muestran las frecuencias relativas.

---

two-way table A table that displays two-variable data by organizing it into rows and columns.

tabla de doble entrada Una tabla que muestran los datos de dos variables por organizándolos en columnas y filas.

		Inside	Outside	Total
Pet	Cats	35	15	50
	Dogs	20	30	50
	Total	55	45	100

Glossary/Glosario

© Houghton Mifflin Harcourt Publishing Company

G40 Glossary/Glosario

unit conversion The process of changing one unit of measure to another.	**conversión de unidades** Proceso que consiste en cambiar una unidad de medida por otra.	
unit conversion factor A fraction used in unit conversion in which the numerator and denominator represent the same amount but are in different units.	**factor de conversión de unidades** Fracción que se usa para la conversión de unidades, donde el numerador y el denominador representan la misma cantidad pero están en unidades distintas.	$\frac{60\ min}{1\ h}$ or $\frac{1\ h}{60\ min}$
unit price A unit rate used to compare prices.	**precio unitario** Tasa unitaria que sirve para comparar precios.	Cereal costs $0.23 per ounce.
unit rate A rate in which the second quantity in the comparison is one unit.	**tasa unitaria** Una tasa en la que la segunda cantidad de la comparación es la unidad.	10 cm per minute

variability The spread of values in a set of data.	**variabilidad** Amplitud de los valores de un conjunto de datos.	The data set {1, 5, 7, 10, 25} has greater variability than the data set {8, 8, 9, 9, 9}.
variable A symbol used to represent a quantity that can change.	**variable** Símbolo que representa una cantidad que puede cambiar.	In the expression $2x + 3$, x is the variable.
Venn diagram A diagram that is used to show relationships between sets.	**diagrama de Venn** Diagrama que muestra las relaciones entre conjuntos.	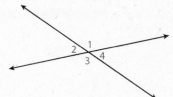
vertex On an angle or polygon, the point where two sides intersect; on a polyhedron, the intersection of three or more faces; on a cone or pyramid, the top point.	**vértice** En un ángulo o polígono, el punto de intersección de dos lados; en un poliedro, el punto de intersección de tres o más caras; en un cono o pirámide, la punta.	A is the vertex of $\angle CAB$.
vertical angles A pair of opposite congruent angles formed by intersecting lines.	**ángulos opuestos por el vértice** Par de ángulos opuestos congruentes formados por líneas secantes.	$\angle 1$ and $\angle 3$ are vertical angles.

Glossary/Glosario

vertical line test A test used to determine whether a relation is a function. If any vertical line crosses the graph of a relation more than once, the relation is not a function.

prueba de la línea vertical Prueba utilizada para determinar si una relación es una función. Si una línea vertical corta la gráfica de una relación más de una vez, la relación no es una función.

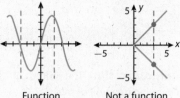

Function Not a function

volume The number of cubic units needed to fill a given space.

volumen Número de unidades cúbicas que se necesitan para llenar un espacio.

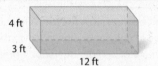

Volume = $3 \cdot 4 \cdot 12 = 144$ ft^3

weighted average A mean that is calculated by multiplying each data value by a weight, and dividing the sum of these products by the sum of the weights.

promedio ponderado Promedio que se calcula por multiplicando cada valor de datos por un peso, y dividiendo la suma de estos productos por la suma de los pesos.

If the data values 0, 5, and 10 are assigned the weights 0.1, 0.2, and 0.7, respectively, the weighted average is:

$$\frac{0(0.1) + 5(0.2) + 10(0.7)}{0.1 + 0.2 + 0.7} = \frac{8}{1}$$

x-axis The horizontal axis on a coordinate plane.

eje x El eje horizontal del plano cartesiano.

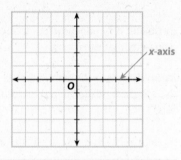

x-axis

x-coordinate The first number in an ordered pair; it tells the distance to move right or left from the origin (0, 0).

coordenada x El primer número de un par ordenado; indica la distancia que debes moverte hacia la izquierda o la derecha desde el origen, (0, 0).

5 is the *x*-coordinate in (5, 3).

x-intercept The *x*-coordinate of the point where the graph of a line crosses the *x*-axis.

intersección con el eje x Coordenada *x* del punto donde la gráfica de una línea cruza el eje *x*.

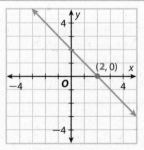

The *x*-intercept is 2.

y-axis The vertical axis on a coordinate plane.

eje y El eje vertical del plano cartesiano.

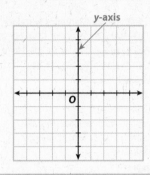

y-coordinate The second number in an ordered pair; it tells the distance to move up or down from the origin (0, 0).

coordenada y El segundo número de un par ordenado; indica la distancia que debes avanzar hacia arriba o hacia abajo desde el origen, (0, 0).

3 is the y-coordinate in (5, 3).

y-intercept The y-coordinate of the point where the graph of a line crosses the y-axis.

intersección con el eje y Coordenada y del punto donde la gráfica de una línea cruza el eje y.

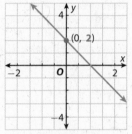

The y-intercept is 2.

Z

zero pair A number and its opposite, which add to 0.

par nulo Un número y su opuesto, cuya suma es 0.

18 and −18

Glossary/Glosario

Index

Index

Index

Index

Index

ASSESSMENT REFERENCE SHEET

TABLE OF MEASURES

Length

1 inch = 2.54 centimeters

1 meter ≈ 39.37 inches

1 mile = 5,280 feet

1 mile = 1,760 yards

1 mile ≈ 1.609 kilometers

1 kilometer ≈ 0.62 mile

Mass/Weight

1 pound = 16 ounces

1 pound ≈ 0.454 kilogram

1 kilogram ≈ 2.2 pounds

1 ton = 2,000 pounds

Capacity

1 cup = 8 fluid ounces

1 pint = 2 cups

1 quart = 2 pints

1 gallon = 4 quarts

1 gallon ≈ 3.785 liters

1 liter ≈ 0.264 gallon

1 liter = 1000 cubic centimeters

FORMULAS

Area

Parallelogram	$A = bh$
Circle	$A = \pi r^2$
Triangle	$A = \frac{1}{2} bh$

Volume

General Prisms	$V = Bh$
Cylinder	$V = \pi r^2 h$
Sphere	$V = \frac{4}{3} \pi r^3$
Cone	$V = \frac{1}{3} \pi r^2 h$

Circumference

Circle	$C = \pi d$ or $C = 2\pi r$

Other

Pythagorean Theorem	$a^2 + b^2 = c^2$